H. P. BLAVATSKY
COLLECTED WRITINGS
VOLUME ONE
1874 — 1878

H. P. BLAVATSKY

COLLECTED WRITINGS

1874-1878

VOLUME ONE

THE THEOSOPHICAL PUBLISHING HOUSE

Wheaton, Ill., U.S.A.

Madras, India   London, England

First Edition 1966
Second Edition 1977

Second edition, 1977, published by the Theosophical Publishing House, Wheaton, Illinois, a department of The Theosophical Society in America.

ISBN: 0-8356-0082-3

PREFACE

[This Preface applies to the entire Edition of H. P. Blavatsky's *Collected Writings*, and not to the present volume only. Together with the Acknowledgments which follow, it w published for the first time in Volume V of the present Series, issued in 1950.]

I

The writings of H. P. Blavatsky, the chief Founder of the modern Theosophical Movement, are becoming with every day more widely known.

They constitute in their totality one of the most astounding products of the creative human mind. Considering their unequalled erudition, their prophetic nature, and their spiritual depth, they must be classed, by friend and foe alike, as being among the inexplicable phenomena of the age. Even a cursory survey of these writings discloses their monumental character.

The best known among them are of course those which appeared in book form and have gone through several editions: *Isis Unveiled* (New York, 1877), *The Secret Doctrine* (London and New York, 1888), *The Key to Theosophy* (London, 1889), *The Voice of the Silence* (London and New York, 1889), *Transactions of the Blavatsky Lodge* (London and New York, 1890 and 1891), *Gems from the East* (London, 1890), and the posthumously published *Theosophical Glossary* (London and New York, 1892), *Nightmare Tales* (London and New York, 1892) and *From the Caves and Jungles of Hindustan* (London, New York and Madras, 1892).

Yet the general public, as well as a great many later theosophical students, are hardly aware of the fact that from 1874 to the end of her life, H. P. Blavatsky wrote incessantly, for a wide range of journals and magazines, and that the combined bulk of these scattered writings exceeds even her voluminous output in book form.

The first articles written by H. P. B. were polemical in nature and trenchant in style. They were published in the best known Spiritualistic journals of the day, such as the *Banner of Light* (Boston, Mass.), the *Spiritual Scientist* (Boston, Mass.), the *Religio-Philosophical Journal* (Chicago, Ill.), *The Spiritualist* (London), *La Revue Spirite* (Paris). Simultaneously, she wrote fascinating occult stories for some of the leading American newspapers, including *The World, The Sun* and *The Daily Graphic,* all of New York.

After she went to India, in 1879, she contributed to *The Indian Spectator, The Deccan Star, The Bombay Gazette, The Pioneer, The Amrita Bazaar Pâtrika,* and other newspapers.

For over seven years, namely during the period of 1879-1886, she wrote serial stories for the well-known Russian newspaper, *Moskovskiya Vedomosty* (Moscow), and the celebrated periodical, *Russkiy Vestnik* (Moscow), as well as for lesser newspapers, such as *Pravda* (Odessa), *Tiflisskiy Vestnik* (Tiflis), *Rebus* (St. Petersburg), and others.

After founding her first theosophical magazine, *The Theosophist* (Bombay and Madras), in October, 1879, she poured into its pages an enormous amount of invaluable teaching, which she continued to give forth at a later date in the pages of her London magazine, *Lucifer,* the short-lived *Revue Théosophique* of Paris, and *The Path* of New York.

While carrying on this tremendous literary output, she found time to engage in polemical discussions with a number of writers and scholars in the pages of other periodicals, especially the *Bulletin Mensuel* of the Société d'Études Psychologiques of Paris, and *Le Lotus* (Paris). In addition to all this, she wrote a number of small pamphlets and Open Letters, which were published separately, on various occasions.

In this general survey no more than mere mention can be made of her voluminous correspondence, many portions of which contain valuable teachings, and of her private *Instructions* which she issued after 1888 to the members of the Esoteric Section.

After 25 years of unremitting research, the individual articles written by H. P. B. in English, French, Russian and Italian, may be estimated at close to *one thousand*. Of special interest to readers is the fact that a considerable number of her French and Russian essays, containing in some cases teachings not stated anywhere else, and never before fully translated into any other language, are now for the first time made available in English.

II

For many years students of the Esoteric Philosophy have been looking forward to the ultimate publication of the writings of H. P. Blavatsky in a collected and convenient form. It is now hoped that this desire may be realized in the publication of the present series of volumes. They constitute a uniform edition of the entire literary output of the Great Theosophist, as far as can be ascertained after years of painstaking research all over the world. These writings are arranged in strictly chronological order according to the date of their original publication in the various magazines, journals, newspapers and other periodicals, or their appearance in book or pamphlet form. Students are thus in a position to trace the progressive unfoldment of H. P. B.'s mission, and to see the method which she used in the gradual presentation of the teachings of the Ancient Wisdom, beginning with her first article in 1874. In a very few instances an article or two appears out of chronological sequence, because there exists convincing evidence that it was written at a much earlier date, and must have been held unprinted for a rather long time. Such articles belong to an earlier date than the date of their actual publication, and have been placed accordingly.

Unless otherwise stated, all writings have been copied *verbatim et literatim* direct from the original sources. In a very few cases, when such source was either unknown, or, if known, was entirely unprocurable, articles have been copied from other publications where they had been reprinted, apparently from original sources, many years ago.

There has been no editing whatsoever of H. P. B.'s literary style, grammar or spelling. Obvious typographical errors, however, have been corrected throughout. Her own spelling of Sanskrit technical terms and proper names has been preserved. No attempt has been made to introduce any uniformity or consistency in these particulars. However, the correct systemic spelling of all Oriental technical terms and proper names, according to present-day scholastic standards, is used in the English translations of original French and Russian material, as well as in the Index wherein it appears within square brackets immediately following such terms or names.*

A systematic effort has been made to verify the many quotations introduced by H. P. B. from various works, and all references have been carefully checked. In every case original sources have been consulted for this verification, and if any departures from the original text were found, these were corrected. Many of the writings quoted could be consulted only in such large Institutions as the British Museum of London, the Bibliothèque Nationale of Paris, the Library of Congress, Washington, D. C., and the Lenin State Library of Moscow. In some cases works quoted remained untraceable. No attempt was made to check quotations from current newspapers, as the transitory nature of the material used did not seem to justify the effort.

Throughout the text, there are to be found many footnotes signed "Ed.," "Editor," "Ed., *Theos.*," or "Editor, *The Theosophist*"; also footnotes which are unsigned. It should be distinctly remembered that all these footnotes are H. P. B.'s own, and are *not* by the Compiler of the present volumes.

All material added by the Compiler—either as footnotes

---

*See explanatory Note on page 442.

or as explanatory comments appended to certain articles—is enclosed within square brackets and signed "Compiler." Obvious editorial explanations or summaries preceding articles or introducing H. P. B.'s comments are merely placed within square brackets.

Occasionally brief sentences appear which are within square brackets, even in the main body of the text or in H. P. B.'s own footnotes. These bracketed remarks are evidently by H. P. B. herself, although the reason for such usage is not readily apparent.

In a very few instances, which are self-evident, the Compiler has added within square brackets an obviously missing word or digit, to complete the meaning of the sentence.

H. P. B.'s text is followed by an Appendix which consists of three sections:

(a) Bibliography of Oriental Works which provides concise information regarding the best known editions of the Sacred Scriptures and other Oriental writings quoted from or referred to by H. P. B.

(b) General Bibliography wherein can be found, apart from the customary particulars regarding all works quoted or referred to, succinct biographical data concerning the less known writers, scholars, and public figures mentioned by H. P. B. in the text, or from whose writings she quotes. It has been thought of value to the student to have this collected information which is not otherwise easily obtainable.

(c) Index of subject matter.

Following the Preface, a brief historical survey will be found in the form of a Chronological Table embodying fully documented data regarding the whereabouts of H. P. B. and Col. Henry S. Olcott, as well as the chief events in the history of the Theosophical Movement, within the period covered by the material contained in any one volume of the Series.

III

The majority of articles written by H. P. Blavatsky, for both magazines and newspapers, are signed by her, either with her own name or with one of her rather infrequent pseudonyms, such as Hadji Mora, Râddha-Bai, Sañjñâ, "Adversary," and others.

There are however, a great many unsigned articles, both in Theosophical journals and elsewhere. Some of these have been included because a most careful study by a number of students thoroughly familiar with H. P. B.'s characteristic literary style, her well-known idiosyncrasies of expression, and her frequent usage of foreign idiom, has shown them to be from H. P. B.'s pen, even though no *irrefutable* proof of this can be advanced. Other unsigned articles are mentioned in early Theosophical books, memoirs and pamphlets, as having been written by H. P. B. In still other cases, clippings of such articles were pasted by H. P. B. in her many *Scrapbooks* (now in the Adyar Archives), with pen-and-ink notations establishing her authorship. Several articles are known to have been produced by other writers, yet were almost certainly corrected by H. P. B. or added to by her, or possibly written by them under her own more or less direct inspiration. These have been included with appropriate comments.

A perplexing problem presents itself in connection with H. P. B.'s writings of which the casual reader is probably unaware. It is the fact that H. P. B. often acted as an amanuensis for her own Superiors in the Occult Hierarchy. At times whole passages were dictated to her by her own Teacher or other Adepts and advanced Chelas. These passages are nevertheless tinged throughout with the very obvious peculiarities of her own inimitable style, and are sometimes interspersed with remarks definitely emanating from her own mind. This entire subject involves rather recondite mysteries connected with the transmission of occult communications from Teacher to disciple.

Preface

At the time of his first contact with the Masters, through the intermediation of H. P. B., A. P. Sinnett sought for an explanation of the process mentioned above and elicited the following reply from Master K. H.:

". . . Besides, bear in mind that these my letters are not written, but *impressed*, or precipitated, and then all mistakes corrected. . . .

". . . I have to think it over, to photograph every word and sentence carefully in my brain, before it can be repeated by precipitation. As the fixing on chemically prepared surfaces of the images formed by the camera requires a previous arrangement within the focus of the object to be represented, for otherwise— as often found in bad photographs—the legs of the sitter might appear out of all proportion with the head, and so on—so we have to first arrange our sentences and impress every letter to appear on paper in our minds before it becomes fit to be read. For the present it is *all* I can tell you. When science will have learned more about the mystery of the lithophyl (or litho-biblion), and how the impress of leaves comes originally to take place on stones, then I will be able to make you better understand the process. But you must know and remember one thing—we but follow and servilely copy Nature in her works."*

In an article entitled "Precipitation", H. P. B., referring directly to the passage quoted above, writes as follows:

"Since the above was written, the Masters have been pleased to permit the veil to be drawn aside a little more, and the *modus operandi* can thus be explained now more fully to the outsider . . .

". . . The work of writing the letters in question is carried on by a sort of psychological telegraphy; the Mahatmas very rarely write their letters in the ordinary way. An electro-magnetic connection, so to say, exists on the psychological plane between a Mahatma and his chelas, one of whom acts as his amanuensis. When the Master wants a letter to be written in this way, he draws the attention of the chela, whom he selects for the task, by causing an astral bell (heard by so many of our Fellows and others) to be rung near him just as the despatching telegraph office signals to the receiving office before wiring the message. The thoughts arising in the mind of the Mahatma are then clothed in words, pronounced mentally, and forced along the astral currents he sends towards the pupil to impinge on the brain of the latter. Thence they are borne by the nerve-currents to the palms of his

---

*A. P. Sinnett. *The Occult World* (orig. ed. London: Trübner and Co., 1881), pp. 143-44. Also *Mah. Ltrs.*, No VI, with small variations.

hand and the tips of his finger, which rest on a piece of magnetically prepared paper. As the thought-waves are thus impressed on the tissue, materials are drawn to it from the ocean of *âkas* (permeating every atom of the sensuous universe), by an occult process, out of place here to describe, and permanent marks are left.

"From this it is abundantly clear that the success of such writings as above described depends chiefly upon these things:— (1) The force and the clearness with which the thoughts are propelled, and (2) the freedom of the receiving brain from disturbance of every description. The case with the ordinary electric telegraph is exactly the same. If, for some reason or other the battery supplying the electric power falls below the requisite strength on any telegraph line or there is some derangement in the receiving apparatus, the message transmitted becomes either mutilated or otherwise imperfectly legible. . . . Such inaccuracies, in fact, do very often arise as may be gathered from what the Mahatma says in the above extract. 'Bear in mind,' says He, 'that these my letters are not written, but *impressed*, or precipitated, and *then all mistakes corrected.*' To turn to the sources of error in the precipitation. Remembering the circumstances under which blunders arise in telegrams, we see that if a Mahatma somehow becomes exhausted or allows his thoughts to wander off during the process or fails to command the requisite intensity in the astral currents along which his thoughts are projected, or the distracted attention of the pupil produces disturbances in his brain and nerve-centres, the success of the process is very much interfered with."*

To this excerpt may be added H. P. B.'s words which occur in her unique article entitled "My Books," published in *Lucifer* the very month of her passing.

". . . Space and distance do not exist for thought; and if two persons are in perfect mutual psycho-magnetic *rapport*, and of these two, one is a great Adept in Occult Sciences, then thought-transference and dictation of whole pages become as easy and as comprehensible at the distance of ten thousand miles as the transference of two words across a room."†

It is of course self-evident that if such dictated passages, long or short, were to be excluded from her *Collected Writings*, it would be necessary to exclude also very large

---

*The Theosophist, Vol. V, Nos. 3-4 (51-52), Dec.-Jan., 1883-84, p. 64.
†*Lucifer*, London, Vol. VIII, No. 45, May 15, 1891, pp. 241-247.

portions of both *The Secret Doctrine* and *Isis Unveiled,* as being either the result of direct dictation to H. P. B. by one or more Adepts, or even actual material precipitated by occult means for her to use, if she chose to do so. Such an attitude towards H. P. B.'s writings would hardly be consistent with either common sense or her own view of things, as she most certainly did not hesitate to append her name to most of the material which had been dictated to her by various high Occultists.

IV

A historical survey of the various steps in the compiling of H. P. B.'s voluminous writings should now be given.

Soon after H. P. B.'s death, an early attempt was made to gather and to publish at least some of her scattered writings. In 1891, resolutions were passed by all the Sections of The Theosophical Society that an "H. P. B. Memorial Fund" be instituted for the purpose of publishing such writings from her pen as would promote "that intimate union between the life and thought of the Orient and the Occident to the bringing about of which her life was devoted."

In 1895, there appeared in print Volume I of "The H. P. B. Memorial Fund Series," under the title of *A Modern Panarion: A Collection of Fugitive Fragments from the pen of H. P. Blavatsky* (London, New York and Madras, 1895, 504 pp.), containing a selection from H. P. B.'s articles in the Spiritualistic journals and a number of her early contributions to *The Theosophist*. It was printed on the H. P. B. Press, 42 Henry Street, Regent's Park, London, N.W., Printers to The Theosophical Society. No further volumes are known to have been published, although it would appear that other volumes in this series were contemplated.

The compiling of material for a uniform edition of H. P. Blavatsky's writings was begun by the undersigned in 1924, while residing at the Headquarters of the Point Loma Theosophical Society, during the administration of Katherine Tingley. For about six years it remained a private project of the Compiler. Some 1,500 pages of typewritten material were collected, copied, and tentatively classified. Many foreign sources of information were consulted for correct data, and a great deal of preliminary work was done.

It was soon discovered in the formative stage of the plan that an analytical study of the early years of the modern Theosophical Movement was essential, not only as a means of discovering what publications had actually published articles from the pen of H. P. B., but also as providing data for running down every available clue as to dates of publication which often had been wrongly quoted.

It was at this particular time that a far-flung international correspondence was started with individuals and Institutions in the hope of eliciting the necessary information. By the end of the summer of 1929, most of this work had been completed in so far as it concerned the initial period of 1874-79.

In August, 1929, Dr. Gottfried de Purucker, then Head of the Point Loma Theosophical Society, was approached regarding the plan of publishing a uniform edition of H. P. B.'s writings. This idea was immediately accepted, and a small Committee was formed to help with the preparation of the material. It was intended from the outset to start publication in 1931, as a tribute to H. P. B. on the Centennial Anniversary of her birth, provided a suitable publisher could be found.

After several possible publishers had been considered, it was suggested by the late Dr. Henry T. Edge—a personal pupil of H. P. Blavatsky from the London days—to approach Rider and Co., in London.

On February 27, 1930, A. Trevor Barker, of London, Transcriber and Compiler of *The Mahatma Letters to A. P. Sinnett,* wrote to Dr. G. de Purucker and among other things advised that he and his friend, Ronald A. V. Morris, had been for some time past working upon a plan of collecting H. P. B.'s magazine articles for a possible series of volumes to be published in the near future. Close contact was immediately established between these gentlemen and the Committee at Point Loma. They first sent a complete list of their material, and in July, 1930, the collected material itself, which consisted mainly of articles from *The Theosophist* and *Lucifer*. While duplicating to a very great extent what had already been collected from these journals, their material contained also a number of valuable items from other sources. In May, 1930, A. Trevor Barker also suggested Rider and Co., of London, as a possible publisher.

In the meantime, namely, on April 1, 1930, the suggestion had been made by the Compiler that this entire work become an Inter-Organizational Theosophical project in which all Theosophical Societies would collaborate. Since this idea dovetailed with the Fraternization Movement inaugurated by Dr. G. de Purucker at the time, it was accepted at once and steps were taken to secure the co-operation of other Theosophical Societies.

On April 24, 1930, a letter was written to Dr. Annie Besant, President, The Theosophical Society (Adyar), asking for collaboration in the compilation of the forthcoming Series. Her endorsement was secured, through the intermediation of Lars Eek, at the Theosophical Convention held in Geneva, Switzerland, June 28—July 1, 1930, at which she presided.

After a period of preliminary correspondence, constructive and fruitful literary teamwork was established with the officials at the Adyar Headquarters. The gracious permission of Dr. Annie Besant to utilize material in the Archives of The Theosophical Society at Adyar, and the wholehearted collaboration of C. Jinarâjadâsa, A. J. Hamerster, Mary K. Neff, N. Sri Ram, and others, extending over a number of years, have been factors of primary importance in the success of this entire effort.

The help of a number of other individuals in different parts of the world was accepted and the work of the compilation took on the more permanent form of an Inter-Organizational Theosophical project, in which many people of various nationalities and Theosophical affiliations co-operated.

While work proceeded on various portions of the mass of material already available, the main effort was directed towards completing Volume I of the Series, which was to cover the period of 1874-1879. This volume proved, in some respects, to be the most difficult to produce, owing to the fact that material for it was scattered over several continents and often in almost unprocurable periodicals and newspapers of that era.

Volume I was ready for the printer in the summer of 1931, and was then sent to Rider and Co., of London, with whom a contract had been signed. Owing to various delays over which the Compiler had no control, it did not go to press until August, 1932, and was finally published in the early part of 1933, under the title of *The Complete Works of H. P. Blavatsky.*

A stipulation was made by the publisher that the name of A. Trevor Barker should appear on the title page of the Volume, as the responsible Editor, owing to his reputation as the Editor of *The Mahatma Letters to A. P. Sinnett* and *The Letters of H. P. Blavatsky to A. P. Sinnett.* This stipulation was agreed to as a technical point intended for business purposes only.

Volume II of the Series was also published in 1933; Volume III appeared in 1935, and Volume IV in 1936. The same year Rider and Co. published a facsimile edition of *Isis Unveiled,* with both volumes under one cover, and uniform with the preceding first four volumes of the *Complete Works.*

Further unexpected delays occurred in 1937, and then came the world crisis resulting in World War II which stopped the continuation of the Series. During the London "blitz," the Offices of Rider and Co. and other Publishing

Houses in Paternoster Row, were destroyed. The plates of the four volumes already published were ruined (as were also the plates of *The Mahatma Letters to A. P. Sinnett* and other works), and, as the edition was only a small one, these volumes were no longer available and have remained so for the last fourteen years.

During the World War period, research work and preparation of material for future publication went on uninterruptedly however, and much new material was discovered. Very rare articles written by H. P. B. in French were unexpectedly found and promptly translated. A complete survey was made of all known writings in her native Russian, and new items were brought to light. This Russian literary output was secured in its entirety, direct from the original sources, the most rare articles being furnished free of charge by the Lenin State Library of Moscow.

The hardships of the economic situation in England, both during and after World War II, made it impossible for Rider and Co. to resume work on the original Series. In the meantime the demand for the writings of H. P. Blavatsky has been steadily growing, and an ever increasing number of people have been looking forward to the publication of an American Edition of her Collected Works. To satisfy this growing demand, the present edition is being launched. Its publication in the seventy-fifth year of the modern Theosophical Movement fills a long-felt need on the American Continent, where the cornerstone of the original Theosophical Society was laid in 1875.

The writings of H. P. Blavatsky are unique. They speak louder than any human commentary, and the ultimate proof of the teachings they contain rests with the disciple himself—when his heart is attuned to the cosmic harmony they unveil before his mind's eye. Like all mystic writings throughout the ages, they conceal vastly more than they reveal, and the intuitive student discovers in them just what he is able to grasp—neither more nor less.

Unchanged by time, unmoved by the phantasmagoria of the world's pageant, unhurt by scathing criticism, unsoiled by the vituperations of trivial and dogmatic minds, these writings stand today, as they did on the day of their first appearance, like a majestic rock amidst the foaming crests of an unruly sea. Their clarion call resounds as of yore, and thousands of heart-hungry, confused and disillusioned men and women, seekers after truth and knowledge, find the entrance to a greater life in the enduring principles of thought contained in H. P. B.'s literary heritage.

She flung down the gauntlet to the religious sectarianism of her day, with its gaudy ritualism and the dead letter of orthodox worship. She challenged entrenched scientific dogmas evolved from minds which saw in Nature but a fortuitous aggregate of lifeless atoms driven by mere chance. The regenerative power of her Message broke the constricting shell of a moribund theology, swept away the empty wranglings of phrase weavers, and checkmated the progress of scientific fallacies.

Today this Message, like the Spring flood of some mighty river, is spreading far and wide over the earth. The greatest thinkers of the day are voicing at times genuine theosophical ideas, often couched in the very language used by H. P. B. herself, and we witness daily the turning of men's minds towards those treasure chambers of the Trans-Himâlayan Esoteric Knowledge which she unlocked for us.

We commend her writings to the weary pilgrim, and to the seeker of enduring spiritual realities. They contain the answer to many a perplexing problem. They open wide portals undreamt of before, revealing vistas of cosmic splendor and lasting inspiration. They bring new hope and courage to the fainthearted but sincere student. They are a comfort and a staff, as well as a Guide and Teacher, to those who are already travelling along the age-old Path. As for those few who are in the vanguard of mankind, valiantly scaling the solitary passes leading to the Gates of Gold, these writings give the clue to the secret knowledge enabling one to lift the heavy bar that must be raised before the Gates admit the pilgrim into the land of Eternal Dawn.

ACKNOWLEDGMENTS

In the course of this literary undertaking, a great deal of volunteer help has been received from many individuals and several distinguished Institutions. Contacts established with them have been the cause of many pleasant associations and friendships of a lasting nature. The Compiler wishes to express his indebtedness to each and every one of them. In particular, a debt of gratitude is due to the following friends and associates:

Gottfried de Purucker, late Leader of the Point Loma Theosophical Society, for his constant encouragement, his invaluable hints concerning H. P. B.'s writings, and the opportunity to share his profound learning on subjects pertaining to Occultism; Henry T. Edge and Charles J. Ryan, for assistance in determining the authorship of many unsigned articles; Bertram Keightley, who, in the closing years of his life, provided valuable information regarding certain articles in the volumes of *Lucifer*, on whose editorial staff he served in H. P. B.'s time; E. T. Sturdy, member of H. P. B.'s Inner Group, for suggestive data and information; C. Jinarâjadâsa, President of The Theosophical Society (Adyar), for his many years of collaboration and his moral and material support; A. J. Hamerster and Mary K. Neff, for their meticulous care in the transcription of material from the Adyar Archives; Marjorie M. Tyberg, whose trained editorial abilities were an important factor in the production of the earlier volumes; Joseph H. Fussell, Sec'y-Gen. of the Point Loma Theosophical Society, for his co-operation in connection with the Society's Archives; A. Trevor Barker and Virginia Barker, London, and Ronald A. V. Morris, Hove, Sussex, for editorial work on portions of the MSS and their role in the business transactions with Rider and Co.; Sven Eek, onetime Manager of the Publications Department, Point Loma, Calif., for valuable assistance in the sale of earlier volumes; Judith Tyberg, for helpful suggestions in connection with Sanskrit technical terms; Helen Morris Koerting, New York; Ernest Cunningham, Philadelphia; Philip Malpas, London; Margaret Guild Conger, Washington, D. C.; Charles E. Ball, London; J. Hugo Tatsch, President, McCoy Publishing Company, New York; J. Emory Clapp, Boston; Ture Dahlin, Paris; T. W. Willans, Australia; W. Emmett Small, Geoffrey Barborka, Mrs. Grace Knoche, Miss Grace Frances Knoche, Solomon Hecht, Eunice M. Ingraham, and others, for research work, checking of references, copying of the MSS and assistance with various technical points connected with the earlier volumes; Mary L. Stanley, London, for painstaking and most able research work at the British Museum; Alexander Petrovich Leino, Helsingfors, Finland, for invaluable assistance in securing original Russian material at the Helsingfors University

Library; William L. Biersach, Jr., and Walter A. Carrithers, Jr., whose thorough knowledge of the historical documents connected with the Theosophical Movement has been of very great assistance; and Mrs. Mary V. Langford, whose most careful and intelligent translation of Russian material provided a major contribution to the entire Series.

The Compiler is also indebted to the following Institutions, and their officials who have contributed information essential to the production of this Series: Stanford University, and the Hoover Institute, Palo Alto, Calif.; British Museum, London; The American-Russian Institute, New York; Avrahm Yarmolinsky, Chief of the Slavonic Division and Paul North Rice, Chief of the Reference Department, New York Public Library; University of California at Los Angeles, Los Angeles, Calif.; Library of Congress, Washington, D. C.; Mary E. Holmes, Librarian, Franklin Library, Franklin, Mass.; Foster M. Palmer, Reference Librarian, Harvard College Library, Cambridge, Mass.; University of Pennsylvania Library, Philadelphia, Pa.; Bibliothèque Nationale, Paris; Lenin State Library, Moscow, U.S.S.R.; Kungliga Biblioteket, Stockholm; Universitetsbiblioteket, Upsala; Boston Public Library; Columbia University Library, New York; Yale University Library, New Haven, Conn.; Grand Lodge Library and Museum, London; American Antiquarian Society, Worcester, Mass.; Public Library, Colombo, Ceylon; The Commonwealth of Massachusetts State Library, Boston, Mass.; The Boston Athenaeum; Imperial Library, Calcutta, India; London Spiritualist Alliance; Massachusetts State Association of Spiritualists, Boston, Mass.; California State Library, Sacramento, Calif.; Library of the Philosophical Research Society, Inc., Los Angeles, Calif.

Other individuals from time to time have contributed in various ways to the success of this literary work. To all of these a debt of appreciation is due, even if their names are not individually mentioned.

BORIS DE ZIRKOFF.
Compiler.

LOS ANGELES, CALIFORNIA, U.S.A.
September 8th, 1950.

[Beginning with Volume VII, the publication of the *Collected Writings* was taken over by The Theosophical Publishing House, Adyar, Madras, India, at the suggestion of our esteemed Brother and Friend, N. Sri Ram, President of The Theosophical Society, Adyar.]

FOREWORD TO VOLUME ONE

Most of the material in the present Volume appeared in print in collected form for the first time in 1933, when it was published by Rider & Co. in London, under the title of *The Complete Works of H. P. Blavatsky*. A considerable portion of the stock of that Volume perished in the London "blitz" during the second World War. As a result of this, these earlier Volumes have been unobtainable for many years.

The material originally published in Volume I has been thoroughly revised; the text has been checked in almost every instance with the original sources of publication, and most of the quoted matter compared with the originals and corrected whenever necessary. Substantial additions have been incorporated in the present Volume, such as H.P.B.'s characteristic marginal pen-and-ink Notes and Comments in her *Scrapbooks* now in the Archives at Adyar, her Travel-Impressions of 1867 jotted down in one of her *Notebooks*, her revealing entries in Col. Olcott's *Diaries* of 1878, and a few articles and brief items from her pen discovered during the last few years. Many explanatory notes and comments have been added by the Compiler to clarify points of Theosophical history. A comprehensive yet succinct outline of H.P.B.'s family background and early life and travels has been prepared especially for this Volume. Biographical and Bibliographical information has been collected in the Appendix with regard to a number of individuals associated with H.P.B. in the formative years of the Theosophical Movement, especially the Co-Founders of the Society, and other personalities she refers to or quotes from.

All in all, the present Volume, far from being merely a second edition of the earlier one, is *de facto* an entirely new Volume, and is intended to set the stage and sound the key-note for the entire Series of the *Collected Writings*.

The Compiler wishes to express his gratitude to all those who have helped in the preparation of this Volume, especially the following friends and associates:

Irene R. Ponsonby who checked all the editorial material and read the page proofs, and whose thorough knowledge of literary style and methods was of inestimable help; Zoltán de Álgya-Pap, of the Adyar Archives, whose willing assistance and painstaking checking of original sources provided a major contribution to the completeness of this Volume; Dara R. Eklund who was responsible for the checking of innumerable quotations in various out of the way publications; Frances Ziegenmeyer who helped with the transcription of microfilm; and Margaret Chamberlain Rathbun who proofread the text of the entire Volume in manuscript.

BORIS DE ZIRKOFF,
Compiler.

LOS ANGELES, CALIFORNIA, U.S.A.
JANUARY 4TH, 1966.

HELENA PETROVNA BLAVATSKY

GENERAL OUTLINE OF HER LIFE PRIOR TO HER PUBLIC WORK.

A definitive edition of the *Collected Writings* of H. P. Blavatsky calls for a brief survey of her early life and her family background, in order to acquaint the reader with the many vicissitudes during that early period when, as far as we know at present, H.P.B. had not yet embarked upon her literary career.

The source material with regard to that period is very fragmentary and uncertain. Her own statements are often contradictory and therefore unreliable, and those of her friends and relatives are often equally confused, with the exception of her sister Vera Petrovna de Zhelihovsky who kept a Diary and was a particularly careful writer.

For some curious reason, many of the uncertainties which could have been at least partially eliminated during the lifetime of various contemporaries, were allowed to remain unchallenged, until too late to do so, owing to the passing of these individuals, or the destruction of documents known to have existed at one time.

All in all, the best that any modern writer can do is to present a fragmentary account with a number of obvious *lacunae* or a choice of possible alternatives, supported by references to early sources of information, leaving the reader to draw his own conclusions as to the most probable course of events.

This, perhaps, is not a unique situation, especially when the *occult* nature of H. P. Blavatsky's career is taken into account. The lives of genuine Occultists throughout the ages are for the most part but little known, and their various moves are, as a rule, uncertain. No complete biographical sketch of any degree of authenticity can be produced in the case of Count de Saint-Germain or Count de Cagliostro, except for certain brief periods in their careers; nor would a biographer fare any better in the case of Apollonius of Tyana, Śaṃkarâchârya, Simon Magus, Zoroaster or Pythagoras.

As time passes, and the constant shifting of scenery on the karmic stage takes its usual course, details are forgotten, individuals vanish into the distant background of historical perspective, and witnesses depart from their former scenes of action, until much is left to mere conjecture and speculation, against the backdrop of a rapidly receding era. It is even more so in the case of those strange and mysterious characters whose lives are woven on a unique pattern, whose mission is devoted to the liberation of men from the thraldom of the senses, and who appear in our midst from time to time as symbols of spiritual freedom, and as living witnesses to the hidden powers of man.

For the "initiates are as hard to catch as the sun-sparkle which flecks the dancing wave on a summer-day. One generation of man may know them under one name in a certain country, and the next, or a succeeding one, see them as someone else in a remote land.

"They live in each place as long as they are needed and then—pass away 'like a breath' leaving no trace behind."

Helena Petrovna Blavatsky was born at Ekaterinoslav, a town on the river Dnieper, in Southern Russia, on the 31st of July, 1831, according to the Julian or so-called "Old Style" Calendar, then current in Russia. According to the Gregorian Calendar the date would have been August 12th. Although no official record has ever been produced of the exact time of her birth, it has been determined with sufficient accuracy by astrological rectification, based on various important events in H.P.B.'s life, to have been 1:42 A.M., local time, which, equated for Greenwich, would be 11:22 P.M., on August 11th, 1831.[1]

The year 1831 was a very bad one in Russia; a widespread epidemic of cholera raged and several members of her parents' household had been victims of the disease. As Helena was born prematurely, and there was fear for the infant's life, an immediate baptism took place. A child who held a candle in the first row behind the officiating priest, set fire to his robes during the ceremony.[2]

Helena's mother was Helena Andreyevna (1814-42), eldest daughter of Andrey Mihailovich de Fadeyev (Dec. 31, 1789-Aug. 28, 1867 o.s.) and Helena Pavlovna, née Princess Dolgorukova (Oct. 11, 1789-Aug. 12, 1860 o.s.).

A. M. de Fadeyev, Helena's maternal grandfather, a Privy Councillor, was at one time Civil Governor of the Province of Saratov and later, for many years (1846-67), Director of the Department of State Lands in the Caucasus, and member of the Council of the Viceroy of the Caucasus, Count Mihail Semyonovich Vorontzov. His *Remin-*

---

[1] *The Theosophist,* Vol. XV, October, 1893, pp. 12-17.
[2] *Ibid.,* Vol. XXX, April, 1909, p. 85.

iscences, 1790-1867[3] is an extremely valuable work giving the entire family background of the de Fadeyevs and much information concerning the various sojourns of H.P.B.'s mother and father, and Helena as a child. The work is also of great importance as a description of Russian life and of many historical personalities of the 19th century.

Helena Pavlovna, Helena's maternal grandmother, whom A. M. de Fadeyev had married in 1813, was the daughter of Prince Paul Vassilyevich Dolgorukov (1755-1837) and Henrietta Adolfovna de Bandré-du-Plessis (d. 1812) who was of French descent.[4] She had married against the wishes of her parents, who objected to her marriage with a commoner, even though he was known to be of great probity. Helena Pavlovna was a very unusual individual, a noted botanist, a woman of scholarly attainments and of great culture, rare

---

[3] *Vospominaniya, 1790-1867* (Russian text), in two parts bound in one volume. Odessa: South-Russian Society for Printing, 1897. Enlarged and supplemented from essays originally published in the *Russkiy Arhiv* (Russian Archive).

[4] The family du Plessis belonged to the old French nobility with the title of Marquis, and was divided into two branches: *Mornay-du-Plessis* and *Bandré-du-Plessis*. One of the members of the latter, being a Huguenot, had to leave France and settle in Saxony. Adolph Franzovich de Bandré-du-Plessis, grandfather of H.P.B.'s grandmother, served first in Saxony but later accepted an invitation to go to Russia, and as a Captain, entered military service there in the beginning of Catherine the Great's reign. He commanded an Army Corps in the Crimean War, became Lieutenant-General, and was a favorite of Field Marshal Suvorov. He also saw diplomatic service in Poland and the Crimea, and was a protégé of the Chancellor, Count Nikita Ivanovich Panin. A highly intelligent and cultured man, he retired in 1790 because of ill health, and resided on his estate of Nizki, in the Province of Mogilev, where he died in 1793.

From his marriage to Helena Ivanovna Briseman-von-Nettig, of the Province of Lifland, he had one daughter, Henrietta Adolfovna. Henrietta was a very beautiful woman but somewhat peculiar and flighty. She married Prince Paul V. Dolgorukov in 1787, she was separated from him after a few years, but rejoined him again some three years before his death. Besides their daughter, Helena Pavlovna, they had a second daughter, Anastassiya Pavlovna (d. 1828) who married Alexander Vassilyevich Sushkov.

These details are from A. M. de Fadeyev's *Reminiscences*, I, 20-22.

endowments for a woman of that period in Russia. She was proficient in history, natural science, archaeology and numismatics, and had some valuable books and collections on these subjects. For many years she corresponded with a number of foreign and Russian scientists, among them Baron F. H. Alexander von Humboldt (1769-1859); Sir Roderick Impey Murchison (1792-1871), British geologist and one of the Founders of the Royal Geographical Society, who went on an extensive expedition to Russia; Christian Steven (1781-1864), the Swedish botanist who engaged in a comprehensive study of Crimean flora and worked in the silk industry of the Caucasus; Otto Wilhelm Hermann von Abich (1806-86), the well-known geologist and explorer; and G. S. Karelin (1801-72), traveller, geographer, ethnologist and explorer of natural science. Helena Pavlovna spoke five languages fluently and was an excellent artist.

Hommaire-de-Hell, traveller and geologist, who spent some seven years in Russia, speaks of Mme. de Fadeyev's hospitality and scholarly attainments in one of his works.[5]

Lady Hester Lucy Stanhope (1776-1839), the famous English traveller who had circled the entire world dressed as a man, says in her book on Russia:

"In that barbarian land I met an outstanding woman-scientist, who would have been famous in Europe, but who is completely underestimated due to her misfortune of being born on the shores of the Volga river, where there was none to recognize her scientific value."

Helena Pavlovna's extensive herbarium was presented after her death to the University of St. Petersburg.[6]

The other children of the de Fadeyevs were: Rostislav Andreyevich

---

[5] Cf. Ignace-Xavier Morand Hommaire-de-Hell (1812-48), *Les steppes de la Mer Caspienne, la Crimée et la Russie méridionale*, etc., Paris, Strassburg, 1843-45, 3 vols. The descriptive part is by his wife Adèle who was a poet and writer in her own right. Chapters XXI and XXII of the French original, and pp. 165-77 of the English translation (*Travels in the Steppes*, etc.; London: Chapman and Hall, 1847), deal with their visit to the Kalmuk prince Tumen'; therein they speak of Madame de Fadeyev and describe the Kalmuk setting and festivities in which H.P.B. herself, as a small girl, took part, as she later recounts in *Isis Unveiled*, II, 600, footnote.

[6] *Vide* "Helena Pavlovna Fadeyeva," by her daughter, Nadezhda A. de Fadeyev, in *Russkaya Starina* (Russian Old Days), Vol. 52, December, 1886, pp. 749-51.

HELENA PETROVNA BLAVATSKY   xxix

(1824-84), Major-General in Artillery, Joint Secretary of State at the Ministry of the Interior, and a noted writer on subjects of military strategy; Nadyezhda Andreyevna (1828-1919), the much beloved aunt of H.P.B., who was only three years her senior, never married and was for some years a member of the Council of The Theosophical Society; Katherine Andreyevna (b. 1819) who married Yuliy F. de Witte and was the mother of the famous statesman, Count Serguey Yulyevich de Witte; and Eudoxia Andreyevna who died in infancy.

Considering the general cultural background, it is not unnatural that Helena Andreyevna, daughter of the Fadeyevs, and mother of H.P.B., should herself have been a very remarkable woman. She was born Jan. 11/23, 1814, near the village of Rzhishchevo, in the Province of Kiev, where the estate of the Dolgorukovs was located. Nurtured in an atmosphere of culture and scholarship, she became a noted novelist, her first work, called *The Ideal*, being published when she was 23. Her marriage, in 1830, at the early age of 16, to a man almost twice her age, Col. Peter Alexeyevich von Hahn,[7] was an unhappy one, owing to incompatibility and the inability on her part to fit into the narrow groove of her husband's military life. Her delicate sensitivity and high ideals made it impossible for her to enjoy the society of people whose ideas and sentiments remained on a very commonplace level. In her novels, she pictured the wretched position of women, their lack of opportunity and education, and voiced the question of their ultimate emancipation. She was the first woman in Russia to do so in literature. Her unhappiness must have contributed to the undermining of her health, and she died from tuberculosis when only 28 years of age.[8]

Helena's father, Captain of Artillery Peter Alexeyevich von Hahn (Gan)—1798-1873—was the son of Lieutenant-General Alexis Gustavo-

---

[7] Written and pronounced in Russian as *Gan*.

[8] Her literary output was large. Her published works include the following: *The Ideal; Utballa, Jelalu'd-din; Theophania Abbiadjio; Medallion; Lubonka; Lozha v Odesskoy opere* (A Box at the Odessa Opera); *Sud svyeta* (The World's Judgement); and *Naprasniy Dar* (A Fruitless Gift). She wrote under the pseudonym of *Zeneida R—va*, and was hailed by the greatest Russian literary critic Byelinsky as a "Russian George Sand." Her *Complete Works* were published in four volumes at St. Petersburg in 1843, a second edition being issued by N. F. Mertz in the same city in 1905.

Vide the comprehensive biographical sketch by Catherine S. Nekrassova entitled "Yelena Andreyevna Gan," in *Russkaya Starina* (Russian vich von Hahn (d. before 1830) and Countess Elizabeth Maksimovna von Pröbsen.[9] The family was descended from an old Mecklenburg family, the Counts Hahn von Rottenstern-Hahn, one branch of which had emigrated to Russia a century or so before. Alexis G. von Hahn was a famous General in the Army of Field Marshal Suvorov and won a decisive battle in the St. Gothard Alps, at a spot named Devil's Bridge, on the River Reuss. He was named Commander of the city of Zürich in Switzerland, during the period of occupation. Not much is known about his wife, H.P.B.'s paternal grandmother, but Vera P. de Zhelihovsky, H.P.B.'s sister, says that it was from her that H.P.B. inherited her "curly hair" and her vivaciousness.[10]

When Helena was born—she was the couple's first child—her father was absent in Poland, at the Russo-Polish war which lasted until September, 1831.

The first ten years of Helena's life were spent in frequent changes from one place of residence to another, partly due to the fact that her father's battery of Horse-Artillery was being transferred from place to place, and partly because of the precarious health of her mother.[11]

In the summer of 1832, her father returned from Poland and they went to live in a small community called Romankovo, in the Province of Ekaterinoslav.[12] Towards the end of 1833, or the beginning of 1834, they moved to Oposhnya, a small place in the Province of Kiev.[13] After

---

Old Days), Vol. LI, August and September, 1886, pp. 335-54, 553-74. A brief account by Lydia P. Bobritsky entitled "Helena Andreevna Hahn," in *The Theosophical Forum*, Vol. XXVI, August, 1948, based primarily upon the Preface to the 2nd edition of her *Complete Works*, St. Petersburg, 1905.

[9] H.P.B.'s father, Peter Alexeyevich, had at least seven brothers and sisters. Among them, Ivan Alexeyevich who was Postmaster-General at St. Petersburg.

[10] Vera P. de Zhelihovsky, *Kak ya bila malen'koy* (When I was Small), 2nd rev. and enl. edition, St. Petersburg, A. F. Devrient, 1894, p. 243.

[11] A. P. Sinnett, *The Letters of H. P. Blavatsky to A. P. Sinnett*, New York, Frederick A. Stokes, 1924, p. 150.

[12] C. S. Nekrassova, "Helena Andreyevna Gan," in *Russkaya Starina*, Vol. LI, August and September, 1886, p. 344.

[13] V. P. de Zhelihovsky, *Moyo otrochestvo* (My Adolescence), St. Petersburg, A. F. Devrient, 3rd ed., p. 76.

other frequent changes of location, they returned to Romankovo for a time.[14]

During this period, Helena's brother Alexander (Sasha) was born; however, he soon became ill and died at Romankovo, where he was buried.[15]

In the same year of 1834, Helena's grandfather, Andrey Mihailovich de Fadeyev became a member of the Board of Trustees for the Colonizers, and moved with his wife to Odessa. Helena went with her mother to stay with them.[16] While there, Helena's sister, Vera, was born on April 17/29, 1835.[17]

Sometime during 1835, Helena and her parents travelled in the Ukraine and in the Provinces of Tula and Kursk.[18] In the Spring of 1836, the family went to St. Petersburg, where the father's battery had been recently transferred.[19] At about this time, A. M. de Fadeyev (Helena's grandfather) was appointed Trustee for the nomadic Kalmuk tribes in the Province of Astrakhan.[20] After a business trip to St. Petersburg, on which his daughter Nadyezhda accompanied him, he left for Astrakhan in May, 1836, or early Summer. Helena, with her mother and sister Vera, went with them, while her father returned to the Ukraine. They remained in Astrakhan for about a year.[21]

In May, 1837, the grandparents, accompanied by Helena, her mother and her sister Vera, went to Zheleznovodsk in the Caucasus, for treatment in the hot water springs.[22]

Later in the same year, Helena, with her mother and sister, resumed their nomadic life, going first to Poltava. It is here that her mother met Miss Antonya Christianovna Kühlwein, who became governess and friend of the family.[23]

---

[14]Nekrassova, *op.cit.*, pp. 346-47.
[15]V. P. de Zhelihovsky, "Helena Andreyevna Gan," in *Russkaya Starina*, Vol. LIII, March, 1887, p. 734; Nekrassova, *op.cit.*, p. 348.
[16]A. M. de Fadeyev, *Vospominaniya*.
[17]Nekrassova, *op.cit.*, pp. 347-48.
[18]Nekrassova, *op.cit.*, pp. 349, 353.
[19]*Ibid.*, pp. 349-50.
[20]Sinnett, *op.cit.*, p. 150; Nekrassova, *op.cit.*, p. 353.
[21]Zhelihovsky, *Ruskaya Starina*, March, 1887, pp. 751-52; de Fadeyev, *Vospominaniya*; Nekrassova, *op.cit.*, p. 354; H.P.B.'s Letter to P. C. Mitra, April 10, 1878; *H.P.B. Speaks*, Vol. 1, p. 109.
[22]Nekrassova, *op.cit.*, p. 556; Zhelihovsky, *op.cit.*, p. 752.
[23]*Ibid.*, p. 500; Zhelihovsky, *op.cit.*, pp. 752-54.

In the Spring of 1838, Helena's mother's condition became more serious, and they moved to Odessa, for mineral water treatments.[24] In June of 1839, the family secured the additional services of an English governess, Miss Augusta Sophia Jeffers, who came from Yorkshire.[25]

In early December of the same year, Helena's grandparents moved to Saratov on the Volga, where A. M. de Fadeyev had become Governor of the Province. Helena, her mother and her sister, Vera, joined them in that city.[26]

In June, 1840, Helena's brother Leonid was born in Saratov (he died Oct. 27/Nov. 9, 1885, at Stavropol').[27] In the Spring of 1841, Helena went with her family to join her father in the Ukraine.[28]. In the early Spring of 1842, they moved to Odessa again, together with the two governesses and Dr. Vassiliy Nikolayevich Benzengr, who attended Helena's mother. In May of the same year, the grandparents de Fadeyev came to Odessa to visit them.[29]

On June 24/July 6, 1842, Helena's mother, Helena Andreyevna von Hahn, died at Odessa, as a result of her protracted illness, and in the Fall of the same year the children went to live with their grandparents in Saratov.[30] They stayed there until the end of 1845, living in the city during the Winter months, and in the neighboring countryside in Summer.[31] It must have been towards the end of this period

---

[24] Zhelihovsky, *Russkaya Starina*, March, 1887, p. 754.

[25] Sinnett, *op.cit.*, pp. 149-50; Sinnett, *Incidents in the Life of H. P. Blavatsky*, London, George Redway, 1886, p. 24; Zhelihovsky, *op.cit.*, p. 756; Nekrassova, *op.cit.*, pp. 562-63.

[26] de Fadeyev, *op.cit.*; Zhelihovsky, *op.cit.*, pp. 762-63; Nekrassova, *op.cit.*, p. 565.

[27] Nekrassova, *op.cit.*, p. 565; Zhelihovsky, *op.cit.*, p. 766.

[28] Nekrassova, *op.cit.*, p. 567.

[29] Zhelihovsky, *op.cit.*, p. 766; Nekrassova, *op.cit.*, p. 573. The period of 1837-42 is described in a very entertaining manner by Vera Petrovna de Zhelihovsky, H.P.B.'s sister, in her book for children entitled *Kak ya bila malen'koy* (When I was Small), 2nd rev. and enl. ed., St. Petersburg, A. F. Devrient, 1894; 269 pp., fig., plates.

[30] Zhelihovsky, *Moyo otrochestvo*, pp. 4-15, 76; Nekrassova, *op.cit.*, p. 573; Sinnett, *Letters, etc.*, pp. 159-60; Sinnett, *Incidents*, etc., pp. 24-25; Zhelihovsky, *Russkaya Starina*, March, 1887, p. 766; Blavatsky, *Isis Unveiled*, II, 600.

[31] Zhelihovsky, *Moyo otrochestvo*, pp. 15-61, 69-160; Zhelihovsky, *Kak ya bila malen'koy*, chapters x and xi.

H. P. BLAVATSKY IN HER EARLY YOUTH

HELENA PAVLOVNA DE FADEYEV
1789-1860
H.P.B.'s maternal grandmother.

ANDREY MIHAILOVICH DE FADEYEV
1789-1867
H.P.B.'s maternal grandfather.

HELENA ANDREYEVNA VON HAHN
1814-1842
H.P.B.'s mother.

VERA PETROVNA DE ZHELIHOVSKY
1835-1896
H.P.B.'s sister.
(*Consult the Bio-Bibliographical Index*)

that H.P.B., then 13, rode a horse which became frightened and bolted—with her foot caught in the stirrup. She felt someone's arms around her body supporting her until the horse was stopped.[32]

On the authority of Helena's sister Vera,[33] it would appear that their father, then living far away and quite alone, and knowing that his children would soon be going to live in the Caucasus with their grandparents, came to see them at Saratov during the Summer of 1845, spending a month there. The family had not seen him for three years and had some difficulty recognizing him, as he had aged and changed greatly. The time of this visit is rather well determined by the fact that Vera says she was then in her "eleventh year."[34]

Sometime before the end of 1845, Helena apparently visited the Ural Mountains and Semipalatinsk with an uncle who had property in Siberia, on the boundary of Mongolia, and made numerous excursions beyond the frontiers.[35]

In January, 1846, Helena's grandfather, A. M. de Fadeyev, was appointed by the Viceroy of the Caucasus, Prince Mihail Semyonovich Vorontzov, to the post of Director of the Department of State Lands in Trans-Caucasia.[36] The last part of the 1845-1846 Winter season, and the Summer of 1846, were spent in and around Saratov.[37]

In the middle of August, 1846, the grandparents and one of the aunts, Miss Nadyezhda A. de Fadeyev, moved to Tiflis in Georgia

---

[32]Madame Pissareva's account in *The Theosophist*, Vol. XXXIV. January, 1913, p. 503.

[33]Zhelihovsky, *Moyo otrochestvo*, pp. 165-68.

[34]Writing to Sinnett (*Letters*, etc., 150) who was importuning her for data regarding her early life, H.P.B. said that she was on a visit to London and France with her father in 1844. It is then that she is supposed to have taken music lessons from Moscheles, and to have lived with her father at Bath. There is no confirmation whatever of any such trip at that time. It should be borne in mind that such a trip would have started from Saratov on the Volga where the family then lived. We have just seen that in the Summer of 1845, in Vera's "eleventh year," they had a visit from their father, who spent only one month with them, and had not seen them for three years. Any trip abroad, which in those days took considerable time, does not seem to fit into the picture at all.

[35]Blavatsky, *Collected Writings*, Vol. VI, pp. 293-94.

[36]Zhelihovsky, *Moyo otrochestvo*, p. 171.

[37]*Ibid.*, pp. 160-73.

(Caucasus), while Helena, Vera, Leonid, their married aunt, Catherine A. de Witte, with her husband and two children, and the two teachers, Mme. Pecqœur and Monsieur Tutardo, moved to a country place on the other side of the Volga, near the village of Pokrovskoye.[38]

They returned to Saratov in the middle of December for the rest of the Winter of 1846-47.[39]

In the beginning of May, 1847, the children, accompanied by Catherine A. de Witte and Antonya Kühlwein started on their journey to Tiflis, to rejoin their grandparents. With no railways or paved roads, such a journey was a very serious venture. They first went down the Volga on the *SS. St. Nicholas,* stopping for two days at Astrakhan. From there they sailed on the *SS. Teheran* along the coast of the Caspian Sea as far as Baku, where they arrived on May 21st o.s., and the very next day started for Tiflis in horse-drawn carriages.[40] On the 23rd they reached Shemaha and remained there for about a month with their grandparents and aunt Nadyezhda, who had come to meet them.[41] In the middle of June the journey to Tiflis was resumed, via Ah-su, the Shemaha pass, and across the river Kura which they forded at Minguichaur, staying a day at Elizabethpol'. They reached Tiflis towards the end of June.[42]

Late in the Summer of the same year the family went to Borzhom, a resort on the estate of Grand Duke Mihail Nikolayevich, and then to the hot baths of Abbas-Tuman, staying at Ahaltzih on their way.[43] They returned to Tiflis at the end of August, and occupied the old Sumbatov mansion through the Winter season of 1847-48.[44]

In the beginning of May, 1848, Helena went with both of her aunts and her uncle Yuliy F. de Witte, to Pyatigorsk and Kislovodsk for "water cures," narrowly escaping disaster from an avalanche between Koyshaur and Kobi.[45] At the end of August they left Pyatigorsk for the German Colony of Elizabethal' to join the rest of the family there, going later to Ekatarinenfeld, a water resort.[46]

The Winter season of 1848-49 was spent at Tiflis in the mansion

---

[38] *Ibid.,* pp. 173 *et seq.,* 198; de Fadeyev, *op.cit.*
[39] Zhelihovsky, *op.cit.,* p. 213.
[40] Zhelihovsky, *Moyo otrochestvo,* pp. 228-46.
[41] *Ibid.,* pp. 249-51.
[42] *Ibid.,* pp. 251-58.
[43] *Ibid.,* pp. 263-66.
[44] *Ibid.,* pp. 269-77.
[45] *Ibid.,* p. 277.
[46] *Ibid.,* pp. 290-92.

of the old Princes Chavchavadze. During that Winter Helena became betrothed to Nikifor Vassilyevich Blavatsky.[47]

In the Spring or early Summer of 1849, Helena appears to have run away from home, possibly following a certain Prince Golitzin, a student of the occult, regarding whom very little information is available. According to Madame M. G. Yermolova, this escapade had some connection with the prospective marriage plans, but the truth about it is not known.[48]

At the end of June, the whole family, including uncle Rostislav, went to Gerger, in the vicinity of Yerivan', and thence to the settlement of Dzhelal-ogli (Kamenka) for the marriage ceremony.[49]

It was there that Helena married N. V. Blavatsky,[50] July 7, 1849,

---

[47] Zhelihovsky, *Moyo otrochestvo*, pp. 293-96.

[48] E. F. Pissareva, *H. P. Blavatsky. A Biographical Sketch* (Russian text), 2nd rev. ed., Geneva, Editorial Offices of *Vestnik*, 1937, pp. 36-38; Madame Pogosky, *The Theosophist*, Vol. XXXIV, July, 1913.

[49] Zhelihovsky, *op.cit.*, pp. 296-98; de Fadeyev, *op.cit.*, II, 113.

[50] Nikifor Vassilyevich Blavatsky was born in 1809, and belonged to the landed gentry of the Province of Poltava in the Ukraine. He attended the Poltava Gymnasium for the Gentry, and became at the end of 1823 a clerk in the Office of the Civil Governor of Poltava. In 1829 he was transferred to Georgia, Caucasus, in the same capacity. In 1830 he served for some months on the Staff of the Commander in Chief, Field Marshal Count Paskevich-Yerivansky, and until 1835 was Assistant Journalist in that Office. He was then temporarily attached to the Office of the Commissary of the Active Army, and in 1839 was transferred to the Office of the Civil Government of Trans-Caucasia. In 1840 he became Inspector of the Police at Shemaha. In 1842-43 he was Head of various *uyezds* in the Caucasus. After a short residence in Persia, he was appointed Nov. 27, 1849, Vice-Governor of the newly formed Province of Yerivan', and governed it during the absence of the Military Governor. In 1857 he was temporarily appointed to an International Committee to investigate controversial issues concerning the frontiers.

In the Summer of 1860 he was given a two months leave of absence and went to Berlin for treatments. This he repeated the following Summer. He resigned as Vice-Governor Nov. 19, 1860, and was assigned to the Central Administration Office of the Viceroy. His resignation from all positions was accepted in Dec., 1864. At that time he had a small estate in the Province of Poltava, and stated in a contemporary document that he was still married. (Cf. *Service Record* leaving with her husband the same day for Darachichag (meaning "valley of flowers"), a mountain resort near Yerivan'.[51] The actual date is given by Sinnett,[52] and may be "old style." She tried to escape during this trip.[53] The months of July and August must have been spent in that resort, where the newly-weds were visited at the end of August by Helena's aunts and grandparents. After a brief visit, they all went to Yerivan', visiting on their way the ancient monastery of Echmiadzin.[54]

The stories of Helena's horseback rides around Mount Ararat and the neighboring countryside probably belong to this period, when she was accompanied by a Kurd tribal chief named Safar Ali Bek Ibrahim Bek Ogli, who was detailed as her personal escort, and who once saved her life.

It is improbable that the real reason or purpose underlying Helena's early and rather strange marriage will ever definitely be known, and it is certainly unwise to accept too readily certain alleged reasons that have been advanced to explain it. According to Madame Pissareva,[55]

---

drawn up in 1864, and which is on file in the Central State Historical Archives of the U.S.S.R.) Throughout his career, N. V. Blavatsky served in civilian capacities, and his civilian rank was no higher than that of Civil Councillor (*statsky sovyetnik*), which was granted to him Dec. 9, 1856.

All efforts to ascertain the year of N. V. Blavatsky's death have proved fruitless. It is known, however, from a letter written by Nadyezhda A. de Fadeyev to H.P.B. and dated October 1/13, 1877, that he was alive then and living in Poltava.

[51] Zhelihovsky, *op.cit.*, pp. 298-99.

[52] Although the year of Helena's marriage has been stated by various writers to have been 1848, and even she herself wrote to Prince Dondukov-Korsakov that it took place "during the Spring of 1848" (*H.P.B. Speaks*, II, 64), nevertheless, a careful month-by-month account of events written by her own sister, Vera Petrovna de Zhelihovsky (*My Adolescence*), establishes the date as 1849. Vera specifically states that when the family went to Gerger for the Summer—and this was prior to Helena's marriage—her cousin, Serguey Yulyevich de Witte (the future Prime Minister), had just been born, and this event occured June 17/29, 1849.

[53] *Incidents*, etc., pp. 56-57.

[54] Zhelihovsky, *op.cit.*, p. 303; Col. Henry S. Olcott, *People from the Other World*, Hartford, Conn., American Publ. Co., 1875, p. 320.

[55] *The Theosophist*, Vol. XXXIV, January, 1913.

this marriage to a middle-aged and unloved man, with whom she could have nothing in common, can be explained by a keen desire to gain more freedom. According to the account of her aunt, Nadyezhda A. de Fadeyev,[56] Helena had been defied one day by her governess to find any man who would be her husband, in view of her temper and disposition. The governess, to emphasize her taunt, said that even the old man she had found so ugly and had laughed at so much, calling him a "plumeless raven," would refuse her as a wife. That was too much for Helena, and three days later she made him propose. This version seems to be somewhat corroborated by H.P.B. herself,[57] although it would appear that she was under the impression she could "disengage" herself just as easily as she had become "engaged."

However, a completely false judgment could result on this subject, unless special attention is given to a letter written by H.P.B. to her friend, Prince Dondukov-Korsakov, in which somewhat obscure but nevertheless half transparent *occult* hints are given in connection with this marriage. The student must be left to his own intuition to unravel the nature of these hints, which H.P.B. very likely did not wish to explain with any degree of detail.[58] Whatever may have been the real reason and purpose, superficial judgment based primarily upon printed or written statements, or the speculations of others, is bound to lead one astray in this matter.

In October 1849, Helena left her husband and started on horseback for Tiflis to rejoin her relatives. The family decided to send her to her father who at the time was apparently in the vicinity of St. Petersburg, having recently remarried.[59] He was to meet her at Odessa. Accompanied by two servants, she was sent by land to catch the steamer at Poti on the Black Sea coast of the Caucasus. Helena contrived in some way or other to miss the boat. Instead, she boarded the English vessel *SS.Commodore*, then in the harbor, and through a liberal outlay of money persuaded the skipper to fall in with her plans. Accompanied by her servants, she took passage for Kerch in the Crimea. The steamer was due to proceed from there to Taganrog, on the Sea of Azov, and thence to Constantinople. Arriving at Kerch, Helena sent her servants ashore to procure apartments and prepare for her landing the following morning. In the night, however, she

---

[56]Sinnett, *Incidents,* etc., p. 54.
[57]Sinnett, *Letters,* etc., p. 157.
[58]*H.P.B. Speaks,* II, 61-65.
[59]Zhelihovsky, *Moyo otrochestvo,* p. 299. He had married Baroness von Lange (d. 1851).

sailed on the *SS. Commodore* for Taganrog and Constantinople.⁶⁰ At this point began a long period of wandering all over the world extremely difficult to trace in any coherent manner.

On arrival at Constantinople, Helena seems to have run into some trouble with the skipper and had to go ashore in a caique with the connivance of the steward. In the city she met an old family friend, a Countess K—(most likely Kisselev).⁶¹

It would seem that the rest of the year 1849 and part of 1850 were spent by Helena travelling in Greece, various parts of Eastern Europe, Egypt and Asia Minor, probably in the company of Countess Kisselev, at least part of the time.⁶² It is possible that during this period she met at Cairo the Copt occultist, Paulos Metamon. Helena's own statement that her life was saved in Greece by an Irishman named Johnny O'Brien may refer to this period also, even though she places this event in 1851.⁶³

The period of 1850-51 presents many uncertainties. Helena must have been in Paris sometime during this period; also in London where she met a friend of the family, Princess Bagration-Muhransky;⁶⁴ she may have made some short tours on the Continent;⁶⁵ she speaks⁶⁶ of being alone in London in the early part of 1851, and living in Cecil St. in furnished rooms, then at the Mivart's (now Claridge's) Hotel with the Princess. After the latter had left, she continued to stay there with her demoiselle de compagnie; she also speaks of having lived in a large hotel somewhere between the City and the Strand.⁶⁷

H.P.B. told Countess Constance Wachtmeister that she met her Teacher, Master M., in the physical body for the first time in London,

---

⁶⁰Sinnett, *Incidents*, etc., pp. 57-58.

⁶¹Sinnett, *op.cit.*, pp. 58-59.

⁶²*Ibid.*, pp. 58-60; Olcott, *Old Diary Leaves*, I, p. 432; *Scrapbook*, Vol. I, p. 48; *The Theosophist*, Vol. V, April, 1884, pp. 167-68; Olcott, *People from the Other World*, pp. 328-32; *Isis Unveiled*, Vol. I, pp. 382, 474.

⁶³H.P.B. to Georgina Johnston, undated but written from London in 1887.

⁶⁴Sinnett, *op.cit.*, p. 61.

⁶⁵*Ibid.*, p. 62.

⁶⁶Sinnett, *Letters*, etc., p. 150.

⁶⁷Sinnett, *Letters*, etc., p. 150; *H.P.B. Speaks*, Vol. II, Adyar, The Theos. Publ. House, 1951, pp. 66-67.

and that this took place in Hyde Park,[68] "in the year of the first Nepal Embassy," as she told Sinnett.[69] The embassy of the Nepal Prime Minister, Prince Jung Bahâdur Koonwar Rânajee, took place in 1850; his party left Calcutta April 7, 1850, and sailed from Marseilles to Calcutta December 19th of the same year. The approximate time when H.P.B. met her Master would therefore be in the Summer of 1850. However, in her *Sketchbook*, now in the Adyar Archives, H.P.B. says that she met her Teacher at Ramsgate, on her twentieth birthday, August 12, 1851. She informed Countess Wachtmeister, however, that "Ramsgate" was a blind.[70] In connection with both of these dates we run into several difficulties. According to the Countess, H.P.B.'s father was in London at the time, and H.P.B. consulted him about the Master's offer to co-operate "in a work which he was about to undertake." From H.P.B.'s sister's account of their youthful years, however, one gathers the impression that their father, who became a widower for a second time in 1851, was then in Russia. Writing to Sinnett,[71] H.P.B. herself says that she was alone in London in 1851, and not with her father. Moreover, the Countess states that, after meeting the Master, H.P.B. soon left London for India.[72] This, however, could refer to the year 1854 when she met her Teacher in London once again.

It is fairly certain or at least probable that H.P.B. went to Canada sometime in the Fall of 1851, to study the Indians, and stayed at Quebec.[73] From there she went to New Orleans, to study the practice of Voodoo; she was warned in a vision of the dangers connected with Voodooism. She then proceeded through Texas to Mexico; she speaks of a Père Jacques, an old Canadian she met in Texas, who saw her through some perils to which she was then exposed. During this period she seems to have received a legacy of some 80,000 rubles from "one of her godmothers."[74] She bought some land in America,

---

[68] Countess Constance Wachtmeister, *Reminiscences of H. P. Blavatsky and "The Secret Doctrine,"* London, Theos. Publ. Society, 1893, pp. 56-58.
[69] Sinnett, *op.cit.*, p. 150.
[70] Wachtmeister, *op.cit.*, p. 58, footnote.
[71] Sinnett, *Letters*, etc., p. 150.
[72] Wachtmeister, *op.cit.*, p. 57.
[73] Sinnett, *Incidents*, etc., p. 62.
[74] According to the tradition of the Greek Orthodox Church, it was permitted to have more than one "godmother" or "godfather," but ordinarily there was only one of each.

but did not remember where and lost all papers connected therewith.[75]

Her travels continued during the year 1852. On her way to South America, H.P.B. met a Hindu chela at Copán, Honduras. She must have travelled extensively through both Central and South America, visiting ancient ruins. She speaks of having "business relations" with an old native priest of Peru, and to have travelled with him or another Peruvian in the interior of the land.[76]

Sometime during 1852 she went to the West Indies; she had written to "a certain Englishman" whom she had met in Germany two years before, and whom she knew to be on the same quest as hers, to join her in the West Indies, in order to go to the Orient together. Both the Englishman and the Hindu chela apparently joined her there, and all three went via the Cape to Ceylon, and thence in a sailing boat to Bombay.[77]

After their arrival at Bombay, the party dispersed. H.P.B. was bent on an attempt to get into Tibet through Nepal alone. This first attempt failed through what she believed to be the opposition of the British Resident. When she tried to cross the Rangît river, she was reported by a guard to Captain C. Murray, who went after her and brought her back. She stayed with Captain and Mrs. Murray for about a month, then left and was heard from as far as Dinâjpur.[78] She says that she stayed in India "nearly two years, receiving money each month from an unknown source."[79]

H.P.B. appears to have gone to Southern India, and thence to Java and Singapore, apparently on her way back to England.[80] From a certain statement of hers, it would appear that she took passage on the *SS. Gwalior* "which was wrecked near the Cape," and was saved with about twenty others.[81]

---

[75]Sinnett, *op.cit.*, pp. 62-65; Letter from H.P.B. to Sydney and Herbert Coryn, November 2, 1889.

[76]Sinnett, *op.cit.*, p. 66; Blavatsky, *Isis Unveiled*, I, 546-48, 595-99.

[77]Sinnett, *Incidents*, etc., pp. 65-66; Sinnett, *Letters*, etc., p. 157.

[78]Sinnett, *Incidents*, etc., p. 66; Olcott, *Old Diary Leaves*, I, 265; *The Theosophist*, Vol. XIV, April, 1893, pp. 429-31: "Traces of H.P.B.," by Col. H. S. Olcott.

[79]*H.P.B. Speaks*, Vol. II, p. 20.

[80]Sinnett, *Incidents*, etc., p. 66.

[81]*H.P.B. Speaks*, Vol. II, p. 20. This steamship, however, could not be identified in the records of Lloyds of London.

HELENA PETROVNA BLAVATSKY

Her sister Vera speaks of her musical talents and of the fact that she was a member of the Philharmonic Society in London. This could have occurred at this period, sometime in 1853.[82]

On September 14/26, 1853, Turkey declared war on Russia, and the English and French Fleets entered the Black Sea in late December. According to the testimony of her sister, H.P.B. was detained in England by a contract, and this was during the Crimean War.[83] Nevertheless, it was not until April 11/23, 1854, that Emperor Nicholas I issued a public Manifesto regarding a declaration of war against England and France. The Allies decided upon an expedition to the Crimea on August 14th, 1854.

It is almost certain that H.P.B. was in London in the Summer of 1854, because she says that she met her Master "in the house of a stranger in England, where he had come in the company of a dethroned native prince." This was undoubtedly Prince Dhuleep Singh, Mahârâja of Lahore.[84] The latter, a son of the famed Ranjît Singh, sailed from India April 19, 1854, accompanied by his guardian, Sir John Login. They arrived at Southampton on the *SS. Colombo,* Sunday, June 18, 1854, and the Prince was presented to the Queen July 1st. If H.P.B.'s statement is not a blind, we have here a fairly accurate date in an otherwise very uncertain period in her travels.

Somewhat later in the Summer or Fall of 1854, H.P.B. set out for America again, landing in New York. She went to Chicago and across the Rockies to San Francisco, with a caravan of emigrants, probably in a covered wagon.[85] It is not clear whether she went to

---

[82]*Rebus,* St. Petersburg, No. 40, 1883, p. 357.
[83]*Ibid.*
[84]"From the Caves and Jungles of Hindostan," Chapter XXI, first published in *Moskovskiya Vedomosty* (Moscow Chronicle), April 29, 1880; *Sir John Login and Dhuleep Singh,* by Lady Login; *Illustrated London News,* Sat., June 24, 1854: "A Distinguished Foreigner"; also issue of July 8, 1854; *The Morning Chronicle,* Monday, June 19, 1854.
[85]Sinnett, *Incidents,* etc., pp. 66-67. It was probably during this trip West that H.P.B. stayed overnight with Mrs. Emmeline Blanche (Woodward) Wells, Editor and Publisher of *The Woman's Exponent,* in Salt Lake City, Utah. Mrs. E. B. Wells (1828-1921) belonged to a Mormon family. We have from her pen a volume of poems, *Musings and Memories* (Salt Lake City: C. Q. Cannon & Sons Co., 1896; 2nd ed., publ. by "The Desert News," 1915). Mrs. Daisie Woods Allen,

South America on this trip, but it is likely that she remained on the American Continent until the Fall of 1855. She then left for India via Japan and the Straits, landing at Calcutta.[86]

H.P.B. engaged in widespread travel throughout India. At Lahore she met a German ex-Lutheran minister by the name of Kühlwein, known to her father (possibly a relative of their governess), and his two companions, the Brothers N——, all of whom had formed the plan to penetrate Tibet under various disguises. They went together through Kashmîr to Leh, the chief city of Ladak, at least part of the time accompanied by a Tartar Shaman who was on his way home to Siberia. According to Sinnett, H.P.B. crossed into Tibetan territory, with the help of this Shaman, while the others were prevented from carrying out their plan.[87] Finding herself in a critical situation, she was rescued by some Lamaist horsemen apprized of the situation by the Shaman's thought.[88]

These adventures have been connected by A. P. Sinnett and other writers with those described in *Isis Unveiled*.[89] The latter narrative concerns the exhibition of psychological powers by a Shaman. This description mentions the neighorhood of Islamâbâd (Anantnag) which is considerably West of Leh, in the Kashmîr Valley, or *away* from Tibetan territory, and curiously enough, the sandy deserts of Mongolia, which geographically are thousands of miles away. Moreover Ladak is spoken of as Central Tibet. All this gives rise to much confusion so that no definite picture can be outlined.

Moreover, we are confronted by various additional difficulties, some of them geographical. Ladak (or Ladakh) and Baltistan are provinces of Kashmîr, and the name of Ladak belongs primarily to the broad valley of the upper Indus, but includes also several surrounding districts in political connection with it. It is bounded North by the Kuenlun range and the slopes of the Karakorum, North-West and West by Baltistan which has been known as Little Tibet, South-

---

who was Mrs. Wells' granddaughter, was told about H.P.B.'s visit by her grandmother who also mentioned the fact that H.P.B. was at the time wearing heavy men's shoes as she intended to travel over rugged country. On the testimony of "old-timers," H.P.B. resided also for a while in Santa Fe, New Mexico, though this may have been during a previous trip.

[86]Sinnett, *Incidents*, etc., p. 67.
[87]Sinnett, *Incidents*, etc., pp. 67-69.
[88]*Ibid.*, pp. 67-72.
[89]Vol. II, pp. 598-602, 626-28.

West by Kashmîr proper, South by what used to be British Himâlayan territory, and East by the Tibetan provinces of Ngari and Rudog. The entire region is very high, the valleys of Rupshu and the South-East being 15,000 feet, and the Indus near Leh some 11,000 feet, while the average height of the surrounding ranges is some 20,000 feet.

Leh (11,550 feet) is the capital of Ladak, and the road to Leh from Srinagar lies up the lovely Sind valley to the sources of the river at the Pass of Zoji La (11,580 ft.) in the Zaskar range. From Leh there are several routes into Tibet, the best known being that from the Indus valley to the Tibetan plateau, by the Chang La, to Lake Pangong and Rudog (14,900 ft.).

The extremes of altitudes with their corresponding harsh climatic conditions, as well as the barrenness of the land must be taken into account.

H.P.B. seems to have travelled also in Burma, Siam and Assam,[90] and must have contracted a "fearful fever" near Rangoon, "after a flood of the Irrawaddy River," but was cured by a native who used an herb.[91]

On May 10, 1857, the Sepoy Mutiny erupted in a revolt at Meerut, but H.P.B. seems to have left India by then; she went in a Dutch vessel from Madras to Java, going there on orders from her Teacher, "for a certain business," as she said.[92]

H.P.B. must have returned to Europe sometime in 1858, possibly in the early part of the year, and travelled through France and Germany, before returning to Russia.[93] In February, 1858, her sister's first husband, Nikolay Nikolayevich de Yahontov, died, and the widow went with her two infant sons to live temporarily with her father-in-law, General N. A. de Yahontov, prior to moving to her own estate. While her sister gives an account of H.P.B.'s unexpected arrival at Pskov on Christmas Night, 1858, it is known from another source[94] that she must have returned to Russian soil somewhat earlier, perhaps in the late Fall of 1858.

This concludes a major cycle in H.P.B.'s career.

---

[90]*The Theosophist*, Vol. XXXI, July, 1910.
[91]Blavatsky, *Isis Unveiled*, II, 621.
[92]Sinnett, *Letters*, etc., p. 151; Sinnett, *Incidents*, etc., p. 72.
[93]Sinnett, *Incidents*, etc., pp. 72, 74.
[94]A letter written by Nikifor V. Blavatsky to Nadyezhda A. de Fadeyev, and dated Nov. 13 (o.s.), 1858. The original is in the Adyar Archives; text was published in *The Theosophist*, Vol. 80, August, 1959.

After a fairly short stay at Pskov, during which H.P.B.'s psychological powers became widely known throughout the neighborhood, and produced quite a stir among the people, she went with her father, and her half-sister Liza,[95] to St. Petersburg, staying at the Hôtel de Paris. This must have been in the Spring of 1859. From there they all went to Rugodevo, in the Novorzhevsky uyezd, in the Province of Pskov, where the estate which her sister had recently inherited from her late husband was located.[96]

While at Rugodevo, H.P.B. became very ill, due to the re-opening of a wound near her heart, received some years before. This illness seems to have been periodic, lasting from three to four days, during which she was often in a deathlike trance. After these attacks she experienced strange and sudden cures.[97]

In the Spring or Summer of 1860, H.P.B. left with her sister Vera for Tiflis, to visit their grandparents; they travelled for about three weeks in a coach drawn by post horses.[98] On their way, they stopped at Zadonsk, Province of Voronezh, in the territory of the Don Cossacks, a place of pilgrimage where the relics of St. Tihon are preserved. They had an interview with Isidore, then Metropolitan of Kiev, whom H.P.B. had known some years earlier when he was Exarch of Georgia. Becoming aware of her psychological powers the nature of which he seemed to understand, Isidore told her prophetically that she would do a great deal of good to her fellowmen if she used these powers with discrimination.[99]

It is known that, while at Tiflis, in the Caucasus, H.P.B. lived for about a year in the house of her grandparents, the old Chavchavadze

---

[95]H.P.B.'s father, Col. Peter A. von Hahn, had married a second time, a Baroness von Lange, by whom he had a daughter, Elizabeth Petrovna (1850-1908); she married Kiril Ivanovich Beliy (d. 1908).

[96]Sinnett, *Incidents*, etc., pp. 91, 115-116; *Rebus*, No. 4, 1885, p. 41; No. 41, 1883, p. 367; No. 44, 1883, p. 397; Letter of H.P.B. to Sydney and Herbert Coryn, Nov. 2, 1889.

[97]Sinnett, *op.cit.*, p. 134; *Rebus*, No. 44, 1883, pp. 399-400.

[98]Sinnett, *op.cit.*, p. 135; Sinnett, *Letters*, etc., p. 151; V. P. Zhelihovsky, Biographical Sketch of H.P.B. in *Lucifer*, London, Vol. XV, November, 1894, p. 206; *Rebus*, No. 46, 1883, p. 418.

[99]Sinnett, *Incidents*, etc., pp. 137-38; *Lucifer*, Vol. XV, November, 1894, p. 207; *Rebus*, No. 46, 1883, p. 418.

mansion. On August 12/24, 1860, her grandmother, Helena Pavlovna de Fadeyev, passed away.[100]

From some sources it would be easy to get the impression that H.P.B.'s marriage to N. V. Blavatsky had been annulled, or at least that steps had been taken to do so. However, in a letter to Prince Dondukov-Korsakov, she states that after returning to Tiflis, she was reconciled with Blavatsky and, after staying with her grandfather, lived with Blavatsky for about a year, on Golovinsky Avenue, in the house of Dobrzhansky.[101]

It would appear from her own statements,[102] that she left Tiflis in 1863, and went for a while to Zugdidi and Kutais, returning thence to Tiflis again, to live for another year with her grandfather.

During these years in the Caucasus, H.P.B. travelled and lived at one time or another in Imeretia, Guriya and Mingreliya, in the virgin forests of Abhasia, and along the Black Sea Coast. She seems to have studied with native *kudyani*, or magicians, and to have become widely known for her healing powers. At one time she was at Zugdidy and Kutais.[103] For a while she was in the military settlement of Ozurgety, in Mingrelia, and even bought a house there.[104] She engaged in commercial enterprises, such as the floating of lumber and the export of nut-tree-spunk.[105] Sometime during this stay in the Caucasus she was thrown from a horse, sustaining a fracture of the spine. It is during this period in her life that her psychological powers became much stronger and she brought them under the complete control of her will.[106] While at Ozurgety, she had a severe illness; on orders of the local physician, she was taken in a native boat down the river Rion to Kutais. She was then transported in a carriage to Tiflis, apparently near death; soon after, however, she had another of her sudden cures, but remained convalescent for some

---

[100]Sinnett, *op.cit.*, pp. 140-143; Gen. P. S. Nikolayev in *Istorichesky Vestnik*, St. Petersburg, Vol. VI, December, 1885, pp. 623-24; *Rebus*, No. 6, 1885, p. 61.
[101]*H.P.B. Speaks*, Vol. II, pp. 152, 156.
[102]*Ibid.*, p. 156.
[103]*H.P.B. Speaks*, Vol. II, p. 156.
[104]Sinnett, *Incidents*, etc., pp. 143-148; Sinnett, *Letters*, etc., p. 156; *Lucifer*, Vol. XV, December, 1894, p. 273.
[105]*Rebus*, No. 46, 1883, p. 418.
[106]Sinnett, *Incidents*, etc., p. 146; *Rebus, loc.cit.*

time.[107] For a while her uncle, Gen. Rostislav A. de Fadeyev, was gravely concerned about her condition.[108] The seriousness and probable *occult* nature of her illness is clearly hinted at when she states that "between the Blavatsky of 1845-65 and the Blavatsky of the years 1865-82 there is an *unbridgeable gulf*."[109]

Just exactly how and under what circumstances H.P.B. acquired a ward by the name of Yury remains wrapped in mystery, except for the fact that she states this was done to protect the honor of another. That this coincided at least approximately with the period in her life now under consideration, is evidenced by a Passport issued to her on August 23(o.s.), 1862, in the city of Tiflis, signed by Orlovsky, Civil Governor. It states that this document was given "in pursuance of a petition presented by her husband, to the effect that she, Mme. Blavatsky, accompanied by their infant ward Yury, proceeds to the provinces of Tauris, Cherson and Pskoff for the term of one year."[110] It is not known whether such a trip was ever undertaken. On the other hand, H.P.B. wrote[111] that during the Summer of 1865 she was at Petrovsk, in the Daghestan region of the Caucasus, where she witnessed one of the ghastly rituals of a native sect. From this we may infer that she was in the Caucasus at least until the Summer of 1865, especially as she definitely states that she "left for Italy in 1865 and never returned again to the Caucasus."[112]

After leaving Russia she began to travel again; no comprehensive account of this period is possible, however, because of contradictory data and often complete lack of definite information.

She may have spent some time travelling in various parts of the Balkans, Servia and the Karpat Mountains, going later to Greece and Egypt.[113] It is probable that she also went to Syria, the Lebanon, and possibly Persia. It may be that it was during this period that she

---

[107]Sinnett, *ibid.*, pp. 148-50; *The Path*, New York, Vol. X, May, 1895, pp. 34-35.

[108]*The Path*, Vol. X, May, 1895, p. 33.

[109]*H.P.B. Speaks*, Vol. II, p. 58.

[110]The original of this Passport was in the Archives of the Point Loma Theosophical Society; a copy of it exists in the Archives at Adyar.

[111]*Isis Unveiled*, Vol. II, p. 568, footnote.

[112]*H.P.B. Speaks*, Vol. II, p. 156. H.P.B.'s sister, however, gives the date of 1864, as appears from H.P.B.'s manuscript translation of her sister's account, "The Truth about H. P. Blavatsky."

[113]Sinnett, *Letters*, etc., p. 151; *Lucifer*, Vol. XV, December, 1894, p. 273.

became a member of the Druzes and possibly of other mystic orders of Asia Minor. She indicated that she had also been in Italy around that time, "studying with a witch," whatever that may mean.[114]

To this period belong her travel-notes written in French and contained in a small Notebook now in the Adyar Archives. Although these notes are undated, H.P.B. mentions one or two historical facts which provide a key to the dating of the trip she describes. It appears that she was at Belgrade when the Turkish garrison yielded the Fort and the commander, Al Rezi Pasha, withdrew from the territory. This was April 13, 1867. H.P.B. travelled by boat on the Danube, and by coach between various towns of Hungary and Transylvania; she visited, among others, Brassó, Szeben, Fehérvár, Kolozsvár, Nagyvárad, Temesvár, Belgrade, Neusatz, Eszék, etc. These travel-notes are the only definite information concerning her whereabouts during a period which presents a great deal of uncertainty.

Later in 1867, H.P.B. apparently went to Bologna, Italy, still having in her care Yury to whom she was greatly attached; he was in poor health and she was trying to save his life.[115] He died, however, and H.P.B. returned to Southern Russia for a very short visit for the purpose of burying her ward, but did not notify her relatives about being in her homeland. She then returned to Italy on the same passport.[116]

After her travels in the Balkan states, she went to Venice,[117] and was definitely present at the battle of Mentana, November 2, 1867, where she was wounded five times; her left arm was broken in two places by a saber stroke, and she had a musket bullet imbedded in her right shoulder and another in her leg.[118]

In the beginning of the year 1868, H.P.B. was in Florence, on her way to India through Constantinople.[119] She went from Florence to Antivari and towards Belgrade, where she waited, on order of her Teacher, in the mountains, before proceeding to Constantinople; she may have been in the Karpat Mountains and Servia once again.[120]

---

[114]Sinnett, *ibid.*, p. 154.
[115]Sinnett, *Letters*, etc., p. 144; Sinnett, *Incidents*, etc., p. 150.
[116]Sinnett, *Letters*, etc., p. 144.
[117]*Ibid.*, p. 144; *The Mahatma Letters to A. P. Sinnett*, p. 478.
[118]Olcott, *Old Diary Leaves*, Vol. I, pp. 9, 263, 264; *Scrapbook*, Vol. I, p. 17; Sinnett, *Letters*, etc., pp. 144, 151, 152, 153. *The Theosophist*, Vol. XV, October, 1893, p. 16.
[119]Sinnett, *op.cit.*, pp. 151-52.
[120]*Ibid.*, p. 152.

She says she was at Belgrade some three months before the murder of the Hospodar, Prince Mihailo Obrenović of Serbia, which took place June 10, 1868.[121]

It is presumed that H.P.B. went via India to some parts of Tibet, and that this was sometime in 1868; mention has been made of her crossing the Kuenlun Mountains and going via Lake Palti (Yamdok-Tso),[122] although geographically this is inconsistent. It is on this journey to Tibet that she met Master K. H. for the first time, and lived in the house of his sister at Shigadze.[123] This may have been the period when she spent some seven weeks in the forests not far from the Karakorum Mountains.[124]

The subject of H.P.B.'s stay in Tibet is wrapped—conceivably for good and sufficient reasons of her own—in considerable mystery. It is probable that we will never know just exactly when and how many times she penetrated this territory. However, to counter any unfriendly critic who may attempt to deny the fact that she was ever in Tibet, we have from her own pen a very specific statement when she wrote:

". . . I have lived at different periods in Little Tibet as in Great Tibet, and . . . these combined periods form more than seven years . . . What I have said, and repeat now, is, that I have stopped in Lamaistic convents; that I have visited Tzi-gadze, the Tashi-Lhünpo territory and its neighbourhood, and that I have been further in, and in such places of Tibet as have never been visited by any other European, and that he can ever hope to visit."[125]

It is important to bear in mind, that while H.P.B. penetrated far into Tibet proper, it does not mean that *every time* she mentions being in Tibet, she necessarily means Tibet proper, as Ladakh used to be known as Little Tibet, and the term Tibet was used in a very general manner.

Towards the end of 1870, namely, on November 11th, her aunt, Miss Nadyezhda Andreyevna de Fadeyev, received the first known letter from Master K. H. stating that H.P.B. was well and would be back in the family before "18 moons" shall have risen.

---

[121] *Ibid.*, pp. 151-53; *Collected Writings*, Vol. I, "A Story of the Mystical."

[122] Sinnett, *Letters*, etc., p. 215.

[123] *Ibid.*, pp. 153, 215.

[124] *The Path*, Vol. IX, January, 1895, p. 299.

[125] *Light*, London, Vol. IV, No. 188, August 9, 1884, pp. 323-24. Cf. *Collected Writings*, Vol. VI, p. 272.

H. P. BLAVATSKY ABOUT 1865-1868

NADYEZHDA ANDREYEVNA DE FADEYEV
1829-1919
H.P.B.'s favorite aunt with whom she kept a steady correspondence through the years, and who visited her many times abroad. This portrait is preserved in the Adyar Archives.

H.P.B. returned to Europe via the Suez Canal which was opened for travel on November 17, 1869, and passed through it sometime towards the end of 1870, possibly in December.[126] She went to Cyprus and Greece and saw Master Hillarion there.[127] She embarked for Egypt at the port of Piraeus, on the *SS Eunomia*, plying between the Piraeus and Nauplia. Ships were provided in those days with guns and gunpowder as a protection against pirates. Between the islands of Dokos and Hydra, in the sight of the island of Spetsai, in the Gulf of Nauplia, the ship's powder magazine blew up, July 4, 1871, with a considerable loss of life; H.P.B., however, was uninjured. The Greek Government provided the survivors passage to their destination, and so H.P.B. finally reached Alexandria, with hardly any means at all. She seems to have won some money, however, on what she calls "No. 27" and went to Cairo sometime in October or November, 1871. She stayed at the Hôtel d'Orient where she met Miss Emma Cutting (later Mme. Alexis Coulomb) who was able to loan her some money for the time being.[128]

H.P.B. remained in Cairo until about April, 1872. During her stay there, she organized what she calls a *Société Spirite*, for the investigation of phenomena; it would appear that this was done against the advice of Paulos Metamon, a well-known Coptic mystic and occultist with whom she was in touch at the time.[129] The society proved a dismal failure within a fortnight, and H.P.B. was nearly shot by an insane Greek who was obsessed.[130] At one time or another, she lived in Bulak, near the Museum.

She then went to Syria, Palestine and Constantinople; she seems to have been at Palmyra; between Baalbek and the river Orontes, she met Countess Lydia Alexandrovna de Pashkov, and went with her to Dair Mar Maroon between the Lebanon and the Anti-Lebanon Mountains.[131]

She reached Odessa and her family sometime in July, 1872, which

---

[126] *The Theosophist*, Vol. XXXIV, July, 1913, p. 476.

[127] Sinnett, *Letters*, etc., p. 153.

[128] Sinnett, *op.cit.*, pp. 153, 215; *Incidents*, etc., p. 157. Also Greek newspapers of the time.

[129] Dr. A. L. Rawson, "Madame Blavatsky: A Theosophical Occult Apology," Frank Leslie's *Popular Monthly*, XXXIII, Feb., 1892.

[130] Sinnett, *Incidents*, etc., pp. 158-69; *The Theosophist*, Vol. XV, Supplement, November, 1883, p. ix; Olcott, *Old Diary Leaves*, I, 23; J. M. Peebles, *Around the World*, 1874, p. 272.

[131] Sinnett, *Incidents*, etc., pp. 167-68; Olcott, *op.cit.*, I, 334-35.

would be some "18 moons" after the receipt of K.H.'s letter. It is difficult to say whether we can credit Witte's statement to the effect that she opened an ink factory and an artificial flower shop at Odessa during her stay there.[132]

There is some inconclusive information to the effect that H.P.B. made a musical tour in Russia and Europe, as "Madame Laura" during 1872-73, but this cannot be considered reliable.[133]

Her stay in Odessa was short, and she left sometime in April of 1873, going first to Bucharest to visit her friend, Mme. Popesco.[134] From there she proceeded to Paris, presumably on orders from her Teacher.[135] She stayed there with her cousin, Nikolay Gustavovich von Hahn, son of her paternal uncle Gustav Alexeyevich, at rue de l'Université 11, and seems to have intended to settle there for some time.[136] According to Dr. L. M. Marquette,[137] she spent her time in painting and writing, and established close ties of friendship with Monsieur and Mme. Leymarie.

One day, very soon after her arrival in Paris, H.P.B. received "orders" from the "Brothers" to go to New York, and sailed the very next day; this must have been towards the end of June, 1873, as she arrived in New York July 7th.[138]

H.P.B. was very short of money, and the Russian Consul refused to loan her any money. She took quarters in a new tenement house, at 222 Madison St., New York, which was a small experiment in co-operative living launched by some forty women workers. The owner of the house, a Mr. Rinaldo, introduced her to two young Jewish friends of his, and these gave her work designing illustrated advertising-cards; she also seems to have tried some ornamental leather work, but

---

[132] Sinnett, *Incidents*, etc., p. 168; *Letters*, etc., pp. 153, 215; *H.P.B. Speaks*, Vol. I, p. 193.
[133] Olcott, *op.cit.*, I, 458 footnote.
[134] Sinnett, *Letters*, etc., pp. 152-54; *Incidents*, etc., p. 169; *H.P.B. Speaks*, Vol. II, p. 23.
[135] *H.P.B. Speaks*, *loc. cit.*
[136] Sinnett, *Letters*, etc., p. 154; Olcott, *op.cit.*, I, p. 20.
[137] Olcott, *op.cit.*, I, pp. 27-28.
[138] Sinnett, *Letters*, etc., p. 154; Olcott, *op.cit.*, I, p. 20; Sinnett, *Incidents*, etc., p. 175; *The Path*, Vol. IX, February, 1895, p. 385.

soon abandoned that and is said to have made artificial flowers and cravats.[139]

Some time later, a widow (possibly Mme. Magnon), offered to share her home in Henry Street with H.P.B. until her financial difficulties ended. She accepted, and together they inaugurated Sunday meetings at this address.[140]

It was on July 15/27, 1873, that H.P.B.'s father, Col. Peter A. von Hahn, passed away after only three days of illness. From a letter written to H.P.B. by her half-sister Liza (dated October 18th, o.s., 1873) her whereabouts were not definitely known to her family at the time, and so the news about the passing of her father reached her after a three months' delay. She also received at the same time some money, as part of her portion of the estate. She then moved to the North-East corner of 14th Street and Fourth Avenue, in a furnished top-floor room, where she seems to have had a small fire.[141] She also lived on Union Square and on East 16th Street.[142]

It would seem that H.P.B. went for a time to Saugus and lived somewhere near the woods; she also visited Buffalo.[143]

On June 22, 1874, H.P.B. entered a partnership agreement, purchasing land near the villages of Newport and Huntington, in Suffolk County, Long Island, in the State of New York. This was to be a partnership with a French lady by the name of Clementine Gerebko, and in July, 1874, H.P.B. moved to the farm.[144] Inevitably, this affair ended in a row and a lawsuit, which, by the way. H.P.B. won when the case was tried by jury, April 26, 1875. Judgment was filed on June 15, 1875, in the Office of the Clerk of Suffolk County.

It was in July of 1874 that Col. Henry Steel Olcott, while working in his New York law office, had an urge to find out what was then going on in contemporary Spiritualism; he bought a copy of the *Banner of Light* edited in Boston, Mass., and read in it the account of the phenomena that were taking place at the Eddy farmhouse in the township of Chittenden, Vermont. He decided to go and see for himself. After staying there three or four days, he returned to New York

---

[139]Olcott, *op.cit.*, I, pp. 20, 472; *The Word*. Vol. XXII, p. 139; Holt. "A Reminiscence of H. P. Blavatsky in 1873," *The Theosophist*, Vol. LIII, December, 1931.
[140]Holt, *loc.cit.*
[141]Holt, *op.cit.*
[142]Olcott, *Old Diary Leaves*, I, p. 30.
[143]Olcott, *op.cit.*, I, p. 440; *H.P.B. Speaks*. Vol. I, p. 193.
[144]Olcott, *op.cit.*, I, pp. 30-31.

and wrote sometime in August an account for the New York *Sun*.[145] Then he received a proposal from the N.Y. *Daily Graphic* to return to Chittenden to investigate the whole affair thoroughly. He accepted this proposal,[146] and returned to the Eddy farmhouse September 17, 1874.

It was on October 14th that H.P.B., acting on instructions received by her,[147] and having read Col. Olcott's accounts in the papers, went to Chittenden, and thus took place the significant meeting of two of the future Co-Founders of The Theosophical Society.

---

[145] *Ibid.*, I, p. 113.
[146] *Ibid.*, I, pp. 1-5.
[417] Letter from H.P.B. to Dr. F. Hartmann, dated April 13, 1886.

CHRONOLOGICAL SURVEY

OF THE CHIEF EVENTS IN THE LIFE OF H. P. BLAVATSKY AND COL. HENRY S. OLCOTT, FROM SEPTEMBER, 1874, TO DECEMBER, 1878, INCLUSIVE.
(the period to which the material in the present volume belongs)

1874

September 17—H. S. Olcott returns to Chittenden, Vt., to report on the séances of the Eddy Brothers for the New York *Daily Graphic;* takes with him the artist, Mr. Kappes, and intends to stay about twelve weeks (*ODL,* I, 1-5).

September 22—H.P.B. signs a U.S.A. Government application form expressing her intention to become naturalized.

October 14—H.P.B. goes to the Eddys' Farm, Chittenden, Vt., and attends her first séance there, at which she calls forth the appearance of Mihalko, a servant of her aunt, Katherine A. de Witte. Came in company of a French-Canadian lady named Boudreau.
  Meets Colonel Henry Steel Olcott after the noon dinner (*ODL,* I, 1-5; *POW,* 293-306).

October 15-24—A number of séances are held during which H.P.B. calls forth a considerable number of "portrait-pictures," as she called them (*POW,* 310-38, 355-60; *ODL,* I, 8-9).
  While at Chittenden, a wound she had just below the heart, incurred sometime during her travels, re-opened slightly (*ODL,* 1-9).

October 25—Most likely date when H.P.B. returned to New York City, her address being 124 East 16th Street (*MPI-R.,* 255).

October 27—H.P.B. writes her first article for the *Daily Graphic,* entitled "Marvellous Spirit Manifestations," which is published Oct. 30th; flays Dr. Geo. M. Beard.

November 4—First letter from Elbridge Gerry Brown, Editor of the *Spiritual Scientist,* in connection with H.P.B.'s article; sends her a copy of the journal.

November (early)—H.P.B. moves to 16 Irving Place, New York. Col. Olcott calls on her there after returning from Chittenden (*ODL,* I, 10).

November (early)—H.P.B. goes on a brief visit to friends in the country; when she returns, she occupies rooms at 23 Irving Place, a few doors from the Lotos Club and on the same side of the street, this being the home of Dr. and Mrs. I. G. Atwood (*ODL*, I, 15; L. C. Holloway in *Word*, XXII, 136).

November 10—H.P.B. writes her second article against Dr. Beard.

November 12—H.P.B. is interviewed by the *Daily Graphic* (*ODL*, I, 31).

November (middle)—H.P.B. writes to Col. Olcott asking him to secure for her an engagement with a New York Journal (*ODL*, 1, 31).

November 14—H.P.B. writes to A. N. Aksakov, telling him she has been translating into Russian Olcott's articles in the *Daily Graphic*; speaks of knowing Andrew Jackson Davis (*MPI-R*, 256-58).

November (after 18th)—Michael C. Betanelly comes from Philadelphia to New York to meet H.P.B. and Col. Olcott; apparently falls in love with H.P.B. (*ODL*, I, 55; Gen. Lippitt in *Religio-Phil. Journal*, April 28, 1878).

November (later part)—H.P.B. leaves New York and goes to stay in Philadelphia, Penna. Her address is at first 1111 Girard St. (*ODL* I, 34). She seems to have gone there mainly to investigate the genuineness of the Holmes as mediums.

December (first two weeks or so)—H.P.B. attends various séances with the Holmeses, as appears from her own articles written during that time.

December 13—H.P.B. and Col. Olcott are both at Hartford, Conn., in connection with Olcott's forthcoming book, *People from the Other World*; she stays there but a couple of days (*MPI-R*, 259).

1875

January 4—Col. Olcott arrives in Philadelphia and joins H.P.B. at 1111 Girard St. He intends to investigate the mediums Holmeses, for which purpose a Committee is formed (*ODL*, I, 35; *POW*, 452).

January 11—On that date, and on the following two days, private séances are held with Mrs. Holmes, at which H.P.B. herself performs certain phenomena (*ODL*, I, 322; *POW*, 459-65).

January 15-19—Col. Olcott is at Hartford, Conn.

January 19-25—Séances held every day (*POW*, 469-78). Col. Olcott holds his last one on the 25th (*POW*, 476-78).

Jan. 29-Feb. 2—Col. Olcott is at Havana, a village in Schuyler Co., N.Y., to investigate the mediumship of Mrs. Eliza J. Compton (*ODL*, I, 35; *POW*, 483-88).

January (last days)—H.P.B. hurts her leg and injures her knee (*Corson*, Letter No. 1, Feb. 9, 1875). At about this time she moves over to the former address of the Holmeses, 825 North 19th St., Philadelphia, after they had gone away.

February 16—H.P.B. writes her second letter to Prof. Hiram Corson, wherein the important statement is made: "I am here, in this country sent by my Lodge, on behalf of *Truth* in modern Spiritualism, and it is my most sacred duty to *unveil what is*, and expose *what is not*. Perhaps, did I arrive here 100 years *too soon* . . ." (*Corson*, Letter No. 2).

February 19—Col. Olcott is at Hartford, Conn. again; writes from there his art.: "The American Katie King" (*Spir. Scientist*, Mch. 4, 1875).

March 1—Col. Olcott is still at Hartford, Conn., in connection with his forthcoming book.

March 11—Approximate date when Col. Olcott's book, *People from the Other World* comes out; publ. by the American Publishing Co., Hartford, Conn.

March 22—By that date, H.P.B. is at 3420 Sansom St., West Philadelphia, which was the address of Michael C. Betanelly (*HPBSp.*, I, 59-60).

March 24—Col. Olcott visits H.P.B. in Philadelphia.

April 3—H.P.B. marries Michael C. Betanelly, a Georgian engaged in export-import business. The ceremony takes place in the First Unitarian Church of Philadelphia, at Chestnut and van Pelt Streets, the Pastor being the Rev. Wm. H. Furness (acc. to Church Records); Col Olcott is in the city, but not present as a witness (*ODL*, I, 56).

April 4 (16 o.s.)—A. N. Aksakov writes to Col. Olcott asking him to find an American medium to be sent to Russia (*ODL*, I, 79-80).

April 17—Most likely date when the famous Circular from the Brotherhood of Luxor is written, with Col. Olcott as amanuensis; publ. in the *Spiritual Scientist*, April 29th (*ODL*, I, 74-76, 102; *facsimile* in *HPBSp.*, I, pp. 18-19).

April (middle)—H.P.B.'s injured leg has been cured by "John King" but the trouble returns owing to lack of rest (*HPBSp.*, I, 71-77).

April 20—Approximate time when Col. Olcott returns to New York from Philadelphia.

April 26—H.P.B. is at Riverhead, Suffolk Co., Long Island, N.Y., in connection with her pending lawsuit; her case is tried on that date by a jury, the judge being C. E. Pratt (*HPBSp.*, II, 175).
H.P.B. wins the suit and returns at once to Philadelphia.

April (or earlier)—H.P.B. was apparently translating into Russian Buckle's *Hist. of Civilization* and Darwin's *Origin of Species*, while her lawsuit was pending, acc. to statement of her lawyer Ivins (*Ransom*, 71 fn.).

April—It is at about this time that A. P. Sinnett, then in London on leave from India, becomes convinced of the reality of spiritualistic phenomena (unpubl. *Autobiography*).

May 1—The most likely time when Col. Olcott received his first letter from Master Serapis (*LMW*, II, Letter No. 12).

May 13—"Important Announcement" publ. in the *Spiritual Scientist* concerning the formation of Col. Olcott's "Miracle Club." (*ODL*, I, 25, 34).

May (middle)—Likely time when Col. Olcott was taken in as a Neophyte by the Brotherhood of Luxor from whom he received a letter (*facsimile* in *LMW*, II, Letter No. 3).

May 21—H.P.B. entrusted with the task of teaching Col. Olcott, but wishes it had been Robert More instead. Her leg is worse and is becoming paralyzed (*HPBSp.*, I, 37 *et seq.*).

May 26—Betanelly writes to Col. Olcott that H.P.B.'s leg is getting paralyzed and may require amputation. Precipitated message on it from "John King" says he will cure it (Adyar Archives).

May 26—Approximate date when H.P.B. sends Betanelly away (*HPBSp.*, I, 80).

May or June—Approximate time when, in the words of Col. Olcott, "a certain wonderful psycho-physiological change happened to H.P.B. that I am not at liberty to speak about, and that nobody has up to the present suspected . . ." (*ODL*, I, 17-18).
Also approximate time when Col. Olcott was transferred to the Indian Section of the Brotherhood.

June 3—The *Spiritual Scientist* (Vol. II, p. 151) announces H.P.B.'s very serious illness. On June 10 (p. 166) it says that the crisis was reached at midnight, June 3rd, and that H.P.B. is now recovering. Her attendants thought her to be dead, as she lay cold, pulseless, and rigid; her injured leg had swollen to twice the natural size and had turned black; her physician had given her up; but within a few hours the swelling subsided and she revived.

CHRONOLOGICAL SURVEY   lvii

June 15—Judgment in H.P.B.'s case against C. Gerebko filed in the office of the clerk, County of Suffolk, N. Y.

June (middle)—Betanelly is back; writes to Gen. Lippitt that H.P.B. is still very ill; sometimes appears to be "dead"; a great puzzle to doctors (*HPBSp.*, I, 93-96).

June—Most of the month H.P.B. is undergoing some grave trial, most likely an initiation, as would appear from Master Serapis' letters to Col. Olcott (*LMW*, II, Nos. 9, 12, 16; *HPBSp.*, II, 179; *Path*, IX, 269-70, 297).

June 30—Col. Olcott is in Boston for the purpose of investigating the remarkable mediumship of Mrs. Thayer. He is guest at the home of Mr. and Mrs. Charles Houghton in the suburb of Roxbury. H.P.B. is much better; plans to join him there (*ODL*, I, 93; *HPBSp.*, I, 97 *et seq.*).

July 4, 6, 7—Col. Olcott attends private *séances* at the Houghtons.

July 7(?)—H.P.B. writes Gen. Lippitt she is leaving for Boston, on a mission to set right damage done to R. D. Owen by Dr. Child (*HPBSp.*, II, 180).

July 9-10—Approximate time when H.P.B. writes her article entitled "A Few Questions to 'Hiraf'," which she calls her "first occult shot." Publ. July 15 and 22 (*ODL*, I, 103 *et seq.*).

July 21—Another *séance* held at the Houghtons in Boston (*ODL*, I, 93 *et seq.*).

July (end)—Most likely time when Col. Olcott returns to New York. H.P.B. seems to have planned going back to Philadelphia, but was dissuaded from doing so by higher authority, as is evident from letters received by Col. Olcott from Master Serapis (*LMW*, II, Nos. 10 and 11). It was suggested to him to take H.P.B. to New York and to watch over her very closely, as she was undergoing great trials.

August—H.P.B. settles at 46 Irving Place, New York; she and Col. Olcott investigate Mrs. Young's phenomena (*ODL*, I, 85-88).

August—Approximate time when William Quan Judge meets H.P.B. (*Path*, VI, p. 66).

August 30—Col. Olcott's first extended written contribution along occult lines, "The Immortal Life," is published in the New York *Tribune* (*ODL*, I, 110 *et seq.*).

Between Aug. 28 and Sept. 4—Gathering held in H.P.B.'s rooms, 46 Irving Place, New York. In H.P.B.'s own words: "On that evening the first idea of the Theos. Society was discussed." (*Vide* Rev. Dr. J. H. Wiggin's account, *The Liberal Christian*, Sept. 4, 1875; H.P.B.'s comments in *Scrapbook*, Vol. I, pp. 54-55; *ODL*, I, 114-15).

September 7, Tuesday—Meeting at H.P.B.'s rooms, for the purpose of hearing a lecture by George H. Felt, engineer and architect, on the subject of "The Lost Canon of Proportion of the Egyptians, Greeks and Romans." About 17 people present. During the discussion which followed, a suggestion is made that a Society be formed to pursue and promote such occult research. (*ODL*, I, 115-21, and *Lucifer*, XII, April, 1893, p. 105, though the two accounts differ somewhat in details; *NCM*, 296).

September 8, Wednesday—Another meeting at H.P.B.'s rooms, during which a Society is more definitely organized, sixteen persons handing in their names for that purpose. Mr. Felt lectures again. Committee of three is appointed to draft a Constitution and Bylaws (*ODL*, I, 121-22; *facsimile* of Minutes, *Path*, IX, frontispiece for April, 1894, and page 1; *Theos.*, XIV, Nov. 1892, pp. 71-75, for Col. Olcott's account of participants; also *Ransom*, 110-15).

September 13—Another meeting at the same address, during which the name of The Theosophical Society is agreed upon (*Hist. Retr.*, p. 2). Mr. Felt gives another lecture (*ODL*, I, 126).

September 15—H.P.B. goes to Albany, N. Y., intending to go from there to visit the Corsons at Ithaca, N. Y. (Letter of Col. Olcott to Prof. Corson, Sept. 14th, *Corson*, 24).

September 17—Most likely date when H.P.B. arrived at the home of the Corsons, to stay for some weeks (*Corson*, 25).

September 20—H.P.B. writing to A. N. Aksakov from Ithaca, N. Y. says she is now writing a large work which, on the advice of "John King," will be called *Skeleton Key to Mysterious Gates* (*MPI-R*, 274).

October 12(?)—H.P.B. returns to New York at about this time.

October 14—*Séance* with Dr. H. Slade in New York, at which Col. Olcott makes some experiments (*Vide* his acc. in *The Spiritualist*, Jan. 28, 1876, p. 45).

October 16—Meeting of The Theosophical Society held in the drawing-rooms of Mrs. Emma Hardinge-Britten, 206 West 38th Street, New York, at 8 p.m., "to organize and elect officers." H.P.B. is present, having returned from Ithaca. After discussion and alterations, the Bylaws were adopted (*ODL*, I, 133-34).

October 30—Meeting of the T.S. held at the same address as the previous one. The Bylaws were discussed again and the final draft adopted. The Mott Memorial Hall, 64 Madison Avenue, New York, was selected as the Society's meeting place. Officers were elected (*ODL*, I, 134-35; *Ransom*, 81-82).

CHRONOLOGICAL SURVEY   lix

November 6—Col. Olcott goes to Boston to attend as guest the annual dinner of the Boston Press Club (*Spir. Sc.* III, p. 115).

November 17—Meeting of the T.S. in Mott Memorial Hall, 64 Madison Ave., N. Y., at which Col. Olcott delivers his Inaugural Address as President of the T.S. (*ODL*, I, 135; Minutes in *Path*, IX, Apr., 1894, pp. 2-3). During the Address, H.P.B. sat among the audience on the North side of the room.

November (end)—H.P.B. and Col. Olcott take two suites of rooms at 433 West 34th Street, New York, she on the first, and he on the second floor. The writing of *Isis Unveiled* proceeds now without interruptions (*ODL*, I, 203; IV, 187).

December 22—Col. Olcott lectures on "Eastern Magic and Western Spiritualism" at Brooklyn Institute, New York (*Spir. Sc.*, Dec. 23, 1875, p. 190).

December 26—H.P.B.'s first article in the N.Y. *Sun*, "A Story of the Mystical," published.

1876

January—E. Gerry Brown begins gradually to withdraw from close collaboration with the Founders (*Ransom*, 71).

January 8—H.P.B., writing to Prof. H. Corson, says that her book is now finished; this is somewhat puzzling, and may refer to a first draft only (*Corson*, 175).

January 12—Wm. Q. Judge invited to assist in the deliberations of the Council of the T.S. Resolution drafted about the T.S. becoming a secret body; to be submitted to the Society at its next regular meeting (*ODL*, I, 145).

January (middle)—Mrs. E. H. Britten's forthcoming work, *Art Magic*, is sent to press (*Spir. Sc.*, Jan. 27, 1876, p. 250).

January (middle)—Approximate time of Charles Sotheran's defection; he resigns from membership in the T.S. and writes against it; has a change of heart six months later and helps with editorial work on *Isis* (*Ransom*, 84).

January—Col. Olcott goes to lecture in Boston, Mass. (*Ransom*, 86). Two of the lectures are held on Jan. 30th.

March 8—Meeting of the T.S. Council; resolved to institute signs of recognition. At about this time the Seal of the T.S. is designed (*ODL*, I, 146).

March 29—Baron de Palm elected on the Council of the T.S. on the resignation of Rev. J. H. Wiggin (*ODL*, I, 149).

April-May—Approximate time when Mrs. Isabelle B. Mitchell, Col. Olcott's sister, her husband and children, come to live in the same apartment house with the Founders (*ODL*, IV, 187; *Ransom*, 90; Holloway in *Word*, XXII, 144-45).

May—The Founders decide on Dr. H. Slade as medium to be sent to Russia, A. N. Aksakov sends $1,000 for his expenses (*ODL*, I, 81 *et seq.*).

May 20—Baron de Palm dies at the Roosevelt Hospital, New York (*ODL*, I, 49). A symbolic memorial service is held in the Masonic Temple, corner of 23rd St., and 6th Ave. (*ODL*, I, 150 *et seq.*).

August (?)—Sometime after de Palm's funeral, H.P.B. and Col. Olcott moved to a flat on the corner of 47th Street and Eighth Avenue. It was here that most of *Isis Unveiled* was written, and it is from here that the Founders left for India (W. Q. Judge in *The Path*, Vol. VIII, pp. 237-39). Some called it the "Lamasery."

August 16—Phenomenon of the passages from the *Dhammapada* precipitated in Col. Olcott's room, endorsed by Serapis (*ODL*, I, 414-15; *LMW*, II, No. 23).

September—H.P.B. "ordered to write *Isis*." This statement contradicts all other evidence on the subject (*ML*, 289).

September-October—Approximate time when the remarkable work entitled *Art Magic* was published, a MS. translated and prepared by Mrs. Emma Hardinge-Britten and attributed to "Chevalier Louis" (*ODL*, I, 185-201).

November 15—Col. Olcott says that from that date there were no more meetings of the T.S. held, and no record in the Society's Minute Book (*Hist. Retr.*, 19).

December 6—Cremation of Baron de Palm's body in the small town of Washington, Wash. Co., Penna.; first cremation in U.S.A. (*ODL*, I, 166 *et seq.*).

December—Most likely time when the room in Mott Memorial Hall was given up, the fees were abolished, and the Bylaws became inoperative (*Ransom*, 90).

1877

January—Approximate time when C. C. Massey and others began meeting together occasionally in London; later in the year, correspondence ensued between them and H.P.B. regarding the formation of a Branch; Miss Kislingbury urges H.P.B. to settle in London (*Ransom*, 100-101).

April 24 (12 old style)—Declaration of war between Russia and Turkey. This gives H.P.B. occasion to write articles in Russian for the *Tiflissky Vestnik*, to help wounded soldiers with the proceeds thereof (*RO*, Nov., 1891, p. 262; *ZhBH*, 15).

May 7—Betanelly writes to H.P.B.; urges her to obtain a divorce (*Theos.*, Aug., 1959).

May 17—Acc. to a letter from J. W. Bouton to Col. Olcott, the first volume of *Isis Unveiled* has been set up and electrotyped; Bouton complains of the high cost of production and of H.P.B.'s constant alterations of the text (*ODL*, I, 216-17).

June 21—*Spiritual Scientist* is temporarily suspended (Vol. VI, p. 186).

July 16—Meeting of the T.S. in connection with powers to be given to Col. Olcott for the work. From this date on, the Council Minute Book records no meetings until Aug. 27, 1878, the final American entry (*Hist. Retr.*, 19).

July—The Founders befriend 13 stranded Muslim Arabs; collect money for them and send them back home with a member of the T.S. (*ODL*, I, 298 et seq.; *Ransom*, 97).

July—Miss Kislingbury, on a visit from England, helps prepare Table of Contents for Vol. II of *Isis*, while Col. Olcott does the one for Vol. I (*Ransom*, 93).

September—Stainton Moses writes to H.P.B. regarding Capt. F. G. Irwin wanting to form a Branch in England (*Ransom*, 98).

September—Approximate time when the first exchange of letters takes place between the Founders and Dayânanda Sarasvatî Swâmi (*ODL*, I, 395; *Ransom*, 98).

September—Approximate time when Dr. Alexander Wilder prepares the Index for *Isis Unveiled* from the advanced sheets; receives a remuneration for this (*Ransom*, 96).

September 29—*Isis Unveiled* is published. 1,000 copies of first printing were exhausted within ten days; first copy off the Press secured by James Robinson, a lawyer, and taken to the newspaper for advance notice. This original ed. has a red binding with a symbolic figure of Isis in gold on the spine. As far as is known, the MSS. was destroyed (*ODL*, I, 225, 294; Holloway in *Word*, XXII, 141; *MPI-R*, p. 287).

October 2—Alexander Y. de Witte, H.P.B.'s cousin, badly injured in head on the Caucasian-Turkish front; dies from the effects of this in 1884; H.P.B. sees this in a vision (*ZhBH*, XV).

November-December—H.P.B. enters into communication with John Yarker, English Freemason in Manchester. He brings to her notice ceremonials belonging to an Order called the Sât Bhai, said to have been started by a Chobî-Brâhmana pandit of Benares. Considerable correspondence ensues (*Ransom*, 99-100).

Dec. 11—Meeting in London of Cobb, Massey, Moses, Kislingbury, to read Col. Olcott's Instructions concerning formation of Branch; some disagreement as to views (*Ransom*, 101-03).

1878

February—The Theos. Soc. decides to make an alliance with the Ârya-Samâja of India (*Ransom*, 103).

February 5—Mûljî Thackersey instructed to organize Bombay Branch of the T.S. (*Ransom*, 103).

February 8—Col. Olcott returns to New York from Boston (*HPBSp.*, I, 112).

February 10—Col. Olcott says that J. W. Bouton offered H.P.B. $5,000 as copyright on an edition of a book in one volume, which would "unveil Isis a little more." H.P.B. refused (*ODL*, I, 295 fn.).

February 11—Monsieur Harrisse draws a portrait of the Master (*HPBSp.*, I, 113).

February 26—Col. Olcott goes to Philadelphia (*Diaries*).

March 7 (Feb. 23 o.s.)—First article of H.P.B.'s published in the Russian newspaper *Pravda* of Odessa; it is dated New York, January 1(13), 1878.

March 11—Artist Thomas Le Clear begins portrait of H.P.B. (*Diaries*).

CHRONOLOGICAL SURVEY   lxiii

March 20—Sworn testimony of Wm. Q. Judge concerning H.P.B.'s precipitation of the portrait of the Tiruvalluvar Yogi. Added testimonies of Dr. L. M. Marquette, Wm. R. O'Donavan and Thos. Le Clear (*Hints*, I, 116-19, ed. of 1909; *HPBSp.*, I, 128; *ODL*, I, 367 *et seq.*).

April—Council of the T.S. meets and gives Col. Olcott full discretionary powers (*Ransom*, 104).

April 2nd or 9th (Tuesday)—Most likely dates when H.P.B. suddenly loses consciousness and does not regain it until five days later. Col. Olcott and his sister, Belle Mitchell, are with her. The Master telegraphs to Col. Olcott from Bombay, not to fear, as H.P.B. will be all right (*Lucifer*, XV, Jan. 1895, p. 364; *Path*, IX, Mch., 1895; *ZhBH.*, p. 15).

April 5—Thomas Alva Edison sends in his signed application for Fellowship in the T.S. (*ODL*, I, 466; *Diaries*).

April 17—H.P.B., Col. Olcott and Sotheran discuss with some Freemasons about constituting the Society as a Masonic body, with Rituals and Degrees (*Ransom*, 103; *ODL*, I, 468).

April—Col. Olcott starts correspondence with High-Priest Sumangala in Ceylon (*Ransom*, 106).

May 3—Col. Olcott wrote his first Circular explaining the origin and plan of the T.S., etc. A packet of these is given to Dr. H. J. Billing to take to London, and another to Countess Lydia A. Pashkoff, to be taken to Japan. Objects are stated in their early form; Brotherhood of Humanity used for the first time (*GB*, 26; *Ransom*, 104; *Diaries*; *ODL*, I, 400).

May 3—First issue of Sotheran's short lived *Echo* (New York) is published (*Diaries*).

May 16—The Founders are directed to make ready for eventual departure for India (*Ransom*, 106).

May 22—Letter from A. Gustam, Record. Sec'y of T.S., "To the Chiefs of the Ârya Samâja," advising them that the Council of the T.S. has accepted the proposal of the Samâja to unite with them. T.S. alters its own title to: "The Theosophical Society of the Ârya Samâja of India." (*Ransom*, 105-06; *ODL*, I, 397).

May 25—Divorce between H.P.B. and Betanelly is granted; he had sued for divorce three years after marriage on grounds of desertion; summonses were served upon H.P.B. in New York; Wm. Q. Judge acted as her counsel (*ODL*, I, 57).

May 27—Italian celebration in New York; unveiling of Mazzini's bust in Central Park; banquet at Lion Park; the Founders present (*Diaries*).

lxiv   BLAVATSKY: COLLECTED WRITINGS

May—Council of T.S. decides to restore initiation fees and to send them to the Ârya Samâja (*Ransom*, 106).

June 4—H.P.B. spends day at Hoboken, N. J., in company with Belle Mitchell and Wimbridge (*Diaries*).

June 16—Col. Olcott goes to Albany, N. Y. (*Diaries*).

June 16—H.P.B. goes to visit Belle Mitchell, returning home June 22 (*Diaries*).

June 24—H.P.B. takes night boat to Troy, N. Y.; goes next day to Albany, N. Y. (*Diaries*).

June 26—H.P.B. and Col. Olcott take night boat to New York, down the Hudson River (*Diaries*).

June 27—First meeting held by the British Theosophical Society, at 38, Great Russell St., London; Cobb represents Col. Olcott; C. C. Massey chosen President; Miss Kislingbury, Secretary (*ED*, 11; *Ransom*, 106-07; *Hist. Retr.*, 11; *ODL*, I, 398, 473 *et seq.*).

June 28—H.P.B. interviewed by the *New York Star*, on her forthcoming naturalization.

June 30—Gen. Abner Doubleday joins the T.S. (*Ransom*, 106).

July 8—H.P.B. is naturalized (*HPBSp.*, I, 114; *ODL*, I, 473; *Ransom*, 108). Col. Olcott leaves for Albany on a mutual business venture with Hartmann.

July 10—Col. Olcott is back in New York (*HPBSp.*, I, 115).

July 13—H.P.B., Col. Olcott and Wimbridge go to East Hampton, Long Island; stop at Capt. Em. Gardiner's Hotel (*ODL*, I, 454; *Diaries*).

July—A. Gustam resigns as Record. Sec'y; Wm. Q. Judge fills the vacancy (*Ransom*, 108).

August 5—Most likely time when the Founders came back from East Hampton to New York by train (*HPBSp.*, I, 116).

August (early)—The Rules of the Ârya Samâja arrive, and prove to be disappointing. The T.S. resumes its original status (*ODL*, I, 398; *Ransom*, 108; *HPBSp.*, I, 116).

August 6—Col. Olcott goes to Albany again (*HPBSp.*, I, 116).

August 27—Meeting of the T.S. in connection with powers delegated to Col. Olcott (*Hist. Retr.*, 19).

September 11—E. Wimbridge prepares H.P.B.'s portrait for engraving (*HPBSp.*, I, 117). Most likely the one which was published in the 5th thousand of *Isis Unveiled*.

September 16—Prince Emil von Sayn-Wittgenstein dies (*Diaries*).

October 9—O'Donavan works on a bronze plaque of H.P.B.; continues on the 10th and 11th (*HPBSp.*, I, 118; *ODL*, I, frontispiece).

October 21—Col. Olcott returns from a trip to Philadelphia (*HPBSp.*, I, 126).

October 22—Orders received from Serapis, through Sahib, "to complete all by the first days of December." (*HPBSp.*, I, 126; *Ransom*, 108).

October 30—Col. Olcott goes again to Philadelphia (*HPBSp.*, I, 130). Comes back on Nov. 2 (*ditto*, 135).

November 14—Master M. conveys orders from Serapis; the Founders have to go the latest between Dec. 15 and 20 (*HPBSp.*, I, 140).

November 20—Vedic ceremony of casting the ashes of Baron de Palm into the sea; this was done in the New York Bay, at 7:45 p.m., an Adept being present (*HPBSp.*, I, 141).

November 21—Orders received to sail Dec. 7 or 17, and to pack up at once (*HPBSp.*, I, 141).

November 25—Miss Rosa Bates leaves for England to await there the arrival of the Founders; two of H.P.B.'s trunks go with her to Liverpool (*Ransom*, 109; *Vania*, 40; *HPBSp.*, I, 142-43).

November 28—Col. Olcott leaves for Fall River (*HPBSp.*, I, 143). Returns Dec. 1st, via Providence (*ditto*, 146).

December 1—Orders received to sell furniture, etc., before 12th (*HPBSp.*, I, 146).

December 2—Col. Olcott goes for the last time to Philadelphia (*HPBSp.*, I, 147).

December 3—Col. Olcott goes to Washington, D.C. (*ditto*, 148).

December 9—H.P.B. goes early in the morning to meet an Adept at the "Battery," a point in New York harbor (*HPBSp.*, I, 153).

December 9—Approximate date on which the auction was held in H.P.B.'s apartment (*HPBSp.*, I, 153).

December 9—Col. Olcott returns home (*HPBSp.*, I, 154).

December 12—Col. Olcott goes to Orange to see his sister (*HPBSp.*, I, 155).

December 13—Col. Olcott goes to Menlo Park, to see Edison about phonograph (*HPBSp.*, I, 156).

December 13—Col. Olcott receives from the President of U.S.A. an autographed letter of recommendation to all U.S. Ministers and Consuls abroad, and a diplomatic passport (*ODL*, I, 479; *HPBSp.*, I, 156).

December 13—Orders seem to have been received at first to sail from Philadelphia, Penna., but this is evidently not carried out (*HPBSp.*, I, 156).

December 17—Col. Olcott buys three tickets on the British steamer *SS Canada*. The Founders and Wimbridge go on board and spend the night there. Captain's name is Sumner (*HPBSp.*, I, 159; *Ransom*, 109).

December 18—Steamer leaves harbor of New York at 2:30 p.m.; then drops anchor off Coney Island waiting for tide (*HPBSp.*, I, 159-60).

December 19—Pilot took steamer across the Sandy Hook bar at about 12:30 p.m. (*HPBSp.*, I, 160; *ODL*, II, 1).

Key to Abbreviations

Autobiogr.—An *Autobiography* of A. P. Sinnett, dated June 3rd, 1912, with additions dated May, 1916, and Jan. 2, 1920, which exists in the form of a typewritten MS. in the Archives of the Mahâtma Letters Trust in London.

Corson—*Some Unpublished Letters of Helena Petrovna Blavatsky.* With an Introduction and Commentary by Eugene Rollin Corson, B.S., M.D. London: Rider & Co. (1929). 255 pp., facs. and ill.

Diaries—Col. Henry Steel Olcott's *Diaries* in the Adyar Archives.

ED—*The Early Days of Theosophy in Europe*, by A. P. Sinnett. London: Theos. Publ. House, 1922. 126 pp.

GB—*The Golden Book of The Theosophical Society*. Ed. by C. Jinarâjadâsa. Adyar: Theos. Publ. House, 1925. xviii, 421 pp., ill.

Hints—*Hints on Esoteric Theosophy*. Issued under the Authority of The Theosophical Society in 1882. Publ. anonymously, but actually written by Allan O. Hume. Nos. 1 and 2.

Hist. Retr.—*A Historical Retrospect of The Theosophical Society, 1875-1896*, by Col. H. S. Olcott. Madras, 1896.

HPBSp.—*H.P.B. Speaks.* Edited by C. Jinarâjadâsa. Adyar, Madras, India: The Theos. Publ. House; Vol. I, 1950; Vol. II, 1951.

LMW—*Letters from the Masters of the Wisdom.* Transcribed and Annotated by C. Jinarâjadâsa. With a Foreword by Annie Besant. *1st Series*, Adyar, Madras: Theos. Publ. House, 1919. 124 pp.; 2nd ed., 1923; 3rd ed., 1945; 4th ed., with new and additional Letters (1870-1900), 1948. viii, 220 pp. —*IInd Series*, Adyar, Theos. Publ. House, 1925; and Chicago: Theos. Press, 1926.

Lucifer—London, 1887, etc.

ML—*The Mahatma Letters to A. P. Sinnett* (from the Mahatmas M. and K. H.). Transcribed, Compiled and with an Introd. by A. T. Barker. London: T. Fisher Unwin, December, 1923; New York: Frederick A. Stokes Co., 1923. xxxv, 492 pp.; 2nd rev. ed., London: Rider & Co., 1926; 8th impression, Rider & Co., 1948; 3rd and rev. ed. Edited by Christmas Humphreys and Elsie Benjamin. Adyar, Madras: The Theos. Publ. House, 1962. xliii, 524 pp. New Index.

MPI—*A Modern Priestess of Isis.* Abridged and Translated on behalf of the Society for Psychical Research from the Russian of Vsevolod S. Soloviov, by Walter Leaf, Litt. D., with Appendices. London: Longmans, Green, and Co., and New York: 15 East 16th St., 1895.

MPI-R—The original Russian work (as above), entitled *Sovremennaya zhritza Isidi*, by V. S. Soloviov. St. Petersburg, 1893; 2nd. ed., N. F. Mertz, 1904. It contains 342 pp. and is somewhat more complete than the English transl. Originally, this material appeared in the *Russkiy Vestnik* (Russian Messenger), Vols. 218-220, 222-223, between Feb. and Dec., 1892.

NCM—*Nineteenth Century Miracles*, by Emma Hardinge-Britten. Manchester, 1883.

ODL—*Old Diary Leaves*, by Col. Henry Steel Olcott. 1st Series. New York and London: G. P. Putnam's Sons, 1895, vii, 491 pp., ill.

Path—*The Path*, Publ. and ed. at New York by Wm. Q. Judge. Vol. I —April, 1886, etc.

POW—*People from the Other World*, by H. S. Olcott. Hartford, Conn.: American Publ. Co., 1875. 492 pp.

Ransom—*A Short History of The Theosophical Society.* Compiled by Josephine Ransom. With a Preface by G. S. Arundale. Adyar, Madras: Theos. Publ. House, 1938. xii, 591 pp.

RO—Russkoye Obozreniye (Russian Review), Moscow Monthly.

Scrapbook—H.P.B.'s *Scrapbooks* in the Adyar Archives.

Spir. Sc.—Spiritual Scientist publ. at Boston, Mass.

Theos.—The Theosophist. Founded by H.P.B. and Col. H. S. Olcott in October, 1879. In progress.

Vania—Madame H. P. Blavatsky, Her Occult Phenomena and the Society for Psychical Research, by K. F. Vania. Bombay: Sat Publ. Co., 1951. xiv, 488 pp.

Word—The Word. Monthly ed. by H. W. Percival. New York: The Theos. Publ. House, Vols. I-XXV, Oct., 1904-Sept., 1917.

ZhBH—Biographical Sketch of H.P.B.'s life and work, by her sister Vera Petrovna de Zhelihovsky, appended to the Russian edition of H.P.B.'s *Enigmatical Tribes of the Blue Hills* and the *Durbar in Lahore,* publ. by V. I. Gubinsky, St. Petersburg, 1893. Sketch covers 56 pp. An Engl. transl. by Mrs. Kirk and Mrs. Lieven appeared in *The London Forum* (incorp. *The Occult Review*), Vols. LX, LXI, LXII, 1935.

GENEALOGICAL TABLE I: DOLGORUKOV; FADEYEV; WITTE.

Prince Feodor Feodorovich Dolgorukov (? -1664)
mar. Anna Vladimirovna Lyapunov (? -1664)

Pr. Grigoriy Feodorovich (1657-1723)
mar. Pr. Marie Ivanovna Galitzin

Children:

- **Pr. Alexis Grig.** (? -1734)
  mar. Praskovya Yuryevna Hilkov
  - **Pr. Ivan Alexeyevich** (1708-exec. 1739)

- **Pr. Serguey Grigoryevich** (? -executed 1739)
  mar. Bar. Martha Petrovna Shaffirov (1697-1762)
  - **Pr. Katherine Alexeyevna** (1712-1745) Betrothed to Emperor Peter II
  - **Pr. Vassiliy Sergueyevich** (? -1807)
    mar. Anastassiya Ivanovna Romodanovsky-Ladizhensky (1735-1823)
    - **Pr. Paul Vassilyevich** (1755-1837)
      mar. Henriette Adolfovna de Bandré-du-Plessis (? -1812)
      - **Pr. Anastassiya Pavl.** (1789-1828)
        mar. Alexander Vassilyevich Sushkov (1790-1831)
      - **Princess Helena Pavlovna** (1789-1860)
        mar. Andrey Mihailovich de Fadeyev (1789-1867)
        - **Helena A.** (1814-1842) mar. Peter von Hahn *(see Table II)*
          - Andrey Y. (1844-1847)
          - Alexander Y. (1846-1884)
          - Boris Y. (1848-1900)
        - **Katherine A.** (1819- ?) mar. Yuliy Feodorovich de Witte (? -1868)
          - [Count] Serguey Yulyevich (1849-1915) mar. (1) Mrs. Spiridonov mar. (2) Matilda Ivanovna Lissanyevich (no issue)
          - Olga Y. (1862?-1918)
        - **Anastassiya A.** (b. and d. 1821)
        - **Rostislav A.** (1824-1884) unmarried
          - Sophia Y. (? -1918) unmarried
        - **Nadyezhda A.** (1829-1919) unmarried

GENEALOGICAL TABLE II: VON HAHN; YAHONTOV; ZHELIHOVSKY.

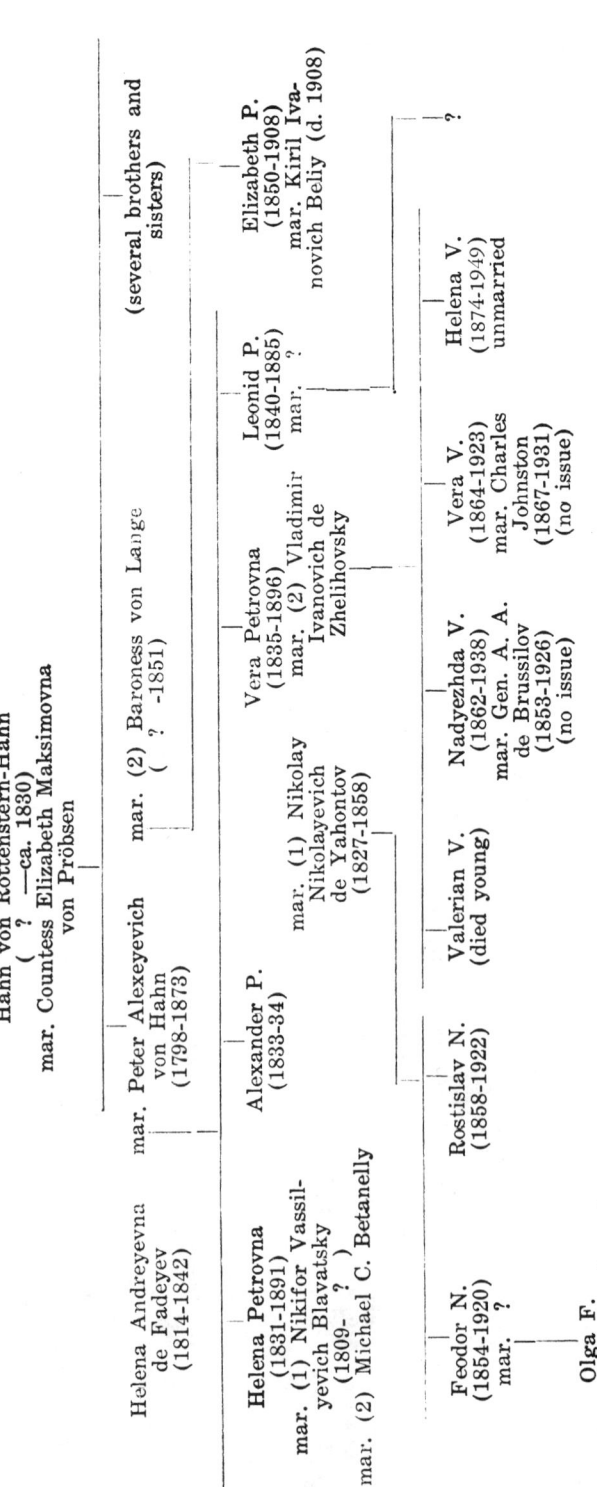

GENEALOGICAL TABLE III: VON HAHN AND THEIR RAMIFICATIONS.

Feodor Gustavovich Hahn von Rottenstern-Hahn (1767- ?) mar. Wilhelmine von Stryk

Karl Gustavovich Hahn von Rottenstern-Hahn (? - ?) mar. Charlotte Feodorovna ?

Alexis Gustavovich Hahn von Rottenstern-Hahn mar. Count. E. M. von Pröbsen

Children of Feodor Gustavovich:

Yevgeniy F. (1807-1874) mar. Yevgeniya Florovna Dolivo-Dobrovolsky

Alexander F. (? -1898) unmarried

Konstantin F. (? - ?) mar. Elizabeth Alexeyevna Nekludov

Children of Karl Gustavovich:

Dmitriy Karlovich von Hahn (1831-1907) mar. Olga Vassilyevna de Dmitriyev (1837-1913)

Peter Alexeyevich von Hahn (1798-1873) mar. Helena A. de Fadeyev

Descendants of Yevgeniy F.:

Serguey D. (1860-1914) mar. Helena Konstantinovna de Stein

Olga D. (1862-1930) mar. Feodor Yossifovich de Knyazhevich (no issue)

Sophia D. (1863- ?) died young

Descendants of Konstantin F.:

Varvara D. (1863-1920) mar. (1) Vladimir Konstantinovich de Pertsov mar. (2) Serguey Grigoryevich de Lishin (no issue)

Descendants of Dmitriy Karlovich:

Vera D. (1868-1920) unmarried

Lydia D. (1874-1960) mar. (1) Mihail Vassilyevich de Zirkoff mar. (2) Boris Petrovich de Bazhenov

Helena Petrovna Blavatsky (see *Table II*)

Children of Serguey D.:

Vladimir S. (died young)

Lydia S. (1884-1922) mar. Feodor Konstantinovich von Baggowuht

Konstantine S. (1893- ?) mar. (1) Nadine de Meller-Zakomelsky mar. (2) ? (no issue)

Child of Lydia D.:

Boris Mihailovich de Zirkoff (1902-)

Children of Lydia S.:

Georgiy F. (1909- ?)

Roman F. (1910- ?)

NOTES ON THE GENEALOGICAL TABLES

The family of the Princes Dolgorukov descends in direct line from St. Mihail Vsevolodovich of Chernigov (ca. 1179-1246), the canonized Prince; hence also from Prince Yaroslav Vladimirovich Mudriy (the Wise: 976-1054) and through him from the semi-legendary Rurik, who is supposed to have been the first "kniaz" or prince of Novgorod.

The great-great-grandson of St. Mihail, Prince Konstantin Ivanovich (d. 1368), ruled over the town of Obolensk, on the Protva river, and was the originator of the Princes Obolensky, a renowned family in the annals of Russia. His younger son was Prince Andrey Konstantinovich Obolensky (middle of XVth century), and it is the latter's son, Prince Ivan Andreyevich, who became known by the nickname of "Dolgorukoy" which meant "long-handed," "far-reaching," and had to do with his ability to detect his enemies wherever they may have been hiding. This was a purely personal characteristic, and therefore, in accordance with Russian grammatical rules, the term could not be applied to the descendants in any other but the genitive case, *i.e.*, *Dolgorukov* in singular, and *Dolgorukovi* in the plural form. However, as time went on, many of the direct descendants of Prince Ivan Andreyevich signed themselves both *Dolgorukoy* and *Dolgorukiy*, the latter being a corruption of the original form of that name. A descriptive name closely akin to this is the Latin name of *Longimanus*.

Prince Ivan Andreyevich "Dolgorukoy' had only one son, Prince Vladimir Ivanovich, and from the latter have originated the four lines of the Princes Dolgorukov, many representatives of which are alive today in various parts of the world, except in the case of the Elder Line which is now extinct.

This elder line stems from Prince Vladimir Ivanovich's son, Semyon Vladimirovich Dolgorukov, and acquired a reputation in the days of his grandson, Prince Ivan Andreyevich, nicknamed "Shiban" (d. 1590) who became a military hero. His grandson, Prince Feodor Feodorovich Dolgorukov (d. 1664) is the first individual of this line indicated on the accompanying Genealogical Table, and it is from him that the line descends down to Princess Helena Pavlovna Dolgorukov (1789-1860), H. P. Blavatsky's maternal grandmother, who had such a marked influence on H.P.B.'s education and upbringing. With this remarkable woman, the Elder Line of the Dolgorukov became extinct.

It is this Elder Line which produced such renowned individuals as Prince Grigoriy Feodorovich (1657-1723) who was ambassador to Poland, and his brother Yakov Feodorovich (1639-1720), the well-known favorite of Peter the Great; Princess Katherine Alexeyevna who

Notes on the Genealogical Tables lxxiii

was betrothed to Czar Peter II; and the unfortunate Prince Serguey Grigoryevich who, together with three of his close relatives, became implicated in a forged testament of Peter II, and other political intrigues, and were executed in 1739. In spite of these sad events, other members of the Dolgorukov Family regained ascendancy and continued through later generations to exercise a decisive influence in Russia.

The third line of the Dolgorukovs produced also some of the most renowned leaders of those days, both in the military and civilian fields; to this line belonged Princess Marie Vladimirovna (d. 1625) who became the wife of Czar Mihail Feodorovich, the First reigning Romanov.

It should be borne in mind that, contrary to erroneous statements made by several theosophical writers, the Dolgorukov Family as such does not include Prince Yuriy Vladimirovich Dolgorukiy (1090-1157), the son of Vladimir Monomah, Grand-Duke of Kiev. Prince Yuriy was the recognized founder of Moscow, and from him were derived the later Princes of Suzdal', Rostov and Moscow.

The von Hahn Family—formerly Hahn von Rottenstern-Hahn— belonged originally to the nobility of Mecklemburg, Germany. When settled in Russia, it dropped its title of Counts, and the name itself, after being spelled for a time as *Hahne*, finally became *Gan*. It is not definitely known when this branch of the German Counts von Hahn emigrated to Russia, but the most likely time was during the reign of Empress Anna Ioanovna (1730-1740). H.P.B. (*Letters to Sinnett*, p. 12) signs herself almost in jest as "*née* Hahn von Rottenstern-Hahn," while her sister Vera referred to the older form of the family name as Hahn-Hahn von der Rohter-Hahn.

H.P.B.'s paternal grandfather, Alexis Gustavovich von Hahn, was a full general who in his earlier years had distinguished himself during the Suvorov campaign, crossing the Swiss Alps, and for a time was Commandant of the city of Zürich. Various members of this family were prominently connected with the administration of the Russian Postal Service. Others became well-known military men and civilian administrators. Among them may be mentioned the following:

Yevgeniy Feodorovich von Hahn was the Presiding Senator of the Senate, and a leading figure in the administration of State-owned properties. His daughter Yevgeniya was court maid-of-honor.

General of Infantry Dmitriy Karlovich von Hahn was the Founder and Commander of the Russian Frontier-Guard Corps, a man of sterling qualities and a trusted adviser under three Emperors.

Serguey Dmitriyevich von Hahn, his son, was a Director of the State Bank, Keeper of the Gold Reserve of the Empire, and Assistant Secretary of Commerce and Industry.

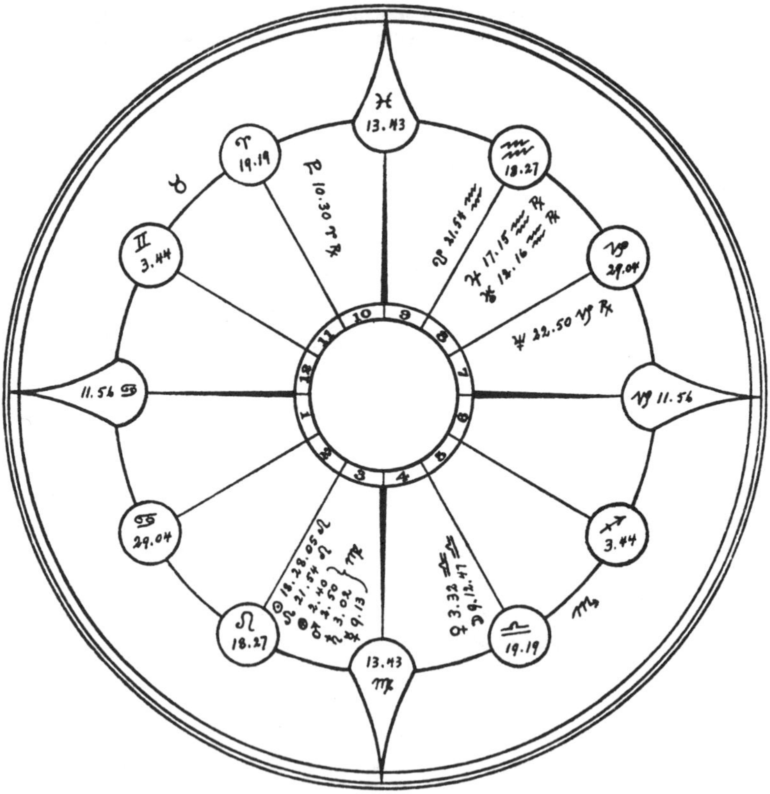

NATAL HOROSCOPE OF H. P. BLAVATSKY

Place of birth: Ekaterinoslav, Russia.
35:01 E. Longitude; 48:27 N. Latitude.
Date of birth:
    July 31, 1831, acc. to Julian Calendar.
    August 12, 1831, acc. to Gregorian Calendar.
Local Time: 1:42:00 A.M.
G.M.T.: 11:21:56 P.M. (Aug. 11th).
Sid. Time: 23:00:43.
Adjusted Calculation Date: Feb. 2. 1831.

TABLE OF CONTENTS

	PAGE
Preface	vii
Foreword	xxiii
H. P. Blavatsky: General Outline of her Life prior to her Public Work	xxv
Chronological Survey	liii
Genealogical Tables	lxix
Notes on the Genealogical Tables	lxxii
Horoscope of H. P. Blavatsky	lxxiv
Table of Contents	lxxv
H. P. Blavatsky's Literary Career	
The Earliest Known Writings	1
H.P.B.'s Sketchbook	2
Légende sur la Belle de Nuit	6
H.P.B.'s Notebook of Travel-Impressions	11

1874

[H.P.B.'s Scrapbooks]	29
Marvellous Spirit Manifestations	30
About Spiritualism	36
From Scrapbook, Vol. I, pp. 7-8	44
From Scrapbook, Vol. I, p. 8	45
[Elbridge Gerry Brown]	45
Madame Blavatsky	46

1875

[H.P.B.'s Role at the Eddy's Homestead]	53
Heroic Women	54
A Card from the Countess Blavatsky	55
The Philadelphia "Fiasco," or Who is Who?	56
From Scrapbook, Vol. I, p. 21	72
Important Note	73
[H.P.B. and the term "Spiritualism"]	74
Who Fabricates?	75

[H.P.B.'s Lawsuit in America] 83
Important to Spiritualists 85
A Budget of Good News 88
From Scrapbook, Vol. I, p. 36 90
[Compiler's Note Concerning Prof. N. P. Wagner] 90
To the Spiritualists of Boston 91
A Word of Advice to the Singing Medium,
    Mr. Jesse Sheppard 92
A Card to the American Public 94
From Scrapbook, Vol. I, p. 58 94
From Scrapbook, Vol. I, p. 39 95
[The "Hiraf" Club and its Historical Background] 95
A Few Questions to "Hiraf ***" 101
"What Are You Going to Do about It?" 119
From Scrapbook, Vol. I, p. 47 120
[Formation of The Theosophical Society] 121
From Scrapbook, Vol. I, p. 57 124
From Madame H. P. Blavatsky to Her Correspondents 126
From Scrapbook, Vol. I, p. 63 133
The Science of Magic 134
From Scrapbook, Vol. I, p. 67 143
A Letter from Madame Blavatsky 143
The Magical Evocation of Apollonius of Tyana 144
From Scrapbook, Vol. I, pp. 77-79 150
An Unsolved Mystery 151
From Scrapbook, Vol. I, pp. 98-99 162
A Story of the Mystical 163

1876

The Luminous Circle 177
Madame Blavatsky Explains 186
From Scrapbook, Vol. I, p. 111 192
From Scrapbook, Vol. I, p. 112 193
From Scrapbook, Vol. I, p. 113 193
From Scrapbook, Vol. I, p. 116 194
A Crisis for Spiritualism 194
From Scrapbook, Vol. I, p. 124 203
The Russian Investigation 204

CONTENTS	lxxvii
"Psychophobia" in Russia	210
Mediums, Beware!	212
From Scrapbook, Vol. I, p. 154	214
From Scrapbook, Vol. I, pp. 155-56	214
The Russian Scientists	215
From Scrapbook, Vol. I, pp. 164-65	220
From Scrapbook, Vol. I, p. 185	220
(New) York Against Lankester	221
Huxley and Slade: Who is More Guilty of "False Pretences"?	226
From Scrapbook, Vol. II, p. 119	233
From Scrapbook, Vol. IV, p. 35	233

1877

Concerning Gods and Interviews	237
From Scrapbook, Vol. IV, p. 54	238
Madame Blavatsky Protests	238
Madame Blavatsky on Fakirs	241
To the Public	245
A Card from Madame Blavatsky	247
Buddhism in America	249
Croquet at Windsor	253
Turkish Barbarities	255
From Scrapbook, Vol. IV, p. 79	260
Washing the Disciples' Feet	261
The Jews in Russia	262
[Isis Unveiled]	264
From Scrapbook, Vol. IV, p. 83	264
"Elementaries"	265
From Scrapbook, Vol. IV, p. 95	271
From Scrapbook, Vol. I, p. 70, and Vol. VII, p. 46	271
Dr. Carpenter, on "Tree-Trickery" and H. P. Blavatsky on Fakir-"Jugglery"	272
From Scrapbook, Vol. IV, p. 108	277
From Scrapbook, Vol. IV, p. 125	278
From Scrapbook, Vol. IV, p. 140	278
[H.P.B. and Her Masonic Diploma]	281

1878

[H.P.B. CORRECTS AN ERROR ABOUT ELEMENTALS]	281
FROM SCRAPBOOK, VOL. IV, p. 163	282
KABALISTIC VIEWS ON "SPIRITS" AS PROPAGATED BY THE THEOSOPHICAL SOCIETY	283
FROM SCRAPBOOK, VOL. IV, pp. 164-65	289
FROM SCRAPBOOK, VOL. IV, pp. 169-72	290
MADAME BLAVATSKY ON THE VIEWS OF THE THEOSOPHISTS	290
A SOCIETY WITHOUT A DOGMA	301
FROM SCRAPBOOK, VOL. IV, p. 176	306
THE AUTHOR OF "ISIS UNVEILED" DEFENDS THE VALIDITY OF HER MASONIC PATENT	307
[H.P.B.'s WRITINGS IN THE RUSSIAN LANGUAGE]	313
FROM SCRAPBOOK, VOL. IV, p. 243	313
DR. SLADE'S FINAL TRIUMPH	314
FROM SCRAPBOOK, VOL. IV, pp. 184-85	319
THE KNOUT	319
MADAME BLAVATSKY ON INDIAN METAPHYSICS	325
FROM SCRAPBOOK, VOL. VII, pp. 56-57	337
THE CAVE OF THE ECHOES	338
"ISIS UNVEILED" AND THE TODAS	353
THE TODAS	354
FOOTNOTES TO "THE SCIENTIFIC HYPOTHESIS RESPECTING MEDIUMISTIC PHENOMENA"	359
FRAGMENTS DE MADAME BLAVATSKY	361
FRAGMENTS FROM MADAME BLAVATSKY	365
THE AKHUND OF SWAT	369
THE THEOSOPHICAL SOCIETY: ITS ORIGIN, PLAN AND AIMS	375
FROM SCRAPBOOK, VOL. VII, pp. 113-14	378
THE ÂRYA SAMÂJ	379
SCIENCE	384
LETTER TO THE EDITOR OF THE "TIFLIS MESSENGER"	385
FROM SCRAPBOOK, VOL. VIII, p. 252	389
LETTER TO THE EDITOR OF "L'OPINIONE NAZIONALE" (And English Translation thereof)	390
PARTING WORDS FROM MADAME BLAVATSKY	393
LA VÉRITABLE MADAME H. P. BLAVATSKY	396
THE REAL MADAME H. P. BLAVATSKY	400

Contents

lxxix

From Scrapbook, Vol. VII, p. 258 403
From Scrapbook, Vol. VII, p. 306 404
From Scrapbook, Vol. V, pp. 77-79 405
From Scrapbook, Vol. V, p. 81 405
The Diaries of H. P. Blavatsky 406
Compiler's Notes on the Diaries 434
Appendix:
    Note on the Transliteration of Sanskrit 442
    General Bibliography (with Biographical Notes) 443
    Index 539

ILLUSTRATIONS

FACING PAGE

H. P. Blavatsky in her Early Youth xxxii
Helena Pavlovna de Fadeyev xxxiii
Andrey Mihailovich de Fadeyev xxxiii
Helena Andreyevna von Hahn xxxiii
Vera Petrovna de Zhelihovsky xxxiii
H. P. Blavatsky about 1865-66 xlviii
Nadyezhda Andreyevna de Fadeyev xlix
Page from H.P.B.'s Scrapbook I 32
Alexander Nikolayevich Aksakov 33
Robert Dale Owen 48
Andrew Jackson Davis 49
Eddy Homestead, Chittenden, Vt. 64
General Francis J. Lippitt 65
"Important Note" 80
H. P. Blavatsky in 1875 81
Fred W. Hinrichs 96
William S. Fales 96
William M. Ivins 96
H. P. Blavatsky in New York Days 97
Hiram Corson 112
The Richardson Cottage, Ithaca, N.Y. 113
Edward Wimbridge 224
George H. Felt 224
Henry J. Newton 224

PRINCE EMIL-K.-L. VON SAYN-WITTGENSTEIN 225
GENERAL ABNER DOUBLEDAY 240
H. P. BLAVATSKY IN 1875 241
HENRY STEEL OLCOTT AS A SOLDIER 304
H. P. BLAVATSKY'S MASONIC DIPLOMA 305
H. P. BLAVATSKY ABOUT 1875-1876 320
WILLIAM STAINTON MOSES 321
H.P.B.'S RESIDENCE AT 302 WEST 47TH STREET, NEW YORK 464
WILLIAM QUAN JUDGE 465
HENRY STEEL OLCOTT 480
DR. ALEXANDER WILDER 481

FACSIMILES

                                                                               PAGE

H.P.B.'S PEN DRAWING OF A SEASIDE VIEW 3
H.P.B.'S PEN DRAWING OF TERESINA MITROVICH 10
CIRCULAR "IMPORTANT TO SPIRITUALISTS" 86
H.P.B.'S NOTE ABOUT ORDERS RECEIVED FROM T.B. 89
H.P.B.'S NOTE ABOUT ORDERS RECEIVED TO ESTABLISH A
    SOCIETY AND TO CHOOSE OLCOTT 95
H.P.B.'S NOTE ABOUT ORDERS FROM SERAPIS 110
MINUTES OF THE MEETING OF SEPTEMBER 8, 1875 125
H.P.B.'S PEN-AND-INK NOTATION CONCERNING ENDREINEK AGARDI 162
PAGE FROM H.P.B.'S DIARY 432

H. P. BLAVATSKY'S LITERARY CAREER
THE EARLIEST KNOWN WRITINGS

[There exists no definite evidence that H.P.B. had ever published any articles, essays or letters to Editors prior to October, 1874. Still the probability of her having written is considerable, as various statements have been made by herself and others which seem to indicate that her literary work began much earlier in life than the year 1874. We may never obtain, however, any conclusive evidence concerning this.

There is, for instance, her own reported statement in an interview given by her to the *Daily Graphic* of New York, and published November 13, 1874, to the effect that she was a contributor to the *Revue des Deux Mondes* of Paris, and acted as correspondent of the *Indépendence Belge* and several Parisian Journals. No record of this exists, however, in the Editorial Offices of these well known periodicals, though it is possible that she may have written under some pseudonym, or merely as "correspondent" from one or another part of the world. The text of this interview is of a rather sensational kind, and embodies a number of errors and misstatements as to names and events. So it cannot be relied upon.

Then there is a statement made around 1956-57 by a very old gentleman, Adolphe de Castro, of Los Angeles, California, who had met H.P.B. in Berlin about 1873, to the effect that she was then reading galley-proofs of some articles she had written in Russian, that he was able to be of help to her with some old Hebrew terms, and that what she was writing was intended either for a Russian paper or for a local Jewish Journal, the most likely one being *Das Zeitung des Judenthums*. The old files of this Journal have been investigated, as far as this could be done in the holdings of the British Museum, but no positive result was obtained.

There is also a statement of hers made to her friend, Alexander Nikolayevich Aksakov, in a letter dated October 28, 1874, to the effect that she translated into Russian a manuscript by a medium

1

named James, and which was supposed to have been the second part of Dickens' unfinished novel, *Edwin Drood*. She would have liked to have had it published in Russian.*

Wm. M. Ivins, H.P.B.'s lawyer in her lawsuit of 1874-75, said that H.P.B. was translating Darwin's *Origin of Species* and H. T. Buckle's *History of Civilization in England*, while the suit was pending.†

All of these various statements may or may not be based on fact. No supporting evidence for them, however, has ever been found.

In the same letter to A. N. Aksakov mentioned above, H.P.B., having just returned to New York from a visit to the farmhouse of the Eddy Brothers, at Chittenden, Vt., says that she has been translating Col. Olcott's articles on the mediumistic phenomena of the Eddy Brothers, which he was then contributing to the pages of the New York *Daily Graphic;* she says that she could send them to Aksakov regularly, together with their accompanying illustrations.‡

It is quite probable that H.P.B. did actually translate all of Col. Olcott's articles as they appeared, because Aksakov wrote to him on April 4/16, 1875, that he had finished reading them. It is these articles of Col. Olcott that were eventually published in book-form, under the title of *People from the Other World* (Hartford, Conn.: American Publishing Co., 1875).††

It is not definitely known what became of H.P.B.'s Russian translation of Col. Olcott's original articles, and there is no evidence that they were ever published in any Russian Journal.]

H.P.B.'S SKETCHBOOK.

[There is in the Archives of The Theosophical Society at Adyar a small booklet, seven by eleven inches, of not more than twenty-six pages, three leaves at least having been torn out. For purposes of identification, we may call it H.P.B.'s *Sketchbook*, as it contains mostly drawings and sketches in both ink and pencil, also

---

Vide Vsevolod S. Solovyov, *A Modern Priestess of Isis*, Engl. transl., London, 1895, p. 227; Russian orig., St. Petersburg, 1904, p. 256.

†Unpublished MS. of Mrs. Laura Holloway-Langford, now destroyed.

‡V. S. Solovyov, *op. cit.*, Engl. tr., pp. 226-27; Russ. orig., p. 256.

††*Old Diary Leaves*, First Series, p. 80. The Colonel speaks of H.P.B.'s translation of his "book." He most likely means his Series of articles as such, because these did not appear in book-form until March, 1875.

mere scrawls and scribbles, with here and there some writing between them.

The first page of the booklet, partly reproduced in *facsimile*, shows in the middle a pen drawing of a seaside view, most likely Ramsgate, England, and a pen-and-ink sketch of a coat of arms, not definitely identified but evidently belonging to one or another branch of the von Hahn Family, as it shows a cock as one of its symbols.

The rest of the page is covered by two columns of two poems in Russian script whose authorship is unknown. At the top of the page H.P.B. has written in Russian: "Indistinct Reminiscences."

The most interesting item on this page is H.P.B.'s French comment written under the seaside sketch and as a footnote. It is as follows:

"Nuit mémorable! Certaine nuit, par un clair de lune qui se couchait à Ramsgate 12 Août, 1851,* lorsque je rencontrais [symbol] le Maître de mes rêves!!"

---

*"Le 12 août—c'est juillet 31 style russe jour de ma naissance —*Vingt ans!*"

[The English equivalent of this is:]

"Memorable night! On a certain night by the light of the moon that was setting at Ramsgate on August 12, 1851,* when I met [symbol] the Master of my dreams!!

---

*"August 12 is July 31 in Russian style, the day of my birth—*Twenty years!*"

[This inscription fixes with a considerable degree of probability the time when this particular booklet was started.

In her *Reminiscences of H. P. Blavatsky and "The Secret Doctrine"* (pp. 57-58) Countess Constance Wachtmeister relates an incident that occurred while H.P.B. was at Würzburg, Germany. It appears that Madame N. A. de Fadeyev, H.P.B.'s aunt, sent her from Russia a box containing various mementoes. Among these was the above-mentioned booklet which the Countess calls a "scrapbook." H.P.B., on seeing the seaside sketch, gave an exclamation of delight and said: "Come and look at this which I wrote in the year 1851, the day I saw my blessed Master." The Countess then quotes the exact French text written by H.P.B. under the sketch. She also adds in a footnote: "On seeing the manuscript I asked why she had written 'Ramsgate' instead of 'London,' and H.P.B. told me that it was a blind, so that anyone casually taking up her book would not know where she had met her Master, and that her first interview with him had been in London as she had previously told me."

The second page of the booklet contains the following brief piece of writing in French:]

. . . Toutes les magnificences de la Nature,—le silence imposant de la nuit, les odeurs des fleurs,—les rayons pâles de la lune à travers les panaches verts des arbres,—les étoiles, fleurs de feu semées dans le ciel, les lucioles, fleurs de feu semées dans l'herbe,—tout cela a été créé pour rendre l'Adepte digne de la NATURE, au moment où, pour la première fois, elle dit à l'Homme, *je t'appartiens,*—mot formé d'un céleste parfum de l'âme, qui s'exale et monte au ciel avec les parfums des fleurs,—moment, le seul de sa vie,— où il est roi, où il est Dieu, moment qu'il paye et qu'il expie par toute une existence de regrets amers.

«Ce moment; c'est le prix de toutes nos misères».

[This text has been altered by H.P.B. at one time or another. The words "l'Adepte digne de la NATURE" are in red ink and are

H.P.B.'s Sketchbook 5

superimposed over the original words "le monde digne de l'homme" written in black ink. The words "elle dit à l'Homme, *je t'appartiens*" are also in red ink and superimposed over the original words "il dit à une femme— je t'aime" written in black ink.]

[English translation of the above:]

. . . . All the glories of Nature—the imposing silence of the night; the aroma of the flowers; the pale rays of the moon through the green tufts of the trees; the stars, flowers of fire strewn over the sky; the glow-worms, flowers of fire strewn over the grass—all these have been created to render the Adept worthy of NATURE, at that moment when for the first time she exclaims to Man, "I am yours,"—words formed of a divine perfume from the soul, which, breathed forth, ascends to heaven together with the perfume of the flowers—the one moment of his life when he is king, when he is God; the moment which he expiates and pays for with a whole life of bitter regrets.

"That moment—it is the price of all our miseries."

[Page 3 of the booklet, aside from meaningless scrawls, contains the following few words also in French:]

La femme trouve son bonheur dans l'acquisition des pouvoirs surnaturels — l'amour — c'est un vilain rêve, un cauchemar.

[English translation of the above:]

Woman finds her happiness in the acquisition of supernatural powers—love is a vile dream, a nightmare.

[Page 4 has more scrawls and the address of a Captain Miller, 1, Dragoon-guards, Aldershot. Page 5 has a pencil drawing of a man's head with his grotesque shadow on the wall, and a poodle sitting upright on his haunches on a table. Page 6 is blank, and pages 7 and 8 contain the beautiful "Légende sur la Belle de Nuit" which is the most important item in this booklet. The text of this Legend written in French is as follows:]

LÉGENDE SUR LA BELLE DE NUIT

Tradition des Steppes.

Tout au commencement de la création du Monde et bien avant le péché qui perdit Ève, un frais buisson vert étendait ses larges feuilles sur le bord d'un ruisseau. Le soleil, jeune à cette époque, fatigué de ses débuts, se couchait lentement, et tirant sur lui ses rideaux de brouillards, enveloppait la terre d'ombres profondes et noires; alors on vit s'épanouir sur une des branches du buisson une modeste fleur; elle n'avait ni la fraîche beauté de la rose; ni l'orgueil superbe et majestueux du beau lys. Humble et modeste elle ouvrit ses pétales, et jeta un regard craintif sur le monde du grand Bouddha. Tout était froid et sombre autour d'elle! Ses compagnes sommeillaient tout autour courbées sur leurs tiges flexibles; ses camarades, mêmes filles du même buisson, se détournaient de son regard; les papillons de nuit, amants volages des fleurs, se reposaient bien un moment sur son sein, puis s'envolaient vers de plus belles. Un gros scarabé faillit la couper en deux en grimpant sans cérémonie sur elle à la recherche d'un gîte nocturne, et la pauvre fleur effrayée de son isolement, et de son abandon au milieu de cette foule indifférente, baissa la tête tristement et laissa tomber une goute de rosée amère. Mais voilà qu'une petite étoile s'alluma dans le ciel sombre; ses brillants rayons vifs et doux percèrent les flots des ténèbres, et soudain la fleur orpheline se sentit vivifiée et rafraîchie comme par une rosée bienfaisante . . . toute ranimée elle leva sa corolle et aperçut l'étoile bienveillante. Aussi reçut-elle ses rayons dans son sein, toute palpitante d'amour et de reconnaissance. Ils l'avaient fait renaître à l'existence.

L'aurore au sourire rose chassa peu à peu les ténèbres et l'étoile fut noyée dans l'océan de lumière que répandit l'astre du jour; des milliers de fleurs courtisanes le saluèrent, se baignant avidement dans ses rayons d'or. Il les versait aussi sur la petite fleur; le grand astre daignait l'envelopper, elle aussi, dans ses baisers de flammes . . . . mais pleine de souvenir de l'étoile du soir, et de son scintillement argentin, la fleur reçut froidement les démonstrations du fier soleil. Elle avait encore devant les yeux la lueur douce et affectueuse de l'étoile; elle sentait encore dans son cœur la goute de rosée bienfaisante et, se détournant des rayons aveuglants du soleil, elle serra ses pétales et se coucha dans le feuillage tout épais du buisson paternel. Depuis lors, le jour devint la nuit pour la pauvre fleur, et la nuit le jour; dès que le soleil apparait, et embrasse de ses flots d'or le ciel et la terre,—la fleur est invisible; mais une fois le soleil couché, et que, perçant un coin de l'horizon obscurci, la petite étoile apparait, la fleur la salue joyeusement, joue avec ses rayons argentins, respire à larges traits sa douce lueur.

Tel est aussi le cœur de beaucoup de femmes. Le premier mot bienveillant, la première caresse affectueuse, tombant sur son cœur endolori s'y enracinent profondément; et se sentant toute émue à une parole amicale, elle reste indifférente aux démonstrations passionnées de l'univers entier. Que le premier soit comme tant d'autres, qu'il se perde dans des milliers d'astres semblables à lui; le cœur de la femme saura le découvrir, de près comme de loin, elle suivra avec amour et intérêt son cours modeste et enverra des bénédictions sur son passage. Elle pourra saluer le fier soleil, admirer son éclat, mais fidèle et reconnaissante, son cœur appartiendra pour toujours à une seule étoile.

[*English translation of the foregoing French text.*]

LEGEND OF THE NIGHT-FLOWER*

TRADITION OF THE STEPPES.

At the very beginning of the creation of the World, and long before the sin which became the downfall of Eve, a fresh green shrub spread its broad leaves on the banks of a rivulet. The sun, still young at that time and tired of its initial efforts, was setting slowly, and drawing its veils of

---

*[This more descriptive name has been chosen for our flower. instead of the very unromantic names of *four-o'clock* and *marvel-of-Peru*, by which it is known.]

mists around him, enveloped the earth in deep and dark shadows. Then a modest flower blossomed forth upon a branch of the shrub. She had neither the fresh beauty of the rose, nor the superb and majestic pride of the beautiful lily. Humble and modest, she opened her petals and cast an anxious glance on the world of the great Buddha. All was cold and dark about her! Her companions slept all around bent on their flexible stems; her comrades, daughters of the same shrub, turned away from her look; the moths, winged lovers of the flowers, rested but for a moment on her breast, but soon flew away to more beautiful ones. A large beetle almost cut her in two as it climbed without ceremony over her, in search for nocturnal quarters. And the poor flower, frightened by its isolation and its loneliness in the midst of this indifferent crowd, hung its head mournfully and shed a bitter dewdrop for a tear. But lo, a little star was kindled in the sombre sky. Its brilliant rays, quick and tender, pierced the waves of gloom. Suddenly the orphaned flower felt vivified and refreshed as by some beneficent dew. Fully restored, she lifted her face and saw the friendly star. She received its rays into her breast, quivering with love and gratitude. They had brought about her rebirth into a new life.

Dawn with its rosy smile gradually dispelled the darkness, and the star was submerged in an ocean of light which streamed forth from the star of day. Thousands of flowers hailed it their paramour, bathing greedily in his golden rays. These he shed also on the little flower; the great star deigned to cover her too with its flaming kisses. But full of the memory of the evening star, and of its silvery twinkling, the flower responded but coldly to the demonstrations of the haughty sun. She still saw before her mind's eye the soft and affectionate glow of the star; she still felt in her heart the beneficent dewdrop, and turning away from the blinding rays of the sun, she closed her petals and went to sleep nestled in the thick foliage of the parent-shrub. From that time on, day became night for the lowly flower, and night became day. As soon as the sun rises and engulfs heaven and earth in its golden rays, the flower becomes invisible; but hardly does the sun set, and the star, piercing a corner of the dark horizon, makes its appearance, than the flower hails it with joy, plays with its silvery rays, and absorbs with long breaths its mellow glow.

Such is the heart of many a woman. The first gracious word, the first affectionate caress, falling on her aching heart, takes root there deeply. Profoundly moved by a friendly word, she remains indifferent to the passionate demonstrations of the whole universe. The first may not differ from many others; it may be lost among thousands of other stars similar to that one, yet the heart of woman knows where to find him, near by or far away; she will follow with love and interest his humble course, and will send her blessings on his journey. She may greet the haughty sun, and admire its glory, but, loyal and grateful, her love will always belong to one lone star.

[Page 9 has two heads in pencil, one *en profile*, the other *en face*, and some numbers and scrawls. Page 10 is blank. Pages 11-14 have faded photographs stuck on them: first a lady with some likeness to H.P.B., possibly her sister Vera Petrovna; then the portraits of H.P.B.'s maternal grandfather and grandmother, Andrey Mihailovich and Helena Pavlovna de Fadeyev, the latter with the date Tiflis, 1855; the last one is of an unidentified younger lady. Page 15 has a hasty pen-and-ink outline of a man; page 16, childish scrawls; page 17, the Greek alphabet with the names of the letters written in Russian script; pages 18 and 19 are occupied with a woman's head in ink and two studies of seemingly Napoleon's head; page 20 is blank; page 21 has some decorative letters; page 22 is blank also; on top of page 23 a Russian sentence written in pencil says: "Thy old copy-book. 1862." It is in the handwriting of H.P.B.'s aunt Nadyezhda.

Page 24—reproduced herewith in *facsimile*— is occupied with pen drawings of Marguerite praying before a crucifix, with hands folded on her breast, and Mephistopheles whispering seductions in her ear, with a caption in pencil:

Teresina Signora Mitrovich. (Faust)

Tiflis 7 Avril, 1862.

The name is that of a Russian singer's wife, herself a singer also. Her husband, Agardi Mitrovich or Metrovich, acquired a notorious fame in H.P.B.'s life through people's slanderous gossip. H.P.B. once saved his life in 1850.

Writing to H.P.B. from Odessa, on November 23 (old style), 1884, Madame Nadyezhda A. de Fadeyev, her aunt, says:

". . . . I can tell him [Col. Olcott] that Mr. Agardi Mitrovich, whom all of us have known so well in Tiflis and at Odessa, and who was a friend to us all, could never have been either your husband or your lover, because he adored his wife who died two years before his own death, poor man, at Cairo; that she is buried in the cemetery of Tiflis, and that your mutual friendship dates from the year when he married his wife. Finally, everybody knows that it is we ourselves who had asked him to go and find you at Cairo, in order to accompany you to Odessa (in the year 1871), and that he died without bringing you back, after which you came back alone . . . ."

These sentences and a few others on other subjects were written in French, with the intention that Col. Olcott could read them and understand their contents.* Madame de Fadeyev's letter quoted above is in the Adyar Archives, together with a large number of other letters from her pen.

Various facts about Mitrovich may be gathered by consulting *The Letters of H. P. Blavatsky to A. P. Sinnett* (pp. 143-44, 147, 148, 189-91). On page 144 of this work, H.P.B. states that she met him "in Tiflis in 1861, again with his wife, who died after I had left in 1865 I believe." This date is of course relevant to the one we find in our *Sketchbook*.

Page 25 contains six strophes, of eight lines each, of a burlesque and somewhat vulgar song in French about the eleven sons of Jacob. Page 26 and last contains only meaningless scrawls.

From the above description of the contents of this *Sketchbook*, it is evident that it belongs to a very early period in H.P.B.'s life, many years prior to the beginning of her literary career.]

H.P.B.'s NOTEBOOK OF TRAVEL-IMPRESSIONS.

[We have seen from the Chronological Survey of H.P.B.'s early life how little information is available about her moves and whereabouts immediately after leaving the Caucasus in 1865. There is, however, in the Adyar Archives a document which throws some light upon this period of H.P.B.'s endless wanderings. It is a special *Notebook* only two-and-a-half by four inches in size, in which she made rather copious notes in black pencil about her impressions while travelling in Eastern Europe. She wrote in French, inserting here and there a few names in Russian. Some parts of the text are faded, a few words are illegible, and the punctuation is somewhat uncertain, but on the whole these notes have been rather well-preserved and are of special interest.

In the pocket attached to the back cover of this *Notebook* there is a Roman Catholic Church Calendar of the year 1851, printed in French, and a small piece of paper bearing the following name written by H.P.B. in Russian:

---

*The original French text of the above-quoted passage is as follows:

«.... Je puis lui dire que Mr. Agardi Mitrovich que nous avons si bien connu tous à Tiflis et à Odessa, et qui était l'ami à nous tous, n'a jamais pu être ni ton mari, ni ton amant, car il adorait sa femme morte deux ans avant sa mort à lui, pauvre homme, au Caire; qu'elle est enterrée à Tiflis, au cimetière, et que Votre amitié mutuelle date de l'année où il a épousé sa femme. Enfin tout le monde sait que c'est nous qui l'avons prié d'aller te chercher au Caire pour t'accompagner à Odessa (l'année 1871) et qu'il est mort sans te ramener, après quoi tu t'es retournée seule ...»

Alexa Berbitz from Belgrade, Serbia.

Pasted on the inner side of the front cover is a red seal made of paper. In the center of it we see the Coat of Arms of Hungary. The inscription around it is in Hungarian: Cs. K. Kizárólagos szabadalmazott fogpapir, Fáczányi Ármin gyógyszerésztöl Pesten (Imperial and Royal Exclusive Patent Paper Seal. From Ármin Fáczányi, Chemist, Budapest).

From the presence of an 1851 Calendar, one could easily infer that these notes belong to the early fifties of last century; but it appears from the context itself that they must have been made during the year 1867, as will be shown in the transcript published below.]

[The superior numbers in the following pages refer to Compiler's Notes appended at the end of the English translation of H.P.B.'s text.]

Kronstadt. Brassó—Transylvania. Hôtel Grüner Baum. Comfortable et bon marché. M. et Mme. Burcheg—professeur de Gymnase. Jeune suisse un peu pédant. Elle joua de la flûte et [est] hongroise. La vieille Mme. Kántor aveugle.—Kronstadt est une des plus jolies petites villes de l'Europe par sa position, sa propreté, et de son élégance. Mais tout près, l'Eau de Borszék y est fameuse.— Venant de *Bucarest* les *Zlapari* vous demandent vos passeports et vous font payer le droit de ne pas examiner vos malles en les bouleversant de leurs mains sales. Population fort mixte des valaques, hongrois et souabes. L'architecture des maisons de villes est entièrement changée. Chaque maison porte la date de la construction sur le toit.[1]

Hermannstadt (Szeben)

Hôtel de Römischer Kaiser. Voleur hongrois. H. Couronne de Hongrie allemand et plus voleur encore. La ville bien moins jolie que Kronstadt est inondée d'officiers autrichiens—Polonais pour la plupart. Régiment Hartmann. Tütch Kapelmeister—Czech. Le soldat violoniste virtuose français. Discussion eternelle sur Mouravieff et *Haynau*.[2] Le conseiller Traposta co-Carbonari ayant déjà reçu un coup de poigne d'une main inconnue. Sa femme compositeur de musique *László Anna*. Le commissaire de police *polonais* partant pour épouser à Bucarest le monstre des foires Flora. Blagueur, menteur et voleur comme polonais et employé autrichien. Église Luthérienne toute sculptée. Beauté unique. Statue St. Nepomucène. 8 h. de Krons.

Karlsburg. Fehérvár (Alba Julia). Ancien camp Romain. Restes et ruines, pour le moment ville juive et forteresse autrichienne. Hôtel de Ung. Krone, Adolf Benedict, juif hongrois. Prétendant être le premier bariton du monde. Bon marché. Le maudit *Kántor!* La société Neeman. Le juif *Lion* Emmanuel Mendl. Violon de dentiste Peterka. 8 h. de diligence.

Klausenburg—(Kolozsvár). Nous gelons en route. Grande ville assez belle. Vieille cathédrale de 700 ans. Beau théâtre. Hôtel *Biasini*. Cher et mal. Directeur Fehérváry. Szephédy. (Mlle Schönberg) juive de Temesvár. Mme. *Nagy Hubert*, Fekete. *Philipovich* M. Le bariton sifflé Heksh.

La baron Bánffy et le Comte Esterházy—grande fureur du pianiste Litolff—le dernier jour de la Terreur de *Robespierre*.[3] Orchestre. La Comtesse Mikes. Le gouverneur général français le Comte *Crenneville*. Fêtes de la Constitution.[4] Canons autrichiens bloqués sur la place. 10 h. de diligence de Karlsburg.

Grosswardein (Nagyvárad). Énorme ville juive. Beaucoup d'hôtels, beaucoup d'églises. Chemin de fer. 24 h. de diligence de *Kolozsvár*.

Debreczen. 6 heures de chemin de fer de G. Ward. Jolie ville. Le plus beau théâtre de Hongrie, plus beau qu'à Pesth. Le cœur de la Hongrie. Tous Hongrois, peu d'allemands. Bal des ouvriers maçons. Bal de *Tzigan*.

Arad. 6 h. de Debreczen par chemin de fer à *Szolnok*. On y couche. De Szolnok autres 6 h. ch. de fer à Arad. Très grande ville. Tous Hongrois. Beaucoup d'aristocratie. Le *pont* près de la forteresse, où l'on a fusillé et pendu en 1849 13 généraux Hongrois. Fêtes de la Constitution. Drapeaux tricolores partout. Les autrichiens s'y cachaient. Petit théâtre infect. M. et Mme. Folinus. Le maestro Caldy. M. et Mme.

*Marzel. Szép Heléna.*⁵ Dalfy, Dalnoly et Mlle *Visconti.*
Mme. *Lukács.* Braves gens.

Temesvár. 8 h. diligence. Charmante ville mais allemande et triste. Hôtels magnifiques. La ville *forteresse* est entourée des 4 côtés par 4 faubourgs communicant à la forteresse par le parc. Le parc *Coronini* est le plus beau. Énorme distance si l'on compte les faubourgs. M. et Mme. *Reiman.* Mme. Kirchberger prima donna admirable Lucretia. Bariton *Malechevsky. Rossi* ténor. Opéra allemand. *Murad* effendi.—Beaucoup de *Serbes.*

Belgrade. 6 h. ch. fer jusqu'à *Bazias,* de là bateau par Danube jusqu'à Belgrade 7 heures. Rencontre avec Mr. Vizkelety. Horrible ville sale, turque, laide, mal pavée mais pleine de ducats. Mme. Anka *Obrenovich,* le Comte *Campo.* Shishkin, Consul russe. *Ignaccio,* Consul d'Italie, Société philharmonique. — M. Feodorovich, *Voulatch. Milovouk* des *Stojan, Svetozar* Vadim Radevoy en masse. Les turcs étaient entrain de vider la forteresse. Rezi Pacha s'en allait par ordre de Sultan et les serbes fêtaient leur liberté. Obrenovich Michael partait pour Constantinople remercier le Sultan.⁶ 101 coups de canon tirés. Chanson Serbe dédiée au Prince. L'infâme Joanovich intendant au Prince. Le métropolite de 28 ans, élevé à Moscou. Hôtel infecte et sale. Bateaux à vapeur allant 2 fois par jour à *Semlin* qui est vis-à-vis.

Pancsova, Autriche. 3 h. de bateau par Danube. Jolie ville propre, population mixte serbes et allemands. Beaucoup d'hôtels et beaux magasins.

Semlin. 3 h. bateau de Pancsova, un trou allemand et serbe. 4 jours à s'embêter à l'hôtel de Venise—attendant le bateau pour Neusatz. Jolie vue sur Belgrade de l'autre côté du Danube. Beaucoup de capitaines de marine, officiers autrichiens faisant l'amour sous les fenêtres — à chaque maison.

Neusatz, Novosad. Ville tout à fait serbe, peu d'hongrois (7 heures de Semlin Danube). Hôtel Grüner Kranz infecte et voleur. Hôtel Elisabeth très beau. *Popovich* rédacteur de journal. Sa femme actrice serbe, beauté splendide. Lue parlant russe et français. Mr. Vizkelety et sa femme 2 filles, Irma et— Braves hongrois. Café de Teremeich Demovladeko. Sa fille Maria. Les frères pravoslavny. Joanovich, Stojanovich et autres. Mr. *Isau* ex-précepteur des enfants du G. D. Michel (Mr. Vermily).

Betchkerek. 2 h. de bateau jusqu'à *Titel,* petit endroit infect sur Theiss et à 2h. du Danube, de là 3 heures par diligence jusqu'à Betchkerek. La ville est sale et laide. Beaucoup de serbes et d'hongrois surtout des juifs. Les derniers veulent les droits égaux aux chrétiens. Députation juive envoyée au ministre hongrois de Pesth. Refus du Cte. Andrássy. Théâtre national serbe, le *Tchizmar.*

Eszek (Slavonie) de Betchkerek à Titel (Wagen). Bateau à vapeur pour Neusatz, jour et coucher la nuit au bateau jusqu'à l'embouchure de *Drava*. On change de bateau et on va par Drava 3 h. jusqu'à *Eszek,* composée de 3 villes qui entourent la forteresse qui est énorme. *Oberstadt,* Neustadt et Unterstadt. Population serbes presque tous, catholiques allemands et hongrois. De 500 à 1000 prisonniers tant politiques que pour autres crimes. Ville très jolie mais fort ennuyeuse. On voit la journée entière des détachements de prisonniers dont les jambes sont enchaînées et suivis de soldats avec leurs fusils—passer par les rues. Il n'y a qu'un mois que les prisonniers politiques italiens 800 en tout furent libérés par réclamation du Gouvt. Italien. Le théâtre dans l'Oberstadt est un vrai bijou, mais tous les directeurs se ruinent car ici la majorité du public sont des officiers qui ne payent que 20 Kr. l'entrée comme partout.[7] Il y a quelques années quand il y eut famine en Serbie et Slavonie que les Auts. proposèrent au peuple *pravoslavny,* de travailler aux grandes routes, moyennant 1 fl. par jour toute l'année—mais à condition—de prendre la religion catholique—autrement on les laissait mourir de faim. Dans la forteresse le meilleur hôtel est *Weisen Wolf,* bon marché. Ici comme dans d'autres villes de la Serbie, Slavonie et Autriche, tous les passants, hommes, femmes, aristocrates ou plèbes vous saluent dans la rue sans vous connaître et les enfants à la vue des personnes de bas étage ajoutent même infailliblement Küss die Hand!—Ce qui m'a fort étonné. O, [nous] subirons toute la journée.

Verchetz, grande ville fort sale—population serbe toute. Grand commerce de vin. *Obradovich* Kosta—tous Russophiles. 2 h. p. équipage la route Weisskirchen. Petite ville charmante toute enterrée dans les vignes. 1 quart d'heure chemin de fer de Verchetz et à 1 quart d'heure de Bu ..... serbes et allemands detestant les uns les autres. *Hôtel de Soleil* bon marché et bon. *Breton, Bouletich* le bâfrent. Environs magnifiques.

Horowitz. Demi village, demi ville, fabriques et ouvriers. La ville est enfouie dans les montagnes (bas Banat) mines d'or mais le gouvernement ayant acheté aux hongrois le terrain n'a plus le moyen d'avoir des ouvriers et on ne trouve que 4-5 ...... d'or par semaine. Ressemble à *Borzhom*.[8] Sign. Scoffa. Mr. Veuv, Bach. Population valaque et allemande. 6 h. de voiture de Weisskirchen.

Rechitza, grande et belle ville à 5 ou 6 énormes fabriques contenant 5 mille ouvriers presque tous prussiens et anglais. Énormes mines de fer. Compagnie française du Crédit Mobilier. Le plus beau pays du monde, une Suisse ..... Mme. *Borz* virtuose de piano. Ses sœurs. La famille *Mack*. 8 h. de voiture de Horowitz. Limite du haut Banat, la plus pittoresque route de l'univers. 14 h. de voiture de Temesvár.

Temesvár—X.

Kikinda. 2 h. de chemin de fer de Temesvár, grande bourgade. Mme. Stoikovich et ses neuf filles. Mr. Stefanovich, le colonel *Anneti-Monti*.

Hazfeld. 1 heure de Kik. chemin de fer.

Mehadia. Bains minéraux, seule et unique rue toute composée d'hôtels splendides et énormes, Hercules Bad, Röber Hôtel. La caverne des brigands dont le souterrain va de Mehadia jusqu'à Orsova. Fameuse légende de Ludwig le chef des brigands qui a donné son nom aux bains. Environs splendides.

Körös-Maros Sebes. Ville de frontière, petite, sale et ennuyeuse.

Lugos, jolie ville hongroise.

[The following four items, written in Russian, are very likely the amounts paid by H.P.B. for her tickets.]

From Vienna to Graz—8-25
From Vienna to Trieste—21-35
From T. to Venice—5-27
From Graz to Laibach—7-20

[On the remaining pages of the *Notebook* we find H.P.B.'s notes of various travelling expenses, most likely both transportation and food; these are written in Russian. She also lists certain monies received by her, but does not indicate their source. On one of the middle pages of the *Notebook* we find a sketch made by H.P.B. showing the geographical position on the map of some of the places she visited during this journey.]

[*Translation of the foregoing French text.*]

Kronstadt. Brassó — Transylvania. Hotel Grüner Baum. Comfortable and cheap. Mr. and Mad. Burcheg—teacher in the Gymnasium. Young Swiss, a bit pedantic. She is Hungarian and plays the flute. Old, blind Mad. Kántor. Kronstadt is one of the nicest small towns in Europe owing to its location, cleanliness and elegance. Quite near to it are the famous mineral waters of Borszék.—Coming from *Bucharest,* the *Zlaparis* ask for your passport, and make you pay for not examining your trunks by turning them inside out with their dirty hands. Very mixed population of Wallachians, Hungarians and Swabians. The architecture of the houses is entirely different. Each house has the date of its construction on the roof.[1]

Hermannstadt (Szeben)
Hotel Römischer Kaiser. A Hungarian thief. Hotel of the Hungarian Crown, German and a still greater thief.

The town is far from being as nice as Kronstadt, and is flooded with Austrian officers, mainly Poles. Regiment Hartmann. The Conductor of the band is Tütch, a Czech. The soldier violinist is a French virtuoso. Eternal discussion about Muraviov and *Haynau*.² Councilman Traposta, co-Carbonari, has already been stabbed by an unknown hand. His wife *László Anna,* is a composer of music. The Chief of Police, a *Pole,* was about to leave for Bucharest, to marry the monster of the fairs, Flora. Being a Pole and an Austrian employee, he is a humbug, a liar, and a thief. Lutheran church, all full of sculptures. Unique beauty. Statue of St. Nepomuk. 8 hours from Kronstadt.

Karlsburg. Fehérvár (Alba Julia). Ancient Roman camp. Remains and ruins. At present a Jewish town and an Austrian Fort. Hotel Ung. Krone. Adolf Benedict, Hungarian Jew, pretending to be the foremost baritone of the world. Cheap. Damned *Kántor!* The Neeman Society. The Jew *Lion* Emmanuel Mendl. Violin of the dentist Peterka. 8 hours by coach.

Klausenburg—(Kolozsvár). We are freezing on our way. A large and rather beautiful town. A 700 years old Cathedral. Nice theatre. Hotel *Biasini.* Expensive and bad. Director Fehérváry. Szephédy. (Miss Schönberg), a Jewess from Temesvár. Mme. *Nagy Hubert,* Fekete. *Philipovich* M. Heksh, the hissed baritone.

The Baron Bánffy and the Count Esterházy — Great success of the pianist Litolff—the last day of the Terreur of *Robespierre*.³ Orchestra. The Countess Mikes. The French Governor-General Count *Crenneville.* Festival of the Constitution.⁴ Austrian cannons jammed on the square. 10 hours by coach from Karlsburg.

Grosswardein (Nagyvárad). Large Jewish town. Many hotels and churches. Railway. 24 hours by coach from *Kolozsvár.*

Debreczen. 6 hours by train from *G. Ward.* Nice town. The most beautiful theatre in Hungary, more beautiful

H.P.B.'s TRAVEL-IMPRESSIONS 19

than in Pesth. The heart of Hungary. All Hungarians, few Germans. Ball of the Masons. Ball of the *Tzigans*.

Arad. 6 hours by train from Debreczen to Szolnok. Spent the night there. From there another 6 hours by train to Arad. A very large town. Entirely Hungarian. Many aristocrats. The *bridge* near the fortress where 13 Hungarian Generals were shot and hanged in 1849. Festival of the Constitution. Tricoloured [Hungarian] flags everywhere. The Austrians hide themselves. A small and unpleasant theatre. Mr. and Mad. Folinus. The maestro Cáldy. Mr. and Mme. *Marzel. Szép Heléna.*[5] Dalfy, Dalnoly and Mlle. *Visconti.* Mme. *Lukács.* Decent people.

Temesvár. 8 hours by coach. A charming place, but German and doleful. Magnificent hotels. The *Fort* is surrounded on all four sides by four suburbs communicating with the Fort through the park. The *Coronini* park is the most beautiful. Enormous distances if one reckons the suburbs. Mr. and Mme. *Reiman.* Mme. Kirchberger, prima donna and admirable Lucretia. Baritone *Malechevsky.* Tenor *Rossi.* German Opera. *Murad* effendi. Many *Serbians.*

Belgrade. 6 hours by train to *Bazias;* thence 7 hours by steamer on the Danube to Belgrade. Meeting with Mr. Vizkelety. Horrible, dirty city, Turkish, ugly, badly paved but full of ducats. Mme. Anka *Obrenović,* the Count *Campo.* Shishkin, the Russian Consul. *Ignaccio,* the Italian Consul. Philharmonic Society—M. Feodorovich, *Voulatch. Milovouk* of the *Stoyans, Svetozar* Vadim Radevoy *en masse.* The Turks were busy evacuating the fortress. Rezi Pasha was about to leave by order of the Sultan, and the Serbs celebrated their freedom. Michael Obrenović was going to Constantinople to thank the Sultan.[6] Cannons were fired 101 times. Serbian song dedicated to the Prince. Joanovich, the wretched superintendent of the Prince. The twenty-eight years old Metropolitan, educated in Moscow. Dirty and disgusting hotel. Steamers twice a day to *Semlin* on the opposite side.

Pancsova, Austria. 3 hours by steamer on the Danube.

Nice, clean town, mixed population of Serbs and Germans. Many hotels and beautiful stores.

Semlin, 3 hours by steamer from Pancsova, a German and Serbian hole. Four days of boredom in the Hotel Venice, awaiting the steamer for Neusatz. Nice view of Belgrade on the opposite bank of the Danube. Many Captains of the Navy. Austrian officers flirting at the windows — in every house.

Neusatz, Novosad. Altogether Serbian town, few Hungarians (7 hours from Semlin along the Danube). Hotel Grüner Kranz, disgusting and thievish. Very nice Hotel Elizabeth. *Popovich,* newspaper editor. His wife—a Serbian actress of outstanding beauty. He speaks Russian and French. Mr. Vizkelety, his wife and two daughters, Irma and— decent Hungarians. Coffee Shop of Teremeich Domovladeko. His daughter Maria. The brothers are Orthodox. Joanovich, Stoyanovich and others. Mr. *Isau,* ex-tutor of the children of Grand Duke Michael (Mr. Vermily).

Becskerek. 2 hours by steamer to *Titel,* a dirty little place on the Theiss and 2 hours from the Danube. From there 3 hours by coach to Becskerek. The town is dirty and unsightly. Many Serbs and Hungarians, mainly Jews. The latter want the same rights as the Christians. Jewish delegation sent to the Hungarian Minister at Pesth. Count Andrássy refused. National Serbian theatre—the *Tchizmar.*

Eszék (Slavonia). From Becskerek to Titel (coach). Steamer to Neusatz, day and night on the steamer down to the mouth of the river *Drava.* Change of steamer and 3 hours upstream on the Drava to *Eszék,* consisting of three parts surrounding the Fort which is enormous. *Oberstadt,* Neustadt and Unterstadt. Almost entirely Serbian population. The Austrians and Hungarians are Catholics. Between 500 and 1,000 prisoners, both political and for other crimes. A very beautiful town, but very boring. One sees the whole day long groups of prisoners in chains marching along the streets, escorted by soldiers armed with rifles. Just a month ago 800 Italian political prisoners were released on demand from the Italian Government. The theatre in Oberstadt is a real gem, but the managers are ruined because the majority of the public here are officers who pay only 20 Kr. for admission, as everywhere else.[7] Some years ago, when there was a famine in Serbia and Slavonia, the Austrians offered to the Orthodox people work, building roads, at the rate of 1 florin per day throughout the year, but on condition of embracing the Catholic faith; otherwise they would be left to starve. In the Fort the best hotel is *Weisen Wolf,* cheap. Here as in other cities of Serbia, Slavonia and Austria, all the passers-by in the streets, men, women, aristocrats and commoners alike, greet you without knowing you; and the children add unfailingly: Küss die Hand—which was a great surprise to me. Well, we'll submit to it all day long.

Verchetz, a very dirty large town, population entirely Serbian. Great trade in wine. *Obradovich* Kosta — all Russophiles. 2 hours by coach to *Weisskirchen.* A charming little town surrounded by vineyards. A quarter of an hour from Verchetz by train and the same from Bu . . . . . Serbians and Austrians detesting each other. *Hôtel de Soleil,* cheap and good. *Breton, Bouletich* and gluttony. Magnificent surroundings.

Horowitz. Half village, half town. Factories and working people. The place is buried in the mountains (Lower Banat); gold mines. The Government, however, having bought the ground from the Hungarians, is unable to get labourers, and one finds but 4 or 5 . . . . . of gold per week. It resembles *Borzhom.*[8] Sigr. Scoffa. Mr. Veuv. Bach. Wallachian and German population. 6 hours by coach from Weisskirchen.

Rechitza. Large and beautiful city with 5 or 6 factories employing five thousand workers, nearly all Prussians and English. Enormous iron ore mines. The French Company of Crédit Mobilier. The most beautiful country in the world, another Switzerland . . . . . . Mme. *Borz,* piano virtuoso. Her sisters. The *Mack* family. 8 hours by coach from Horowitz. Boundary of the High Banat, the most picturesque route in the universe. 14 hours by coach from Temesvár.

Temesvár—X.

Kikinda. Two hours by train from Temesvár; large village. Mme. Stoykovich and her nine daughters. Mr. Stefanovich, Colonel *Anneti-Monti.*

Hatzfeld. One hour by train from Kikinda.

Mehadia. Mineral baths. Only one street consisting of enormous and splendid hotels. Hercules Bad. Röber Hotel. The cave of the brigands with a tunnel reaching from Mehadia to Orsova. Famous legend about Ludwig, the chief of the brigands, who has given his name to the Spa. Splendid surroundings.

Körös-Maros Sebes. Frontier town, small, dirty and boring.

Lugos, nice Hungarian town.

[The following four items, written in Russian, are very likely the amounts paid by H.P.B. for her tickets:]

From Vienna to Gratz—8-25
From Vienna to Trieste—21-35
From T. to Venice—5-27
From Gratz to Laibach—7-20

———

[The following Notes may be of interest in connection with H.P.B.'s Travel-Impressions:

[1]These dates are laid out in tiles of a different color.
[2]Julius Jacob Haynau (1786-1853), Austrian General, the natural son of the landgrave—afterwards elector—of Hesse-Cassel, William IX. Of violent temper and fanatical hatred of revolutionary movements, he was the most cruel oppressor of the Hungarians after the National Uprising against Austria in 1848-49.
[3]Henri (Charles) Litolff, French pianist and composer, born in London Feb. 6, 1818; died at Bois-le-Combes, near Paris,

Aug. 6, 1891. His father was an Alsatian soldier taken prisoner by the English in the Peninsular War, who had settled in London and had married an English woman. In 1831, Litolff was brought to Moscheles and taken gratis as pupil, on account of great ability. He appeared in Covent Garden Theatre, July 24, 1832. Married when seventeen and settled for a while in France, he led a wandering life for a number of years, marrying later for a second time. In 1861, he started the "Collection Litolff," a cheap and accurate edition of classical music. He married once again, this time Countess de la Rochefoucault. There are about 115 works attributed to him, among them the Operas "Die Braut von Kynast" and "Les Templiers." His overtures "Robespierre" and "Girondisten" were composed for Wolfgang Robert Griepenkerl's (1810-1868) dramas bearing these titles. "Robespierre" dates from sometime between 1849 and 1853.

[4]The first Hungarian responsible Ministry was formed on February 17, 1867; as a consequence of this, the Office of the Governor-General in Transylvania ceased to function. The last Governor-General was Folliol-Crenwille (or Crenneville). This explains what H.P.B. meant by the "festival of the Constitution."

[5]The operetta Helen of Troy.

[6]Prince Michael Obrenović III (1838-68), the youngest son of Prince Miloš Obrenović I, received the keys of the Fortress in Belgrade on April 13, 1867, from Al Rezi Pasha. Before this actually took place, Prince Michael had been to Constantinople to thank the Sultan.

The above information has been verified in the Hungarian State Archives, so that there can be no doubt that H.P.B. was in Belgrade at this specific time. Consult also Jenö Horváth, *History of Diplomacy*, Vol. I, p. 188, in connection with these political events.

[7]One hundred Kreutzers make 1 Florin.

[8]Small settlement in the former Tiflis Province of the Caucasus, about 2600 feet above sea level; it is famous for its hot mineral waters and has been frequented for many years by tubercular people.]

[Many of the towns and localities visited by H.P.B. in the course of her travels have changed their names since. In order to help the student in identifying them on the map, the following Table has been prepared which shows the earlier and the present-day names of the various places:

German	Hungarian	Rumanian (*today*)	Serbo-Croatian (*today*)
Kronstadt	Brassó	Braşov	
	Borszék	Borsec	
Hermannstadt (on river Zibin)	Szeben (Nagyszeben)	Sibiu	
Karlsburg (formerly Weissenburg)	Gyulafehérvár	Alba Julia	
Klausenburg (on Little Szamos)	Kolozsvár	Cluj	
Grosswardein (on river Körös)	Nagyvárad	Oradea (or Oradea Mare)	
Debrezin	Debrecen		
	Szolnok (on confluence of Tisza and Zagyva)		
	Arad	Arad	
	Temesvár (on Béga Canal)	Timişoara	
	Báziás (on Danube)	Bazias	
	Pancsova (on mouth of Temes into Danube)		Pančevo
Semlin	Zimony (on Danube)		
Neusatz (Novosad)	Ujvidék		Novi Sad
	Titel (on Tisza)		
	Becskerek Nagybecskerek (on Béga Canal)		Zrenyanin

H.P.B.'s Travel-Impressions 25

Esseg (on Drava)	Eszék	Osijek
Werschitz (on Theresien Canal)	Versecz	Vršac
Weisskirchen	Fehértemplom	Bela Crkva
Orawitza	Oravicabánya	Oravitsa
Reschitza	Resicabánya	Reşitsa Montana
	Nagykikinda	Veliki-Kikinda
Hatzfeld	Zsombolya	Jimbolia
	Mehadia (on Bela)	
Kreuz	Körös	Križevci
	Lugos (on Temes)	Lugoj
	Sebes	
	Badara	
Fünfkirchen	Pécs	
Agram (on river Medveščak)	Zágráb	Zagreb
Carlo Karlstadt (on Kulpa)	Károlyváros	Karlovac
Fiume		Rijeka-Sušak
Jägerhorn	Zombor	Sombor

—*Compiler.*]

[There are also in the Adyar Archives eight small *Notebooks*, numbered 1 to 8, in which H.P.B. made various notations, copied quotations from various writings and references to works she had apparently consulted. Here and there appears some original material from her own pen, mainly on the subject of occult teachings, such as the lokas and the states of consciousness. There are also some translated passages from French and other books. Much of this material belongs to the period when she was working on *Isis Unveiled;* some of it refers to *The Secret Doctrine;* and one of the *Notebooks* has reference to *The Key to Theosophy*. It is obvious, therefore, that none of this material belongs to her early years, and whatever there is from her own pen in these *Notebooks* will be found in later volumes of the present Series.]

1874

H.P.B.'S SCRAPBOOKS

[Beginning in 1874, and for about ten years, H.P.B. pasted a wide variety of cuttings from newspapers and magazines into Scrapbooks. There are twenty-four of them in the Archives of The Theosophical Society at Adyar, India. Every newspaper reference to the T.S. and its work, and any account thought to be of consequence for historical purposes, was pasted in these Scrapbooks. This included also cuttings of H.P.B.'s own articles and letters to Editors which had been published, and some of Col. Olcott's contributions to various Journals of the day.

H.P.B. appended pen-and-ink and pencil remarks and comments to various statements in the text of these articles; many of these comments are humorous and are enhanced by cartoons, either drawn by herself or pasted in from some other magazine or paper, frequently with her own additions. Here and there appears some important statement of her own, not to be found anywhere else in her writings.

In the pages that follow, the reader will find all pertinent comments by H.P.B. introduced in their approximate chronological sequence, which at times is not easy to determine; some of H.P.B.'s annotations may have been added later than the time when any given article was published.—*Compiler.*]

[The first article definitely known to be from the pen of H.P.B. is the one in the New York *Daily Graphic*, entitled "Marvellous Spirit Manifestations," with which the present Volume opens:]

MARVELLOUS SPIRIT MANIFESTATIONS

A SECOND IDA PFEIFFER WITH THE EDDYS — APPARITIONS OF GEORGIANS, PERSIANS, KURDS, CIRCASSIANS, AFRICANS, AND RUSSIANS — WHAT A RUSSIAN LADY THINKS OF DR. BEARD.

[*The Daily Graphic*, New York, Vol. V, October 30, 1874, p. 873]

The following letter was addressed to a contemporary journal by Mme. Blavatsky, and was handed to us for publication in *The Daily Graphic*, as we have been taking the lead in the discussion of the curious subject of Spiritualism.

EDITOR, *The Daily Graphic*.

Aware in the past of your love of justice and fair play, I most earnestly solicit the use of your columns to reply to an article of Dr. G. M. Beard in relation to the Eddy family in Vermont. He, in denouncing them and their spiritual manifestations in a most sweeping declaration, would aim a blow at the entire spiritual world of today. His letter appeared this morning (October 27th). Dr. George M. Beard has for the last few weeks assumed the part of the "roaring lion" seeking for a medium "to devour." It appears that today the learned gentleman is more hungry than ever. No wonder, after the failure he has experienced with Mr. Brown, the "mind-reader," at New Haven.

I do not know Dr. Beard personally, nor do I care to know how far he is entitled to wear the laurels of his profession as an M.D.; but what I do know is that he may never hope to equal, much less to surpass, such men and *savants* as Crookes, Wallace, or even Flammarion, the French astronomer, all of whom have devoted years to the investigation of Spiritualism. All of them came to the conclusion that, supposing even the well-known phenomenon of materialization of spirits did not prove the identity of the persons whom they purported to represent, it was not, at all events, the work of mortal hands; still less was it a *fraud*.

Now to the Eddys. Dozens of visitors have remained there for weeks and even for months; not a single *séance* has taken place but some of them realized the personal presence of a friend, a relative, a mother, father, or dear departed child. But lo! here comes Dr. Beard, stops less than two days, applies his powerful electrical battery, under which the spirit does not even wink or flinch, closely examines the cabinet (in which he finds nothing), and then turns his back and declares most emphatically "that he wishes it to be perfectly understood that if his scientific name ever appears in connection with the Eddy family, it must be only to expose them as the greatest frauds who cannot do even good trickery." *Consummatum est!* Spiritualism is defunct. *Requiescat in pace!* Dr. Beard has killed it with one word. Scatter ashes over your venerable but silly heads, oh Crookes, Wallace and Varley! Henceforth you must be considered as demented, psychologized, and lunatics, and so must it be with the many thousands of Spiritualists who have seen and talked with their friends and relatives departed, recognizing them at Moravia, at the Eddys', and elsewhere throughout the length and breadth of this continent. But is there no escape from the horns of this dilemma? Yea, verily, Dr. Beard writes thus: "When your correspondent returns to New York I will teach him on any convenient evening to do all that the Eddys do." Pray why should a *Daily Graphic* reporter be the only one selected by G. M. Beard, M.D., for initiation into the knowledge of so clever a "trick"? In such a case why not publicly denounce this universal trickery, and so benefit the whole world? But Dr. Beard seems to be as partial in his selections as he is clever in detecting said tricks. Didn't the learned doctor say to Colonel Olcott while at the Eddys' that three dollars' worth of second-hand drapery would be enough for him to show how to materialize all the spirits that visit the Eddy homestead?

To this I reply, backed as I am by the testimony of hundreds of reliable witnesses, that all the wardrobe of Niblo's Theatre would not suffice to attire the number of spirits that emerge night after night from an empty little closet.

Let Dr. Beard rise and explain the following fact if he can: I remained fourteen days at the Eddys'. In that short period of time I saw and recognized fully out of 119 apparitions seven spirits. I admit that I was the only one to recognize them, the rest of the audience not having been with me in my numerous travels throughout the East, but their various dresses and costumes were plainly seen and closely examined by all.

The first was a Georgian boy, dressed in the historical Caucasian attire, the picture of whom will shortly appear in *The Daily Graphic*.* I recognized and questioned him in Georgian upon circumstances known only to myself. I was understood and answered. Requested by me in his mother tongue (upon the whispered suggestion of Colonel Olcott) to play the "Lezguinka," a Circassian dance, he did so immediately upon the guitar.

Second. A little old man appears. He is dressed as Persian merchants generally are. His dress is perfect as a national costume. Everything is in its right place, down to the "babouches" that are off his feet, he stepping out in his stockings. He speaks his name in a loud whisper. It is "Hassan Aga," an old man whom I and my family have known for twenty years at Tiflis. He says, half in Georgian and half in Persian, that he has got a "big secret to tell me," and comes at three different times, vainly seeking to finish his sentence.

Third. A man of gigantic stature emerges forth, dressed in the picturesque attire of the warriors of Kurdistan. He does not speak, but bows in the Oriental fashion, and lifts up his spear ornamented with bright-coloured feathers, shaking it in token of welcome. I recognize him immediately as Saffar Ali Bek, a young chief of a tribe of Kurds, who used to accompany me in my trips around Ararat in Armenia on horseback, and who on one occasion saved my life.† More, he bends to the ground as though picking up a handful of

---

* [This boy was Michalko Guegidze, of Kutais, Georgia, who was a servant in the household of Katherine de Witte. See in connection with this subject Col. H. S. Olcott's work, *People from the Other World*, Hartford, Conn., 1875, pp. 298 *et seq.*—*Compiler.*]

† [Safar Ali Bek Ibrahim Bek Ogli, mentioned by Col. Olcott in his *People from the Other World*, p. 320.—*Compiler.*]

PORTION OF A PAGE OF H.P.B.'S SCRAPBOOK I

(See page 34 of the present volume for transcription of her pen-and-ink remarks.)

ALEXANDER NIKOLAYEVICH AKSAKOV
1823-1903
(Consult the *Bio-Bibliographical Index* for biographical sketch.)

mould and scattering it around, presses his hand to his bosom—a gesture familiar only to the tribes of the Kurdistan.

Fourth. A Circassian comes out. I can imagine myself at Tiflis, so perfect is his costume of "nouker" (a man who either runs before or behind one on horseback). This one speaks. More, he corrects his name, which I pronounced wrongly on recognizing him, and when I repeat it he bows, smiling, and says in the purest guttural Tartar, which sounds so familiar to my ear, "Tchoch yachtchi" (all right), and goes away.

Fifth. An old woman appears with a Russian headgear. She comes out and addresses me in Russian, calling me by an endearing term that she used in my childhood. I recognize an old servant of my family, a nurse of my sister.

Sixth. A large powerful negro next appears on the platform. His head is ornamented with a wonderful *coiffure,* something like horns wound about with white and gold. His looks are familiar to me, but I do not at first recollect where I have seen him. Very soon he begins to make some vivacious gestures, and his mimicry helps me to recognize him at a glance. It is a conjurer from Central Africa. He grins and disappears.

Seventh and last. A large grey-haired gentleman comes out attired in the conventional suit of black. The Russian decoration of Saint Ann hangs suspended by a large red moiré ribbon with two black stripes—a ribbon, as every Russian will know, belonging to said decoration. This ribbon is worn around his neck. I feel faint, for I think of recognizing my father. But the latter was a great deal taller. In my excitement I address him in English, and ask him: "Are you my father?" He shakes his head in the negative, and answers as plainly as any mortal man can speak, and in Russian, "No; I am your uncle." The word "diadia" has been heard and remembered by all the audience. It means "uncle."

But what of that? Dr. Beard knows it to be but a pitiful

trick, and we must submit in silence. People that know me know that I am far from being credulous. Though a Spiritualist of many years' standing,* I am more sceptical in receiving evidence from paid mediums than many unbelievers. But when I receive such evidence as I received at the Eddys', I feel bound on my honour, and under the penalty of confessing myself a moral coward, to defend the mediums, as well as the thousands of my brother and sister Spiritualists, against the conceit and slander of one man who has nothing and no one to back him in his assertions. I now hereby finally and publicly challenge Dr. Beard to the amount of $500 to produce before a public audience and under the same conditions the manifestations herein attested, or, failing this, to bear the ignominious consequences of his proposed *exposé*.

—H. P. BLAVATSKY.
124 East Sixteenth Street, October 27.

[In H.P.B.'s *Scrapbook*, Vol. I, the above article is pasted on page 5, in three separate columns, together with the Press Cutting mentioning her arrival at the Eddy Homestead on Oct. 14, 1874, as may be seen on the accompanying illustration. H.P.B.'s comment at the top of the page reads:]

The curtain is raised. — H.S.O.'s acquaintance on October 14, 1874, with H.P.B. at Chittenden. H. S. Olcott is a — *Rabid Spiritualist*, and H. P. Blavatsky is an *occultist* — one who laughs at the supposed agency of Spirits! (but all the same pretends to be one herself).

[To the date of the article H.P.B. added in pen and ink: 1874; and she also wrote the following footnote under column 3:]

#They may be the *portraits* of the dead people then repro . . . . . (they certainly are *not* Spirits or Souls) yet a *real* . . . . . nomenon produced by the Elementaries. H.P.B.

---

*[When H.P.B. pasted the cutting of this article in her *Scrapbook*, Vol. I, p. 5, she rubbed out the words "a Spiritualist," substituted for them the words "an Occultist," and underlined in blue the entire sentence.—*Compiler*.]

Marvellous Spirit Manifestations

[The sign introducing the footnote is missing in the actual article; there are, however, blue underlinings and quotation marks in connection with the word "spirits," in the 4th and 5th paragraphs of the text, made by H.P.B., and to which her footnote may refer.]

[In A. P. Sinnett's well-known work, *Incidents in the Life of H. P. Blavatsky* (New York: J. W. Bouton, 1886), pp. 131-33, there occurs a rather important statement, as well as a direct quote of H.P.B.'s own words, bearing upon the *séances* at the Eddy Brothers. Mr. Sinnett says that H.P.B.

". . . . has tried with the most famous mediums to evoke and communicate with those dearest to her, and whose loss she had deplored, but could never succeed. 'Communications and messages' she certainly did receive, and got their signatures, and on two occasions their *materialized forms*, but the communications were couched in a vague and gushing language quite unlike the style she knew so well. Their signatures, as she has ascertained, were obtained from her own brain; and *on no* occasion, when the presence of a relation was announced and the form described by the medium, who was ignorant of the fact that Mme. Blavatsky could *see* as well as any of them, has she recognized the 'spirit' of the alleged relative in the host of spooks and elementaries that surrounded them (when the medium was a genuine one of course). Quite the reverse. For she often saw, to her disgust, how her own recollections and brain-images were drawn from her memory and disfigured in the confused amalgamation that took place between their reflection in the medium's brain which instantly sent them out, and the shells which *sucked them in* like a sponge and objectivized them— '*a hideous shape with a mask on* in my sight,' she tells us."

H.P.B. herself goes on to say:]

Even the materialized form of my uncle at the Eddy's was the picture; it was I who sent it out from my own mind, as I had come out to make experiments without telling it to any one. It was like an empty outer envelope of my uncle that I seemed to throw on the medium's astral body. I saw and followed the process. I knew Will Eddy was a genuine medium, and the phenomenon as real *as it could be,* and, therefore, when days of trouble came for him, I defended him in the papers. In short, for all the years of experience in America I never succeeded in identifying, in one single instance, those I wanted to see.

It is only in my dreams and personal visions that I was brought in direct contact with my own blood relatives and friends, those between whom and myself there had been a strong mutual *spiritual* love . . . . . For certain psycho-magnetic reasons, too long to be explained here, *the shells of those spirits* who loved us best will not, with a very few exceptions, approach us. They have no need of it since, unless they were irretrievably wicked, they have us with them in Devachan, that state of bliss in which the *monads* are surrounded with all those, and that, which they have loved—objects of spiritual aspirations as well as human entities. "Shells" once separated from their higher principles have nought in common with the latter. They are not drawn to their relatives and friends, but rather to those with whom their terrestrial, sensuous affinities are the strongest. Thus the shell of a drunkard will be drawn to one who is either a drunkard already or has a germ of this passion in him, in which case it will develop it by using his organs to satisfy the craving; one who died full of sexual passion for a still living partner will have its shell drawn to him or her, etc. We Theosophists, and especially occultists, must never lose sight of the profound axiom of the Esoteric Doctrine which teaches us that it is we, the living, who are drawn toward the spirits—but that the latter can never, even though they would, descend to us, or rather into our sphere.

ABOUT SPIRITUALISM*

[*The Daily Graphic*, New York, Vol. VI, November 13, 1874, pp. 90-91]

To the Editor of *The Daily Graphic*:

As Dr. Beard has scorned (in his scientific grandeur) to answer the challenge sent to him by your humble ser-

---

*[In her *Scrapbook*, Vol. I, p. 6, where this article is pasted in, H.P.B. wrote across the top of the page:
My 2nd letter to *N. Y. Graphic,* November 14, 1874.
—*Compiler.*]

vant in the number of *The Daily Graphic* for the 30th of October last, and preferred instructing the public in general rather than one "credulous fool" in particular, let her come from Circassia or Africa, I fully trust you will permit me to use your paper once more, in order that by pointing out some very spicy peculiarities of this amazingly scientific exposure, the public might better judge to whose door the aforesaid elegant epithet could be more appropriately laid.

For a week or so an immense excitement, a thrill of sacrilegious fear, if I am allowed this expression, ran through the psychologized frames of the Spiritualists of New York. It was rumored in ominous whispers that G. Beard, M.D., the Tyndall of America, was coming out with his peremptory exposure of the Eddys' ghosts, and—the Spiritualists trembled for their gods!

The dreaded day has come; the number of *The Daily Graphic* for November the 9th is before us. We have read it carefully, with respectful awe—for *true* science has always been an authority for us (weak-minded fool though we may be), and so we handled the dangerous exposure with a feeling somewhat akin to the one of a fanatic Christian opening a volume of "Büchner." We perused it to the last; we turned the page over and over again, vainly straining our eyes and brain to detect therein one word of scientific proof or a solitary atom of overwhelming evidence that would thrust into our spiritualistic bosom the venomous fangs of doubt. But no; not a particle of reasonable explanation or a scientific evidence that what we have all seen, heard, and felt at the Eddys' was but delusion. In our feminine modesty, still allowing the said article the benefit of the doubt, we disbelieved our own senses, and so devoted a whole day to the picking up of sundry bits of criticism from judges that we believed more competent than ourselves, and at last came collectively to the following conclusion:

The Daily Graphic has allowed Dr. Beard in its magnanimity nine columns of its precious pages to prove—what? Why, the following: First, that he, Dr. Beard, according to his own modest assertions (see columns second and third), is more entitled to occupy the position of an actor entrusted with characters of simpletons (Molière's *Tartuffe* might fit him perhaps as naturally) than to undertake the difficult part of a Prof. Faraday *vis-à-vis* the Chittenden D. D. Home.

Secondly, that notwithstanding the learned doctor was "overwhelmed already with professional labours" (a nice and cheap *réclame,* by the way) and scientific researches, he gave the latter another direction, and so went to the Eddys'. That arrived there he played with Horatio Eddy, for the glory of science and the benefit of humanity, the difficult character of a "dishevelled simpleton," and was rewarded in his scientific research by finding on the said suspicious premises a professor of bumps, "a poor harmless fool"! Galileo, of famous memory, when he detected the sun in its involuntary imposture, chuckled certainly less over his triumph than does Dr. Beard over the discovery of this "poor fool" No. 1. Here we modestly suggest that perhaps the learned doctor had no business to go so far as Chittenden for that.

Further, the doctor, forgetting entirely the wise motto *"non bis in idem,"* discovers and asserts throughout the length of his article that all the past, present, and future generations of pilgrims to the "Eddy homestead" are collectively fools, and that every solitary member of this numerous body of Spiritualistic pilgrims is likewise "a weak-minded, credulous fool"! Query—The proof of it, if you please, Dr. Beard? Answer—Dr. Beard has said so, and Echo responds, Fool!

Truly miraculous are thy doings indeed, O Mother Nature! The cow is black and its milk is white! But then, you see, those ill-bred, ignorant Eddy brothers have allowed their credulous guests to eat up all the "trout" caught by Dr. Beard and paid by him seventy-five cents per pound as a penalty; and that fact alone might have turned him a little—how shall we say, sour, prejudiced? No; erroneous in his statement will answer better.

For erroneous he is, not to say more. When, assuming

an air of scientific authority, he affirms that the *séance-room* is generally so dark that one cannot recognize at three feet distance his own mother, he says what is not true. When he tells us further that he saw through a hole in one of the shawls and the space between them all the manoeuvres of Horatio's arm, he risks to find himself belied by thousands who, weak-minded though they may be, are not blind for all that, neither are they confederates of the Eddys, but far more reliable witnesses in their simple-minded honesty than Dr. Beard is in his would-be scientific and unscrupulous testimony. The same when he says that no one is allowed to approach the spirits nearer than twelve feet distance, still less to touch them, except the "two simple-minded, ignorant idiots" who generally sit on both ends of the platform. To my knowledge many other persons have sat there besides those two.

Dr. Beard ought to know this better than anyone else, as he has sat there himself. A sad story is in circulation, by the way, at the Eddys'. The records of the spiritual *séances* at Chittenden have devoted a whole page to the account of a terrible danger that has threatened for a moment to deprive America of one of her brightest scientific stars. Dr. Beard, admitting a portion of the story himself, perverts the rest of it, as he does everything else in his article. The doctor admits that he has been badly struck by the guitar, and, not being able to bear the pain, "jumped up" and broke the circle. Now it clearly appears that the learned gentleman has neglected to add to the immense stock of his knowledge the first rudiments of "logic." He boasts himself of having completely blinded Horatio and others as to the real object of his visit. What should then Horatio pummel his head for? The spirits were never known before to be as rude as that. But then Dr. B. does not believe in their existence and so puts the whole thing to Horatio's door. He forgets to state, though, that a whole shower of missiles were thrown at his head, and that, "pale as a ghost"—so says the tale-telling record— the poor scientist surpassed for a moment the "fleet-footed Achilles" himself in the celerity with which he took to his heels. How strange if Horatio, not suspecting him still, left him standing at two feet distance from the shawl? How very logical?

It becomes evident that the said neglected logic was keeping company at the time with old mother Truth at the bottom of her well, not being wanted, none of them, by Dr. Beard. I myself have sat upon the upper step of the platform for fourteen nights by the side of Mrs. Cleveland. I got up every time "Honto" approached me to an inch of my face in order to see her the better. I have touched her hands repeatedly as other spirits have been touched, and even embraced her nearly every night. Therefore, when I read Dr. Beard's preposterous and cool assertion that "a very low order of genius is required to obtain command of a few words in different languages and so to mutter them to credulous Spiritualists," I feel every right in the world to say in my turn that such a scientific exposure as Dr. Beard has come out with in his article does not require any genius at all; *per contra,* it requires the most ridiculous faith on the part of the writer in his own infallibility, as well as a positive confidence in finding in all his readers what he elegantly terms "weak-minded fools." Every word of his statement, when it is not a most evident untruth, is a wicked and malicious insinuation, built on the very equivocal authority of one witness against the evidence of thousands.

Says Dr. Beard, "I have proved that the life of the Eddys is one long lie; the details need no further discussion." The writer of the above lines forgets, by saying these imprudent words, that some people might think that "like attracts the like." He went to Chittenden with deceit in his heart and falsehood on his lips, and so, judging his neighbour by the character he assumed himself, he takes everyone for a knave when he does not put him down as a fool. Declaring so positively that he has proved it, the doctor forgets one trifling circumstance, namely, that he has proved nothing whatever.

Where are his boasted proofs? When we contradict him by saying that the *séance*-room is far from being as dark as he pretends it to be, and that the spirits have repeatedly called out themselves through Mrs. Eaton's voice for more light, we only say what we can prove before any jury. When Dr. Beard says that all the spirits are personated by W. Eddy, he advances what would prove to be a greater conundrum for solution than the apparition of spirits themselves. There he falls right away into the domain of Cagliostro: for if Dr. B. has seen five or six spirits in all, other persons, myself included, have seen one hundred and nineteen in less than a fortnight, nearly all of whom were differently dressed. Besides, the accusation of Dr. Beard implies the idea to the public that the artist of *The Daily Graphic* who made the sketches of so many of those apparitions, and who is not a "credulous Spiritualist" himself, is likewise a humbug, propagating to the world what he did not see, and so thrusting at large the most preposterous and outrageous lie.

When the learned doctor will have explained to us how any man in his shirt-sleeves and a pair of tight pants for an attire can possibly conceal on his person (the cabinet having been previously found empty) a whole bundle of clothes, women's robes, hats, caps, headgears, and entire suits of evening dress, white waistcoats and neckties included, then he will be entitled to more belief than he is at present. That would be a proof indeed, for, with all due respect to his scientific mind, Dr. Beard is not the first Oedipus that had thought of catching the Sphinx by its tail and so unriddle the mystery. We have known more than one "weak-minded fool," ourselves included, that has laboured under a similar delusion for more than one night, but all of us were finally obliged to repeat the words of the great Galileo, *Eppur si muove!* and give it up.

But Dr. Beard, he does not give it up. Preferring to keep a scornful silence as to any reasonable explanation, he hides the secret of the above mystery in the depths of his profoundly scientific mind. "His life is given to scientific researches," you see; "his physiological knowledge and neuro-physiological learning are immense," for he says so, and skilled as he is in combating fraud by still greater fraud (see column the eighth), spiritualistic humbug has no more mysteries for him. In five minutes this scientist has done more towards science than all the rest of the scientists put together have done in years of labour, and "would feel ashamed if he had not." (See same column.) In the overpowering modesty of his learning he takes no credit upon himself for having done so, though he has discovered the astounding, novel fact of the "cold benumbing sensation." How Wallace, Crookes, and Varley, the naturalist-anthropologist, the chemist and electrician, will blush with envy in their old country! America alone is able to produce on her fertile soil such quick and miraculous intellects. *Veni, vidi, vici!* was the motto of a great conqueror. Why would not Dr. Beard select for his crest the same? And then, not unlike the Alexanders and the Caesars of the antiquity (in the primitive simplicity of his manners), he abuses people so elegantly, calling them "fools" when he cannot find a better argument.

A far more wise mind than Dr. Beard (shall he dispute the fact?) has suggested, centuries ago, that the tree was to be judged according to its fruits. Spiritualism, notwithstanding the desperate efforts of more scientific men than himself, stands its ground without flinching for more than a quarter of a century. Where are the fruits of the tree of science that blossoms on the soil of Dr. Beard's mind? If we are to judge of them by his article, then, verily, the said tree needs more than usual care. As for the fruits, it would appear that they are as yet in the realms of "sweet delusive hope." But then, perhaps, the doctor was afraid to crush his readers under the weight of his learning (true merit has been in all days modest and unassuming), and that accounts for the learned doctor withholding from us any scientific proof of the fraud that he pretends exposing, except the above-mentioned fact of the "cold benumbing sensation." But how Horatio can keep his hand and arm ice-cold under a warm shawl for half an hour at a time, in summer as well as in any other season, and that without having some ice concealed about his person, or how he can prevent it from thawing—all the above is a mystery that Dr. Beard doesn't reveal for the present. Maybe he will tell us something of it in his book that he advertises in the article. Well, we only hope that the former will be more satisfactory than the latter.

I will add but a few words before ending my debate with Dr. Beard for ever. All that he says about the lamp concealed in a bandbox, the strong confederates, etc., exists but in his imagination, for the mere sake of argument, we suppose. "False in one, false in all," says Dr. Beard on column the sixth. These words are a just verdict to his own article.

Here I will briefly state what I reluctantly withheld up to the present moment from the knowledge of all such as Dr. Beard. The fact was too sacred in my eyes to allow it to be trifled with in newspaper gossiping. But now, in order to settle the question at once, I deem it my duty as a Spiritualist to surrender it to the opinion of the public.

On the last night that I spent with the Eddys I was presented by George Dix and Mayflower with a silver decoration, the upper part of a medal with which I was but too familiar. I quote the precise words of the spirit: "We bring you this decoration, for we think you will value it more highly than anything else. You shall recognize it, for it is the badge of honour that was presented to your father by his Government for the campaign of 1828, between Russia and Turkey. We got it through the influence of your uncle, who appeared to you here this evening. We brought it from your father's grave at Stavropol. You shall identify it by a certain sign known to yourself." These words were spoken in the presence of forty witnesses. Colonel Olcott will describe the fact and give the design of the decoration.*

I have the said decoration in my possession. I know it as having belonged to my father. More, I have identified it by a portion that, through carelessness, I broke myself

---

* [See H.P.B.'s explanation on pp. 203-04 of the present Volume. On page 357 of Col. Olcott's work *People from the Other World* may be found the drawing of both the buckle and the decoration itself.
—*Compiler.*]

many years ago, and, to settle all doubt in relation to it, I possess the photograph of my father (a picture that has never been at the Eddys', and could never possibly have been seen by any of them) on which this medal is plainly visible.

Query for Dr. Beard: How could the Eddys know that my father was buried at Stavropol; that he was ever presented with such a medal, or that he had been present and in actual service at the time of the war of 1828?

Willing as we are to give every one his due, we feel compelled to say on behalf of Dr. Beard that he has not boasted of more than he can do, advising the Eddys to take a few private lessons of him in the trickery of mediumship. The learned doctor must be expert in all such trickeries. We are likewise ready to admit that in saying as he did that "his article would only confirm the more the Spiritualists in their belief" (and he ought to have added, "convince no one else"), Dr. Beard has proved himself to be a greater "prophetic medium" than any other in this country!

H. P. BLAVATSKY.

23 Irving Place.

[In H.P.B.'s *Scrapbook*, Vol. I, pp. 6-7, where the above article is pasted, H.P.B. added in pen and ink under her signature:]

So much in defence of *phenomena,* as to whether these Spirits are *ghosts* is another question.

H.P.B.

[In H.P.B.'s *Scrapbook*, Vol. I, pp. 7-8, there is a cutting from *The Daily Graphic* of November 1874, which deals with the visit of a Mr. Brown, the "mind reader," to the Eddys' Homestead. Mr. Brown relates how one of the "spirits" brought to H.P.B. one of the decorations which had belonged to her father, and says that "Madame was overwhelmed with gratitude."

H.P.B. underlined the word *overwhelmed* and added at the end of the article in pen and ink:]

Overwhelmed—be switched! . . . . not my father's pet, if you please. H. P. Blavatsky is never "overwhelmed."

[In *Scrapbook*, Vol. I, p. 8, the account of Mr. Brown is followed immediately by an article entitled "Unpractical Spirits," presumably also from *The Daily Graphic*. It is signed with the initials "I.F.F." which obviously stand for Irvin Francis Fern. H.P.B. added the following remarks in pen and ink:]

Bravo! Irvin Francis Fern—a great Occultist. He is RIGHT but we have to defend phenomena & prove it too before we teach them *philosophy*.

[ELBRIDGE GERRY BROWN]

[It is interesting and significant to bear in mind that at the earliest stage of the modern Theosophical effort, in addition to H. P. Blavatsky and Col. Henry S. Olcott, a third individual had been selected by the Teachers to play an important part in the initial work. This individual was Elbridge Gerry Brown, a young American who was Editor of the *Spiritual Scientist* of Boston, Mass.

A careful perusal of letters received by Col. Olcott from the Adept-Brother who signed himself *Serapis* throws a good deal of light on this early plan. The Egyptian Section of the Brotherhood, under whose special care the earliest stage of the Movement had been placed, appears to have intended a broadening and deepening of contemporary Spiritualism, to be achieved by the introduction into its midst of a larger philosophy. Fraudulent phenomena had to be sifted from genuine ones, and the true occult explanation of the latter was to be attempted. In the beginning, E. Gerry Brown evidently responded to these ideals and plans.

The day after H.P.B. had published her letter to the Editor of *The Daily Graphic*, in its issue of November 13, 1874, E. Gerry Brown wrote her a letter, the original of which is pasted in H.P.B.'s *Scrapbook*, Vol. III, p. 259. It runs as follows:

"Mme. H. P. Blavatsky.

"I have read your article in the *Daily Graphic*, and am so much pleased with the statements therein, and the powerful refutations of Dr. Beard's so-called 'arguments,' that I hasten to acknowledge to you, as editor of the *Scientist*, my gratitude for the service you have done Spiritualism in re-opening the eyes of the skeptical world.

"Should you ever be in Boston, I beg that you will grant

me permission, to call on you that I may learn more of the Eddy Family from one who has had so wonderful an experience and presents it in so interesting and attractive style.

"I have taken the liberty, to send you a copy of the *Scientist*.

"Hoping you will pardon my enthusiasm, which thus seeks expression, I have the honor to subscribe myself,
with respect,
truly yours
Gerry Brown."

9 Bromfield Street,
Boston.

No further developments seem to have taken place for some time. According to Col. Olcott's account, in his *Old Diary Leaves*, Vol. I, pp. 72-73, it was not until the first quarter of 1875 that he and H.P.B. became seriously interested in E. Gerry Brown's journal. H.P.B. herself, in an undated letter written to Prof. Hiram Corson in the Spring of 1875 calls the efforts of Brown to his attention, speaks of the persecution he had been subjected to, and voices her intention to help Brown with his Journal and to secure his collaboration. She also suggests to Prof. Corson to write for the *Spiritual Scientist*.*]

[The following excerpt from a letter is the first item from H.P.B.'s pen in the pages of the *Spiritual Scientist*:]

MADAME BLAVATSKY

Her Experience—Her Opinion of American Spiritualism and American Society.

[*Spiritual Scientist*, Boston, Vol. I, December 3, 1874, pp. 148-9]

From a letter received from Mme. Blavatsky last week we make the following extracts, want of space alone preventing us from publishing it entire. It is written in her usual lively and entertaining style, and her opinions expressed are worthy of careful study, many of them being fully consistent with the true state of affairs. She says:

As it is, I have only done my duty: first, towards Spiritualism, that I have defended as well as I could from the

---

*Cf. E. R. Corson, *Some Unpublished Letters of H. P. Blavatsky*, letter No. 8.

attacks of imposture under its too transparent mask of science; then, towards two helpless, slandered "mediums"—the last word becoming fast in our days the synonym of "martyr"; secondly, I have contributed my mite in opening the eyes of an indifferent public to the real, intrinsic value of such a man as Dr. Beard. But I am obliged to confess that I really do not believe in having done any good—at least, any practical good—to Spiritualism itself; and I never hope to perform such a feat as that were I to keep on bombarding for an eternity all the newspapers of America with my challenges and refutations of the lies told by the so-called "scientific exposers."

It is with a profound sadness in my heart that I acknowledge this fact, for I begin to think there is no help for it. For over fifteen years have I fought my battle for the blessed truth; I have travelled and preached it—though I never was born for a lecturer—from the snow-covered tops of the Caucasian Mountains, as well as from the sandy valleys of the Nile. I have proved the truth of it practically and by persuasion. For the sake of Spiritualism I have left my home, an easy life amongst a civilized society, and have become a wanderer upon the face of this earth. I had already seen my hopes realized, beyond the most sanguinary [*sic*] expectations, when, in my restless desire for more knowledge, my unlucky star brought me to America.

Knowing this country to be the cradle of modern Spiritualism, I came over here from France with feelings not unlike those of a Mohammedan approaching the birthplace of his prophet. I had forgotten that "no prophet is without honor save in his own country." In the less than fourteen months that I am here, sad experience has but too well sustained the never-dying evidence of this immortal truth!

What little I have done towards defending my belief, I am ever ready to do it over and over again, as long as I have a breath of life left in me. But what good will it ever do? We have a popular and wise Russian saying that "one Cossack on the battlefield is no warrior." Such is my case, together with many other poor, struggling wretches, every one of whom, like a solitary watch, sent far ahead in advance of the army, has to fight his own battle, and defend the entrusted post, unaided by no one but himself. There is no union between Spiritualists, no *"entente cordiale,"* as the French say. Judge Edmonds said, some years ago, that they numbered in their ranks over eleven million in this country alone; and I believe it to be true, in which case it is but to be the more deplored. When one man—as Dr. Beard did and will do it yet—dares to defy such a formidable body as that, there must be some cause for it. His insults, gross and vulgar as they are, are too fearless to leave one particle of doubt that if he does it, it is but because he knows too well that he can do so with impunity and perfect ease. Year after year the American Spiritualists have allowed themselves to be ridiculed and slighted by everyone who had a mind to do so, protesting so feebly as to give their opponents the most erroneous idea of their weakness. Am I wrong, then, in saying that our Spiritualists are more to be blamed than Dr. Beard himself in all this ridiculous polemic? Moral cowardice breeds more contempt than the "familiarity" of the old motto. How can we expect such a scientific sleight-of-hand as he is to respect a body that does not respect itself? We ourselves brought upon our heads that shower of abuse lavished by his hand with the dexterity and ability of a drunken London cockney.

My humble opinion is, that the majority of our Spiritualists are *too much* afraid for their "respectability" when called upon to confess and acknowledge their "belief." Will you agree with me, if I say that the dread of the social Areopagus is so deeply rooted in the hearts of your American people, that to endeavour to tear it out of them would be undertaking to shake the whole system of society from top to bottom? "Respectability" and "fashion" have brought more than one utter materialist to select (for mere show) the Episcopalian and other wealthy churches. But Spiritualism is not "fashionable," as yet, and that's where the trouble is. Notwithstanding its immense and daily increasing numbers, it has not won, till now, the right of citizenship. Its chief leaders are *not* clothed in gold and purple

ROBERT DALE OWEN
1801-1877
(From W. G. Langworthy Taylor's *Katie Fox*, New York, 1933.
Consult the *Bio-Bibliographical Index* for biographical sketch.)

ANDREW JACKSON DAVIS
1826-1910
From Sir A. Conan Doyle's *History of Spiritualism*, London, 1926.
Consult the *Bio-Bibliographical Index* for biographical sketch.)

and fine raiments; for not unlike Christianity in the beginning of its era, Spiritualism numbers in its ranks more of the humble and afflicted ones, than of the powerful and wealthy of this earth. Spiritualists belonging to the latter class will seldom dare to step out on the arena of publicity and boldly proclaim their belief in the face of the whole world; that hybridous monster, called "public opinion," is too much for them; and what does a Dr. Beard care for the opinion of the poor and the humble ones? He knows but too well, that his insulting terms of "fools" and "weak-minded idiots," as his accusations for credulousness, will never be applied to themselves by any of the proud castes of modern "Pharisees"; Spiritualists, as they know themselves to be, and have perhaps been for years, if they deign to notice the insult at all, it will be but to answer him as the cowardly apostle did before them, "Man, I tell thee, I know him not!"

St. Peter was the only one of the remaining eleven that denied his Christ thrice before the Pharisees; that is just the reason why, of all the apostles, he is the most revered by the Catholics, and has been selected to rule over the most wealthy as the most proud, greedy and hypocritical of all the churches in Christendom! And so, half Christians and half believers in the new dispensation, the majority of those eleven millions of Spiritualists stand with one foot on the threshold of Spiritualism, pressing firmly with the other one the steps leading to the altars of their "fashionable" places of worship, ever ready to leap over under the protection of the latter in hours of danger. They know that under the cover of such immense "respectability" they are perfectly safe. Who would presume or dare to accuse of "credulous stupidity" a member belonging to certain "fashionable congregations"? Under the powerful and holy shade of any of those "pillars of truth" every heinous crime is liable to become immediately transformed into but a slight and petty deviation from strict Christian virtue. Jupiter, for all his numberless "Don Juan"-like frolics, was not the less considered for it by his worshippers as the "Father of Gods"!

1875

[H.P.B.'S ROLE AT THE EDDYS' HOMESTEAD]

[In H.P.B.'s *Scrapbook*, Vol. I, pp. 11-12, a cutting is pasted from *The Spiritualist* of January 1, 1875. It is entitled "Materialized Spirit Forms" and is an article written by Benjamin Coleman who deals with Robert Dale Owen's opinion on the genuineness of the phenomena of materialization. The following parts were commented upon by H.P.B.:

"The Countess' presence at several of the Eddy séances led to most surprising manifestations, including the appearance of several spirits of persons known to her in foreign countries."

H.P.B. marked this sentence with blue pencil and added at the side in pen and ink:]

Yes; for I have called them out MYSELF.

H.P.B.

[The last sentence of the article: "These American facts, coupled with our own, should have an important bearing in correcting the errors of both science and theology"—was continued by H.P.B. who added in pen and ink:]

—and—*Spiritualism* please add. Belief in the agency of "Spirits" or disembodied souls in these phenomena is as foolish & irrational as belief in the agency of the Holy Ghost in the fabrication of Jesus—if the latter ever lived.

H. P. Blavatsky.

[The following two items, entitled "Heroic Women" and "A Card from the Countess Blavatsky," appear as cuttings from a newspaper in H.P.B.'s *Scrapbook*, Vol. I, p. 17. The name and date of the newspaper do not appear in print, but H.P.B. wrote in ink above the first cutting: "From the N. Y. Mercury, Jan. 18, 1875."

It is probable that these two items appeared one week apart from each other, but the actual dates have remained somewhat uncertain, as the files of both the New York *Mercury* and *Sunday Mercury* have not been located, and therefore could not be verified.

Words that are underlined have been underscored by H.P.B. herself in her *Scrapbook*. Her various comments at the side of the cuttings appear as footnotes.]

HEROIC WOMEN

A Petticoated Staff Officer of Garibaldi—Strange and Striking Career—A Former Companion Whose History Reads Like Romance.

It is not often that two heroines appear at the same time before the public, yet Helen P. Blavatsky and Clementine Gerebko have entered the legal arena in order to have a slight business misunderstanding settled by Judge Pratt of the Supreme Court, Brooklyn. Both of these ladies possess a romantic and remarkable record.

Helena P. Blavatsky, who is about forty years [of] age,* at the age of seventeen married a Russian nobleman then in his seventy-third year. For many years† they resided together at Odessa, and finally a legal separation‡ was effected. The husband died recently in his ninety-seventh year. The widow is now a resident of the City of New York, and is highly accomplished. She converses and writes fluently in Russian, Polish, Romaic, Low Dutch, German, French, Spanish, Italian, Portuguese and English. She has translated the works of Darwin and the Treatise of Buckle on Civilization in England into the Russian language. She is thoroughly versed in Darwinian theory, is a firm believer in Wallace's scientific spiritualism, and is a member of the Order of Rosicrucians.

Her life has been one of many vicissitudes, and the area of her experiences is bounded only by the world. It is said that she visited this country with a party of tourists. On her return to Europe she married†† and in the struggle for liberty fought under the victorious standard of Garibaldi. She won renown for unflinching bravery in many hard-fought battles, and was elevated to a high position on the staff of the great general. She still bears the scars of many wounds she received in the conflict. Twice her horse was shot under her, and

---

*a fib.
†a *lie*—was with him but for three weeks.
‡legal, because he died.
††whom? when!! how!?

she escaped hasty death only by her coolness and matchless skill."
Altogether Madame Blavatsky is

AN ASTONISHING WOMAN

A CARD FROM THE COUNTESS† BLAVATSKY‡

To the Editors of the N. Y. *Sunday Mercury*.

In last Sunday's issue I read an article headed "Heroic Women," and find that I figure therein as the primary heroine. My name is H. P. Blavatsky. I decline the honor of a comparison with "the latter heroine" C. Gerebko, and proceed to explain some of the statements of the said article. If I married a Russian "nobleman" I never resided with him anywhere; for three weeks after the sacrifice I left him for reasons plausible enough in my eyes, as in those of the "puritan" world. I do not know if he died at the advanced age of ninety-seven as for the last twelve years†† this noble patriarch has entirely vanished out of my sight and memory. But I beg leave to say that I never was married again, for this one solitary case of "conjugal love" has proved too much for me. I did not get acquainted with Mrs. Gerebko at the residence of the Russian consul; I never had the honor of visiting this gentleman, but upon business in his office. I know Mr. G.'s family in Odessa, and he never rose above the rank of a captain of a private steamer belonging to Prince Worontzoff. I was residing at Tiflis when Mrs. Gerebko came there in 1866 from Teheran (Persia), and heard of her as well as others did

---

*Every word is a *lie*. Never was on "Garibaldi's staff." Went with friends to Mentana to help shooting the Papists and got shot myself. Nobody's business—least of any a d — d reporter's.

†["the Countess" scored out in ink by H.P.B.]

‡Answered a long letter but they inserted but this paragraph and added LIES.—H.P.B.

††["for the last twelve years" scored out and substituted for it at the side: since then.]

daily for about two months. She married Gerebko at Kutais. When they arrived in this country, a year ago, they did not purchase a beautiful residence, but simply bought a farm of six acres of land at Northport for the modest sum of $1,000. My unlucky star brought me in contact with her about the latter part of June last. She represented to me her farm as giving a revenue of nearly $2,000 yearly, and induced me to go into partnership with her on the following terms: I had to give her $1,000 and pay half of the expenses that might occur, for which sum I bought of her the right on the half of the yearly profit of everything. We made the contract for three years, and it was recorded. I paid the money, and went to live with them. The first month I spent nearly $500 for buildings and otherwise; at the expiration of which month she prayed to be released of the contract, as she was ready to pay me my money back. I consented, and gave her permission to sell at auction all we had except the farm land and buildings, and we both came to New York in view of settlement. She was to give me a promissory note or a mortgage on the property to the amount of the sum due by her, and that immediately after our coming to New York. Alas! three days after we had taken lodging in common, on one fine afternoon, upon my returning home, I found that the fair countess had left the place, neglecting to pay me back her little bill of $1,000. I am now waiting patiently for the opinion of an American jury.

H. P. BLAVATSKY,
124 East Sixteenth Street.

THE PHILADELPHIA "FIASCO," OR WHO IS WHO?

[*Banner of Light,* Boston, Vol. XXXVI, January 30, 1875, pp. 2-3]

A few weeks ago, in a letter, extracts from which have appeared in the *Spiritual Scientist* of December 3rd, I alluded to the deplorable lack of accord between American Spiritualists, and the consequences of the same. At that time I had just fought out my useless battle with a foe who, though beneath my own personal notice, had insulted all the Spiritualists of this country, as a body, in a caricature of a so-called scientifice *exposé*. In dealing with him I dealt but with one of the numerous "bravos" enlisted in the army of the bitter opponents of our belief, and my task was, comparatively speaking, an easy one, if we take it for granted that falsehood can hardly withstand truth, as the latter will ever speak for itself. Since that day the scales have turned; prompted now as then, by the same love of justice and fair play, I feel compelled to throw [down] my glove once more in our defence, seeing that so few of the adherents to our cause are bold enough to accept that duty, and so many of them show the white feather of pusillanimity.

I indicated in my letter that such a state of things, such a complete lack of harmony, and such cowardice, I may add, among our ranks, subjected the Spiritualists and the cause to constant attacks from a compact, aggressive public opinion, based upon ignorance and wicked prejudice, intolerant, remorseless and thoroughly dishonest in the employment of its methods. As a vast army, amply equipped, may be cut to pieces by an inferior force well trained and handled, so Spiritualism, numbering its hosts by millions, and able to vanquish every reactionary theology by a little directed effort, is constantly harassed, weakened, impeded by the convergent attacks of pulpit and press, and by the treachery and cowardice of its trusted leaders. It is one of these professed leaders that I propose to question today, as closely as my rights, not only as a widely known Spiritualist, but a resident of the United States, will allow me. When I see the numbers of believers in this country, the broad basis of their belief, the impregnability of their position, and the talent that is embraced within their ranks, I am disgusted at the spectacle that they manifest at this very moment, after the Katie King—how shall we say—fraud? By no means, since the last word of this sensational comedy is far from being spoken.

There is not a country on the face of our planet, with a

jury attached to its courts of justice, but gives the benefit of the doubt to every criminal brought within the law, and a chance to be heard and tell *his* story.

Is such the case between the pretended "spirit-performer," the alleged bogus Katie King, and the Holmes mediums? I answer most decidedly *no*, and mean to prove it, if no one else does.

I deny the right of any man or woman to wrench from our hands all possible means of finding out the truth. I deny the right of any editor of a daily newspaper to accuse and publish accusations, refusing at the same time to hear one word of justification from the defendants, and so, instead of helping people to clear up the matter, leaving them more than ever to grope their way in the dark.

The biography of "Katie King" has come out at last; a sworn certificate, if you please, equally endorsed (under oath?) by Dr. Child,* who throughout the whole of this "burlesque" epilogue has ever appeared in it, like some inevitable *deus ex machina*. The whole of this made-up elegy (by whom? evidently not by Mrs. White) is redolent with the perfume of erring innocence, of Magdalene-like tales of woe and sorrow, and tardy repentance and the like, giving us the abnormal idea of a pickpocket in the act of robbing our soul of its most precious, thrilling sensations; the carefully-prepared explanations on some points that appear now and then as so many stumbling-blocks in the way of a seemingly fair *exposé*, do not preclude, nevertheless, through the whole of it, the possibility of doubt, for many awkward semblances of truth, partly taken from the confessions of that fallen angel, Mrs. White, and partly —most of them we should say—copied from the private notebook of her "amanuensis," give you a fair idea of the veracity of this *sworn* certificate. For instance, according

---

* [In her *Scrapbook*, Vol. I, p. 19, where the cutting of this article is pasted, H.P.B. added the following remark in pen and ink:

Child was a *confederate*. He took money . . . . . lmes' séance. He is a ra . . . l.

The last word may be *rascal.—Compiler.*]

to her own statement and the evidence furnished by the *habitués* of the Holmeses, Mrs. White having never been present at any of the dark circles (her alleged acting as Katie King excluding all possibility, on her part, of such a public exhibition of flesh and bones), how comes she to know so well, in every particular, about the tricks of the mediums, the programme of their performances, etc.? Then, again, Mrs. White, who remembers so well—by rote we may say—every word exchanged between Katie King and Mr. Owen, the spirit and Dr. Child, has evidently forgotten *all that was ever said* by her in her bogus personation to Dr. Fellger;* *she does not even remember a very important secret* communicated by her to the latter gentleman! What an extraordinary combination of memory and absence of mind at the same time! May not a certain memorandum book, with its carefully noted contents, account for it, perhaps? The document is signed, under oath, with the name of a *non*-existing spirit, Katie King. . . . Very clever!

All protestations of innocence or explanations sent in by Mr. or Mrs. Holmes, written or verbal, are peremptorily refused publication by the press. No respectable paper dares take upon itself the responsibility of such an unpopular cause.

The public feels triumphant; the clergy, forgetting, in the excitement of their victory, the Brooklyn scandal, rub their hands and chuckle; a certain exposer of materialized spirits and mind-reading, like some monstrous anti-spiritual *mitrailleuse*, shoots forth a volley of missiles, and sends a condoling letter to Mr. Owen; Spiritualists, crestfallen, ridiculed and defeated, feel crushed *for ever* under the pretended exposure and that overwhelming, pseudonymous evidence. . . . The day of Waterloo has come for us, and sweeping [away] the last remnants of the defeated army, it remains for us to ring our own death-knell. . . . Spirits, beware! Henceforth, if you lack prudence, your materialized forms

---

*[A well-known and highly respected Philadelphia physician—Dr. Adolphus Fellger.—*Compiler*.]

will have to stop at the cabinet doors, and in perfect tremor melt away from sight, singing in chorus Poe's *Nevermore!*

One would really suppose that the whole belief of us Spiritualists hung at the girdles of the Holmeses, and that in case they should be unmasked as tricksters, we might as well vote our immortality an old woman's delusion.

Is the scraping off of a barnacle the destruction of a ship? But, moreover, we are not sufficiently furnished with any plausible proofs at all.

Colonel Olcott is here, and has begun investigations. His first tests with Mrs. Holmes alone, for Mr. Holmes is lying sick at Vineland, have proved satisfactory enough in his eyes, to induce Mr. Owen to return to the spot of his first love, namely, the Holmes' cabinet. He began by tying Mrs. Holmes up in a bag, the string drawn tightly round her neck, knotted and sealed in the presence of Mr. Owen, Col. Olcott and a third gentleman. After that the medium was placed in the empty cabinet, which was rolled away into the middle of the room, and it was made a *perfect impossibility for her to use her hands.* The door being closed, hands appeared in the aperture, then the outlines of a face came, which gradually formed into the classical head of John King, turban, beard and all. He kindly allowed the investigators to stroke his beard, touch his *warm* face, and patted their hands with his. After the *séance* was over, Mrs. Holmes, with many tears of gratitude, in the presence of the three gentlemen, assured Mr. Owen *most solemnly* that she had spoken many a time to Dr. Child about "Katie" leaving her presents in the house and dropping them about the place, and that she—Mrs. Holmes —wanted Mr. Owen to know it; but that the Doctor had given her most peremptory orders to the contrary, forbidding her to let the former know it, his precise words being; "Don't do it; it's useless; *he must not know it!*" I leave the question of Mrs. Holmes' veracity as to this fact for Dr. Child to settle with her.

On the other hand, we have the woman, Eliza White, exposer and accuser of the Holmeses, who remains up to the present day a riddle and an Egyptian mystery to every man and woman of this city, except to the clever and equally invisible party—a sort of protecting deity—who took the team in hand, and drove the whole concern of "Katie's" materialization to destruction, and at what he considered such a first-rate way. She is not to be met, or seen, or interviewed, or even spoken to by anyone, least of all by the ex-admirers of "Katie King" herself, so anxious to get a peep at the modest, blushing beauty who deemed herself worthy of personating the fair spirit. Maybe it's rather dangerous to allow them the chance of comparing for themselves the features of both? But the most perplexing fact of this most perplexing imbroglio is that Mr. R. D. Owen, by his own confession to me, *has never, not even on the day of the exposure, seen Mrs. White, or talked to her, or had otherwise the least chance to scan her features close enough for him to identify her.* He caught a glimpse of her general outline but once, viz., at the mock *séance* of the 5th of December, referred to in her biography, when she appeared to half a dozen witnesses (invited to testify and identify the fraud) emerging *de novo* from the cabinet, with her face *closely covered with a double veil*(!), after which the sweet vision vanished and appeared no more! Mr. Owen adds that he is not prepared to swear to the identity of Mrs. White and Katie King.

May I be allowed to inquire as to the necessity of such a profound mystery, after the promise of a public exposure of all the fraud? It seems to me that the said exposure would have been far more satisfactory if conducted otherwise. Why not give the fairest chance to R. D. Owen, the party who has suffered the most on account of this disgusting swindle—if swindle there is—to compare Mrs. White with *his* Katie? May I suggest again that it is perhaps because the spirit's features are but too well impressed on his memory, poor, noble, confiding gentleman! Gauze dresses and moonshine, coronets and stars can possibly be counterfeited, in a half-darkened room, while features, answering line for line to the "spirit Katie's" face, are not so easily made up; the latter require *very clever* preparations. A *lie* may be easy enough for a smooth tongue, but no *pug nose* can lie itself into a *classical one.*

A very honorable gentleman of my acquaintance, a fervent admirer of the "spirit Katie's" beauty, who has seen and addressed her at two feet distance about *fifty* times, tells me that on a certain evening, when Dr. Child begged the spirit to let him see her tongue (did the honourable doctor want to compare it with Mrs. White's tongue—the lady having been his patient?), she did so, and upon her opening her mouth, the gentleman in question assures me that he plainly saw, what in his admiring phraseology he terms "the most beautiful set of teeth—two rows of pearls." He remarked* most particularly those teeth. Now there are some wicked, slandering gossips, who happen to have cultivated *most intimately* Mrs. White's acquaintance in the happy days of her innocence, before her fall and subsequent *exposé,* and they tell us very bluntly (we beg the penitent angel's pardon, we repeat but a hearsay), that this lady can hardly number among her other natural charms, the rare beauty of *pearly teeth,* or a *perfect, most beautifully formed hand and arm.* Why not show her teeth at once to the said admirer, and so shame the slanders? Why shun "Katie's" best friends? If we were so anxious as she seems to be to prove "who is who," we would surely submit with pleasure to the operation of showing our teeth, yea, even in a court of justice. The above fact, trifling as it may seem at first sight, would be considered as a very important one by any intelligent juryman in a question of personal identification.

Mr. Owen's statement to us is corroborated by "Katie King" herself in her biography, a sworn document, remember, in the following words: "She consented to have an interview with some gentlemen who had seen her personating the spirit, *on condition that she would be allowed*

---

* [H.P.B. uses on many occasions the word "remarked" when she actually means "noticed." It is an unconscious translation of the French word "remarquer" which means "to notice."—*Compiler.*]

to keep a veil over her face all the time she was conversing with them."*

Now pray why should these "too credulous, weak-minded gentlemen," as the immortal Dr. Beard would say, be subjected again to such an extra strain on their blind faith? We should say that that was just the proper time to come out and prove to them what was the nature of the mental aberration they were labouring under for so many months. Well, if they do swallow this new *veiled* proof they are welcome to it. *Vulgus vult decipi—decipiatur!* But I expect something more substantial before submitting in guilty silence to be laughed at. As it is, the case stands thus:

According to the same biography (same column) the mock *séance* was prepared and carried out—to everyone's heart's content—through the endeavours of the amateur detective, who by the way, if any one wants to know, is a Mr. W. O. Leslie, a contractor or agent for the Baltimore, Philadelphia and New York Railroad, residing in this city. If the Press, and several of the most celebrated victims of the fraud, are under bond of secrecy with him, *I am not*, and mean to say what I know. And so the said *séance* took place on the 5th of December last, which fact appearing in a sworn evidence, implies that Mr. Leslie had wrested from Mrs. White the confession of her guilt at least several days previous to that date, though the precise day of the "amateur's" triumph is very cleverly withheld in the *sworn* certificate. Now comes a new conundrum.

On the evening of the 2nd and 3rd of December, at two *séances* held at the Holmeses', I, myself, in the presence of Robert Dale Owen and Dr. Child (chief manager of those performances, from whom I got on the same morning an admission card), together with twenty more witnesses, saw the spirit of Katie step out of the cabinet twice, in full form and beauty; and I can swear in any court of justice that she did not bear the least resemblance to Mrs. White's portrait.

**Philadelphia Inquirer,* January 11, 1875, 4th column, "Katie King's Biography."

As I am unwilling to base my argument upon any other testimony than my own, I will not dwell upon the alleged apparition of Katie King at the Holmeses' on the 5th of December, to Mr. Roberts and fifteen others, among whom was Mr. W. H. Clarke, a reporter for *The Daily Graphic,* for I happened to be out of town, though, if this fact is demonstrated, it will go far against Mrs. White, for on that precise evening, and at the same hour, she was exhibiting herself as the *bogus* Katie at the mock *séance.* Something still more worthy of consideration is found in the most positive assertion of a gentleman, a Mr. Westcott, who on that evening of the 5th, on his way home from the real *séance,* met in the car Mr. Owen, Dr. Child and his wife, all three returning from the mock *séance.* Now it so happened that this gentleman mentioned to them about having just seen the spirit Katie come out of the cabinet, adding "he thought she never looked better"; upon hearing which Mr. Robert Dale Owen stared at him in amazement, and all the three looked greatly perplexed.

And so I here but insist on the apparition of the spirit at the medium's house on the evenings [of] the 2nd and 3rd of December, when I witnessed the phenomenon, together with Robert Dale Owen and other parties. It would be worse than useless to offer or accept the poor excuse that the confession of the woman White, her exposure of the fraud, the delivery to Mr. Leslie of all her dresses and presents received by her in the name of Katie King, the disclosure of the sad news by this devoted gentleman to Mr. Owen, and the preparation of the mock *séance* cabinet and other important matters, had all of them taken place on the 4th; the more so, as we are furnished with most positive proofs that Dr. Child at least, if not Mr. Owen, knew all about Mr. Leslie's success with Mrs. White several days beforehand. Knowing then of the fraud, how could Mr. Leslie allow it to be still carried on, as the fact of Katie's apparition at the Holmeses' on the 2nd and 3rd of December proves it to have been the case? Any gentleman, even with a very moderate degree of honour about him, would never allow the public to be fooled and de-

THE EDDY HOMESTEAD, CHITTENDEN, VERMONT
Here H.P.B. and Col. H. S. Olcott met each other, October 14, 1874.
(From Col. H. S. Olcott's *People from the Other World*, Hartford, Conn., 1875.)

GENERAL FRANCIS J. LIPPITT
1812-1902
(From his *Reminiscences*, Providence, R.I., 1902. Consult the *Bio-Bibliographical Index* for biographical data.)

The Philadelphia "Fiasco" 65

frauded any longer, unless he had the firm resolution of catching the *bogus* spirit on the spot and proving the imposition. But no such thing occurred; quite the contrary; for Dr. Child, who had constituted himself from the first not only chief superintendent of the *séances,* cabinet and materialization business, but also cashier and ticket-holder (paying the mediums at first ten dollars per *séance,* as he did, and subsequently fifteen dollars, and pocketing the rest of the proceeds), on that same evening of the 3rd *took the admission money* from every visitor as quietly as he ever did. I will add furthermore, that I, *in propria persona,* handed him on that very night a five-dollar bill, and that he (Dr. Child) kept the whole of it, remarking that the balance could be made good to us by *future séances.*

Will Dr. Child presume to say that getting ready, as he then was, in company with Mr. Leslie, to produce the *bogus* Katie King on the 5th of December, he knew nothing, as yet, of the fraud on the 3rd?

Further; in the same biography (Chapter viii, Column the 1st), it is stated that, immediately upon Mrs. White's return from Blissfield, Mich., she called on Dr. Child, and offered to expose the whole humbug she had been engaged in, but that he would not listen to her. Upon that occasion *she was not veiled,* as indeed there was no necessity for her to be, since by Dr. Child's own admission she had been a patient of his, and under his medical treatment. In a letter from Holmes to Dr. Child, dated Blissfield, August 28th, 1874, the former writes:

"Mrs. White says you and the friends were very rude, 'wanted to look into all our boxes and trunks, and break open locks. What were you looking for, or expecting to find?' "

All these several circumstances show in the clearest possible manner that Dr. Child and Mrs. White were on terms much more intimate then than that of casual acquaintance, and it is the height of absurdity to assert that if Mrs. White and Katie King were identical, the fraud was not perfectly well known to the "Father Confessor" [see narrative of John and Katie King, p. 45]. But a sidelight is thrown upon this comedy from the pretended biography of John King and his daughter Katie, written at *their dictation in his own office* by Dr. Child himself. This book was given out to the world as an authentic revelation from these two spirits. It tells us that they stepped in and stepped out of his office, day after day, as any mortal being might, and after holding brief conversations, followed by long narratives, they fully endorsed the genuineness of their own apparitions in the Holmes' cabinet. Moreover, the spirits appearing at the public *séances*, corroborated the statements which they made to their amanuensis in his office; the two dovetailing together, and making a consistent story. Now, if the Holmes' Kings were Mrs. White, who were the spirits visiting the Doctor's office? and if the spirits visiting *him* were genuine, who were those that appeared at the public *séances?* In which particular has the "Father Confessor" defrauded the public? In selling a book containing false biographies or exposing bogus spirits at the Holmeses? Which or both? Let the Doctor choose.

If his conscience is so tender as to force him into print with his certificate and affidavits, why does it not sink deep enough to reach his pocket, and compel him to refund to us the money obtained by him under false pretenses? According to his own confession, the Holmeses received from him, up to the time they left town, about $1,200, for four months of daily *séances*. That he admitted every night as many visitors as he could possibly find room for—sometimes as many as *thirty-five*—is a fact that will be corroborated by every person who has seen the phenomena more than once. Furthermore, some six or seven reliable witnesses have told us that the modest fee of $1 was only for the *habitués*; too curious or over-anxious visitors having to pay sometimes as much as $5, and in one instance $10. This last fact I give under all reserve, not having had to pay so much as that myself.

Now let an impartial investigator of this Philadelphia imbroglio take a pencil and cast up the profit left after paying the mediums in this nightly spirit speculation lasting many months. The result would be to show that the business of a spirit "Father Confessor" is, on the whole, a very lucrative one.

Ladies and Gentlemen of the spiritual belief, methinks we are all of us between the horns of a very wonderful dilemma. If you happen to find your position comfortable, *I do not,* and so will try to extricate myself.

Let it be perfectly understood, though, that I do not intend in the least to undertake at present the defense of the Holmeses. They may be the greatest frauds for what I know or care. My only purpose is to know for a certainty to whom I am indebted for my share of ridicule—small as it may be, luckily for me. If we Spiritualists are to be laughed at, and scoffed, and ridiculed, and sneered at, we ought to know at least the reason why. Either there was a fraud or there was none. If the fraud is a sad reality, and Dr. Child by some mysterious combination of his personal cruel fate has fallen the first victim to it, after having proved himself so anxious for the sake of his honour and character to stop at once the further progress of such a deceit on a public that had hitherto looked on him alone as the party responsible for the perfect integrity and genuineness of a phenomenon so fully endorsed by him, in all particulars, why does not the Doctor come out the first and help us to the clue of all this mystery? Well aware of the fact that the swindled and defrauded parties can at any day assert their rights to the restitution of moneys laid out by them solely on the ground of their entire faith in him they had trusted, why does he not sue the Holmeses, and so prove his own innocence? He cannot but admit, that in the eyes of some initiated parties, his case looks far more ugly as it now stands, than the accusation under which the Holmeses vainly struggle. Or, if there was *no fraud,* or if it is not fully proved, as it cannot well be on the shallow testimony of a nameless woman, signing documents with pseudonyms, why then all this comedy on the part of the principal partner in the "Katie materialization" business? Was not Dr. Child the institutor, the promulgator, and we may say the creator of what proves to have been but a *bogus* phenomenon, after all? Was not *he* the advertising agent of this incarnated humbug—the Barnum of this spiritual show? And now, that he has helped to fool not only Spiritualists but the world at large, whether as a confederate himself or one of the weak-minded fools—no matter, as long as it is demonstrated that it was he that helped us to this scrape—he imagines that by helping to accuse the mediums, and expose the fraud, by fortifying with his endorsement all manner of bogus affidavits and illegal certificates from non-existing parties, he hopes to find himself henceforth perfectly clear of responsibility to the persons he has dragged after him into this infamous swamp!

We must demand a legal investigation. We have the right to insist upon it, for we Spiritualists have bought this right at a dear price: with the lifelong reputation of Mr. Owen as an able and reliable writer and trustworthy witness of the phenomena, who may henceforth become a doubted and ever-ridiculed visionary by skeptical wiseacres. We have bought this right with the prospect that all of us, whom Dr. Child has unwillingly or otherwise (time will prove it) fooled into belief in his Katie King, will become for a time the butts for endless raillery, satires and jokes from the press and ignorant masses. We regret to feel obliged to contradict on this point such an authority in all matters as *The Daily Graphic*, but if orthodox laymen rather decline to see this fraud thoroughly investigated in a court of justice, for fear of the Holmeses becoming entitled to the crown of martyrs, we have no such fear as that, and repeat with Mr. Hudson Tuttle that "better perish the cause with the impostors, than live such a life of eternal ostracism, with no chance for justice or redress."

Why in the name of all that is wonderful, should Dr. Child have all the laurels of this unfought battle, in which the attacked army seems forever doomed to be defeated without so much as a struggle? Why should he have all the material benefit of this materialized humbug, and R. D. Owen, an honest Spiritualist, whose name is universally respected, have all the kicks and thumps of the skeptical press?

Is this fair and just? How long shall we Spiritualists be turned over like so many scapegoats to the unbelievers, by cheating mediums and speculating prophets? Like some modern shepherd Paris, Mr. Owen fell a victim to the snares of this pernicious, newly materialized Helen; and on him falls heaviest the present reaction that threatens to produce a new Trojan war. But the Homer of the Philadelphia *Iliad*—the one who has appeared in the past as the elegiac poet and biographer of that same Helen, and who appears in the present kindling up the spark of doubt against the Holmeses, till, if not speedily quenched, it might become a roaring ocean of flames—he that plays at this present hour the unparalleled part of a chief justice presiding *at his own* trial and deciding *in his own* case—Dr. Child, we say, turning back on the spirit-daughter of his own creation, and backing the mortal, illegitimate offspring furnished by somebody, is left unmolested! Only fancy, while R. D. Owen is fairly crushed under the ridicule of the exposure, Dr. Child, who has endorsed false spirits, now turns state's evidence and endorses as fervently spirit-certificates, swearing to the same in a Court of Justice!

If ever I may hope to get a chance of having my advice accepted by some one anxious to clear up all this sickening story, I would insist that the whole matter be forced into a real Court of Justice and unriddled before a jury. If Dr. Child is, after all, an honest man whose trusting nature was imposed upon, he must be the first to offer us all the chances that lay in his power of getting at the bottom of all these endless "whys" and "hows." If he does not, in such a case, we will try for ourselves to solve the following mysteries:

First. Judge Allen, of Vineland, now in Philadelphia, testifies to the fact that when the cabinet, made up under the direct supervision and instructions of Dr. Child, was brought home to the Holmeses, the doctor worked at it himself, unaided, one whole day, and with his own tools, Judge Allen being at the time at the medium's, whom he was visiting. If there was a trapdoor or "two cut boards" connected with it, who did the work? Who can doubt that such a clever machinery, filed in a way and so as to baffle frequent and close examinations on the part of the skeptics, requires an experienced mechanic, of more than ordinary ability? Further, unless well paid, he could hardly be bound to secrecy. Who paid him? Is it Holmes out of his ten-dollar nightly fee? We ought to ascertain it.

Second. If it is true — as two persons are ready to swear — that the party, calling herself Eliza White, *alias* "Frank," *alias* Katie King, and so forth, is no widow at all, having a well-materialized husband, who is living, and who keeps a drinking saloon in a Connecticut town; for in such case the fair widow has perjured herself and Dr. Child has endorsed the perjury. We regret that he should endorse the statements of the former as rashly as he accepted the fact of her materialization.

Third. Affidavits and witnesses (five in all) are ready to prove that on a certain night, when Mrs. White was visibly in her living body, refreshing her penitent stomach in company with impenitent associates in a lager beer saloon, having no claims to patrician "patronage," Katie King, in her spirit-form, was as visibly seen at the door of her cabinet.

Fourth. On one occasion, when Dr. Child (in consequence of some prophetic vision, maybe) invited Mrs. White to his own house, where he locked her up with the inmates, who entertained her the whole of the evening, for the sole purpose of convincing (he always seems anxious to convince somebody of something) some doubting skeptics of the reality of the spirit-form, the latter appeared in the *séance*-room and talked with R. D. Owen in the presence of all the company. The Spiritualists were jubilant that night, and the Doctor the most triumphant of them all. Many are the witnesses ready to testify to the fact, but Dr. Child, when questioned, seems to have entirely forgotten this important occurrence.

Fifth. Who is the party whom she claims to have engaged to personate General Rawlins? Let him come out and swear to it, so that we will all see his great resemblance to the defunct warrior.

Sixth. Let her name the friends from whom she borrowed the costumes to personate "Sauntee" and "Richard." They must prove it under oath. Let them produce the dresses. Can she tell us where she got the shining robes of the second and third spheres?

Seventh. Only some portions of Holmes' letters to "Frank" are published in the biography: some of them for the purpose of proving their co-partnership in the fraud at Blissfield. Can she name the house and parties with whom she lodged and boarded at Blissfield, Michigan?

When all of the above questions are answered and demonstrated to our satisfaction, then, and only then, shall we believe that the Holmeses are the only guilty parties to a fraud, which, for its consummate rascality and brazenness, is unprecedented in the annals of Spiritualism.

I have read some of Mr. Holmes' letters, whether original or forged, no matter; and blessed as I am with good memory, I well remember certain sentences that have been, very luckily for the poetic creature, suppressed by the blushing editor as being too vile for publication. One of the most modest of the paragraphs runs thus:

"Now, my advice to you, Frank, *don't crook your elbow* too often; no use doubling up and squaring your fists again," etc., etc. Oh, Katie King!

Remember, the above is addressed to the woman who pretends to have personated the spirit of whom R. D. Owen wrote thus: "I particularly noticed this evening the ease and harmony of her motions. In Naples, during five years, I frequented a circle famed for courtly demeanour; but never in the best-bred lady of rank accosting her visitors, have I seen Katie out-rivalled." And further: "A well-known artist of Philadelphia, after examining Katie, said to me that he had seldom seen features exhibiting more classic beauty. 'Her movements and bearing,' he added, 'are the very ideal of grace!'"

Compare for one moment this admiring description with

the quotation from Holmes' letter. Fancy an ideal of classic beauty and grace crooking her elbow in a lager beer saloon, and—judge for yourselves!

H. P. BLAVATSKY.

1111 *Girard Street, Philadelphia.*

[In H.P.B.'s *Scrapbook*, Vol. I, p. 21, there is pasted a short printed announcement concerning the visit of Col. H. S. Olcott to Boston. H.P.B. added to it in her handwriting the date of January 20, 1875.

To the sentence which states that "Dr. Gardiner announced that Col. Olcott's subjects next Sunday would be 'Human and Elementary Spirits' in the afternoon, and in the evening 'Ancient Magic and Modern Spiritualism,' " H.P.B. added in pen and ink the following remarks:]

The "Spirits" wrote anonymous letters to Dr. Gardiner and threatened to kill—Col. Olcott if he lectured against them. They did *not* kill him though, — guess didn't know how, the sweet "angels"! . . .

[In H.P.B.'s *Scrapbook*, Vol. I, between pages 20 and 21, may be found the manuscript of the following "Important Note" in H.P.B.'s own handwriting. It is undated, but its last paragraph places it as being prior to the formation of The Theosophical Society. The accompanying illustration reproduces this "Note" just as it appears on two small separate sheets of paper in H.P.B.'s *Scrapbook*.

Her words show better than anything else the pathos of her situation, and the complex psychological and spiritual difficulties she was working under even at that early period in the history of the Movement. On what specific purpose she was sent to America is stated here beyond any doubt.]

IMPORTANT NOTE

Yes. I am sorry to say that I *had* to identify myself during that shameful exposure of the *mediums* Holmes with the Spiritualists. I had to save the situation, for I was sent from Paris on purpose to America to *prove* the phenomena and their reality and—show the fallacy of the Spiritualistic theories of "Spirits." But how could I do it best? I did not want people at large to know that I could *produce the same thing at will*. I had received ORDERS to the contrary, and yet, I had to keep alive the reality, the genuineness and *possibility* of such phenomena in the hearts of those who from *Materialists* had turned *Spiritualists* and now, owing to the exposure of several mediums fell back again, returned to their skepticism. This is why, selecting a few of the faithful, I went to the Holmeses and helped by M∴ and *his power*, brought out the face of John King and Katie King in the astral light, produced the phenomena of materialization and—allowed the Spiritualists at large to believe it was done thro' the mediumship of Mrs. Holmes. She was terribly frightened herself, for she knew that *this once* the apparition was real. Did I do wrong? The world is not prepared yet to understand the philosophy of Occult Sciences—let them assure themselves first of all that there are beings in an invisible world, whether "Spirits" of the dead or *Elementals*; and that there are hidden powers in man, which are capable of making a *God* of him on earth.

When I am dead and gone people will, perhaps, appreciate my disinterested motives. I have pledged my word to help people on to *Truth* while living and—will keep my word. Let them abuse and revile me. Let some call me a MEDIUM and a Spiritualist, and others an *impostor*. The day will come when posterity will learn to know me better.

Oh poor, foolish, credulous, wicked *world!*

M∴ brings orders to form a Society — a secret Society like the Rosicrucian Lodge. He promises to help.

H.P.B.

[H.P.B. AND THE TERM "SPIRITUALISM"]

[A great deal of misunderstanding on the subject of H.P.B.'s relation to modern Spiritualism arises from the fact that H.P.B. herself, as well as some of the students of her writings, use the word "Spiritualism" in more than one meaning.

Whenever H.P.B. states that she is a Spiritualist, that her early life has been devoted to the defence of the cause of Spiritualism, and other similar and cognate expressions, she does not mean the *beliefs* of ordinary mediums and of those among their numerous followers who share them. It is very important to bear in mind that a recognition of the genuineness of certain mediumistic phenomena on the part of H.P.B.—*phenomena which she herself could duplicate at will and in full consciousness*—never implied an acceptance of current *beliefs* in the manifestation of so-called "spirits" and their participation in *séance* phenomena. There is abundant evidence of this in the words of H.P.B. herself.

Speaking of herself as a Spiritualist and a follower of Spiritualism, H.P.B. meant what she called *"ancient* Spiritualism" and Spiritualism according to the "ancient Alexandrian way."

In *The Theosophical Glossary*, in a paragraph definitely written in her own style, *Spiritualism* is defined as follows:

"In philosophy, the state or condition of mind opposed to materialism or a *material conception* of things. Theosophy, a doctrine which teaches that all which exists is animated or informed by the Universal Soul or Spirit, and that not an atom in our universe can be outside of this omnipresent Principle— is *pure* Spiritualism. As to the belief that goes under that name, namely, belief in the constant communication of the living with the dead, whether through the mediumistic powers of oneself or a so-called *medium*—it is no better than the materialization of spirit, and the degradation of the human and the divine souls. Believers in such communications are simply dishonouring the dead and performing constant sacrilege. It was well called 'Necromancy' in days of old. But our modern Spiritualists take offence at being told this simple truth."

It is advisable to keep the above definition in mind when reading H.P.B.'s early articles on the subject of mediums and phenomena contained in the present volume.—*Compiler.*]

WHO FABRICATES?

SOME LIGHT ON THE KATIE KING MYSTERY—MORE EVIDENCE—A STATEMENT, AT LAST, WHICH SEEMS CONSISTENT WITH CIRCUMSTANCES—A LETTER FROM MADAME BLAVATSKY.*

[*Spiritual Scientist*, Boston, Vol. II, April, 1875, pp. 44-5]

In the last *Religio-Philosophical Journal* (for February 27th), in the Philadelphia department, edited by Dr. Child, under the most poetical heading of "After the Storm comes the Sunshine," we read the following:

"I have been waiting patiently for the excitement in reference to the Holmes fraud to subside a little. I will now make some further statements and answer some questions."

Further:

"The stories of my acquaintance with Mrs. White are all fabrications."

Further still:

"I shall not notice the various reports put forth about my pecuniary relations, farther than to say, there is a balance due to me for money loaned to the Holmeses."

I claim the right to answer the above three quotations, the more so, that the second one consigns me most unceremoniously to the ranks of the *liars*. Now, if there is, in my humble judgment, anything more contemptible than a cheat, it is certainly a *liar*. The rest of this letter—editorial—or whatever it may be, is unanswerable, for reasons that will be easily understood by whoever reads it. When the petulant Mr. Pancks [in *Little Dorrit*] spanked the benevolent Christopher Casby, this venerable patriarch only mildly lifted up his blue eyes heavenward, and smiled more benignly than ever. Dr. Child, tossed about and as badly spanked by public opinion, smiles as sweetly as Mr. Casby,

---

*[In her *Scrapbook*, Vol. I, p. 23, H.P.B. appended a footnote to the cutting of this article, stating:]

Ordered to expose Dr. Child. I did so. The D' is a hypocrite, a liar & a fraud.

H.P.B.

talks of "sunshine," and quiets his urgent accusers by assuring them that "it is all fabrications."

I don't know whence Dr. Child takes his "sunshine" unless he draws it from the very bottom of his innocent heart.

For my part, since I came to Philadelphia, I have seen little but slush and dirt, slush in the streets, and dirt in this exasperating Katie King mystery.

I would strongly advise Dr. Child not to accuse *me* of "fabrication," whatever else he may be inclined to ornament me with. What I say I can *prove,* and am ever willing to do so at any day. If he is innocent of all participation in this criminal fraud, let him "rise and explain." If he succeeds in clearing his record, I will be the first to rejoice and promise to offer him publicly my most sincere apology, for the "erroneous suspicions" I labor under respecting his part in the affair; but he must first prove that he is thoroughly innocent. Hard words prove nothing and he cannot hope to achieve such a victory by simply accusing people of "fabrications." If he does not abstain [from] applying epithets unsupported by substantial proofs, he risks, as in the game of shuttlecock and battledore, the chance of receiving the missile back, and maybe that it will hurt him worse than he expects.

In the article in question he says:

"The stories of my acquaintance with Mrs. White are all fabrications. I did let her in two or three times, but the entry and hall were so dark that it was impossible to recognize her or anyone. I have seen her several times and knew that she looked more like Katie King than Mr. (?) or Mrs. Holmes . . ."

Mirabile dictu! This beats our learned friend, Dr. Beard! The latter denies, point-blank, not only "materialization," which is not yet actually proved to the world, but also every spiritual phenomenon. But Dr. Child denies being acquainted with a woman, whom he confesses himself to have seen "several times," received in his office, where she was seen repeatedly by others, and yet at the same time admits that he "knew she looked like Katie King," etc. By the way, we have all laboured under the impression that Dr. Child admitted in *The Inquirer* that he saw Mrs. White for the first time, and recognized her as Katie King, only on that morning when she made her affidavit at the office of the justice of [the] peace. A "fabrication" most likely. In the *R.-P. Journal* for October 27th, 1874, Dr. Child wrote thus:

"Your report does not for a moment shake my confidence in our Katie King, as she comes to me every day and talks to me. On several occasions Katie had come to me and requested Mr. Owen and myself to go there (meaning to the Holmes) and she would come and tell us just what she had told me alone."

Did Dr. Child ascertain where Mrs. White was at the time of the spirits' visits to him?

"As to Mrs. White, I know her well. I have on many occasions let her into the house. I saw her here at the time the manifestations were going on in Blissfield. She has since gone to Massachusetts."

And still the Doctor assures us he was not acquainted with Mrs. White. What signification does he give to the word "acquaintance" in such a case? Did he not go in the absence of the Holmeses to their house and talk with her and even *quarrel* with the woman? Another fabricated story, no doubt. I defy Dr. Child to print again, if he dare, such a word as fabrication in relation to myself, after he has read a certain statement that I reserve for the last.

In all this pitiful, humbugging romance of an "exposure" by a too material she-spirit, there has not been given us a single reasonable explanation of even so much as one solitary fact. It began with a bogus biography, and threatens to end in a *bogus* fight, since every single duel requires, at least, two participants, and Dr. Child prefers extracting sunshine from the cucumbers of his soul and letting the storm subside, to fighting like a man for his own fair name. He says that "he shall not notice" what people say about his little speculative transactions with the Holmeses. He assures us that *they* owe him money. Very likely, but it does not alter the alleged fact of his having paid $10 for every *séance* and pocketing the balance. Dare he say that he did not do it? The Holmeses say otherwise; and the statements in writing of various witnesses corroborate them.

The Holmeses may be scamps in the eyes of certain persons, and the only ones in the eyes of the more prejudiced; but as long as their statements have not been proven false, their word is as good as the word of Dr. Child; aye, in a court of justice even, the "Mediums Holmes" would stand just on the same level as any spiritual prophet or clairvoyant who might have been visited by any same *identical* spirits that visited the former. So long as Dr. Child does not legally prove them to be cheats and himself innocent, why should not they be as well entitled to belief as himself?

From the first hour of the Katie King mystery, if people have accused *them*, no one so far as I know—not even Dr. Child himself—has proved, or even undertaken to prove the innocence of their ex-cashier and recorder. The fact that every word of the ex-leader and president of the Philadelphian Spiritualists would be published by every spiritual paper (and here we must confess to our wonder, that he does not hasten much to avail himself of this opportunity) while any statement coming from the Holmeses would be pretty sure of rejection, would not necessarily imply the fact that they *alone* are guilty; it would only go towards showing, that notwithstanding the divine truth of our faith and the teachings of our invisible guardians, some Spiritualists have not profited by them, to learn impartiality and justice.

These "mediums" are persecuted; so far, it is but justice, since they themselves admitted their guilt about the photography fraud, and *unless it can be shown that they were thereunto controlled by lying spirits*, their own mouths condemn them; but what is less just, is, that they are slandered and abused on all points and made to bear *alone,* all the weight of a crime, where *confederacy* peeps out from every page of the story. No one seems willing to befriend them —these two helpless uninfluential creatures, who, if they sinned at all, perhaps sinned through weakness and ignorance—to take their case in hand and by doing justice to them, do justice at the same time to the cause of truth. If their guilt should be as evident as the daylight at noon,

Who Fabricates?

is it not ridiculous that their partner Dr. Child should show surprise at being so much as suspected! History records but one person, the legitimate spouse of the great Caesar —whose name has to remain enforced by law [as] above suspicion; methinks, that if Dr. Child possesses some natural claims to his self-assumed title of Katie King's "Father Confessor," he can have none whatever to share the infallibility of Madame Caesar's virtue. Being pretty sure as to this myself, and feeling, moreover, somewhat anxious to swell the list of pertinent questions, which are called by our disingenuous friend "fabrications," with at least ONE FACT, I will now proceed to furnish your readers with the following:

"Katie's" picture has been, let us say, proved a fraud, an imposition on the credulous world, and is Mrs. White's portrait. This counterfeit has been proved by the beauty of the "crooking elbow," in her bogus autobiography (the proof sheets of which Dr. Child was seen correcting) by the written confession of the Holmeses and—lastly by Dr. Child himself.

Out of the several bogus portraits of the supposed spirit, the most spurious one, has been declared—mostly on the testimony endorsed by Dr. Child and "over his signature" —to be the one where the pernicious and false Katie King is standing behind her *medium*.

The operation of this delicate piece of imposture, proved so difficult as to oblige the Holmeses to take into the secret of the conspiracy the photographer.

Now Dr. Child denies having anything whatever to do with the sittings for those pictures. He denies it most emphatically, and goes so far as to say (we have many witnesses and proofs to that), that he was out of town, four hundred miles away, when the said pictures were taken. And so he was, bless his dear prophetic soul! Meditating and chatting with the nymphs and goblins of Niagara Falls, so that, when he pleads an *alibi,* it's no "fabrication" but the truth for once.

Unfortunately for the veracious Dr. Child, "whose character and reputation for truthfulness and moral integrity no one doubts."

(Here we quote the words of "Honesty" and "Truth," transparent pseudonyms of an "amateur" for detecting, exposing and writing under the cover of secrecy, who tried to give a friendly push to the doctor in two articles—but failed in both.)—

Unfortunately for H. T. Child, we say, he got inspired in some evil hour to write a certain article, and forgetting the wise motto, *Verba volant, scripta manent,* to publish it in *The Daily Graphic* on the 16th of November last, together with the portraits of John and Katie King.

Now for this bouquet of the endorsement of a fact by a truthful man, "whose moral integrity no one can doubt."

To the Editor of *The Daily Graphic.*

On the evening of July 20th, after a large and successful *séance,* in which Katie had walked out into the room in the presence of thirty persons and *had disappeared* and *reappeared in full view,* she remarked to Mr. Leslie and myself that if we, with four others whom she named, would remain after the *séance,* she would like to try for her photograph. We did so, and there were present six persons besides the photographer. I had procured two dozen magnesium spirals and when all was ready, she opened the door of the cabinet and stood in it, while Mr. Holmes on one side, and I upon the other, burned these, making a brilliant light. We tried two plates, but neither of them were satisfactory.

Another effort was made on the 23rd of July, which was successful. *We* asked her if she would try to have it taken by daylight. She said she would. *We sat with shutters open* at four o'clock p.m. In a few moments, Katie appeared at the aperture and said she was ready. She asked to have one of the windows closed, and that we should hold a shawl to screen her. As soon as the camera was ready she came out and walked behind the shawl to the middle of the room, a distance of six or eight feet, where she stood in front of the camera. She remained in that position until the first picture was taken, when she retired to the cabinet.

Mr. Holmes proposed that she should permit him to sit in front of the camera, and should come out and place her hand upon his shoulder. To this she assented and desired all present *to avoid looking into her eyes,* as this disturbed the conditions very much....

The second picture was then taken in which she stands behind Mr. Holmes. When the camera was closed, she showed great signs of weakness, and it was necessary to assist her back to the cabinet, *and when she got to the door she appeared ready to sink to the floor and disappeared(?). The cabinet door was opened, but she was not to be seen.*

"IMPORTANT NOTE"
Pasted by H.P.B. in her *Scrapbook*, Vol. I, pp. 20-21.
(See page 73 of the present volume for transcription.)

H. P. BLAVATSKY IN 1875
Photograph by Beardsley, Ithaca, N.Y.

In a few minutes she appeared again, and remarked that she had not been sufficiently materialized and said she would like to try again, if *we* could wait a little while. *We* waited about fifteen minutes, when she rapped on the cabinet, signifying that she was ready to come out. She did so, and *we* obtained the *third* negative.

(Signed) Dr. H. T. Child.

And so, Dr. Child, *we* have obtained this, *we* did that, and *we* did many other things. Did you? Now, besides Dr. Child's truthful assertions about his being out of town, *especially at the time this third negative was obtained*, we have the testimony of the photographer, Dr. Selger, and other witnesses to corroborate the fact. At the same time, I suppose that Dr. Child will not risk a denial of his own article. I have it in my possession and keep it, together with many others as curious, printed like it, and *written* in black and white. Who fabricates stories? Can the doctor answer?

How will he creep out of this dilemma? What rays of his spiritual "sunshine" will be able to dematerialize such a contradictory fact as this one? Here we have an article taking up two spacious columns of *The Daily Graphic,* in which he asserts as plainly as possible, that *he was present himself* at the sittings of Katie King for her portrait; that the spirit came out boldly, *in full daylight,* that *she disappeared* on the threshold of the cabinet, and that *he,* Dr. Child, helping her back to it on account of her great weakness, saw that there was *no one* in the said cabinet, *for the door remained opened.* Who did he help? Whose fluttering heart beat against his paternal arm and waistcoat? Was it the bonny Eliza? Of course, backed by such reliable testimony, of such a truly trustworthy witness, the pictures sold like *wildfire.* Who got the proceeds? Who kept them? If Dr. Child was not in town when the pictures were taken, then this article is an "evident fabrication." On the other hand, if what he says in it is truth, and he was present at all, at the attempt of this bogus picture taking, then he certainly must have known "who was who, in 1874," as the photographer knew it, and as surely it did not require Argus-eyes to recognize *in full daylight,* with only one shutter partially closed, a materialized, ethereal spirit, from a common, "elbow-crooking" mortal woman, whom, though *not acquainted with her,* the doctor still "knew her well."

If our self-constituted leaders, our prominent recorders of the phenomena, will humbug and delude the public with such reliable statements as this one, how can we Spiritualists wonder at the masses of incredulous scoffers that keep on politely taking us for "lunatics" when they do not very rudely call us "liars and charlatans" to our faces? It is not the occasionally cheating "mediums" that have impeded or can impede the progress of our cause; it's the exalted exaggerations of some fanatics on one hand and the deliberate, unscrupulous statements of those, who delight [in] dealing in "wholesale fabrications" and "pious frauds" that have arrested the unusually rapid spreading of Spiritualism in 1874, and brought it to a dead stop in 1875. For how many years to come yet, who can tell?

In his "After the Storm the Sunshine," the Doctor makes the following melancholy reflection:

"It has been suggested that going into an atmosphere of fraud, such as surrounds these mediums (the Holmeses) and *being sensitive* [O, poor Yorick!] I was more liable to be deceived than others."

We shudder indeed at the thought of the exposure of so much sensitiveness to so much pollution! Alas, soiled dove! How very sensitive must a person be who picks up such evil influences that they actually force him into the grossest of fabrications, and which make him invent stories and endorse facts that he has not and could not have seen. If Dr. Child, victim to his too sensitive nature, is liable to fall so easily as that under the control of wicked "Diakka" our friendly advice to him is, to give up Spiritualism as soon as possible, and join the Young Men's Christian Association; for then, under the protecting wing of the true Orthodox Church, he can begin a regular fight, like a second St. Anthony, with the Orthodox Devil. Such Diakka, as he fell in with at the Holmeses, must beat Old Nick by long odds, and if he could not withstand them by the unaided strength of his own pure soul, he may with "bell, book and candle," and the use of holy water, be more fortunate in a tug with Satan;

crying as other "Father Confessors" have heretofore, *"Exorciso vos in nomine Lucis!"* and signifying his triumph, with a robust *"Laus Deo!"*

H. P. BLAVATSKY.

Philadelphia, March, 1875.*

[H.P.B.'S LAWSUIT IN AMERICA]

[When H.P.B. lived for a time in Brooklyn, N. Y. with the French people who came to the United States when she did, she was induced to invest in two parcels of land at the East end of Long Island. One of these tracts was in the North part of Huntington, and the other in the neighborhood of the village of Northport, near Huntington, both in the Suffolk County.

From the existing Court Records, it appears that this land had been purchased by a certain Clementine Gerebko, the deed of conveyance being dated June 2nd, 1873, in other words prior to H.P.B.'s arrival in the United States, July 7, 1873.

On June 15/27, 1873, H.P.B.'s father, Col. Peter Alexeyevich von Hahn, died at Stavropol' in the Caucasus, and sometime in the Fall of the same year H.P.B. received a sum of money as part of her inheritance. It is apparently that sum of money that H.P.B. was induced to invest in the above-mentioned land. On June 22nd, 1874, she entered into co-partnership with Clementine Gerebko for the purpose of working the land and farm at Northport. The co-partnership was to commence on July 1, 1874, and continue for the period of three years. Clause 3 of the Articles states that Clementine Gerebko put the use of the farm into the co-partnership as off-set against the sum of one thousand dollars paid by H.P.B., and Clause 4 states that "all proceeds for crops, poultry, produce, and other products raised on the said farm shall be divided equally, and all expenses" equally shared. The title of the land was reserved to Clementine Gerebko.†

H.P.B. went to live on the farm, but very soon found herself in litigation with Clementine Gerebko as to the validity of the

---

*[In her *Scrapbook,* Vol. I, p. 23, H.P.B. made a notation on top of the page indicating that this article was written March 16, 1875. —*Compiler.*]

†Cf. H. S. Olcott, *Old Diary Leaves,* Vol. I, pp. 30-31.

agreement of the defendant to execute a mortgage to the plaintiff, and returned to New York.

The law firm of Bergen, Jacobs and Ivins of Brooklyn, N.Y. represented H.P.B. Her case was tried by a jury on Monday, April 26, 1875, before Judge Calvin E. Pratt, in the Supreme Court of Suffolk County, at Riverhead. She won the suit and recovered the sum of $1146 and costs of the action. The Judgment, dated June 1, 1875, was filed on June 15 in the Office of the Clerk of Suffolk County, N.Y.

From the recollections of William M. Ivins, Attorney at Law, who became a very good friend of H.P.B.'s, we learn some of the circumstances of this curious trial. He wrote:

"Long Island in those days was a long ways from Brooklyn, for travelling facilities were limited. The calendar of this particular term was very slow, and all the parties were kept there waiting their turn to be heard. As many of the documents and witnesses were French, and there was no interpreter to the court, William S. Fales, a student in the law firm of General Benjamin Tracy, was made special interpreter, and he reported H.P.B.'s testimony which was given in French. For two weeks the Judge, the lawyers, clerks, clients and interpreter were guests in a dull country hotel. . . ."*

Ivins, in addition to being a brilliant lawyer, was a bookworm with a phenomenal memory. More as a joke than in earnest, he deluged his client with Occultism, Gnosticism, Cabalism and white and black magic. Fales, taking his key from Ivins, gave long dissertations on mystical arithmetic, astrology, alchemy, mediaeval symbolism, Neo-Platonism, Rosicrucianism and quaternions. It is a great pity that none of this was apparently recorded, and therefore cannot be recovered from the Court Records.

Another sidelight on this interesting episode may be derived from a passage in a work of Charles R. Flint entitled *Memories of an Active Life*. He writes:

"The circumstances of the trial were interesting, for Madame, who was her own principal witness, testified quite contrary to the way in which her attorneys assumed she would testify. Ivins had associated with him in the trial Fales, who was then a law student. As cautious lawyers, they had gone over the testimony with Madame before the trial, and had advised her as to what points she should emphasize; but, to their great discomfiture, on the witness stand she took the bit in her teeth and galloped along lines of evidence quite opposed to their

---

*Recorded by Mrs. Laura Holloway-Langford in a handwritten manuscript now unfortunately destroyed.

instructions, giving as a reason, when they complained of her testimony, that her 'familiar,' whom she called Tom[John] King, stood at her side (invisible to everyone but her), and prompted her in her testimony. After the court had taken the matter under advisement, Madame left the city, but wrote several letters to Ivins asking him as to the progress of the suit, and finally astonished him by a letter giving an outline of an opinion which she said the court would render in the course of a few days, in connection with a decision in her favor. In accordance with her prediction, the court handed down a decision sustaining her claim upon grounds similar to those which she had outlined in her letter."*

—*Compiler.*]

IMPORTANT TO SPIRITUALISTS

[In the issue of April 29, 1875, there was published in the *Spiritual Scientist* a Circular entitled "Important to Spiritualists" facsimile of which is reproduced herewith. In an Editorial which appears in the same issue, E. Gerry Brown, writing under the heading "A Message from Luxor," had the following to say:

"The readers of the *Scientist* will be no more surprised to read the circular which appears on our front page than we were to receive the same by post . . . . . Who may be our unknown friends of the 'Committee of Seven,' we do not know, nor who the 'Brotherhood of Luxor'; but we do know that we are most thankful for this proof of their interest, and shall try to deserve its continuance. Can anyone tell us of such a fraternity as the above? And what Luxor is meant? . . . It is time that some 'Power,' terrestrial or supernal, came to our aid, for after twenty-seven years of spiritual manifestations, we know nothing about the laws of their occurrence . . . . We cannot help regarding this as an evil of magnitude, and if we could only be satisfied that the appearance of this mysterious circular is an indication that the Eastern Spiritualistic Fraternity is about to lift the veil that has so long hid the Temple from our view, we in common with all other friends of the cause, would hail the event with joy. It will be a blessed day for us when the order shall be, SIT LUX."

---

*Charles R. Flint, *Memories of an Active Life*. New York and London: G. P. Putnam's Sons, 1923. xviii, 349 pp. This excerpt is from Chapter IX entitled "A Society for Testing Human Credulity," pp. 115-32.

IMPORTANT TO SPIRITUALISTS.

THE spiritual movement resembles every other in this respect: that its growth is the work of time, and its refinement and solidification the result of causes working from within outward. The twenty-seven years which have elapsed since the rappings were first heard in Western New York, have not merely created a vast body of spiritualists, but moreover stimulated a large and constantly increasing number of superior minds into a desire and ability to grasp the laws which lie back of the phenomena themselves.

UNTIL the present time these advanced thinkers have had no special organ for the interchange of opinions. The leading spiritual papers are of necessity compelled to devote most of their space to communications of a trivial and purely personal character, which are interesting only to the friends of the spirits sending them, and to such as are just beginning to give attention to the subject. In England the London *Spiritualist*, and in France the *Revue Spirite*, present to us examples of the kind of paper that should have been established in this country long ago—papers which devote more space to the discussion of principles, the teaching of philosophy, and the display of conservative critical ability, than to the mere publication of the thousand and one minor occurrences of private and public circles.

IT is the standing reproach of American Spiritualism that it teaches so few things worthy of a thoughtful man's attention; that so few of its phenomena occur under conditions satisfactory to men of scientific training; that the propagation of its doctrines is in the hands of so many ignorant, if not positively vicious, persons; and that it offers, in exchange for the orderly arrangements of prevailing religious creeds, nothing but an undigested system of present and future moral and social relations and accountability.

THE best thoughts of our best minds have heretofore been confined to volumes whose price has, in most instances, placed them beyond the reach of the masses, who most needed to be familiar with them. To remedy this evil, to bring our authors into familiar intercourse with the great body of spiritualists, to create an organ upon which we may safely count to lead us in our fight with old superstitions and mouldy creeds, a few earnest spiritualists have now united.

INSTEAD of undertaking the doubtful and costly experiment of starting a new paper, they have selected the *Spiritual Scientist*, of Boston, as the organ of this new movement. Its intelligent management up to the present time, by Mr. E. GERRY BROWN, and the commendable tone that he has given to its columns, make comparatively easy the task of securing the co-operation of the writers whose names will be a guarantee of its brilliant success. Although the object has been agitated only about three weeks, the Committee have already received promises from several of our best known authors to write for the paper, and upon the strength of those assurances many subscriptions have been sent in from different cities. The movement is not intended to undermine or destroy any of the existing spiritualistic journals: there is room for all, and patronage for all.

THE price of the *Spiritual Scientist* is $2.50 per annum, postage included. A person sending five yearly subscriptions, is entitled to a copy for himself without extra charge. Subscriptions may be made through any respectable agency, or by direct communication with the editor, E. GERRY BROWN, No. 18 Exchange Street, Boston, Mass.

For the Committee of Seven,

BROTHERHOOD OF LUXOR.

IMPORTANT TO SPIRITUALISTS 87

Writing about this Circular in his *Old Diary Leaves*, Vol. I, pp. 74-76, Col. Olcott says:

"I wrote every word of this circular myself, alone corrected the printer's proofs, and paid for the printing. That is to say, nobody dictated a word that I should say, nor interpolated any words or sentences, nor controlled my action in any visible way. I wrote it to carry out the expressed wishes of the Masters that we — H.P.B. and I — should help the Editor of the [*Spiritual*] *Scientist* at what was to him, a difficult crisis, and used my best judgment as to the language most suitable for the purpose. When the circular was in type at the printer's and I had corrected the proofs, and changed the arrangement of the matter into its final paragraphs, I enquired of H.P.B. (by letter) if she thought I had better issue it anonymously or append my name. She replied that it was the wish of the Masters that it should be signed thus: '*For the Committee of Seven*, BROTHERHOOD OF LUXOR.' And so it was signed and published. She subsequently explained that our work, and much more of the same kind, was being supervised by a Committee of seven Adepts belonging to the Egyptian group of the Universal Mystic Brotherhood. Up to this time she had not even seen the circular, but now I took one to her myself and she began to read it attentively. Presently she laughed, and told me to read the acrostic made by the initials of the six paragraphs. To my amazement, I found that they spelt the name under which I knew the (Egyptian) adept under whose orders I was then studying and working.* Later, I received a certificate, written in gold ink, on a thick green paper, to the effect that I was attached to this 'Observatory,' and that three (named) Masters had me under scrutiny. This title, Brotherhood of Luxor, was pilfered by the schemers who started, several years later, the gudgeon-trap called 'The H.B.of L.' The existence of the real lodge is mentioned in Kenneth Mackenzie's *Royal Masonic Cyclopaedia* (p. 461).

"Nothing in my early occult experience during this H.P.B. epoch, made a deeper impression on my mind than the above acrostic . . ."

When H.P.B. pasted a copy of this Circular in her *Scrapbook*, Vol. I, p. 29 (originally 23), she wrote above the title:]

Sent to E. Gerry Brown by the order of S*** and T*** B*** — of Lukshoor. (Published and Issued by Col. Olcott by order of M ∴)

---

*[Tuitit, or Tuitit Bey. See *Letters from the Masters of the Wisdom*. Second Series. Letter No. 3.—*Compiler*.]

[At the end of this, Col. Olcott added, most likely long afterwards, in blue pencil now too faint for reproduction:]

(but unconscious of any exterior agency. H.S.O.)

[At the bottom of the Circular, H.P.B. wrote as follows:]

Several hundred dollars out of our pockets were spent on behalf of the Editor, and he was made to pass through a minor "diksha." This proving of no avail—the Theosophical Society was established.—[*Script*] (See pages further)— The man might have become a POWER, he preferred to remain an Ass. *De gustibus non disputandum est.*

[From H.P.B.'s own words concerning the establishment of the T.S., it would appear that these remarks of hers were added to the clipping in pen and ink at some later time than the actual appearance of the Circular.]

[In H.P.B.'s *Scrapbook*, Vol. I, p. 27, may be found a cutting from the *Spiritual Scientist* of May 27, 1875, the text of which is as follows:

A BUDGET OF GOOD NEWS

The organization of Col. Olcott's 'Miracle Club' is progressing satisfactorily. Applications are daily received from those wishing to join, but few selections have been positively made; as it is desired that the Club should be composed of men of such standing, and scientific, and other attainments, as shall afford to the public a perfect guarantee of the trustworthiness of any conclusions they may reach.

The medium who is to sit with the investigators, being actively interested in certain business operations, has been temporarily called from New York. Meanwhile in anticipation of the commencement of his report of the séances of the Miracle Club, Col. Olcott authorises the announcement that he will contribute to the *Scientist* some of the results of his winter's reading, in the form of a series of articles entitled "What the Ancients knew, and what the Moderns think they know." This popular author in addition to what he gleaned in his researches among the splendid collections of the "Watkinson Library of Reference," in Hartford, has recently had access to some ancient manuscripts, furnished him by "one who knows *when* and *how*," as the phrase goes; and our readers may count upon both entertainment and instruction in the papers which will appear in this Journal.

We shall also begin at once the publication of a most important paper contributed by N. Wagner, Professor of Zoology in the University of St. Petersburg, and the Huxley of Russia; it gives the results of recent séances held with a French medium, named Brédif, by Prof. Wagner and two other professors of equal eminence. The document, which will appear in three successive chapters, has been translated from the Russian language for this paper by Madame Blavatsky, the accomplished lady, to whose trenchant pen several American journals are indebted for recent contributions which have elicited the highest praise for the elegance of their style and the vigour of their argument.

At the end of this cutting, H.P.B. wrote the following in pen and ink:]

An attempt in consequence of *orders* received from T*** B*** through P*** personating J.K. [symbol]. Ordered to

begin telling the public the *truth* about the phenomena & their mediums. And *now* my martyrdom will begin! I will have all the Spiritualists against me in addition to the Christians & the Skeptics! Thy Will, oh M∴ be done!

H.P.B.

[In H.P.B.'s *Scrapbook*, Vol. 1, p. 36, may be found another cutting from the *Spiritual Scientist* of May 27, 1875, the text of which is as follows:

"It is rumoured that one or more Oriental Spiritualists of high rank have just arrived in this country. They are said to possess a profound knowledge of the mysteries of illumination, and it is not impossible that they will establish relations with those whom we are accustomed to regard as the leaders in Spiritualistic affairs. If the report be true, their coming may be regarded as a great blessing; for after a quarter century of phenomena, we are almost without a philosophy to account for them or control their occurrence. Welcome to the Wise Men of the East, if they have really come to worship at the cradle of our new Truth."

H.P.B. underlined in red pencil the word "Spiritualist," and wrote on the margin, lengthwise up the page, also in red pencil:]

At . . . & Ill. . . . passed thro' New York & Boston; thence thro' California & Japan back. M∴ appearing in *Kama-Rupa* daily.

[The abbreviations most likely stand for Atrya and Illarion (or Hilarion), two of the Adept-Brothers.]

COMPILER'S NOTE

[To this period belongs chronologically H.P.B.'s English translation of a Report issued by Professor Nikolay Petrovich Wagner (1829-1907) of the Universities of Moscow and St. Petersburg, concerning *séances* with the medium Brédif. This Report was originally published in the *Vestnik Yevropy* (European Herald). H.P.B.'s translation appeared in the *Spiritual Scientist* of Boston, Mass., Vol. II, June 3, 10 and 17, 1875, pp. 145-47, 157-59, and 169-71 respectively. It was entitled: "Another Eminent Convert.—The Report of Prof. Wagner of the Imperial University of St. Petersburg, Russia.—The Results of Recent Séances."—*Compiler*.]

TO THE SPIRITUALISTS OF BOSTON

[*Spiritual Scientist*, Boston, Vol. II, June 24, 1875, p. 183]

The following, just received, explains itself. As will be seen by the editorial columns full particulars will be published next week.

E. GERRY BROWN, ESQ., Editor, *Spiritual Scientist*, Boston.

In a private letter received by me from A. N. Aksakoff, Counselor of State in the private Chancellery of the Emperor of Russia, at St. Petersburg, and a circular—"Appeal to Mediums"—both sent by me to the Consul-General of Russia in New York for verification and certification, I, the undersigned, am entrusted by A. N. Aksakoff to select several of the best American mediums for physical manifestations and other phenomena, and invite them to St. Petersburg, with the object to have the Spiritual Phenomena investigated by a special committee of scientists, appointed by the Imperial University of St. Petersburg, under the presidency of the Chief Professor of the said University, D. I. Mendeleyeff. The investigations are to take place twice a week and during no less a period than six months.

All the expenses of the mediums who will accept the invitation are to be defrayed by the said committee, and terms by those of the mediums, who will be selected here and accepted as genuine, to be sent to St. Petersburg, to the President of Committee, Professor Mendeleyeff.

Therefore, I appoint and name as my sole deputy at Boston, for the selection of such mediums, E. Gerry Brown, Esq., Editor of the *Spiritual Scientist,* and beg of him to take the necessary steps for it immediately.

H. P. BLAVATSKY.

Philadelphia, June 22nd, 1875.

A WORD OF ADVICE TO THE SINGING MEDIUM, MR. JESSE SHEPPARD

[*Spiritual Scientist*, Boston, Vol. II, July 8, 1875, p. 209]

I am truly sorry that a spiritualist paper like the *Religio-Philosophical Journal,* which claims to instruct and enlighten its readers, should suffer such trash as Mr. Jesse Sheppard is contributing to its columns to appear without review. I will not dwell upon the previous letter of this very gifted personage, although everything he has said concerning Russia and life at St. Petersburg might be picked to pieces by any one having merely a superficial acquaintance with the place and the people; nor will I stop to sniff at his nosegays of high-sounding names—his Princess Bulkoffs and Princes This and That—which are as preposterously fictitious as though, in speaking of Americans, some Russian singing medium were to mention his friends Prince Jones or Duke Smith, or Earl Brown—for if he chooses to manufacture noble patrons from the oversloppings of his poetic imagination, and it amuses him or his readers, no great harm is done. But when it comes to his saying the things he does in the letter of July 3rd, in that paper, it puts quite a different face upon the matter. Here he pretends to give historical facts—but which never existed. He tells us of things he saw *clairvoyantly,* and his story is such a tissue of ridiculous, gross anachronisms that they not only show his utter ignorance of Russian history, but are calculated to injure the Cause of Spiritualism by throwing doubt upon all clairvoyant descriptions. Secondarily in importance they destroy his own reputation for veracity, stamp him as a trickster, and a false writer, and bring the gravest suspicion upon his claim to possess any mediumship whatever.

What faith can anyone, acquainted with the rudiments of history, have in a medium who sees a mother (Catherine II) giving orders to strangle her son (Paul I) when we all know that the Emperor Paul ascended the throne upon the decease of the very mother whom the inventive genius of this musical prodigy makes guilty of infanticide.

A Word of Advice to the Singing Medium

Permit me, O! young seer, as a Spiritualist and a Russian somewhat read in the history of my country, to refresh your memory. Spiritualism has been laughed at quite enough recently in consequence of such pious frauds as yours, and as Russian *savants* are about to investigate the subject, we may as well go to them with clean hands. The journal which gives you its hospitality goes to my country, and its interests will certainly suffer if you are allowed to go on with your embroidery and spangle-work without rebuke. Remember, young poetico-historian, that the Emperor Paul was the paternal grandfather of the present Tsar,* and every one who has been at St. Petersburg knows that the "old palace," which to your spiritual eye, wears such "an appearance of dilapidation and decay, worthy of a castle of the Middle Ages," and the one where your Paul was strangled, is an everyday, modern-looking, respectable building, the successor of one which was pulled down early in the reign of the late Emperor Nicholas, and known from the beginning until now as the Pavlovsky Military College for the "Cadets." And the two assassins, begotten in your clairvoyant loins—PETRESKI and KOFSKI! Really now, Mr. Sheppard, the gentlemanly assassins ought to be very much obliged to you for these pretty aliases!

It is fortunate for you, dear Sir, that it did not occur to you to discuss these questions in St. Petersburg, and that you evolved your history from the depths of your own consciousness, for in our autocratical country one is not permitted to discuss the little unpleasant verses of the Imperial family history, and the rule would not be relaxed for a Spanish Grandee, or even that more considerable personage, an American singing medium. An attempt on your part to do so would assuredly have interfered with your grand concert, under imperial patronage, and might have led to your journeying to the borders of Russia under an armed escort befitting your exalted rank.

H. P. BLAVATSKY.

---

*[Alexander II.]

A CARD TO THE AMERICAN PUBLIC

[*Spiritual Scientist,* Boston, Vol. II, July 8, 1875, p. 211]

In compliance with the request of the Honourable Alexander Aksakoff, Counselor of State in the Imperial Chancellery at St. Petersburg, the undersigned hereby gives notice that they are prepared to receive applications from physical mediums who may be willing to go to Russia, for examination before the Committee of the Imperial University.

To avoid disappointment, it may be well to state, that the undersigned will recommend no mediums whose personal good character is not satisfactorily shown; nor any who will not submit themselves to a thorough scientific test of their mediumistic powers, in the city of New York, prior to sailing; nor any who cannot exhibit most of their phenomena in a lighted room, to be designated by the undersigned, and with such ordinary furniture as may be found therein.

Approved applications will be immediately forwarded to St. Petersburg, and upon receipt of orders thereon from the Scientific Commission or its representative, Mr. Aksakoff, proper certificates and instructions will be given to accepted applicants, and arrangements made for defraying expenses.

Address the undersigned, in care of E. Gerry Brown, Editor of the *Spiritual Scientist,* 18 Exchange Street, Boston, Mass, who is hereby authorized to receive personal applications from mediums in the New England States.

HENRY S. OLCOTT.
HELENA P. BLAVATSKY.

[In H.P.B.'s *Scrapbook,* Vol. I, p. 58, may be found at the bottom of the page the following important note written by H.P.B. in pen and ink:]

Orders received from India direct to establish a philosophico-religious Society and choose a name for it—also to choose Olcott. July 1875.

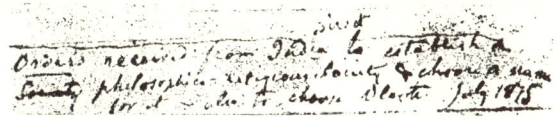

[In H.P.B.'s *Scrapbook*, Vol. I, p. 39, several cuttings are pasted consisting of articles by Col. H. S. Olcott written for the *Spiritual Scientist* about July 15, 1875. One of these, entitled "Mutterings of a Storm," deals with the crisis of Spiritualism, and Col. Olcott ends it with the following remarks concerning the Journal:

"Already some of the best and brightest minds among our psychologists have come to our assistance, and no paper in the world has a more talented corps of contributors. Already friends gather around us, send us money, exert themselves, without our solicitation, to get subscribers, and our young enterprise stands upon 'rock bottom'."

Along the side of this article, H.P.B. wrote in pen and ink:]

The Editor and *Medium* Gerry Brown has thanked us for our help. Between Col. Olcott & myself, H.P.B., we have spent over a 1000 dollars given him to pay his debts & support his paper. Six months later he became our *mortal* enemy, because only we declared our unbelief in *Spirits*. Oh grateful mankind...

H.P.B.

[THE "HIRAF" CLUB AND ITS HISTORICAL BACKGROUND]

[Mention has already been made of the names of William M. Ivins and William S. Fales, two attorneys at law who represented H.P.B. in her court-case at Riverhead, Long Island, N. Y. As these two individuals, together with several of their friends, played an important part in H.P.B.'s literary activity at its very inception, the following excerpt from the work of Charles R. Flint, *Memories of an Active Life*, from which we already had occasion to quote, will be of interest to the reader. Mr. Flint writes:

"For several years I was a member of the Philologian Debating Society of the Brooklyn Polytechnic, and out of this organization grew what was probably the most extraordinary secret body the world has ever known. Among the members of the Philologian were Dr. Henry Van Dyke, the famous author; Charles F. Chichester, who became Treasurer of the Century Company; Frederick W. Hinrichs, the political reformer; and William E. S. Fales, who was regarded by everyone as a man of genius.

"None of his friends can ever forget Fales, the many-sided, with his massive head and his blond curls, his high, broad forehead and square jaw, deep chest and steel muscles. Six feet of splendid physical manhood, he loved to display his powers and often exhibited his mountainous biceps. But though he might have excelled as an athlete, his herculean strength was more than equalled by his wonderful mental equipment. Books had been his friends from childhood, and he loved to 'ponder over many a quaint and curious volume of forgotten lore.' Research, a natural flow of language, a brilliant fancy, and a glowing imagination, led him naturally to literary composition.

"Like champagne, he was often effervescent, sparkling, and overflowing. Much that he emitted was like froth, but much, too, was substantial and weighty. He even had his periods of gloom. He would deliver a talk on the history of Satan, and follow it with a paper on the origin of obscene words. This, in turn, would be succeeded by a lugubrious poem on death, or on the final 'wreck of matter and the crash of worlds.' While in addition to exercising his skill in the realm of the imagination, he was addicted to mathematics and scientific research.

"But despite his gifts, Fales lacked purpose and the will for sustained effort. He was conscious that he could surpass most men if he cared to exert himself. This circumstance, as in the case of the hare and the tortoise, frequently caused his failure, a duller competitor securing the victory.

"He often said that life was a joke and he generally appeared to make this epigram the maxim of his career. Thus, while he was recognized by his fellows in the Columbia School of Mines, as the most brilliant mathematician that school had ever had, and as a student who in less time than any other could accomplish a given task, after leading his class in the first year he fell to the middle in the second year, and failed of graduation in the third. An enraged father sent him to Brazil to follow a business career. Tiring of that after a year's absence, he returned to New York and to Columbia, where he passed his examinations and received his degree after a very

FREDERICK W. HINRICHS

WILLIAM E. S. FALES

WILLIAM M. IVINS
1851-1915
(The two upper photographs are from Charles R. Flint's *Memories of an Active Life*, New York and London, 1923. The portrait of W. M. Ivins is from *The National Cyclopaedia of American Biography*, Vol. XXX. Consult pp. 95-100, and the *Bio-Bibliographical Index* for biographical data.)

H. P. BLAVATSKY IN NEW YORK DAYS

brief period of study. From the School of Mines he went to the School of Law. Indeed, there is little that he did not attempt.

"For a while he taught a class of small boys at a Sunday School, and he filled their pockets with—cigars. He challenged a missionary to compete with him in a petition to Heaven. He lacked reverence, absolutely.

"He was a great debater; but quite conscienceless, for he would volunteer on either side of a controversy, whatever his opinion as to the real merits of the question. There seemed to be no subject upon which he was unprepared to speak interestingly and with effect.

"It seemed to his associates in the Milton Literary Association that there was no height to which he might not have climbed, had he been governed by a high purpose. Hinrichs has preserved many of Fales' letters. These two men were different in their ideals, but each had the warmest affection for the other. Fales had a big heart, and much is pardoned one who is generous.

"In 1868 the Milton Literary Association was organized and with this association the Philologian Society was merged. Its incorporators were A. Augustus Healy—for many years President of the Brooklyn Institute of Arts and Sciences—myself, and other members of the Philologian Society.

"For six years the Milton Association met weekly in the rooms of the Hamilton Literary Society, of which Seth Low was the most prominent member, and which subsequently became the Hamilton Club. The Milton was an exclusive society, no one being admitted until he had been pronounced intellectually fit by an unanimous vote of the members. In its conceit, it black-balled no less a personnage than Hon. William M. Ivins who was afterwards generally regarded as one of the most brilliant men in the city of New York, and who, at a later period, was admitted to the membership of the Milton. We debated all questions concerning the heavens above, the earth beneath, and the waters under the earth.

"After six years the Miltonians became engrossed in professional and business affairs and the meetings of the Association were discontinued, but reunion dinners were held every few years. At one of these reunions Ivins arose, and to the surprise of all, disclosed the existence of an organization named 'Hiraf,' which, he said, had been created more than thirty-five years before, 'for the purpose of testing human credulity!' The name 'Hiraf' was an acrostic made up of the first letters of the names of five Miltonians.

"*H* stood for Frederick W. Hinrichs, the man who probably ran for more important public offices, without being elected, than any man in the United States. In 1896 he ran for Lieutenant-Governor of New York on the Gold Democratic ticket; in 1897 for President of the Borough of Brooklyn, on the Seth Low Fusion ticket; in 1898 for Attorney-General of the State of New York, on a Citizens' ticket which was to have been headed by Theodore Roosevelt; in 1903 for Comptroller of the City of New York, on a Fusion ticket, headed by Seth Low for mayor. In 1904 he was nominated for Governor of New York by a faction of the Democratic Party, and the nomination was seconded by his brother Miltonian, A. Augustus Healy. He is generally known for his independent speech and his consistent opposition to political machines.

"*I* stood for William M. Ivins, who was one of the ablest lawyers in New York. He became City Chamberlain, and was one of the leaders who brought about the adoption of the secret ballot. Governor Charles T. Hughes appointed him chairman of a charter commission, and he was most active in drawing a proposed new charter for Greater New York—which a prominent politician told me was 'the best charter that could have been drawn for the people, but the worst for the politicians, and, therefore, would never be adopted.' At the request of Governor Hughes, Ivins drew the laws under which the public utilities commissions have been appointed. On behalf of the City he acted as counsel in the investigations of Tammany Hall; and he also ran for Mayor of New York City.

"*R* stood for James C. Robinson, whose part in the activities of the 'Hiraf' is evidenced by a letter which I will quote on a succeeding page.

"*A* stood for Charles Frederick Adams, an able and learned lawyer practicing in New York.

"*F* stood for William E. S. Fales.

"That evening we learned from Ivins that the 'Hiraf' in its efforts to test human credulity and to contribute to behavioristic psychology, conceived the idea of sending an article to a Boston magazine, the *Spiritual Scientist,* which was one of the most important spiritistic publications in the United States. The article was prepared by four members of the 'Hiraf,' who without consultation with one another, wrote psychic and esoteric sentences which were transmitted to Fales, who was known as the 'conjunctor,' and whose duty it was to combine into a more or less consistent whole the efforts of the various contributors . . . . . .

"Although the 'Hiraf' article was written by young men upon the threshold of their careers, partly as an exercise in mental gymnastics, or even as a literary hoax, nevertheless we must be struck by the fact that recent advances in science and some of the arts make us believe that the time is not far distant when some of the dreams and visions which have been entertained by theologians, philosophers, and prophets in the past may be realized.

". . . . . parties interested in the theosophic movement have insisted that whatever the origin of the 'Hiraf' utterances may have been, the authors were, without their knowledge, inspired, by a power over and beyond them, to utter words of weight and possibly prophecy.

"Whatever adverse opinion may still be entertained as to Madame Blavatsky and her cult, it cannot be denied that her teachings contain much that is interesting, even elevating, and that she has managed to affect many, many thousands, from India in the east to California in the west."*

Further details concerning this matter may be gathered from a letter written by Frederick W. Hinrichs to C. Jinarâiadâsa, dated from 140 Liberty Street, Manhattan, New York, May 2, 1923, and which is now in the Adyar Archives. Mr. Hinrichs says:

". . . . The writers of the 'Hiraf' article are William M. Ivins, William E. S. Fales and myself. There were two others of our number who took a lively interest in our philosophic and theological discussions,—but they contributed little or nothing to the production. One was Charles F. Adams,—the other James Robinson. Of the group of five, all are dead but myself. The name 'Hiraf' was made up of the initial letters of our five names. I always thought that Adams had contributed some portion of the essay,—but, shortly before his death, in reading over the article with me, he said that he could not recognize that any part of it was his. All of us were young lawyers at the time, or students of the law, with exception of Robinson, who was a clerk in a commercial concern. Fales received the fragments prepared by Ivins and myself and, together with his own contribution, welded the three into one. Fales, Ivins and I wrote without consultation with one another on such topics as suggested themselves to us, after we separated one evening. We five often met at the house of Fales (a many-sided genius) to read, to discuss literature, especially philosophic literature, and cognate matters . . . . . ·

---

*C. R. Flint, *Memories of an Active Life*, pp. 115-32.

". . . . We young men had little reverence, some learning and some power of expression, and, at the meeting referred to, jocularly suggested to one another the writing of a mystic article on Theosophy, esoteric science and what not. I had been reading *Zanoni*, a book on Rosicrucianism, and the life of Paracelsus,—so that I wrote, especially, along those lines. The Madame [H.P.B.] claimed to be a Rosicrucian and, when Fales received my contribution and Ivins' contribution (this latter on recent phases of philosophical thought), he (Fales), without any consultation with either Ivins or myself, dubbed the article, which he compounded out of our three or four separate unrelated contributions—'Rosicrucianism.' Fales also created the acrostic 'Hiraf' out of our initials, and added five stars, probably suggested by three stars appended to an article which has previously appeared in the Madame's paper. We all laughed heartly over the compounded article and sent it to the Madame in Boston. She published it in two numbers of her periodical, as I recall it, and wrote two very flattering editorials on 'Hiraf.' Our production provoked considerable comment, and called forth some correspondence from different widely separated quarters, some of which correspondence appeared in the Madame's paper.

"I have been told by Theosophists here, that we young men had written better than we knew, and that we were probably inspired by higher powers. Of this, I know nothing, *although this may be so*. Certain it is, that 'Hiraf' has been quite extensively quoted as authority in various printed publications . . . ."

Such were the curious circumstances which provided the background to the publication of the article entitled "Rosicrucianism" in the *Spiritual Scientist*, Vol. II, July 1 and 8, 1875, pp. 202 and 212-13 respectively.

A brief item from the pen of Colonel Olcott introduced the "young author" to the reading public in rather laudable terms, and promised a reply from "a most competent hand."

The article drew from H.P.B. an immediate reply which was her first major contribution on the subject of Occultism, a literary production which she herself called "My first *Occult* Shot." The text of this reply, in the words of Col. Olcott (*Old Diary Leaves*, I, 103), "laid open the whole field of thought since ploughed up by the members, friends, and adversaries of the Theosophical Society."—*Compiler*.]

A FEW QUESTIONS TO "HIRAF***"

AUTHOR OF THE ARTICLE "ROSICRUCIANISM"

By Madame H. P. Blavatsky

[*Spiritual Scientist*, Boston, July 15 and 22, 1875, pp. 217-18, 224, 236-7]*

Among the numerous sciences pursued by the well-disciplined army of earnest students of the present century, none has had less honors or more scoffing than the oldest of them—the science of sciences, the venerable mother-parent of all our modern pigmies. Anxious, in their petty vanity, to throw the veil of oblivion over their undoubted origin, the self-styled, positive scientists, ever on the alert, present to the courageous scholar who tries to deviate from the beaten highway traced out for him by his dogmatic predecessors, a formidable range of serious obstacles.

As a rule, Occultism is a dangerous, double-edged weapon for one to handle, who is unprepared to devote his whole life to it. The theory of it, unaided by serious practice, will ever remain in the eyes of those prejudiced against such an unpopular cause, an idle, crazy speculation, fit only to charm the ears of ignorant old women. When we cast a look behind us, and see how, for the last thirty years, modern Spiritualism has been dealt with, notwithstanding the occurrence of daily, hourly proofs which speak to all our senses, stare us in the eyes, and utter their voices from "beyond the great gulf," how can we hope that Occultism, or Magic, which stands in relation to Spiritualism as the Infinite to the Finite, as the cause to the effect, or as

---

* [Along the side of this title, in H.P.B.'s *Scrapbook*, Vol. I, p. 41, where the cutting is pasted, may be found H.P.B.'s remark in pen and ink:

My first *Occult* Shot
                H.P.B.

—Compiler.]

unity to multifariousness, how can we hope, I say, that it will easily gain ground where Spiritualism is scoffed at? One who rejects *a priori*, or even doubts, the immortality of man's soul can never believe in its Creator, and blind to what is heterogeneous in his eyes, will remain still more blind to the proceeding of the latter from Homogeneity. In relation to the Cabala, or the compound mystic textbook of all the great secrets of Nature, we do not know of anyone in the present century who could have commanded a sufficient dose of that moral courage which fires the heart of the true adept with the sacred flame of propagandism—to force him into defying public opinion, by displaying familiarity with that sublime work. Ridicule is the deadliest weapon of the age, and while we read in the records of history of thousands of martyrs who joyfully braved flames and faggots in support of their mystic doctrines in the past centuries, we would scarcely be likely to find one individual in the present times, who would be brave enough even to defy ridicule by seriously undertaking to prove the great truths embraced in the traditions of the Past.

As an instance of the above, I will mention the article on Rosicrucianism, signed "Hiraf." This ably-written essay, notwithstanding some fundamental errors, which, though they are such would be hardly noticed except by those who had devoted their lives to the study of Occultism in its various branches of practical teaching, indicates with certainty to the practical reader that, for theoretical knowledge, at least, the author need fear few rivals, still less superiors. His modesty, which I cannot too much appreciate in his case—though he is safe enough behind the mask of his fancy pseudonym—need not give him any apprehensions. There are few critics in this country of Positivism who would willingly risk themselves in an encounter with such a powerful disputant, on his own ground. The weapons he seems to hold in reserve, in the arsenal of his wonderful memory, his learning, and his readiness to give any further information that enquirers may wish for, will undoubtedly scare off every theorist, unless he is perfectly sure of himself, which few are. But book learning—and here I refer only to the subject of Occultism—vast as it may be, will always prove insufficient even to the analytical mind, the most accustomed to extract the quintessence of truth, disseminated throughout thousands of contradictory statements, unless supported by personal experience and practice. Hence, Hiraf can only expect an encounter with some one who may hope to find a chance to refute some of his bold assertions on the plea of having just such a slight *practical* experience. Still, it must not be understood that these present lines are intended to criticize our too modest essayist. Far from poor, ignorant me be such a presumptuous thought. My desire is simply to help him in his scientific but, as I said before, rather hypothetical researches, by telling a little of the little I picked up in my long travels throughout the length and breadth of the East—that cradle of Occultism—in the hope of correcting certain erroneous notions he seems to be labouring under, and which are calculated to confuse uninitiated sincere enquirers, who might desire to drink at his own source of knowledge.

In the first place, Hiraf doubts whether there are in existence, in England or elsewhere, what we term regular colleges for the neophytes of this Secret Science. I will say from personal knowledge that such places there are in the East—in India, Asia Minor, and other countries, As in the primitive days of Socrates and other sages of antiquity, so now, those who are willing to learn the Great Truth will find *the chance* if they only "try" to meet someone to lead them to the door of one "who knows *when* and *how*." If Hiraf is right about the seventh rule of the Brotherhood of the Rosy Cross which says that "the Rose-crux *becomes* and is not made," he may err as to the exceptions which have ever existed among other Brotherhoods devoted to the pursuit of the same secret knowledge. Then again, when he asserts, as he does, that Rosicrucianism is almost forgotten, we may answer him that we do not wonder at it, and add, by way of parenthesis, that, strictly speaking, the

Rosicrucians do not now even exist, the last of that Fraternity having departed in the person of Cagliostro.*

Hiraf ought to add to the word Rosicrucianism "that particular sect," at least, for it was but a sect after all, one of many branches of the same tree.

By forgetting to specify that particular denomination, and by including under the name of Rosicrucians all those who, devoting their lives to Occultism, congregated together in Brotherhoods, Hiraf commits an error by which he may unwittingly lead people to believe that the Rosicrucians having disappeared, there are no more Cabalists practicing Occultism on the face of the earth. He also becomes thereby guilty of an anachronism,† attributing to the Rosicrucians the building of the Pyramids and other majestic monuments, which indelibly exhibit in their architecture the symbols of the grand religions of the Past. For it is not so. If the main object in view was and still is alike with all the great family of the ancient and modern Cabalists, the dogmas and formulae of certain sects differ greatly. Springing one after the other from the great Oriental mother-root, they scattered broadcast all over the world, and each of them desiring to outrival the other by plunging deeper and deeper into the secrets jealously guarded by Nature, some of them became guilty of the greatest heresies against the primitive Oriental Cabala.

While the first followers of the secret sciences, taught to the Chaldaeans by nations whose very name was never breathed in history, remained stationary in their studies, having arrived at the maximum, the Omega of the knowledge permitted to man, many of the subsequent sects separated from them, and, in their uncontrollable thirst for more knowledge, trespassed the boundaries of truth, and fell into fictions. In consequence of Pythagoras—so says Iamblichus—having by sheer force of energy and daring

---

*Knowing but little about Occultism in Europe I may be mistaken; if so, any one who knows to the contrary will oblige me by correcting my error.

†The same mistake pervades the whole of that able book, *The Rosicrucians*, by Hargrave Jennings.

A FEW QUESTIONS TO "HIRAF"

penetrated into the mysteries of the Temple of Thebes, and obtained therein his initiation, and afterwards studied the sacred sciences in Egypt for twenty-two years, many foreigners were subsequently admitted to share the knowledge of the wise men of the East, who, as a consequence, had many of their secrets divulged. Later still, unable to preserve them in their purity, these mysteries were so mixed up with fictions and fables of the Grecian mythology that truth was wholly distorted.

As the primitive Christian religion divided, in course of time, into numerous sects, so the science of Occultism gave birth to a variety of doctrines and various brotherhoods. So the Egyptian Ophites became the Christian Gnostics, shooting forth the Basilideans of the second century, and the original Rosicrucians created subsequently the Paracelsists, or Fire-Philosophers, the European Alchemists, and other physical branches of their sect. (See Hargrave Jennings' *The Rosicrucians*.) To call indifferently every Cabalist a Rosicrucian, is to commit the same error as if we were to call every Christian a Baptist on the ground that the latter are also Christians.

The Brotherhood of the Rosy Cross was not founded until the middle of the thirteenth century, and notwithstanding the assertions of the learned Mosheim, it derives its name, neither from the Latin word *Ros* (dew), nor from a cross, the symbol of Lux. The origin of the Brotherhood can be ascertained by any earnest, *genuine* student of Occultism, who happens to travel in Asia Minor, if he chooses to fall in with some of the Brotherhood, and if he is willing to devote himself to the head-tiring work of deciphering a Rosicrucian manuscript—the hardest thing in the world, for it is carefully preserved in the archives of the very Lodge which was founded by the first Cabalist of that name, but which now goes by another name. The founder of it, a German Reuter [Knight], by the name of Rosencranz, was a a man who, after acquiring a very suspicious reputation through the practice of the Black Art, in his native place, reformed in consequence of a vision. Giving up his evil practices, he made a solemn vow, and went on foot to

Palestine, in order to make his *amende honorable* at the Holy Sepulchre. Once there, the Christian God, the meek, but well-informed Nazarene—trained as he was in the high school of the Essenes, those virtuous descendants of the botanical as well as astrological and magical Chaldaeans—appeared to Rosencranz, a Christian would say, in a vision, but I would suggest, in the shape of a materialized spirit. The purport of this visitation, as well as the subject of their conversation, remained forever a mystery to many of the Brethren; but immediately after that, the ex-sorcerer and Reuter disappeared, and was heard of no more till the mysterious sect of Rosicrucians was added to the family of Cabalists, and their powers aroused popular attention, even among the Eastern populations, indolent, and accustomed as they are to live among wonders. The Rosicrucians strove to combine together the most various branches of Occultism, and they soon became renowned for the extreme purity of their lives and their extraordinary powers, as well as for their thorough knowledge of the secret of the secrets.

As alchemists and conjurers they became proverbial. Later (I need not inform Hiraf precisely when, as we drink at two different sources of knowledge), they gave birth to the more modern Theosophists, at whose head was Paracelsus, and to the Alchemists, one of the most celebrated of whom was Thomas Vaughan (seventeenth century) who wrote the most practical things on Occultism, under the name of Eugenius Philalethes. I know and can prove that Vaughan was, most positively, "made before he became."

The Rosicrucian Cabala is but an epitome of the Jewish and the Oriental ones combined, the latter being the most secret of all. The Oriental Cabala, the practical, full, and *only* existing copy, is carefully preserved at the headquarters of this Brotherhood in the East, and, I may safely vouch, will never come out of its possession. Its very existence has been doubted by many of the European Rosicrucians. One who wants "to become" has to hunt for his knowledge through thousands of scattered volumes, and pick up facts and lessons, bit by bit. Unless he takes the nearest way and consents "to be made," he will never become a practical

Cabalist, and with all his learning will remain at the threshold of the "mysterious gate." The Cabala may be used and its truths imparted on a smaller scale now than it was in antiquity, and the existence of the mysterious Lodge, on account of its secrecy, doubted; but it does exist and has lost none of the primitive secret powers of the ancient Chaldaeans.* The lodges, few in number, are divided into sections and known but to the Adepts; no one would be likely to find them out, unless the sages themselves found the neophyte worthy of initiation. Unlike the European Rosicrucians, who, in order "to become and not be made," have constantly put into practice the words of St. John, who says, "Heaven suffereth violence, and the violent take it by force," and who have struggled alone, violently robbing Nature of her secrets, the Oriental Rosicrucians (for such we will call them, being denied the right to pronounce their

---

*For those who are able to understand intuitionally what I am about to say, my words will be but the echo of their own thoughts. I draw the attention of such only, to a long series of inexplicable events which have taken place in our present century; to the mysterious influence directing political cataclysms; the doing and undoing of crowned heads; the tumbling down of thrones: the thorough metamorphosis of nearly the whole of the European map, beginning with the French Revolution of '93, predicted in every detail by the Count de St.-Germain, in an autograph MS., now in possession of the descendants of the Russian nobleman to whom he gave it, and coming down to the Franco-Prussian War of the latter days. This mysterious influence called "chance" by the skeptic and Providence by Christians, may have a right to some other name. Of all these degenerated children of Chaldaean Occultism, including the numerous societies of Freemasons, only one of them in the present century is worth mentioning in relation to Occultism, namely, the "Carbonari." Let some one study all he can of that secret society, let him think, combine, deduce. If Raymond Lully, a Rosicrucian, a Cabalist, could so easily supply King Edward I of England with six millions sterling to carry on war with the Turks in that distant epoch, why could not some secret lodge in our day furnish, as well, nearly the same amount of millions to France, to pay their national debt—this same France, which was so wonderfully, quickly defeated, and as wonderfully set on her legs again. Idle talk!— people will say. Very well, but even an hypothesis may be worth the trouble to consider sometimes.

true name), in the serene beatitude of their divine knowledge, are ever ready to help the earnest student struggling "to become" with practical knowledge, which dissipates, like a heavenly breeze, the blackest clouds of sceptical doubt.

Hiraf is right again when he says that "knowing that their mysteries, if divulged," in the present chaotic state of society, "would produce mere confusion and death," they shut up that knowledge within themselves. Heirs to the early heavenly wisdom of their first forefathers, they keep the keys which unlock the most guarded of Nature's secrets, and impart them only gradually and with the greatest caution. But still they *do* impart sometimes! Once in such a *cercle vicieux*, Hiraf sins likewise in a certain comparison he makes between Christ, Buddha, and Khong-foo-tse, or Confucius. A comparison can hardly be made between the two former wise and spiritual *Illuminati*, and the Chinese philosopher. The higher aspirations and views of the two Christs can have nothing to do with the cold, practical philosophy of the latter; brilliant anomaly as he was among a naturally dull and materialistic people, peaceful and devoted to agriculture from the earliest ages of their history. Confucius can never bear the slightest comparison with the two great Reformers. Whereas the principles and doctrines of Christ and Buddha were calculated to embrace the whole of humanity, Confucius confined his attention solely to his own country; trying to apply his profound wisdom and philosophy to the wants of his countrymen, and little troubling his head about the rest of mankind. Intensely Chinese in patriotism and views, his philosophical doctrines are as much devoid of the purely poetic element, which characterizes the teachings of Christ and Buddha, the two divine types, as the religious tendencies of his people lack in that spiritual exaltation which we find, for instance, in India. Khong-foo-tse has not even the depth of feeling and the slight spiritual striving of his contemporary, Lao-tse. Says the learned Ennemoser: "The spirits of Christ and Buddha have left indelible, eternal traces all over the face of the world. The doctrines of Confucius can be mentioned only as the most brilliant proceedings of cold human reasoning." C. F. Haug, in his *Allgemeine Geschichte*,* has depicted the Chinese nation perfectly, in a few words: their "heavy, childish, cold, sensual nature explains the peculiarities of their history." Hence any comparison between the first two reformers and Confucius, in an essay on Rosicrucianism, in which Hiraf treats of the Science of Sciences and invites the thirsty for knowledge to drink at her inexhaustible source, seems inadmissible.

Further, when our learned author asserts so dogmatically that the Rosicrucian learns, though *he never* uses, the secret of immortality in earthly life, he asserts only what he himself, in his practical inexperience, thinks impossible. The words "never" and "impossible" ought to be erased from the dictionary of humanity, until the time at least when the great Cabala shall all be solved, and so rejected or accepted. The "Count de Saint-Germain" is, until this very time, a living mystery, and the Rosicrucian Thomas Vaughan another one. The countless authorities we have in literature, as well as in oral tradition (which sometimes is the more trustworthy) about this wonderful Count's having been met and recognized in different centuries, is no myth. Anyone who admits one of the practical truths of the Occult Sciences taught by the Cabala, tacitly admits them all. It must be Hamlet's "to be or not to be," and if the Cabala is true, then Saint-Germain need be no myth.

But I am digressing from my object, which is, firstly, to show the slight differences between the two Cabalas—that of the Rosicrucians and the Oriental one; and, secondly, to say that the hope expressed by Hiraf to see the subject better appreciated at some future day than it has been till now, may perhaps become more than a hope. Time will show many things; till then, let us heartily thank Hiraf for this first well-aimed shot at those stubborn scientific runaways, who, once before the Truth, avoid looking her in the face, and dare not even throw a glance behind them, lest they should be forced to see that which would greatly lessen their

---

* [Stuttgart, 1841, p. 127.]

self-sufficiency. As a practical follower of Eastern Spiritualism, I can confidently wait for the time when, with the timely help of those "who know," American Spiritualism, which even in its present shape has proved such a sore in the side of the materialists, will become a science and a thing of mathematical certitude, instead of being regarded only as the crazy delusion of epileptic monomaniacs.

The first Cabala in which a mortal man ever dared to explain the greatest mysteries of the universe, and show the keys to "those masked doors in the ramparts of Nature through which no mortal can ever pass without rousing dread sentries never seen upon this side of her wall," was compiled by a certain Shimon Ben Yochai, who lived at the time of the second Temple's destruction. Only about thirty years after the death of this renowned Cabalist, his MSS. and written explanations, which had till then remained in his possession as a most precious secret, were used by his son Rabbi Eleazar and other learned men. Making a compilation of the whole, they so produced the famous work called *Zohar* (God's splendour). This book proved an inexhaustible mine for all the subsequent Cabalists, their source of information and knowledge, and all more recent and genuine Cabalas were more or less carefully copied from the former. Before that, all the mysterious doctrines had come down in an unbroken line of merely oral traditions as far back as man could trace himself on earth. They were scrupulously and jealously guarded by the Wise Men of Chaldaea, India, Persia and Egypt, and passed from one initiate to another, in the same purity of form as when handed down to the first man by the angels, students of God's great Theosophic Seminary. For the first time since the world's creation, the secret doctrines, passing through Moses who was initiated in Egypt, underwent some slight alterations. In consequence of the personal ambition of this great prophet-medium, he succeeded in passing off his familiar spirit, the wrathful "Jehovah," for the spirit of God himself, and so won undeserved laurels and honors. The same influence prompted him to alter some of the principles of the great oral Cabala in order to make them the more secret. These principles were laid out in symbols by him in the first four books of the *Pentateuch*, but for some mysterious reasons he withheld them from *Deuteronomy*. Having initiated his seventy Elders in his own way, the latter could give but what they had received themselves, and so was prepared the first opportunity for heresy, and the erroneous interpretations of the symbols. While the Oriental Cabala remained in its pure primitive shape, the Mosaic or Jewish one was full of drawbacks, and the keys to many of the secrets—forbidden by the Mosaic law—purposely misinterpreted. The powers conferred by it on the initiates were formidable still, and of all the most renowned Cabalists, King Solomon and his bigoted parent, David, notwithstanding his penitential psalms, were the most powerful. But still the doctrine remained secret and purely oral, until, as I have said before, the days of the second Temple's destruction. Philologically speaking, the very word Cabala is formed from two Hebrew words, meaning *to receive*, as in former times the initiate received it orally and directly from his Master, and the very Book of the *Zohar* was written out on received information, which was handed down as an unvarying stereotyped tradition by the Orientals, and altered through the ambition of Moses, by the Jews.

If the primitive Rosicrucians learned their first lessons of wisdom from Oriental masters, not so with their direct descendants, the fire-philosophers or Paracelsists; for in many things the Cabala of the latter *Illuminati* proves to be degenerated into a twin sister of the Jewish. Let us compare. Besides admitting the "*Shedim*," or intermediate spirits of the Jews—the elementary ones, which they divide into four classes, those of the air, of the water, the fire, and of minerals—the Christian Cabalist believes like the Jewish, in Asmodeus, the *Ever-accursed One*, or our good friend the orthodox Satan. Asmodeus, or Asmodi, is the chief of the elementary goblins. This doctrine alone differs considerably from the Oriental philosophy, which denies that the great Ain-soph (the Endless or Boundless) who made his existence known through the medium of the spiritual substance sent forth from his Infinite Light—the eldest of the ten Intelligences or Emanations—the first Sephira—could ever create an endless, macrocosmal evil. It (Oriental philosophy) teaches us that, though the first three spheres out of seven—taking it for granted that our planet comes in fourth—are inhabited by elementary or future *men* (this might account for the modern doctrine of Re-incarnation, perhaps) and, though until they become such men they are beings without immortal souls in them and but the "grossest purgations of the celestial fire," still they do not belong to Eternal Evil. Every one of them has the chance in store of having its matter *reborn* on this "fourth sphere," which is our planet, and so have "the gross purgation" purified by the Immortal Breath of the Aged of the Aged, who endows every human being with a portion of his boundless self. Here, on our planet, commences the first spiritual transition, from the Infinite to the Finite, of the elementary matter which first proceeded from the pure Intelligence, or God, and also the operation of that pure Principle upon this material purgation. Thus begins the immortal man to prepare for Eternity.

In their primitive shape, the elementary spirits, so often mistaken in modern Spiritualism for the undeveloped or unprogressed spirits of our dead, stand in relation to our planet as we stand in relation to the Summer Land. When we use the term "disembodied spirit," we only repeat what the elementary ones most certainly think or say of us human beings, and if they are as yet devoid of immortal souls, they are, nevertheless, gifted with instinct and craft, and we appear as little material to them as the spirits of the fifth sphere appear to us. With our passage into each subsequent sphere, we throw off something of our primitive grossness. Hence, there is eternal progress—physical and spiritual—for every living being. The transcendental knowledge and philosophy of the greatest Oriental Cabalists never penetrated beyond a certain mark, and the Hermetist, or rather Rosicrucian, if we would be precise, never went farther than to solve the majestic, but more limited problems of the Jewish Cabala, which we can divide thus:

PROFESSOR HIRAM CORSON
1828-1911
(From W. T. Hewett's *Cornell University: A History*, New York, 1905. Consult the *Bio-Bibliographical Index*, for biographical sketch.)

THE RICHARDSON COTTAGE
Temporarily occupied by the Corsons in 1875, when H.P.B. visited them. Part of *Isis Unveiled* was written here.
(From E. R. Corson's *Some Unpublished Letters of Helena Petrovna Blavatsky*, London, 1929.)

1. The nature of the Supreme Being:

2. The origin, creation, and generation of the Universe, the *Macrocosmos;*

3. The creation, or generation, of *outflowing* of angels and man;

4. The ultimate destiny of angels, man, and the Universe; or the *inflowing;*

5. To point out to humanity the real meaning of the whole of the Hebrew Scriptures.

As it is, the real, the complete Cabala of the first ages of humanity is in possession, as I said before, of but a few Oriental philosophers; where they are, who they are, is more than is given me to reveal. Perhaps I do not know it myself, and have only dreamed it. Thousands will say it is all imagination; so be it. Time will show. The only thing I can say is that such a body exists, and that the location of their Brotherhoods will never be revealed to other countries, until the day when Humanity shall awake in a mass from its spiritual lethargy, and open its blind eyes to the dazzling light of Truth. A too premature discovery might blind them, perhaps forever. Until then, the speculative theory of their existence, will be supported by what people erroneously believe to be *supernal* facts. Notwithstanding the selfish, sinful opposition of science to Spiritualism in general, and that of the scientists in particular, who, forgetting that their first duty is to enlighten Humanity, instead of that, allow millions of people to lose themselves and drift about like so many disabled ships, without pilot or compass, among the sandbanks of superstition; notwithstanding the toy-thunderbolts and harmless anathemas hurled around by the ambitious and crafty clergy, who, above all men, ought to believe in spiritual truths; notwithstanding the apathetic indifference of that class of people who prefer believing in nothing, pretending the while to believe in the teachings of their churches, which they select according to their best notions of respectability and fashion; notwithstanding all these things, Spiritualism will rise above all, and its progress can be as little helped as the dawn of the morning or the rising of the sun. Like the former, will the glorious Truth arise among all these black clouds gathered in the East; like the latter, will its brilliant light pour forth upon awakening humanity its dazzling rays. These rays will dissipate these clouds and the unhealthy mists of a thousand religious sects which disgrace the present century. They will warm up and recall into new life the millions of wretched souls who shiver and are half frozen under the icy hand of killing skepticism. Truth will prevail at last, and Spiritualism, the new world's conqueror, reviving, like the fabulous Phoenix out of the ashes of its first parent, Occultism, will unite for ever in one Immortal Brotherhood all antagonistic races; for this new St. Michael will crush for ever the dragon's head—of Death!

I have but a few words more to say before I close. To admit the possibility of anyone becoming a practical Cabalist (or a Rosicrucian, we will call him, as the names seem to have become synonymous) who simply has the firm determination to "become" one, and hopes to get the secret knowledge through studying the Jewish Cabala, or every other one that may come into existence, without actually being initiated by another, and so being "made" such by someone who "knows," is as foolish as to hope to thread the famous labyrinth without the clue, or to open the secret locks of the ingenious inventors of the mediaeval ages, without having possession of the keys. If the Christian New Testament, the easiest and youngest of all the Cabalas known to us, has presented such immense difficulties to those who would interpret its mysteries and secret meanings (which, were they only once studied with the key of modern Spiritualism, would open as simply as the casket in Aesop's fable), what hope can there be for a modern Occultist, learned only in theoretical knowledge, to ever attain his object? Occultism without practice will ever be like the statue of Pygmalion, and no one can animate it without infusing into it a spark of the sacred Divine Fire. The Jewish Cabala, the only authority of the European Occultist, is all based on the secret meanings of the Hebrew scriptures, which, in their turn, indicate the keys to them, by signs *hidden* and unintelligible to the uninitiated. They afford no hope for the adepts to solve them practically. The Seventh Rule of the Rosicrucian "who became, but was not made" has its secret meaning, like every other phrase left by the Cabalists to posterity, in writing. The words: "The dead letter killeth," which Hiraf quotes, can be applied in this case with still more justice than to the Christian teachings of the first apostles. A Rosicrucian had to struggle ALONE, and toil long years to find some of the preliminary secrets—the A B C of the great Cabala—only on account of his ordeal, during which were to be tried all his mental and physical energies. After that, if found worthy, the word "Try" was repeated to him for the last time before the final ceremony of the ordeal. When the High Priests of the Temple of Osiris, of Serapis, and others, brought the neophyte before the dreaded Goddess Isis, the word "Try" was pronounced for the last time; and then, if the neophyte could withstand that final mystery, the most dreaded as well as the most trying of all horrors for him who knew not what was in store for him; if he bravely "lifted the veil of Isis," he became an initiate, and had naught to fear more. He had passed the last ordeal, and no longer dreaded to meet face to face the inhabitants from "over the dark river."

The only cause for the horror and dread we feel in the presence of death, lies in its unsolved mystery. A Christian will always fear it, more or less; an initiate of the secret science, or a *true* Spiritualist, never; for both of the latter have lifted the veil of Isis, and the great problem is solved by both, in theory and in practice.

Many thousand years ago the wise King Solomon declared that "There is nothing new under the Sun," and the words of this very wise man ought to be repeated till the farthest ends of time. There is not a science, nor a modern discovery in any section of it, but was known to the Cabalists thousands of years since. This will appear a bold and ridiculous assertion, I know; and one apparently unconfirmed by any authority. But I will answer that where truth stares one in the face, there can be no other authority than one's senses. The only authority I know of, lies scattered throughout the East. Besides, who would ever dare, in the ever-changing, ever-discovering Europe, or adolescent America, to risk proclaiming himself as an authority? The scientist, who was an authority yesterday, becomes by the mere lucky chance a contemporary discoverer, a worn-out hypothesist. How easily the astronomer of today forgets that all his science is but the picking up of crumbs left by the Chaldaean astrologers. What would not modern physicians, practitioners of their blind and lame science of medicine, give for a part of the knowledge of botany and plants—I won't say of the Chaldaeans—but even of the more modern Essenians. The simple history of the Eastern people, their habits and customs, ought to be a sure guarantee that what they once knew, they cannot have totally forgotten. While Europe has changed twenty times its appearance, and been turned upside down by religious and political revolutions and social cataclysms, Asia has remained stationary. What was, two thousand years ago, exists now with very little variation. Such practical knowledge as was possessed by the ancients could not die out so soon with such a people. The hope of finding remnants even of such wisdom as Ancient Asia possessed, ought to tempt our conceited modern science to explore her territory.

And thus is it that all we know of what we profess and live upon, comes to us from the scorned, despised Occultism of the East. Religion and sciences, laws and customs—all of these, are closely related to Occultism, and are but its result, its direct products, disguised by the hand of time, and palmed upon us under new pseudonyms. If people ask me for the proof, I will answer that it does not enter my province to teach others what they can learn themselves with very little difficulty, provided they give themselves the trouble to read and think over what they read. Besides, the time is near when all the old superstitions and the errors of centuries must be swept away by the hurricane of Truth. As the prophet Mohammed, when he perceived that the mountain would not come to him, went himself towards the mountain, so Modern Spiritualism made its unexpected appearance from the East, before a skeptical world, to terminate in a very near future the oblivion into which the ancient secret wisdom had fallen.

Spiritualism is but a baby now, an unwelcome stranger, whom public opinion, like an unnatural foster mother, tries to crush out of existence. But it is growing, and this same East may one day send some experienced, clever nurses to take care of it. The immediate danger of Salem tragedies has passed away. The Rochester knockings, tiny as they were, awoke some vigilant friends, who, in their turn, aroused thousands and millions of jealous defenders for the true Cause. The most difficult part is done; the door stands ajar; it remains for such minds as Hiraf invites to help earnest truth-seekers to the key which will open for them the gates, and aid them to pass the threshold dividing this world from the next, "without rousing the dread sentries never seen upon this side of her wall." It belongs to the exact knowledge of the Occultist to explain and alter much of what seems "repulsive" in Spiritualism, to some of the too delicate Orthodox souls. The latter may object the more to Spiritualistic phenomena, on the ground that Cabalism is mixed up with it. They will begin to prove that Occultism, *if it does exist*, is the forbidden "Black Art," the sorcery for which people were burnt, not so long ago. In such a case I will humbly reply, that there is nothing in nature but has two sides to it. Occultism is certainly no exception to the rule, and is composed of *White* and *Black* magic. But so is Orthodox religion, likewise. When an Occultist is a real Rosicrucian, he is a thousand times purer and nobler, and more divine, than any of the holiest Orthodox priests; but when one of the latter gives himself up to the turbulent demon of his own vile passions, and so rouses all the fiends, they shout with joy at the sight of such a perversity. In what, pray, is this Orthodox priest better than the blackest of all the sorcerers' dealings with the Elementary "Dweller," or with the "Diakka" of A. J. Davis?

Verily, we have *White* and *Black* Christianity, as well as White and Black magic.

O, you very Orthodox priests and clergymen of various creeds and denominations, you who are so intolerant towards Spiritualism, this purest of the Children of Ancient Magic, can you tell me why, in such a case, you practice daily yourselves, all the most prominent rites of magic in your churches, and follow the antetypes of the very ceremonies of Occultism? Can you light a taper, or illuminate your altars with circles of wax lights, for instance, and not repeat the rites of magic? What is your altar with the vertical burning candles, but the modern mimicry of the original magic monolith with the Baal fires upon it? Don't you know that by doing so you are following right in the steps of the ancient fire-worshippers, the Persian Heathen Ghebers? And your Pope's sparkling mitre, what is it but the direct descendant of the Mithraic Sacrifice, symbolical covering invented for the heads of the high priests of this very Occultism in Chaldaea? Having passed through numerous transformations it now rests in its last (?) Orthodox shape, upon the venerable head of your successor of St. Peter. Little do the devout worshippers of the Vatican suspect, when they lift up their eyes in mute adoration upon the head of their God on Earth, the Pope, that what they admire, is after all, but the caricatured head-dress, the Amazon-like helmet of Pallas Athene, the heathen goddess Minerva! In fact, there is scarcely a rite or ceremony of the Christian Church that does not descend from Occultism.

But say or think what you will, you cannot help that which was, is, and ever will be, namely, the direct communication between the two worlds. We term this intercourse modern Spiritualism, with the same right and logic as when we say the "New World," in speaking of America.

I will close by startling, perhaps, even Orthodox Spiritualists by reaffirming that all who have ever witnessed our modern materializations of genuine spirit-forms, have, unwittingly, become the initiated neophytes of the Ancient Mystery; for each and all of them have solved the problem of Death, have "lifted the veil of Isis."

[At the end of this article, in her *Scrapbook*, Vol. I, p. 45, where the cutting was pasted, H.P.B. wrote in pen and ink the following:]

Shot No. 1—Written by H.P.B. by express orders from S *** (See first result in the query from a *learned!!* Mason —art: "Rosicrucianism," back of the page.

[*The parenthesis is not closed in the original.*]

[In her *Scrapbook*, Vol. III, H.P.B. pasted the cuttings of this long article again. It occupies pages 241-245 therein. She signed the article in pen and ink: H. P. Blavatsky, June 1875.]

"WHAT ARE YOU GOING TO DO ABOUT IT?"

[*Spiritual Scientist*, Boston, Vol. II, July 22, 1875, p. 235]

A most outrageous swindle was perpetrated upon the public last Sunday evening, at the Boston Theatre. Some persons with no higher aspirations in the world, than a lust for a few dollars to fill their pockets depleted by unsuccessful cheap shows, advertised a "*Séance*" and engaged as "Mediums" some of the most impudent impostors with which the world is cursed. They furthermore abused public confidence by causing it to be understood that these people were to appear before the Scientific Commission at St. Petersburg.

Is it not about time that some Society in Boston should be sufficiently strong financially, and have members who will have the requisite energy TO ACT, in an emergency like this? Common sense would dictate what might be done, and a determined WILL would overcome all obstacles. Spiritualism needs a Vigilance Committee. Public opinion will justify any measures that will tend to check this trifling. "Up, and At Them" should be the watchword, until we have rid Society of these pests and their supporters.

The Press of Boston are disposed to be fair towards Spiritualists. But if Spiritualists do not care enough for Spiritualism to defend it from tricksters who have not sufficient skill to merit them the title of jugglers, how can they expect any different treatment than that it is receiving?

As a proof of the sincerity of the Boston Press, and also in support and further explanation of the above, we might mention that the following card sent to all the Morning Dailies, was accepted and printed in Tuesday's edition.

BOSTON, *July* 19*th,* 1875.

Sir,—The undersigned desire to say that the persons who advertised a so-called spiritualistic exhibition, at the Boston Theatre, last evening, were guilty of false representations to the public. We are alone empowered by the Academy of Sciences attached to the Imperial University of St. Petersburg, Russia, to select the mediums who shall be invited by that body to display their powers during the forthcoming scientific investigation of Spiritualism, and Mr. E. Gerry Brown, editor *Spiritual Scientist* of this city, is our only authorized **Deputy.**

Neither "F. Warren," "Prof. J. T. Bates," "Miss Suydam," "Mrs. S. Gould," nor "Miss Lillie Darling," has been selected, or are at all likely to be selected for that honor.

As this swindle may be again attempted, we desire to say, once for all, that no medium accepted by us will be obliged to exhibit his powers to earn money to defray his expenses, nor will any such exhibition be tolerated. The Imperial University of St. Petersburg makes this investigation in the interest of science; not to assist charlatans to give juggling performances in theatres, upon the strength of our certificates.

HENRY S. OLCOTT.
H. P. BLAVATSKY.

[In H.P.B.'s *Scrapbook,* Vol. I, p. 47, there is a cutting of an article from the *Spiritual Scientist* of July 22, 1875, entitled "Mrs. Holmes Caught Cheating." On the free space between the two columns, H.P.B. wrote in pen and ink the following remarks:]

She swore to me in Philadelphia that if I only saved her that once she would NEVER resort to cheating & trickery again. I *saved* her but upon receiving her solemn oath.— And now she went out of greed for money to produce her *bogus* manifestations again. M ∴ forbid me to help her. Let her receive her *fate*—the vile, fraudulent liar!

H.P.B.

[FORMATION OF THE THEOSOPHICAL SOCIETY]

[In H.P.B.'s *Scrapbook*. Vol. I. pp. 54-55, there is a cutting from a weekly journal, *The Liberal Christian*, of Saturday, September 4, 1875, which consists of an article entitled "Rosicrucianism in New York." It is unsigned but is known to have been written by the Rev. Dr. J. H. Wiggin, the Editor of that Journal. Starting with a superficial survey of Rosicrucian ideas, Dr. Wiggin goes on to relate the circumstances under which he had recently met H. P. Blavatsky. He says:

"It was just after Col. Olcott's astounding stories in the *Sun* about the floral gifts received from the spirits through a Boston medium, that I was kindly bidden by my friend, Mr. Sotheran, of the *American Bibliopolist*, to meet both Madame and the Colonel the following evening in Irving Place; with permission to bring some friends . . ."

According to Dr. Wiggin's account, there were present at this gathering: Col. Olcott, *Il Conte*, "the secretary once of Mazzini," Charles Sotheran, Judge M. of New Jersey, his wife, Mr. M., a Boston gentleman, and H. P. Blavatsky, who, he says, was "the centre of the group."

To the cutting in her *Scrapbook*, H.P.B. appended the following remarks in pen and ink:]

Written by Rev. Dr. Wiggin. This article provoked the wrath of Rev. Dr. Bellows; hence he wrote another one, on "Sorcery and Necromancy" and pitched into us.

[H.P.B. then drew a blue line from the title along the cutting to the bottom on the right edge of page 55 and added in pen and ink the following significant remark:]

On that evening the first idea of the Theos. Society was discussed.

[To this, Col. Olcott added the following note, possibly at a later date:]

For a much better account see a quotation on p. 296 of E. H. Britten's *Nineteenth Century Miracles,* London 1883.

[Unfortunately, Col. Olcott's remark confuses the issue. What he has in mind is a report of the gathering that took place in H.P.B.'s quarters, at 46 Irving Place, on Tuesday, September 7, 1875, which was published in one of the New York Dailies and reprinted in *The Spiritual Scientist* a year later. Some seventeen people were present at this meeting, and George H. Felt, an engineer and architect, gave a lecture on "The Lost Canon of Proportion of the Egyptians." It is this account that was included in Mrs. Emma Hardinge-Britten's work, and it is obvious, of course, that Dr. Wiggin could not have reported it in the September 4th issue of his Journal.

We have seen that Dr. Wiggin specifically mentions Col. Olcott's stories in the New York *Sun*. This has reference to his article entitled "Ghosts That Are Ghosts," published in the *Sun* of Wednesday, August 18, 1875, in which he outlines at considerable length the remarkable mediumship of Mrs. Mary Baker Thayer of Boston, whose phenomena consisted mainly of *apports* of flowers and birds. Somewhat prior to the above-mentioned date, Col. Olcott had occasion personally to investigate the genuineness of her powers and remained thoroughly convinced of their *bona fides*.

From Dr. Wiggin's words it would appear that the gathering he describes took place fairly soon after Col. Olcott's published account of Mrs. Thayer's phenomena. As no mention of any such gathering occurs in *The Liberal Christian* of Saturday, August 28th, it is likely that it took place sometime between August 28th and September 4th.

In mentioning this earlier gathering, but giving no date, Col. Olcott (*Old Diary Leaves*, I, 114-15) speaks of it as having taken place "during the previous week," and identifies one of the persons present as Signor Bruzzesi, who may have been the same personage as "Il Conte" of Dr. Wiggin. By "previous week" he means the period between August 29th and September 4th.

There seems to be no reason, however, to doubt the fact that the *actual* formation of the Theosophical Society took place on September 7th, 1875, even though, in Col. Olcott's own words "no official memorandum exists of the persons actually present on that particular evening," and "no official record by the Secretary of the attendance at this first meeting survives" (*op. cit.*, pp. 114, 118).

Formation of the Theosophical Society 123

In a book which belonged to H.P.B. and is now in the Library at Adyar, entitled *A Guide to Theosophy*—a Collection of Select Articles which was published by Tukaram Tatya in Bombay in 1887, we find on page 51 the Objects and Rules of the T.S., as revised in 1886. Among other things, the account states that the Society was formed at New York, U.S. of America, 17 November, 1875. To this H.P.B. appended a footnote in pen and ink:]

Formally; Yet in truth it was founded on 7th Sept. 1875 at my house in 46 Irving Place New York.

[On page 79 of Vol. 1 of H.P.B.'s *Scrapbook*, there is another cutting from *The Liberal Christian* of September 25, 1875. It is a report of the Meeting of September 7, 1875, entitled "The Cabala." It describes Mr. Felt's lecture and mentions the formation of the Theosophical "Club." It speaks of Dr. Pancoast of Philadelphia as a very wise occultist, and refers to his statement to the effect that ancient occultists "could summon long departed 'spirits from the vasty deep,' and compel them to answer questions." To this H.P.B. appended the following remark in pen and ink:]

Not "departed Spirits or souls" but the "Elementals" the beings living in the Elements.

[We must bear in mind that Col. Olcott, when writing the First Series of his *Old Diary Leaves*, did so from memory, as his actual Diaries of the period 1874-78 had mysteriously disappeared. Speaking of the gathering on September 7th, he says that during the animated discussion which followed Felt's lecture,

". . . the idea occurred to me [Olcott] that it would be a good thing to form a society to pursue and promote such occult research, and, after turning it over in my mind, I wrote on a scrap of paper the following:
'*Would it not be a good thing to form a Society for this kind of study?*'
—and gave it to Judge, at the moment standing between me and H.P.B., sitting opposite, to pass over to her. She read it and nodded assent...."

On the other hand, Annie Besant, writing in *Lucifer* (Vol. XII, April, 1893, p. 105) about the formation of the T.S., says that

". . . she [H.P.B.] has told me herself how her Master bade her found it, and how at His bidding she wrote the suggestion of starting it on a slip of paper and gave it to W. Q. Judge to pass to Colonel Olcott; and then the Society had its first beginning . . ."

While these two contradictory accounts are somewhat perplexing to the historian, we must bear in mind that neither of them is based on any actual document or written contemporary account. What is of particular importance and interest, however, is the fact that H.P.B. herself, as we have seen earlier in the present Volume, concluded her "Important Note" pasted in her *Scrapbook*, I, pp. 20-21, with the statement that ". . . M∴ brings orders to form a Society—a secret Society like the Rosicrucian Lodge. He promises to help." In addition to that, she specifically states having received *orders* from India "to establish a philosophico-religious Society" and to "choose Olcott," and dates this notation "July 1875."

It is evident, therefore, that the impending formation of such a Society was already "in the air," so to say, a considerable time prior to the gathering at which it was first broached.]

[In addition to H.P.B., Col. Olcott and W. Q. Judge, the other "formers" of the Theosophical Society, to use Col. Olcott's own expression, were: Charles Sotheran, Dr. Charles E. Simmons, Herbert D. Monachesi, Charles C. Massey, W. L. Alden, George H. Felt, D. E. de Lara, Dr. W. Britten, Mrs. Emma Hardinge-Britten, Henry J. Newton, John Storer Cobb, J. Hyslop, and H. M. Stevens.

The reader should consult the Bio-Biographical Index at the end of the present Volume, under the respective names. A special effort has been made to collect as much information as was possible to obtain concerning at least some of these individuals. A few of them have remained untraced.—*Compiler*.]

[In H.P.B.'s *Scrapbook*, Vol. I, p. 57, an article by Col. Olcott is pasted in, entitled "Spiritualism Rampant." It is dated September 7, 1875, and deals with the Elementary Spirits and their personations. H.P.B. pasted at the side of this article three small coloured cartoons: a very fat man with an enormous head; three bottles of whiskey with faces on corks; and the head of a clown with squinting eyes. Under them, H.P.B. wrote in pen and ink:]

The present generation of men gradually evolving from—plants, vegetables, fish and becoming finally Whiskey bottles, —the "Embryonic man" or ancestor of the present race.

Formation of the Theosophical Society

Meeting held at No. 46 Irving Place on Wednesday Evening, September 8th, 1875.

In consequence of a proposal of Col. Henry S. Olcott, that a society be formed for the study and elucidation of Occultism, the Cabala &c., the ladies and gentlemen then and there present resolved themselves into a meeting, and, upon motion of Mr. W. Q. Judge it was

Resolved, that Col. H. S. Olcott take the chair.

Upon motion it was also

Resolved, that Mr. W. Q. Judge, act as secretary.

The Chair then called for the names of those persons present, who would agree to found and belong to a society such as had been mentioned. The following persons handed their names to the secretary:

Col. Olcott, Mme. H. P. Blavatsky, Chas. Sotheran, Dr. Chas. E. Simmons, H. D. Monachesi, C. C. Massey of London, W. L. Alden, G. H. Felt, D. E. de Lara, Dr. Britten, Mrs. E. H. Britten, Henry J. Newton, John Storer Cobb, J. Hyslop, W. Q. Judge, H. M. Stevens.

Upon motion of Herbert D. Monachesi, it was

Resolved, that a committee of three be appointed by the chair, to draft a constitution and by-laws, and to report the same at the next meeting.

Upon motion it was

Resolved, that the chair be added to the committee.

The Chair then appointed Messrs. H. J. Newton, H. M. Stevens, and C. Sotheran to be such committee.

Upon motion it was

Resolved, that we now adjourn until Monday Septr 13th, at the same place, at 8 P. M.

H. S. Olcott, Chairman.
William Q. Judge, Secretary.

FROM MADAME H. P. BLAVATSKY TO HER CORRESPONDENTS

AN OPEN LETTER SUCH AS FEW CAN WRITE

[*Spiritual Scientist*, Boston, Vol. III, September 23, 1875, pp. 25-7]

Being daily in receipt of numerous letters—written with the view of obtaining advice as to the best method of receiving information respecting Occultism, and the direct relation it bears to modern Spiritualism, and not having sufficient time at my disposal to answer these requests, I now propose to facilitate the mutual labor of myself and correspondents, by naming herein a few of the principal works treating upon *magiism,* and the mysteries of such modern Hermetists.

To this I feel bound to add, respecting what I have stated before, to wit: that would-be aspirants must not lure themselves with the idea of any possibility of their becoming practical Occultists by mere book-knowledge. The works of the Hermetic Philosophers were never intended for the masses, as Mr. Charles Sotheran,* one of the most learned members of the Society *Rosae Crucis,* in a late essay, thus observes: "Gabriele Rossetti in his *Disquisitions on the Antipapal spirit, which produced the Reformation,* shows that the art of speaking and writing in a language which bears a double interpretation, is of very great antiquity; that it was in practice among the priests of Egypt, brought from thence by the Manichees, whence it passed to the Templars and Albigenses, spread over Europe, and brought about the Reformation."

The ablest book that was ever written on Symbols and Mystic Orders, is most certainly Hargrave Jennings' *The Rosicrucians,* and yet it has been repeatedly called "obscure trash" in my presence, and that too, by individuals who were most decidedly well-versed in the rites and mysteries of modern Freemasonry. Persons who lack even the latter knowledge, can easily infer from this, what would be the

---

*[See the Bio-Bibliographical Index for information concerning him.—*Compiler.*]

amount of information they might derive from still more obscure and mystical works than the latter; for if we compare Hargrave Jennings' book with some of the mediaeval treatises and ancient works of the most noted Alchemists and Magi, we might find the latter as much more obscure than the former—as regards language—as a pupil in celestial Philosophy would the Book of the Heavens, if he should examine a far distant star with the naked eye, rather than with the help of a powerful telescope.

Far from me, though, the idea of disparaging in anyone the laudable impulse to search ardently after Truth, however arid and ungrateful the task may appear at first sight; for my own principle has ever been to make the Light of Truth, the beacon of my life. The words uttered by Christ eighteen centuries ago: "Believe and you will understand," can be applied in the present case, and repeating them with but a slight modification, I may well say: "Study and you will believe."

But to particularize one or another Book on Occultism, to those who are anxious to begin their studies in the hidden mysteries of nature is something, the responsibility of which, I am not prepared to assume. What may be clear to one who is intuitional, if read in the same book by another person, might prove meaningless. Unless one is prepared to devote to it his whole life, the superficial knowledge of Occult Sciences will lead him surely to become the target for millions of ignorant scoffers to aim their blunderbusses, loaded with ridicule and chaff, against. Besides this, it is in more than one way dangerous to select this science as a mere pastime. One must bear forever in mind the impressive fable of Oedipus, and beware of the same consequences. Oedipus unriddled but one-half of the enigma offered him by the Sphinx, and caused its death; the other half of the mystery avenged the death of the symbolic monster, and forced the King of Thebes to prefer blindness and exile in his despair, rather than face what he did not feel himself pure enough to encounter. He unriddled the man, the form, and had forgotten God—the idea.

If a man would follow in the steps of Hermetic Philosophers, he must prepare himself beforehand for martyrdom. He must give up personal pride and all selfish purposes, and be ready for everlasting encounters with friends and foes. He must part, once for all, with every remembrance of his earlier ideas, on all and on everything. Existing religions, knowledge, science must rebecome a blank book for him, as in the days of his babyhood, for if he wants to succeed he must learn a new alphabet on the lap of Mother Nature, every letter of which will afford a new insight to him, every syllable and word an unexpected revelation. The two hitherto irreconcilable foes, science and theology—the Montecchi and Capuletti of the nineteenth century—will ally themselves with the ignorant masses, against the modern Occultist. If we have outgrown the age of stakes, we are in the heyday, *per contra,* of slander, the venom of the press, and all these mephitic *venticelli* of calumny, so vividly expressed by the immortal Don Basilio.* To Science, it will be the duty, arid and sterile as a matter of course—of the Cabalist to prove that from the beginning of time there was but one positive Science—Occultism; that it was the mysterious lever of all intellectual forces, the Tree of Knowledge of good and evil of the Allegorical Paradise, from whose gigantic trunk sprang in every direction boughs, branches and twigs, the former shooting forth straight enough at first, the latter, deviating with every inch of growth, assuming more and more fantastical appearances, till at last one after the other, lost its vital juice, got deformed, and, drying up, finally broke off, scattering the ground afar with heaps of rubbish. To Theology, the Occultist of the future will have to demonstrate, that the Gods of the Mythologies, the Elohim of Israel as well as the religious, theological mysteries of Christianity, to begin with the Trinity, sprang from the sanctuaries of Memphis and Thebes; that their mother Eve is but the spiritualized Psyche of old, both of them paying a like penalty for their curiosity, descending to Hades or Hell, the latter to bring back to

---

*[A calumniating niggardly bigot in de Beaumarchais' *Barber of Seville* and *Marriage of Figaro.—Compiler.*]

earth the famous Pandora's box—the former, to search out and crush the head of the serpent—symbol of time and evil; the crime of both expiated by the Pagan Prometheus and the Christian Lucifer; the first, delivered by Hercules—the second conquered by the Saviour.

Furthermore, the Occultist will have to prove to the Christian Theology, publicly, what many of its priesthood are well aware of in secret—namely, that their God on earth was a Cabalist, the meek representative of a tremendous Power, which, if misapplied, might shake the world to its foundations; and that, of all their evangelical symbols, there is not one but can be traced up to its parent fount. For instance, their Incarnated Verbum or *Logos* was worshipped at His birth by the three Magi, led on by the star, and received from them the gold, the frankincense and myrrh, the whole of which is simply an excerpt from the Cabala our modern theologians despise, and the representation of another and still more mysterious "Ternary,"* embodying allegorically in its emblems, the highest secrets of the Cabala.

A clergy, whose main object ever has been to make of their Divine Cross the gallows of Truth, and Freedom, could not do otherwise than try and bury in oblivion the origin of that same cross, which, in the most primitive symbols of the Egyptians' magic, represents the key to Heaven. Their anathemas are powerless in our days, the multitude is wiser; but the greatest danger awaits us just in that latter direction, if we do not succeed in making the masses remain at least neutral—till they come to know better—in this forthcoming conflict between Truth, Superstition and Presumption; or, to express it in other terms, Occult Spiritualism, Theology and Science. We have to fear neither the miniature thunderbolts of the clergy, nor the unwarranted negations of Science. But Public Opinion, this invisible, intangible, omnipresent, despotic tyrant; this thousand-headed Hydra—the more dangerous for being composed of indi-

---

*The Ternarius or Ternary, the Symbol of perfection in antiquity, and the Star, the Cabalistic sign of the Microcosm.

vidual mediocrities—is not an enemy to be scorned by any would-be Occultist, courageous as he may be. Many of the far more innocent Spiritualists have left their sheepskins in the clutches of this ever-hungry, roaring lion—for he is the most dangerous of our three classes of enemies. What will be the fate, in such a case, of an unfortunate Occultist, if he once succeeds in demonstrating the close relationship existing between the two? The masses of people, though they do not generally appreciate the science of truth, or have real knowledge, on the other hand are unerringly directed by mere instinct; they have intuitionally—if I may be allowed to express myself—the sense of what is formidable in its genuine strength. People will never conspire except against *real* Power. In their blind ignorance, the Mysteries and the Unknown have been, and ever will be, objects of terror for them. Civilization may progress, human nature will remain the same throughout all ages. Occultists, beware!

Let it be understood, then, that I address myself but to the truly courageous and persevering. Besides the danger expressed above, the difficulties to becoming a practical Occultist in this country, are next to insurmountable. Barrier upon barrier, obstacles in every form and shape will present themselves to the student; for the Keys of the Golden Gate leading to the Infinite Truth, lie buried deep, and the gate itself is enclosed in a mist which clears up only before the ardent rays of implicit Faith. Faith alone, one grain of which as large as a mustard-seed, according to the words of Christ, can lift a mountain, is able to find out how simple becomes the Cabala to the initiate, once that he has succeeded in conquering the first abstruse difficulties. The dogma of it is logical, easy and absolute. The necessary union of ideas and signs; the trinity of words, letters, numbers, and theorems; the religion of it can be compressed into a few words: "It is the Infinite condensed in the hand of an infant," says Éliphas Lévi. Ten ciphers, 22 alphabetical letters, one triangle, a square and a circle. Such are the elements of the Cabala, from whose mysterious bosom sprang all the religions of the past and present; which endowed all the Free Masonic associations with their symbols and secrets, which alone can reconcile human reason with God and Faith, Power with Freedom, Science with Mystery, and which has alone the keys of the present, past and future.

The first difficulty for the aspirant lies in the utter impossibility of his comprehending, as I said before, the meaning of the best books written by Hermetic Philosophers. The latter who mainly lived in the mediaeval ages, prompted on the one hand by their duty towards their brethren, and by their desire to impart to them and their successors only, the glorious truths, and on the other very naturally desirous to avoid the clutches of the blood-thirsty Christian Inquisition, enveloped themselves more than ever in mystery. They invented new signs and hieroglyphs, renovated the ancient symbolical language of the high-priests of antiquity, who had used it as a sacred barrier between their holy rites and the ignorance of the profane, and created a veritable Cabalistic slang. This latter, which continually blinded the false neophyte, attracted towards the science only by his greediness for wealth and power which he would have surely misused were he to succeed, is a living, eloquent, clear language; but it is and can become such, only to the true disciple of Hermes.

But were it even otherwise, and could books on Occultism, written in a plain and precise language, be obtained, in order to get initiated in the Cabala, it would not be sufficient to understand and meditate on certain authors. Galatinus and Pico della Mirandola, Paracelsus and Robertus de Fluctibus do not furnish one with the key to the practical mysteries. They simply state what can be done and why it is done; but they do not tell one *how* to do it. More than one philosopher who has by heart the whole of the Hermetic literature, and who has devoted to the study of it upwards of thirty or forty years of his life, fails when he believes he is about reaching the final result. One must understand the Hebrew authors, such as *Sepher Yetzîrah*, for instance; learn by heart the great book of the *Zohar* in its original tongue; master the *Kabbalah Denudata*, from the Collection of 1684 (Paris);* follow up the Cabalistic Pneumatics at first, and then throw oneself headlong into the turbid waters of that mysterious unintelligible ocean, called the *Talmud*,† this compilation of "absurd monstrosities" according to some blind profanes, the final key to all the Hermetists in its dogmatic and allegorical signs.

Were I to name two of the books, which contain the most of the occult information which was derived and utilized by the greatest Cabalists of the mediaeval ages—Paracelsus was one of them—I might astonish many of my correspondents "craving for knowledge," and they might let it pass unnoticed. Adepts more learned than I will nevertheless endorse the truths of my assertion. For prudence sake I prefer quoting from a book, written by one of our greatest modern Occultists.

"Among the sacred books of the Christians," says Éliphas Lévi, "there exist two works, which, strange to say, the Infallible Church does not even pretend to understand and never tried to explain: the *Prophecy of Ezekiel* and the *Apocalypse*; two Cabalistic treatises, reserved, without doubt, for the commentaries of the Magi Kings; books closed with the seven seals to the faithful Christian; but perfectly clear to the Infidel initiated in the Occult Sciences."

Thus, the works on Occultism were not, I repeat, written for the masses, but for those of the Brethren who make the solution of the mysteries of the Cabala the principal object of their lives, and who are supposed to have conquered the first abstruse difficulties of the Alpha of Hermetic Philosophy.

---

*[This is the work of Baron Christian Knorr von Rosenroth (1636-89), the first volume of which was published at Sulzbach, 1677-78, and the second at Frankfurt, 1684. It contains several treatises of the *Zohar* translated into Latin and published together with the Hebrew text.—*Compiler.*]

†Immanuel Deutsch found it otherwise, and in his celebrated *Quarterly Review Essay* eulogizes the *Talmud* as the repository of vast stores of information for the philosophical student, placing it in certain respects above even the Old Testament itself.—ED., *Spiritual Scientist.*

To fervent and persevering candidates for the above science, I have to offer but one word of advice, "Try and become." One single journey to the Orient, made in the proper spirit, and the possible emergencies arising from the meeting of what may seem no more than the chance acquaintances and adventures of any traveller, may quite as likely as not throw wide open to the zealous student, the heretofore closed doors of the final mysteries. I will go farther and say that such a journey, performed with the omnipresent idea of the one object, and with the help of a fervent will, is sure to produce more rapid, better, and far more practical results, than the most diligent study of Occultism in books—even though one were to devote to it dozens of years. In the name of Truth,

Yours,
H. P. BLAVATSKY.

[Herbert D. Monachesi, one of the original Founders of the T.S., had written an article entitled "Proselyters from India" which was published in *The Sunday Mercury* of New York, October 3rd, 1875, acc. to H.P.B.'s pen and ink notation. In it he praised the religions of India and China. The article was unsigned, but H.P.B. identified the author by inserting his name at the end of the cutting pasted in her *Scrapbook*, Vol. I, p. 63. She also wrote the following remarks in pen and ink between the two columns of the article:]

Our original programme is here clearly defined by Herbert Monachesi, F.T.S., one of the Founders. The Christian and Scientists must be made to respect their Indian betters. The Wisdom of India, her philosophy and achievement *must* be made known in Europe & America & the English be made to respect the natives of India & Tibet more than they do.

H. P. B.

THE SCIENCE OF MAGIC

PROOFS OF ITS EXISTENCE—MEDIUMS IN
ANCIENT TIMES, ETC., ETC.

By Mme. H. P. Blavatsky.*

[*Spiritual Scientist*, Boston, Vol. III, October 14, 1875, pp. 64-65]

Happening to be on a visit to Ithaca, where spiritual papers in general, and the *Banner of Light* in particular, are very little read, but where, luckily, the *Scientist* has found hospitality in several houses, I learned through your paper of the intensely interesting, and very erudite attack in an editorial of the *Banner*, on "Magic"; or rather on those who had the *absurdity* to believe in Magic. As hints concerning myself—at least in the fragment I see—are very decently veiled, and, as it appears, Col. Olcott alone, just now, is offered by way of a pious Holocaust on the altar erected to the angel-world by some Spiritualists, who seem to be terribly in earnest, I will—leaving the said gentleman to take care of himself, provided he thinks it worth his trouble—proceed to say a few words only, in reference to the alleged *non-existence* of Magic.

Were I to give anything on my own authority, and base my defence of Magic only on what I have seen *myself*, and *know* to be true in relation to that science, as a resident of many years' standing in India and Africa, I might, perhaps, risk to be called by Mr. Colby—with that unprejudiced, spiritualized politeness, which so distinguishes the venerable editor of the *Banner of Light*—"an irresponsible woman"; and that would not be for the first time either. Therefore, to his astonishing assertion that no *magic* whatever either exists or has existed in this world, I will try to find as good authorities as himself, and maybe, better ones,

---

*[This article was written by H.P.B. as a reply to Mr. Colby who denied in the *Banner of Light* the existence of Magic. After the cutting had been pasted in her *Scrapbook*, Vol. I, pp. 70-71, H.P.B. made some pen and ink remarks and additions, which are shown herewith in footnotes appended as indicated by H.P.B. herself.—*Compiler*.]

and thus politely proceed to contradict him on that particular point.

Heterodox Spiritualists, like myself, must be cautious in our days and proceed with prudence, if they do not wish to be persecuted with all the untiring vengeance of that mighty army of "Indian Controls" and "Miscellaneous Guides" of our bright Summer Land.

When the writer of the editorial says, that "he does not think it at all improbable that there are humbugging spirits who try to fool certain aspirants to Occult knowledge, with the notion that there is such a thing as magic"(?) then, on the other hand, I can answer him that I, for one, not only think it probable, but I am perfectly sure, and can take my oath to the certainty, that more than once, spirits, who were either elementary or very unprogressed ones, calling themselves Theodore Parker, have been most decidedly *fooling* and disrespectfully *humbugging* our most esteemed Editor of the *Banner of Light* into the notion that the Apennines were in Spain, for instance.

Furthermore, supported in my assertions by thousands of intelligent Spiritualists, generally known for their integrity and truthfulness, I could furnish numberless proofs and instances where the Elementary Diakka, *Esprits malins et farfadets,* and other such-like unreliable and ignorant denizens of the spirit-world, arraying themselves in pompous, world-known and famous names, suddenly gave the bewildered witnesses such deplorable, unheard-of, slip-slop trash, and betimes something worse, that more than one person who, previous to that, was an earnest believer in the spiritual philosophy, has either silently taken to his heels; or, if he happened to have been formerly a Roman Catholic, has devoutly tried to recall to memory with which hand he used to cross himself, and then cleared out with the most fervent exclamation of *Vade retro, Satanas!* Such is the opinion of every educated Spiritualist.

If that indomitable Attila, the persecutor of modern Spiritualism, and mediums, Dr. G. Beard, had offered such a remark against Magic, I would not wonder, as a too profound devotion to blue pill and black draught is generally considered the best antidote against mystic and spiritual speculations; but for a firm Spiritualist, a believer in invisible, mysterious worlds, swarming with beings, the true nature of which is still an unriddled mystery to everyone—to step in and then sarcastically reject that which has been proved to exist and believed in for countless ages by millions of persons, wiser than himself, is too audacious! And that skeptic is the editor of a leading Spiritual paper! A man, whose first duty should be, to help his readers to seek—untiringly and perseveringly—for the TRUTH in whatever form it might present itself; but who takes the risk of dragging thousands of people into error, by pinning them to his personal rose-water faith and credulity. Every serious, earnest-minded Spiritualist must agree with me, in saying, that if modern Spiritualism remains, for a few years only, in its present condition of chaotic anarchy, or still worse, if it is allowed to run its mad course, shooting forth on all sides, idle hypotheses based on superstitious, groundless ideas, then will the Dr. Beards, Dr. Marvins, and others, known as scientific (?) skeptics, triumph indeed.

Really, it seems to be a waste of time to answer such ridiculous, ignorant assertions as the one which forced me to take up my pen. Any well-read Spiritualist, who finds the statement "that there ever was such a science as magic, has never been proved, nor ever will be," will need no answer from myself, nor anyone else, to cause him to shrug his shoulders and smile, as he probably has smiled, at the wonderful attempt of Mr. Colby's spirits to reorganize geography by placing the Apennines in Spain.

Why, man alive, did you never open a book in your life, besides your own records of Tom, Dick and Harry descending from upper spheres to remind their Uncle Sam that he had torn his gaiters or broken his pipe in the Far West?

Did you suppose that Magic is confined to witches riding astride broomsticks and then turning themselves into black cats? Even the latter superstitious trash, though it was never called Magic, but Sorcery, does not appear so great an absurdity for one to accept, who firmly believes in the transfiguration of Mrs. Compton* into Katie Brinks. The laws of nature are unchangeable. The conditions under which a medium can be transformed, entirely absorbed in the process by the spirit, into the semblance of another person, will hold good whenever that spirit or rather *force* should have a fancy to take the form of a cat.

The exercise of *magical* power is the exercise of *natural* powers, but SUPERIOR to the ordinary functions of Nature. A miracle is not a violation of the laws of Nature, except for ignorant people. Magic is but a *science,* a profound knowledge of the Occult forces in Nature, and of the laws governing the visible or the invisible world. Spiritualism in the hands of an adept becomes Magic, for he is learned in the art of blending together the laws of the Universe, without breaking any of them and thereby violating Nature. In the hands of an experienced medium, Spiritualism becomes UNCONSCIOUS SORCERY; for, by allowing himself to become the helpless tool of a variety of spirits, of whom he knows nothing save what the latter permit him to know, he opens, unknown to himself, a door of communication between the two worlds, through which emerge the blind forces of Nature lurking in the astral light, as well as good and bad spirits.

A powerful mesmerizer, profoundly learned in his science, such as Baron Du Potet, Regazzoni, Pietro d'Amicis of Bologna, are *magicians,* for they have become the adepts, the initiated ones, into the great mystery of our Mother Nature. Such men as the above-mentioned—and such were Mesmer and Cagliostro—*control* the spirits instead of allowing their subjects or themselves to be controlled by them; and Spiritualism is safe in their hands. In the absence of experienced Adepts though, it is always safer for a naturally clairvoyant medium to trust to good luck and chance, and try to judge of the tree by its fruits. Bad spirits will seldom

---

*[In her *Scrapbook,* Vol. I, p. 32, H.P.B. added the following remarks to a cutting describing *séances* with Mrs. Compton:

This Mrs. Compton is a real *wonderful* medium. She is a true electric battery worked by the Elementals.
—*Compiler.*]

communicate through a pure, naturally good and virtuous person; and it is still more seldom that pure spirits will choose impure channels. Like attracts like.

But to return to Magic. Such men as Albertus Magnus, Raymond Lully, Cornelius Agrippa, Paracelsus, Robert Fludd, Eugenius Philalethes, Khunrath, Roger Bacon and others of similar character, in our skeptical century, are generally taken for visionaries; but so, too, are Modern Spiritualists and mediums—nay worse, for charlatans and poltroons; but never were the Hermetic Philosophers taken by anyone for fools and idiots, as, unfortunately for ourselves and the Cause, every unbeliever takes ALL of us believers in Spiritualism to be. Those Hermeticists and philosophers may be disbelieved and doubted now, as everything else is doubted, but very few doubted their knowledge and power during their lifetime, for they always could prove what they claimed, having command over those forces which *now command* helpless mediums. They had their science and demonstrated philosophy to help them to throw down ridiculous negations, while we sentimental Spiritualists, rocking ourselves to sleep with our "Sweet By-and-By," are unable to recognize a spurious phenomenon from a genuine one, and are daily deceived by vile charlatans. Even though doubted then, as Spiritualism is in our day, still these philosophers were held in awe and reverence, even by those who did not implicitly believe in their Occult potency, for they were giants of intellect. Profound knowledge, as well as cultured intellectual powers, will always be respected and revered; but our mediums and their adherents are laughed and scorned at, and we are all made to suffer, because the phenomena are left to the whims and pranks of self-willed and other mischievous spirits, and we are utterly powerless in controlling them.

To doubt Magic is to reject History itself as well as the testimony of ocular witnesses thereof, during a period embracing over 4,000 years. Beginning with Homer, Moses, Hermes, Herodotus, Cicero, Plutarch, Pythagoras, Apollonius of Tyana, Simon the Magician, Plato, Pausanias, Iamblichus, and following this endless string of great men, historians and philosophers, who all of them either believed in magic or were magicians themselves, and ending with our modern authors, such as W. Howitt, Ennemoser, H. R. Gougenot des Mousseaux, Marquis de Mirville and the late Éliphas Lévi, who was a magician himself—among all these great names and authors, we find but the solitary Mr. Colby, Editor of the *Banner of Light,* who ignores that there ever was such a science as *Magic.* He innocently believes the whole of the sacred army of Bible prophets, commencing with Father Abraham, including Christ, to be merely mediums; in the eyes of Mr. Colby they were all of them acting under control! Fancy Christ, Moses, or an Apollonius of Tyana, controlled by an Indian guide!! The venerable editor ignores, perhaps, that spiritual mediums were better known in those days to the ancients, than they are now to us, and he seems to be equally unaware of the fact that the inspired Sibyls, Pythonesses, and other mediums, were entirely guided by their High Priest and those who were initiated into the Esoteric Theurgy and mysteries of the Temples. Theurgy was *magic;* as in modern times, the Sibyls and Pythonesses WERE MEDIUMS; but their High Priests were magicians. All the secrets of their theology, which included *magic,* or the art of invoking ministering spirits, were in their hands. They possessed the science of DISCERNING SPIRITS; a science which Mr. Colby does not possess at all—to his great regret no doubt. By this power they controlled the spirits at will, allowing but the good ones to absorb their mediums. Such is the explanation of *magic*—the real, existing, *White* or sacred magic, which ought to be in the hands of science now, and would be, if science had profited by the lessons which Spiritualism has inductively taught for these last twenty-seven years.

That is the reason why no trash was allowed to be given by unprogressed spirits in the days of old. The oracles of the sibyls and inspired priestesses could never have affirmed Athens to be a town in India, or jumped Mount Ararat from its native place down to Egypt.

If the skeptical writer of the editorial had, moreover, devoted less time to little prattling Indian spirits and more to profitable lectures, he might have learned perhaps at the same time, that the ancients had their illegal mediums—I mean those who belonged to no special Temple, and thus the spirits controlling them, unchecked by the expert hand of the magician, were left to themselves, and had all the opportunity possible to perform their capers on their helpless tools; that such mediums were generally considered *obsessed* and *possessed,* which they were in fact; in other words, and according to the Bible phraseology, "they had the seven devils in them." Furthermore, these mediums were ordered to be put to death, for the intolerant Moses, the magician, who was learned in the wisdom of Egypt, had said, "Thou shalt not suffer a witch to live."* Alone, the Egyptians and Greeks, even more humane and just than Moses, took such into their Temples, and when found unfit for sacred duties of prophecy [they] *were cured,* in the same way as Jesus Christ cured Mary of Magdala and many others, by "casting out the seven devils." Either Mr. Colby and Co. must completely deny the miracles of Christ,† the Apostles, Prophets, Thaumaturgists, and Magicians, and so deny point-blank every bit of the sacred and profane histories, or he must confess that there is a POWER in this world which can command spirits, at least the bad and unprogressed ones, the elementary and Diakka. The *pure ones,* the disembodied, will never descend to our sphere, unless attracted by a current of powerful sympathy and love, or on some useful mission.

Far from me the thought of casting odium and ridicule on our‡ medium. I am†† myself a Spiritualist, if, as says Colonel Olcott, a firm belief in our souls‡‡ immortality and *the knowledge* of a constant possibility for us to communicate with the spirits of our departed and loved ones, either through honest, pure mediums, or by means of the Secret Science, constitutes a Spiritualist. But§ I am not of

---
* [*Exodus,* xxii, 18.]
† if he ever lived—which is more than doubtful.
‡ [Corrected to "all."] †† [Corr. to "am not."]
‡‡ [Corrected to "spirits."] § [Corrected to "And."]

THE SCIENCE OF MAGIC 141

those fanatical Spiritualists, to be found in every country, who blindly accept the claims of every spirit,* for I have seen too much of various phenomena, undreamed of in America. I *know* that MAGIC does exist, and 10,000 editors of Spiritual papers cannot change my belief in what I know. There is a white and a black magic; and no one who has ever travelled in the East, can doubt it, if he has taken the trouble to investigate. My faith being firm I am, therefore, ever ready to support and protect any honest medium—aye, and even occasionally one who appears *dishonest;* for I know but too well, what helpless tools and victims such mediums are in the hands of unprogressed, invisible beings. I am furthermore aware of the malice and wickedness of the elementary, and how far they can inspire not only a sensitive medium, *but any other person* as well. Though I may be an "irresponsible woman" in the eyes of those who are but "too responsible" for the harm they do to EARNEST Spiritualists by their unfairness, one-sidedness, and spiritual sentimentalism, I feel safe to say, that generally I am quick enough to detect whenever a medium is cheating *under control,* or cheating consciously.

Thus magic exists and has existed ever since prehistoric ages. Begun in history with the Samathracian mysteries, it followed its course uninterruptedly, and ended for a time with the expiring theurgic rites and ceremonies of christianized Greece; then reappeared for a time again with the Neo-Platonic, Alexandrian school, and passing, by initiation, to sundry solitary students and philosophers, safely crossed the mediaeval ages, and notwithstanding the furious persecutions of the Church, resumed its fame in the hands of such adepts as Paracelsus and several others, and finally died out in Europe with the Count de St.-Germain and Cagliostro, to seek refuge from the frozen-hearted skepticism in its native country of the East.

In India, magic has never died out, and blossoms there as well as ever. Practised, as in ancient Egypt, only within

---

* [Enclosed in quotes: "spirit."]

the secret enclosure of the Temples, it was, and still is, called the "sacred science." For it is a science, based on natural occult forces of Nature; and not merely a blind belief in the poll-parrot talking of crafty, elementary ones, ready to forcibly prevent *real, disembodied* spirits from communicating with their loved ones whenever they can do so.

Some time since, a Mr. Mendenhall devoted several columns in the *Religio-Philosophical Journal,* to questioning, cross-examining, and criticizing the mysterious Brotherhood of Luxor. He made a fruitless attempt at forcing the said Brotherhood to answer him, and thus unveil the sphinx. I can satisfy Mr. Mendenhall. The BROTHERHOOD OF LUXOR is one of the sections of the Grand Lodge of which *I am a member.* If this gentleman entertains any doubt as to my statement—which I have no doubt he will—he can, if he chooses, write to *Lahore* for information. If perchance, the *Seven of the Committee* were so rude as not to answer him, and would refuse to give him the desired information, I can then offer him a little business transaction. Mr. Mendenhall, as far as I remember, has two wives in the spirit world. Both of these ladies materialize at M. Mott's, and often hold very long conversations with their husband, as the latter told us of several times, and over his own signature; adding, moreover, that he had no doubt whatever of the identity of the said spirits. If so, let one of the departed ladies tell Mr. Mendenhall the name of that section of the Grand Lodge I belong to. For *real, genuine, disembodied* spirits, if both are what they claim to be, the matter is more than easy; they have but to enquire of other spirits, look into my thoughts, and so on; for a disembodied entity, an immortal spirit, it is the easiest thing in the world to do. Then, if the gentleman I challenge, though I am deprived of the pleasure of his acquaintance, tells me the true name of the section—which name three gentlemen in New York, who are accepted neophytes of our Lodge, know well—I pledge myself to give to Mr. Mendenhall the true statement concerning the Brotherhood, which is not composed of spirits, as he may think, but of *living* mortals, and I will, moreover, if he desires to, put him in direct communication with the Lodge as I have done for others. *Methinks, Mr. Mendenhall will answer that no such name can be given correctly by the spirits, for no such Lodge or either Section exists at all, and thus close the discussion.

[In H.P.B.'s *Scrapbook*, Vol. I, p. 67, there is a cutting from the *Spiritual Scientist* of October 21, 1875, which deals with remarks made by a certain Dr. G. Bloede, who went to the trouble of warning people against the newly-formed Theosophical Society and the work of Mrs. Emma Hardinge-Britten entitled *Art Magic*, as enemies of Spiritualism. H.P.B. appended in pen and ink the following side-remark:]

And now I am accused by Dr. Bloede, an ardent Spiritualist, of being the *paid tool of the Jesuits* to pull down *Spiritualism!!!*

A LETTER FROM MADAME BLAVATSKY

[*Spiritual Scientist*, Boston, Vol. III, November 4, 1875, p. 104]

To the Editor of the *Spiritual Scientist*:

Sir,—In my country, and in every other recognized as civilized, except America, a man who defames and slanders a woman innocent of crime, however humble she may be, is contemned as a coward. What should European gentlemen think of American manhood, when they read in the Spiritualist journals of the United States, such false, cowardly and unmannerly assaults upon a foreign-born lady, a life-long Spiriutalist, and NOT A PROFESSIONAL MEDIUM,

---

* [H.P.B. added on the margin:

And so he did and—abused me in a vile way in the papers for my offer. The *Spirits* proved to be ignoramuses!!

It is most likely, however, that this refers to the *last* sentence of the article.—*Compiler.*]

as those against myself, which have recently appeared? My great offences are, that I have told the truth, but not all the truth, about certain dishonourable persons, who taint the name of American Spiritualism, by association with it; and given a very imperfect glimpse of the wonders of Magic, which, in common with a hundred other travellers, I have been made acquainted with in the course of extended travels through the East. These malicious assaults upon my reputation, harm only those who have attacked me; for my antecedents are too well known to require a formal defence at my hands. But I blush as a Spiritualist for the impression which they must inevitably produce, as to the ribaldry and licence permissible in American journalism towards a woman. If it can bear the opprobrium I have nothing to say.

Meanwhile, as answer to numerous questions and criticisms, I send you the following translation of a chapter from one of Lévi's books.

H. P. BLAVATSKY.

THE MAGICAL EVOCATION OF APOLLONIUS OF TYANA

A CHAPTER FROM ÉLIPHAS LÉVI.*

Translated by Mme. H. P. Blavatsky.

[*Spiritual Scientist*, Boston, Vol. III, November 4, 1875, pp. 104-5]

We have already said that in the Astral Light the images of persons and things are preserved. It is also in this light that can be evoked the forms of those who are no longer in our world, and it is by its means that are effected the mysteries of necromancy which are as *real* as they are denied.

The Cabalists, who have spoken of the spirit-world, have simply related what they have seen in their evocations.

Éliphas Lévi Zahed (these Hebrew names translated are: Alphonse-Louis Constant), who writes this book, has evoked and he has seen.

---

*[Chapter XIII in his *Dogme et Rituel de la Haute Magie*, pp. 276-92 in the 6th edition, Paris, 1920.—*Compiler*.]

EVOCATION OF APOLLONIUS OF TYANA

Let us first tell what the masters have written of their visions or intuitions in what they call the *light of glory*.

We read in the Hebrew book, *The Revolution of the Souls*,* that there are souls of three kinds: the daughters of Adam, the daughters of the angels, and the daughters of sin. There are also, according to the same book, three kinds of spirits: captive spirits, wandering spirits, and free spirits. Souls are sent in couples. There are, however, souls of men which are born single, and whose mates are held captive by Lilith and Naemah, the queens of *Strygis*;† these are the souls which have to make future expiations for their rashness, in assuming a vow of celibacy. For example, when a man renounces from childhood the love of woman, he makes the spouse who was destined for him the slave of the demons of lust. Souls grow and multiply in heaven as well as bodies upon earth. The immaculate souls are the offspring of the union of the angels.

Nothing can enter into Heaven, except that which is of Heaven. After death, then, the divine spirit which animated the man, returns alone to Heaven, and leaves upon earth and in the atmosphere two corpses. One, terrestrial and elementary; the other, aerial and sidereal; the one lifeless already, the other still animated by the universal movement of the soul of the world (Astral light), but destined to die gradually, absorbed by the astral powers which produced it. The earthly corpse is visible: the other is invisible to the eyes of the terrestrial and living body, and cannot be perceived except by the influences of the astral or *translucid* light, which communicates its impressions to the nervous system, and thus affects the organ of sight, so as to make it see the forms which are preserved, and the words which are written in the book of vital life.

When a man has lived well, the astral corpse or spirit evaporates like a pure incense, as it mounts towards the higher regions; but if a man has lived in crime, his astral body, which holds him prisoner, seeks again the objects of passions, and desires to resume its course of life. It torments the dreams of young girls, bathes in the steam of spilt blood, and hovers about the places where the pleasures of its life flitted by; it watches continually over the treasures which it possessed and concealed; it exhausts itself in unhappy efforts to make for itself material organs and live evermore. But the stars attract and absorb it; it feels its intelligence weakening, its memory is gradually lost, all its being dissolves . . . its old vices appear to it as incarnations, and

---

*[Reference here is to Isaac ben Solomon Loria's *Commentarius in librum Zeniutha. Tractatus de revolutionibus animarum*, which may be found in the second volume of Knorr von Rosenroth's *Kabbala Denudata*, etc.; the first volume of this work appeared at Sulzbach in 1677-78, and the second at Frankfurt a. M. in 1684.—*Compiler.*]

†A word applied by the Valaginians and Orientals to a certain kind of unprogressed elementary spirits.—*Ed.* [H.P.B.]

pursue it under monstrous shapes; they attack and devour. . . . The unhappy wretch thus loses successively all the members which served its sinful appetites; then it dies a second time and for ever, because it then loses its personality and its memory. Souls, which are destined to live, but which are not yet entirely purified, remain for a longer or shorter time captives in the Astral body, where they are refined by the odic light which seeks to assimilate them to itself and dissolve. It is to rid themselves of this body that suffering souls sometimes enter the bodies of living persons, and remain there for a while in a state which the Cabalists call *Embryonic.*

These are the aerial phantoms evoked by necromancy. These are the larvae, substances dead or dying, with which one places himself *en rapport;* ordinarily they cannot speak except by the ringing in our ears, produced by the nervous quivering of which I have spoken, and usually reasoning only as they reflect upon our thoughts or dreams.

But to see these strange forms one must put himself in an exceptional condition, partaking at once of sleep and death; that is to say, one must magnetize himself and reach a kind of lucid and wakeful somnambulism. Necromancy, then, obtains real results, and the evocations of magic are capable of producing veritable apparitions. We have said that in the great magical agent, which is the Astral light, are preserved all the impressions of things, all the images formed, either by their rays or by their reflections; it is in this light that our dreams appear to us, it is this light which intoxicates the insane and sweeps away their enfeebled judgment into the pursuit of the most fantastic phantoms. To see without illusions in this light it is necessary to push aside the reflections by a powerful effort of the will, and draw to oneself only the rays. To dream waking is to see in the Astral light; and the orgies of the witches' Sabbath, described by so many sorcerers upon their criminal trials, do not present themselves to them in any other manner. Often the preparations and the substances employed to arrive at this result were horrible, as we have seen in the chapters devoted to the ritual; but the results were never doubtful. Things of the most abominable, fantastic, and impossible description were seen, heard, and touched. . . .

In the Spring of the year 1854, I went to London to escape from certain family troubles and give myself up, without interruption, to science. I had introductory letters to eminent persons interested in supernatural manifestations. I saw several, and found in them, combined with much politeness, a great deal of indifference or frivolity. Immediately they demanded of me miracles, as they would of a charlatan. I was a little discouraged, for to tell the truth, far from being disposed to initiate others into the mysteries of ceremonial magic, I had always dreaded for myself the illusions and fatigues thereof; besides, these ceremonies demand materials at once expensive and hard to collect together. I, therefore, buried myself in the study of the High Cabala, and thought no more of the English adepts until one day, upon en-

Evocation of Apollonius of Tyana   147

tering my lodging, I found a note with my address. This note contained the half of a card, cut in two, and upon which I recognized, at once, the character of Solomon's Seal and a very small bit of paper upon which was written in pencil: "Tomorrow, at three o'clock, before Westminster Abbey, the other half of this card will be presented you." I went to this singular rendezvous. A carriage was standing at the place. I held in my hand, with seeming indifference, my half of the card; a servant approached, and opening the carriage door, made me a sign. In the carriage was a lady in black whose bonnet was covered with a very thick veil; she beckoned to me to take a seat beside her, at the same time showing me the other half of the card which I had received. The footman closed the door, the carriage rolled away; and the lady having raised her veil I perceived a person whose eyes were sparkling and extremely piercing in expression. "Sir," said she to me, with a very strong English accent, "I know that the law of secrecy is very rigorous among adepts; a friend of Sir Bulwer Lytton, who has seen you, knows that experiments have been requested of you, and that you have refused to satisfy their curiosity. Perhaps you have not the necessary things: I wish to show you a complete magic cabinet; but I demand of you in advance the most inviolable secrecy. If you do not give this promise upon your honor I shall order the coachman to reconduct you to your house." I promised what was required, and I show my fidelity in mentioning neither the name, the quality, nor the residence of this lady, whom I soon recognized as an initiate, not precisely of the first degree, but of a very high one. We had several long conversations, in the course of which she constantly insisted upon the necessity of practical experiments to complete initiation. She showed me a collection of magical robes and instruments, even lent me some curious books that I needed; in short, she decided *to try* at her house the experiment of a complete evocation, for which I prepared myself during twenty-one days, by scrupulously observing the practices indicated in the XIIIth chapter of the "Ritual."

All was ready by the 24th of July; our purpose was to evoke the phantom of the Divine Apollonius and interrogate him as to two secrets, of which one concerned myself, and the other interested this lady. She had at first intended to assist at the evocation, with an intimate friend; but at the last moment, this lady's courage failed, and, as three persons, or one, are strictly required for magical rites, I was left alone. The cabinet prepared for the evocation was arranged in the small tower, four concave mirrors were properly disposed, and there was a sort of altar, whose white marble top was surrounded by a chain of magnetized iron. Upon the white marble was chiselled and gilded the sign of the pentagram; and the same sign was traced in different colors upon a fresh white lambskin, which was spread under the altar. In the centre of the marble slab, there was a little brazier of copper, containing charcoal of elm and laurel wood;

another brazier was placed before me, on a tripod. I was clothed in a white robe, something like those used by our Catholic priests, but longer and more full, and I wore upon my head a crown of verbena leaves interwoven in a golden chain. In one hand I held a naked sword, and in another the Ritual. I lighted the two fires, with the substances requisite and prepared, and I began at first in a low voice, then louder by degrees, the invocations of the Ritual. The smoke spread, the flame flickered and made to dance all the objects it lighted, then went out. The smoke rose white and slow from the marble altar. It seemed as if I had detected a slight shock of earthquake, my ears rang and my heart beat rapidly. I added some twigs and perfumes to the braziers, and when the flame rose, I saw distinctly, before the altar, a human figure, larger than life size, which decomposed and melted away. I recommenced the evocations, and placed myself in a circle which I had traced in advance of the ceremony between the altar and the tripod; I saw then the disc of the mirror facing me, and which was behind the altar becoming illuminated by degrees, and a whitish form there developed itself, enlarging and seeming to approach, little by little. I called three times upon Apollonius, at the same time closing my eyes; and, when I re-opened them a man was before me, completely enveloped in a shroud, which seemed to me rather gray than white; his face was thin, sad and beardless, which did not seem to convey to me the idea which I had previously formed of Apollonius. I experienced a sensation of extraordinary cold, and when I opened my mouth to question the phantom, it was impossible for me to articulate a sound. I then put my hand upon the sign of the Pentagram, and I directed towards him the point of the sword, commanding him mentally by that sign, not to frighten me but to obey. Then the form became confused, and suddenly disappeared. I commanded it to reappear; upon which I felt it pass near me, like a breath, and something having touched the hand which touched the sword, I felt my arm instantly stiffened, as far as the shoulder. I thought I understood that this sword offended the spirit, and I planted it by the point in the circle near me. The human figure then re-appeared, but I felt such a weakness in my limbs, and such exhaustion seize hold of me, that I took a couple of steps to seat myself. As soon as I was in my chair, I fell into a profound slumber, accompanied by dreams, of which, upon returning to myself, I had only a vague and confused remembrance. For several days my arm was stiff and painful. The apparition had not spoken to me, but it seemed that the questions which I wished to ask it, answered themselves in my mind. To that of the lady, an interior voice replied in me, "Dead!" (it concerned a man of whom she wished to have some intelligence). As to myself I wished to know, if reconciliation and pardon would be possible between two persons, of whom I thought, and the same interior echo pitilessly answered, "Dead!"

I relate these facts exactly as they happened, not forcing them upon the faith of any one. The effect of this first experiment upon me, was something inexplicable. I was no longer the same man. . . .

I twice repeated in the course of a few days, the same experiment. The result of these two other evocations, was to reveal to me two cabalistic secrets, which might, if they were known by everyone, change in a short time the foundations and laws of the whole society. . . . I will not explain by what physiological laws, I saw and touched; I simply assert, that I did see and touch, that I saw clearly and distinctly, without dreaming, and that is enough to prove the efficacy of magic ceremonies. . . .

I will not close this chapter without noticing the curious belief of certain Cabalists, who distinguish apparent from real death, and think that they seldom occur simultaneously. According to their story the greatest part of persons buried are alive, and many others, whom we think living, are, in fact, dead. Incurable insanity, for instance, would be, according to them, an incomplete but *real* death, which leaves the earthly body under the exclusive instinctive control of the astral or sidereal body. When the human soul experiences a shock too violent for it to bear, it would separate itself from the body and leave in its place the animal soul, or in other words, the astral body, which makes of human wreck something in one sense less living than even an animal. Dead persons of this kind can be easily recognized by the complete extinction of the affectional and moral senses; they are not bad, they are not good; they are dead. These beings, who are the poisonous mushrooms of the human species, absorb as much as they can the vitality of the living; that is why their approach paralyzes the soul, and sends a chill to the heart. These corpse-like beings prove all that has ever been said of the vampires, those dreadful creatures who rise at night and suck the blood from the healthy bodies of sleeping persons. Are there not some beings in whose presence one feels less intelligent, less good, often even less honest? Does not their approach quench all faith and enthusiasm, and do they not bind you to them by your weaknesses, and slave you by your evil inclinations, and make you gradually lose all moral sense in a constant torture?

These are the dead whom we take for the living persons; these are the vampires whom we mistake for friends!

EXPLANATORY REMARKS

So little is known in modern times of Ancient Magic, its meaning, history, capabilities, literature, adepts and results, that I cannot allow what precedes to go out, without a few words of explanation. The ceremonies and paraphernalia so minutely described by Lévi, are calculated and were intended to deceive the superficial reader. Forced by an irresistible impulse to write what he knew, but fearing to be dangerously explicit, in this instance, as everywhere throughout his works, he magnifies unimportant details and slurs over things of greater moment. True, Oriental Cabalists need no preparation, no costumes, apparatus, coronets or war-like weapons: these appertain to the Jewish Cabala, which bears the same relation to its simple Chaldaean prototype as the ceremonious observances of the Romish Church to the simple worship of Christ and his apostles. In the hands of the true adept of the East, a simple wand of bamboo with seven joints, supplemented by their ineffable wisdom and indomitable will-power, suffices to evoke spirits and produce the miracles authenticated by the testimony of a cloud of unprejudiced witnesses. At this *séance* of Lévi's, upon the reappearance of the phantom, the daring investigator saw and heard things, which in his account of the first trial, are wholly suppressed, and in that of the others merely hinted at. I know this from authorities which cannot be questioned.

Suppose that the *criticasters* of the *"Banner"* and the *"ir-Religio,"* who, every week, occupy themselves with shooting off their little pop-guns at the Elementary Spirits evoked in their literature by Colonel Olcott and myself, should try their hand at some of the simplest ceremonies given to neophytes, to sharpen their wisdom-teeth upon, before undertaking to amuse and instruct the world with their wit and wisdom. Shoot away, good friends, you amuse yourselves and hurt nobody else.

[A copy of the *Preamble and By-Laws of The Theosophical Society* is pasted in H.P.B.'s *Scrapbook*, Vol. I, pp. 77-79. On top of the first column, above the title, H.P.B. wrote in blue pencil:]

The Child is
    born!
        Hosannah!

AN UNSOLVED MYSTERY
[*Spiritual Scientist*, Vol. III, November 25, 1875, pp. 133-35]

The circumstances attending the sudden death of M. Delessert, inspector of the *Police de Sûreté,* seems to have made such an impression upon the Parisian authorities that they were recorded in unusual detail. Omitting all particulars except what are necessary to explain matters, we reproduce here the undoubtedly strange history.

In the fall of 1861 there came to Paris a man who called himself Vic de Lassa, and was so inscribed upon his passport. He came from Vienna, and said he was a Hungarian, who owned estates on the borders of the Banat, not far from Zenta. He was a small man, aged thirty-five, with pale and mysterious face, long blonde hair, a vague, wandering blue eye, and a mouth of singular firmness. He dressed carelessly and ineffectively, and spoke and talked without much *empressement.* His companion, presumably his wife, on the other hand, ten years younger than himself, was a strikingly beautiful woman, of that dark, rich, velvety, luscious, pure Hungarian type which is so nigh akin to the gipsy blood. At the theatres, on the Bois, at the cafés, on the boulevards, and everywhere that idle Paris disports itself, Madame Aimée de Lassa attracted great attention and made a sensation.

They lodged in luxurious apartments on the Rue Richelieu, frequented the best places, received good company, entertained handsomely, and acted in every way as if possessed of considerable wealth. Lassa had always a good balance *chez* Schneider, Reuter et Cie., the Austrian Bankers in Rue de Rivoli, and wore diamonds of conspicuous lustre.

How did it happen then, that the Prefect of Police saw fit to suspect Monsieur and Madame de Lassa, and detailed Paul Delessert, one of the most *rusé* inspectors of the force, to "pipe" him? The fact is, the insignificant man with the splendid wife was a very mysterious personage, and it is the habit of the police to imagine that mystery always hides either the conspirator, the adventurer, or the charlatan. The conclusion to which the Prefect had come in regard to M. de Lassa was that he was an adventurer and charlatan too. Certainly a successful one, then, for he was singularly unobtrusive and had in no way trumpeted the wonders which it was his mission to perform, yet in a few weeks after he had established himself in Paris the *salon* of M. de Lassa was the rage, and the number of persons who paid the fee of 100 francs for a single peep into his magic crystal, and a single message by his spiritual telegraph, was really astonishing. The secret of this was that M. de Lassa was a conjurer and diviner, whose pretensions were omniscient and whose predictions always came true.

Delessert did not find it very difficult to get an introduction and admission to de Lassa's *salon*. The receptions occurred every other day—two hours in the forenoon, three hours in the evening. It was evening when Inspector Delessert called in his assumed character of M. Flabry, *virtuoso* in jewels and a convert to Spiritualism. He found the handsome parlors brilliantly lighted, and a charming assemblage gathered of well-pleased guests, who did not at all seem to have come to learn their fortunes or fates, while contributing to the income of their host, but rather to be there out of complaisance to his virtues and gifts.

Mme. de Lassa performed upon the piano or conversed from group to group in a way that seemed to be delightful, while M. de Lassa walked about or sat in his insignificant, unconcerned way, saying a word now and then, but seeming to shun everything that was conspicuous. Servants handed about refreshments, ices, cordials, wines, etc., and Delessert could have fancied himself [to have] dropped in upon a quite modest evening entertainment, altogether *en règle,* but for one or two noticeable circumstances which his observant eyes quickly took in.

Except when their host or hostess was within hearing, the guests conversed together in low tones, rather mysteriously, and with not quite so much laughter as is usual on such occasions. At intervals a very tall and dignified footman would come to a guest, and, with a profound bow, present him a card on a silver salver. The guest would then go out, preceded by the solemn servant, but when he or she returned to the *salon*—some did not return at all—they invariably wore a dazed or puzzled look, were confused, astonished, frightened, or amused. All this was so unmistakably genuine, and de Lassa and his wife seemed so unconcerned amidst it all, not to say distinct from it all, that Delessert could not avoid being forcibly struck and considerably puzzled.

Two or three little incidents, which came under Delessert's own immediate observation, will suffice to make plain the character of the impressions made upon those present. A couple of gentlemen, both young, both of good social condition, and evidently very intimate friends, were conversing together and *tutoying* one another at a great rate, when the dignified footman summoned Alphonse. He laughed gaily. "Tarry a moment, *cher* Auguste," said he, "and thou shalt know all the particulars of this wonderful fortune!" "*Eh bien!*" responded Auguste, "may the oracle's mood be propitious!" A minute had scarcely elapsed when Alphonse returned to the *salon*. His face was white and bore an appearance of concentrated rage that was frightful to witness. He came straight to Auguste, his eyes flashing, and bending his face toward his friend, who changed colour and recoiled, he hissed out, "Monsieur Lefébure, *vous êtes un lâche!*" "Very well, Monsieur Meunier," responded Auguste, in the same low tone, "to-morrow morning at six o'clock!" "It is settled, false friend, execrable traitor! *À la mort!*" rejoined Alphonse, walking off. "*Cela va sans dire!*" muttered Auguste, going towards the hat-room.

A diplomatist of distinction, representative at Paris of a neighboring state, an elderly gentleman of superb *aplomb* and most commanding appearance, was summoned to the oracle by the bowing footman. After being absent about five minutes he returned, and immediately made his way through the press to M. de Lassa, who was standing not far from the fireplace, with his hands in his pockets, and a look of utmost indifference upon his face. Delessert standing near, watched the interview with eager interest. "I am exceedingly sorry," said General Von ——, "to have to absent myself so soon from your interesting *salon,* M. de Lassa, but the result of my *séance* convinces me that my dispatches have been tampered with." "I am sorry," responded M. de Lassa, with an air of languid but courteous interest, "I hope you may be able to discover which of your servants has been unfaithful." "I am going to do that now," said the General, adding, in significant tones, "I shall see that both he and his accomplices do not escape severe punishment." "That is the only course to pursue, Monsieur le Comte." The ambassador stared, bowed, and took his leave with a bewilderment on his face that was beyond the power of his tact to control.

In the course of the evening M. de Lassa went carelessly to the piano, and, after some indifferent vague preluding, played a remarkably effective piece of music, in which the turbulent life and buoyancy of bacchanalian strains melted gently, almost imperceptibly away, into a sobbing wail of regret and languor, and weariness and despair. It was beautifully rendered, and made a great impression upon the guests, one of whom, a lady, cried, "How lovely, how sad! Did you compose that yourself, M. de Lassa?" He looked towards her absently for an instant, then replied: "I? Oh, no! That is merely a reminiscence, madame." "Do you know who did compose it, M. de Lassa?" enquired a *virtuoso* present. "I believe it was originally written by Ptolemy Auletes, the father of Cleopatra," said M. de Lassa, in his indifferent, musing way, "but not in its present form. It has been twice re-written to my knowledge; still, the air is substantially the same." "From whom did you get it, M. de Lassa, if I may ask?" persisted the gentleman. "Certainly! certainly! The last time I heard it played was by Sebastian Bach; but that was Palestrina's — the present—version. I think I prefer that of Guido of Arezzo— it is ruder, but has more force. I got the air from Guido himself." "You—from—Guido!" cried the astonished gentleman, "Yes, monsieur," answered de Lassa, rising from the piano with his usual indifferent air. *"Mon Dieu!"* cried the *virtuoso,* putting his hand to his head after the manner of

An Unsolved Mystery 155

Mr. Twemlow, "*Mon Dieu!* that was in Anno Domini 1022!" "A little later than that—July 1031, if I remember rightly," courteously corrected M. de Lassa.

At this moment the tall footman bowed before M. Delessert, and presented the salver containing the card. Delessert took it and read: "*On vous accorde trente-cinq secondes, M. Flabry, tout au plus!*" Delessert followed the footman from the *salon* across the corridor. The footman opened the door of another room and bowed again, signifying that Delessert was to enter. "Ask no questions," he said briefly; "Sidi is mute." Delessert entered the room and the door closed behind him. It was a small room, with a strong smell of frankincense pervading it. The walls were covered completely with red hangings that concealed the windows, and the floor was felted with a thick carpet. Opposite the door, at the upper end of the room near the ceiling, was the face of a large clock; under it, each lighted by tall wax candles, were two small tables containing, the one an apparatus very like the common registering telegraph instrument, the other a crystal globe about twenty inches in diameter, set upon an exquisitely wrought tripod of gold and bronze intermingled. By the door stood Sidi, a man jet black in colour, wearing a white turban and burnous, and having a sort of wand of silver in one hand. With the other, he took Delessert by the right arm above the elbow, and led him quickly up the room. He pointed to the clock, and it struck an alarm; he pointed to the crystal. Delessert bent over, looked into it and saw—a facsimile of his own sleeping-room, everything photographed exactly. Sidi did not give him time to exclaim, but still holding him by the arm, took him to the other table. The telegraph-like instrument began to click-click. Sidi opened the drawer, drew out a slip of paper, crammed it into Delessert's hand, and pointed to the clock, which struck again. The thirty-five seconds were expired. Sidi, still retaining hold of Delessert's arm, pointed to the door and led him towards it. The door opened, Sidi pushed him out, the door closed, the tall footman stood there bowing, the interview with the oracle was over. Delessert glanced at the piece of paper in his hand. It was a printed scrap, capital letters, and read simply: "To M. Paul Delessert: The policeman is always welcome; the spy is always in danger!"

Delessert was dumbfounded a moment to find his disguise detected; but the words of the tall footman, "This way, if you please, M. Flabry," brought him to his senses. Setting his lips, he returned to the *salon*, and without delay sought M. de Lassa. "Do you know the contents of this?" asked he, showing the message. "I know everything, M. Delessert," answered de Lassa, in his careless way. "Then perhaps you are aware that I mean to expose a charlatan, and unmask a hypocrite, or perish in the attempt?" said Delessert. "*Cela m'est égal, monsieur,*" replied de Lassa. "You accept my challenge, then?" "Oh! it is a defiance, then?" replied de Lassa, letting his eye rest a moment upon Delessert, "*mais oui, je l'accepte!*" And thereupon Delessert departed.

Delessert now set to work, aided by all the forces the Prefect of Police could bring to bear, to detect and expose this consummate sorcerer, whom the ruder processes of our ancestors would easily have disposed of—by combustion. Persistent enquiry satisfied Delessert that the man was neither a Hungarian nor named de Lassa; that no matter how far back his power of "reminiscence" might extend, in his present and immediate form he had been born in this unregenerate world in the toy-making city of Nuremberg; that he was noted in boyhood for his great turn for ingenious manufactures, but was very wild, and a *mauvais sujet*. In his sixteenth year he had escaped to Geneva and apprenticed himself to a maker of watches and instruments. Here he had been seen by the celebrated Robert Houdin, the *prestidigitateur*. Houdin, recognizing the lad's talents, and being himself a maker of ingenious automata, had taken him off to Paris and employed him in his own workshops, as well as an assistant in the public performances of his amusing and curious *diablerie*. After staying with Houdin some years, Pflock Haslich (which was de Lassa's right name) had gone East in the suite of a Turkish Pasha, and after many years' roving, in lands where he could not be traced under a cloud of pseudonyms, had finally turned up in Venice, and come thence to Paris.

Delessert next turned his attention to Mme. de Lassa. It was more difficult to get a clue by means of which to know her past life; but it was necessary in order to understand enough about Haslich. At last, through an accident, it became probable that Mme. Aimée was identical with a certain Mme. Schlaff, who had been rather conspicuous among the *demi-monde* of Buda. Delessert posted off to that ancient city, and thence went into the wilds of Transylvania to Medgyes. On his return, as soon as he reached the telegraph and civilization, he telegraphed the Prefect from Karcag: "Don't lose sight of my man, nor let him leave Paris. I will run him in for you two days after I get back."

It happened that on the day of Delessert's return to Paris the Prefect was absent, being with the Emperor at Cherbourg. He came back on the fourth day, just twenty-four hours after the announcement of Delessert's death. That happened, as near as could be gathered, in this wise: the night after Delessert's return he was present at de Lassa's *salon* with a ticket of admittance to a *séance*. He was very completely disguised as a decrepit old man, and fancied that it was impossible for any one to detect him. Nevertheless, when he was taken into the room, and looked into the crystal, he was actually horror-stricken to see there a picture of himself, lying face down and senseless upon the side-walk of a street; and the message he received read thus: "What you have seen will be Delessert, in three days. Prepare!" The detective, unspeakably shocked, retired from the house at once, and sought his own lodgings.

In the morning he came to the office in a state of extreme dejection. He was completely unnerved. In relating to a brother inspector what had occurred, he said: "That man can do what he promises, I am doomed!"

He said that he thought he could make a complete case out against Haslich *alias* de Lassa, but could not do so without seeing the Prefect, and getting instructions. He would tell nothing in regard to his discoveries in Buda and in Transylvania—said that he was not at liberty to do so—and repeatedly exclaimed: "Oh! if M. le Préfet were only here!" He was told to go to the Prefect at Cherbourg, but refused, upon the ground that his presence was needed in Paris. He time and again averred his conviction that he was a doomed man, and showed himself both vacillating and irresolute in his conduct, and extremely nervous. He was told that he was perfectly safe, since de Lassa and all his household were under constant surveillance; to which he replied; "You do not know the man." An inspector was detailed to accompany Delessert, never lose sight of him night and day, and guard him carefully; and proper precautions were taken in regard to his food and drink, while the guards watching de Lassa were doubled.

On the morning of the third day, Delessert, who had been staying chiefly indoors, avowed his determination to go at once and telegraph to M. le Préfet to return immediately. With this intention he and his brother-officer started out. Just as they got to the corner of the Rue de Lancry and the Boulevard, Delessert stopped suddenly and put his hand to his forehead.

"My God!" he cried, "the crystal! the picture!" and he fell prone upon his face, insensible. He was taken at once to a hospital, but only lingered a few hours, never regaining his consciousness. Under express instructions from the authorities, a most careful, minute, and thorough autopsy was made of Delessert's body by several distinguished surgeons, whose unanimous opinion was, that the cause of his death was apoplexy, due to fatigue and nervous excitement.

As soon as Delessert was sent to the hospital, his brother-inspector hurried to the Central Office, and de Lassa, together with his wife and every one connected with the establishment, were at once arrested. De Lassa smiled contemptuously as they took him away. "I knew you were coming; I prepared for it. You will be glad to release me again."

It was quite true that de Lassa had prepared for them.

When the house was searched, it was found that every paper had been burned, the crystal globe was destroyed, and in the room of the *séances* was a great heap of delicate machinery broken into indistinguishable bits. "That cost me 200,000 francs," said de Lassa, pointing to the pile, "but it has been a good investment." The walls and floors were ripped out in several places, and the damage to the property was considerable. In prison neither de Lassa nor his associates made any revelations. The notion that they had something to do with Delessert's death was quickly dispelled, in a legal point of view, and all the party but de Lassa were released. He was still detained in prison, upon one pretext or another, when one morning he was found hanging by a silk sash to the cornice of the room where he was confined—dead. The night before, it was afterwards discovered, "Madame" de Lassa had eloped with a tall footman, taking the Nubian Sidi with them.

De Lassa's secrets died with him.

[In the next issue of the *Spiritual Scientist*, namely, December 2, 1875, p. 151, the following Editorial Note was published:]

"An Unsolved Mystery"

"It is an interesting story,—that article of yours in today's *Scientist*. But is it a record of facts, or a tissue of the imagination? If true, why not state the source of it; in other words, specify your authority for it?"

The above is not signed, but we would take the opportunity to say, that the story, "An Unsolved Mystery," was published because we considered the main points of the narrative,—the prophecies, and the singular death of the officer—to be psychic phenomena, that have been, and can be again produced. Why quote "authorities"? The Scriptures tell us of the death of Ananias, under the stern rebuke from Peter; here we have a phenomenon of a similar nature. Ananias is supposed to have suffered instant death from fear. Few can realize this power, governed by spiritual laws; but those who have trod the boundary line, and KNOW some few of the things that CAN be done, will see no great mystery in this, or the story published last week. We are not speaking in mystical tones. Ask the powerful mesmerist if there is danger that the subject may pass out from his control? If he could will the spirit out, never to return? It is capable of demonstration, that the mesmerist can act on a subject at a distance of many miles; and it is no less certain that the majority of mesmerists know little or nothing of the laws that govern their powers.

It may be a pleasant dream to attempt to conceive of the beauties of the spirit-world; but the time can be spent more profitably in a study of the spirit itself, and it is not necessary that the subject for study should be in the spirit-world.

[In the same issue of the *Spiritual Scientist,* on page 147, there appeared the following letter to the Editor which throws further light upon this remarkable story:]

"AN UNSOLVED MYSTERY"

To the Editor of the *Spiritual Scientist.*

Sir:—

I am quite well aware of the source from whence originated the facts woven into the highly interesting story entitled "An Unsolved Mystery," which appeared in No. 12, Vol. III, of your paper. I was myself at Paris at the time of the occurrences described, and personally witnessed the marvellous effects produced by the personage who figures in the anecdote as M. de Lasa. The attention you are giving to the subject of Occultism meets with the hearty approbation of all initiates—among which class it is idle for me to say whether I am or am not included.

You have opened to the American public a volume crammed, from cover to cover, with accounts of psychic phenomena surpassing in romantic interest the more wonderful experiences of the present day Spiritualism; and before long your paper will be quoted all over the world as their chief repository. Before long, too, the numerous writers in your contemporary journals, who have been gloating over the supposed discomfiture of your Russian friends, Mme. Blavatsky and the President of the Philosophical Académie, will have the laugh turned upon them, and wish they had not been so hasty in committing themselves to print. The same number which contains de Lassa's story, has, in an article on "Occult Philosophy," a suggestion that the supposed materialized spirit-forms, recently seen, may be only the simulacra of deceased people, resembling those individuals, but who are no more the real spirits than is the "photograph in your album" the sitter.

Among the notable personages I met in Paris at the time specified, was the venerable Count d'Ourches, then a hale, old gentleman nearly ninety years of age. His noble parents perished on the scaffold in the Reign of Terror, and the events of that bloody epoch were stamped indelibly upon his memory. He had known Cagliostro and his wife, and had a portrait of that lady, whose beauty dazzled the courts of Europe. One day he hurried breathlessly into the apartment of a certain nobleman, residing on the Champs Élysées, holding this miniature in his hand and exclaiming, in great excitement: *"Mon Dieu!*—she has returned—it is she!—Madame Cagliostro is here!" I smiled at seeing the old Count's excitement, knowing well what he was about to say. Upon quieting himself he told us he had just attended a séance of M. de Lasa, and had recognized in his wife the original of the miniature, which he exhibited, adding that it had come into his possession with other effects left by his martyred father. Some of the facts concerning the de Lasa are detailed very erroneously, but I shall not correct the errors.

I am aware that the first impulse of the facetious critics of Occultism will be to smile at my hardihood in endorsing, by implication, the possibility that the beautiful Madame de Lasa, of 1861, was none other than the equally beautiful Madame Cagliostro of 1786; at the further suggestion that it is not at all impossible that the proprietor of the crystal globe and clicking telegraph, which so upset the nerves of Delessert, the police spy, was the same person, who, under the name of Alessandro di Cagliostro, is reported by his lying biographers to have been found dead in the prison of Sant' Angelo.

These same humorous scribblers will have additional provocation to merriment when I tell you that it is not only probable, but likely, that this same couple may be seen in this country before the end of the Centennial Exhibition, astounding alike professors, editors, and Spiritualists.

The initiates are as hard to catch as the sun-sparkle which flecks the dancing wave on a summer day. One generation of men may know them under one name in a certain country, and the next, or a succeeding one, see them as someone else in a remote land.

They live in each place as long as they are needed and then—pass away "like a breath" leaving no trace behind.

ENDREINEK AGARDI, of Koloswar.

[In H.P.B.'s *Scrapbook*, Vol. I, p. 83, where the above Letter to the Editor of the *Spiritual Scientist* is pasted as a clipping, the author of it is identified as a pupil of Master M. The town formerly known as Kolozsvár was at that time within the boundaries of Hungary; it is now known as Cluj and is in the Transylvanian District of Rumania; its German equivalent was Klausenburg.

H.P.B. also says that the story, "An Unsolved Mystery" was written from the narrative of the Adept known as Hillarion, who sometimes signed himself Hillarion Smerdis, though the Greek original has only one "l" in it, as a rule. H.P.B. drops the initial mark of an aspirate and uses merely the initial letter "I" as would be the case in Slavonic languages.

The *facsimile* of H.P.B.'s pen-and-ink notation in her *Scrapbook* is appended herewith.

> The initiates are as hard to catch as the sun-sparkle which flecks the dancing wave on a summer day. One generation of man may know them under one name in a certain country, and the next, or a succeeding one, see them as some one else in a remote land.
> They live in each place as long as they are needed and then—pass away "like a breath" leaving no trace behind.
> ENDREINEK AGARDI, of Koloswar. **F.TS**

Written from J. **** Narrative — & pupil of M∴

It is a curious fact that when Peter Davidson, F.T.S., published in *The Theosophist* (Vol. III, Feb. and March, 1882) an Old Tale about the Mysterious Brothers, which he transcribed from an eighteenth century work, he concluded his account with the following words:

". . . . those mysterious 'beings' termed Brothers, Rosicrucians, etc., have been met with in every clime, from the crowded streets of 'Civilized'(!) London, to the silent crypts of crumbling temples in the 'uncivilized' desert; in short, wherever a mighty and beneficent purpose may call them or where genuine merit may attract them from their hermetic reticence, for one generation may recognize them by one name in a certain country, and the succeeding, or another generation meet them as someone else in a foreign land." —*Compiler*.]

[Professor Hiram Corson of Ithaca, N.Y., in an article dated December 26, 1875, and published in the *Banner of Light* under the title of "The Theosophical Society and its President's Inaugural Address," sharply criticizes Col. Olcott's Presidential Address of November 17, 1875, especially those portions of it which refer to Spiritualism. To the cutting of this article, as pasted in her *Scrapbook*, Vol. I, pp. 98-99, H.P.B. appended the following remarks:]

Oh, poor Yorick—we know him well! Aye even to having frequently seen him go to bed with his silk hat and dirty boots on. Hiram Yorick must have been drunk when he wrote this article.

See H. S. Olcott's answer on page 112.

A STORY OF THE MYSTICAL

Told by a Member of the Theosophical Society.*

A DREAD SCENE IN EASTERN NECROMANCY — VENGEANCE MARVELLOUSLY WROUGHT BY OCCULT METHODS—MYSTERIES—THE SCÎN-LÂC.

[*The Sun*, New York, Vol. XLIII, No. 104, December 26, 1875]

To the Editor of *The Sun*.
Sir,—
One morning in 1868 Eastern Europe was startled by news of the most horrifying description. Michael Obrenovitch, reigning Prince of Serbia, his aunt, the Princess Catherine, or Katinka, and her daughter, had been murdered in broad daylight, near Belgrade, in their own garden, the

---

*[This story was republished by H.P.B. in *The Theosophist*, Vol. IV, January, 1883, pp. 99-101, under the title of "Can the 'Double' Murder?" She prefaced it with the following Editorial Note:

"The story which follows was written by the editor of this magazine some years ago at the request of a literary friend in America, and published in a leading journal of New York. It is reprinted because the events actually occurred, and they possess a very deep interest for the student of psychological science. They show in a marked degree the enormous potentiality of the human will upon mesmeric subjects whose whole being may be so imbued with an imparted intellectual preconception that the 'double,' or *mayavi-rupa*, when projected transcorporeally, will carry out the mesmerizer's mandate with helpless subserviency. The fact that a mortal wound may be inflicted upon the inner man without puncturing the epidermis will be a novelty only to such readers as have not closely examined the records and noted the many proofs that death may result from many psychical causes besides the emotions whose lethal power is universally conceded."
—*Compiler*.]

assassin or assassins remaining unknown.* The Prince had received several bullet shots and stabs, and his body was actually butchered; the Princess was killed on the spot, her head smashed, and her young daughter, though still alive, was not expected to survive. The circumstances are too recent to have been forgotten, but in that part of the world, at that time, the case created a delirium of excitement.

In the Austrian dominions and in those under the doubtful protectorate of Turkey, from Bucharest down to Trieste, no high family felt secure. In those half-oriental countries every Montecchi has its Capuletti, and it was rumored that the bloody deed was perpetrated by the Prince Kara-Georgevitch, an old pretender to the modest throne of Serbia, whose father had been wronged by the first Obrenovitch. The Jaggos of this family were known to nourish the bitterest hatred toward one whom they called a usurper, and "the shepherd's grandson." For a time, the official papers of Austria were filled with indignant denials of the charge that the treacherous deed had been done or procured by Kara-Georgevitch, or "Czerno-Georgiy," as he is usually called in those parts. Several persons, innocent of the act, were, as is usual in such cases, imprisoned, and the real murderers escaped justice. A young relative of the victim, greatly beloved by his people, a mere child, taken

---

*[Mihailo Obrenović (1823-68) was the youngest son of Prince Miloš Obrenović (1780-1860). After the abdication of his father in 1839, and the death of his elder brother, Milan Obrenović, the same year, he ascended the throne of Serbia. His ambitious program of self-assertion abroad and reforms within, alienated Turkey and Austria. Heavy taxation imposed upon the people strengthened the party which had forced his father to abdicate. In August, 1842, Vučić, the leader of the malcontents, forced him to leave Serbia, and Alexander Karageorgević was elected in his place. In 1858 Alexander was dethroned in his turn, and Miloš Obrenović recalled to the throne. On his death in 1860, Mihailo succeeded him. His policy was wise and moderate; he entertained plans for a union of various Slavonic tribes in South-East Europe, and obtained the withdrawal of the last Turkish garrisons from Serbia April 18, 1867. On May 29/June 10, 1868, he was assassinated in the park of Koshutnyak, at Topcider, near Belgrade.—*Compiler.*]

for the purpose from a school in Paris, was brought over in ceremony to Belgrade and proclaimed Hospodar of Serbia.* In the turmoil of political excitement the tragedy of Belgrade was forgotten by all but an old Serbian matron, who had been attached to the Obrenovitch family, and who, like Rachel, would not be consoled for the death of her children. After the proclamation of the young Obrenovitch, the nephew of the murdered man, she had sold out her property and disappeared; but not before taking a solemn vow on the tombs of the victims to avenge their deaths.

A VAMPIRE

The writer of this truthful narrative had passed a few days at Belgrade, about three months before the horrid deed was perpetrated, and knew the Princess Katinka. She was a kind, gentle and lazy creature at home; abroad she seemed a Parisian in manners and education. As nearly all the personages who will figure in this true story are still living, it is but decent that I should withhold their names, and give only initials.

The old Serbian lady seldom left her house, going out but to see the Princess occasionally. Crouched on a pile of pillows and carpeting, clad in the picturesque national dress, she looked like the Cumaean Sibyl in her days of calm repose. Strange stories were whispered about her occult knowledge, and thrilling accounts circulated sometimes among the guests assembled round the fireside of my modest inn. Our fat landlord's maiden aunt's cousin had been troubled for some time past by a wandering vampire, and had been bled nearly to death by the nocturnal visitor; and while the efforts and exorcisms of the parish pope had been of no avail, the victim was luckily delivered

---

[This was Milan Obrenović (1854-1901), son of Miloš Jevremović Obrenović (1829-1861), the nephew of Prince Miloš (1780-1860), and by his cousin Mihailo, educated at Bucharest and Paris, and placed on the throne under a regency in 1868.—*Compiler.*]

by Gospoja P—, who had put to flight the disturbing ghost by merely shaking her fist at him, and shaming him in his own language. It was in Belgrade that I learned for the first time this highly interesting fact for philology, namely, that spooks have a language of their own. The old lady, whom I will call Gospoja P———, was generally attended by another personage destined to be the principal actress in our tale of horror. It was a young gypsy girl, from some part of Rumania, about fourteen years of age. Where she was born, and who she was, she seemed to know as little as anyone else. I was told she had been brought one day by a party of strolling gypsies, and left in the yard of the old lady; from which moment she became an inmate of the house. She was nicknamed "the sleeping girl," as she was said to be gifted with the faculty of apparently dropping asleep wherever she stood, and speaking her dreams aloud. The girl's heathen name was Frosya.

About eighteen months after the news of the murder had reached Italy, where I was at the time, I was travelling over the Banat, in a small wagon of my own, hiring a horse whenever I needed it, after the fashion of this primitive, trusting country. I met on my way an old Frenchman, a scientist, travelling alone after my own fashion, but with the difference that while he was a pedestrian I dominated the road from the eminence of a throne of dry hay, in a jolting wagon. I discovered him one fine morning, slumbering in a wilderness of shrubs and flowers, and had nearly passed over him, absorbed as I was, in the contemplation of the surrounding glorious scenery. The acquaintance was soon made, no great ceremony of mutual introduction being needed. I had heard his name mentioned in circles interested in mesmerism, and knew him to be a powerful adept of the school of Du Potet.

THE QUEEN OF CLAIRVOYANTS

"I have found," he remarked in the course of the conversation, after I had made him share my seat of hay, "one of the most wonderful subjects in this lovely Thebaide.

I have an appointment to-night with the family. They are seeking to unravel the mystery of a murder by means of the clairvoyance of the girl. . . . She is wonderful; very, very wonderful!"

"Who is she?" I asked.

"A Rumanian gypsy. She was brought up, it appears, in the family of the Serbian reigning Prince, who reigns no more, for he was very mysteriously mur——. Holoah, take care! Diable, you will upset us over the precipice!" he hurriedly exclaimed, unceremoniously snatching from me the reins, and giving the horse a violent pull.

"You do not mean Prince Obrenovitch?" I asked, aghast.

"Yes, I do; and him precisely. To-night I have to be there, hoping to close a series of *séances* by finally developing a most marvellous manifestation of the hidden power of human spirit, and you may come with me. I will introduce you; and, besides, you can help me as an interpreter, for they do not speak French."

As I was pretty sure that if the somnambule was Frosya, the rest of the family must be Gospoja P——, I readily accepted. At sunset we were at the foot of the mountain, leading to the old castle, as the Frenchman called the place. It fully deserved the poetical name given it. There was a rough bench in the depths of one of the shadowy retreats, and as we stopped at the entrance of this poetical place, and the Frenchman was gallantly busying himself with my horse on the suspicious-looking bridge which led across the water to the entrance gate, I saw a tall figure slowly rise from the bench and come toward us. It was my old friend, Gospoja P——, looking more pale and more mysterious than ever. She exhibited no surprise at seeing me, but simply greeting me after the Serbian fashion, with a triple kiss on both cheeks, she took hold of my hand and led me straight to the nest of ivy. Half reclining on a small carpet spread on the tall grass with her back leaning against the wall, I recognized our Frosya.

THE ENTRANCEMENT

She was dressed in the national costume of the Valachian women, a sort of gauze turban intermingled with various gilt medals and bands on her head, white shirt with opened sleeves, and petticoats of variegated colours. Her face looked deadly pale, her eyes were closed, and her countenance presented that stony, sphinx-like look which characterizes in such a peculiar way the entranced clairvoyant somnambule. If it were not for the heaving motion of her chest and bosom, ornamented by rows of medals and bead necklaces which feebly tinkled at every breath, one might have thought her dead, so lifeless and corpse-like was her face. The Frenchman informed me that he had sent her to sleep just as we were approaching the house, and that she now was as he had left her the previous night: he then began busying himself with the *sujet,* as he called Frosya. Paying no further attention to us, he shook her by the hand, and then making a few rapid passes, stretched out her arm and stiffened it. The arm, as rigid as iron, remained in that position. He then closed all her fingers but one—the middle finger—which he caused to point at the evening star, which twinkled in the deep blue sky. Then he turned round and went over from right to left, throwing on some of his fluids here, again discharging them at another place; busying himself with his invisible but potent fluids, like a painter with his brush when giving the last touches to a picture.

The old lady, who had silently watched him, with her chin in her hand the while, put out her thin, skeleton-looking hand on his arm and arrested it, as he was preparing himself to begin the regular mesmeric passes.

"Wait," she whispered, "till the star is set, and the ninth hour completed. The Vourdalaki* are hovering around; they may spoil the influence."

"What does she say?" inquired the mesmerizer, annoyed at her interference.

---

*[Also known as *vlukolak* and *vukodlak* among Slavonian people. —Compiler.]

I explained to him that the old lady feared the pernicious influences of the Vourdalaki.

"Vourdalaki? What's that, the Vourdalaki?" exclaimed the Frenchman. "Let us be satisfied with Christian spirits, if they honor us to-night with a visit, and lose no time for the Vourdalaki."

I glanced at the Gospoja. She had become deathly pale, and her brow was sternly knitted over her flashing black eyes.

"Tell him not to jest at this hour of the night!" she cried. "He does not know the country. Even the Holy Church may fail to protect us, once the Vourdalaki aroused. What's this?" pushing with her foot a bundle of herbs the botanizing mesmerizer had laid near on the grass. She bent over the collection and anxiously examined the contents of the bundle, after which she flung the whole in the water.

"It must not be left here," she firmly added; "these are the St. John's plants, and they might attract the wandering ones."

Meanwhile the night had come, and the moon illuminated the landscape with a pale, ghostly light. The nights in the Banat are nearly as beautiful as in the East, and the Frenchman had to go on with his experiments in the open air as the "pope" of the Church had prohibited such in his tower, which was used as the parsonage, for fear of filling the holy precincts with the heretical devils of the mesmerizer, which, he remarked, he would be unable to exorcise on account of their being foreigners.

OCCULT DETECTIVE WORK

The old gentleman had thrown off his travelling blouse, rolled up his shirt sleeves, and now striking a theatrical attitude began a regular process of mesmerization. Under his quivering fingers the odile fluid actually seemed to flash in the twilight. Frosya was placed with her figure facing the moon, and every motion of the entranced girl was discernible as in daylight. In a few minutes large drops of perspiration appeared on her brow and slowly rolled down her pale face, glittering in the moonbeams. Then she moved uneasily about and began chanting a low melody, to the words of which the Gospoja, anxiously bent over the unconscious girl, was listening with avidity and trying to catch every syllable. With her thin finger on her lips, her eyes nearly starting from their sockets, her frame motionless, the old lady seemed herself transfixed into a statue of attention. The group was a remarkable one, and I regretted that I was not a painter. What followed was a scene worthy to figure in "Macbeth." At one side the slender girl, pale and corpse-like, writhing under the invisible fluid of him who for the hour was her omnipotent master; at the other the old matron, who, burning with her unquenched desire of revenge, stood like the picture of Nemesis, waiting for the long-expected name of the Prince's murderer to be at last pronounced. The Frenchman himself seemed transfigured, his gray hair standing on end; his bulky, clumsy form seemed to have grown in a few minutes. All theatrical pretence was now gone; there remained but the mesmerizer, aware of his responsibility, unconscious himself of the possible results, studying and anxiously expecting. Suddenly Frosya, as if lifted by some supernatural force, rose from her reclining posture and stood erect before us, motionless and still again, waiting for the magnetic fluid to direct her. The Frenchman, silently taking the old lady's hand, placed it in that of the somnambulist, and ordered her to put herself *en rapport* with the Gospoja.

"What seest thou, my daughter?" softly murmured the Serbian lady. "Can your spirit seek out the murderers?"

"Search and behold!" sternly commanded the mesmerizer, fixing his gaze upon the face of the subject.

"I am—on my way—I go," faintly whispered Frosya, her voice seeming not to come from herself, but from the surrounding atmosphere.

THE MYSTIC DOUBLE

At this moment something so extraordinary took place that I doubt my ability to describe it. A luminous shadow, vapor-like, appeared closely surrounding the girl's body. At first about an inch in thickness, it gradually expanded, and, gathering itself, suddenly seemed to break off from the body altogether, and condense itself into a kind of semi-solid vapor, which very soon assumed the likeness of the somnambule herself. Flickering about the surface of the earth, the form vacillated for two or three seconds, then glided noiselessly toward the river. It disappeared like a mist dissolved in the moonbeams, which seemed to absorb and imbibe it altogether.

I had followed the scene with intense attention. The mysterious operation, known in the East as the evocation of the *scîn-lâc** was taking place before my own eyes. To doubt was impossible, and Du Potet was right in saying that mesmerism is the conscious magic of the ancients, and spiritualism the unconscious effect of the same magic upon certain organisms.

As soon as the vaporous double had soaked itself through the pores of the girl, the Gospoja had, by a rapid motion of the hand which was left free, drawn from under her pelisse something which looked to us suspiciously like a small stiletto, and placed it as rapidly in the girl's bosom. The action was so quick that the mesmerizer, absorbed in his work, had not remarked it,† as he afterwards told me. A few minutes elapsed in a dead silence. We seemed a group of petrified persons. Suddenly a thrilling and trans-piercing cry burst from the entranced girl's lips. She bent forward, and snatching the stiletto from her bosom, plunged it furiously around her in the air, as if pursuing imaginary foes. Her mouth foamed, and incoherent, wild exclamations

---

* [H.P.B. seems to imply that this is an Eastern term, while in reality it is an Anglo-Saxon one. *Scîn-lâc* means magic, necromancy and sorcery, as well as a magical appearance, a spectral form, a deceptive appearance or a phantom (*phantasma*). *Scîn-lâeca* is a magician or sorcerer, and *scîn-lâece*, a sorceress. The art by means of which illusory appearances are produced was known as *scînn-craeft*. From the Anglo-Saxon *scînan*, to shine, was also derived the term *scîn-fold* used for the idea of the Elysian fields.—*Compiler*.]

† [H.P.B. must have often thought in French, even when writing English. This is a case in point. She means "had not noticed it," but uses the equivalent of the French word "remarquer" which carries a different meaning in English.—*Compiler*.]

broke from her lips, among which discordant sounds I discerned several times two familiar Christian names of men. The mesmerizer was so terrified that he lost all control over himself, and instead of withdrawing the fluid, he loaded the girl with it still more.

"Take care!" exclaimed I. "Stop! You will kill her or she will kill you!"

But the Frenchman had unwittingly raised subtle potencies of nature, over which he had no control. Furiously turning round, the girl struck at him a blow which would have killed him, had he not avoided it by jumping aside, receiving but a severe scratch on the right arm. The poor man was panic-stricken. Climbing with an extaordinary agility for a man of his bulky form on the wall over her, he fixed himself on it astride, and gathering the remnants of his will power, sent in her direction a series of passes. At the second, the girl dropped the weapon and remained motionless.

"What are you about?" hoarsely shouted the mesmerizer in French, seated like some monstrous night goblin on the wall. "Answer me: I command you!"

"I did—but what she—whom you ordered me to obey—commanded me do," answered the girl in French, to my amazement.

"What did the old witch command you?" irreverently asked he.

VENGEANCE SATISFIED

"To find them—who murdered—kill them—I did so—and they are no more!—avenged—avenged! They are——"

An exclamation of triumph, a loud shout of infernal joy rang loud in the air, and awakening the dogs of the neighboring villages a responsive howl of barking began from that moment like a ceaseless echo of the Gospoja's cry.

"I am avenged. I feel it, I know it. My warning heart tells me that the fiends are no more." And she fell panting on the ground, dragging down in her fall the girl, who allowed herself to be pulled down as if she were a bag of wool.

"I hope my subject did no further mischief to-night. She is a dangerous as well as a very wonderful subject!" said the Frenchman.

We parted. Three days after that I was at T——, and as I was sitting in the dining-room of a restaurant waiting for my lunch I happened to pick up a newspaper, and the first lines I read ran thus:

"VIENNA, 186—. TWO MYSTERIOUS DEATHS. Last evening, at 9:45, as P—— was about to retire, two of the gentlemen in waiting suddenly exhibited great terror, as though they had seen a dreadful apparition. They screamed, staggered, and ran about the room holding up their hands as if to ward off the blows of an unseen weapon. They paid no attention to the eager questions of the Prince and suite, but presently fell writhing upon the floor, and expired in great agony. Their bodies exhibited no appearance of apoplexy, nor any external marks of wounds; but wonderful to relate, there were numerous dark spots and long marks upon the skin, as though they were stabs and slashes made without puncturing the cuticle. The autopsy revealed the fact that beneath each of these mysterious discolorations there was a deposit of coagulated blood. The greatest excitement prevails, and the faculty are unable to solve the mystery."

HADJI MORA.*

---

*[In her *Scrapbook*, Vol. I, p. 118, H.P.B. pasted a cutting of this story and signed her name under this pseudonym. Concerning the veracity of the facts outlined by H.P.B., and other data relevant to this story, the student is referred to H.P.B.'s letter written to A. P. Sinnett in the early part of 1886 and numbered Letter No. LXI, in the volume entitled *The Letters of H. P. Blavatsky to A. P. Sinnett*, published in 1924.

Some years later, when this story was republished in *The Theosophist*, Vol. IV, January, 1883, John Yarker, the well-known Mason, wrote a brief account of similar experiences he had had with sensitives (*ibid.*, March, 1883, pp. 149-50). To his inquiry as to the genuineness of the narrative, H.P.B. added in a footnote: "We assure our learned correspondent that every word of our narrative is true." —*Compiler.*]

1876

THE LUMINOUS CIRCLE*

Wonderful Powers of the Divining Girl of Damascus.

A Theosophical Tale told by an Old Traveller in the Far East. — A Magic Moon. — What was Seen Therein. — The Dervishes of Constantinople. — A Dwarf's Transformation.

[*The Sun*, New York, Vol. XLIII, No. 111, January 2, 1876]

We were a small party of merry travellers. We had arrived at Constantinople a week before from Greece, and had devoted fourteen hours a day to running up and down the steep hills of Pera, visiting bazaars, climbing to the tops of minarets, and fighting our way through armies of hungry dogs, traditional masters of the streets of Stamboul. Nomadic life is infectious, they say, and no civilization is strong enough to destroy the charm of unrestrained freedom when it has once been tasted. For the first three days my spaniel, Ralph, had kept at my heels, and behaved like a tolerably well-educated quadruped. He was a fine fellow, my travelling companion and most cherished friend; I was afraid to lose him, and so kept a good watch over his incomings and outgoings. At every impudent attack by his Mohammedan fellow creatures, whether demonstrations of friendship or hostility, he would merely draw in his tail between his legs, and seek in a dignified and modest manner protection under one or the other wing of our little party. He had shown from the first a decided aversion to bad company, and so, having become assured of his discretion, by the end of the third day I relinquished my vigilance. This neglect was speedily followed by punishment. In an unguarded moment he listened to the voice of some canine

---

*[In her *Scrapbook*, Vol. I, p. 118, H.P.B. made a notation in blue pencil above this title to the effect that this was her "2nd story." —Compiler.]

siren, and the last I saw of him was his bushy tail vanishing around the corner of a dirty, crooked street.

Greatly annoyed, and determined to recover him at all hazards, I passed the remainder of the day in a vain search. I offered twenty, thirty, forty francs reward for him. About as many vagabond Maltese began a regular chase, and toward night we were assailed in our hotel by the whole troop, every man of them with a mangy cur in his arms, which he tried his best to convince me was the dog I had lost. The more I denied, the more solemnly they insisted, one of them actually going down upon his knees, snatching from his bosom an old corroded image of the Virgin, and swearing with a solemn oath that the Queen of Heaven herself had appeared to him and kindly shown him which dog was mine. The tumult had increased so as to threaten a riot, when finally our landlord had to send for a couple of kavasches from the nearest police station, who expelled the army of bipeds and quadrupeds by main force. I was the more in despair, as the headwaiter, a semi-respectable old brigand, who, judging by appearances, had not passed more than a half-dozen years in the galleys, gravely assured me that my pains were all useless, as my spaniel was undoubtedly devoured and half digested by this time, the Turkish dogs being very fond of their toothsome Christian brothers.

The discussion was held in the street, at the door of the hotel, and I was about to give up the search for that night, when an old Greek lady, a Phanariote, who had listened attentively to the fracas from the steps of a neighboring house, approached our disconsolate group and suggested to Miss H., one of our party, that we should inquire of the Dervishes concerning the fate of Ralph.

"And what can the Dervishes know about my dog?" inquired I, in no mood to joke.

THE "HOLY MEN"

"The holy men know all, Kyrea (madam)!" answered she, somewhat mysteriously. "Last week I was robbed of my new satin pelisse, which my son had brought me from

Brusa, and, as you all see, there I have it on my back again."

"Indeed? Then the holy men have also metamorphosed your new pelisse into an old one, I should say," remarked a gentleman of our company, pointing to a large rent in the back, which had been clumsily mended with pins.

"And it is precisely that which is most wonderful," quietly answered the Phanariote, not in the least disconcerted. "They showed me in the luminous circle the quarter of the town, the house, and even the room in which the Jew who stole it was preparing to rip and cut my garment into pieces. My son and I had barely the time to run over to the Kalindjikoulosek quarter and save my property. We caught the thief in the very act, and both instantly recognized him as the man shown us by the Dervishes in the magic moon. He confessed, and is in prison now."

Not understanding what she meant by the luminous circle and magic moon, but not a little mystified by her account of the divining powers of the "holy men," we felt so satisfied that the story was not wholly a fabrication that we decided to go and see for ourselves on the following morning.

The monotonous cry of the Muezzin from the top of a minaret had just proclaimed the noon of the day as we, descending from the heights of Pera to the port of Galata, with difficulty elbowed our way through the unsavory crowds of the commercial quarter of the town. Before we reached the docks we had been half deafened by the shouts and incessant, ear-piercing noises, and the Babel-like confusion of tongues. In this part of the city it is useless to expect to be guided by either house numbers or names of streets. The location of any desired place is indicated by its relative proximity to some other conspicuous building, such as a Mosque, bath or European storehouse; for the rest one has to put his faith in Allah and his prophet.

DERVISHES AT HOME

It was with the greatest difficulty, therefore, that we finally found the British shipchandler's store in the rear of which we were to look for the place of our destination.

Our hotel guide knew about the Dervishes as little as ourselves; but at last a Greek urchin, in all the simplicity of primitive undress, consented for a modest copper *bakshish,* to lead us to the dancers.

We arrived at last, and were shown into a gloomy and vast hall, which appeared to me like a vacated stable. It was long and narrow, the floor was thickly strewn with sand, as in a *manège,* and it was lighted only through small windows under the cornices of the ceiling. The Dervishes had finished their morning performances, and were evidently resting from their exhausting labors. They looked completely prostrated, some lying about in corners, others sitting on their heels, staring vacantly, in mute contemplation of the Invisible Divinity, as we were informed. They appeared to have lost all power of speech and hearing, for none of them responded to our questions until a gaunt, giant-limbed fellow, in a tall pointed cap, which made him appear over seven feet high, emerged from an obscure nook.

Informing us that he was the chief, he remarked that the holy brethren, being in the act of receiving orders for further ceremonies of the day from Allah himself, must not be disturbed. But when the interpreter had explained to him the object of our visit, which concerned himself alone, he being the sole proprietor of the "divining rod," his objections vanished, and he extended his hand for the alms. Upon being gratified, he beckoned two of our party, signifying that he could not accommodate more at once, and led the way.

THE SIBYL'S RETREAT

Plunging after him into the darkness of what seemed a half-subterranean passage, we were led to the foot of a tall ladder reaching to a chamber under the roof. We scrambled up after our guide and found ourselves in a wretched garret, of moderate size, destitute of all furniture. The floor, however, was carpeted with a thick layer of dust, and cobwebs festooned the walls in profusion. In one corner we perceived something which I mistook, at first, for a bundle of old rags; but the heap presently moved, got on its legs, advanced to the middle of the room, and stood before us, the most extraordinary-looking creature that I ever beheld. Its sex was female, but it was impossible to decide whether she was a woman or a child. She was a hideous-looking dwarf, with a head so monstrously developed that it would have been too big for a giant; the shoulders of a grenadier; the bosom of a Normandy wet nurse; and the whole supported on two short, lean, spider-looking legs, which trembled under the disproportionate size of the trunk as she advanced. She had a grinning countenance, like the face of a satyr, and it was ornamented with letters and signs from the *Koran,* painted in bright yellow. On her forehead was a blood-red crescent; her head was crowned with a dusty *tarboosh;* the lower extremities covered with large Turkish trousers; the upper portion of the body wrapped in dirty white muslin, barely sufficient to conceal one-half of its deformities. This creature rather let herself drop than sat down, in the middle of the floor, and as her weight came upon the rickety boards it sent up a thick cloud of dust, which invaded our throats and set us to coughing and sneezing. This was the famous Tatmos, known as the Damascus Oracle!

THE MAGICIAN AT WORK

Without losing time in idle talk, the Dervish produced a piece of chalk, and traced round the girl a circle about six feet in diameter. Fetching from behind the door twelve small copper lamps, and filling them with a dark liquid contained in a vial which he drew from his bosom, he placed them symmetrically around the magic circle. He then broke a chip of wood from the half-ruined panel of the door, which bore evident marks of many a similar depredation, and, holding the chip between his thumb and finger, began blowing on it at regular intervals, alternating with mutterings of weird incantation; suddenly, and to all appearance without any apparent cause for its ignition, there appeared a spark on the chip, and it blazed up like a dry match. He lit the twelve lamps at this self-generated flame. During this process, Tatmos, who until then had sat altogether unconcerned and motionless, removed her yellow *babouches* off from her naked feet, and throwing them into a corner, disclosed, as an additional beauty, a sixth toe on each deformed foot. The Dervish then reached over into the circle, and, seizing the dwarf's ankles, gave a jerk as if he had been lifting a bag of corn, raised her clear off the ground, and stepping back, held her head downward. He shook her as one might a sack to pack its contents, the motion being regular and easy. He then swung her to and fro like a pendulum until the necessary momentum was acquired, when, letting go one foot and seizing the other with both hands, he made a powerful, muscular effort and whirled her round in the air as if she had been an Indian club.

My companion had shrunk back into a corner in fear. Round and round the Dervish swung his living burden, she remaining perfectly passive. The motion increased in rapidity, until the eye could hardly follow her body in its circuit. This continued perhaps for two or three minutes, until gradually slackening the motion, he stopped it, and in an instant had landed the girl upon her knees in the middle of the lamp-lit circle. Such was the Eastern method of mesmerization as practised among the Dervishes.

IN A TRANCE

And now the dwarf seemed entirely oblivious of external objects, and in a deep trance. Her head and jaw dropped upon her chest, her eyes were glazed and staring, and altogether her appearance was hideous. The Dervish then carefully closed the wooden shutters of the only window, and we would have been in total obscurity but that there was a hole bored in it, through which entered a bright ray of sunlight, which shot through the darkened room and shone upon the girl. He arranged her drooping head so that the ray should fall directly upon the crown, after which, motioning us to remain silent, he folded his arms upon his bosom, and fixing his gaze upon the bright spot, became as motionless as an image of stone. I, too, riveted my eyes upon the same spot, and followed the proceeding with in-

The Luminous Circle

tense interest, for I had seen something similar before, and knew what beautiful phenomena to expect.

By degrees the bright patch, as if it had drawn through the sunbeam a greater splendor from without and condensed it within its own area, shaped itself into a brilliant star, which from its focus sent out rays in every direction.

A curious optical effect then occurred. The room, which previously had been partially lighted by the sunbeam, grew darker and darker as the star increased in radiance, until we found ourselves in an Egyptian gloom. The star twinkled, trembled, and turned, at first with a slow, gyratory motion, then faster and faster, expanding and increasing its circumference at every rotation until it formed a brilliant disc, and we lost sight of the dwarf as if she herself had been absorbed into its light. Having gradually attained a vertiginous velocity, as the girl had when whirled by the Dervish, the motion began decreasing, and finally merged into a feeble vibration, like the shimmer of moonbeams on rippling water. Then it flickered for a moment longer, emitted a few last flashes, and assuming the density and irridescence of an immense opal, it remained motionless. The disc now radiated a moon-like lustre, soft and silvery, but instead of illuminating the garret, this seemed only to intensify the darkness. Its edge was not penumbrous, but, on the contrary, sharply defined like that of a silver shield.

THE MAGICAL SHIELD

All being now ready the Dervish without uttering a word, or removing his gaze from the disc, stretched out a hand and taking hold of mine, he drew me to his side and pointed to the illuminated shield. Looking at the place indicated, we saw dark patches appear like those upon the moon. These gradually formed themselves into figures, which began moving about till they came out in high relief in their natural colors. They neither appeared like a photograph nor an engraving; still less like reflection of images on a mirror; but as if the disc were a cameo and they were raised above its surface and then endowed with life and motion. To my astonishment and my friend's consternation we recognized the bridge leading from Galata to Stamboul, spanning the Golden Horn from the new to the old city. There were the people hurrying to and fro, steamers and gay caiks gliding on the blue Bosphorus; the many-colored buildings, villas and palaces reflected in the water; and the whole picture illuminated by the noonday sun.

It passed like a panorama; but so vivid was the impression that we could not tell whether it or ourselves were in motion. All was bustle and life, but not a sound broke the oppressive stillness. It was noiseless as a dream. It was a phantom picture. Street after street and quarter after quarter succeeded each other; there was the Bazaar, with its narrow, roofed passages, the small shops on each side, the coffee house, with gravely-smoking Turks; and as either they or we glided past them, one of the smokers upset the narghile and coffee of another, and a volley of soundless invectives caused us great amusement. So we travelled with the picture until we came to a large building, which I recognized as the Palace of the Minister of Finance. In a ditch behind the house and close by to a Mosque, lying in a pool of mud, with his silken coat all bedraggled, lay my poor Ralph! Panting and crouching down as if exhausted, he seemed dying; and near him were gathered some sorry-looking curs who lay blinking in the sun and snapping at the flies!

I had seen all that I desired, although I had not breathed a word about the dog to the Dervish, and had come more out of curiosity than with the idea of any success. I was impatient to leave at once to recover Ralph; but as my companion besought me to remain a little while longer, I reluctantly consented.

THINKING OF HIM

The scene faded away, and Miss H—— placed herself in her turn nearer by the side of the gigantic Dervish.

"I will think of *him*," whispered she into my ear, with that sentimental tone which young ladies generally assume when referring to a "him."

A long stretch of sand; a blue sea, with white caps dancing in the sun; a great steamer, ploughing her way along past a desolate shore, and leaving a milky track behind her. The deck is full of life; then men busy forward; the cook, with his white cap and apron, coming out of his galley; uniformed officers moving about; passengers on the quarter deck flirting, lounging, or reading; and a young man we both recognize comes forward and leans over the taffrail. It is—*him!*

Miss H—— gives a little gasp, blushes and smiles, and concentrates her thoughts again. The picture of the steamer fades away in its turn; the magic moon remains for a few seconds pictureless. But new spots appear on its luminous face; we see a library slowly emerging from its depths—a library with green carpet and hangings, and book-shelves around three sides of the room. Seated in an armchair by the table, under the chandelier, is an old gentleman writing. His grey hair is brushed back from his forehead, his face is smooth-shaven, and his countenance has an expression of benignity.

"Father!" joyfully exclaims Miss H——.

The Dervish makes a hasty motion to enjoin silence. The light on the disc quivers, but resumes its steady brilliancy once more.

WONDERFUL

We are back in Constantinople now; and out of the pearly depths of the shield forms our own apartment in the hotel. There are our papers and books lying upon the bureau, my friend's travelling-hat in a corner, her ribbons hanging on the glass, and on the bed the very dress which she had exchanged when we started out on our memorable expedition. No detail was lacking to make the identification complete; and, to prove that we were not seeing something conjured up in our own imaginations, there lay upon the dressing case two sealed letters, the very handwriting upon which my friend recognizes. They were from a very dear relative of hers, from whom she had expected to hear at Athens, but had been disappointed. The scene faded away, and we now see her brother's room, with himself lying upon the lounge, and the servant bathing his head, which, to our horror, we see bleeding!

We had left the boy perfectly well one hour before; but upon seeing his picture my companion uttered a cry of alarm, and seizing me by the hand dragged me towards the door. Down below we rejoined our guide, and hurried back to our hotel.

The boy had fallen downstairs and cut himself badly on the forehead; in the room, on the writing desk were the two letters which had been forwarded from Athens, letters she had seen in the disc and recognized, and the arrival of which had been so impatiently expected. Ordering the carriage, I drove hurriedly to the Minister of Finance, and alighting with the guide went right to the ditch I had never seen but in the magic room. In the middle of the pool, badly mangled, half famished, but still alive, lay my beautiful spaniel, Ralph!

HADJI MORA.

MADAME BLAVATSKY EXPLAINS

A RAP AT THE "LUTHER"-ANS—HER OPINION OF THE
EDDYS—MEDIUMS CRITICIZED.

[*Spiritual Scientist*, Boston, Vol. III, January 6, 1876, pp. 208-9]

To the Editor of the *Spiritual Scientist*:

Dear Sir,—For the last three months one has hardly been able to open a number of the *Banner*, or the other papers, without finding one or more proofs of the fecundity of the human imagination in the condition of hallucination. The Spiritualist camp is in an uproar, and the clans are gathering to fight imaginary foes. The tocsin is sounded; danger signals shoot, like flaming rockets, across the hitherto serene sky, and warning cries are uttered by vigilant sentries posted at the four corners of the "angel-girt world." The reverberations of this din resound even in the daily press.

One would think that the last day of judgment had come for American Spiritualism.

Why all this disturbance? Simply because two humble individuals have spoken a few wholesome truths. If the grand beast of the *Apocalypse* with its seven heads, and the word "Blasphemy" written upon each, had appeared in heaven, there would hardly have been so much commotion there, as this; and there seems to be a concerted effort to pitch Colonel Olcott and myself, coupled like a pair of Hermetic Siamese twins, into the school of the Diakka.* Occultism seems to the superstitious, as ominous as a comet with fiery tail, and the precursor of war, plagues and other calamities. They seem to think that if they do not crush us, we will destroy Spiritualism.

I have no time to waste, and what I now write is not intended for the benefit of such persons as these, whose soap-bubbles, however pretty, are sure to burst of themselves, but to set myself right with many most estimable Spiritualists for whom I feel a sincere regard.

If the spiritual press of America were conducted upon a principle of doing even justice to all, I would send your contemporaries copies of this letter, but their course in the past has made me, whether rightly or not, feel as if no redress could be had outside of your columns. I shall be only too glad if their treatment in this case gives me cause to change my opinion that they and their slandering theorists are inspired by the biblical devils who left Mary Magdalene and returned to the land of the "Sweet By-and-By."†

---

* [When the cutting of this article was pasted in H.P.B.'s *Scrapbook*, Vol. I, p. 108, she corrected the word "school" to read "Scheol" and added the following footnote in pen and ink:

Scheol—the hell of the Jews—you donkey printer.
—*Compiler.*]

† [A hymn by Ira David Sankey (1840-1908), in which occur the following lines:
"In the sweet by-and-by,
We shall meet on that beautiful shore."
—*Compiler.*]

To begin, I wish to unhook my name from that of Col. Olcott, if you please, and declare that as he is not responsible for my views or actions, neither am I for his. He is bold enough and strong enough to defend himself under all circumstances, and has never allowed his adversaries to strike without knocking out two teeth to their one. If our views on Spiritualism are in some degree identical, and our work in the Theosophical Society pursued in common, we are, notwithstanding, two very distinct entities and mean to remain such. I highly esteem Colonel Olcott, as every one does who knows him. He is a gentleman; but what is more in my eyes, he is an honest and true man, and an *unselfish* Spiritualist, in the proper sense of that word. If he now sees Spiritualism in another light than Orthodox Spiritualists would prefer, they themselves are only to blame. He strikes at the rotten places of their philosophy, and they do all they can to cover up the ulcers, instead of trying to cure them. He is one of the truest and most unselfish friends that the cause has today in America, and yet he is treated with an intolerance that could hardly be expected of anybody above the level of the rabid Moodys and Sankeys. Surely, facts speak for themselves, and a faith so pure, angelic and unadulterated as American Spiritualism is claimed to be, can have nothing to fear from Heresiarchs. A house built on the rock stands unshaken by any storm. If the New *Luther*-an Church can prove all its "controls, guides and visitors from behind the Shining River," to be disembodied spirits, why all this row? That's just where the trouble lies; they cannot prove it. They have tasted these fruits of Paradise, and while finding some of them sweet and refreshing because gathered and brought by *real* angel friends, so many others have proved sour and rotten to the core, that to escape an uncurable dyspepsia, many of the best and most sincere Spiritualists have left the communion without asking for a letter of dismissal.

This is not Spiritualism; it is as I say, a New *Luther*-an Church, and really, though the late Oracle of the *Banner of Light* was evidently a pure and true woman—for the breath of calumny, this raging demon of America, has never been able to soil her reputation, and though certainly she was a wonderful medium—still I don't see why a Spiritualist should be ostracized, only, because after having given up St. Paul, he or she does not strictly adhere to the doctrines of St. Conant.

The last number of the *Banner* contained a letter from a Mr. Saxon, criticizing some expressions in a recent letter of Colonel Olcott, to the New York *Sun,* in defence of the Eddys. The only part which concerned me is this:

> Surely, some magician with his or *her* Cabalistic Presto! Change! has worked sudden and singular revolutions in the mind of this disciple of Occultism, this gentleman who "is" and "is not" a Spiritualist.

As I am the only she-Cabalist in America, I cannot be mistaken as to the author's meaning; so I cheerfully pick up the glove. While I am not responsible for the changes in the barometer of Col. Olcott's spirituality (which, I notice, usually presage a storm), I am for the following facts: Since I left Chittenden, I have constantly and fearlessly maintained against every one, beginning with Dr. Beard, that their apparitions are genuine and powerful. Whether they are "spirits of hell or goblins damned," is a question quite separate from that of their mediumship. Col. Olcott will not deny that when we met at Chittenden for the first time, and afterwards—and that more than once—when he expressed suspicions about the genuineness of May-Flower and George Dix, the spirits of Horatio's dark *séances,* I insisted that so far as I could judge, they were genuine spirits.* He will also no doubt admit, since he is an eminently truthful man, that when the ungrateful behaviour of the Eddys, towards whom every visitor at the Homestead will testify that he was kinder than a brother—had made him ready to express his indignation, I interfered in their behalf, and begged that he would never confound mediums with other people as to their responsibility. Mediums have tried to shake my opinions of the Eddy boys, offering in two cases that I can recall, to go to Chittenden with me

---

*[In her *Scrapbook*, Vol. I, p. 108, H.P.B. corrected the word "spirits" to read "phenomena."—*Compiler.*]

and expose the fraud. I acted the same with them that I did with the Colonel. Mediums have tried likewise to convince me that Mr. Crookes' Katie King was but Miss F. Cook walking about, while a wax-bust, fabricated in her likeness and covered with her clothes, lay in the cabinet, representing her as entranced. Other mediums, regarding me as a fanatical Spiritualist, who would even be ready to connive at fraud rather than see the cause hurt by an exposure, have let, or pretended to let, me into the secrets of the mediumship of their fellow mediums, and sometimes incautiously into their own. My experience shows that the worst enemies of mediums are mediums. Not content with slandering each other, they assail and traduce their warmest and most unselfish friends.

Whatever objection any one may have to me on account of country, religion, occult study, rudeness of speech, cigarette smoking, or any other peculiarity, my record in connection with Spiritualism for long years does not show me as making money by it, or gaining any other advantage direct or indirect. On the contrary: those who have met me in all parts of the world (which I have circumnavigated three times) will testify that I have given thousands of dollars, imperilled my life, defied the Catholic Church, where it required more courage to do so than the Spiritualists seem to show about encountering Elementaries, and in camp and court, on the sea, in the desert, in civilized and savage countries, I have been, from first to last, the friend and champion of the mediums. I have done more: I have often taken the last dollar out of my pocket and even necessary clothes off my back to relieve their necessities.

And how do you think I have been rewarded? By honors, emoluments, and social position? Have I charged a fee for imparting to the public or individuals what little knowledge I have gathered in my travels and studies? Let those who have patronized our principal mediums answer. I have been slandered in the most shameful way, and the most unblushing lies circulated about my character and antecedents by the very mediums whom I have been defending at the risk of being taken for their confederate when their tricks have been detected. What has happened in American cities is no worse nor different from what has befallen me in Europe, Asia, and Africa. I have been injured temporarily in the eyes of good and pure men and women, by the libels of mediums whom I never saw, and who never were in the same city with me at the same time. Of mediums who made me the heroine of shameful histories whose action was alleged to have occurred when I was in another part of the world, far away from the face of a white man. Ingratitude and injustice have been my portion since I had first to do with spiritual mediums. I have met here with [a] few exceptions, but very, very few.

Now, what do you suppose has sustained me throughout? Do you imagine that I could not see the disgusting frauds mixed up with the most divine genuine manifestations? Could I, having nothing to gain in money, power, or any other consideration, have been content to pass through all these dangers, suffer all this abuse, and receive all these injurious insults, if I saw nothing in Spiritualism but what these critics of Col. Olcott and myself can see? Would the prospect of an eternity passed in the angel-girt world, in company with unwashed Indian guides and military controls, with Aunt Salleys and Professor Websters, have been inducement enough? No, I would prefer annihilation to such a prospect! It was because I knew that through the same golden gates which swung open to admit the elementary and those unprogressed human spirits who are worse if anything than they, have often passed the real and purified forms of the departed and blessed ones. Because, knowing the nature of these spirits and the laws of mediumistic control, I have never been willing to hold my calumniators responsible for the great evil they did, when they were often simply the unfortunate victims of obsession by unprogressed spirits. Who can blame me for not wishing to associate with or receive instruction from spirits who, if not far worse, were no better nor wiser than I? Is a man entitled to respect and veneration simply because his body is rotting under ground, like that of a dog? To me the grand object of my life was attained and the immortality of our spirit demonstrated. Why should I turn necromancer and evoke the dead, who could neither teach me nor make me better than I was? It is a more dangerous thing to play with the mysteries of life and death than most Spiritualists imagine. Let them thank God for the great proof of immortality afforded them in this century of unbelief and materialism; and if divine Providence has put them on the right path, let them pursue it by all means, but not stop to pass their time in dangerous talk indiscriminately with every one from the other side. The land of spirits, the Summer Land as they call it here, is a *terra incognita*—no believer will deny it; it is vastly more unknown to every Spiritualist, as regards its various inhabitants, than a trackless virgin forest of Central Africa; and who can blame the pioneer settler if he hesitates to open his door to a knock, before assuring himself whether the visitor be man or beast?

Thus, just because of all that I have said above I proclaim myself a true Spiritualist; because my belief is built upon a firm ground, and that no exposure of mediums, no social scandal affecting them or others, no materialistic deductions of exact science, or sneers and denunciations of scientists can shake it. The truth is coming slowly to light, and I shall do my best to hasten its advent. I will breast the current of popular prejudice and ignorance. I am prepared to endure slander, foul insinuations, and insult in the future as I have in the past. Already, one spiritual editor, to most effectually demonstrate his spirituality, has called me a witch. I have survived, and hope to do so if two or two score more should do the same; but whether I ride the air to attend my Sabbath or not, one thing is certain: I will not ruin myself to buy broomsticks upon which to chase after every lie set afloat by editors or mediums.

H. P. BLAVATSKY.

[In H.P.B.'s *Scrapbook*, Vol. I, p. 111, may be found a cutting from the *Banner of Light* of January 15, 1876. The author, F.H.C., announces Col. Olcott's lecture in Boston on Jan. 30th, and deals with the subject of Col. Olcott and the Elementaries.

He quotes from his Inaugural Address the statement concerning Mr. Felt who had promised, by simple chemical means, to exhibit the race of beings which people the elements. At the side of the cutting, H.P.B. remarked in pen and ink:]

And Mr. Felt *has done it* in the presence of nine persons in all.

[In H.P.B.'s *Scrapbook*, Vol. I, p. 112, there is pasted a cutting from the *Banner of Light*, of January 15, 1876, which is a Letter of Charles Sotheran to the Editor, in which he explains the reasons for his resignation from the Theosophical Society and indulges in some very uncomplimentary remarks about H.P.B. On the left margin of this article, H.P.B. wrote in pen and ink:]

This did not prevent Mr. Sotheran to come 6 months after that and beg my pardon, and beg on his knees to be taken into the Society again as will be proved further.

[Col. H. S. Olcott replied in the pages of the *Spiritual Scientist* to the very outspoken criticism of Prof. Hiram Corson in regard to his Inaugural Address of November 17, 1875. He protested against the rather rude and unfair remarks of Prof. Corson. The last paragraph of his reply is quoted below, and the italicized words in it are those which have been underlined by H.P.B. when she pasted the cutting of this reply in her *Scrapbook*, Vol. I, p. 113:]

"As for the Theosophical Society, our present *e*xperience with a *certain person*, who shall be nameless since his conduct has been such as to forfeit his right to recognition, has been a lesson that we mean to profit by. We are considering a proposition to organize ourselves into a *secret society** *so that we may pursue our studies* uninterrupted by the falsehoods and inpertinences of outside parties. When we have secured the proof palpable of the Unseen Universe and its laws, we may publish it to the world, unless we should then be satisfied that some other critic as courteous and fair as Mr. Corson would denounce us as guilty of 'assumption,' 'pretention,' or 'brag.' "

[On the right margin of the column, H.P.B. inserted the following note in pen and ink which refers to the asterisk she inserted in Olcott's text:]

Till the row with Sotheran the Society was *not* a secret one, as will be seen by this. But he began to revile our experiments & denounce us to Spiritualists & impede the Society's progress & it was found necessary to make it *secret*.

[Below the signature of Col. Olcott, H.P.B. pasted a small colored picture, showing a big monkey sitting and searching diligently for parasites on the neck of a little monkey child. Above the head of the big monkey, just under the signature, she pasted the six-pointed star with an open eye in the center of it, and wrote the following explanation in pen and ink:]

Pres^t Moloney in his future capacity of the Hindu Hanuman tenderly searching for and delivering his younger Brothers of the *Enemy*-parasite.

[In the *Banner of Light* of February 12, 1876, Louisa Andrews wrote an article entitled "Professor Crookes still Faithful to his Conviction," in which she said that "it is especially gratifying to know that this gentleman is still firmly grounded in the faith."
To this H.P.B. appended the following footnote when she pasted the cutting into her *Scrapbook*, Vol. I, p. 116:]

Firmly "grounded" in his faith in the phenomena—perfectly sceptical as to their being produced by *disembodied* "Spirits"! Nei!—O, sweet sugar-plum Louisa. . . . .

A CRISIS FOR SPIRITUALISM

THE JESUITS BEGINNING TO SHOW THEIR HANDS—WHAT THE MEDIUM HOME IS DOING FOR MOTHER CHURCH.

[*Spiritual Scientist,* Boston, Vol. IV, March 23, 1876, pp. 32-34]

To the Editor of the *Spiritual Scientist*:

The crisis which thoughtful minds have long anticipated for Spiritualism is approaching at last. The Cause is being mortally wounded in the house of its friends. To what a pass things have come may be inferred from the fact that an occultist, upon whose back all the sins of the community have been piled, is left to denounce the behavior of one of its greatest mediums. Home endorses the greatest outrage of modern times—the imprisonment of the poor martyr of Mazas. He does more; he charges felony—which could not be proved even by the prosecutors—upon an innocent man who lies in jail. Wolves will not tear a wounded comrade until life is extinct; but this medium, *par excellence,* who, in contradiction to everyone else, tells of himself that he is "very truthful" (see *Boston Herald,* March 12th) cannot even show the moderation of these animals. Hardly have the prison gates closed behind Leymarie, that unfortunate victim of Jesuitism and ecclesiastical vengeance; hardly has the sincere petition of thousands of the most respected of Spiritualists for the clemency of MacMahon been sent on its way to Paris, when a brother medium, gloating over his misfortune, assails his reputation, and clasps hands with the devilish persecutors of Spiritualism.

Let whoever doubts the innocence of the poor editor of the *Revue Spirite,* read the "Procès" against the Spiritists. Let him assure himself that, notwithstanding the best efforts of his detractors, and the French police, not one single accusation could be maintained against him, of either dishonesty or double dealing. Every locality of Paris where Leymarie had lived with his family was searched in vain for damaging information against him; abundant testimony in favor of his perfect integrity of character were the only responses gathered by the spies. This is what J. Mace, the commissary of Police, handed to M. Lachaud, the counsel for Leymarie, and the following words closed the testimony of that official, read publicly in the Court of Justice:

> Leymarie left only good remembrances in the Rue de Provence and the Rue Vivienne. . . . The Leymarie couple had always taken care of their old and invalid parents; their life was throughout simple and modest. . . . They have a boy and a girl, and bring up their children very decently. . . . If Leymarie was a bad business man, on the other hand he is an excellent father to his family, and his morality is above suspicion. He behaves well and works untiringly; and the sole object of his life is to rehabilitate himself.
>
> (Signed) Commissary of Police, J. MACE.

The "rehabilitation" consisted in paying off the debts he had contracted in consequence of business misfortunes culminating in his failure, some years ago.

And this poor father of a family, this most ardent apostle of Spiritual faith, who now suffers in prison for the fraudulent dealings of a knave, is coolly and publicly stigmatized by D. D. Home as "no better than Buguet"—who is condemned by every honest person as a swindler, a liar, and a tool of the persecuting party. One of the shrewdest detectives of Paris is forced to testify that "his morality is above suspicion," but a brother medium, a man who boasts of a faith purer and higher than Christianity itself, traduces him. He spits in the face of unmerited misfortune; he covers with mud a reputation left unpolluted even by the Roman Catholic persecution; and delights in kicking a man prostrated by injustice. A man felled to the ground by the powerful enemies of that very faith of which Home constitutes himself the immaculate champion!

True, we must not forget that years ago D. D. Home became a renegade to our spiritual faith; that he besought on his knees Father Ventura di Raulica, of Rome, to receive him into the *Holy* Mother Church. True again, the Prelate spurned him, saying:

I wish to have nothing to do with M. Home, he is thoroughly *demonized*. . . . Let him remain where he is, under the care of Father de Ravignan; he can be in no better hands than those of this priest. . . .*

And our great medium did remain in the hands of the Catholic Priests, until purged of his mediumship, he became a Papist himself—after having confessed *his* "guides" to be *devils*. Home repudiates this fact in his truthful memoirs† — more crowded with phenomena unauthenti-

---

*Gougenot des Mousseaux, *La magie au dix-neuvième siècle*, etc., new ed., Paris, 1864, p. 23.

†[D. D. Home, *Incidents in My Life*, Fifth edition, 1864. pp. 137-38.]

cated by witnesses, than of the other kind—he particularly insists that he could not have promised to renounce spiritual manifestations and *did not* do so. He narrates very poetically his loss of *powers*, his longing for spiritual consolation when life seemed to him "a blank," and tells us *why* he became a Roman Catholic. But I am prepared to prove that he *could not* have been baptized and received into the Latin Church without renouncing first his "spirits" as *demons*. Every Parish Priest can prove it as well.

The present is a categorical proposition, not a mere hypothetical assertion. For him less than for any other heretic, would the Church have changed her time-honored rites and ceremonies? No Spiritualist—let alone a world-famous medium like him—could be accepted into the bosom of the Holy Mother Church without *First,* renouncing Satan and all his works; *Second,* passing through the ceremony of exorcism; *Third,* spitting upon these spirits who had controlled him without possessing diplomas from the Holy See. Therefore, the only logical deduction from these facts is that Home became first a renegade to his Mother's Faith; then to Spiritualism; after that he backed out of Catholicism; and now, true to his antecedents, he becomes naturally a Judas to his brothers. Moreover, by working so evidently in the interest of the Roman Catholic Church, *he cannot* escape being identified with her champions whether open or *secret*. Others besides himself have a "wonderful memory" and have been in Rome. But fortunately we are not left solely to conjecture, to prove the falsity of his negations. In one of the ablest magazines issued by the Roman Catholic clergy we find it stated:

> The Church has declared the practice of Spiritism, evocation of spirits, consulting them, or holding communication with them—that is, necromancy—to be unlawful, and she prohibits it to all her children in the most positive manner, as may be seen in the case of the American, or rather Scotchman, Daniel Home, the most famous of modern mediums, and the most dangerous.*

Catholic World, Vol. IX, p. 290.

And this is the man who tells us that when he started out on his "glorious mission" his spirit mother hailed him with these words:

My child . . . be truthful and truth-loving. . . . Yours is a glorious mission—you will convince the infidel, cure the sick, and console the weeping.*

If the glorious mission of consoling the weeping consists in smashing the reputation of every brother medium; in backbiting a man hardly escaped from prison, like poor, young Firman; in cruelly turning the knife in the bleeding wounds of Leymarie; in safely defaming the grave of Éliphas Lévi—a dead man who cannot defend himself; in slandering and vilifying a woman, Firman's mother, who is also said to have passed away, and whom he calls a "drunken, low, vile wretch," then, verily, the mission of a spiritual medium proves itself a "glorious one"!

To those who may think that these words of mine are dictated by a personal malevolence for a man, who for these last six months has been dragging my name in all the ditches of calumny, I will answer, that if I alone was the sufferer I never would have paid the slightest attention either to his verbal or published calumnies. Not a word has been uttered by me in print, since he began throwing slurs upon me, for being called by Colonel Olcott a "wonderful medium"; a title to which I never laid the slightest claim. If people, ignorant of the psychological laws, were hallucinated enough to take me for a "wonderful medium" I am not responsible for it. I, at least, neither practised mediumship nor pretended to it. But I would ask the general question: what, supposing that I *had* been a medium, or an occultist, or a magician, or a witch, has that fact to do with either my family, my adventures, or my reputation for morality? If by destroying the character of mediums Mr. Home could wipe out their powers, I can understand that he might do some good to the cause by driving out all mediums *less pure, truthful,* and *magnanimous* than himself.

---

*Home, *op. cit.*, pp. 25-26.

But as it is, I can only see, in common with other sensible people, that his course is dictated by his obligations to a POWER hostile to *all* mediums, and approved by a petty vanity only to be appeased by the immolation of a fresh victim each day.

If it would have added to his malicious happiness he might have accused me, for what I care, of an intrigue with Anti-Christ himself, and insinuated, in[to] the bargain, that the latter "knew me to his sorrow." I would never have gone to the trouble of answering him. But, upon reading the second part of his letter published by his accommodating friend Dr. Bloede, my spirit revolted in me against such inhumanity. Any amount of wrong done by him to me, who until now, have always defended him, would have been venial, in comparison with his parricidal, fratricidal and sacrilegious attacks upon the suffering mediums, and dead as well as living persons. What is my individual reputation, my personal happiness, when compared to our great cause? This Cause of Truth, for the acceptance of which, by Science and the Christian World, I am ready to lay down my life without a moment's hesitation. Those who know me, well know I speak sincerely and say but what I feel. Because I study Occultism, or *Ancient Spiritualism,* I am thought an enemy to the cause pure and simple. Never was there a more erroneous impression. My only object is to demonstrate Spiritualism mathematically, to *force* it upon Science; and how can we expect the world to receive its grand truths, while it is left in the hands of those who, through ignorance of its philosophy based on scientific principles, do it more wrong than good by their blind fanaticism, and who stone its most ardent supporters besides?

Every day sees a reinforcement of our doctrine that mediums are controlled by spirits of more than one kind. All metaphysical Occultism aside, it rests upon strictly logical conclusions drawn from well-established syllogisms. To use an expression of Victor Hugo, God is demonstrated to us mathematically; God, therefore, is the Great Unit—the Monad, the Alpha and Omega, the Symbol of Universal Harmony which represents Divinity. According to Pythagoras, this Unit implies "Peace, Order, Justice and Harmony, and is Indivisible." Such is true Spiritualism. As soon as the Unit becomes *Two* or the *Duad,* it is the "origin of Contrast, Diversity, Inequality, Divisibility, Separation." Such Modern Spiritualism threatens to become. Two, taken by itself, is, in Occultism, the Evil Principle—a number of bad augury, characterizing Disorder, Confusion and Dissension; nevertheless, two are indispensable in Nature, but they must be maintained in equilibrium, by keeping to the geometrical straight line—symbolical of impartiality. *Daemon est Deus inversus.*

Let us now trace the imaginary line and make it the beam of a scale, in the two pans of which are placed equal units, respectively representing good and evil, light and shadow, spirit and matter, God and Devil. So long as these opposite forces act only upon their internal segments, and do not trespass upon their external ones; so long as we keep on the strict line between the two, we will be in the right path. For the Law of Compensation is strict and impartial justice, and justice means punishment of transgression, as well as the reward of welldoing. If an offence should go unpunished, it would be as unjust as for a good deed to go unrewarded. Mercy without justice would imply weakness, and to suffer even goodness to be carried to extremes without check, would suggest an idea incompatible with a mathematically demonstrated and Harmonious Deity.

If we can believe in a God at all, it is in one who is the embodiment of Harmony; and, as we see, harmony can only exist where there is a just equilibrium. Such a God the Egyptians symbolized in a cubical stone with a true and square surface at each of its sides. Theoretically, it represented good as well as evil, and thus the union of God-Spirit and God-matter was indicated in this admirably concrete Image. If either side had protruded the fraction of an inch, nay, a hair's breadth, beyond the exact square, there would be no symmetry, and the stone could not have represented Deity. So, too, if either pan of our imaginary scale goes down, the descending unit becomes Evil; and Unity, or God, is conquered by the Duad, or Devil.

Now for our conclusions: if Home had confined his abuse to myself, who claims to be neither infallible nor immaculate, but have ever furnished, on the contrary, the choicest tit-bits of scandal, to palates like his, by my manner of life, no one could complain. Even I might have conceded that this great medium had been given to act as the scourge of the Law of Compensation, and humbly accepted my punishment. But, he now includes me among a number of victims, two of whom—Leymarie and Firman—have already been victimized by human "Justice," upon the testimony of a self-confessed perjurer. Thus, by stepping into the shoes of another executioner, he makes the already unbalanced scales to kick the beam. Harmony is destroyed, but the occult theorem is demonstrated. To paraphrase in the form of a syllogism our three propositions, we may say:

Major Premise: Like attracts like; good and pure spirits are only attracted by harmony. Bad ones by discord.

Minor Premise: Mr. Home is in antagonism with his brother mediums, and moved by feelings, the reverse of good.

Conclusion: Ergo, Mr. Home's "guides" can only be *dark* spirits; or, as his Mother Church would call them—Devils.

To state it more mathematically still; Mr. Home, by his malevolence, destroys the perfect square of Harmony, and draws evil to himself. He disfigures the former into a right-angled triangle, and, thus becoming a monstrous mediumistic *hypotenuse,* subtends the right angle of dissension, and forcing it through all the mediums who come in his way, impales them unmercifully upon its sharp point.

This is what we call testing spirits and mediums by the Occult Pythagorean and the Euclidean-mathematical method!

I was accused in the *Banner,* by our sagacious Dr. Bloede, of being a secret emissary of the Jesuits; and now, this poor, deluded, but sincere Spiritualist, walks right into the snare set by the very agent and pupil of Father de Ravignan! The tree is known by its fruits. The world of Spiritualists cannot content itself until worshipping D. D. Home as the only spiritual medium, the immaculate agent of the Invisible Spirit-Land. Rumor whispers that he has lost his powers. We have his own confession in his book (*Incidents in My Life*) what mental consolation he resorts to when the loss of power leaves in his life "a blank." Who will dare say that his letters and publications do not tend towards helping the Catholic clergy in their foul, secret conspiracy against Spiritism and Spiritualism? Leymarie was sentenced against all justice, either human or divine. His sentence, and the mode of administering justice will remain for ever a stain on the French Magistrature, and just at the moment when hundreds of honest hearts beat in expectation of the poor man's pardon—just when Firman, escaping from the clutches of a prejudiced law, tries his best to rehabilitate himself, there comes a denunciation from an *authority* on mediumship. A book which the Catholic organ significantly calls "the most dangerous," exposing *dark séance*-ism, *rope-tying*-ism, and every *ism* except *Home*-ism, is suspended over our doomed heads, like the sword of Damocles. The moment for its appearance is calculated with a wonderful precision. It comes just in time after the trial of the French Spiritists. It will force thousands to shrink from investigating that which is proved to be 80 per cent a fraud by Mr. Home himself, and thousands of others to break off every connection with such a "low, shameful *ism*." Finally, if we may judge the future from the past and present, this book will be the cruelest blow at the character of the poor mediums that they have ever been called to suffer from.

Would to God that D. D. Home, the immaculate medium, purified as he is now by the Catholic baptism, would fill up his book with all the disreputable rumors, either truthful or lying, about myself alone, that he can collect. It is my fervent prayer that he would cast his venomous slime solely upon my selected person; for, verily, I have a broad back, and can stand any amount of abuse from such world-famous scandal-mongers as he is known to be. But if he is yet worthy the name of a human being; if all charity and compassion has not died out of that heart which seems to be in full possession of the wickedest fiends; if he does not wish to disgust the world with Spiritualism, then— let him abstain from slandering his brother mediums. For, I prophesy that the forthcoming book, to use the words of one of the most respected correspondents of spiritual papers, will prove an "ASSASSINATION," not a warfare.*

H. P. BLAVATSKY.

[In H.P.B.'s *Scrapbook*, Vol. 1, p. 124, there is a cutting from the Boston *Sunday Herald* of March, 1876. It is a letter from Dr. G. Bloede to the Editor of the paper. Under the subtitle of "Home's Doubts of the Mediumship of Mme. Blavatsky," the writer quotes from Col. Olcott's *People from the Other World* in which he speaks of H.P.B. as "one of the most remarkable mediums in the world," but adds that "at the same time her mediumship is totally different from that of any person I ever met, for, instead of being controlled by spirits to do their will, it is she who seems to control them to do her bidding." Dr. Bloede comments on this by saying: "If we find that Mr. Home's opinion of that eminent foreigner essentially differs from that of Col. Olcott, in regard to her supposed mediumship as well as otherwise, we must not disregard the fact that he knew her as early as 1858." To this H.P.B. appended the following remarks in pen and ink:]

Home doubting *my* mediumship proved that he is a genuine and even a reliable medium. H. P. Blavatsky was NEVER a medium except, perhaps, in her earliest youth.

[The next paragraph of the same article deals with the burying of Russian dignitaries (in this case H.P.B.'s father) with their decorations, Dr. Bloede quoting Col. Olcott again on this subject. He also quotes D. D. Home who provides the testimony that no such custom exists in Russia. The decorations are carried as far as the tomb, and are later returned to the Government. At this point, H.P.B. added the following in pen and ink:]

And who ever thought or said they were! It is *not* a decoration but a *buckle,* you Spiritualistic fool. It ought to

---

*[Consult the Bio-Bibliographical Index, s. v. HOME, for further data about this medium.—*Compiler.*]

be remembered also, that Mr. D. D. Home who was twice tried for swindling (Mrs. Lyon once) never—knew or even *saw* me in his whole life, but, has certainly gathered most carefully the dirtiest gossip possible about Nathalie *Blavatsky*. Home is a liar and poor Dr. Bloede was turned into a *cat* by this mediumistic *monkey* to draw the chestnuts for him out of the fire, as the *Sp. Scientist* says.

[In connection with another cutting on the subject of D. D. Home and his relation to Spiritualism, H.P.B. makes the following brief remark in her *Scrapbook*:]

and Mr. Home is an irresponsible medium.

THE RUSSIAN INVESTIGATION

ANOTHER DISGRACE FOR SCIENCE.—THE ST. PETERSBURG PROFESSORS IMITATE THOSE OF HARVARD AND LONDON. — A. N. AKSAKOFF'S NOBLE PROTEST.

[*Spiritual Scientist*, Boston, Vol. IV, April 27, 1876, pp. 85-7]

To the Editor of the *Spiritual Scientist*:

Dear Sir,—In advices just received from St. Petersburg, I am requested to translate and forward to the *Scientist* for publication, the protest of the Honorable Alexander Aksakoff, Imperial Counsellor of State, against the course of the professors of the university respecting the spiritualistic investigation. The document appears, in Russian, in the *Vedomosty*, the official journal of St. Petersburg. This generous, high-minded, courageous gentleman has done the possible, and even the impossible, in order to open the spiritual eyes of those incurable moles who fear the daylight of truth as the burglar fears the policeman's "bull's eye."

The heartfelt thanks and gratitude of every Spiritualist ought to be forwarded to this noble defender of the cause, who regretted neither his time, trouble nor money to help the propagation of the truth.

H. P. BLAVATSKY.

New York, April 19th, 1876.

TO THE COMMISSION APPOINTED BY THE SOCIETY OF PHYSICAL SCIENCES OF THE ST. PETERSBURG UNIVERSITY, FOR THE INVESTIGATION OF MEDIUMISTIC MANIFESTATIONS.

According to my promise to the Commission to help them in extending their invitations to mediums, I have neglected no effort to the accomplishment of the said purpose. Nevertheless but few mediums have shown any desire to come to Russia, and those who did were unsuitable for a preliminary examination, as their mediumistical powers were not of a nature to afford any chance to investigate physical phenomena. Finally, and for reasons previously detailed to the commission, I concluded to bring with me from England the two Petty boys. The mediumistic powers of these boys proved too weak, not only for them to be tested by a committee but even at private *séances* in my own house. Having obtained no manifestations worthy of any attention at all—as already published by me—at the committee's investigation, after four *séances* I declined to waste any more of its time in investigating the Petty boys.

Immediately after that, on the 15th of December last, Professor Mendeleyeff delivered his lecture on Spiritism. The haste exhibited by him on this occasion, the precipitancy with which the failures of the four *séances* were reviewed, when the Scientific Commission had just adopted a resolution to make not less than *forty* experimental examinations, did not agree, in my opinion, with the impartial and serious character which we have the right to expect in a truly scientific investigation. This lecture did not appear in print, and it was therefore impossible to either reply to its *errors* or to point out its one-sidedness. But in what was declared by Mr. Mendeleyeff, the attitude of the commission toward the object of their examination was very clearly defined. Prof. Mendeleyeff—at whose suggestion the commission was organized, and under whose direction it acted—openly avowed himself an enemy of Spiritualism. The commission, acting in unity with Mr. Mendeleyeff, was evidently anxious that the results of its further investigations should prove as fruitless as the results of the first four *séances* with the Petty boys. The difficulties in the way of obtaining an impartial examination multiplied tenfold; and for my part I felt fully that it would be useless for me to attempt any further assistance to the commission. But as I had already taken steps to invite here other mediums, and had succeeded in inducing a lady to come—who is possessed of remarkable mediumistic powers, and perfectly answers the requirements of the commission's investigation—I decided upon proceeding further. I hoped that I might be mistaken as to the predispositions of the commission. Furthermore, I desired to ascertain how it would conduct its investigations when it had to do with a true medium in the full acceptation of this word, and one moreover who was not professional. This lady was totally independent as to her social and financial position, and had consented to take part in such an unpopular position merely for the sake of promoting the scientific object ostensibly in view.

I had the honor of introducing this medium to the commission in the person of Mrs. C. From the very beginning of the *séances*, the physical manifestations which characterize this lady's mediumship—namely, loud raps, movements and levitations of the table—occurred with great strength. Of the experimental *séances*, we had in this second series of four—on the 11th, 25th, 27th and 29th of January. The *séance* at which the medium, by reason of sickness, could not attend was, although the commission had been notified twenty-four hours beforehand, counted by its members as one of the forty which it had bound itself to hold.

During the experiments of this second member series, we learned the following:

1. The commission failed to act up to its resolution of May the 9th, 1875, that immediately after each *séance* a report should be written out and signed by the witnesses on both sides. Instead of that, the reports were filed several days later, and not in the presence of witnesses, but were presented to them for signature when already prepared by the commission, and when they could not be altered in any particular.

2. The plan itself of these reports underwent a thorough change. The commission saw fit to accept the private testimony of persons not belonging to the commission, but who may be said to have been present at the *séances*, since they had been eavesdropping and peeping through the keyholes. Such uncalled-for and personal testimony, based on subjective impressions, either amounts to nothing at a scientific investigation and therefore is inadmissible, or if the contrary, then the commission itself was useless, for it was organized, we must suppose, for the very reason of replacing such personal and subjective evidence with unanimous and impersonal experiment.

3. Having found room for personal evidence of its own choosing, the commission nevertheless rejected my offer to select a lady of their acquaintance for the purpose of examining the feet of the lady medium, under the pretext that *personal* testimony was not convincing.

4. The reports of the experimental commission were drawn carelessly and inaccurately. It is impossible to gather any definite idea in these reports either of the manifestations which took place or of the condition under which they occurred. Some of the narrative does not coincide with what happened, while some manifestations that transpired are not even mentioned. All this is demonstrated in the individual reports made by myself and other witnesses.

5. As to the reports for publication, the commission resolved neither to allow them to be carried to the private domiciles of the

witnesses for signature, nor to furnish copies, nor to allow such to be taken by the witnesses who were present. Such an order of procedure compelled the witnesses who were appointed to watch the interests of the medium, to present their own private reports, and was as strange as it was embarrassing.

In view of such a state of affairs, in my report of February the 5th, I had the honor to explain to the commission that before we could proceed with the experiments at all, the witnesses for the medium must be permitted to acquaint themselves previously with the general reports, which had not been as yet presented to us for signature, as well as with the private reports of the outside members of the commission.

After that, on the 13th of February, I read in the rooms of the Physical Society the protocol (or report) of the third *séance* of January the 27th. As to the report of the fourth *séance*, I learned that it was not yet even filled up. Concerning the private reports, Mr. Mendeleyeff informed me that the committee had neither assigned any particular time nor order for their presentation. Thus, it remained for us witnesses to advance without knowing what lay in wait for us. At the same time the little of which we had assured ourselves was of a nature to make it very difficult for us to proceed. Of all the reports which had appeared, the most prominent were two extended ones by Mr. Mendeleyeff. They embodied a long series of undemonstrated affirmations which tended to convey to every reader the impression that all the manifestations mentioned in the reports were simply tricks consciously performed by the hands and feet of the medium. And in the report of Mr. Bobileff, who, as well as Mr. Mendeleyeff, attended but two *séances*, we see indicated a *full conviction* of the spuriousness of the phenomena, and that the medium produced them *herself* at will by muscular contraction. Moreover, the observations upon which both of these gentlemen try to base their conclusions as to what took place at the *séances* were not communicated by them to the other witnesses present, thus making it impossible for them to either verify or correct that which was suspicious. I am quite ready to admit that what took place was very far from being surrounded with such conditions as to warrant the commission after only *four séances* to come to a final conclusion favorable to the genuineness of mediumistic phenomena. If, after the forty *séances* agreed upon, an unfavorable report had been made upon the basis that the experiments had been unsatisfactory, then the decision might have been respected by every one. But in view of the methods to which the commission has now stooped, all further investigation, at least with the present medium, is impossible. I have no right to leave Mrs. C. in ignorance of what people write about her, and these writings consist of dishonorable attempts to prove that she is an impostor. Under the circumstances I do not feel myself warranted in any longer subjecting a private person, and especially a lady, to such uncalled-for accusations, which to anyone who feels himself to be innocent of intended fraud are highly insulting.

Thus, this series of investigations, with an undoubtedly good medium, has shown me very clearly, that the conclusion to which I arrived after hearing Mr. Mendeleyeff's lecture as to the *preconceived intentions* of our commission was correct.

But, apart from the above reason, there are two more which preclude the possibility of my having anything more to do with the Scientific Commission.

So far back as on the 10th of November last, I reported to the committee that the term fixed by them—namely, May 1876—was too short to enable us to bring mediums to St. Petersburg; and therefore begged to be informed whether I ought to continue corresponding with foreign mediums who might consent to come here after this term. In consequence of this, the committee discussed the matter in my presence, and decided to change the term of investigation into a definite number of *séances*. I was then notified that the commission had decided upon having not less than forty *séances, excluding* the months of vacations. Professor Butleroff then left with me the commission, both of us believing that there had been established a clear understanding between the members and ourselves that these forty *séances* were exclusive of the May term.

Under this impression I proceeded with my arrangements with mediums, and succeeded in engaging the services of one of the greatest and most famous American mediums, Dr. H. Slade, who agreed to reach here towards the fall.

To my amazement I learned that on the 15th of January the commission had met again, to discuss the subject of the term, and had decided that the forty *séances* must be confined to the month of May, 1876.

Upon what grounds the committee came to such a conclusion, clearly contrary to the interest of the investigation itself, is more than I can tell; but the fact is that we have no mediums in readiness for them. Mrs. C. only promised to remain until the 1st of March. Moreover, neither myself nor anyone else could have guaranteed to the commission for May, the forty *séances* to which they had consented to sacrifice themselves.

The second reason is, that after the *séance* with Mrs. C., the commission, at the meeting of January the 15th, had resolved that "with a view to save time with mediums, they would experiment only with apparatus prepared by themselves." And after *séance* No. 3, the commission categorically demanded that they should immediately proceed to crucial tests, with the appliance of their own various apparatuses. Such a resolution and demand on their part upset everything. Every investigation in the domain of Nature must be divided into two definite periods: the *preliminary* period of the *authentication* of every manifestation by means of observation, and the final period of investigation. It is an easy matter to note a fact; it is very difficult to investigate and verify it. Thousands of people testify that the mediumistic phenomena exist; it is the duty of the commission, if they once undertook such a social question, to stoop to the level of the crowd, and first see that which the crowd sees, and in the same manner as it sees it; and only when familiar with the superficial aspect of the question to apply the apparatus which the case seems to suggest. No one prevented the committee—even had they followed the method of the crowd—from arriving at an unfavorable conclusion. But the demand—after holding but three *séances*, and when the manifestations had hardly begun—for crucial tests with apparatuses, when the members of the commission themselves could not be aware what set of complete apparatus might be required—was something which it was impossible not to regard as diametrically opposed to the idea of a regular course of determined experiments.

In the present most deplorable state of affairs, a negative result of the investigation, obtained through the apparatus furnished by the commission, would not stand as a proof of the uselessness of the said apparatus itself, but be taken as a demonstration of the non-existence of the mediumistic force. Therefore, every step which might be conceded by those who defend the reality of the mediumistic manifestations would only compromise our affair.

It is unwarranted on the part of Professor Mendeleyeff to reproach us, witnesses, that "in our writings we lay a great stress on the value of scientific experiments, and when they are offered to us, we obstinately refuse them and demand an adherence to the valueless testimony of the *school of the crowd*." To clear away, once for all, every misunderstanding, I deem it a duty to say that we do not in the least reject the *scientific*, that is, experimental and instrumental methods of investigation for the manifestations. We only assert that such a method is liable to bring to no great result until after a sufficient acquaintance with the phenomena, by way of ordinary observation. I am fully authorized to believe, that if the committee had continued their ordinary *séances* with Mrs. C., accepting such conditions as are generally adopted by the "crowd" for the prevention of fraud, the several kinds of phenomena, such as raps, movements and levitation of the table, might have been displayed to such a satisfactory degree as to force the commission to see in them "manifestations worthy of investigation." The happiest issue of the promised forty *séances* could not have been greater than this; but this alone might have forced the commission to undertake further experiments.

In consideration of all the foregoing facts, any further interference on my part becomes, as I have said, impossible. But as it is more than evident that the investigation undertaken by the commission did not primarily depend on my personal help, therefore I may be left to hope that it will find means to select the help of other persons in order to bring their experiments to a fuller and more satisfactory result. My personal trouble I certainly do not regret, for I considered it my duty to comply with the invitation of the Society of Physical Sciences. So far as I could, and my knowledge went, I have fulfilled my promise; and at the same time a very important object—at least for myself—has been obtained: *the attitude of our commission towards the subject, and the object of their investigation has been made clear.*

In conclusion I beg leave to add that so long as the commission hold to the policy of flatly denying the phenomena, and see in them only charlatanry, they will neither attain to the object of their researches which was sketched in the first offer made by Mr. Mendeleyeff, nor will they satisfy those who certify to the existence of such manifestations. The committee forgets that the mediumistic power has its origin, force and support in domestic circles and in their own experiments against which the policy of negation and fraud is powerless. Such questions which have attained a social importance, cannot be solved by negation and an ignorance of them. Let Science and knowledge be on the side of the negators and skeptics, but upon the other side we have the conviction in the reality of facts; which conviction we have obtained by *the evidence of our senses and by reason.*

A. AKSAKOFF.

St. Petersburg, March 4th, 1876.

Translated and prepared with the notes and explanations, for the *Spiritual Scientist,* by "BUDDHA."

"PSYCHOPHOBIA" IN RUSSIA

[*Banner of Light,* Boston, Vol. XXXIX, No. 5, April 29, 1876, p. 8]

To the Editor of the *Banner of Light:*

Dear Sir,—I have received from St. Petersburg the protests of Professor Butleroff and the Honorable Alexander Aksakoff, with a request from the latter gentleman that I will translate for our spiritual papers their just criticisms upon the action of the University Commission for the investigation of spiritual phenomena. I forward you the Butleroff paper.

The Commission has acted so unfairly at the preliminary *séances,* that these two gentlemen have declined to have anything more to do with it. Dr. Slade was about to sail for Europe under a contract to place himself at the disposal of the Commission (God help him!) but by the last mail instructions have been received by us to terminate this contract and make a new one. Dr. Slade having consented to the terms, will visit St. Petersburg, but will *not* have anything to do with the Commission.

I deeply regret that Russian men of science should have shown themselves as narrow-minded and unfair as the Willis persecutors of 1857, and the lofty souls of the Royal Society, who declined the invitation of the Dialectical Society.

The documents appear in Russian, in the official journals of St. Petersburg. The evidence seems to show that the epidemic which, for the lack of another name, I propose to call PSYCHOPHOBIA, has attacked the scientists of my country as soon as the investigation of phenomenal Spiritualism and mediumism threatened to turn successful.

Respectfully yours,

H. P. BLAVATSKY.

New York, April 21*st,* 1876.

[This article is followed by H.P.B.'s translation of Prof. Butleroff's Paper addressed to the Commission appointed by the Society of Physical Sciences of the St. Petersburg University for the investigation of the spiritual phenomena. At one point, H.P.B. appended the following outspoken footnote:]

If I did not have it from Mr. Aksakoff himself, I would have been disposed to indignantly deny the charge that Russian scientists could stoop to the dirty methods of the police-spy. They had so little confidence, it appears, in their own experience and their ingenious apparatus, that they posted persons not officially connected with the Commission to peep through cracks and key holes!

MEDIUMS, BEWARE!

[*Banner of Light*, Boston, Vol. XXXIX, No. 7, May 13, 1876, p. 8]

To the Editor of the *Banner of Light:*

Dear Sir,—I take the earliest opportunity to warn mediums generally—but particularly American mediums—that a plot against the cause has been hatched in St. Petersburg. The particulars have just been received by me from one of my foreign correspondents, and may be relied upon as authentic.

It is now commonly known that Professor Wagner, the geologist, has boldly come out as a champion for mediumistic phenomena. Since he witnessed the wonderful manifestations of Brédif, the French medium, he has issued several pamphlets, reviewed at great length Colonel Olcott's *People from the Other World,* and excited and defied the anger of all the Scientific Psychophobists of the Imperial University. Fancy a herd of mad bulls rushing at the *red* flag of a *picador,* and you will have some idea of the effect of Wagner's Olcott pamphlet upon his colleagues!

Chief among them is the Chairman of the Scientific Commission which has just exploded with a report of what they did *not* see, at *séances never* held! Goaded to fury by the defense of Spiritualism, which they had intended to quietly butcher, this individual suddenly took the determination to come to America, and is now probably on his way. Like a Samson of science, he expects to tie our foxes of mediums together by the tails, set fire to them and turn them into the corn of those Philistines, Wagner and Butleroff.

Let me give mediums a bit of friendly caution. If this Russian Professor should turn up at a *séance,* keep a sharp eye upon him, and let everyone do the same; give him no private *séances* at which there is not present at least one truthful and impartial Spiritualist. Some scientists are not to be trusted. My correspondent writes that the Professor "goes to America to create a great scandal, burst up Spiritualism and turn the laugh on Prof. Wagner, Messrs. Aksakoff and Butleroff." The plot is very ingeniously contrived: he is coming here under the pretext of the Centennial, and will attract as little attention as possible among the mediums.

But, Mr. Editor, what if he should meet the fate of Hare and become a Spiritualist! What a wailing would there not be in the Society of Physical Sciences! I shudder at the mortification which should await my poor countrymen.

But another distinguished Russian scientist is also coming, for whom I bespeak a very different reception. Professor Kittara, the greatest technologist of Russia, and a member of the Emperor's Privy Council, is *really* sent by the government to the Centennial. He is deeply interested in Spiritualism, very anxious to investigate it, and will bring the proper credentials from Mr. Aksakoff. The latter gentleman writes me that every civility and attention will be shown Professor Kittara, as his report, if favorable, will have a tremendous influence upon public opinion.

The unfairness of the University Commission has, it seems, produced a reaction. I translate the following from a paper which Mr. Aksakoff has sent me:

From the St. Petersburg "Birzheviya Vedomosty"

We hear that the Commission for the investigation of mediumism, which was formed by the Society of Physical Sciences attached to the University, is preparing to issue a report of its *labors* [?!]. It will appear as an appendix to the monthly periodical of the Chemical and Physical Societies. Meanwhile, another Commission is being formed, but this time its members will not be supplied from the "Physical Science Society," but from the Medical Society. Nevertheless, several members of the former will be invited to join, as well as the friends of mediumism, and others who would be able to offer important suggestions *pro* or *con*. We hear that the formation of this new Commission is warmly advocated, its necessity having been shown in the breach of faith by the "Physical Science Society," its failure to hold the promised forty *séances*, its premature adoption of unfair conclusions, and the strong prejudices of the members.

Let us hope that this new organization may prove more honorable than its predecessor (peace to its ashes!).

H. P. Blavatsky.

[In H.P.B.'s *Scrapbook*, Vol. I, pp. 143-154, there are a number of cuttings from various papers in connection with the burial of Baron de Palm which took place May 28, 1876. This ceremony and the subsequent cremation of the body are fully described by Col. Olcott in his *Old Diary Leaves*, Vol. I, pp. 147-184.

There is in the *Scrapbook*, Vol I, p. 154, a much faded photograph of the Baron; on both sides of the picture, H.P.B. wrote in pen and ink as follows:]

Baron
Henry
de Palm
"Principally
famous as
a corpse"
Buried May
28, 1876

Joseph
Louis
Member
and Fellow
of the
Theos. Society
Cremated
December 6,
76

[In connection with an exaggerated newspaper account of the Baron's alleged estate, H.P.B. marked certain passages in blue pencil and wrote:]

The *Society* paid for the funeral.

[In her *Scrapbook*, Vol. I, pp. 155-56, H.P.B. pasted a cutting from the *Newark Daily Journal* of June 2, 1876. The Editor calls the special attention of the readers to an exposition of Spiritualism by Frederic Thomas of the Theosophical Society of New York. He says that "it will be found full of interest," to which H.P.B. added in pen and ink:]

and of prejudiced statements, unverified hypotheses and deliberate *lies*. Mr. Fred Thomas, once a member of the Theosophical Society, was made to resign after this article. Sergeant Cox of London to whom he sent it, treated its author with the utmost contempt.

THE RUSSIAN SCIENTISTS

EXCITEMENT IN ST. PETERSBURG.—A PROTEST BY THE HIGHEST NOBILITY OF THE EMPIRE.—THE SEVEREST REBUKE A SCIENTIFIC BODY EVER HAD.

[*Banner of Light*, Boston, Vol. XXXIX, June 24, 1876, p. 8]

Special Correspondence of the *Banner of Light*.

NEW YORK, *June* 15*th,* 1876.

Dear Sir,—By the last Russian mail I received the highly important document which I enclose. It is the sharpest rebuke that a scientific body ever had within my remembrance. The Commission for the investigation of the spiritual phenomena was composed of our most eminent scientists, and when they agreed to devote forty *séances* to the investigation of what they term "mediumistic manifestations," every one expected them to make good their promise. The country was as sure that the bottom of the thing would be reached as they would have been if Wagner had undertaken to report on zoology, Butleroff on chemistry, Mendeleyeff himself on physics. But when, after four miserable sittings, Mendeleyeff prostituted his great reputation to pander to ignorant prejudice, the whole influential class of the Empire rose in indignation. The best papers in the country—which had not a shade of sympathy with or knowledge of Spiritualism—agreed as to the insufficiency of his arguments and the injustice of his conclusions upon the facts stated. One of them declares that Mohammed did not have half as good a basis for Mohammedanism as the Spiritists for Spiritualism, and that the matter *must be* investigated thoroughly and impartially. A universal laugh was raised at the Commission's assertion that all the mediumistic phenomena can be explained by mechanical contrivances hid beneath the medium's petticoats!

The names attached to this protest represent the best blood of Russia. It is the most influentially signed document, probably, that ever appeared in an official journal of my country. It represents a large part of our wealth, intellect and family influence. Some of the names will be recognized by your readers as historical, and as having shed lustre upon the Russian name the wide world over. Its effect upon the scientists, as I learn from private letters, has been amusing and wholesome. Mendeleyeff has been forced into a corner, like a fugitive rat, and is now preparing his defense in the shape of a book, we are told! Professor Wagner's favorable review of Colonel Olcott's *People from the Other World* has contributed largely toward creating the excitement in the ranks of our enemies.

The Russians are waiting eagerly to see Dr. Slade's phenomena. A contract has been signed today, which binds him to report in St. Petersburg on the 1st of November next, and remain there three months. The Theosophical Society, as you are aware, has made a very careful and patient investigation. Two out of three *skeptics* on the Committee were converted beyond backsliding, and the manifestations were found *genuine*. A copy of the official report was duly forwarded to St. Petersburg, as a sedative for the Russian psychophobists.

H. P. BLAVATSKY.

The following document was sent to the office of the St. Petersburg *Vedomosty,* accompanied by this letter:

Mr. Editor,—On the 25th of March last, the Scientific Commission organized for the investigation of the mediumistic phenomena published its report; and a month later, namely, on the 24th and 25th of April, Professor Mendeleyeff delivered two lectures about Spiritualism. In the absence of popular appreciation of the Commission, Mr. Mendeleyeff undertook the trouble of himself pronouncing a panegyric upon its activity! At his last lecture, he expressed the idea that in the reports of the Commission, Truth asserted itself with resistless force, and society, suddenly dazzled by its light, involuntarily bowed its head before the verdict of science. The following protest, signed by over one hundred and thirty persons, testifies to the fact that in our society, notwithstanding the opinion of Mr. Mendeleyeff, there *are* persons who can distinguish a difference between Science and his Commission.

The insufficiency of the verbal reports of the latter has become evident even to our public papers. What follows is a new evidence of this fact.

In its April number, the *Otechestveniya Zapisky*, with a bearing of quite an Olympic pride toward Spiritism (very amusing, by the way), confesses, nevertheless, that the Commission of the Physical Society, which had undertaken to expose and crush out of existence spiritual phenomena, did not at all attain its object. According to a very just remark of the said Review, the Commission vainly endeavors to conceal its true character of a police-detective agency, and surrounds itself with a scientific lustre. Its evident object was to condemn "a heresy," and not to make a scientific investigation: *that* it plainly never had in view. Therefore, the *Otechestveniya Zapisky* calls the members of the Commission "the modern fathers of orthodox science," who, zealous for the welfare of true science, determined to convene an Ecumenical Council of orthodox scientists, to sit in judgment on the "heretical doctrine," with the full assurance that no one will dare to dispute the infallibility of its predetermined and oral verdict.

We believe that the above opinion, which issues from the very stronghold of the avowed enemies of Spiritism, reflects in a manner which cannot be improved, the general opinion respecting the pretended "investigations" of the Commission.

V. MARKOFF.

PROTEST AGAINST THE CONCLUSIONS OF THE COMMISSION FOR INVESTIGATING MEDIUMISM.

The learned Commission organized for the examination of mediumistic phenomena, had for its object—if we may credit the assertion of Mr. Mendeleyeff which appeared in the *Golos* (No. 137, 1875)—to carefully investigate "these manifestations," and thereby "render a great and universal public service."

From the public lecture of Mr. Mendeleyeff we learned that the principal object of the Commission's labour was to be the following mediumistic phenomena: Movements of inanimate objects, with and *without* contact of hands; levitation of various objects; the alteration of their weight; movements of objects and percussive sounds therein, indicating an *intelligent* producing cause, by conversations or responses—a phenomenon which the Commission termed *dialogistic;* writing produced by inanimate objects, or *psychographical* phenomena; and finally, the formation and apparition of detached members of the human frame, and of full forms, named by the Commission *mediumo-plastic phenomena*. To the investigation of these manifestations the Commission pledged itself to devote *not less* than *forty séances*.

It now announces in its Report of March 21st (*Golos*, No. 85, 1876) that it has finished its labors, that "its object is attained," and that its unanimous verdict is that "mediumistic phenomena are produced either by unconscious movements or *conscious fraud,*" and that the "Spiritist doctrine is nothing but superstition."

This verdict of the Commission is based, according to its own declaration, upon *eight séances,* at the first four of which there were no mediumistic phenomena at all, and at the last four, the Commission only saw a few movements of the table and heard a few raps! But where are the promised experiments of the Commission with movements of objects without contact, the alteration of weight of bodies, the *dialogistic, psychographic and mediumo-plastic* wonders? Of the limited programme of investigation which the Commission prescribed for itself, it appears that it did not carry out even the fourth part. But on the other hand, without the slightest warrant, it busied itself with the doctrine of Spiritism, which did not enter in its programme at all.

Therefore, we, the undersigned, deem it our duty to declare that by such a superficial and hasty treatment of the grave subject under investigation, the Commission has by no means solved the problem which it undertook to demonstrate. It evidently did not gather data enough to warrant it in either accepting or rejecting the occurrence of mediumistic phenomena.

Having confined itself to but eight *séances,* the Commission had no reasonable warrant to declare its labors finished; still less had it the right, after only eight *séances,* to pronounce an authoritative opinion either *pro* or *con.* Having undertaken this investigation in the interest of a certain portion of society, the Commission has not satisfied this interest; it has left society in its former state of uncertainty as to phenomena whose reality has been vouched by so many witnesses worthy of credit and the highest esteem.

Therefore, we, the undersigned, feel compelled to express a hope, that this investigation of spiritual phenomena promised in the name of science may be pushed to its legitimate conclusion, in a manner commensurate with the dignity and exactness of true science, if not by the same persons who have already pronounced their verdict, even as to things that they *did not* see, then by others who are prepared to make a more patient and careful investigation. Only such an one can render "a great and universal public service."

V. S. AVDAKOFF
PRINCE BAGRATION
N. BAHMETYEFF
J. BALASHOFF
A. BARDSKY
A. BARIKOVA
B. BARTENEVA
P. N. BASHMAKOVA
L. BONVEY

M. BORISSOVA
D. BUNYAKOVSKAYA
E. CHELISHCHEFF
M. CHELISHCHEFF
N. CHUYKO
VLADIMIR CHUYKO
J. DANILOFF
L. DANILOFF
Z. DUROVA

N. Djoga
E. Evreinova
M. P. Gedeonoff
M. Genzo
Princess Golitzina-
  Prozorofskaya
U. Gran
N. Gredyakin
M. Gredyakova
D. Grigorovich
G. Ignatyeff
E. Ivanoff
Baron A. Jomini
F. Kalinina
F. Kalinoff
V. Kishkin
S. Kislinsky
F. Klimoff
Count Komarovsky
Count A. Komarovsky
E. Konstantin
V. Kressenko
V. Krusey
Prince A. Kurakin
Prince B. Kurakin
Prince M. Kurtzevich
E. Lansserey
J. Lapshin
E. Lavrova
N. Leskoff
F. Levshin
N. Lvoff
N. S. Makarevskaya
A. Makarevsky
E. Malohovetz
F. Malohovetz
S. Manuhin
P. Marchenko
V. Markoff
N. Matveyeff
P. May
Baron N. Meyendorff
G. Meyer
A. Miller
P. P. Miller
A. A. Moiseyeff
G. Montandre

S. N. Moskaleff
V. Nicksenstein
A. Ober
Princess N. Obolenskaya
Prince O. Obolensky
P. Orloff
Prince Paskevich
Princess Paskevich
T. Passek
P. Pelshoff
J. K. Peltzer
F. F. Pritvitz
K. F. Pritvitz
E. A. Pirogoff
A. B. Polovtzeff
A. U. Polubinsky
J. B. Prejentzoff
V. Pribitkoff
E. Pribitkova
W. Pribitkova
V. Rossolovky
J. Rumin
V. I. Safonoff
J. O. Schmidt
K. A. Semenoff
A. W. Semenova
A. Serebryakoff
Prince A. Shahovskoy
V. Shchago
A. Shchenovky
N. Shcherbacheff
Prince A. Shcherbatoff
N. Skorodumoff
E. Skropotova
U. Smolensky
A. P. Soloton
A. Starojevsky
A. Stepanoff
E. Stoletoff
Count Grégoire S. Stroganoff
Countess Mary Stroganoff
Prince Suvoroff
Prince K. Suvoroff
Count Tatishcheff
E. Teminskaya
A. Tokmacheff
Countess A. Tolstaya

F. Toman
S. Torneus
Prince A. Troubetzkoy
A. Tutkovsky
L. Unger
Prince Uroussoff
Princess A. Vassilchikova
E. Vlassova
Princess Vorontzova
P. Weimarn
K. Witt
Prince E. Wittgenstein
E. Zagrafo
A. Zinovieff
D. Zinovieff
A. Zinovieva

[The *Spiritual Scientist* published "A Letter from D. D. Home" in its issue of July 6, 1876. The letter was written in self-defence against an anonymous "Comte" who attacked Home because he insulted a lady. In the first paragraph of this letter, Home writes as follows:

"I have ever striven to be an honest man, and *I never condescended to write an anonymous letter,* or to make charges sotto voce against anyone. What I say I can prove:* I sign my name. Sign yours!"

H.P.B. pasted the cutting in her *Scrapbook*, Vol. I, pp. 164-65, underlined as shown above, added an asterisk, and wrote in pen and ink the following remarks:]

Except in the case of anonymous and infamous letters sent to a poor lady at Geneva, traced to him (D. D. Home) and for which an English officer, a friend of Prince Wittgenstein went to flog him. His behaviour was so cowardly that the officer left in disgust, "without even whipping him a little" adds the Prince who wrote the facts to Col. Olcott.

[In H.P.B.'s *Scrapbook*, Vol. I, p. 185, there is a cutting which gives an account most likely from the *Boston Herald* of October, 1876, of various "materializations" produced by Mrs. Bennett, a medium, and of how she was finally exposed as a trickster. To this H.P.B. added the following in pen and ink:]

This is the same Mrs. Bennett whose mediumship was so strongly believed in by Epes Sargent. He wrote me a letter and sent a picture made in the dark by this cheat of the departed daughter of one of his friends. The picture was unanimously *recognized*. "The best test that was ever given" wrote poor Epes Sargent to his correspondents.

(NEW) YORK AGAINST LANKESTER
A NEW WAR OF THE ROSES — DEGENERATION OF SPECIES —
A THEOSOPHIST COMES TO THE DEFENSE OF A MEDIUM.

[*Banner of Light*, Boston, Vol. XL, No. 3, October 14, 1876]

To the Editor of the *Banner of Light:*

Sir,—Despite the constant recurrence of new discoveries by modern men of science, an exaggerated respect for authority and an established routine among the educated class retards the progress of *true* knowledge. Facts, which, if observed, tested, classified and appreciated would be of inestimable importance to science, are summarily cast into the despised limbo of supernaturalism. To these conservatives the experience of the past serves neither as an example nor a warning. The overturning of a thousand cherished theories finds our modern philosopher as unprepared for each new scientific revelation as though his predecessors had been infallible from time immemorial.

The protoplasmist should at least, in modesty, remember that his past is one vast cemetery of dead theories; a desolate Potter's Field wherein exploded hypotheses lie in ignoble oblivion like so many executed malefactors, whose names cannot be pronounced by the next of kin without a blush.

The nineteenth century is essentially the age of demolition. True, science takes just pride in many revolutionary discoveries, and claims to have immortalized the epoch by forcing from Dame Nature some of her most important secrets. But for every inch she illumines of the narrow and circular path within whose limits she has hitherto trodden, what boundless stretches have been left behind unexplored? Worst is that science has not simply withheld her light from these regions that seem dark (but are not), but her votaries try their best to quench the light of other people under the pretext that they are not authorities, and their friendly beacons are but "will-o'-the-wisps." Prejudice and preconceived ideas have entered the public brain, and, cancer-like, are eating it to the core. Spiritualism—or, if some for whom the word has become so unpopular prefer it, the universe of spirit—is left to fight out its battle with the world of matter, and the crisis is at hand.

Half-thinkers, and aping, would-be philosophers, in short, that class which is unable to penetrate events any deeper than their crust, and which measures every day's occurrence by its present aspect, unmindful of the past and careless of the future, heartily rejoice over the latest rebuff given to phenomenalism in the Lankester-Donkin offensive and defensive alliance, and the pretended exposure of Slade. In this hour of would-be *Lancastrian* triumph, a change should be made in English heraldic crests. The Lancasters were always given to creating dissensions and provoking strife among peaceable folk. From ancient York the War of Roses is now transferred to Middlesex; and Lankester (whose name is a corruption) instead of uniting himself with the hereditary foe, has joined his idols with those of Donkin (whose name is evidently also a corruption). As the hero of the hour is not a knight, but a zoologist, deeply versed in the science to which he devotes his talents, why not compliment his ally by quartering the red rose of Lancaster with the downy thistle so delicately appreciated by a certain prophetic quadruped who seeks for it by the wayside? Really, Mr. Editor, when Mr. Lankester tells us that all those who believe in Dr. Slade's phenomena "are lost to reason," we must accord to biblical animals a decided precedence over modern ones. The ass of Balaam had at least the faculty of perceiving spirits, while some of those who bray in our academies and hospitals show no evidence of its possession. Sad degeneration of species!

Such persons as these bound all spiritual phenomena in nature by the fortunes and mishaps of mediums—each new favorite, they think, must of necessity pull down in his fall an unscientific hypothetical "unseen universe," as the tumbling red Dragon of the *Apocalypse* drew with his tail the third part of the stars of heaven. Poor blind moles! They perceive not that by inveighing against the "craze" of such phenomenalists as Wallace, Crookes, Wagner and Thury, they only help the spread of *true* Spiritualism. We millions of lunatics really ought to address a vote of thanks to the "dishevelled" Beards who make supererogatory efforts to appear as stupid clodpoles to deceive the Eddys and Lankesters simulating "astonishment and intense interest" the better to cheat Dr. Slade. More than any advocates of phenomenalism, they bring its marvels into public notice by their pyrotechnic exposures.

As one entrusted by the Russian Committee with the delicate task of selecting a medium for the coming St. Petersburg experiments, and as an officer of the Theosophical Society, which put Dr. Slade's powers to the test in a long series of *séances,* I pronounce him not only a genuine medium, but one of the best and least fraudulent mediums ever developed. From personal experience, I can not only testify to the genuineness of his slate-writing, but also to that of the materializations which occur in his presence. A shawl thrown over a chair (which I was invited to place *wherever I chose*) is all the cabinet he exacts, and his apparitions immediately appear, and that in gaslight.

No one will charge *me* with a superfluous confidence in the personality of materializing apparitions, or superabundance of love for them; but honour and truth compel me to affirm that those who appeared to me in Slade's presence were real phantoms, and not "made up" confederates or dolls. They were evanescent and filmy, and the only ones I have seen in America which have reminded me of those which the adepts of India evoke. Like the latter, they formed and dissolved before my eyes, their substance rising mist-like from the floor, and gradually condensing. Their eyes moved and their lips smiled; but as they stood near me their forms were so transparent that I could see through them the objects in the room. These I call *genuine spiritual* substances, whereas the opaque ones that I have seen elsewhere were nothing but animated forms of matter—whatever they be—with sweating hands and a peculiar odour which I am not called upon to define at this time.

Everyone knows that Dr. Slade is not acquainted with foreign languages, and yet at our first *séance*, three years ago, on the day after my arrival in New York, where no one knew me, I received upon his slate a long communication in Russian.* I had purposely avoided giving either to Dr. Slade, or his partner, Mr. Simmons, any clue to my nationality, and while, from my accent, they would of course have detected that I was not an American, they could not possibly have known from what country I came. I fancy that if Dr. Lankester had allowed Slade to write on both knees and both elbows successively or simultaneously, the poor man would not have been able to turn out a Russian message by trick and device.

In reading the accounts in the London papers it has struck me as very remarkable that this "vagrant" medium, after baffling such a host of *savants,* should have fallen so easy a victim to the *zoologico-osteological* brace of scientific detectives. Fraud, that neither the "psychic" Serjeant Cox; nor the "unconsciously cerebrating" Carpenter; nor the wise Wallace; nor the experienced M. A. (Oxon.); nor the cautious Lord Rayleigh, who, mistrusting his own acuteness, employed a professional juggler to attend the *séance* with him; nor Professor Carter-Blake; nor a host of other competent observers could detect, was seen by the eagle eyes of the Lankester-Donkin *gemini* at a single glance. There has been nothing like it since Beard, of electro-hay-fever and Eddy fame, denounced the faculty of Yale for a set of asses, because they would not accept his divinely inspired revelation of the secret of mind-reading, and pitied the imbecility

---

*[The actual date of H.P.B.'s arrival in New York, namely, July 7, 1873, is given in A. P. Sinnett's *Incidents in the Life of H. P. Blavatsky,* p. 175. It is also implied by H.P.B. herself in a letter to her aunt, Nadyezhda A. de Fadeyev (*The Path,* New York, Vol. IX, February, 1895, p. 385), written the day she became a citizen of the United States, July 8, 1878, "five years and one day since I came to America," as she says therein.—*Compiler.*]

EDWARD WIMBRIDGE
See *Bio-Bibliographical Index*
for data.

GEORGE H. FELT
See *Bio-Bibliographical Index*
for data.

HENRY JOTHAM NEWTON
1823-1895
See *Bio-Bibliographical Index* for biographical sketch.
(The above three portraits are from the Adyar Archives.)

PRINCE EMIL-KARL-LUDWIG VON SAYN-WITTGENSTEIN
1824-1878
(From Emma Hardinge-Britten's *Nineteenth Century Miracles*, London, 1883. Consult the *Bio-Bibliographical Index* for biographical data.)

of that "amiable idiot," Colonel Olcott, for trusting his own two-months' observation of the Eddy phenomena in preference to the electric doctor's single *séance* of an hour.

I am an American citizen in embryo, Mr. Editor, and I cannot hope that the English magistrates of Bow Street will listen to a voice that comes from a city proverbially held in small esteem by British scientists. When Professor Tyndall asks Professor Youmans if the New York carpenters could make him a screen ten feet long for his Cooper Institute lectures, and whether it would be necessary to send to Boston for a *cake of ice* that he wished to use in the experiments; and when Huxley evinces grateful surprise that a "foreigner could express himself in your [our] language, in such a way as to be so readily intelligible, to all appearance," by a New York audience, and that those clever chaps—the New York reporters—could report him despite his accent, neither New York witnesses nor New York "spooks" can hope for a standing in a London court, when the defendant is prosecuted by English scientists. But fortunately for Dr. Slade, British tribunals are not inspired by the Jesuits, and so Slade may escape the fate of Leymarie. He certainly will, if he is allowed to summon to the witness stand his Owasso and other devoted "controls," to write their testimony inside a double slate, furnished and held by the magistrate himself. This is Dr. Slade's golden hour: he will never have so good a chance to demonstrate the reality of phenomenal manifestations and make Spiritualism triumph over skepticism; and we who know the doctor's wonderful powers, are confident that he *can* do it, if he is assisted by those who in the past have accomplished so much through his instrumentality.*

H. P. BLAVATSKY,
Corresponding Secretary of the Theosophical Society.

New York, October 8th, 1876.

---

* [Consult the *Bio-Bibliographical Index* of the present volume for other data concerning Dr. Slade.—*Compiler*.]

HUXLEY AND SLADE: WHO IS MORE GUILTY OF "FALSE PRETENCES"?

[*Banner of Light*, Boston, Vol. XL, No. 5, October 28, 1876, p. 1]

To the Editor of the *Banner of Light*:

Sir,—As I see the issue that has been raised by Dr. Hallock with Mr. Huxley, it suggests to me the comparison of two men looking at the same distant object through a telescope. The Doctor, having taken the usual precautions, brings the object within close range where it can be studied at one's leisure; but the naturalist, having forgotten to remove the cap, sees only the reflection of his own image.

Though the materialists may find it hard to answer even the brief criticisms of the Doctor, yet it appears that Mr. Huxley's New York lectures—as they present themselves to me in their naked desolation—suggest one paramount idea which Dr. Hallock has not touched upon. I need scarcely say to you, who must have read the report of these would-be iconoclastic lectures, that this idea is one of the "false pretenses" of modern science. After all the flourish which attended his coming, all the expectations that had been aroused, all the secret apprehensions of the church and the anticipated triumph of the materialists, what did he teach us that was really *new* or so extremely suggestive? Nothing, positively *nothing*. Exclude a sight of his personality, the sound of his well-trained voice, the reflection of his scientific glory, and the result may be summed up thus: "*Cr.: Thomas H. Huxley,* £1,000."

Of him it may be said, as it has of other teachers before, that what he said that was new was not true; and that which was true was not new. Without going into details, for the moment it suffices to say that the materialistic theory of evolution is far from being demonstrated, while the thought that Mr. Huxley does *not* grasp—*i.e.,* the *double* evolution of spirit and matter—is imparted under the form of various legends in the oldest parts of the *Rig-Veda* (the *Aitareya-Brâhmana*). Only the benighted

Hindus, it seems, made the trifling improvement over modern science, of hooking a First Cause on the further end of the chain of evolution.

In the Chaturhôtri Mantra (Book V, ch. iv, § 23, of the *Aitareya-Brâhmana*) the Goddess Earth (*iyam*), who is termed the Queen of the Serpents (*sarpa-râjñî*), for she is the mother of everything that moves (*sarpat*), was in the beginning of time completely *bald*. She was nothing but *one round head,* which was soft to the touch (*i.e.*, a "gelatinous mass"). Being distressed at her baldness, she called for help to the great Vâyu, the Lord of the *airy* regions; she prayed him to teach her the *Mantra* (invocation or sacrificial prayer, a certain part of the Veda), which would confer on her the magical power of creating things (generation). He complied, and then as soon as the Mantra was pronounced by her "in the proper metre" she found herself covered with hair (vegetation). She was now hard to the touch, for the *Lord of the air had breathed upon her*—(the globe had cooled). She had become of a variegated or motley appearance, and suddenly acquired the power to produce out of herself every animate and inanimate form, and *to change one form to another.* "Therefore in like manner," says the sacred book, "the man who has such a knowledge [of the Mantras]* obtains the faculty of assuming any shape or form he likes."

It will scarcely be said that this allegory is capable of more than one interpretation, viz.: that the ancient Hindus many centuries before the Christian era taught the doctrine of evolution. Martin Haug, the Sanskrit scholar, asserts that the *Vedas* were already in existence from 2,000 to 2,200 B.C.

Thus, while the theory of evolution is nothing new, and may be considered a proven fact, the new ideas forced upon the public by Mr. Huxley are only undemonstrated hypotheses; and as such, liable to be exploded the first fine day upon the discovery of some new fact. We find no admission of this, however, in Mr. Huxley's communications to the public, but the unproved theories are enunciated with

---

* [Square brackets are H.P.B.'s.—*Compiler.*]

as much boldness as though they were established scientific facts corroborated by unerring laws of nature. Notwithstanding that, the world is asked to revere the great Evolutionist, only because he stands under the shadow of a great name.

What is this but one of the many *false pretences* of the Sciolists? And yet Huxley and his admirers charge the believers in the evolution of spirit with the same crime of false pretences, because, forsooth, our theories are as yet undemonstrated. Those who believe in Slade's spirits are "lost to reason," while those who can see embryonic man in Huxley's "gelatinous mass," are accepted as the progressive minds of the age. Slade is arraigned before the magistrate for taking $5 from Lankester, while Huxley triumphantly walks away with $5,000 of American gold in his pockets, which was paid him for imparting to us the mirific fact that man evolved from the hind toe of a pedactyl horse!

Now, arguing from the standpoint of strict justice, in what respect is a Materialistic theorist any better than a Spiritualistic one? And in what degree is the evolution of man—independent of Divine and Spiritual interference—better proven by the toe-bone of an extinct horse, than the evolution and survival of the human spirit by the writing upon a screwed-up slate by some unseen power or powers? And yet again, the soulless Huxley sails away laden with flowers like a fashionable corpse, conquering and to conquer in fresh fields of glory, while the poor medium is haled before a police magistrate as a "vagrant and a swindler," without proof enough to sustain the charge before an unprejudiced tribunal.

There is good authority for the statement that psychological science is a debatable land upon which the modern physiologist hardly dares to venture. I deeply sympathize with the embarrassed student of the physical side of nature. We all can readily understand how disagreeable it must be to a learned theorist ever aspiring for the elevation of his hobby to the dignity of an accepted scientific truth, constantly to receive the lie direct from his remorseless and untiring antagonist—psychology. To see his cherished materialistic theories become every day more untenable, until they are reduced to the condition of mummies swathed in shrouds, self-woven and inscribed with a farrago of pet sophistries, is indeed—hard.

And yet in their self-satisfying logic these Sons of Matter reject every testimony but their own; the divine entity of the Socratic *daïmonion,* the ghost of Caesar, and Cicero's *divinum quiddam,* they explain by epilepsy; and the prophetic oracles of the Jewish *Bath-Kol* are set down as hereditary hysteria!

And now, supposing the great *protoplasmist* to have proved to the general satisfaction that the present horse is an effect of gradual development from the *Orohippus,* or four-toed horse of the Eocene formation, which, passing further through the Miocene and Pliocene periods, has become the modern honest *Equus,* does Huxley thereby prove that man has also developed from a one-toed human being? For nothing short of that could demonstrate his theory. To be consistent he must show that while the horse was losing at each successive period a toe, man has in reversed order acquired an additional one at each new formation; and, unless we are shown the fossilized remains of man in a series of one-, two-, three-, and four-toed anthropoid apelike beings antecedent to the present perfected *Homo,* what does Huxley's theory amount to? Nobody doubts that everything has evolved out of something prior to itself. But, as it is, he leaves us hopelessly in doubt whether it is man who is a *hipparionic* or equine evolution, or the antediluvian *Equus* that evolved from the primitive genus *Homo!*

Thus, to apply the argument to Slade's case, we may say that, whether the messages on his slate indicate an authorship among the returning spirits of antediluvian monkeys, or the Bravos and Lankestrian ancestors of our day, he is no more guilty of *false pretences* than the $5,000 Evolutionist. Hypothesis, whether of scientist or medium, is no false pretence; but *unsupported assertion is,* when people are charged money for it.

If, satisfied with the osseous fragments of a Hellenized or Latinized skeleton, we admit that there is a physical evolution, by what logic can we refuse to credit the possibility of an evolution of spirit? That there are two sides to the question, no one but an utter Psychophobist will deny. It may be argued that even if the Spiritualists have demonstrated their bare facts, their philosophy is incomplete, since it has missing links. But no more have the Evolutionists. They have fossil remains which prove that once upon a time the ancestors of the modern horse were blessed with three and even four toes and fingers, the fourth answering "to the little finger of the human hand," and that the *protohippus* rejoiced in "a fore-arm." Spiritualists in their turn exhibit entire hands, arms and even bodies in support of their theory that the dead still live and revisit us. For my part I cannot see that the osteologists have the better of them. Both follow the inductive or purely scientific method, proceeding from particulars to universals; thus Cuvier, upon finding a small bone, traced around it imaginary lines until he had built up from his prolific fancy a whole mammoth. The data of scientists are no more certain than those of Spiritualists; and while the former have but their modern discoveries upon which to build their theories, Spiritualists may cite the evidence of a succession of ages, which began long prior to the advent of modern science.

An inductive hypothesis, we are told, is demonstrated when the facts are shown to be in an entire accordance with it. Thus, if Huxley possesses conclusive evidence of the evolution of man in the genealogy of the horse, Spiritualists can equally claim that proof of the evolution of spirit out of the body is furnished in the materialized, more or less substantial, limbs that float in the dark shadows of the cabinet, and often in full light; a phenomenon which has been recognized and attested by numberless generations of wise men of every country. As to the pretended superiority of modern over ancient science, we have only the word of the former for it. This is also an hypothesis; better evidence is required to prove the fact. We have but to turn to Wendell Phillips' lecture on the Lost Arts* to have a certain right to doubt the assurance of modern science.

Speaking of evidence, it is strange what different and arbitrary values may be placed upon the testimony of different men equally trustworthy and well-meaning. Says the parent of protoplasm:

> It is impossible that one's practical life should not be more or less influenced by the views which we may hold as to what has been the past history of things. One of them is *human testimony* in its various shapes—all testimony of eye-witnesses, traditional testimony from the lips of those who have been eye-witnesses, and the testimony of those who have put their impressions into writing or into print.

On just such testimony, amply furnished in the Bible (evidence which Mr. Huxley rejects), and in many other less problematical authors than Moses, among whom may be reckoned generations of great philosophers, theurgists, and laymen, Spiritualists have a right to base their fundamental doctrines. Speaking further of the broad distinction to be drawn between the different kinds of evidence, some being more valuable than others, because given upon grounds not clear, upon grounds illogically stated, and upon such as do not bear thorough and careful inspection, the same gelatinist remarks:

> For example, if I read in your history of Tennessee [Ramsay's], that one hundred years ago this country was peopled by wandering savages, my belief in this statement rests upon the conviction that Mr. Ramsay was actuated by the same sort of motives that men are now; . . . that he himself was, like ourselves, not inclined to make false statements. . . . If you read Caesar's *Commentaries*, wherever he gives an account of his battles with the Gauls, you place a certain amount of confidence in his statements. You take his testimony upon this. *You feel that Caesar would not have made these statements unless he had believed them to be true.*

Profound philosophy! precious thoughts! gems of condensed, gelatinous truth! long may it stick to the American

---

*[Lecture of about 1838-39 which was delivered by this great orator and writer about two thousand times under various circumstances. It was published in booklet form by Lee and Shepherd, Boston, Mass., and T. Dillingham. New York, in 1884. 23 pages.—*Compiler.*]

mind. Mr. Huxley ought to devote the rest of his days to writing primers for the feeble-minded adults of the United States. But why select Caesar as the type of the trustworthy witness of ancient times? And, if we must implicitly credit his reports of battles, why not his profession of faith in augurs, diviners and apparitions? For, in common with his wife, Calphurnia, he believed in them as firmly as any Modern Spiritualist in his mediums and phenomena.

We also feel that no more than Caesar would such men as Cicero and Herodotus and Livy and a host of others "have made these false statements" or reported such things "unless they believed them to be true."

It has already been shown that the doctrine of evolution, as a whole, was taught in the *Rig-Veda,* and I may also add that it can be found in the most ancient of the *Books of Hermes.* This is bad enough for the claim to originality set up by our modern scientists; but what shall be said when we recall the fact that the very pedactyl horse, the finding of whose footprints has so overjoyed Mr. Huxley, was mentioned by ancient writers (Herodotus and Pliny, if I mistake not), and was once outrageously laughed at by the French Academicians? Let those who wish to verify the fact read Salverte's *Des Sciences Occultes,* translated by Anthony Todd Thomson.*

Some day, proofs as conclusive will be discovered of the reliability of the ancient writers as to their evidence on psychological matters. What Niebuhr, the German materialist, did with Livy's *History,* from which he eliminated every one of the multitude of facts there given of phenomenal "Supernaturalism," scientists now seem to have tacitly agreed to do with all the ancient, mediaeval and modern authors. What they narrate, that can be used to bolster up the physical part of science, scientists accept and sometimes cooly appropriate without credit; what supports the spiritualistic philosophy, they incontinently reject as mythical and contrary to the order of nature. In such cases "evidence"

---

*[Entitled *The Philosophy of Magic.* New York: Harper and Brothers, 1847. 2 vols.—*Compiler.*]

and the testimony of "eye-witnesses" count for nothing. They adopt the contrary course to Lord Verulam, who, arguing on the properties of amulets and charms, remarks that, "we should not reject all this kind, because it is not known how far those contributing to superstition depend on *natural causes."*

There can be no real enfranchisement of human thought, nor expansion of scientific discovery, until the existence of spirit is recognized, and the *double* evolution accepted as a fact. Until then, false theories will always find favour with those who, having forsaken "the God of their fathers," vainly strive to find substitutes in nucleated masses of matter. And of all the sad things to be seen in this era of "shams," none is more deplorable—though its futility is often ludicrous—than the conspiracy of certain scientists to stamp out spirit by their one-sided theory of evolution, and destroy Spiritualism by arraigning its mediums upon the charge of "false pretences."

H. P. BLAVATSKY.

[In H.P.B.'s *Scrapbook*, Vol III, p. 119, there is an undated cutting from the *Spiritual Scientist* which treats of opinions on spirit return among the ancients. H.P.B. wrote a footnote in pen and ink which says:]

Mind is the quintessence of the Soul—and having joined its divine Spirit *Nous*—can return no more on earth— IMPOSSIBLE.

[In H.P.B.'s *Scrapbook*, Vol. IV, p. 35, there is pasted a cutting from the New York *Sun* of December 17, 1876. It is a brief communication from Col. H. S. Olcott who repudiates the charge of having received $8,000 from Baron de Palm, and proves that the expenses of the funeral and the cremation were paid by him and Mr. Henry J. Newton; he says that "not a Dollar has been, nor ever will be realized from the Baron's estate." H.P.B. marked this article and wrote on the margin in blue pencil:]

Letter proving how much the Baron left us.

1877

CONCERNING GODS AND INTERVIEWS

[*The World*, New York, January 24, 1877]

To the Editor of *The World:*

Sir,—In my benighted country such a thing as an "interview" is unknown. Had I been aware of its dangers, I would have tried to use magic enough to impress my words upon the intelligent young gentleman who called upon me yesterday in your behalf. As it is, I find in his "report" a little error that is calculated to give my very esteemed antagonists, the theologians, a poor opinion of my Biblical scholarship. He makes me put into the mouth of Jehovah the injunction, "Fear the gods." What I did say was that in *Exodus*, xxii, 28, Jehovah commands, "Thou shalt not revile the gods"; and that, attempting to break its force, some commentators interpret the word to mean the "rulers."

As I have had the opportunity of knowing many rulers, in many different countries, and never knew one to be "a god," I made so bold as to express my wonder at such an elastic interpretation.

The theologians do not imitate the moderation of the "Lord God," but "revile the gods" of other people without stint, especially the "gods" (spirits) of the Spiritualists. As none of their writers have thought of availing themselves of this weapon of defense, I thought it no more than fair to introduce it in my "Veil of Isis,"* for their benefit as well as

---

* [*The Veil of Isis* was to be the original title of H.P.B.'s first large work, but on May 8, 1877, J. W. Bouton, the Publisher, wrote to H.P.B. saying that another work had already been published with this title. He and Charles Sotheran suggested a change of title to *Isis Unveiled*. The suggestion was accepted by H.P.B. By that time, however, the running head of Volume I had already been printed, and it stands as "Veil of Isis" throughout the first Volume, as it would have cost too much to alter it. The introductory section "Before the Veil" retained its original title also.

The work to which Bouton referred is: *The Veil of Isis. The Mysteries of the Druids*. By W. Winwood Reade. London: Chas. J. Skeet, 1861, 250 pp.—*Compiler.*]

that of the "heathen" to whom you are so kindly sending missionaries to convert them. Hoping that I am not trespassing upon the hospitality of your columns in asking the insertion of these few lines,

I am, Sir, your obedient servant,
H. P. BLAVATSKY,
A benighted Buddhist, and the Corresponding Secretary of the Theosophical Society.

New York, January 23rd.

[In H.P.B.'s *Scrapbook*, Vol. IV, p. 54, there is pasted a cutting from the *Banner of Light*, dated by H.P.B. herself as of March, 1887. It bears the title: "Art Magic—Explanation Desired!" The writer, William Emmette Coleman, of Leavenworth, Kansas, asks for an explanation concerning the difference between the original price of Mrs. Emma Hardinge-Britten's *Art Magic* for subscribers ($5.00), and the price advertised then ($3.00) for sale to the general public.

H.P.B. wrote in blue pencil at the left side of the cutting:]

Actually Emma H. Britten surreptitiously published 1,500 copies (through Wheat & Cornette, N.Y.).

[and at the right side of the cutting:]

I was an original subscriber for *two* copies.

MADAME BLAVATSKY PROTESTS

[*The World*, New York, April 6, 1877]

To the Editor of *The World:*

Sir,—There was a time when the geocentric theory was universally accepted by Christian nations, and if you and I had been carrying on our little philological and psychological controversy, I should have bowed in humility to the dictum of an authority so "particularly at home" in "the mysticism of the Orient." But despite all modifications of our astronomical system, I am no heliolater, though I do subscribe for the *Sun* as well as *The World*. I feel no more bound to "cajole" or "conciliate" the one than to suffer my feeble taper to be extinguished by the draught made by the other in its diurnal rush through journalistic space.

As near as I can judge from your writing there is this difference between us, that I write from personal experience and you upon information and belief. My authorities are my eyes and ears, yours obsolete works of reference and the pernicious advice of a spontaneously-generated "lampsakano," who learned his mysticism from the detached head of one Dummkopf. (See the *Sun* of March 25th.) My assertions may be corroborated by any traveller, as they have been by the first authorities. Elphinstone's *Kingdom of Kabul*, etc., was published sixty-two years ago (1815);* his *The History of India* thirty-six years ago. If the latter is the "standard text book" for British civil servants it certainly is not for native Hindoos, who perhaps know as much of their philosophy and religion as he. In fact, a pretty wide reading of European "authorities" has given me a very poor opinion of them, since no two agree. Sir William Jones, whose shoestrings few Orientalists are worthy to untie, made, himself, very grave mistakes, which are now being corrected by Max Müller and others. He knew nothing of the *Vedas* (see Max Müller's *Chips*, Vol. I, p. 183), and even expressed his belief that Buddha was the same as the Teutonic deity Wodan or Odin, and Sâkya—another name of Buddha —the same as Shishac, a king of Egypt! Why, therefore, could not Elphinstone make a mess of such subtle religious distinctions as the innumerable sects of Hindoo mystics present?

I am charged with such ignorance that I imagine the fakirs to be "holy mendicants of the religion of Brahmâ," while you "say they are not of the religion of Brahmâ at all, but Mahometans." Does this precious piece of information come also from Elphinstone? Then I give you a Roland

---

*[The original title of this work by Mounstuart Elphinstone was: *An Account of the Kingdom of Caubul, and its Dependencies in Persia, Tartary, and India*, etc., London, 1815.—Compiler.]

for your Oliver. I refer you to James Mill's *The History of British India* (Vol. I, p. 283; London, 1858). You say "those seeking ready-made information can find our statements corroborated in any encyclopaedia." Perhaps you refer to Appleton's? Very well. In the article on James Mill (Vol. II, p. 501)* you will find it saying that his *India* was the first complete work on the subject. "It was without a rival as a source of information, and the justice of its views appeared in the subsequent measures for the government of that country." Now, Mill says that the fakirs are a sect of Brahmanism; and that their penances are prescribed by the *Laws of Manu*. Will your Lamp-sickener, or whatever the English of that Greek may be, say that Manu was a Mahometan? And yet that would be no worse than your clothing the fakirs—who belong, as a rule, to the Brahman pagodas—in yellow, the color exclusively worn by Buddhist lamas,† and breeches which form part of the costume of the Mahometan dervishes. Perhaps it is a natural mistake for you Lampsakanoi, who rely upon Elphinstone for your facts and have not visited India, to confound the Persian dervishes with the Hindoo fakirs. But "while the lamp holds out to burn," read Louis Jacolliot's *Bible in India*, just out, and learn from a man who has passed twenty years in India that your correspondent is neither a fool nor a liar.

You charge me with saying that a fakir is a "worshipper of God." I say I did not, as the expression I used, "fakir is a *loose* word," well proves. It was a natural mistake of the

---

* [Reference is probably to the *Appleton's Cyclopaedia of Biography*. It is not known what edition H.P.B. had in mind. In the 1872 edition, although the above wording does not occur, the ideas expressed about Mill's work are equally laudable.—*Compiler*.]

† [This must be a *lapsus calami* on the part of H.P.B. Yellow is worn by Buddhist monks of the Southern School but not by Tibetan Lamas. The Bhikkus of the Theravâda School have, since the foundation of the Order by the Buddha, worn three robes of various shades of orange or yellow. Members of the Gelug-pa Order of Tibetan Buddhism, founded in the fourteenth century by Tsong-kha-pa, wear on special occasions yellow hats as distinct from the red hats worn by other sects, and on certain festive occasions yellow silk over their maroon robes.—*Compiler*.]

GENERAL ABNER DOUBLEDAY
1819-1893
(Consult the *Bio-Bibliographical Index* for biographical sketch.)

H. P. BLAVATSKY IN 1875
Photograph by Beardsley, Ithaca, N.Y.

reporter, who did not employ stenography at our interview. I said, "A *Svâmi* is one who devotes himself entirely to the service of God." All Svâmis of the Nir-Narrain sect are fakirs, but all fakirs are not necessarily Svâmis. I refer you to Coleman's *The Mythology of the Hindus* (p. 244), and to the *Asiatic Journal*. Coleman says precisely what Louis Jacolliot says, and both corroborate me. You very obligingly give me a lesson in Hindustani and the Devanagari, and teach me the etymology of "guru," "Fakir," "Gosain," etc. For answer I refer you to John Shakespear's large *Hindustani-English Dictionary*. I may know less English than you Lampsakanoi, but I do know of Sanskrit and Hindustani more than can be learned on Park Row.

As I have said in another communication, I did not invite the visits of reporters, nor seek the notoriety which has suddenly been thrust upon me. If I reply to your criticisms —rhetorically brilliant, but wholly unwarranted by the facts —it is because I value your good opinion (without caring to cajole you), and at the same time cannot sit quiet and be made to appear alike devoid of experience, knowledge and truthfulness.

Respectfully, but still rebelliously, yours,
H. P. BLAVATSKY.

Monday, April 2nd, 1877.

MADAME BLAVATSKY ON FAKIRS

[*Banner of Light*, Boston, Vol. XLI, April 21, 1877, p. 8]

To the Editor of *The Sun:*

Sir,—However ignorant I may be of the laws of the solar system, I am, at all events, so firm a believer in heliocentric journalism that I subscribe for *The Sun*. I have, therefore, seen your remarks in to-day's *Sun* upon my "iconoclasm."

No doubt it is a great honor for an unpretentious foreigner to be thus crucified between the two greatest celebrities of your chivalrous country—the truly good Deacon Richard Smith, of the blue gauze trousers, and the nightingale of the willow and the cypress, G. Washington Childs, A.M. But I am not a Hindu fakir, and therefore cannot say that I enjoy crucifixion, especially when unmerited. I would not even fancy being swung round the "tall tower" with the steel hooks of your satire metaphorically thrust through my back. I have not invited the reporters to a show. I have not sought notoriety. I have only taken up a quiet corner in your free country, and, as a woman who has travelled much, shall try to tell a Western public what strange things I have seen among Eastern peoples. If I could have enjoyed this privilege at home, I should not be here. Being here, I shall, as your old English proverb expresses it, "Tell the truth and shame the devil."

The World reporter who visited me wrote an article which mingled his souvenirs of my stuffed apes and my canaries, my tiger-heads and palms, with aerial music and the flitting *doppelgängers* of adepts. It was a very interesting article, and certainly intended to be very impartial. If he made me appear to deny the immutability of natural law, and inferentially to affirm the possibility of miracle, it is due to my faulty English or to the carelessness of the reader.

There are no such uncompromising believers in the immutability and universality of the laws of nature as students of occultism. Let us then, with your permission, leave the shade of the great Newton to rest in peace. It is not the principle of the law of gravitation, or the necessity of a central force acting toward the sun, that is denied, but the assumption that behind the law which draws bodies toward the earth's centre, and which is our most familiar example of gravitation, there is not another law, equally immutable, that under certain conditions appears to counteract it. If but once in a hundred years a table or a fakir is seen to rise in the air, without a visible mechanical cause, then that rising is a manifestation of a natural law of which our scientists are yet ignorant. Christians believe in miracles; occultists credit them even less than pious scientists—Sir David Brewster, for instance. Show an occultist an unfamiliar phenomenon, and he will never affirm *a priori* that it is either a trick or a miracle. He will search for the cause in the region of causes.

There was an anecdote about Babinet, the astronomer, current in Paris in 1854, when the great war was raging between the Academy and the "waltzing tables." This skeptical man of science had proclaimed in the *Revue des Deux Mondes* (January 15, 1854, p. 414) that the levitation of furniture without contact "was simply as impossible as perpetual motion." A few days later, during an experimental *séance,* a table was levitated, without contact, in his presence. The result was that Babinet went straight to a dentist to have a molar tooth extracted, which the iconoclastic table, in its aerial flight, had seriously damaged. But it was too late to recall his article.

I suppose nine men out of ten, including editors, would maintain that the undulatory theory of light is one of the most firmly established. And yet, if you will turn to page 22 of *The New Chemistry* (New York, 1876), by Professor Josiah P. Cooke, Jr., of Harvard University, you will find him saying: "I cannot agree with those who regard the wave theory of light as an established principle of science. . . . [it] requires a combination of qualities in the ether of space, which I find it difficult to believe are actually realized." What is this but iconoclasm?

Let us bear in mind that Newton himself received the corpuscular theory of Pythagoras and his predecessors, from whom he learned it, and that it was only *en désespoir de cause* that later scientists accepted the wave theory of Descartes and Huyghens. Kepler maintained the magnetic nature of the sun. Leibnitz ascribed the planetary motions to agitations of an ether. Borelli anticipated Newton in his discovery, although he failed to demonstrate it as triumphantly. Huyghens and Boyle, Horrocks and Hooke, Halley and Wren, all had ideas of a central force acting toward the sun, and of the true principle of diminution of action of the force in the ratio of the inverse square of the distance.

The last word has not yet been spoken with respect to gravitation; its limitations can never be known until the nature of the sun is better understood. They are just beginning to recognize (see Professor Balfour Stewart's lecture at Manchester, entitled *The Sun and the Earth,* and Professor A. M. Mayer's lecture, *The Earth a Great Magnet*) the intimate connection between the sun's spots and the position of the heavenly bodies. The interplanetary magnetic attractions are but just being demonstrated. Until gravitation is understood to be simply magnetic attraction and repulsion, and the part played by magnetism itself in the endless correlations of forces in the ether of space—that "hypothetical medium," as Webster terms it, I maintain that it is neither fair nor wise to deny the levitation of either fakir or table. Bodies oppositely electrified attract each other; similarly electrified, repulse each other. Admit, therefore, that any body having weight, whether man or inanimate object, can by any cause whatever, external or internal, be given the same polarity as the spot on which it stands, and what is to prevent its rising?

Before charging me with falsehood when I affirm that I have seen both men and objects levitated, you must first dispose of the abundant testimony of persons far better known than my humble self. Mr. Crookes, Professor Thury of Geneva, Louis Jacolliot, your own Dr. Gray and Dr. Warner, and hundreds of others, have, first and last, certified to the fact of levitation.

I am surprised to find how little even the editors of your erudite contemporary, *The World,* are acquainted with Oriental metaphysics in general, and the trousers of Hindu fakirs in particular. It was bad enough to make those holy mendicants of the religion of Brahmâ graduate from the Buddhist Lamaseries of Tibet; but it is unpardonable to make them wear baggy breeches in the exercise of their religious functions. This is as bad as if a Hindu journalist had represented the Rev. Mr. Beecher entering his pulpit in the scant costume of the fakir—the *dhoti,* a cloth about the loins; "only that and nothing more." To account, therefore, for the oft-witnessed, open-air levitations of the *Svâmis* and *Gurus* upon the theory of an iron frame concealed beneath the clothing, is as reasonable as Monsieur Babinet's explanation of the table-tipping and tapping as "unconscious ventriloquism."

You may object to the act of disembowelling, which I am compelled to affirm I have seen performed. It is, as you say, "remarkable"; but still not miraculous. Your suggestion that Dr. Hammond should go and see it is a good one. Science would be the gainer, and your humble correspondent be justified. Are you, however, in a position to guarantee that he would furnish the world of skeptics with an example of "veracious reporting," if his observation should tend to overthrow the pet theories of what we loosely call science?

Yours very respectfully,
H. P. BLAVATSKY.

New York, March 28th, 1877.

TO THE PUBLIC

[*Banner of Light*, Vol. XLI, No. 4, April 21, 1877, p. 8]

At a meeting of the Theosophical Society, held this day, the statement having been read from a London journal that D. D. Home, the medium, will devote some portion of his forthcoming work to "The Theosophical Society; its vain quest for sylphs and gnomes," and other matters pertaining to the organization, a committee was appointed to make known the following facts:

1. The Theosophical Society has been from the first a secret organization.

2. The communication of any particulars as to its affairs, except by direct authority, would be a dishonorable act.

3. The medium in question cannot possibly have any knowledge of these matters, except from persons who have long ceased to be members, and have violated their obligations, or persons discredited and disgraced at a very early period in the history of the Society. Therefore, whatever statements he may publish cannot be relied upon or verified.

Whether this Society, or sections, or individual members have seen "Elementary" or other spirits at its meetings, concerns themselves alone. They will act as judges themselves when any phenomena have occurred that are suitable to give to the public. That magical phenomena do sometimes happen in presence of members of the Society when strangers can witness them, may be inferred from the editorial description which appeared in the New York *World* of Monday last.

The Theosophical Society is quietly prosecuting those subjects which interest the members, careful to neither infringe upon any person's rights nor to transcend its own legitimate field. In advance, therefore, of an authoritative report of its own doings, it is unprofitable to pass judgement upon biased inferences made by third parties upon the allegations either of those who do not know the truth, or such as by an act of treachery have proved themselves incapable of speaking it.

H. S. OLCOTT, *President.*
R. B. WESTBROOK, D.D., *Vice Pres.*
PROF. ALEX. WILDER, M.D., *Vice Pres.*
H. P. BLAVATSKY, *Cor. Sec.*
EMMA HARDINGE-BRITTEN.
G. L. DITSON, M.D.
H. J. BILLING, M.D.
L. M. MARQUETTE, M.D.
W. Q. JUDGE (*Counsel*).
H. D. MONACHESI.
MORTIMER MARBLE.
SOLON J. VLASTO.
J. F. OLIVER.

} *Committee of the Theosophical Society.*

[*Official Copy*]

New York, March 30th, 1877.

A. GUSTAM, *Secretary.*

A CARD FROM MADAME BLAVATSKY

[*The World*, New York, May 6, 1877]*

To the Editor of *The World:*

Sir,—Since the first month of my arrival in America I began, for reasons mysterious but perhaps intelligible, to provoke hatred among those who pretend to be on good terms with me, if not the best of friends. Slanderous reports, vile insinuations, innuendo, have rained about me. For more than three years I have kept silent, although the least of the offenses attributed to me was calculated to excite the loathing of a person of my disposition. I have rid myself of a number of these retailers of slander, but finding that I was actually suffering in the estimation of friends whose good opinion I valued, I adopted a policy of seclusion. For two years my world has been in my apartments, and for an average of at least seventeen hours a day I have sat at my desk with my books and manuscripts as my companions. During this time many highly valued acquaintances have been formed with ladies and gentlemen who have sought me out without expecting me to return their visits. I am an old woman, and I feel the need of fresh air as well as any one, but my disgust for the lying, slanderous world that we find outside of "heathen" countries has been such that in seven months I believe I have been out but three times.

But no retreat is secure against the anonymous slanderer who uses the United States mail. Letters have been received by my trusted friends containing the foulest aspersions upon myself. At various times I have been charged with (1)

---

* [Also published in the New York *Sun*, under the title "Various Slanders Refuted," as appears from H.P.B.'s *Scrapbook*, Vol. IV, p. 61.—*Compiler.*]

drunkenness; (2) forgery; (3) being a Russian spy; (4) with being an anti-Russian spy; (5) with being no Russian at all, but a French adventuress; (6) of having been in jail for theft; (7) of being the mistress of a Polish count in Union Square; (8) with murdering seven husbands; (9) with bigamy; (10) of being the mistress of Colonel Olcott; (11) also of an acrobat. Other things might be mentioned, but decency forbids.

Since the arrival of Wong Chin Foo the game has recommenced with double activity. I have received anonymous letters and others, and newspaper slips, telling infamous stories about him; on his part he has received communications about us, one of which I beg you to insert:

May 4th.
Does the disciple of Buddha know the character of the people with whom he is at present residing? The surroundings of a teacher of morality and religion should be moral. Are his so? On the contrary, they are people of very doubtful reputation, as he can ascertain by applying at the nearest police station.

A FRIEND.

Of Wong Chin Foo's merits or shortcomings I know nothing except that since his arrival his conversation and behavior have impressed me favorably. He appears to me a very earnest and enthusiastic student. However, he is a man, and is able to take care of himself, although, like me, a foreigner. But I wish to say for myself just this: that I defy any person in America to come forward and prove a single charge against my honor. I invite everyone possessed of such proofs as will vindicate them in a court of justice to publish them over their own signatures in the newspapers. I will furnish to everyone a list of my several residences, and contribute towards paying detectives to trace my every step. But I hereby give notice that if any more unverifiable slanders can be traced to responsible sources, I will invoke the protection of the law, which, on the theory of your national Constitution, was made for heathen as well as

Christian denizens. And I further notify slanderers of a speculative turn that no blackmail is paid at No. 302 West Forty-seventh Street.

Respectfully,
H. P. BLAVATSKY.*

May 5th, 1877.

BUDDHISM IN AMERICA

SOME PHILOLOGICAL AND THEOLOGICAL REMARKS FROM MME. BLAVATSKY.

[*The Sun,* New York, Vol. XLIV, No. 255, May 13, 1877]

To the Editor of *The Sun:*

Sir,—As, in your leading article of May 6th, I am at one moment given credit for knowing something about the religion of the Brahmans and Buddhists, and, anon, of being a pretender of the class of Jacolliot, and even his plagiarist, you will not wonder at my again knocking at your doors for hospitality. This time I write over my own signature, and am responsible, as I am not under other circumstances.

No wonder that the "learned friend" at your elbow was reminded "of the utterances of one Louis Jacolliot." The paragraphs in the very able account of your representative's interview, which relate to "Adhima and Heva" and "Jezeus Christna," were translated bodily, in his presence, from the French edition of the *Bible in India.* They were read, moreover, from the chapter entitled, "Bagaveda-Gita," which, doubtless, most American scholars have read. Jacolliot spells the name Bagaveda instead of Bhagavad as you put it, kindly correcting me. In so doing, in my humble opinion, he is right, and the others are wrong; were it but

---

*[In her *Scrapbook,* Vol. IV, p. 61, H.P.B. marked in red pencil most of this paragraph and also added the words:
What I am
—Compiler.]

for the reason that the Hindus themselves so pronounced it—at least those of Southern India, who speak either the Tamil language or other dialects. Since we seek in vain among Sanskrit philologists for any two who agree as to the spelling or meaning of important Hindu words, and scarcely two as to the orthography of this very title, I respectfully submit that neither "the French fraud" nor I are chargeable with any grave offense in the premises.

For instance, Professor Whitney, your greatest American Orientalist, and one of the most eminent living, spells it Bagavata; while his equally great opponent, Max Müller, prefers Bagavadgita, and half a dozen others spell it in as many different ways, as naturally, each scholar, in rendering the Indian words into his own vernacular, follows the national rule of pronunciation; and so, you will see, that Professor Müller in writing the syllable *ad* with an A does precisely what Jacolliot does in spelling it *ed,* the French E having the same sound as the English A, before a consonant. The same holds good with the name of the Hindu Saviour, which by different authorities is spelled Krishna, Crisna, Khristna and Krisna; everything, in short, but the right way—Christna. Perhaps you may say that this is mere hypothesis. But since every Indianist follows his own fancy, in his phonetic transcriptions, I do not know why I may not exercise my best judgment, especially as I can give good reasons to support it.

You affirm that there "never was a Hindu reformer named Jezeus Christna"; and, although I confined my affirmation of his existence to the authority of Jacolliot at the interview in question, I now assert on my own responsibility that there was, and is, a personage of that name recognized and worshipped in India, and that he is not Jesus Christ. Christna is a Brahmanical deity, and, except by the Brahmans, is recognized by several sects of the Jainas. When Jacolliot says Jezeus Christna he only shows a little clumsiness in phonetic rendering, and is nearer right than many of his critics. I have been at the festivals of Janmotsar, in commemoration of the birth of Christna (which is their Christmas), and have heard thousands of voices shouting: "Jas-i-Christna! Jasas-wi-Christna!" Translated, they are: *Jas-i*—renowned, famous; and *Jasas-wi*—celebrated, or divinely renowned, powerful; and *Christna,* sacred. To avoid being again contradicted, I refer the reader to any Hindostanee dictionary. All the Brahmans with whom I have talked on the subject spoke of Christna either as Jas-i-Christna, or Jadar-Christna, or again used the term, *Jadu-pati,* Lord of Yadavas, descendant of Yadu, one of the many titles of Christna in India. You see, therefore, that it is but a question of spelling.

That Christna is preferable to Krishna can be clearly shown under the rules laid down by Burnouf and others upon the authority of the pundits. True, the initial of the name in Sanskrit is generally written *K;* but the Sanskrit *k* is strongly aspirated; it is a guttural expiration whose only representation is the Greek *Chi.* In English, therefore, the *k* instead of having the sound of *k* as in *King* would be even more aspirated than the *h* in heaven. As in English the Greek word is written Christos in preference to H'ristos, which would be nearer the mark, so with the Hindu deity; his name under the same rule should be written Christna, notwithstanding the possible unwelcomeness of the resemblance.

Mr. Textor de Ravisi, a French Catholic Orientalist, and for ten years Governor of Karikal (India), Jacolliot's bitterest opponent in religious conclusions, fully appreciated the situation. He would have the name spelt *Krishna,* because (1) most of the statues of this god are black, and *Krishna* means black; and (2) because the real name of Christna "was Kaneya, or Caneya." Very well; but black is *Krishna.* And if not only Jacolliot, but the Brahmans themselves, are not to be allowed to know as much as their European critics, we will call in the aid of Volney and other Orientalists, who show that the Hindu deity's name is formed from the radical *Chris,* meaning sacred, as Jacolliot shows it. Moreover, for the Brahmans to call their God the "black one" would be unnatural and absurd; while to style him the sacred, or *pure essence,* would be perfectly appropriate to their notions. As to the name being Caneya, Mr. Textor de Ravisi, in suggesting it, completes his own discomfiture. In escaping Scylla he falls into Charybdis. I suppose no one will deny that the Sanskrit Canya means Virgin; for even in modern Hindostanee the Zodiacal sign of *Virgo* is called Kaniya. Christna is styled Caneya, as having been born of a virgin. Begging pardon, then, of the "learned friend" at your elbow, I reaffirm that if there "never was a Hindu reformer named Jezeus Christna," there was a Hindu Saviour, who is worshipped unto this day as Jas-i-Christna, or, if it better accords with his pious preferences, Jas-i-Kristna.*

When the 84,000 volumes of the *Dharma-Khanda,* or sacred books of the Buddhists, and the thousands upon thousands of ollas of Vedic and Brahmanical literature, now known by their titles only to European scholars, or even a tithe of those actually in their possession are translated, and comprehended, and agreed upon, I will be happy to measure swords again with the *solar* pundit who has prompted your severe reflections upon your humble subscriber.

Though, in common with various authorities, you stigmatize Jacolliot as a "French fraud," I must really do him the justice to say that his Catholic opponent, de Ravisi, said of his *Bible in India,* in a report made at the request of the Société Académique de St. Quentin, that it is written "with good faith, of absorbing interest, *a learned work* on known facts and with familiar arguments."

Ten years' residence and studies in India were enough to fit him to give an opinion. Unfortunately, however, in America it is but too easy to gain the reputation of "a fraud" in much less time.

Respectfully,

H. P. BLAVATSKY.

---

*[Owing to the fact that the Slavonic pronunciation of "J" is equivalent to "Y," H.P.B. sometimes uses "J" for the Devanâgarî character "Ya," as is the case in this article where the terms should be *Yaś-i-Kṛishṇa, Yaśas-vin,* etc.—*Compiler.*]

CROQUET AT WINDSOR

[In H.P.B.'s *Scrapbook*, Vol. IV, pp. 67-68 (old numbering Vol. II, pp. 49-50) may be found a cutting from *The Illustrated Weekly*, Saturday, June 2, 1877, an American journal published in New York in 1875-77. The cutting contains a rather celebrated poem of Ivan Sergueyevich Turguenyev entitled "Croquet at Windsor," translated by H.P.B. into English, at the special request of her aunt, Nadyezhda A. de Fadeyev, as appears from one of her letters to H.P.B. now in the Adyar Archives. This poem, in its original Russian, acquired a wide notoriety during the Russo-Turkish War of 1877-78.]

The proud Queen sits stately on Windsor's green lawn,
    Her ladies at croquet are playing;
She watches their game as the evening creeps on,
    And smiles as the balls go a-straying.

They roll through the wickets; the arches are passed,
    The strokes are so bold and so steady—
There's scarcely a miss . . . stop! the Queen, all aghast,
    As though stricken with death seems already.

She sees, as in vision, the balls disappear,
    And corpse-heads, all ghastly and bleeding,
Roll toward her, where, speechless and palid with fear,
    She shudders, and watches their speeding.

Heads frosted, and heads of the young and the fair;
    Heads of children, whose innocent prattle
Was drowned in the hell-storm that swept through the air
    When their village was sacked in the battle.

And lo! the Queen's daughter—youngest, fairest of all,
    Instead of the red ball, is throwing
A babe's gory head, which comes rolling, to fall
    At her feet, with its lifeblood still flowing!

The head of a babe, pinched with torture and white—
   And its golden locks dabbled with gore;
The lips speak reproach, though the eyes lack their sight—
   Till the Queen shrieks: "Torment me no more!"

She calls her physician to come to her aid,
   "Quick, quick!" she cries, "quick to my cure!"
He quietly answers: "You may well be afraid,
   You've been reading the papers, I'm sure.

"THE TIMES with Bulgarian horrors is filled—
   Tells of Servian martyrs and Christian despair;
No wonder your majesty dreams of the killed;
   Take these drops, and come in from the chill of the air."

She's housed: but as plunged in a revery still,
   She sits with her eyes cast reflectively down,
O horror! her heart with new terror grows chill,
   For she sees to her knees the blood spread on her gown!

"Quick! Wash it away, for I fain would forget,
   Wash! Wash, British rivers and waters, this gore!"
No, no, haughty Queen, though that stain is still wet,
   'Tis of innocent blood, and will fade never more!

New York, May 25, 1877.

TURKISH BARBARITIES

WHAT MME. BLAVATSKY HAS HEARD DIRECTLY FROM THE FRONT.

[*The World*, New York, August 13, 1877]

To the Editor of *The World*.

Sir: The Sublime Porte has had the sublime effrontery to ask the American people to execrate Russian barbarity. It appeals for sympathy on behalf of helpless Turkish subjects at the seat of war. With the memories of Bulgaria and Servia still fresh, this seems the climax of daring hypocrisy. Barely a few months ago the reports of Mr. Schuyler and other impartial observers of the atrocities of Bashi-Bazouks sent a thrill of horror through the world. Perpetrated under official sanction, they aroused the indignation of all who had hearts to feel. In today's paper I read another account of pretended Russian cruelties, and your able and just editorial comments upon the same. Permit one who is, perhaps, in a better position than any other private person here to know what is taking place at the front, to inform you of certain facts derived from authentic sources. Besides receiving daily papers from St. Petersburg, Moscow, Tiflis and Odessa, I have an uncle, a cousin and a nephew in active service,* and nearly every steamer brings me accounts of military movements from eyewitnesses. My cousin and nephew have taken part in all the bloody engagements in Turkish Armenia up to the present time, and were at the siege and capture of Ardahan. Newspapers may suppress, color or exaggerate facts; the private letters of brave soldiers to their families rarely do.

---

*[These were General Rostislav Andreyevich de Fadeyev, brother of H.P.B.'s mother; Alexander Yulyevich de Witte, son of H.P.B.'s aunt, Katherine Andreyevna de Witte; and Rostislav Nikolayevich de Yahontov, son of H.P.B.'s sister, Vera Petrovna, by her first marriage.—*Compiler*.]

Let me say then that during this campaign the Turkish troops have been guilty of such fiendish acts as make me pray that my relatives may be killed rather than fall into their hands. In a letter from the Danube, corroborated by several correspondents of German and Austrian papers, the writer says: "On June 20th we entered Kozlovetz, a Bulgarian town of about two hundred houses, which lies three or four hours distant from Sistova. The sight which met our eyes made the blood of every Russian soldier run cold, hardened though he is to such scenes. On the principal street of the deserted town were placed in rows 140 beheaded bodies of men, women and children. The heads of these unfortunates were tastefully piled in a pyramid in the middle of the street. Among the smoking ruins of every house we found half-burned corpses, fearfully mutilated. We caught a Turkish soldier, and to our questions he reluctantly confessed that their chiefs had given orders not to leave a Christian place, however small, before burning it and putting to death every man, woman and child."

On the first day that the Danube was crossed some foreign correspondents, among them that of the *Cologne Gazette,* saw several bodies of Russian soldiers whose noses, ears, hands, etc., had been cut off, while the genital organs had been stuffed into the mouths of the corpses. Later three bodies of Christian women were found—a mother and two daughters—whose condition makes one almost drop the pen in horror at the thought. Entirely nude, split open from below to the navel, their heads cut off; the wrists of each corpse were tied together with strips of skin and flesh flayed from the shoulder down, and the corpses of the three martyrs were similarly bound to each other by long ribbons of flesh dissected from their thighs.

A correspondent writes from Sistovo: "The Emperor continues his daily visits to the hospitals and passes whole hours with the wounded. A few days ago His Majesty, accompanied by Colonel Wellesley, the British military attaché, visited two unfortunate Bulgarians who died on the night following. The skull of one of them was split open both laterally and vertically, by two sword-cuts, an eye was torn out, and he was otherwise mutilated. He explained, as well as he could, that several Turks seizing him, demanded his money. As he had none, four of the party held him fast while the fifth, brandishing his sword, and repeating all the time, 'There, you Christian dog, there's your cross for you!' first split his skull from the forehead to the back of the head, and then crosswise, from ear to ear. While the Emperor was listening to these details the greatest agony was depicted upon his face. Taking Colonel Wellesley by the arm, and pointing to the Bulgarian, he said to him in French, 'See the work of your protégés!' The British officer blushed and was much confused."

The special correspondent of the London *Standard*, describing his audience with the Grand Duke Nicholas, Commander-in-Chief, on the 7th of July, says that the Grand Duke communicated to him the most horrifying details about the cruelties committed at Dobruja. A Christian, whose hands were tied with strips of his own skin cut from the length of both his arms, and his tongue cut out from the root, was laid at the feet of the Emperor, and died there before the eyes of the Czar and the British agent, the same Colonel Wellesley, who was in attendance. Turning to the latter, His Majesty, with a stern expression, asked him to inform his Government of what he had just seen for himself. "From the beginning of the war," says the correspondent, "I have heard of quite a number of such cases, but never witnessed one myself. After the personal assurances given to me by the Grand Duke, it is no longer possible to doubt that the Turkish officers are unable to control their irregular troops."

The correspondent of the *Syeverniy Vestnik* had gone the rounds of the hospitals to question the wounded soldiers. Four of them, belonging to the Second Battalion of Minsk Rifles, testified with the most solemn asseverations that they had seen the Turks approach the wounded, rob them, mutilate their bodies in the most cruel way and finish them with the bayonet. They themselves have avoided this fate only by feigning death.

It is a common thing for wounded Turks to allure Russian soldiers and members of the sanitary corps to their assistance and, as they bend over them, to kill with a revolver or dagger those who would relieve them. A case like this occurred under the eye of one of my correspondents in Turkish Armenia and was in all the Russian papers. A sergeant's assistant (a *sanitar*) was dispatched under such circumstances; thereupon a soldier standing by killed the assassin.

My cousin, Major Alexander Y. Witte, of the Sixteenth Nizhegorodsky Dragoons, one of the most gallant soldiers in the army of Loris-Melikoff, and who has just been decorated by the Grand Duke, under the authority of the Emperor, with a golden sword inscribed "For Bravery," says that it is becoming positively dangerous to relieve a wounded Turk.* The people who robbed and killed the wounded in the hospital at Ardahan upon the entry of the Russian troops were the Karapapahs, Mussulmans and the supposed allies of the Turks. During the siege they prudently awaited the issue from a safe distance. As soon as the Russians conquered, the Karapapahs flew like so many tigers into the town, slaying the wounded Turks, robbing the dead, pillaging houses, bringing the horses and mules of the fleeing enemy into the Russian camp, and swearing allegiance to the Commander-in-Chief. The Cossacks had all the trouble in the world to prevent their new allies from continuing the greatest excesses. To charge, therefore, upon the Russians the atrocities of these cowardly jackals (a nomadic tribe of brigands) is an impudent lie of Mukhtar Pasha, whose falsifications have become so notorious that some Parisian papers have nick-

---

* [Alexander Yulyevich de Witte (1846-1877) was the second son of Yuliy Feodorovich de Witte and Katherine Andreyevna de Fadeyev, sister of H.P.B.'s mother. He was a younger brother of Serguey Yulyevich de Witte who became Prime Minister of Russia. According to Vera P. de Zhelihovsky, in her brief biographical account of H.P.B.'s life (See Preface to the Russian edition of H.P.B.'s "Enigmatical Tribes of the Blue Hills," p. xv), he was at the time a Major in the Nizhegorodsky Dragoons and suffered a painful contusion in an engagement on Oct. 2, 1877. This developed into heavy migraines, and he died in 1884 from the aftereffects of the injuries.—*Compiler*.]

named him "Blageur Pasha." His dispatches are only matched in mendacity by those of the Spanish commanders in Cuba.

The stupidity of charging such excesses upon the Russian army becomes apparent when we remember that the policy of the Government from the first has been to pay liberally for supplies, and win the goodwill of the people of the invaded provinces by kindness. So marked and successful has this policy proved in General Loris-Melikoff's field of operations, that the anti-Russian papers of England, Austria and other countries have denounced it as Russian "craft."

With the Danubian forces is the Emperor in person—liberator of millions of serfs, and the mildest and most just sovereign who has ever occupied the throne of any country. As he won the love of his whole people and the adoration of his army, by his sense of justice and benevolent regard, I ask you, if he is likely to countenance any cruel excesses? While the cowardly Abdul-Hamid hides in the alcoves of his harem, and of the Imperial Princes none have taken the field, the Czar follows his army step by step, submits to comparatively severe and unaccustomed hardships, and exposes his health and life against all the remonstrances and prayers of Prince Gortchakoff. His four sons are all in active service, and the son of the Grand Duke Nicholas was decorated at the crossing of the Danube for personal courage, having exposed his life for hours under a shower of bullets.

I only ask the American people to do justice to their long-tried and unfaltering friends, the Russians. However politicians may have planned, the Russian people have entered this war as a holy crusade to rescue millions of helpless Slavonians—their brothers—of the Danube from Turkish cruelty. The people have dragged the Government to the field. Russia is surrounded by false neutrals, who but watch the opportunity to fly at her throat; and, shameful fact! the blessing of the Pope rests upon the Moslem standards, and his curse against his fellow Christians has been read in all the Catholic churches. For my part, I care a great deal less even than my countrymen for his blessings or curses, for, besides other reasons, I regard this war not as one of

Christian against Moslem, but as one of humanity and civilization against barbarism. This is the view of the Catholic Czechs of Bohemia. So great was their indignation at what they rightly considered the dishonor of the Roman Catholic Church, that on the 4th of July—anniversary of the martyrdom of John Huss*—notwithstanding the efforts of the police, they repaired in multitudes to the heights of Smichovo, Beraun and other hills around Prague and burnt at the stake the portraits and wax effigies of the Pope and the Prince Archbishop Schwartzenberg, and the Papal discourse against the Russian Emperor and army, singing the while Slavonian national songs, and shouting, "Down with the Pope!" "Death to the Ultramontanes!" "Hurrah for the Czar-Liberator!"

All of which shows that there are good Catholics among the Slavonians, at least, who rightly hold in higher estimation the principles of national solidarity than foolish dogmas of the Vatican, even though backed by pretended infallibility.

Respectfully,
H. P. BLAVATSKY.

August 9.

[In H.P.B.'s *Scrapbook*, Vol. IV, p. 79, there is a cutting from the *Banner of Light* of September 8, 1877. It is a very appreciative review by Dr. G. Bloede of some advance sheets of *Isis Unveiled*. H.P.B. wrote at the bottom of the first column:]

This is the same Dr. Bloede who a year before abused us & Theosophy & then made my acquaintance, begged my pardon &—joined us, and ever remained a friend.

---

*[In 1415.—*Compiler.*]

WASHING THE DISCIPLES' FEET

[*The Sun,* New York, Vol. XLIV, No. 350, August 16, 1877]

To the Editor of *The Sun:*

Sir: At the ceremony of "feet-washing" which occurred at Limwood Camp ground, August 8th, and is described in *The Sun* of today, Elder Jones, of Mechanicsburg, Pa., professed to give the history of this ancient custom. The report says:

> He claimed that its origin did not date anterior to the coming of Christ; neither was the matter of cleanliness to be thought of in this connection. Its observance was due exclusively to the fact that it was a scriptural injunction; it originated in Christ's example, and it devolved upon his hearers to follow this example. Numerous scriptural passages were quoted in support of this argument.

The reverend gentleman is in error. The ceremony was first performed by the Hindoo Christna (or Krishna), who washed the feet of the Brahmins, as an example of humility, many thousand years anterior to the Christian era. Chapter and verse will be given, if required, from the Brahmanical books. Meanwhile, the reader is referred to the Rev. John P. Lundy's *Monumental Christianity,* p. 154.

H. P. BLAVATSKY.

New York, August 12th.

THE JEWS IN RUSSIA
[*The World*, New York, September 25, 1877]

It is to be regretted that your incandescent contemporary, *The Sun,* should have no better sources of information. It stated on Saturday last that "in Russia the persecution of the Israelites is continued, with nearly all its ancient cruelty. They are not permitted to reside in many of the greatest cities. Kief and Novgorod, as well as Moscow, are forbidden to them, and even in the rural districts they are burdened with multiform exactions."

This is the reverse of correct, as is the further statement that "they have been robbed and oppressed in Bulgaria by the Russians." The murdering and plundering at the seat of war, it is now pretty well settled, has been done by the Turks exclusively, and, notwithstanding that the English and other Turkophile organs have diligently cast the blame upon the Russians, the plot of the Ottoman Government, thanks to the honest old Emperor of Germany, is now discovered. The Turks are convicted of systematic lying, and nearly every country, including England herself, has sent its protest to the Sublime Porte against her atrocities. As to the condition of Israelites in Russia, it has immensely improved since the accession of Alexander II to the throne of his father. For more than ten years they have been placed on jury duty, admitted to the bar and otherwise accorded civil rights and privileges. If social disabilities still linger, we are scarcely the ones to chide, in view of our Saratoga and Long Branch custom, and the recent little unpleasantness between Mr. Hilton and the descendants of the "chosen people."

If your neighbor would take the trouble to ask any traveller or Russian Israelite now in America it would learn that Kief, as well as other "greatest cities" are full of Jews; that in fact there are more Jews than Gentiles in the first named of those cities. Pretty much all trade is in their hands, and they furnish even all the olive oil that is permanently burnt at the *rakas* (shrines) of the 700 orthodox saints whose beatified mummies fill up the Catacombs of Kief, and the wax for the candles on all the altars; and it is again the Jews who keep the dram-shops, or *kabak,* where the faithful congregate after service to give a last filip to their devotional ardor. It is barely four months since the chief Rabbi of Moscow published in the official *Vedomosty* an earnest address to his co-religionists throughout the empire to remind them that they were Russians by nativity, and called upon them to display their patriotism in subscriptions for the wounded, prayers in the synagogues for the success of the Russian arms and all other practical ways. In 1870, during the *émeute* in Odessa, which was caused by some Jewish children throwing dirt into the church on Easter night, and which lasted more than a week, the Russian soldiers shot and bayonetted twelve Christian Russians and not a single Jew; while—and I speak as an eyewitness — over two hundred rioters were publicly whipped by order of the Governor-General, Kotzebue,* of whom none were Israelites. That there is a hatred between them and the more fanatical Christians is true, but the Russian Government can be no more blamed for this than the British and American Governments because Orangemen and Catholics mutually hate, beat, and occasionally kill each other.

H. P. BLAVATSKY.

New York, September 24th.

---

*[Count Paul Kotzebue, Governor-General of Odessa and later of Warsaw.—*Compiler.*]

[ISIS UNVEILED]

[It is here chronologically that the two volumes of H.P.B.'s first great work, *Isis Unveiled*, belong. In a letter addressed to her friend, Alexander Nikolayevich Aksakov, and dated October 2, 1877, she says: ". . . My work has appeared. It was born, the dear thing, last Saturday, September 29 . . ."* She also says that the first edition—most likely the first printing or "run"—consisted of 1,000 copies, and these were sold in two days, so that some of the subscribers had to wait a week or more until another "run" could be made ready.

Isis Unveiled was published in Two Volumes by J. W. Bouton, 706 Broadway, New York, and also bears the imprint of Bernard Quaritch, London. Its subtitle is: "A Master-Key to the Mysteries of Ancient and Modern Science and Theology." The original edition has a dark red binding with the title, author's name and a symbolic figure of Isis on the spine in gold.

Consult Col. Olcott's *Old Diary Leaves*, First Series, for his interesting account of the manner in which this work was written. And the more comprehensive outline appended to the edition of *Isis Unveiled* as part of the present Series.—Compiler.]

[In H.P.B.'s *Scrapbook*, Vol. IV, p. 83, there is a cutting concerning Dr. J. M. Peeble's travels in India and Africa. He looks upon Buddhists as being Spiritualists, and suggests that millions of Spiritualistic tracts be distributed among them to enlighten them on the subject of "angel ministry."
To this H.P.B. added the following remarks in pen and ink:]

Heaven save the mark! It is not enough for the poor Hindus to be pestered with Christian missionaries, but they must have the affliction of being bombarded with tracts and lectures of *modern* Spiritualism. Of Spiritualism of which they and their forefathers were just masters and professors for the last several millenniums.

---

*Translated from the Russian original in the work of Vsevolod S. Solovyov, *Sovremennaya Zhritsa Isidi* (Modern Priestess of Isis), St. Petersburg, 1904, p. 287. Cf. English transl. by Walter Leaf, London, 1895, p. 276.

"ELEMENTARIES"

A LETTER FROM THE CORRESPONDING SECRETARY OF THE THEOSOPHICAL SOCIETY.

[*Religio-Philosophical Journal*, Chicago, Vol. XXIII, Nov. 17, 1877]

Editor, *Journal:*

Dear Sir,—I perceive that of late the ostracized subject of the Kabalistic "elementaries," is beginning to appear in the orthodox spiritual papers, pretty often. No wonder; Spiritualism and its philosophy are progressing, and they will progress, despite the opposition of some very learned ignoramuses who imagine the cosmos rotates within the academic brain. But if a new term is once admitted for discussion the least we can do is to first clearly ascertain what that term means; we students of the Oriental philosophy count it a clear gain that Spiritualist journals on both sides of the Atlantic are beginning to discuss the subject of subhuman and earth-bound beings, even though they ridicule the idea. Only do those who ridicule it know what they are talking about? Having never studied the Kabalist writers, it becomes evident to me that they confound the "elementaries"—disembodied, vicious, and earth-bound, yet human spirits, with the "elementals," or nature-spirits.

With your permission, then, I will answer an article by Dr. Woldrich, which appeared in your *Journal* of the 27th inst., and to which the author gives the title of "Elementaries." I freely admit that owing to my imperfect knowledge of English at the time I first wrote upon the elementaries, I may have myself contributed to the present confusion, and thus brought upon my doomed head the wrath of Spiritualists, mediums, and their "guides" into the bargain. But now I will attempt to make my meaning clear. Éliphas Lévi applies equally the term "elementary" to earthbound human spirits and to the creatures of the elements.

This carelessness on his part is due to the fact that as the human elementaries are considered by the Kabalists as having irretrievably lost every chance of immortality, they therefore, after a certain period of time, become no better than the elementals who never had any soul at all. To disentangle the subject, I have, in my *Isis Unveiled,* shown that the former should alone be called "elementaries," and the latter "elementals" (Before the Veil, Vol. I, pp. xxix-xxx).

Dr. Woldrich, in imitation of Herbert Spencer, attempts to explain the existence of a popular belief in nature-spirits, demons and mythological deities, as the effect of an imagination untutored by science, and wrought upon by misunderstood natural phenomena. He attributes the legendary sylphs, undines, salamanders and gnomes, four great families, which include numberless subdivisions, to mere fancy; going, however, to the extreme of affirming that by long practice one can acquire "that power which disembodied spirits have of materializing apparitions by his will." Granted that "disembodied spirits" have sometimes that power, but if disembodied, why not embodied spirit also, *i.e.,* a yet living person who has become an adept in occultism through study? According to Dr. Woldrich's theory an embodied spirit or magician can create only subjectively, or to quote his words —"he is in the habit of summoning, that is, bringing up to his imagination his familiar spirits, which, having responded to his will, he will consider as real existences."

I will not stop to inquire for the proofs of this assertion, for it would only lead to an endless discussion. If many thousands of Spiritualists in Europe and America have seen materialized objective forms which assure them they were the spirits of once living persons, millions of Eastern people throughout the past ages have seen the Hierophants of the temples, and even now see them in India, also evoking, without being in the least mediums, objective and tangible forms, which display no pretensions to being the souls of disembodied men. But I will only remark that, as Dr. Woldrich tells us that, though subjective and invisible to others, these forms are palpable, hence objective to the clairvoyant, no scientist has yet mastered the mysteries of even the physical sciences sufficiently to enable him to contradict, with anything like plausible or incontrovertible proofs, the assumption that because a clairvoyant sees a form remaining subjective to others, this form is nevertheless neither a hallucination nor a fiction of the imagination. Were the persons present endowed with the same clairvoyant faculty, they would everyone of them see this "creature of hallucination" as well; hence there would be sufficient proof that it had an objective existence. And this is how the experiments are conducted in certain psychological training schools, as I call such establishments in the East. One clairvoyant is never trusted. The person may be honest, truthful, and have the greatest desire to learn only that which is real, and yet mix the truth unconsciously and accept an elemental for a disembodied spirit, and *vice versa*. For instance, what guarantee can Dr. Woldrich give us that "Hoki" and "Thalla," the guides of Miss May Shaw, were not simply creatures produced by the power of imagination? This gentleman may have the word of his clairvoyant for this; he may implicitly and very deservedly trust her honesty when in her normal state; but the fact alone that a medium is a passive and docile instrument in the hands of some invisible and mysterious powers, ought to make her irresponsible in the eyes of every serious investigator. It is the spirit, or these invisible powers, he has to test, not the clairvoyant's; and what proof has he of their trustworthiness that he should think himself warranted in coming out as the exponent of a philosophy based on thousands of years of practical experience, the iconoclast of experiments performed by whole generations of learned Egyptian Hierophants, Guru-Brahmans, adepts of the sanctuaries, and a whole host of more or less learned Kabalists, who were all trained Seers? Such an accusation, moreover, is dangerous ground for the Spiritualists themselves. Admit once that a magician creates his forms only in fancy, and as a result of hallucination, and what becomes of all the guides, spirit friends, and the *tutti quanti* from the sweet Summerland crowding around the trance medium and seers? Why these would-be disembodied entities should be considered more identified than the elementals, or as Dr. Woldrich terms them, "elementaries"—of the magician, is something which could scarcely bear investigation.

From the standpoint of certain Buddhist schools, your correspondent may be right. Their philosophy teaches that even our visible universe assumed an objective form as a result of the fancy followed by the volition or the will of the unknown and supreme adept, differing from Christian theology, however, inasmuch as they teach that instead of calling out our universe from nothingness, he had to exercise this will upon pre-existing matter, eternal and indestructible as to invisible substance, though temporary and ever-changing as to forms. Some higher and still more subtle metaphysical schools of Nepal even go so far as to affirm—on very reasonable grounds too—that this pre-existing and self-existent substance or matter (Svabhavat) is itself without any other creator or ruler; when in the state of activity it is *Pravritti*, a universal creating principle; when latent and passive, they call this force *Nivritti*. As for something eternal and infinite, for that which had neither beginning nor end, there can be neither past nor future, but everything that was and will be, IS, therefore there never was an action or even thought, however simple, that is not impressed in imperishable records on this substance called by the Buddhists Svabhavat, by the Kabalists astral light. As in a faithful mirror this light reflects every image, and no human imagination could see anything outside that which exists impressed somewhere on the eternal substance. To imagine that a human brain can conceive of anything that was never conceived of before by the "universal brain," is a fallacy, and a conceited presumption. At best, the former can catch now and then stray glimpses of the "eternal thought" after these have assumed some objective form, either in the world of the invisible or visible universe. Hence the unanimous testimony of trained seers goes to prove that there are such creatures as the elementals; and that though the elementaries have been at some time human spirits, they, having lost every connection with the purer immortal world, must be recognized by some special term which would draw a distinct line of demarcation between them and the true and genuine disembodied souls which have henceforth to remain immortal. To the Kabalists and the adepts, especially in India, the difference between the two is all important, and their tutored minds will never allow them to mistake the one for the other; to the untutored medium they are all one.

Spiritualists have never accepted the suggestions and sound advice of certain of their seers and mediums. They have regarded Mr. Peebles' "Gadarenes" with indifference; they have shrugged their shoulders at the "Rosicrucian" fantasies of P. B. Randolph, and his "Ravalette" has made none of them the wiser; they have frowned and grumbled at A. Jackson Davis' "Diakka"; and finally lifting high the banner have declared a murderous war of extermination to the Theosophs and Kabalists. What are now the results?

A series of exposures of fraudulent mediums that have brought mortification to their endorsers and dishonor upon the cause; identification by genuine seers and mediums of pretended spirit-forms that were afterwards found to be mere personations by living cheats—which goes to prove that in such instances at least, outside of clear cases of confederacy the identifications were due to illusion on the part of the said seers; spirit-babes discovered to be battered masks and bundles of rags; obsessed mediums driven by their guides to drunkenness and immorality of conduct— the practices of free love endorsed and even prompted by alleged immortal spirits; sensitive believers forced to the commission of murder, suicide, forgery, embezzlement and other crimes; the overcredulous led to waste their substance in foolish investments and the search after hidden treasures; mediums fostering ruinous speculations in stocks; free loveites parted from their wives in search of other female affinities; two continents flooded with the vilest slanders, spoken and sometimes printed by mediums against other mediums; *incubi* and *succubi* entertained as returning angel-husbands or wives; mountebanks and jugglers protected by scientists and the clergy and gathering large audiences to witness imitations of the phenomena of cabinets, the reality of which genuine mediums themselves and spirits are powerless to vindicate by giving the necessary test-conditions; *séances* still held in Stygian darkness where even genuine phenomena can readily be mistaken for the false and false for the real; mediums left helpless by their angel guides, tried, convicted and sent to prison and no attempt made to save them from their fate by those, who, if they are spirits having the power of controlling mortal affairs, ought to have enlisted the sympathy of the heavenly hosts in behalf of their mediums in the face of such crying injustice; other faithful Spiritualist lecturers and mediums broken down in health and left unsupported by those calling themselves their patrons and protectors. Such are some of the features of the present situation, the black spots of what ought to become the grandest and noblest of all religious philosophies —freely thrown by the unbelievers and materialists into the teeth of every Spiritualist; no intelligent person of the latter class need go outside of his own personal experience to find examples like the above. Spiritualism has not progressed and is not progressing, and will not progress until its facts are viewed in the light of the Oriental philosophy.

Thus, Mr. Editor, your esteemed correspondent, Dr. Woldrich, may be found guilty of two erroneous propositions. In the concluding sentence of his article he says:

> I know not whether I have succeeded in proving the "elementary" a myth, but at least I hope that I have thrown some more light upon the subject to some of the readers of the *Journal*.

To this I would answer: (1) He has not proved at all the "elementary a myth," since the elementaries are with a few exceptions the earth-bound guides and spirits in which he believes together with every other Spiritualist; (2) Instead of throwing light upon the subject the Doctor has but darkened it the more; (3) Such explanations and careless exposures do the greatest harm to the future of Spiritualism and greatly serve to retard its progress, by teaching its adherents that they have nothing more to learn.

Sincerely hoping that I have not trespassed too much on the columns of your esteemed *Journal,* allow me to sign myself, dear Sir, yours respectfully,

H. P. BLAVATSKY,
Corresponding Secretary of the Theosophical Society.

New York.

[In H.P.B.'s *Scrapbook,* Vol. IV, p. 95, there is a cutting from the *Religio-Philosophical Journal* with an article by E. Gerry Brown on Elementaries and Elementals. It is Brown's reaction to H.P.B.'s own article entitled "Elementaries" in the same Journal, and he is defending the Spiritualistic viewpoint. H.P.B. wrote the following remarks in pen and ink:]

Bravo Gerry Brown! Good and noble from a *friend* who not long ago called us his *benefactors*!! E. G. Brown a *medium,* a *sensitive,* c'est tout dire.

[In her *Scrapbook,* Vol. I, p. 70, H.P.B. pasted the last portion of an article by Emily Kislingbury entitled "Spiritualism in America," published in *The Spiritualist* of London, December 14, 1877. Above the cutting, H.P.B. wrote in ink:]

Address delivered by our friend and Brahmabodhini—Emily Kislingbury before the B. N. Asson of Spiritualists in London December 1877.
Complimentary bits from it—to poor H.P.B. (poor Violet!)

[The last parenthetical remark is in blue pencil and might have been added by Col. Olcott.]

[In her *Scrapbook,* Vol. VII, p. 46, H.P.B. pasted another article by the same writer and wrote the following remarks on a small card decorated with coloured flowers:]

Emily Kislingbury, one of the few redeeming features of Humanity.

DR. CARPENTER ON "TREE-TRICKERY" AND H. P. BLAVATSKY ON FAKIR-"JUGGLERY"

[*Religio-Philosophical Journal*, Chicago, Vol. XXIII, December 22, 1877, p. 8]

A wise saying that which affirms that he who seeks to prove too much, in the end proves nothing. Professor W. B. Carpenter, F.R.S. (and otherwise alphabetically adorned), furnishes a conspicuous example in his strife with men better than himself. His assaults accumulate bitterness with every new periodical he makes his organ; and in proportion with the increase of his abuse his arguments lose force and cogency. And, forsooth, he nevertheless lectures his antagonists for their lack of "calm discussion," as though he were not the very type of controversial nitroglycerine! Rushing at them with his proofs, which are "incontrovertible" only in his own estimation, he commits himself more than once. By one of such committals I mean to profit today, by citing some curious experience of my own.

My object in writing the present is far from that of taking any part in this onslaught upon reputations. Messrs. Wallace and Crookes are well able to take care of themselves. Each has contributed in his own specialty towards real progress in useful knowledge more than Dr. Carpenter in his. Both have been honored for valuable original researches and discoveries, while their accuser has been often charged of being no better than a very clever compiler of other men's ideas. After reading the able rejoinders of the "defendants," and the scathing review of the Mace-swinging Professor Buchanan, everyone—except his friends, the psychophobists—can see that Dr. Carpenter is completely floored. He is as dead as the traditional doornail.

In the December Supplement of the *Popular Science Monthly,* I find (p. 116) the interesting admission that a poor Hindu juggler can perform a feat that quite takes the great Professor's breath away! In comparison, the mediumistic phenomena of Miss Nichol (Mrs. Guppy) are of no account. "The celebrated 'tree-trick,'" says Dr. Carpenter, "which most people who have been long in India have seen, as described by several of our most distinguished civilians and scientific officers, is simply the greatest marvel I [he] ever heard of. That a mango tree should first shoot up to a height of six inches, from a grassplot to which the conjurers had no previous access, beneath an inverted cylindrical basket, whose emptiness has been previously demonstrated, and that this tree should appear to grow in the course of half an hour from six inches to six feet, under a succession of taller and yet taller baskets, quite beats Miss Nichol."

Well, I should think it did. At any rate it beats anything that any F.R.S. can show by daylight or dark, in the Royal Institution or elsewhere. Would not one think that such a phenomenon so attested and occurring under circumstances that preclude trickery, would provoke scientific investigation? If not, what would? But observe the knot hole through which an F.R.S. can creep out. "Does Mr. Wallace," ironically asks the Professor, "attribute this to a spiritual agency? or, like the world in general [of course meaning the world that science created and Carpenter energizes] and the performers of the 'tree-trick' in particular, does he regard it as a piece of clever jugglery?"

Leaving Mr. Wallace—if he survives this Jovian thunderbolt—to answer for himself, I have to say for the "performers," that they would respond with an emphatic "*No*" to both interrogatories. The Hindu jugglers neither claim for their performance a "spiritual agency," nor admit it to be a "trick of clever jugglery." The ground they take is that the tricks are produced by certain powers inherent in man himself, which may be used for a good or bad purpose. And the ground that I, humbly following after those whose opinion is based on really exact psychological experiments and knowledge take, is that neither Dr. Carpenter nor his bodyguard of scientists, though their titles stream after their names like the tail after a kite, have as yet the slightest conception of these powers. To acquire even a superficial knowledge of them, they must change their scientific and philosophical methods. Following after Wallace and Crookes they must begin with the A B C of Spiritualism, which, meaning to be very scornful, Dr. Carpenter terms "the centre of enlightenment and progress." They must take their lessons not alone from the true but as well from spurious phenomena, from what his (Carpenter's) chief authority, the "arch priest of the new religion," properly classifies as "Delusions, Absurdities and Trickeries." After wading through all this, as every intelligent investigator has had to do, he may get some glimpses of truth. It is as useful to learn what the phenomena are not, as to find out what they are.

Dr. Carpenter has two patent keys warranted to unlock every secret door of the mediumistic cabinet. They are labelled "expectancy" and "prepossession." Most scientists have some picklock like this. But to the "tree-trick" they scarcely apply; for neither his "distinguished civilians" nor "scientific officers," could have expected to see a stark naked Hindu, on a strange grassplot, in full daylight make a mango grow six feet from the seed in half an hour; their "prepossessions" would be all against it. It can't be a "spiritual agency," it must be "jugglery." Now, Maskelyne and Cooke, two clever English jugglers, have been keeping the mouths and eyes of all London wide open with their exposures of Spiritualism. They are admired by all the scientists, and at Slade's trial figured as expert witnesses for the prosecution. They are at Dr. Carpenter's elbow. Why does he not call them to explain this clever jugglery, and make Messrs. Wallace and Crookes blush with shame at their own idiocy? All the tricks of the trade are familiar to them; where can science find better allies? But we must insist upon identical conditions. The "tree-trick" must not be performed by gaslight on the platform of any Egyptian Hall, nor with the performers in full evening dress. It must be in broad daylight, on a strange grassplot to which the conjurers had no previous access. There must be no machinery, no confederates. White cravats and swallow-tailed coats must be laid aside and the English champions appear in the primitive apparel of Adam and Eve—a tight-fitting "coat of skin," and with the single addition of a *dhoti,* or a breech cloth seven inches wide. The Hindus do all this, and we only ask fair play. If they raise a mango sapling under these circumstances, Dr. Carpenter will be at perfect liberty to beat with it the last remnant of brains out of the head of any "crazy Spiritualist" he may encounter. But until then, the less he says about Hindu jugglery the better for his scientific reputation.

It is not to be denied that in India, China and elsewhere in the East there are veritable jugglers who exhibit tricks. Equally true is it that some of these performances surpass any with which Western people are acquainted. But these are neither "fakirs" nor the performers of the "mango tree" marvel, as described by Dr. Carpenter. Even this is sometimes imitated both by Indian and European adepts in sleight-of-hand, but under totally different conditions. Modestly following in the rear of the "distinguished civilians" and "scientific officers," I will now narrate something which I have seen with my own eyes.

While at Cawnpoor, en route to Benares, the holy city, a lady, my travelling companion, was robbed of the entire contents of a small trunk. Jewellery, dresses, and even her notebook, containing a diary which she had been carefully compiling for over three months, had mysteriously disappeared, without the lock of the valise having been disturbed. Several hours, perhaps a night and a day had passed since the robbery, as we had started at daybreak to explore some neighboring ruins, yet freshly allied with the Nana Sahib's reprisals on the English. My companion's first thought was to call upon the local police—mine for the help of some native gosâin (a holy man supposed to be informed of everything) or at least a "jâdûgar" or conjurer. But the ideas of civilization prevailed, and a whole week was wasted in fruitless visits to the "chabutara" (police house) and interviews with the "kotwal"— its chief. In despair, my expedient was at last resorted to, and a gosâin procured. We occupied a small bungalow at the extreme end of one of the suburbs, on the right bank of the Ganges, and from the verandah a full view of the river was had, which at that place was very narrow.

Our experiment was made on that verandah, in the

presence of the family of the landlord—a half-caste Portuguese from the South—my friend and myself, and two freshly imported Frenchmen, who laughed outrageously at our superstition. Time, three o'clock in the afternoon. The heat was suffocating, but notwithstanding, the holy man—a coffee-colored, living skeleton—demanded that the motion of the punkah (hanging fan worked by a cord) should be stopped. He gave no reason, but it was because the agitation of the air interferes with all delicate magnetic experiments. We had all heard of the "rolling-pot," as an agency for the detection of theft in India, a common iron pot being made under the influence of a Hindu conjurer, to roll of its own impulse, without any hand touching it, to the very spot where the stolen goods are concealed. The gosâîn proceeded otherwise. He first of all demanded some article that had been latest in contact with the contents of the valise; a pair of gloves was handed him. He pressed them between his thin palms, and rolling them over and over again; then dropped them on the floor, and proceeded to turn himself slowly around, with arms outstretched and fingers expanded, as though he were seeking the direction in which the property lay. Suddenly, he stopped with a jerk, sank gradually to the floor and remained motionless, sitting cross-legged and with his arms still outstretched in the same direction, as though plunged in a cataleptic trance. This lasted for over an hour, which in that suffocating atmosphere, was to us one long torture. Suddenly the landlord sprang from his seat to the balustrade, and began instantly looking towards the river, in which direction our eyes also turned. Coming from whence, or how, we could not tell; but out there, over the water, and near its surface, was a dark object approaching. What it was we could not make out; but the mass seemed impelled by some interior force to revolve, at first slowly, but then faster and faster as it drew near. It was as though supported on an invisible pavement, and its course was in a direct line as the bee flies. It reached the bank, disappeared again among the high vegetation, and anon, rebounding with force as it leaped over the low garden wall, flew rather than rolled on the verandah and dropped with a heavy thud under the extended palms of the gosâîn. A violent, convulsive tremor shook the frame of the old man, as with a deep sigh he opened his half-closed eyes. All were astounded, but the Frenchmen stared at the bundle with an expression of idiotic terror in their eyes! Rising from the ground the holy man opened the tarred canvas envelope and within were found all the stolen articles down to the least thing. Without a word, or waiting for thanks, he salaamed low to the company and disappeared through the doorway before we recovered from our surprise. We had to run after him a long way before we could press upon him a dozen rupees, which blessings he received in his wooden bowl.

This may appear a very surprising and incredible story to Europeans and Americans who have never been in India. But we have Dr. Carpenter's authority for it, that even his "distinguished civilian" friends and "scientific officers," who are as little likely to sniff out anything mystical there, with their aristocratic noses, as Dr. Carpenter to see it with his telescopic, microscopic, double-magnifying scientific eyes in England, have witnessed the mango "tree-trick," which is still more wonderful. If the latter is "clever jugglery" the other—must be, too. Will the white-cravated and swallow-tailed gentlemen of Egyptian Hall please show the Royal Society how either is done?

H. P. BLAVATSKY.

[Sometime in December, 1877, W. J. Colville, a trance medium, was giving trance-addresses in London. A cutting pasted in H.P.B's *Scrapbook*, Vol. IV, p. 108, tells that his guides lectured the Sunday before against the views of the Theosophists, as laid down by Col. Olcott. Under this statement, H.P.B. wrote in pencil:]

Oh poor miserable Moloney! We must be disreputable and wrong in our views indeed to have thus lecturing against the latter the sweet denizens of the Sugary Spheeeres!!!...

[In her *Scrapbook*, Vol. IV, p. 125, H.P.B. pasted a cutting from the New York *World* of April 4, 1874, entitled "Incremation." It is most likely that the following remarks written by her in red pencil (much faded) were made at a later period, probably about the end of 1877:]

A PAGE FAR BACK—H. S. Olcott's idea on "Cremation" so far back as 1874; which proves that the cremation of the Baron was not due to theosophical ideas alone.

[In the same *Scrapbook*, Vol. IV, p. 140, H.P.B. pasted a cutting concerning the exposure of the medium James M. Choate whose alleged phenomenal flowers were hidden in his handkerchief. It appears that the medium, "without making any explanation," departed "by the back entrance." H.P.B. added the following suggestion in pen and ink:]

Insist upon thoroughly searching every "Medium," and thus two-thirds of them will do likewise—and disappear through the back door . . .

1878

[H.P.B. AND HER MASONIC DIPLOMA]

[In connection with an article by George Corbyn entitled "Rosicrucianism" and published in the *Spiritual Scientist*, criticising the article by "Hiraf" as well as H.P.B.'s reply thereto, H.P.B. wrote in her *Scrapbook*, Vol. III, p. 256, as follows:]

I am sorry Mr. Corbyn is so ignorant of Masonry. Since this was written I have received from the Sovereign Grand Master General of the A. and P. Rite of England and Wales a diploma of 32nd Degree.

H.P.B.
N. Y. Jan.
1878

[H.P.B. CORRECTS AN ERROR ABOUT ELEMENTALS]

[In her *Scrapbook*, Vol. IV, p. 152, H.P.B. pasted a cutting from the London *Spiritualist* of January 18, 1878, which contains "Some Personal Experiences in Mediumship" from the pen of Baroness Adelma von Vay (Countess Wurmbrand). Although the writer expresses her admiration for H.P.B. in connection with *Isis Unveiled*, she says, however: "While our elementaries are spirits doing penance for past sin, and preparing themselves for a better state of existence, *her elementals are souls which have already lost their spirits*, and will themselves, in process of time, become annihilated."
Underlining the sentence italicized above, H.P.B. wrote in pen and ink as follows:]

Quite the reverse. Never said such a thing and the "Isis" is there to show the mistake. Either the fair Baroness has not read it (with) attention, or she did not understand it.

[In H.P.B.'s *Scrapbook*, Vol. IV, p. 163, there is a cutting from the London *Spiritualist* of January 25, 1878. It is a Letter to the Editor from Dr. J. M. Peebles, who is attempting to prove that there *are* Hindu Spiritualists by quoting the words of Peary Chand Mittra who used the expression "the nobleness of Spiritualism." To this H.P.B. appended the following remarks in pen and ink:]

Yes, the nobleness of *Spiritualism*—not of modern *Phenomenalism*, great difference. Ask Peary Chand Mittra whether he would accept "materialized" spooks with sweating and corpse-stinking bodies for his dear "departed ones"? and see what he will answer . . . That our friend Peebles has always had a tendency to confer the name of Spiritualist on every one he met, the following is a proof.

[Here H.P.B. drew a line to a cutting on the same page entitled "Is Longfellow a Spiritualist?" in which Longfellow declines to be considered as such. H.P.B. then continues her remark thus:]

(See what Peary Chand Mittra writes on the subject of materialization. February 8, 1878.)

[Underneath H.P.B. pasted a printed picture showing the enormous figure of a native woman. The title is: "Cuzco Costumes—Woman of the Lower Order," to which picture H.P.B. added the comment:]

at some future date—a "materialized" Angel.

KABALISTIC VIEWS ON "SPIRITS" AS PROPAGATED BY THE THEOSOPHICAL SOCIETY

[*Religio-Philosophical Journal*, Chicago, Vol. XXIII, January 26, 1878, p. 2]

Editor, *Journal:*

Dear Sir,—I must beg you to again allow me a little space for the further elucidation of a very important question—that of the "Elementals" and the "Elementaries." It is a misfortune that our European languages do not contain a nomenclature expressive of the various grades and conditions of spiritual beings. But surely I cannot be blamed for either the above linguistic deficiency, or because some people do not choose or are unable to understand my meaning! I cannot too often repeat that in this matter I claim no originality. My teachings are but the substance of what many kabalists have said before me, which, today, I mean to prove with your kind permission.

I am accused (1) of "turning somersaults" and jumping from one idea to another. The defendant pleads—not guilty. (2) Of coining not only words, but philosophies out of the depths of my consciousness: defendant enters the same plea. (3) Of having repeatedly asserted that "intelligent spirits other than those who have passed through an earth experience in a human body were concerned in the manifestations known as the phenomena of Spiritualism:" true, and defendant repeats the assertion. (4) Of having advanced, in my bold and unwarranted theories, "beyond the great Éliphas Lévi himself." Indeed? Were I to go even as far as he (see his *La Science des Esprits*), I would deny that a single so-called spiritual manifestation is more than hallucination, produced by soulless Elementals, whom he calls "Elementary." (See *Dogme et Rituel de la Haute Magie*.)

I am asked, "What proof is there of the existence of the elementals?" In my turn, I will inquire, what proof is there of "diakkas," "guides," "bands," and "controls"? And yet these terms are all current among Spiritualists. The unanimous testimony of innumerable observers and competent experimenters furnishes the proof. If Spiritualists cannot or will not go to those countries where they are living, and these proofs are accessible, they, at least, have no right to give the lie direct to those who have seen both the adepts and the proofs. My witnesses are living men, teaching and exemplifying the philosophy of hoary ages; theirs, these very "guides" and "controls" who, up to the present time, are at best hypothetical, and whose assertions have been repeatedly found, by Spiritualists themselves, contradictory and false.

If my present critics insist that since the discussion of this matter began a disembodied soul has never been described as an "elementary," I merely point to the number of the London *Spiritualist* for February 18th, 1876, published nearly two years ago, in which a correspondent, who has certainly studied occult sciences, says: "Is it not probable that some of the elementary spirits of an evil type are those spirit-bodies which, only recently disembodied, are on the eve of an eternal dissolution, and which continue their temporary existence only by vampirizing those still in the flesh? They had existence; they never attained to being." Note two things: that human elementaries are recognized as existing, apart from the gnomes, sylphs, undines and salamanders—beings purely elemental; and that annihilation of the soul is regarded as potential.

Says Paracelsus, in his *Philosophia Sagax*: "The current of astral light with its peculiar inhabitants, gnomes, sylphs, etc., is transformed into human light at the moment of the conception, and it becomes the first envelope of the soul— its grosser portion; combined with the most subtle fluids, it forms the sidereal (astral, or ethereal) phantom—the inner man."* And Éliphas Lévi: "The astral light is saturated with

---

*[Reference is to the work entitled: *Astronomia magna: oder die gantze Philosophia sagax der grossen und kleinen Welt*, Frankfurt, Hieronymus Feyerabends, 1571. British Museum: 531.n.23, 1st ed.— *Compiler.*]

souls which it discharges in the incessant generation of beings
. . . At the birth of a child, they influence the four temperaments of the latter—the element of the gnomes predominates in melancholy persons; of the salamanders in the sanguine; of the undines, in the phlegmatic; of the sylphs, in the giddy and bilious. . . . These are the spirits which we designate under the term of occult elements." (*Dogme et Rituel de la Haute Magie*, Vol. II, chapter on the conjuration of the four classes of elementaries.) "Yes, yes," he remarks (in Vol. I, *op. cit.*, p. 164), "these spirits of the elements do exist. Some wandering in their spheres, others trying to incarnate themselves, others again already incarnated and living on earth. These are vicious and imperfect men."

Note that we have here described to us more or less "intelligent spirits other than those who have passed through an earth experience in a human body." If not intelligent, they would not know how to make the attempt to incarnate themselves. Vicious elementals, or elementaries, are attracted to vicious parents; they bask in their atmosphere, and are thus afforded the chance by the vices of the parents to perpetuate in the child the paternal wickedness. The unintellectual "elementals" are drawn in unconsciously to themselves; and in the order of nature, as component parts of the grosser astral body or soul, determine the temperament. They can as little resist as the animalcules can avoid entering into our bodies in the water we swallow.

Of a third class, out of hundreds that the Eastern philosophers and kabalists are acquainted with, Éliphas Lévi, discussing spiritistic phenomena, says: "They are neither the souls of the damned nor guilty; the elementary spirits are like children curious and harmless, and torment people in proportion as attention is paid to them." These he regards as the sole agents in all the meaningless and useless physical phenomena at *séances*. Such phenomena will be produced unless they be dominated "by wills more powerful than their own." Such a will may be that of a living adept, or as there are none such at Western spiritual *séances*, these ready agents are at the disposal of every strong, vicious, earth-bound, human elementary who has been attracted to the place. By such they can be used in combination with the astral emanations of the circle and medium, as stuff out of which to make materialized spirits.

So little does Lévi concede the possibility of spirit-return in objective form, that he says: "The good deceased come back in our dreams; the state of mediumism is an extension of dream, it is somnambulism in all its variety and ecstasies. Fathom the phenomenon of sleep and you will understand the phenomena of the spirits"; and again: "According to one of the great dogmas of the kabala, the spirit despoils itself in order to ascend, and thus would have to reclothe itself to descend. There is but one way for a spirit already liberated to manifest itself again on earth—it must get back into its body and resurrect. This is quite another thing from hiding under a table or a hat. That is why necromancy is horrible. It constitutes a crime against nature. . . . We have admitted in our former works the possibility of vampirism, and even tried to explain it. The phenomena now actually occurring in America and Europe unquestionably belong to this fearful malady. . . . The mediums do not, it is true, eat the flesh of corpses [like one Sergeant Bertrand], but they breathe in throughout their whole nervous organism the phosphoric emanations of putrefied corpses, or spectral light. They are not vampires, but they evoke vampires. For this reason, they are nearly all debilitated and sick."*

Do those in Europe and America, who have heretofore described the cadaverous odor that, in some cases, they have noticed as attending materialized spirits, appreciate the revolting significance of the above explanation?

Henry Khunrath was a most learned kabalist, and the greatest authority among mediaeval occultists. He gives, in one of the clavicles of his *Amphitheatrum Sapientiae Aeternae*, illustrative engravings of the four great classes of elementary spirits, as they presented themselves during an evocation of ceremonial magic, before the eyes of the

---

*[*La Science des esprits*, pp. 241-42, 253-54 in ed. of 1909.]

magus, when, after passing the threshold, he lifts the "Veil of Isis." In describing them, Khunrath corroborates Éliphas Lévi. He tells us they are disembodied, vicious men, who have parted with their divine spirits and become elementary. They are so termed, "because attracted by the earthly atmosphere, and are surrounded by the earth's elements." Here Khunrath applies the term "elementary" to human doomed souls, while Lévi uses it, as we have seen, to designate another class of the same great family—gnomes, sylphs, undines, etc.—sub-human entities.

I have before me a manuscript, intended originally for publication but withheld for various reasons. The author signs himself "Zeus," and is a kabalist of more than twenty-five years' standing. This experienced occultist, a zealous devotee of Khunrath, expounding the doctrine of the latter, also says that the kabalists divided the spirits of the elements into four classes corresponding to the four temperaments in man.

It is charged against me as a heinous offense that I aver that some men lose their souls and are annihilated. But this last-named authority, "Zeus," is equally culpable, for he says, "They (the kabalists) taught that man's spirit descended from the great ocean of spirit, and is therefore, *per se*, pure and divine; but its soul or capsule, through the (allegorical) fall of Adam, became contaminated with the world of darkness, or the world of Satan (evil), of which it must be purified, before it could ascend again to celestial happiness. Suppose a drop of water enclosed within a capsule of gelatine and thrown in the ocean; so long as the capsule remains whole, the drop of water remains isolated: break the envelope, and the drop becomes a part of the ocean, its individual existence has ceased. So it is with the spirit, so long as its ray is enclosed in its plastic mediator or soul, it has an individual existence. Destroy this capsule (the astral man, who then becomes an elementary), which destruction may occur from the consequences of sin, in the most depraved and vicious, and the spirit returns back to its original abode—the individualization of man has ceased." "This militates," he adds, "with the idea of progression, that

Spiritualists generally entertain. If they understood the law of harmony, they would see their error. It is only by this law that individual life can be sustained; and the farther we deviate from harmony the more difficult it is to regain it." To return to Lévi, he remarks (*Dogme et Rituel de la Haute Magie,* Vol. I, p. 319), "When we die, our interior light (the soul) ascends, agreeably to the attraction of its star (the spirit), but it must first of all get rid of the coils of the serpent (earthly evil—sin); that is to say, of the unpurified astral light, which surrounds and holds it captive, unless, by the force of will, it frees and elevates itself. This immersion of the living soul in the dead light (the emanations of everything that is evil, which pollute the earth's magnetic atmosphere, as the exhalation of a swamp does the air) is a dreadful torture; the soul freezes and burns therein, at the same time."

The kabalists represent Adam as the Tree of Life, of which the trunk is humanity; the various races, the branches; and individual men, the leaves. Every leaf has its individual life, and is fed by the one sap; but it can live through the branch, as the branch itself draws its life through the trunk. "The wicked," says the Kabala, "are the dead leaves and the dead bark of the tree. They fall, die, are corrupted, and changed into manure, which returns to the tree through the root."

My friend, Miss Emily Kislingbury, of London, Secretary of the British National Association of Spiritualists, who is honored, trusted and beloved by all who know her, sends me a spirit-communication obtained, in April, 1877, through a young lady, who is one of the purest and most truthful of her sex. The following extracts are singularly *à propos* to the subject under discussion: "Friend, you are right. Keep our Spiritualism pure and high, for there are those who would abase its uses. But it is because they know not the power of Spiritualism. It is true, in a sense, that the spirit can overcome the flesh, but there are those to whom the fleshly life is dearer than the life of the spirit; they tread on dangerous ground. For the flesh may so outgrow the spirit, as to withdraw from it all spirituality, and man become as a beast of the field, with no saving power left. These are they whom the Church has termed "reprobate," eternally lost, but they suffer not, as the Church has taught —in conscious hells. They merely die, and are not; their light goes out, and has no conscious being." (Question): "But is this not annihilation?" (Answer): "It amounts to annihilation; they lose their individual entities, and return to the great reservoir of spirit—unconscious spirit."

Finally, I am asked: "Who are the trained seers?" They are those, I answer, who have been trained from their childhood in the pagodas, to use their spiritual sight; those whose accumulated testimony has not varied for thousands of years as to the fundamental facts of Eastern philosophy; the testimony of each generation corroborating that of each preceding one. Are these to be trusted more, or less, than the communications of "bands," each of whom contradicts the other as completely as the various religious sects, which are ready to cut each other's throats, and of mediums, even the best of whom are ignorant of their own nature, and unsubjected to the wise direction and restraint of an adept in psychological science?

No comprehensive idea of nature can be obtained except by applying the law of harmony and analogy in the spiritual as well as in the physical world. "As above, so below," is the old Hermetic axiom. If Spiritualists would apply this to the subject of their own researches, they would see the philosophical necessity of there being in the world of spirit as well as in the world of matter, a law of the survival of the fittest.

Respectfully,
H. P. BLAVATSKY.

[In H.P.B.'s *Scrapbook*, Vol. IV, pp. 164-65, there is a cutting from the *Banner of Light* of February 2, 1878, being an article by Charles Sotheran entitled "Honours to Madame Blavatsky." The writer defends H.P.B., her work *Isis Unveiled*, and the Masonic Diploma which she received from John Yarker. To this H.P.B. appended the following remark in pen and ink:]

Mr. C. Sotheran who so abused me and the Society has now returned to it again confessing his *mistake* and making *Puja* to me again—Oh humanity ! !

H.P.B.

[In her *Scrapbook*, Vol. IV, pp. 169-72, H.P.B. pasted a cutting from the *Banner of Light* of February 2, 1878, in which Dr. J. M. Peebles speaks again of the Buddhists and remarks that "as all English speaking nations are nominally Christians, so in a broad, general sense all Buddhists are Spiritualists." H.P.B. marked the quoted sentence and wrote in blue pencil a side-remark:]

How can they be Spiritualists you goose when they *do not* believe in the existence of the "Soul"? Three *lies* for you!

MADAME BLAVATSKY ON THE VIEWS OF THE THEOSOPHISTS

[*The Spiritualist*, London, February 8, 1878, pp. 68-69] *

Sir,

Permit an humble Theosophist to appear for the first time in your columns, to say a few words in defence of our beliefs. I see in your issue of December 21st ultimo, one of your correspondents, Mr. J. Croucher, makes the following very bold assertions:

> Had the Theosophists thoroughly comprehended the nature of the soul and spirit, and its relation to the body, they would have known that if the soul once left the body, it could not return. The spirit can leave, but if the soul once leaves, it leaves for ever.

---

*[In her *Scrapbook*, Vol. III, p. 197, H.P.B. wrote the following remarks in blue pencil, in connection with a tribute to W.H. Harrison, the Editor of *The Spiritualist*:

Very true. The best, most scientific and impartial of all Spiritual papers.

—*Compiler.*]

This is so ambiguous that, unless he uses the term "soul" to designate only the vital principle, I can only suppose that he falls into the common error of calling the astral body, spirit, and the immortal essence, "soul." We, Theosophists, as Colonel Olcott has told you, do *vice versa*.

Besides the unwarranted imputation to us of ignorance, Mr. Croucher has an idea (peculiar to himself) that the problem which has heretofore taxed the powers of the metaphysicians in all ages has been solved in our own. It is hardly to be supposed that Theosophists or any others "thoroughly" comprehend the nature of the soul and spirit, and their relation to the body. Such an achievement is for Omniscience; and we Theosophists, treading the path worn by the footsteps of the old sages in the moving sands of exoteric philosophy, can only hope to approximate the absolute truth. It is really more than doubtful whether Mr. Croucher can do better, even though an "inspirational medium," and experienced "through constant sittings with one of the best trance mediums" in your country. I may well leave to time and Spiritual philosophy to entirely vindicate us in the far hereafter. When any Oedipus of this or the next century shall have solved this eternal enigma of the Sphinx-man, every modern dogma, not excepting some pets of the Spiritualists, will be swept away, as the Theban monster, according to the legend, leaped from his promontory into the sea, and was seen no more.

As early as February 18th, 1876, your learned correspondent, "M. A. (Oxon.)," took occasion, in an article entitled "Soul and Spirit," to point out the frequent confusion of the terms by other writers. As things are no better now, I will take the opportunity to show how sorely Mr. Croucher, and many other Spiritualists of whom he may be taken as the spokesman, misapprehended Colonel Olcott's meaning, and the views of the New York Theosophists. Colonel Olcott neither affirmed nor dreamed of implying that the immortal spirit leaves the body to produce the medial displays. And yet Mr. Croucher evidently thinks he did, for the word "spirit" to him means the inner astral man or double. Here is what Colonel Olcott did say, double commas and all:

> That mediumistic physical phenomena are not produced by pure spirits, but by "souls" embodied or disembodied, and usually with the help of elementals.

Any intelligent reader must perceive that, in placing the word "souls" in quotation marks, the writer indicated that he was using it in a sense not his own. As a Theosophist, he would more properly and philosophically have said for himself "astral spirits," or "astral men," or doubles. Hence, the criticism is wholly without even a foundation of plausibility. I wonder that a man could be found who, on so frail a basis, would have attempted so sweeping a denunciation. As it is, our President only propounded the *trine* of man, like the ancient and Oriental philosophers and their worthy imitator Paul, who held that the physical corporeity, the flesh and blood, was permeated and so kept alive by the *psychê*, the soul or astral body. This doctrine, that man is trine—spirit, or *Nous*, soul and body—was taught by the Apostle of the Gentiles more broadly and clearly than it has been by any of his Christian successors (see *1 Thess.*, v, 23). But having evidently forgotten or neglected to "thoroughly" study the transcendental opinions of the ancient philosophers and the Christian Apostles upon the subject, Mr. Croucher views the soul (*psychê*) as spirit (*Nous*) and *vice versa*.

The Buddhists, who separate the three entities in man (though viewing them as one when on the path to Nirvana), yet divide the soul into several parts, and have names for each of these and their functions. Thus confusion is unknown among them. The old Greeks did likewise, holding that *psychê* was *bios*, or physical life, and it was *thumos*, or passional nature, the animals being accorded but a lower faculty of the soul-instinct. The soul or *psychê* is itself a combination, *consensus* or unity of the *bios*, or physical vitality, the *epithumia* or concupiscible nature, and the *phren, mens,* or mind. Perhaps the *animus* ought to be included. It is constituted of ethereal substance, which pervades the whole universe, and is derived wholly from the soul of the world—*Anima Mundi* or the Buddhist Svabhavat—which is *not* spirit; though intangible and impalpable, it is yet, by comparison with spirit or pure abstraction—objective matter. By its complex nature, the soul may descend and ally itself so closely to the corporeal nature as to exclude a higher life from exerting any moral influence upon it. On the other hand, it can so closely attach to the *nous* or spirit, as to share its potency, in which case its vehicle, physical man, will appear as a God even during his terrestrial life. Unless such union of soul and spirit does occur, either during this life or after physical death, the individual man is not immortal as an entity. The *psychê* is sooner or later disintegrated. Though the *man* may have gained "the whole world," he has lost his "soul." Paul, when teaching the *anastasis*, or continuation of individual spiritual life after death, set forth that there was a physical body which was raised in incorruptible substance. The spiritual body is most assuredly *not* one of the bodies, or visible or tangible *larvae*, which form in circle-rooms, and are so improperly termed "materialized spirits." When once the *metanoia*, the full developing of spiritual life, has lifted the spiritual body out of the psychical (the disembodied, corruptible astral man, what Colonel Olcott calls "soul"), it becomes, in strict ratio with its progress, more and more an abstraction for the corporeal senses. It can influence, inspire, and even communicate with men subjectively; it can make itself felt, and even, in those rare instances, when the clairvoyant is perfectly pure and perfectly lucid, seen by the inner eye (which is the eye of the purified *psychê*—soul). But how can it ever manifest objectively?

It will be seen, then, that to apply the term "spirit" to the materialized *eidola* of your "form-manifestations," is grossly improper, and something ought to be done to change the practice, since scholars have begun to discuss the subject. At best, when not what the Greeks termed *phantasma*, they are but *phasma*, or apparitions.

In scholars, speculators, and especially in our modern *savants*, the psychical principle is more or less pervaded by the corporeal, and "the things of the spirit are foolishness and impossible to be known" (*1 Cor.,* ii, 14). Plato was then right, in his way, in despising land-measuring, geometry, and arithmetic, for all these overlooked all high ideas. Plutarch taught that at death Proserpine separated the body and the soul entirely, after which the latter became a free and independent *demon* (*daïmon*). Afterward, the good underwent a second dissolution: Demeter divided the *psychê* from the *nous* or *pneuma*. The former was dissolved after a time into ethereal particles—hence the inevitable dissolution and subsequent annihilation of the man who at death is purely psychical; the latter, the *nous,* ascended to its higher Divine power and became gradually a pure, Divine spirit. Kapila, in common with all Eastern philosophers, despised the purely psychical nature. It is this agglomeration of the grosser particles of the soul, the mesmeric exhalations of human nature imbued with all its terrestial desires and propensities, its vices, imperfections, and weakness, forming the astral body—which can become objective under certain circumstances—which the Buddhists call *skandhas* (the groups), and Colonel Olcott has for convenience termed the "soul." The Buddhists and Brahmanists teach that the man's individuality is not secured until he has passed through and become disembarrassed of the last of these groups, the final vestige of earthly taint. Hence their doctrine of the metempsychosis, so ridiculed and so utterly misunderstood by our greatest Orientalists. Even the physicists teach us that the particles composing physical man are, by evolution, reworked by nature into every variety of inferior physical form. Why, then, are the Buddhists unphilosophical or even unscientific, in affirming that the semi-material *skandhas* of the astral man (his very *ego,* up to the point of final purification) are appropriated to the evolution of minor astral forms (which, of course, enter into the purely physical bodies of animals) as fast as he throws them off in his progress toward *Nirvâna?* Therefore, we may correctly say, that so long as the disembodied man is throwing off a single particle of these *skandhas,* a portion of him is being reincarnated in the bodies of plants and animals. And if he, the disembodied astral man, be so material that "Demeter" cannot find even one spark of the *pneuma* to carry up to the "divine power," then the individual, so to speak, is dissolved, piece by piece, into the crucible of evolution, or, as the Hindus allegorically illustrate it, he passes thousands of years in the bodies of impure animals. Here we see how completely the ancient Greek and Hindu philosophers, the modern Oriental schools, and the Theosophists, are ranged on one side, in perfect accord; and the bright array of "inspirational mediums" and "spirit guides" stand in perfect discord on the other. Though no two of the latter, unfortunately, agree as to what is and what is not truth, yet they do agree with unanimity to antagonize whatever of the teachings of the philosophers we may repeat!

Let it not be inferred, though, from all this, that I, or any other real Theosophist, undervalue true Spiritual phenomena or philosophy, or that we do not believe in the communication between pure mortals and pure spirits, any less than we do in communication between bad men and bad spirits, or even of good men with bad spirits under bad conditions. Occultism is the essence of Spiritualism, while modern or popular Spiritualism I cannot better characterize than as adulterated, unconscious magic. We go so far as to say that all the great and noble characters, all the grand geniuses—the poets, painters, sculptors, musicians—all who have worked at any time for the realization of their highest ideal, irrespective of selfish ends—have been Spiritually inspired; not mediums, as many Spiritualists call them—passive tools in the hands of controlling guides—but incarnate, illuminated souls, working consciously in collaboration with the pure disembodied human and newly-embodied high Planetary Spirits, for the elevation and spiritualization of mankind. We believe that everything in material life is most intimately associated with Spiritual agencies. As regards psychical phenomena and mediumship, we believe that it is only when the passive medium has given place, or rather grown into, the conscious mediator, that he can discern between spirits good and bad. And we do believe, and know also, that while the incarnate man (though the highest adept) cannot vie in potency with the pure disembodied spirits, who, freed of all their *skandhas*, have become subjective to the physical senses, yet he can perfectly equal, and can far surpass in the way of phenomena, mental or physical, the average "spirit" of modern mediumship. Believing this, you will perceive that we are better Spiritualists, in the true acceptation of the word, than so-called Spiritualists, who, instead of showing the reverence we do to true spirits—gods—debase the name of spirit, by applying it to the impure, or, at best, imperfect beings who produce the majority of the phenomena.

The two objections urged by Mr. Croucher against the claim of the Theosophists, that a child is but a duality at birth, "and perhaps until the sixth or seventh year," and that some depraved persons are annihilated at some time after death, are (1) that mediums have described to him his three children, "who passed away at the respective ages of two, four, and six years"; and (2) that he has known persons who were "very depraved" on earth come back. He says:

> These statements have been afterwards confirmed by glorious beings who come after, and who have proved by their mastery of the laws which are governing the universe, that they are worthy of being believed.

I am really happy to learn that Mr. Croucher is competent to sit in judgment upon these "glorious beings," and give them the palm over Kapila, Manu, Plato, and even Paul. It is worth something, after all, to be an "inspirational medium." We have no such "glorious beings" in the Theosophical Society to learn from; but it is evident that while Mr. Croucher sees and judges things through his emotional nature, the philosophers whom we study took nothing from any glorious being that did not perfectly accord with the universal harmony, justice, and equilibrium of the manifest plan of the universe. The Hermetic axiom, "as below, so above," is the only rule of evidence accepted by the Theosophists. Believing in a spiritual and invisible universe, we cannot conceive of it in any other way than as completely dovetailing and corresponding with the material, objective universe; for logic and observation alike teach us that the latter is the outcome and visible manifestation of the former, and that the laws governing both are immutable.

In his letter of December 7th, Colonel Olcott very appropriately illustrates his subject of potential immortality by citing the admitted physical law of the survival of the fittest. The rule applies to the greatest as to the smallest things—to the planet equally with the plant. It applies to man. And the imperfectly developed manchild can no more exist under the conditions prepared for the perfected types of its species, than can an imperfect plant or animal. In infantile life, the higher faculties are not developed, but, as everyone knows, are only in the germ, or rudimentary. The babe is an animal, however "angelic" he may, and naturally enough, ought to appear to his parents. Be it ever so beautifully molded, the infant body is but the jewel-casket preparing for the jewel. It is bestial, selfish, and, as a babe, nothing more. Little of even the soul, Psychê, can be perceived except as vitality is concerned; hunger, terror, pain, and pleasure appear to be the principal of its conceptions. A kitten is its superior in everything but possibilities. The grey neurine of the brain is equally unformed. After a time mental qualities begin to appear, but they relate chiefly to external matters. The cultivation of the mind of the child by teachers can only affect this part of the nature—what Paul calls natural or psychical, and James and Jude sensual or psychical. Hence the words of *Jude* [verse 19], "psychical, having not the spirit," and of Paul:

> The psychical man receiveth not the things of the spirit, for to him they are foolishness; the spiritual man discerneth [*1 Cor.*, ii, 14].

It is only the man of full age, with his faculties disciplined to discern good and evil, whom we can denominate spiritual, noetic, intuitive. Children developed in such respects would be precocious, abnormal—abortives.

Why, then, should a child who has never lived other than an animal life; who never discerned right from wrong; who never cared whether he lived or died—since he could not understand either of life or death—become individually immortal? Man's cycle is not complete until he has passed through the earthlife. No one stage of probation and experience can be skipped over. He must be a man before he can become a spirit. A dead child is a failure of nature —he must live again; and the same *psyché* re-enters the physical plane through another birth. Such cases, together with those of congenital idiots, are, as stated in *Isis Unveiled*,* the only instances of human reincarnation. If every child-duality were to be immortal, why deny a like individual immortality to the duality of the animal? Those who believe in the trinity of man know the babe to be but a duality—body and soul; and the individuality which resides only in the psychical is, as we have seen proved by the philosophers, perishable. The completed trinity only survives. Trinity, I say, for at death the astral form becomes the outward body, and inside a still finer one evolves, which takes the place of the *psyché* on earth, and the whole is more or less overshadowed by the *nous*. Space prevented Colonel Olcott from developing the doctrine more fully, or he would have added that not even all of the elementaries (human) are annihilated. There is still a chance for some. By a supreme struggle these may retain their third and higher principle, and so, though slowly and painfully, yet ascend sphere after sphere, casting off at each transition the previous heavier garment, and clothing themselves in more radiant spiritual envelopes, until, rid of every finite particle, the trinity merges into the final Nirvana, and becomes a unity—a God.

A volume would scarce suffice to enumerate all the varieties of elementaries and elementals; the former being so called by some Kabalists (Henry Khunrath, for instance) to indicate their entanglement in the terrestial elements which hold them captive, and the latter designated by that name to avoid confusion, and equally applying to those which go to form the astral body of the infant, and to the

---

* [Vol. I, p. 351.]

stationary nature-spirits proper. Éliphas Lévi, however, indifferently calls them all "Elementary," and "souls." I repeat again, it is but the wholly psychical, disembodied astral man, which ultimately disappears as an individual entity. As to the component parts of his *psychê*, they are as indestructible as the atoms of any other body composed of matter.

That man must indeed be a true animal who has not, after death, a spark of the divine *ruach* or *nous* left in him to allow him a chance of self-salvation. Yet there are such lamentable exceptions; not alone among the depraved, but also among those who, during life, by stifling every idea of an after-existence, have killed in themselves the last desire to achieve immortality. It is the will of man, his all-potent will, that weaves his destiny, and if a man is determined in the notion that death means annihilation, he will find it so. It is among our commonest experiences that the determination of physical life or death depends upon the will. Some people snatch themselves by force of determination from the very jaws of death; while others succumb to insignificant maladies. What man does with his body he can do with his disembodied *psychê*.

Nothing in this militates against the images of Mr. Croucher's children being seen in the Astral Light by the medium, either as actually left by the children themselves, or as imagined by the father to look when grown. The impression in the latter case would be but a *phasma*, while in the former it is a *phantasma*, or the apparition of the indestructible impress of what once really was.

In days of old the "mediators" of humanity were men like Krishna, Gautama Buddha, Jesus, Paul, Apollonius of Tyana, Plotinus, Porphyry, and the like of them. They were adepts, philosophers—men who, by struggling their whole lives in purity, study, and self-sacrifice, through trials, privations, and self-discipline, attained divine illumination and seemingly superhuman powers. They could not only produce all the phenomena seen in our times, but regarded it as a sacred duty to cast out "evil spirits" or demons, from the unfortunate who were obsessed. In other words, to rid the medium of their days of the "elementaries."

But in our time of improved psychology every hysterical sensitive blooms into a seer, and behold! there are mediums by the thousand! Without any previous study, self-denial, or the least limitation of their physical nature, they assume, in the capacity of mouthpieces of unidentified and unidentifiable intelligences, to outrival Socrates in wisdom, Paul in eloquence, and Tertullian himself in fiery and authoritative dogmatism. The Theosophists are the last to assume infallibility for themselves, or recognize it in others; as they judge others, so they are willing to be judged.

In the name, then, of logic and common sense, before bandying epithets, let us submit our differences to the arbitrament of reason. Let us compare all things, and, putting aside emotionalism and prejudice as unworthy of the logician and the experimentalist, hold fast only to that which passes the ordeal of ultimate analysis.

H. P. BLAVATSKY.

New York, January 14th, 1878.

[In connection with the above article, a sentence from a letter of Master K. H. written to A. P. Sinnett in the Fall of 1882, may be of interest (*The Mahatma Letters*, etc., p. 289):

"It was H.P.B. who, acting under the orders of Atrya (one whom you do not know) was the first to explain in the *Spiritualist* the difference there was between *psychê* and *nous*, *nefesh* and *ruach*—Soul and Spirit. She had to bring the whole arsenal of proofs with her, quotations from Paul and Plato, from Plutarch and *James*, etc. before the Spiritualists admitted that the theosophists were right . . ."

—Compiler.]

A SOCIETY WITHOUT A DOGMA
[*The Spiritualist*, London, February 8th, 1878, pp. 62-63] *

Times have greatly changed since the winter of 1875-6, when the establishment of the Theosophical Society caused the grand army of American Spiritualists to wave banners, clang steel, and set up a great shouting. How well we all remember the putting forth of "Danger Signals," the oracular warnings and denunciations of numberless mediums! How fresh in memory the threats of "angel-friends" to Dr. Gardiner, of Boston, that they would kill Colonel Olcott if he dared call them "Elementaries" in the lectures he was about delivering!† The worst of the storm has passed. The hail of imprecations no longer batters around our devoted heads; it is but raining now, and we can almost see the rainbow of promised peace spanning the sky.

Beyond doubt, much of this subsidence of the disturbed elements is due to our armed neutrality. But still, I judge that the gradual spread of a desire to learn something more as to the cause of the phenomena must be taken into account. And yet the time has not quite come when the lion (Spiritualism) and the lamb (Theosophy) are ready to lie down together—unless the lamb is willing to lie inside the lion. While we held our tongues we were asked to speak, and when we spoke—or rather our President spoke—the hue and cry was raised once more. Though the popgun fusillade and the dropping shots of musketry have mostly ceased, the defiles of your Spiritual Balkans are defended by your heaviest Krupp guns. If the fire were directed only against Colonel Olcott there would be no occasion for me to bring up the reserves. But fragments from both of the bombs which your able gunner and our mutual friend,

---
* [Square brackets in this article are H.P.B.'s own.—*Compiler.*]
† [See p. 72 in the present Volume.]

"M. A. (Oxon.)," has exploded, in his two letters of January 4th and 11th, have given me contusions—under the velvet paw of his rhetoric I have felt the scratch of challenge!

At the very beginning of what must be a long struggle, it is imperatively demanded that the Theosophical position shall be unequivocally defined. In the last of the above two communications, it is stated that Colonel Olcott transmits "the teaching of the learned author of *Isis Unveiled,* the *master key to all problems* [?]." Who has ever claimed that the book was that, or anything like it? Not the author, certainly. The title? A misnomer for which the publisher is unpremeditatedly responsible; and, if I am not mistaken, "M. A. (Oxon.)" knows it. My title was the *Veil of Isis,* and that headline runs through the entire first volume. Not until that volume was stereotyped did any one recollect that a book of the same name was before the public. Then, as a *dernière ressource,* the publisher selected the present title.

"If he [Olcott] be not the rose, at any rate he has lived near it," says your learned correspondent. Had I seen this sentence apart from the context, I would never have imagined that the unattractive old party, superficially known as H. P. Blavatsky, was designated under this poetical Persian simile. If he had compared me to a bramble-bush, I might have complimented him upon his artistic realism. "Colonel Olcott," he says, "of himself would command attention; he commands it still more on account of the store of knowledge to which he has had access." True, he has had such access, but by no means is it confined to my humble self. Though I may have taught him a few of the things that I had learned in other countries (and corroborated the theory in every case by practical illustration), yet a far abler teacher than I could not in three brief years have given him more than the alphabet of what there is to learn before a man can become wise in spiritual and psycho-physiological things. The very limitations of modern languages prevent any rapid communication of ideas about Eastern philosophy. I defy the great Max Müller himself to translate Kapila's *Sûtras* so as to give their real meaning. We have seen what the best European authorities can do with the Hindu metaphysics; and what a mess they have made of it, to be sure! The Colonel corresponds directly with Hindu scholars, and has from them a good deal more than he can get from so clumsy a preceptor as myself.

Our friend, "M. A. (Oxon.)," says that Colonel Olcott "comes forward to enlighten us"—than which scarce anything could be more inaccurate. He neither comes forward nor pretends to enlighten anyone. The public wanted to know the views of the Theosophists, and our president attempted to give, as succinctly as possible in the limits of a single article, some little glimpse of so much of the truth as he had learned. That the result would not be wholly satisfactory was inevitable. Volumes would not suffice to answer all the questions naturally presenting themselves to an enquiring mind; a library of quartos would barely obliterate the prejudices of those who ride at the anchor of centuries of metaphysical and theological misconceptions—perhaps even errors. But, though our president is not guilty of the conceit of pretending to "enlighten" Spiritualists, I think he has certainly thrown out some hints worthy of the thoughtful consideration of the unprejudiced.

I am sorry that "M. A. (Oxon.)" is not content with mere suggestions. Nothing but the whole naked truth will satisfy him. We must "square" our theories with his facts, we must lay our theory down "on exact lines of demonstration." We are asked, "Where are the seers? What are their records? and (far more important), how do they verify them to us?" I answer, the seers are where "Schools of the Prophets" are still extant, and they have their records with them. Though Spiritualists are not able to go in search of them, yet the philosophy they teach commends itself to logic, and its principles are mathematically demonstrable. If this be not so, let it be shown.

But, in their turn, Theosophists may ask, and do ask, where are the proofs that the medial phenomena are exclusively attributable to the agency of departed "spirits"? Who are the "seers" among mediums blessed with an infallible lucidity? What "tests" are given that admit of no alternative explanation? Though Swedenborg was one of the greatest of seers, and churches are erected in his name, yet except to his adherents what proof is there that the "spirits" objective to his vision—including Paul—promenading in hats, were anything but the creatures of his imagination? Are the spiritual potentialities of the living man so well comprehended that mediums can tell when their own agency ceases, and that of outside influences begins? No, but for all answer to our suggestions that the subject is opened to debate, "M. A. (Oxon.)" shudderingly charges us with attempting to upset what he designates as "a cardinal dogma of our faith"—*i.e.*, the faith of the Spiritualists.

Dogma? Faith? These are the right and left pillars of every soul-crushing theology. Theosophists have no dogmas, exact no blind faith. Theosophists are ever ready to abandon every idea that is proved erroneous upon strictly logical deductions; let Spiritualists do the same. Dogmas are the toys that amuse and can satisfy but unreasoning children. They are the offspring of human speculation and prejudiced fancy. In the eye of true philosophy it seems an insult to common sense that we should break loose from the idols and dogmas of either Christian or heathen exoteric faith to catch those of a church of Spiritualism. Spiritualism must either be a true philosophy, amenable to the tests of the recognized criterion of logic, or be set up in its niche beside the broken idols of hundreds of antecedent Christian sects. Realizing as they do the boundlessness of the absolute truth, Theosophists repudiate all claims to infallibility. The most cherished preconceptions, the most "pious hope," the strongest "master passion," they sweep aside like dust from their path, when their error is pointed out. Their highest hope is to approximate the truth; that they have succeeded in going a few steps beyond the Spiritualists, they think proved in their conviction that they know nothing in comparison with what is to be learned; in their sacrifice of every pet theory and prompting of emotionalism at the shrine of Fact; and in their absolute and unqualified repudiation of everything that smacks of "dogma."

With great rhetorical elaboration "M. A. (Oxon.)"

HENRY STEEL OLCOTT
1832-1907
The portrait shows him in the days of his military service. It is preserved in the Adyar Archives.
(Consult the *Bio-Bibliographical Index* for a comprehensive biographical outline.)

H.P.B.'s MASONIC DIPLOMA
(Reproduced from *H.P.B. Speaks*, Vol. II, published by The Theosophical Publishing House, Adyar, Madras, India, 1951.)

paints the result of the supersedure of Spiritualistic by Theosophic ideas. In brief, he shows Spiritualism a lifeless corpse—"a body from which the soul has been wrenched, and for which most men will care nothing." We submit that the reverse is true. Spiritualists wrench the soul from *true* Spiritualism by their degradation of spirit. Of the infinite they make the finite; of the divine subjective they make the human and limited objective. Are Theosophists materialists? Do not their hearts warm with the same "pure and holy love" for their "loved ones" as those of Spiritualists? Have not many of us sought long years "through the gate of mediumship to have access to the world of spirit"—and vainly sought? The comfort and assurance modern Spiritualism could not give us we found in Theosophy. As a result we believe far more firmly than many Spiritualists—for our belief is based on knowledge—in the communion of our beloved ones with us; but not as materialized spirits with beating hearts and sweating brows.

Holding such views as we do as to logic and fact, you perceive that when a Spiritualist pronounces to us the words dogma and facts, debate is impossible, for there is no common ground upon which we can meet. We decline to break our heads against shadows. If fact and logic were given the consideration they should have, there would be no more temples in this world for exoteric worship, whether Christian or heathen, and the *method* of the Theosophists would be welcomed as the only one insuring action and progress—a progress that cannot be arrested, since each advance shows yet greater advances to be made.

As to our producing our "Seers" and "their records"—one word. In *The Spiritualist* of January 11th, I find Dr. Peebles saying that in due time he "will publish such facts about the Dravida Brâhmans as I am [he is] permitted. I say permitted because some of these occurred under the promise and seal of secrecy." If ever the casual wayfarer is put under an obligation of secrecy, before he is shown some of the less important psycho-physiological phenomena, is it not barely possible that the Brotherhood to which some Theosophists belong, has also doctrines, records, and phenomena, that cannot be revealed to the profane and the indifferent, without any imputation lying against their reality and authoritativeness? This, at least, I believe, "M. A. (Oxon.)" knows. As we do not offensively obtrude ourselves upon an unwilling public, but only answer under compulsion, we can hardly be denounced as contumacious if we produce to a promiscuous public, neither our "Seers" nor "their records." When Mahomet is ready to go to the mountain it will be found standing in its place.

And that no one that makes this search may suppose that we Theosophists send him to a place where there are no pitfalls for the unwary, I quote from the famous *Commentary on the Bhagavad-Gîtâ* of our brother Hurrychund Chintamon, the unqualified admission that "In Hindostan, as in England, there are doctrines for the learned and dogmas for the unlearned; strong meat for men, and milk for babes; facts for the few, and fictions for the many; realities for the wise, and romances for the simple; esoteric truth for the philosopher, and exoteric fable for the fool." Like the philosophy taught by this author in the work in question, the object of the Theosophical Society "is the cleansing of Spiritual truth."

H. P. BLAVATSKY.

New York, January 20th, 1877.*

[Page 176 of H.P.B.'s *Scrapbook,* Vol. IV, is occupied with various cuttings dealing with the Masonic Diploma granted to H.P.B. The *Providence Journal* announces on Feb. 4, 1878, that the *Franklin Register* will have a discussion of the genuineness of being a Freemason. To this H.P.B. remarks in pen and ink:]

From the *Providence Daily Journal,* the best daily paper in New England. Its editor is Senator Anthony. U. S. Senator.

---

*[An obvious error for 1878.—*Compiler.*]

THE AUTHOR OF *ISIS UNVEILED* DEFENDS THE VALIDITY OF HER MASONIC PATENT
[*Franklin Register*, Franklin, Mass., February 8, 1878] *

EDITORIAL.—We are gratified to be able to present to the readers of the *Register* this week, the following highly-characteristic letter, prepared expressly for our Paper by Madame H. P. Blavatsky, the authoress of *Isis Unveiled*. In this letter the lady defends the validity of her diploma as a Mason, reference to which was had in our issue of January 18th. The immediate cause of the letter from Madame B. was the multiplication of attacks upon her claim to that distinguished honour both before and since the publication mentioned.

The field is open for a rejoinder; and we trust that a champion will appear, to defend that which she so vigorously and bravely assails.

That the subject-matter in controversy may be seen at a glance by those who may not be regular readers of our paper, we again print the text of her diploma.

[*See the Facsimile appended herewith*]

To the Editor of *The Franklin Register.*

Dear Sir,

I am obliged to correct certain errors in your highly complimentary editorial in *The Register* of January 18th. You say that I have taken "the regular degrees in Masonic Lodges" and attained high dignity in the order, and further add: "Upon Madame B. has recently been conferred the diploma of the thirty-third Masonic Degree, from the oldest Masonic body in the world."

If you will kindly refer to my *Isis Unveiled* (Vol. II, p. 394), you will find me saying: "We are under neither

---

* [The full name of this paper was *Franklin Register and Norfolk County Journal* and as far as is known, it was a weekly. Its Editor and Publisher in 1878 was James M. Stewart. Apart from a few copies, no complete files of it have ever been located, and the text of H.P.B.'s article has been copied from a cutting pasted by her in her *Scrapbook*, Vol. IV, pp. 174-75 (old numbering, Vol. II, 96-97).—*Compiler.*]

promise, obligation, nor oath, and therefore violate no confidence"—reference being made to *Western* Masonry, to the criticism of which the chapter is devoted; and full assurance is given that I have never taken "the regular degrees" in any *Western* Masonic Lodge. Of course, therefore, having taken no such degree, I am not a thirty-third degree Mason. In a private note, also in your most recent editorial, you state that you find yourself taken to task by various Masons, among them one who has taken thirty-three degrees—which include the "Ineffable"—for what you said about me. My Masonic experience—if you will so term membership in several Eastern Masonic Fraternities and Esoteric Brotherhoods—is confined to the Orient. But, nevertheless, this neither prevents my knowing, in common with all Eastern "Masons," everything connected with Western Masonry (including the numberless humbugs that have been imposed upon the Craft during the last half century) nor, since the receipt of the diploma from the "Sovereign Grand Master," of which you publish the text, my being entitled to call myself a Mason. Claiming nothing, therefore, in Western Masonry but what is expressed in the above diploma, you will perceive that your Masonic mentors must transfer their quarrel to John Yarker, jun., P.M., P.Mk.M., P.Z., P.G.C. and M.W.S.—K.T. and R.C., K.T.P., K.H., and K.A.R.S., P.M.W., P.S.G.C., and P.S.Dai., A. and P. Rite, to the man, in short, who is recognized in England and Wales and the whole world, as a member of the Masonic Archaeological Institute; as Honorary Fellow of the London Literary Union; of Lodge No. 227, Dublin; of the Bristol College of Rosicrucians; who is Past Grand Maréchal of the Temple; Member of the Royal Grand Council of Ancient Rites—time immemorial; Keeper of the Ancient Royal Secrets; Grand Commander of Mizraim, Ark Mariners, Red Cross of Constantine, Babylon, and Palestine; R. Grand Superintendent for Lancashire; Sovereign Grand Conservator of the Ancient and Primitive Rite of Masonry, thirty-third and last degree, etc., from whom the Patent issued.

Your "Ineffable" friend must have cultivated his spiritual

perceptions to small purpose in the investigation and contemplation of the "Ineffable Name," from the fourth to the fourteenth degrees of that gilded humbug, the A. and A. Rite, if he could say that there is "no authority for a derivation through the charter of the Sovereign Sanctuary of America, to issue this patent."

He lives in a veritable Crystal Palace of Masonic glass, and must look out for falling stones. Brother Yarker says, in his *Notes on the Scientific and Religious Mysteries of Antiquity* (p. 149), that the "Grand Orient, derived from the Craft Grand Lodge of England, in 1725, and latterly, works and recognizes the following Rites, appointing representatives with Chapters *in America* and elsewhere: 1. French Rite. 2. Rite of Heredom. 3. A. and A. Rite. 4. Rite of Kilwinning. 5. Philosophical Rite. 6. *Rite du Régime rectif*. 7. Rite of Memphis. 8. Rite of Mizraim. All under a Grand College of Rites."

The A. and P. Rite was originally chartered in America, November 9th, 1856, with David McClellan as G. M. [see Kenneth Mackenzie's *The Royal Masonic Cyclopaedia*, p. 43], and in 1862 submitted entirely to the Grand Orient of France. In 1862 the Grand Orient *vised* and sealed the American Patent of Seymour as G.M., and mutual representatives were appointed, down to 1866, when the relations of the G.O. with America were ruptured, and the American Sovereign Sanctuary took up its position, "in the bosom" of the Ancient Cerneau Council of the "Scottish Rite" of 33 degrees, as John Yarker says, in the above quoted work. In 1872 a Sovereign Sanctuary of the Rite was established in England, by the American Grand Body, with John Yarker as Grand Master. Down to the present time the legality of Seymour's Sanctuary has never been disputed by the Grand Orient of France, and reference to it is found in Marconis de Nègres books.

It sounds very grand, no doubt, to be a thirty-second degreeist, and an "Ineffable" one into the bargain; but read what Robert B. Folger, M. D., Past Master thirty-third, says himself in his *The Ancient and Accepted Scottish Rite, in Thirty-Three Degrees*: "In reference to the other degrees, five or six in number, which are additional, those (with the exception of the Thirty-third, which was manufactured at Charleston) were all in the possession of the Grand Orient before, but were termed, like a great many others, 'obsolete'."

And further, he asks: "Who were the persons who formed this Supreme Council of the Thirty-third degree? And where did they get that degree, or the power to confer it? . . . Their Patents have never been produced nor has any evidence ever yet been given, that they came in possession of the Thirty-third degree in a regular and lawful manner" (pp. 92, 95, 96).

That an American Rite, thus spuriously organized, declines to acknowledge the Patent of an English Sovereign Sanctuary, duly recognized by the Grand Orient of France, does not at all invalidate my claim to Masonic honours. As well might Protestants refuse to call the Dominicans Christians, because they—the Protestants—broke away from the Catholic Church and set up for themselves, as for A. and A. Masons of America to deny the validity of a Patent from an English A. and P. Rite body. Though I have nothing to do with American modern Masonry, and do not expect to have, yet, feeling highly honoured by the distinction conferred upon me by Brother Yarker, I mean to stand for my chartered rights, and to recognize no other authority than that of the high Masons of England, who have pleased to send me this unsolicited and unexpected testimonial of their approval of my humble labours.

Of a piece with the above is the ignorant rudeness of certain critics who pronounce Cagliostro an "impostor" and his desire of engrafting Eastern Philosophy upon Western Masonry "charlatanism." Without such a union Western Masonry is a corpse without a soul. As Yarker observes, in his *Notes on the Scientific and Religious Mysteries of Antiquity* [p. 157]:

". . . As the Masonic fraternity is now governed, the Craft is fast becoming the paradise of the *bon vivant* . . . the manufacturer of paltry masonic tinsel . . . and the masonic 'Emperor' and other charlatans who make power or money out of the aristocratic pretensions which they have tacked on to our institutions—*ad captandum vulgus* . . ."

Respectfully,
H. P. BLAVATSKY.

[The above article from the pen of H.P.B. was preceded by articles written by others in the January 18 and February 1 issues of *The Franklin Register*. Unfortunately, they have not been preserved, and so cannot be consulted.

The circumstances under which H.P.B. received her Masonic Patent are described as follows by John Yarker who issued it:

"In the year 1872 I printed, at my own cost, a small book entitled, *Notes on the Scientific and Religious Mysteries of Antiquity; the Gnosis and Secret Schools of the Middle Ages; Modern Rosicrucianism; and the various Rites and Degrees of Free and Accepted Masonry*. At this time, I was Grand Master of the Ancient and Primitive Rite of Memphis, 95°; and before that of the combined Scottish Rite of 33°, and Mizraim of 90°; and among our initiates, 32°-94°, was Brother Charles Sotheran who left England and settled at New York. This brother lent a copy of the book just named to Madame Blavatsky, and she was good enough to refer to it in her *Isis Unveiled*, with some complimentary remarks . . .

"However, at the request of Bro. Sotheran I sent Madame Blavatsky the certificate of the female branch of the Sat Bhai (Seven Brothers, or seven birds of a species, which always fly by sevens); it was a system organized at Benares in India by the Pundit of the 43rd Rifles, and brought to England by Major J. H. Lawrence-Archer, 32°-94°. This led to a letter from Col. H. S. Olcott, setting forth the very superior qualities of Madame to the certificate sent, and vouching that she was proficient in all masonic sciences. On the 20th of August, 1877, the, then newly established Theosophical Society of New York sent me by the hands of Col. Cobb a certificate of Honorary membership accompanied by a pretty gold Jewel of the Crux Ansata of Egypt entwined with a serpent in green enamel.

"Both the Rites of Memphis and Mizraim as well as the Grand Orient of France possessed a branch of Adoptive Masonry, popular in France in the eighteenth and nineteenth centuries, and of which, in later years, the Duchess of Bourbon held the rank of Grand Mistress. We accordingly sent H.P.B.

on the 24th of November, 1877, a certificate of the highest rank, that of a Crowned Princess 12°, said to have been instituted at Saxe, in the last quarter of the eighteenth century. The publication of this certificate led to newspaper questions and attack. *The Franklin Register* of 1st of February, 1878, contained an article by Bro. Leon Hynemann vouching for the reality of my signature, and another by Bro. Charles Sotheran who vouched for the possession by H.P.B. of Masonic initiation, and this was followed the next week (8th of February) by a slashing article from the pen of Madame herself against her calumniators...."*

The facsimile of the Diploma shows it to be the standard ornate form of the *Ancient and Primitive Rite*, the name and degrees being filled in in pen and ink. The Diploma states, however, that the degrees and titles conferred upon H.P.B. are those of the *Rite of Adoption*. The various *Rites of Adoption* were not recognized as being Masonry by the Masonic bodies of France, Great Britain, and America. Guillemain de Saint-Victor, French Masonic writer, author of *Handbook of the Women Freemasons or the True Freemasonry of Adoption*, is quoted in Mackey's *Encyclopaedia of Freemasonry* as follows:

"It is a virtuous amusement by which we recall a part of the mysteries of our religion; and the better to reconcile humanity with the knowledge of its Creator, after we have inculcated the duties of virtue, we deliver ourselves up to the sentiments of a pure and delightful friendship by enjoying in our Lodges the pleasure of society—pleasure which among us is always founded on reason, honor, and innocence."

A full discussion of Adoptive Masonry and the other Rites mentioned in the article may be found in the *Encyclopaedia of Freemasonry* by Albert G. Mackey, ed. by Robert I. Clegg. Chicago: The Masonic History Co., 1929.—*Compiler.*]

---

*Universal Masonry, Vol. I, No. 4, October, 1910.

[H.P.B.'S WRITINGS IN RUSSIAN]

[As far as could be ascertained, as a result of long and far-reaching search, the first of a series of Letters written by H.P.B. in her native Russian language was published in the Odessa newspaper *Pravda* (Truth), No. 45, February 23 (March 7), 1878. It was entitled: "From Across the Sea, from Beyond the Blue Ocean." As appears, however, from H.P.B.'s own entry in Col. H. S. Olcott's Diary on February 7, 1878, she must have written at least four other articles or Letters to the Editor, as she states that four of them had been definitely lost, according to word received by her from Madame N. A. de Fadeyev. Thus, it is most likely that her Russian literary contributions were started sometime in the later part of 1877. Early in 1878, she also began to write for the *Tiflisskiy Vestnik* (Tiflis Messenger). There is evidence to show that H.P.B. contributed some of her remuneration to the cause of the Russian soldiers wounded in the Russo-Turkish War of 1877-78, and that she also relinquished some of it to the benefit of her sister Vera Petrovna who must have been in need at the time.

All of H.P.B.'s Russian writings in English translation may be found in a separate volume of the present Series.—*Compiler*.]

[In H.P.B.'s *Scrapbook*, Vol. IV, p. 243, there is pasted a cutting from *The Spiritualist* of March 8, 1878. It is a very biased and hostile criticism from a lady Spiritualist entitled "Mrs. Showers on *Isis Unveiled*." Above the title H.P.B. wrote in ink:]

This is the abuse *I receive for defending* the philosophy of India and the East in *Isis*.

DR. SLADE'S FINAL TRIUMPH

[*Banner of Light*, Boston, Vol. XLII, March 9, 1878, p. 4]

To the Editor of the *Banner of Light:*

I have just received from the Hon. Alexander Aksakoff, of St. Petersburg, a letter dated February 7th, the substance of which he desires me to make known to the readers of the *Banner of Light.* This generous and brave gentleman begins with a cry of triumph: "I hasten to send you," he says, "most welcome, most consoling news! That unfortunate medium (Slade), our martyr, has finally received a full verdict of acquittal at the University of Leipzig. Three professors have had a whole series of most remarkable *séances* with him. Their experiments and investigations were crowned with striking success!"

It appears that Professor Zöllner, the great "astrophysicist"—as he is called in Germany—after numerous experiments to test his theory about what he calls "the fourth dimension of space" (whatever he may mean by that—I have not read his book), came to the conclusion that some of the mediumistic phenomena are possible. As I understand it, he assigns certain beings to each of four divisions of space, and holds that, "such beings, to whom the *fourth* division is accessible, could, for instance, make knots in an endless rope by a certain natural process and without a break of the continuity." Mr. Aksakoff says that these conclusions were published by Zöllner in August, 1877. Considering his high scientific rank, Spiritualists and Theosophists ought to feel thankful for even such small favors: the former, because he admits the possibility of *any* phenomena; the latter because his *Vierdimmensionale Wesen*—literally translated, "four-dimensional beings"—bear a very strong family resemblance to the now famous Elementaries and Elementals of the Theosophical Society.

What the Professor inferred upon theory in August last, he saw demonstrated in practice on the 17th of December. On a simple rope which he brought to the *séance,* and the ends of which were tied together and sealed by him, four knots were tied in a few minutes by "beings of some kind, while he, Zöllner, held the rope in his own hand." "Thus a fact *a priori,*" says Mr. Aksakoff, "which rested on a previously unsupported hypothesis, was practically proved and demonstrated. It is useless for me to enter into lengthy arguments," he adds, "as to the enormous benefit which these Leipzig experiments will assuredly confer upon Spiritualism: it is the first purely scientific hypothesis for the explanation of some of its phenomena, and it will undoubtedly fling wide open for them the portals of science."

This experiment is fully described, with engraved illustrations, in a volume just issued by Professor Zöllner, *Wissenschaftliche Abhandlungen*, I, Leipzig, 1878. He had subsequently extremely interesting experiments, which doubtless will be fully illustrated in a second volume. Mr. Aksakoff says that "all this was kept a profound secret from the public, until the appearance of the book . . . but I knew of the success of the experiment some time ago." The obligation of secrecy, under which our friend Mr. Simmons, as well as Dr. Slade himself, was placed, is now made plain.

Although Slade had been in St. Petersburg but a few days, lengthy reports of his wonderful phenomena had appeared in two of the most skeptical of the daily papers— the *Novoye Vremya* of January 17th, and the *St. Petersburg News* of January 20th. Both writers declined to attribute the phenomena they had seen to jugglery. We do not believe in spirits, they say, but we feel incompetent to explain the manifestations, therefore give them merely as *facts,* occurring in full daylight, at a table chosen at random by ourselves, in the hotel where the Doctor lives, and as facts admitting of no explanation upon any known hypothesis. One of the writers was lifted up perpendicularly, chair and all, until his knees came in contact with the lower edge of the table. Writing was produced under the hand of the investigator; ghostly hands were felt while the hands of everyone were on the table; an old harmonicon, brought by Mr. Aksakoff, was played upon—once without contact—and then, when Dr. Slade's hands and feet were in full view, it leaped on the knees of a skeptic, or rather was gently laid upon them, with precautions against hurting him. One of the writers was pinched, as he says, "very painfully."

Of course the Doctor's Owasso, Brédif's Jacko, the Chinawoman spirit, and even Katie King, all got a scratch from these editors. They do not like the explanations given them; they would prefer not to hear such "made-up stories" as the biography of Slade, as told by Mr. Simmons and himself—it appears "too artificial." And yet, both writers confess their amazement, and are at a loss what to think. We may expect a lively time in St. Petersburg. The war between Russia and Turkey being over, there loom up the portents of a great strife between the invisible "four-dimensional beings" and the skeptics who inhabit this muddy sphere of the lowest dimension.

The *News* reports an interesting episode of Slade's experience at Berlin, which is of quite a political and religious character. "Allie" and "Owasso" were the indirect (or shall we say direct?) means of disturbing Prince Bismarck's equanimity, and even getting him into trouble. I will give the story as nearly in the language of the paper as the necessity for condensation permits. In Berlin there are more "Spiritists than in St. Petersburg, and no wonder, as the arrival of Slade, who is considered the greatest medium after Home (?), stirred up the liveliest interest." As usual, parties were formed for and against Slade. The opponents of Spiritism felt indignant, and—again as usual—began exposing him. Hermann, the well-known Berlin juggler, promised through the press to show the public how it was all done.

Another Berlin juggler, Bellachini,* still more famous than Hermann, then stepped in and began investigating, with the determination "to expose the fraud." The inquiry

---

* [Samuel Bellachini, Court Conjurer to the Emperor of Germany. —Compiler.]

of the latter was quite protracted, after which he published in the daily papers, over his own signature, the fact that the phenomena which take place in Slade's presence can by no means be included among the tricks of jugglery. The reader may well imagine the scandal which this confession created. Bellachini was abused from every side, and charged with having been "fooled" by a Yankee, who could not even speak German.

The fight raged fiercely, passions were excited, and finally the affair was transplanted into the domain of politics. It must be known that the defenders of Dr. Slade and Spiritualism had found hospitality in the columns of the clerical party, while their opponents bombarded them from within the stronghold of the national liberal press. Prince Bismarck, who was quietly resting at Varzin, and felt quite innocent of having any leaning towards mediumism, was dragged into the fight and had to pay the damages. The clerical party pestered the great Chancellor by reviving a long forgotten story. Thus the matter assumed a political character, and was carried into the Landtag. The clergy had profited by the appearance of the new and incontestably genuine phenomena to claim recognition for their old miracle of the appearance of the Virgin Mary in the Marringen Community. It appears that the devout believers in this "miracle" had come in crowds to pray at the spot where the apparition had been seen, and had been badly treated by the local police. The old complaints were now revived. Minister Friedenthal, in the Landtag, defending the police pronounced both the clerical "Miracle" and the mediumistic phenomena dangerous frauds. The clericalist deputy Boehm demanded the punishment of the police and damages for the insulted community. Windthorst, the well-known orator, of the church party, claimed recognition for both miracle and phenomena, pointing out that even such men as Schopenhauer, Fichte and others, did not deny their possibility. The fight was lively for a time. Bismarck was annoyed and the public scandalized by this clerical impudence which was provoked by Dr. Slade's spirits.

All this led to Professor Virchow himself coming out with

an offer to investigate Slade's phenomena. But the celebrated medium felt, most probably, if anything, still more annoyed to play a part which, though political, was at best a thankless one. He refused point-blank, remarking that he did not feel justified in trusting a scientist who belonged to that party of progressionists which had so bitterly attacked him. Then it was that the American medium was *advised* to leave Berlin.

And no wonder! A man who had encountered Science (?) in the persons of a Lankester and his Donkin had good reasons for avoiding any more such intimacies. And now he is reaping laurels in St. Petersburg. If Spiritualism should be the gainer by his present demonstrations of his marvelous powers before Mr. Aksakoff's committee, its friends will at least have to put this fact to the credit of the Theosophical Society as a counterpoise against the thousand-and-one sins that have been laid at its door, that it knew how to select among American mediums the one best of all fitted to convince the most hard-headed of European skeptics.

H. P. Blavatsky.

[W. Emmette Coleman rather violently attacked both H.P.B. and Col. Olcott, in the pages of the *Religio-Philosophical Journal* of February 16, 1878, writing under the title of "Sclavonic Theosophy Versus American Spiritualism." Among other things, he made the following statement:

"The turning point of Col. Olcott's destiny occurred when he was at Chittenden. Meeting there the masculine-feminine Sclavonic Theosoph from Crim-Tartary, the erudite collaborator of *Isis Unveiled* (which work, as Youmans and other able critics affirm, unveils nothing), he soon became a willing victim to her intense psychological power, and from that day to this he has been the mouthpiece for her utterances, the obsequious tool and slave of Her Occultic Highness."

[At the end of the cutting pasted in her *Scrapbook*, Vol. IV, pp. 184-85, H.P.B. wrote in pen and ink:]

This prominent "Spiritualist" is not content, as it seems, of being thought a good natured though irascible ass.—Out he must show himself in print a LIAR and a BLACKGUARD! Oh—unhappy Spiritualism!

[She also added in pencil:]

(See for my answer on page 133, The Knout)

[H.P.B.'s Answer, printed below, may be found pasted in her *Scrapbook*, Vol. IV, p. 235.]

THE KNOUT

AS WIELDED BY THE GREAT RUSSIAN THEOSOPHIST.

[*Religio-Philosophical Journal*, Chicago, Vol. XXIV, March 16, 1878, p. 8]

Mr. Editor:

I have read some of the assaults upon Colonel Olcott and myself, that have appeared in the *Journal*. Some have amused me, others I have passed by unread; but I was quite unprepared for the good fortune that lay in store for me in the embryo of the paper of February 16th. The "Protest" of Mr. W. Emmette Coleman, entitled "Sclavonic Theosophy *versus* American Spiritualism," is the musky rose in an odoriferous bouquet. Its pungent fragrance would give the nose-bleed to a sensitive whose olfactories would withstand the perfume of a garden full of the Malayan flower-queen —the tuberose; and yet, my tough, pug, Mongolian nose, which has smelled carrion in all parts of the world, proved itself equal even to this emergency.

"From the sublime to the ridiculous," says the French proverb, "there is but a single step." From sparkling wit to dull absurdity, there is no more. An attack, to be effective, must have an antagonist to strike, for to kick against something that exists only in one's imagination, wrenches man or beast. Don Quixote fighting the "air-drawn" foes in his windmill, stands for ever the laughingstock of all generations, and the type of a certain class of disputants, that, for the moment, Mr. Coleman represents.

The pretext for two columns of abuse—suggesting, I am sorry to say, parallel sewers—is that Miss Emily Kislingbury, in an address before the B.N.A. of Spiritualists, mentioned Colonel Olcott's name in connection with a leadership of Spiritualism. I have the report of her remarks before me, and find that she neither proposed Colonel Olcott to American Spiritualists as a leader, nor said that he had wanted "leadership," wanted it now, or could ever be persuaded to take it. "It is seriously proposed," says Mr. Coleman, "by our trans-atlantic sister, Miss Kislingbury, that American Spiritualists should select as their guardian guide—Col. H. S. Olcott!!" If anyone is entitled to this wealth of exclamation points it is Miss K., for the charge against her from beginning to end is simply an unmitigated falsehood. Miss K. merely expressed the personal opinion that a certain gentleman for whom she had a deserved friendship, would have been capable, at one time, of acting as a leader. This was her private opinion, to which she had as good a right as either of her defamers—who, in a cowardly way, try to use Colonel Olcott and myself as sticks to break her head with—have to their opinions. It may or may not have been warranted by the facts—that is immaterial. The main point is, that Miss K. has not said one word that gives the slightest pretext for Mr. Coleman attacking her on this question of leadership. And yet, I am not surprised at his course; for this brave, noble-hearted, truthful and spotless lady occupies too impregnable a position to be assailed, except by indirection. Some one had to pay for her plain speaking about American Spiritualism. What better scapegoat than Olcott and Blavatsky, the twin "theosophical gorgons"!

What a hullabaloo is raised, to be sure, about Spiritualists declining to follow our "leadership." In my "Buddhistico-Tartaric" ignorance, I have always supposed that some-

H.P.B. ABOUT 1875-1876

WILLIAM STAINTON MOSES
1839-1892
(From Sir A. Conan Doyle's *History of Spiritualism*, London, 1926.
Consult the *Bio-Bibliographical Index* for biographical sketch.)

thing must be offered before it can either be indignantly spurned or even respectfully declined. Have we offered to lead Spiritualists by the nose or other portions of their anatomy? Have we ever proclaimed ourselves as "teachers," or set ourselves up as infallible "guides"? Let the hundreds of unanswered letters that we have received from Spiritualists, be our witness. Let us even include two letters from Mr. W. Emmette Coleman, Fort Leavenworth, Kansas, calling attention to his published articles of January 13th, 20th, 27th, and February 3rd (four papers), inviting controversy. He says, in his communication of January 23rd, 1877, to Colonel Olcott, "I am in search of truth"—therefore he has not all the truth. He asks him to answer certain "interrogatories"—therefore, our opinions are admitted to have some weight. He says: "This address"—the one he wants us to read and express our opinion upon—"was delivered some time since; if of more recent date, I [he] might modify somewhat."

Now, Olcott's *People from the Other World* was published January, 1875;* Mr. Coleman's letter to the Colonel was written in January, 1877; and his present "protest" to the *Journal* appeared February, 1878. It puzzles me to know how a man "in search of truth" could lower himself so far as to hunt for it in the coat pockets of an author whose work is "clearly demonstrative of the utterly unscientific character of his researches, full of exaggerations, inaccuracies, marvelous statements recorded at second hand without the slightest confirmation, lackadaisical sentimentalities, egotistical rhodomontade and grammatical inelegancies and solecisms." To go to a man for "truth," who is characterized by "the most fervid imagination and brilliant powers of invention," according to Mr. Emmette Coleman, shows Mr. Coleman in a sorry light indeed! His only excuse can be that in January, 1877, when he invited Colonel Olcott to discuss with him—despite the fact that the Theosophical Society had been established in 1875, and all our "heresies" were

---

*[More likely about March 11th, 1875.—*Compiler.*]

already in print—his estimation of his intellectual powers was different from what it is now, that Mr. Coleman's "address" has been left two years unread and unnoticed. Does this look like our offering ourselves as "leaders"? We address the great body of intelligent American Spiritualists. They have as much a right to their opinions as we to ours; they have no more right than we to falsely state the positions of their antagonists. But their would-be champion, Mr. Coleman, for the sake of having an excuse to abuse me, pretends to quote (see column 2, paragraph 1) from something I have published, a whole sentence that I defy him to prove I ever made use of. This is downright literary fraud and dishonesty. A man who is in "search of truth" does not usually employ a falsehood as a weapon.

Good friends, whose inquiries we have occasionally but rarely answered, bear us witness that we have always disclaimed anything like "leadership"; that we have invariably referred you to the same standard authors whom we have read, the same old philosophers which we have studied. We call on you to testify that we have repudiated dogmas and dogmatists, whether living men or disembodied spirits. As opposed to materialists, theosophists are Spiritualists, but it would be as absurd for us to claim the leadership of Spiritualism as for a Protestant priest to speak for the Romish Church, or a Romish cardinal to lead the great body of Protestants, though both claim to be Christians! Recrimination seems to be the life and soul of American journalism, but I really thought that a *Spiritualistic* organ had more congenial matter for its columns than such materialistic abuse as the present "Fort Leavenworth" criticism!

One chief aim of the writer seems to be to abuse *Isis Unveiled*. My publisher will doubtless feel under great obligation for giving it such a notoriety just now, when the fourth edition* is ready to go to press. That the fossilized reviewers of the *Tribune* and *Popular Science Monthly*—both ad-

---

*[Rather the fourth *printing* of the same original edition; the word "edition" has been often used in a rather loose manner.—*Compiler*.]

mitted advocates of materialistic science, and unsparingly contemptuous denunciators of Spiritualism—should, without either having read my book, brand it as Spiritualistic moonshine, was perfectly natural. I should have thought that I had written my first volume, holding up modern science to public contempt for its unfair treatment of psychological phenomena, to small purpose, if they had complimented me. Nor was I at all surprised that the critic of the New York *Sun* permitted himself the coarse language of a partisan and betrayed his ignorance of the contents of my book by terming me a "Spiritualist." But I am sorry that a critic like Mr. Coleman, who professes to speak for the Spiritualists and against the materialists, should range himself by the side of the flunkeys of the latter, when at least twenty of the first critics of Europe and America, not Spiritualists, but well-read scholars, should have praised it even more unstintedly than he has bespattered it. If such men as the author of *The Great Dionysiak Myth* and *Poseidon*,* writing a private letter to a fellow archeologist and scholar, which he thought I would never see, says the design of my book is "simply colossal," and that the book "is really a marvelous production" and has his "entire concurrence" in its views about: "(1) The wisdom of the ancient sages; (2) The folly of the merely material philosopher [the Emmette Colemans, Huxleys and Tyndalls]; (3) The doctrine of Nirvana; (4) Archaic monotheism," etc.; and when the London *Public Opinion* calls it "one of the most extraordinary works of the Nineteenth Century," in an elaborate criticism; and when Alfred R. Wallace says, "I am amazed at the vast amount of erudition displayed in the chapters, and the great interest of the topics on which they treat—your book will open up to many Spiritualists a whole world of new ideas, and cannot fail to be of the greatest value in the inquiry which is now being so earnestly carried on," Mr. Coleman really appears in the sorry light of one who abuses for the mere sake of abusing.

What a curious psychological power I must have! All the

---

*[Robert Brown, Jr.]

Journal writers, from the talented editor down to Mr. Coleman, pretend to account for the blind devotion of Colonel Olcott for Theosophy, the over-partial panegyric of Miss Kislingbury, the friendly recantation of Dr. G. Bloede, and the surprisingly vigorous defense of myself by Mr. C. Sotheran, and other recent events, on the ground of my having psychologized them all into the passive servitude of hoodwinked dupes! I can only say that *such* psychology is next door to a miracle. That I could influence men and women of such acknowledged independence of character and intellectual capacity, would be at least more than any of your lecturing mesmerizers or "spirit controls" have been able to accomplish. Do you not see, my noble enemies, the logical consequences of such a doctrine? Admit that I can do that, and you admit the reality of *magic,* and my powers as an adept. I never claimed that magic was anything but psychology practically applied. That one of your mesmerizers can make a cabbage appear a rose, is only a lower form of the power you all endow me with. You give an old woman—whether forty, fifty, sixty, or ninety years old (some swear I am the latter, some the former), it matters not; an old woman whose "Kalmuco-Buddhisto-Tartaric features," even in youth, never made her appear pretty; a woman, whose ungainly garb, uncouth manners and masculine habits are enough to frighten any bustled and corseted fine lady of fashionable society out of her wits—you give [her] such powers of fascination as to draw fine ladies and gentlemen, scholars and artists, doctors and clergymen, to her house by the scores, to not only talk philosophy with her, not merely to stare at her as though she were a monkey in red flannel breeches, as some of them do, but to honor her in many cases with their fast and sincere friendship and grateful kindness! Psychology! If that is the name you give it, then, although I have never offered myself as a teacher, you had better come, my friends, and be taught at once the "trick" (gratis, for unlike other psychologizers, I never yet took money for teaching anybody anything), so that hereafter you may not be deceived into recognizing as— what Mr. Coleman so graphically calls "the sainted dead of earth"—those pimple-nosed and garlic-breathing beings who climb ladders through trap-doors and carry tow wigs and battered masks in the penetralia of their underclothing.

H. P. BLAVATSKY.

"The masculino-feminine Sclavonic Theosoph, from Crim-Tartary"—
a title which does more credit to Mr. Coleman's vituperative ingenuity than to his literary accomplishments.

MADAME BLAVATSKY ON INDIAN METAPHYSICS

[*The Spiritualist*, London, March 22, 1878, pp. 140-41] *

Sir,

Two peas in the same pod are the traditional symbol of mutual resemblance, and the time-honoured simile forced itself upon me when I read the twin letters of our two masked assailants in your paper of February 22nd. In substance they are so identical that one would suppose the same person had written them simultaneously with his two hands, as Paul Morphy will play you two games of chess, or Kossuth dictate two letters at once. The only difference between these two letters—lying beside each other on the same page, like two babes in one crib—is, that "M. A. (Cantab.)'s" is brief and courteous, while "Scrutator's" is prolix and uncivil.

By a strange coincidence both these sharp-shooters fire from behind their secure ramparts a shot at a certain "learned occultist" over the head of Mr. C. C. Massey, who quoted some of that personage's views, in a letter published May 10th, 1876. Whether in irony or otherwise, they hurl

---

*[Square brackets in the body of this article are H.P.B.'s own. —*Compiler*.]

the views of this "learned occultist" at the heads of Colonel Olcott and myself, as though they were missiles that would floor us completely. Now, the "learned occultist" in question is not a whit more, or less, learned than your humble servant, for the very simple reason that we are identical. The extracts published by Mr. Massey, by permission, were contained in a letter from myself to him. Moreover, it is now before me, and, save one misprint of no consequence, I do not find in it a word that I would wish changed. What is said there I repeat now over my own signature—the theories of 1876 do not contradict those of 1878 in any respect, as I shall endeavour to prove, after pointing out to the impartial reader the quaking ground upon which our two critics stand. Their arguments against Theosophy—certainly "Scrutator's"—are like a verdant moss, which displays a velvety carpet of green, without roots, and with a deep bog below.

When a person enters a controversy over a fictitious signature, he should be doubly cautious, if he would avoid the accusation of abusing the opportunity of the mask to insult his opponents with impunity. Who or what is "Scrutator"? A clergyman, a medium, a lawyer, a philosopher, a physician (certainly not a metaphysician), or what? *Quien sabe?* He seems to partake of the flavour of all, and yet to grace neither. Though his arguments are all interwoven with sentences quoted from our letters, yet in no case does he criticize merely what is written by us, but what he thinks we *may* have meant, or what the sentences *might* imply. Drawing his deductions, then, from what existed only in the depths of his own consciousness, he invents phrases, and forces constructions upon which he proceeds to pour out his wrath. Without meaning to be in the least personal—for, though propagating "absurdities" with "utmost effrontery," I would feel sorry and ashamed to be as impertinent with "Scrutator" as he is with us—yet, hereafter, when I see a dog chasing the shadow of his own tail, I will think of his letter.

In my doubts as to what this assailant might be, I invoked the help of Webster to give me a possible clue in the pseudonym. "Scrutator," says the great lexicographer, "is one who scrutinizes," and "scrutiny" he derives from the Latin *scrutari,* "to search even to the rags"; which *scrutari* itself he traces back to a Greek root, meaning "trash, trumpery." In this ultimate analysis, therefore, we must regard the *nom de plume,* while very applicable to his letter of February 22nd, very unfortunate for himself; for at best it makes him a sort of literary *chiffonnier,* probing in the dust-heap of the language for bits of hard adjectives to fling at us. I repeat that, when an anonymous critic accuses two persons of "slanderous imputations" (the mere reflex of his own imagination), and of "unfathomable absurdities," he ought, at least, to make sure (1) that he has thoroughly grasped what he is pleased to call the "teachings" of his adversaries; and (2) that his own philosophy is infallible. I may add, furthermore, that when that critic permits himself to call the views of other people—not yet half-digested by himself—"unfathomable absurdities," he ought to be mighty careful about introducing as arguments into the discussion sectarian absurdities far more "unfathomable" and which have nothing to do with either science or philosophy.

> I suppose [gravely argues "Scrutator"] a babe's brain is soft, and a quite unfit tool for intelligence, otherwise Jesus could not have lost His intelligence when He took upon Himself the body and the brain of a babe [!!?].

The very opposite of Oliver Johnson evidently, this Jesus-babe of "Scrutator's."

Such an argument might come with a certain force in a discussion between two conflicting dogmatic sects, but if picked "even to rags," it seems but "utmost effrontery"—to use "Scrutator's" own complimentary expression—to employ it in a philosophical debate, as if it were either a scientific or historically proved fact! If I refused, at the very start, to argue with our friend "M. A. (Oxon.)," a man whom I esteem and respect as I do few in this world, only because he put forward a "cardinal dogma," I shall certainly lose no time in debating Theosophy with a tattering Christian, whose "scrutinizing" faculties have not helped him beyond the acceptance of the latest of the world's *Avatars,* in all its unphilosophical dead letter meaning, without even suspecting its symbolical significance. To parade in a would-be philosophical debate the exploded dogmas of any church, is most ineffectual, and shows, at best, a great poverty of resource. Why does not "Scrutator" address his refined abuse, *ex cathedra,* to the Royal Society, whose Fellows doom to annihilation every human being, Theosophist or Spiritualist, pure or impure?

With crushing irony he speaks of us as "our teachers." Now, I remember having distinctly stated in a previous letter that we have *not* offered ourselves as teachers, but, on the contrary, decline any such office—whatever may be the superlative panegyric of my esteemed friend, Mr. O'Sullivan, who not only sees in me "a Buddhist priestess" (!), but, without a shadow of warrant of fact, credits me with the foundation of the Theosophical Society and its Branches! Had Colonel Olcott been half as "psychologised" by me as a certain American Spiritualist paper will have it, he would have followed my advice and refused to make public our "views," even though so much and so often importuned in different quarters. With characteristic stubbornness, however, he had his own way, and now reaps the consequence of having thrown his bomb into a hornet's nest. Instead of being afforded opportunity for a calm debate, we get but abuse, pure and simple—the only weapon of partisans. Well, let us make the best of it, and join our opponents in picking the question "to rags." Mr. C. C. Massey comes in for his share, too, and, though fit to be a leader himself, is given by "Scrutator" a chief!

Neither of our critics seems to understand our views (or his own) so little as "Scrutator." He misapprehends the meaning of Elementary, and makes a sad mess of spirit and matter. Hear him say that elementary

> is a new-fangled and ill-defined term . . . not yet two years old!

This sentence alone proves that he forces himself into the

discussion, without any comprehension of the subject at issue. Evidently, he has neither read the mediaeval nor modern Kabalists. Henry Khunrath is as unfamiliar to him as the Abbé Constant. Let him go to the British Museum, and ask for the *Amphitheatrum Sapientiae Aeternae* of Khunrath. He will find in it illustrative engravings of the four great classes of elementary spirits, as seen during an evocation of ceremonial magic by the Magus who lifts the *Veil of Isis*. The author explains that these are disembodied vicious men, who have parted with their divine spirits, and become as beasts. After reading this volume, "Scrutator" may profitably consult Éliphas Lévi, whom he will find using the words "Elementary Spirits" throughout his *Dogme et Rituel de la Haute Magie,* in both senses in which we have employed it. This is especially the case where (Vol. I, p. 262 *et seq.*) he speaks of the evocation of Apollonius of Tyana by himself. Quoting from the greatest Kabalistic authorities, he says:

> When a man has lived well, the astral cadaver evaporates like a pure incense, as it mounts towards the higher regions; but if a man has lived in crime, his astral cadaver, which holds him prisoner, seeks again the objects of his passions and desires to resume its earthly life. It torments the dreams of young girls, bathes in the vapour of spilt blood, and wallows about the places where the pleasures of his life flitted by; it watches without ceasing over the treasures which it possessed and buried: it wastes itself in painful efforts to make for itself material organs [materialize itself] and live again. But the stars attract and absorb it; its memory is gradually lost, its intelligence weakens, all its being dissolves . . . The unhappy wretch loses thus in succession all the organs which served its sinful appetites. Then it [this astral body, this "soul," this all that is left of the once living man] dies a second time and for ever, for it then loses its personality and its memory. Souls which are destined to live, but which are not yet entirely purified, remain for a longer or shorter time captive in the astral cadaver, where they are refined by the odic light, which seeks to assimilate them to itself and dissolve. It is to rid themselves of this cadaver that suffering souls sometimes enter the bodies of living persons, and remain there for a time in a state which the Kabalists call embryonic [*embryonat*]. These are the aerial phantoms evoked by necromancy [and I may add, the "materialized Spirits" evoked by the unconscious necromancy of incautious mediums, in cases where the forms are not transformations of their own doubles];

these are larvae, substances dead or dying with which one places himself *en rapport*.

Further Lévi says (*op. cit.,* p. 164):

> The astral light is saturated with elementary souls . . . Yes, yes, these spirits of the elements do exist. Some wandering in their spheres, others trying to incarnate themselves, others, again, already incarnated and living on earth; these are vicious and imperfect men.

And in the face of this testimony (which he can find in the British Museum, two steps from the office of *The Spiritualist!*) that since the Middle Ages the Kabalists have been writing about elementaries, and their potential annihilation, "Scrutator" permits himself to arraign Theosophists for their "effrontery" in foisting upon Spiritualists a "new-fangled and ill-defined term" which is "not yet two years old"!!

In truth, we may say that the idea is older than Christianity, for it is found in the ancient Kabalistic books of the Jews. In the olden time they defined three kinds of "souls" —the daughters of Adam, the daughters of the angels, and those of sin; and in the book of *The Revolution of the Souls* three kinds of "spirits" (as distinct from material bodies) are shown—the captive, the wandering and the free spirits. If "Scrutator" were acquainted with the literature of Kabalism, he would know that the term elementary applies not only to one principle or constituent part, to an elementary primary substance, but also embodies the idea which we express by the term elemental—that which pertains to the four elements of the material world, the first principles or primary ingredients. The word "elemental," as defined by Webster, was not current at the time of Khunrath, but the idea was perfectly understood. The distinction has been made, and the term adopted by Theosophists for the sake of avoiding confusion. The thanks we get are that we are charged with propounding, in 1878, a different theory of the "elementaries" from that of 1876!

Does anything herein stated, either as from ourselves, or Khunrath, or Lévi, contradict the statement of the "learned occultist" that:

> Each atom, no matter where found, is imbued with that vital prin-

ciple called spirit . . . Each grain of sand, equally with each minutest atom of the human body, has its inherent latent spark of the divine light?

Not in the least. "M. A. (Cantab.)" asks, "How then, can a man *lose* this divine light, in part or in whole, as a rule before death, if each minutest atom of the human body has its inherent latent spark of the divine light?" Italicizing some words, as above, but omitting to emphasize the one important word of the sentence, *i.e.*, "latent," which contains the key to the whole mystery. In the grain of sand, and each atom of the human material body, the spirit is *latent,* not active; hence, being but a correlation of the highest light, something concrete as compared with the purely abstract, the atom is vitalized and energized by spirit, without being endowed with distinct consciousness. A grain of sand, as every minutest atom, is certainly "imbued with that vital principle called spirit." So is every atom of the human body, whether physical or astral, and thus every atom of both, following the law of evolution, whether of objective or semi-concrete astral matter, will have to remain eternal throughout the endless cycles, indestructible in their primary, elementary constituents. But will "M. A. (Cantab.)" for all that, call a grain of sand, or a human nail-paring, consciously immortal? Does he mean us to understand him as believing that a fractional part, as a fraction, has the same attributes, capabilities, and limitations as the whole? Does he say that because the atoms in a nail-paring are indestructible as atoms, therefore the body, of which the nail formed a part, is of necessity, as a conscious whole, indestructible and immortal?

Our opponents repeat the words Trinity, Body, Soul, Spirit, as they might say the cat, the house, and the Irishman inhabiting it—three perfectly dissimilar things. They do not see that, dissimilar as the three parts of the human trinity may seem, they are in truth but correlations of the one eternal essence—which is no essence; but unfortunately the English language is barren of adequate expression, and, though they do not see it, the house, the physical Irishman, and the cat are, in their last analysis, one. I verily begin to suspect that they imagine that spirit and matter are two, instead of one! Truly says Vishnu Bawa Brahmachâri, in one of his essays in Marathi (1869), that

> The opinion of the Europeans that matter is "Padârtha" (an equivalent for the "pada," or word "Abhâva," *i.e., Ahey,* composed of two letters, "Ahe," meaning *is,* and "nahin," *not*), whereas "Abhâva" is no "Padârtha," is foolishly erroneous!"

Kant, Schopenhauer and Hartmann seem to have written to little effect, and Kapila will be soon pronounced an antiquated ignoramus. Without at all ranging myself under Schopenhauer's banner, who maintains that in reality there is neither spirit nor matter, yet I must say that if ever he were studied, Theosophy would be better understood.

But can one really discuss metaphysical ideas in an European language? I doubt it. We say "spirit," and behold, what confusion it leads to! Europeans give the name spirit to that something which they conceive as apart from physical organization, independent of corporeal, objective existence; and they call spirit also the airy, vaporous essence, alcohol. Therefore, the New York reporter who defined a materialized Spirit as "frozen whiskey," was right, in his way. A copious vocabulary, indeed, that has but one term for God and for alcohol! With all their libraries of metaphysics, European nations have not even gone to the trouble of inventing appropriate words to elucidate metaphysical ideas. If they had, perhaps one book in every thousand would have sufficed to really instruct the public, instead of there being the present confusion of words, obscuring intelligence, and utterly hampering the Orientalist, who would expound his philosophy in English. Whereas, in the latter language, I find but one word to express, perhaps, twenty different ideas, in the Eastern tongues, especially Sanskrit, there are twenty words or more to render one idea in its various shades of meaning.

We are accused of propagating ideas that would surprise the "average" Buddhist. Granted, and I will liberally add that the average Brahminist might be equally astonished. We never said that we were either Buddhists or Brahminists in the sense of their popular exoteric theologies. Buddha, sitting on his lotus, or Brahmâ, with any number of teratological arms, appeal to us as little as the Catholic Madonna, or the Christian personal God, which stare at us from cathedral walls and ceilings. But neither Buddha nor Brahmâ represent to their respective worshippers the same ideas as these Catholic icons, which we regard as blasphemous. In this particular, who dares say that Christendom, with its boasted civilization, has outgrown the fetishism of the Fijians? When we see Christians and Spiritualists speaking so flippantly and confidently about God and the materialization of "spirit," we wish they might be made to share a little in the reverential ideas of the old Aryas.

We do not write for "average" Buddhists, or average people of any sort. But I am quite willing to match any tolerably educated Buddhist or Brahman against the best metaphysicians of Europe, to compare views on God and on man's immortality.

The ultimate abstract definition of this—call it God, force, principle, as you will—will ever remain a mystery to Humanity, though it attain to its highest intellectual development. The anthropomorphic ideas of Spiritualists concerning spirit are a direct consequence of the anthropomorphic conceptions of Christians as to the Deity. So directly is the one the outflow of the other, that "Scrutator's" handiest argument against the duality of a child and potential immortality is to cite "Jesus who increased in wisdom as his brain increased."

Christians call God an Infinite Being, and then endow Him with every finite attribute, such as love, anger, benevolence, mercy! They call Him All-Merciful, and preach eternal damnation for three-fourths of humanity in every church; All-Just, and the sins of this brief span of life may not be expiated by even an eternity of conscious agony. Now, by some miracle of oversight, among thousands of mistranslations in the "Holy" Writ, the word "destruction," the synonym of annihilation, was rendered correctly in the King James' version, and no dictionary can make it read either damnation, or eternal torment. Though the Church consistently put down the "destructionists," yet the impartial will scarcely deny that they come nearer than their persecutors to believing what Jesus taught and what is consistent with justice, in teaching the final annihilation of the wicked.

To conclude, then, we believe that there is but one indefinable principle in the whole universe, which being utterly incomprehensible by our finite intellects, we prefer rather to leave undebated, than to blaspheme its majesty with our anthropomorphic speculations. We believe that all else which has being, whether material or spiritual, and all that may have existence, actually or potentially in our idealism, emanates from this principle. That everything is a correlation in one shape or another of this Will and Force; and hence, judging of the unseen by the visible, we base our speculations upon the teachings of the generations of sages who preceded Christianity, fortified by our own reason.

I have already illustrated the incapacity of some of our critics to separate abstract ideas from complex objects, by instancing the grain of sand and the nail-paring. They refuse to comprehend that a philosophical doctrine can teach that an atom imbued with divine light, or a portion of the great Spirit, in its latent stage of correlation, may, notwithstanding its reciprocal or corresponding similarity and relations to the one indivisible whole, be yet utterly deficient in self-consciousness. That it is only when this atom, magnetically drawn to its fellow atoms, which had served in a previous state to form with it some lower complex object, is transformed at last, after endless cycles of evolution, into MAN —the apex of perfected being, intellectually and physically, on our planet—in conjunction with them becomes, as a whole, a living soul, and reaches the state of intellectual self-consciousness. "A stone becomes a plant, a plant an animal, an animal a man, and man a spirit," say the Kabalists. And here again, is the wretched necessity of translating by the word "spirit" an expression which means a celestial, or rather ethereal, transparent man—something diametrically opposite to the man of matter, yet a man. But if man is the crown of evolution on earth, what is he in the initiatory stages of the next existences—that man who, at his best, even when he is pretended to have served as a habitation for the Christian God, Jesus, is said by Paul to have been "made a little lower than the angels"? But now we have every astral spook transformed into an "angel"! I cannot believe that the scholars who write for your paper —and there are some of great intelligence and erudition who think for themselves; and whom exact science has taught that *ex nihilo nihil fit*; who know that every atom of man's body has been evolving by imperceptible gradations, from lower into higher forms, through the cycles— accept the unscientific and illogical doctrine that the simple unshelling of an astral man transforms him into a celestial spirit and "angel" guide.

In Theosophical opinion a spirit is a ray, a fraction of the whole; and the Whole being Omniscient and Infinite, its fraction must partake, in degree, of the same abstract attributes. Man's "spirit" must become the drop of the ocean, called "Iśvara-Bhava"—the "I am one body, together with the universe itself" (I am in my Father, and my Father is in me), instead of remaining but the "Jiva-Bhava," the body only. He must feel himself not only a part of the Creator, Preserver and Destroyer, but of the soul of the three, the Parabrahma, who is above these, and is the vitalizing, energizing, and ever-presiding Spirit. He must fully realize the sense of the word "Sahajânanda," that state of perfect bliss in Nirvâna, which can only exist for the It, which has become co-existent with the "formless and actionless present time." This is the state called "Vartamana," or the "Ever Still Present," in which there is neither past nor future, but one infinite eternity of present. Which of the controlling "spirits," materialized or invisible, have shown any signs that they belong to the kind of real spirits known as the "Sons of Eternity"? Has the highest of them been able to tell even as much as our own Divine *Nous* can whisper to us in moments when there comes the flash of sudden prevision? Honest communicating "intelligences" often answer to many questions: "We do not know; this has not been revealed to us." This very admission proves that, while in many cases on their way to knowledge and perfection, yet they are but embryonic, undeveloped "spirits"; they are inferior even to some living Yogis who, through abstract meditation, have united themselves with their personal individual Brahmâ, their Âtman, and hence have overcome the "Ajñâna," or lack of that knowledge as to the intrinsic value of one's "self," the *Ego,* or self-being, so recommended by Socrates and the Delphic commandment.

London has been often visited by highly intellectual, educated Hindus. I have not heard of any one professing a belief in "materialized spirits"—as spirits. When not tainted with Materialism, through demoralizing association with Europeans, and when free from superstitious sectarianism, how would one of them, versed in the Vedânta, regard these apparitions of the circle? The chances are that, after going the rounds of the mediums, he would say: "Some of these may be survivals of disembodied men's intelligences, but they are no more spiritual than the average man. They lack the knowledge of 'Dhyânânta,' and evidently find themselves in a chronic state of 'Mâyâ,' *i.e.,* possessed of the idea that 'they are that which they are not.' The 'Vartamana' has no significance for them, as they are cognizant but of the 'Vishama' [that which, like the concrete numbers in mixed mathematics, applies to that which can be numbered]. Like simple, ignorant mortals, they regard the shadow of things as the reality, and *vice versa,* mixing up the true light of the 'Vyatireka' with the false light or deceitful appearance—the 'Anvaya.' . . . In what respect, then, are they higher than the average mortal? No; they are not spirits, not 'Devas,' . . . they are astral 'Dasyus'."

Of course, all this will appear to "Scrutator" "unfathomable absurdities," for, unfortunately, few metaphysicians shower down from Western skies. Therefore, so long as our English opponents will remain in their semi-Christian ideas, and not only ignore the old philosophy, but the very terms it employs to render abstract ideas; so long as we are forced to transmit these ideas in a general way—particularly being impracticable without the invention of special words—it will be unprofitable to push discussion to any great length. We would only make ourselves obnoxious to the general reader, and receive from other anonymous writers such unconvincing compliments as "Scrutator" has favoured us with.

H. P. BLAVATSKY.

New York, March 7th, 1877.*

[In H.P.B.'s *Scrapbook*, Vol. VII, pp. 56-57, there is pasted a cutting from *The Spiritualist* of London, dated March 29, 1878. It is an article by G. Damiani regarding "The Manifestations in Naples of the Alleged Spirit of Nana Sahib." H.P.B. wrote the following remarks at the end of this article:]

How interesting—were it not for the fact that there is every reason *to believe* that Nana Sahib is still alive.

---

* [An obvious error for 1878.—*Compiler*.]

THE CAVE OF THE ECHOES*

AN APPALLING TALE OF RETRIBUTIVE JUSTICE INFLICTED BY AN EARTHBOUND "SPIRIT."

BY H. P. BLAVATSKY.

[*Banner of Light*, Boston, Vol. XLII, March 30, 1878, p. 2]

In the older countries of Europe and Asia there frequently occur examples of interference by the dead with the living, to which American Spiritualists are as yet comparative strangers. The experience of many generations has taught the higher, equally with the lower classes, to accept this intervention as a fixed fact. With this difference, however, that as a rule, the former acknowledging the reality of the phenomena, find, to escape ridicule, a convenient loophole by attributing them to strange coincidences, while the latter, with less learning but more intuition, have no difficulty in divining the real cause. Tales calculated to freeze the blood with horror circulate in many of the lands I have visited, and more than once, instances of the reward and punishment of good or evil deeds by occult agency have come under my own observation.

The story I am about to relate has the merit of being perfectly true. The family is well-known in that portion of the Russian dominions where the scene is located. The circumstance was witnessed by one of my relatives, upon whom it made an impression that he carried to his grave.

---

* [In her *Scrapbook*, Vol. I, p. 119, where the cuttings of this story are pasted, H.P.B. wrote in pen and ink:

3d story (Killed on account of being too horrible . . .)

She most likely means by this that the New York *Sun* refused to publish it at the time her 1st and 2nd stories appeared therein.

This story was republished by H.P.B. in *The Theosophist*, Vol. IV, April, 1883, pp. 164-66, and later appeared in a Russian version— most likely from H.P.B.'s own pen—in *Rebus* (Riddle), Vol. V, January 5, 12 and 19, 1886. The latter version is somewhat fuller, even though it lacks some of the paragraphs of the English text.—*Compiler*.]

The Cave of the Echoes

My object in telling it is to illustrate one of the many phases of psychological science studied by Theosophists, and which must be studied by whoever would inform himself thoroughly upon the relations of living man with the silent world of shadows—that bourne from which . . . *some travellers do return.* . . .

It may be taken as a case of mediumship of a most striking kind—in short, a *transfiguration*. It differs only in degree from that of Mrs. Markee—formerly Compton—witnessed and described by Colonel Olcott in his work, and one of the most astounding ones on record.* The physical body of Mrs. Compton was transformed alternately into the shapes of a dwarfish girl and a tall Indian chief. In the present instance the haunting soul of an old man enters a child's body, and temporarily re-incarnating itself, becomes the agent of inexorable destiny. The intelligent reader will need no further hint to enable him to trace the lesson which my veracious narrative conveys.†

In one of the distant governments of Russia, in a small town on the very borders of Siberia, a mysterious tragedy occurred some twenty years ago—a tragedy which haunts the memory of the older inhabitants of the district to this very day, and is recounted but in whispers to the inquisitive traveller.

About six versts from the little town of P——, famous for the wild beauty of its scenery, and for the wealth of its inhabitants—generally proprietors of mines and iron foundries—stood an old and aristocratic mansion. Its household consisted of the master, a rich old bachelor, and his brother, a widower and the father of two sons and three daughters. It was known that the proprietor, Mr. Izvertzoff, had adopted his brother's children, and, having formed an especial attachment for his eldest nephew, Nicholas, had made him the sole heir to his numerous estates.

---

* [*Vide* Col. H. S. Olcott, *People from the Other World*, Hartford, Conn., 1875, pp. 479 *et seq.*—*Compiler*.]

† [The opening paragraphs, up to here, do not occur in the Russian version of this story.—*Compiler*.]

Time rolled on. The uncle was getting old, the nephew coming of age. Days and years had passed in monotonous serenity, when, on the hitherto clear horizon of the quiet family appeared a cloud. On an unlucky day one of the nieces took it into her head to study the zither. The instrument being of purely Teutonic origin, and no teacher for that specialty residing in the neighborhood, the indulgent uncle sent to St. Petersburg for both. After diligent search only one such professor could be found willing to trust himself in such close proximity to Siberia. It was an old German artist, who, sharing equally his earthly affections between his instrument and a pretty blonde daughter, would part with neither. And thus it came to pass that, one fine morning, the old professor arrived at the mansion with his zithercase under one arm, and his fair Minchen leaning on the other.

From that day the little cloud began growing rapidly; for every vibration of the melodious instrument found a responsive echo in the old bachelor's heart. Music awakens love, they say, and the work begun by the zither was completed by Minchen's blue eyes. At the expiration of six months the niece had become an expert zitherplayer and the uncle was desparately in love. One morning, gathering his adopted family around him, he embraced them all very tenderly, promised to remember them in his will, and wound up by declaring his unalterable resolution to marry the blue-eyed Minchen. After which he fell upon their necks and wept in silent rapture. The family also wept: but it was for another cause. Having paid this tribute to self-interest, they tried their best to rejoice, for the old gentleman was sincerely beloved. Not all of them rejoiced, though. Nicholas, who had equally felt himself heart-smitten by the pretty Germain maid, and who found himself at once defrauded of his belle and his uncle's money, neither rejoiced nor consoled himself, but disappeared for the whole day.

STARTING ON A LONG JOURNEY.

Meanwhile Mr. Izvertzoff gave orders to prepare his travelling carriage for the following morning. It was whispered that he was going to the government town at some distance from here, with the intention of altering his will. Though very wealthy he had no superintendent on his estate, but kept his books himself. The same evening, after supper, he was heard in his room scolding angrily at his body-servant who had been in his service for over thirty years. This man, Ivan, was a native of Northern Asia, from Kamchatka. Brought up by the family in the Christian religion, he was thought very much attached to his master. But when the tragic circumstances I am about to relate had brought all the police force to the spot, it was remembered that Ivan was drunk on that night; that his master, who had a horror of this vice, had paternally thrashed him and turned him out of the room; and that Ivan had been seen reeling out of the door and heard to mutter threats.

There was on the estate of the Izvertzoffs a great cavern, which excited (and still excites) the curiosity of all who visited it. A pine forest, which began nearly at the garden gate, climbed by steep terraces a long range of rocky hills, which it covered with a belt of impenetrable verdure. The grotto leading to the place, which people called the "Cave of the Echoes," was situated about half a mile from the mansion, from which it appeared as a small excavation in the hillside, almost hidden by luxuriant plants. Still it was not so masked as to prevent any person entering it from being readily seen from the terrace of the house. Inside the grotto, the explorer finds at the rear of an ante-chamber a narrow cleft, having passed which he emerges into a lofty cavern, feebly lighted through fissures in a ceiling fifty feet high. The cavern itself is immense, capable of easily holding two or three thousand people. A part of it was, at the time of my story, paved with flags, and often used in the summer by picnic parties as a ball-room. Of an irregular oval shape, it gradually narrows into a broad corridor, which runs several miles underground, intercepted here and there by other chambers as large and lofty as the ballroom, but, unlike that, inaccessible except by boat, as they are full of water. These natural basins have the reputation of being unfathomable.

THE ECHOES.

On the margin of the first of these was a small platform, with several mossy rustic seats arranged on it, and it is from this spot that the phenomenal echoes were heard in all their weirdness. A word pronounced in a whisper or a sigh seemed caught up by endless, mocking voices, and instead of diminishing in volume, as honest echoes generally do, the sound grew louder at every successive repetition, until at last it burst forth like the repercussion of a pistol shot, and receded in a plaintive wail down the corridor.

On the evening in question, Mr. Izvertzoff had mentioned his intention of having a dancing party in the cave on his wedding day, which he had fixed for an early date. On the following morning, while preparing for his departure, he was seen by his family entering the grotto, accompanied only by the Siberian. Half an hour later Ivan returned to the mansion for a snuffbox which his master had forgotten in his room, and went back with it to the cave. An hour later the whole household was startled with his loud cries. Pale, and dripping with water, Ivan rushed in like a madman and declared that Mr. Izvertzoff was nowhere to be found in the grotto. Thinking he had fallen into one of the lakes, he had dived into the first basin in search of him, and got nearly drowned himself.

The day passed in vain attempts to find the body. The police filled the house, and louder than the rest in his despair seemed Nicholas, the nephew, who had returned home only in time to hear the sad tidings.

A dark suspicion fell upon Ivan, the Siberian. He had been struck by his master the night before, and had been heard to swear revenge. He had accompanied him alone to the cave, and when his room was searched a casket full of rich family jewelry, known to have been carefully kept in old Izvertzoff's apartment, was found under Ivan's bedding. Vainly did the man call God to witness that the casket had been handed to him in charge by his master himself, just before they proceeded to the cave; that it was the latter's purpose to have the jewelry reset, as he intended it for a wedding present for his bride, and that he, Ivan, would willingly give his own life to recall that of his benefactor, if he knew him to be dead. No heed was paid to him, however, and he was arrested upon the charge of foul murder, though no definite sentence could be passed on him, as, under the old Russian law, a criminal cannot be sentenced for any crime, however conclusive the evidence, unless he confesses his guilt; yet the poor man had the prospect of prison for the whole of his life, unless he did confess.

A MARRIAGE.

After a week spent in useless search the family arrayed themselves in deep mourning, and, as the will as originally drawn remained without a codicil, the whole of the estate passed into the hands of the nephew. The old teacher and his fair daughter bore this sudden reverse of fortune with true Germanic phlegm, and prepared to depart. Taking again his zither under one arm, the father was about to lead his Minchen by the other, when the nephew stopped him by offering himself as groom instead of his departed uncle. The change was found an agreeable one, and, without much ado, the young couple were married.

Ten years roll away again, and we find the happy family at the beginning of 1855. The fair, blue-eyed Minchen had become fat and vulgar. From the day of the old man's disappearance Nicholas had been morose and retired in his habits. Many wondered at the change in him, for now he was never seen to smile. It seemed as if his only aim in life, since the catastrophe, was to find out his uncle's murderer or rather to bring Ivan to confess his guilt. But the man still persisted that he was innocent.

An only son had been born to the young couple, and it was hoped that this would have brought a ray of sunshine to the father's heart. But it was such a weak and puny little creature that it seemed scarce able to catch its breath; and so, according to the Russian custom in such cases, the family priest was called to christen it the same evening, lest, dying, it might go to the place prepared for unbaptized infants by Christian theology. The family and servants were gathered at the ceremony in the large reception room of the house, and the priest was about to dip the babe thrice in the water, when he was seen to stop abruptly, turn deadly pale, and stare into vacancy, while his hands shook so violently that he almost dropped the child into the baptismal font. At the same time, the nurse, who stood at the end of the first row of spectators, gave a wild shriek, and pointing to the direction of the library room used by the old Izvertzoff, ran away in terror. No one could understand the panic of these two personages, for, except them, no one had seen anything extraordinary. Some had remarked the library door swing slowly open, but it must have been caused by the wind, which was now wailing all through the old mansion. After the ceremony, the priest, corroborated by the hysterically sobbing maid, solemnly averred that he had seen, for one moment, the apparition of the deceased master upon the threshold of his library, then swiftly glide toward the font, and instantly disappear. Both witnesses described the spectre as having on its features an expression of menace. The priest, after crossing himself and muttering prayers, insisted that the whole family should have Masses said for the space of seven weeks for the repose of the "troubled soul."*

It was a strange child, this babe of Nicholas and Minchen, and seemed to have an uncanny atmosphere about it. Small, delicate, and ever ailing, his frail life appeared to hang by a thread as he grew. When his features were in repose, his resemblance to his grand uncle was so striking that the members of the family often shrank from him in terror. It was the pale, shrivelled face of a man of sixty upon the shoulders of a child of nine years. He was never seen to either laugh or play; but, perched in his high chair, gravely sat, folding his arms in a way peculiar to the late Izvertzoff. He would remain so for hours, motionless and drowsy. His nurse was often seen furtively crossing herself, at night, upon approaching him; and not one of his attendants would consent to sleep alone with him in the nursery. His father's

---

* [This entire scene is lacking in the Russian version of the story. —*Compiler.*]

THE CAVE OF THE ECHOES 345

behaviour toward him was still more strange. He seemed to love him passionately, and yet to hate him bitterly at moments. He never embraced or caressed the boy, but would pass long hours watching him, with livid cheek and staring eye, as he sat quietly in a corner, in his goblin-like, old-fashioned way. The child had never left the estate, and few outside the family knew him.

A MYSTERIOUS TRAVELLER.

About the middle of July, a tall Hungarian traveller, preceded by a great reputation for eccentricity, wealth, and most extraordinary mesmeric powers, arrived at P—— from Kamchatka, where, as was rumoured, he had resided for some time, surrounded by Shamans. He settled in the little town, with one of this sect, and was said to experiment in mesmerism on this North Siberian "sorcerer," as he was called by the inhabitants. He gave dinners and parties, and during such receptions, invariably exhibited his Shaman of whom he felt very proud. One day, the notables of P—— made an unexpected invasion of the domain of Nicholas Izvertzoff, and requested of him the loan of his "Cave" for an evening entertainment. Nicholas consented with great reluctance, and with still greater hesitancy was he prevailed upon to join the party, among whom was my own relative.

The first cavern and the platform beside the bottomless lake glittered that evening with lights. Hundreds of flickering torches and lamps, stuck in the clefts of the rocks, illuminated the place, and drove the shadows from the mossy nooks and corners, where they had been undisturbed for many years. The stalactites on the walls sparkled brightly, and the sleeping echoes were suddenly awakened by a confusion of joyous laughter and conversation. The Shaman, who was never lost sight of by his friend and patron, sat in a corner, half entranced as usual. Crouched on a projecting rock, about midway between the entrance and the water, with his orange-yellow wrinkled face, flat nose, and thin beard, he looked more like an ugly stone idol than a human being. Many of the company pressed round him and received correct answers from the oracle to their questions, the

Hungarian cheerfully submitting his mesmerized "subject" to cross examination.

A LOVING NEPHEW.

Suddenly one of the party, a lady, thoughtlessly remarked that it was in that very cave that old Mr. Izvertzoff had so unaccountably disappeared ten years before. The foreigner appeared interested, and desired to learn more of the mysterious circumstances. Nicholas was sought in the crowd, and led before the eager group. He was the host, and he found it impossible to refuse the narrative demanded by a sympathizing guest. He repeated the sad tale in a trembling voice, with a pallid cheek, and a tear was seen to glitter in his feverish eye. The company was greatly affected, and encomiums upon the behaviour of the loving nephew, who so honoured the memory of his uncle and benefactor, freely circulated in sympathetic whispers. Suddenly the voice of Nicholas became choked, his eyes started from their sockets, and, with a suppressed groan, he staggered back. Every eye in the crowd followed with curiosity his haggard look, as it remained riveted upon a weazened little face that peeped from behind the back of the Shaman.

"Where do you come from? Who brought you here, child?" lisped out Nicholas, as pale as death itself.

"I was in bed, papa; this man came to me and brought me here in his arms," simply answered the boy, pointing to the Shaman, beside whom he stood on the rock, and who, with his eyes closed, kept swaying himself to and fro like a living pendulum.

"That is very strange," remarked one of the guests; "why, the man has never moved from his place!"

"Good God! What an extraordinary resemblance!" muttered an old resident of the town, a friend of the dead man.

"You lie, boy!" fiercely exclaimed the father. "Return to your bed; this is no place for you...."

"Come, come," interposed the Hungarian, with a strange expression of authority on his face, and encircling with his arm, as if in protection, the slender, childish figure. "The little fellow has seen my Shaman's double, which roams sometimes far away from his body, and has mistaken the astral man for the outward phantom itself. Let the child remain with us awhile."

At these strange words the guests stared at each other in mute surprise, and some of them looked upon the speaker with real terror.

UNRAVELING THE MYSTERY AT LAST.

"By the bye," continued the Hungarian, with a very peculiar firmness of accent, and addressing the public rather than any one in particular, "why should we not try to unravel the mystery hanging over that tragedy, with the help of the clairvoyant powers of my Shaman? Is the suspected party still lying in prison? . . . What? . . . not confessed till now? This is indeed strange. But now we will learn the truth in a few minutes. . . . My Shaman's second sight, when properly directed, never errs. Let all keep silent!"

He then approached the Tehuktchene, and making as though drawing an imaginary circle with his hand around himself, the Shaman, and boy, immediately began his operations over the subject without so much as asking the consent of the master of the place. The latter stood rooted to the spot as if petrified with horror, and unable to articulate a sound. Except by him, the suggestion was met with general approbation, and the "Police-Master," Colonel S——, was the first to approve the idea.

"Ladies and gentlemen," then said the mesmerizer in amiable tone, "allow me for this once to proceed otherwise than I generally do. I will employ the method of native magic. It is more appropriate to this wild place, and, I dare say, we will find it far more effective than our European mode of mesmerization."

Without waiting for an answer he drew from a bag that, as he explained, never left his person, first, a small drum, and then two little vials—one full of liquid, the other empty. With the contents of the former he sprinkled the Shaman, who fell to trembling and nodding more violently than ever. The air was filled with the perfumes of spicy odors, and the atmosphere itself seemed to become clearer. Then, to the horror of those present, he approached the Shaman, and taking a miniature, antiquated-looking knife from his bosom, quietly plunged the sharp steel into the man's forearm and drew blood from it, which he caught in the empty vial. When it was half-filled he pressed the orifice of the wound with his thumb, and stopped the flow as easily as if he had corked a bottle; after which he sprinkled the blood over the little boy's head. He then suspended the drum from his neck, and with two ivory drumsticks which were covered with strange carved letters and signs, he began beating a sort of reveille—he said to drum up the Shaman's "spirits."

MAGICAL WONDERS.

The bystanders, half shocked and half terrified at these extraordinary proceedings, eagerly, yet half timidly, crowded around him, and for a few moments a dead silence reigned throughout the lofty cavern. Nicholas, with his face livid and corpse-like, stood speechless as before.

And now the mesmerizer magician had placed himself between the Shaman and the platform, and continued slowly drumming. The first notes were muffled, and vibrating so softly in the air that they awakened no echo; only the Shaman quickened still more his pendulum-like motion, and the child became restless. The mysterious drummer then began a low chant, slow, impressive and solemn.

As the unknown words issued from his lips, the flames of the torches, lamps and candles wavered and flickered, until they began dancing in rhythm with the chant. A cold wind came wheezing from the dark corridors beyond the water, leaving a plaintive echo in its trail. Then a sort of nebulous vapor, which seemed to ooze from the rocky ground and walls, gathered about the Shaman and the boy. Around the latter the aura was silvery and transparent, but the cloud which enveloped the former was red and sinister. Approaching nearer the platform, the adept beat a louder call on his drum, and this time the echo caught it up with terrific effect. It reverberated near and far in incessant peals; one wail followed another, louder and louder, until the thundering roar seemed the chorus of a thousand demon voices rising from the fathomless depths of the dark lake. The water itself, whose tranquil surface, illuminated by many lights, had previously been smooth as a sheet of glass, became suddenly agitated, as if a powerful gust of wind had swept over its face.

Another chant and a roll of the drum, and the mountain trembled to its foundation with the cannon-like peals which rolled through the dark and distant corridors. The Shaman's body rose two yards in the air, and, nodding and swaying, he sat, self-suspended, like a hideous apparition. But the transformation which now occurred in the boy chilled everyone with fear as they speechlessly watched the scene. The silvery cloud about the child now seemed to lift him, too, into the air; but, *unlike the Shaman, his feet never left the ground.* The little boy began to grow as if the work of years was to be miraculously accomplished in a few seconds. He became tall and large, and his senile features grew older, in harmony with the body. A few more seconds and the youthful form had entirely disappeared: *it was totally absorbed in another individuality!* and, to the horror of those present who had been familiar with his appearance, this individuality was old Izvertzoff! . . .

THE PHANTOM.

On his left temple was a large, gaping wound, from which trickled great drops of blood. The *phantom* now moved directly in front of Nicholas, who, with his hair standing erect, gazed at his own son, transformed into his uncle, with the look of a raving madman. This sepulchral silence was broken by the Hungarian, who, addressing the child phantom, asked him in solemn voice: "In the name of Them who have all powers, answer the truth, and nothing but the truth. Restless soul, was thy body lost by accident, or foully murdered?"

The spectre's lips moved, but it was the echo from afar which answered in lugubrious shouts:

"Murdered! Murde-red! Mur-de-red!"

"Where? How? By whom?" asked the adept.

The apparition pointed a finger at Nicholas, and without

removing its gaze or lowering its arm, retreated backward slowly towards the lake. At every step it took, the young Izvertzoff, as if compelled by some irresistible fascination, advanced a step toward it, until the phantom reached the edge of the water, and the next moment was seen gliding on its surface. It was a fearful, ghostly scene!

When Nicholas had come to within two steps of the brink of the watery abyss, a violent convulsion ran through the frame of the guilty man. Flinging himself upon his knees, he clung to one of the rustic seats with a desperate clutch, and, staring wildly, uttered one long, piercing cry of agony, which rang through the ears of the crowd, but was unable to arouse even one of them from the lethargy into which they seemed all plunged. Like one in the clutches of a nightmare, they saw, heard, and remembered all, but were unable to stir a finger. The phantom now remained motionless on the water, and, bending its extended hand, slowly beckoned the assassin to come. Crouched in abject terror, the wretched man shrieked until the cavern rang again:

"I did not . . . no, I did not murder you! . . ."

Then came a splash, and now there was the boy in the dark water, struggling for his life in the middle of the lake, with the same motionless, stern apparition brooding over him, from whose very substance the child seemed to have dropped out.

"Papa! papa! save me!—I am drowning!" cried the piteous little voice amid the uproar of the echoes.

"My boy!" shrieked Nicholas in the accents of a maniac, springing to his feet, "My boy! save, oh, save him! . . . Yes, I confess—I am the murderer! . . . I killed him!"

"Killed . . . him . . . killed . . . killed! . . ." repeated hundreds of echoes like peals of laughter from a legion of infuriated demons.

Another splash, and the phantom suddenly disappeared. With one cry of unutterable terror the company, released from the spell which had hitherto paralyzed them, rushed toward the platform to the rescue of both father and child. But their feet were rooted to the ground anew as they beheld amid the swirling eddies a whitish, shapeless mass, an elongated mist, wrapping the murderer in tight embrace, and slowly sinking into the bottomless lake! . . .

On the morning after these occurrences, when, after a sleepless night, some of the party went to the residence of the Hungarian gentleman, they found it closed and deserted. He and the Shaman had disappeared. To add to the general consternation, the Izvertzoff mansion took fire on that same night, and was completely destroyed. The archbishop himself performed the ceremony of exorcism, but the locality is considered accursed to this day.

The government investigated the facts, and—ordered silence.

And now a few words in conclusion.* I hope that, whoever else may be disposed to question the possibility of an occurrence like the above, it will not be the intelligent Spiritualist. Not a feature in my narrative but finds in the records of mediumship its parallel. The apparition of the astral form like that of old Izvertzoff at the baptism is an everyday affair with clairvoyants. If the child was transformed into a man, in the sight of a crowd of people, so has a child-apparition been seen to emerge from Dr. Monck's side, and many children to step out of William Eddy's cabinet. If elongation of the body occurred in the boy's case, the same thing is alleged of various mediums. If a "spirit"—according to the accepted phraseology, an "astral man" as we term it—crowding out the undeveloped soul of the newly-born *dual* creature, took possession of his body, so have hundreds of other earth-bound souls obsessed the bodies of mediums. Interchange of "souls" has been noticed in living men unacquainted with each other, and even residing at opposite points of the globe. This may happen either from disease, which generally loosens the bonds between the astral and the physical man, or in consequence of some other

---

*[These concluding remarks do not appear in the Russian version of the story.—*Compiler.*]

occult condition. The levitation of the Shaman is no more a matter of wonder; and if his "double" wandered from his entranced body, so has the same phenomenon been oft reported in Spiritualistic papers as happening under our own observation. This Russian episode but confirms what investigators of modern phenomena have experienced. In it, throughout a period of ten years, the whole plot is developed by a real disembodied "spirit." Earth-bound, he burned for a just but fiendish revenge, the planning and execution of which constituted certainly an insurmountable impediment to the progress and purification of the troubled soul. The "Elementals" play no part in my story, except when thrown into violent perturbation by the sounds of the magical drum and the *incantations* of the adept. The action of these creatures was limited to the flickering of the flames, the disturbance of the water in the lake, and the intensification of the awakened echoes. The phenomena at P—— were produced and controlled by an adept-psychologist, working *for, with,* and *through* a disembodied soul, upon a deliberate plan for the accomplishment of a cruel vengeance, which, though charged to the account of the unhappy, restless astral man, yet accomplished the ends of the unerring law of Retribution in punishing the guilty and rescuing the innocent.

Let the Spiritualist who would pronounce magic an exploded superstition, compare the methods of the "magician" with those of the "circle." The latter derives its very name from the most common arrangement of the sitters, required by the "spirits" themselves. This is found *philosophical* and *necessary* by the Spiritualists. To ensure the formation of a circular magnetic current, the sitters are obliged to take hold of hands. Most generally the medium will complain of being affected if this magnetic chain is broken. Instances are known where instruments floating in the air have fallen upon the breaking of this current. The "magician" either draws with chalk a circle around the spot where the occult forces are to be concentrated to produce phenomena, as Baron Du Potet is known by all France to do—or forms one in thought, by *will power;* and this cannot be broken unless his WILL gives way. The rhythmic drum beats of the "magician" and his *incantations* are but another and more perfected form of the singing and music-playing of modern circles. In a word, the modern *séance* could be and should be made a school of magic, or philosophical, controllable Spiritualism. *Verb. sap.*

New York, 1878.

ISIS UNVEILED AND THE TODAS

[*The Spiritualist,* London, April 5, 1878, pp. 161-62]

To the Editor of *The Spiritualist.*

Sir,

I have read the communications of "H.M." in your paper of the 8th inst. I would not have mentioned the "Todas" at all in my book, if I had not read a very elaborate octavo work in 271 pages, by William E. Marshall, Lieut.-Col. of Her Majesty's Bengal Staff Corps, entitled, *A Phrenologist Among the Todas,* copiously illustrated with photographs of the squalid and filthy beings to whom "H.M." refers. Though written by a staff officer, assisted "by the Rev. Friedrich Metz, of the Basel Missionary Society, who had spent upwards of twenty years of labours" among them, and "the only European able to speak the obscure Toda tongue," the book is so full of misrepresentations—though both writers appear to be sincere—that I wrote what I did.

What I said I knew to be true, and I do not retract a single word. If neither "H.M." nor Lieut.-Col. Marshall, nor the Rev. Mr. Metz have penetrated the secret that lies behind the dirty huts of the aborigines they have seen, that is their misfortune, not my fault.

H. P. BLAVATSKY.

New York, March 18th, 1878.

THE TODAS

[*The Spiritualist*, London, April 12, 1878]

Sir,

For my answer to the sneer of your correspondent "H.M." about my opinion of the Todas (*The Spiritualist*, March 8), a few lines sufficed. I only cared to say that what I have written in *Isis Unveiled* was written after reading Colonel Wm. E. Marshall's *A Phrenologist among the Todas*, and in consequence of what, whether justly or not, I believe to be the erroneous statements of that author. Writing about Oriental psychology, its phenomena and practitioners, as I did, I would have been ludicrously wanting in common sense if I had not anticipated such denials and contradictions as those of "H.M." from every side. How would it profit the seeker after this Occult knowledge to face danger, privations, and obstacles of every kind to gain it, if, after attaining his end, he should not have facts to relate of which the profane were ignorant? A pretty set of critics the ordinary travellers or observers, even though what Dr. Carpenter euphemistically calls a "scientific officer," or "distinguished civilian," when, confessedly every European unfurnished with some mystical passport, is debarred from entering any orthodox Brahman's house, or the inner precincts of a pagoda. How we poor Theosophists should tremble before the scorn of those modern Daniels when the cleverest of them has never been able to explain the commonest "tricks" of Hindu jugglers, to say nothing of the phenomena of the Fakirs! These very *savants* answer the testimony of Spiritualists with an equally lofty scorn, and resent as a personal affront the invitation to even attend a *séance*.

I should therefore have let the "Todas" question pass, but for the letter of "Late Madras C.S." in your paper of the 15th. I feel bound to answer it, for the writer plainly makes me out to be a liar. He threatens me, moreover, with the thunderbolts that a certain other officer has concealed in his library closet.

It is quite remarkable how a man who resorts to an *alias,* sometimes forgets that he is a gentleman. Perhaps such is the custom in your civilized England, where manners and education are said to be carried to a superlative elegance; but not so in poor, barbarous Russia, which a good portion of your countrymen are just now preparing to strangle (if they can). In my country of Tartaric Cossacks and Kalmucks, a man who sets out to insult another, does not usually hide himself behind a shield. I am sorry to have to say this much, but you have allowed me, without the least provocation, and upon several occasions, to be unstintedly reviled by correspondents, and I am sure that you are too much of a man of honour to refuse me the benefit of an answer.

"Late Madras C.S." sides with Mrs. Showers in the insinuation that I never was in India at all. This reminds me of a calumny of last year, originating with "spirits" speaking through a celebrated medium at Boston, and finding credit in many quarters. It was, that I was *not* a Russian, did not even speak that language, but was merely a French adventuress. So much for the infallibility of some of the sweet "angels"! Surely, I will neither go to the trouble of exhibiting to any of my masked detractors, of this or the other world, my passports *viséed* by the Russian embassies half a dozen times, on my way to India and back. Nor will I demean myself to show the stamped envelopes of letters received by me in different parts of India. *Such* an accusation makes me simply laugh, for my word is, surely, as good as that of anybody else. I will only say that more's the pity that an English officer, who was "fifteen years in the district," knows less of the Todas than I, who, he pretends, never was in India at all. He calls *gopura* a "tower" of the pagoda. Why not the roof, or anything else, as well? *Gopura* is the sacred pylon, the pyramidal gateway by which the pagoda is entered; and yet I have repeatedly heard the people of Southern India call the pagoda itself a *gopura.* It may be a careless mode of expression employed among the vulgar; but when we come to consult the authority of the best Indian lexicographers we find it accepted. In John Shakespear's *Hindustani-English Dictionary* (edition of 1849, p. 1727) the word *gopura* is rendered as "an idol temple of the Hindus." Has "Late Madras C.S.," or any of his friends, ever climbed up into the interior, so as to know who or what is concealed there? If not, then perhaps his fling at me was a trifle premature. I am sorry to have shocked the sensitiveness of such a philological purist, but, really, I do not see why, when speaking of the temples of the Todas—whether they exist or not—even a Brahman Guru might not say that they had their *gopuras*. Perhaps he, or some other brilliant authority in Sanskrit and other Indian languages, will favour us with the etymology of the word? Does the first syllable, *go* or *gu*, relate to the *roundness* of these "towers," as my critic calls them (for the word *go* does mean something round), or to *gopa*, a cowherd, which gave its name to a Hindu caste, and was one of the names of Krishna, *go-pâla*, meaning the cowherd? Let these critics carefully read Colonel Marshall's work, and see whether the pastoral tribe, whom he saw so much, and discovered so little about, whose worship (exoteric, of course) is all embraced in the care of the sacred cows and buffaloes; the distribution of the "*divine* fluid" —milk; and whose seeming adoration, as the missionaries tell us, is so great for their buffaloes, that they call them the "gift of God," could not be said to have their *gopuras*, though the latter were but a cattle-pen, a *tirîêri*, the *mand*, in short, into which the phrenological explorer crawled alone by night with infinite pains and—neither saw nor found *anything*! And because he found nothing he concludes they have *no* religion, *no* idea of God, *no* worship. About as reasonable an inference as Dr. W. B. Carpenter might come to if he had crawled into Mrs. Showers' *séance*-room some night when all the "angels" and their guests had fled, and straightway reported that among Spiritualists there are neither mediums nor phenomena.

Colonel Marshall I find far less dogmatic than his admirers. Such cautious phrases as "I believe," "I could not ascertain," "I believe it to be true," and the like, show his desire to find out the truth, but scarcely prove conclusively that he has found it. At best it only comes to this, that Colonel Marshall believes one thing to be true, and I look upon it differently. He credits his friend the missionary, and I believe my friend the Brahman, who told me what I have written. Besides, I explicitly state in my book (see *Isis Unveiled*, Vol. II, pp. 614, 615):

> . . . as soon as their [the Todas]* solitude was profaned by the avalanche of civilization . . . the Todas began moving away to other parts as unknown and more inaccessible than the Nîlgiri hills had formerly been.

The Todas, therefore, of whom my Brahman friend spoke, and whom Captain W. L. D. O'Grady, late manager of the Madras Branch Bank at Ootacamund, tells me he has seen specimens of, are not the degenerate remnants of the tribe whose phrenological bumps were measured by Colonel Marshall. And yet, even what the latter writes of these, I, from personal knowledge, affirm to be in many particulars inaccurate. I may be regarded by my critics as over-credulous, but this is surely no reason why I should be treated as a liar, whether by late or living Madras authorities of the "C.S." Neither Captain O'Grady, who was born at Madras and was for a time stationed on the Nîlgiri Hills, nor I, recognized the individuals photographed in Colonel Marshall's book as Todas. Those we saw wore their dark brown hair very long, and were much fairer than the Badagas, or any other Hindus, in neither of which particulars do they resemble Colonel Marshall's types. "H.M." says:

> The Todas are brown, coffee-coloured, like most other natives.

But turning to Appleton's *New American Cyclopaedia* (Vol. XII, p. 173), we read:

> These people are of a *light complexion,* having strongly-marked Jewish features, and have been supposed by many to be one of the lost tribes.

"H.M." assures us that the places inhabited by the Todas

---

* [Square brackets in this article are H.P.B.'s own.—*Compiler.*]

are not infested by venomous serpents or tigers; but the same *Cyclopaedia* remarks that:

> The base of these mountains . . . is clothed with a dense forest swarming with wild animals of all descriptions, among which elephants and tigers are numerous.

But the "Late" (defunct?—is your correspondent a disembodied angel?) "Madras C.S." attains to the sublimity of the ridiculous when, with biting irony in winding up, he says:

> All good spirits, of whatever degree, astral or elementary, . . . prevent his [Captain R. F. Burton's] ever meeting with *Isis*—rough might be the unveiling!

Surely—unless that military Nemesis should tax the hospitality of some American newspaper, conducted by politicians—he could never be rougher than this Madras Grandison! And then, the idea of suggesting that, after having contradicted and made sport of the greatest authorities of Europe and America, to begin with Max Müller and end with the Positivists, in both my volumes, I should be appalled by Captain Burton, or the whole lot of captains in Her Majesty's service—though each carried an Armstrong gun on his shoulder and a *mitrailleuse* in his pocket—is positively superb! Let them reserve their threats and terrors for my Christian countrymen.

Any moderately equipped sciolist (and the more empty-headed, the easier) might tear *Isis* to shreds, in the estimation of the vulgar, with his sophisms and presumably authoritative analysis, but would that prove him to be right, and me wrong? Let all the records of medial phenomena, rejected, falsified, slandered, and ridiculed, and of mediums terrorized, for thirty years past, answer for me. I, at least, am not of the kind to be bullied into silence by such tactics, as "Late Madras" may in time discover; nor will he ever find me skulking behind a *nom de plume* when I have insults to offer. I always have had, as I now have, and trust ever to retain the courage of my opinions, however unpopular or erroneous they may be considered; and there are not

Showers enough in Great Britain to quench the ardour with which I stand by my convictions.

There is but one way to account for the tempest which, for four months, has raged in *The Spiritualist* against Colonel Olcott and myself, and that is expressed in the familiar French proverb— "*Quand on veut tuer son chien, on dit qu'il est enragé.*"

H. P. BLAVATSKY.

New York, March 24th, 1878.

FOOTNOTES TO "THE SCIENTIFIC HYPOTHESIS RESPECTING MEDIUMISTIC PHENOMENA"

[*Banner of Light*, Boston, Vol. XLII, April 20, 1878]

[In compliance with his request, H.P.B. translated from the Russian A. N. Aksakoff's article entitled "The Scientific Hypothesis Respecting Mediumistic Phenomena" and published in the *St. Petersburg Vedomosti*. She added two footnotes of her own to the translation; we include below portions of Aksakoff's article to which these footnotes refer.]

. . . Geometrical figures *not* distinguishable by our thought (similar in form, size, and the mutual relation of their parts) should not be distinguishable by our *sensuous perception* either; they must be brought into such relations with us as would make them identical in the effects they produce upon us. This condition is satisfied by *planes* (or figures of two dimensions), symmetrical figures, but it is not satisfied by equally regular *solids* (figures which embrace the three dimensions). Two equal triangles can always be made to perfectly fit each other by turning over one of them, *i.e.*, through a process accomplished which involves the aid of the third dimension; but if we move these triangles in a *plane* only, that is to say, using but two dimensions, we would never succeed in making them fit each other, so that one of these would completely occupy the place of the other.

I think that perhaps I can make Mr. Aksakoff's meaning

a little clearer by stating the proposition in the following terms: in the case of plane figures, *i.e.*, of two dimensions only (length and breadth) when they are of perfect equivalence, we can verify that equivalence to sensuous perception by the aid of the third dimension of thickness; or otherwise expressing it, by the simple act of superposition whereby our senses verify the equivalence; but in the case of solid bodies of perfect equivalence, these possessing the third dimension already, it is obvious that there is no position of superposition which will enable our sensuous perception to verify the equivalence.

> This experiment in the domain of mediumship [to establish Zöllner's hypothesis of the existence of a fourth dimension of space] has nothing substantially new in it; it belongs to a long series of phenomena which exhibit what is generally described as the passage of matter through matter.

The employment of the term "dimension" to express this "passage of matter through matter," appears to me as likely to lead to a great confusion of ideas. It would be made much more comprehensible to the general reader if Zöllner were to apply the term quality equally to length, breadth, thickness and permeability. But at best, the present discussion affords one more example of the fact I have repeatedly pointed out, that the European languages are wretchedly poor in words to express metaphysical and psychological ideas in comparison with the Oriental tongues. The property which we have here clumsily designated as a "fourth" dimension of space is known throughout the whole East by appropriate and specific terms, among not only scholars but the very "jugglers" who make boys disappear from beneath baskets. If Western scientists would familiarize themselves a little more with the Pythagorean *Tetraktys,* or even with the algebraical "unknown quantity" in its transcendental meaning, all difficulties in the way of accepting Zöllner's hypothesis would disappear.

FRAGMENTS DE MADAME BLAVATSKY
[*La Revue Spirite*, Paris, avril, 1878]

Les Spiritualistes Saxons font assez confusion entre l'esprit et le périsprit. Peut-être ne distinguent-ils pas l'un de l'autre, désignant le premier par le mot âme, le second par celui d'esprit. Les Théosophes font le contraire; pour eux, l'esprit proprement dit, le *Nous,* est l'esprit. Le périsprit ou *Psyché,* l'âme.

Les Théosophes n'admettent point de dogmes, c'est-à-dire d'idées, de principes préconçus, auxquels tout doive être subordonné. Ils cherchent la vérité avec sagesse et bonne foi, et sont disposés à l'accepter d'où qu'elle vienne, fut-ce au prix du sacrifice de ce qu'ils ont jusqui'ici admis. Quoiqu'ils disent en ce moment, ils sont loin de penser avoir tout résolu. Une telle prétention serait de l'omniscience, elle serait absurde. Le jour où un nouvel Oedipe aura trouvé l'*entière* solution de cette énigme des siècles: "Qu'est-ce l'homme?" ce jour là, dogmes anciens et modernes, approximations spiritualistes elles-mêmes, comme le Sphinx antique, se précipiteront dans l'Océan de l'oubli.

Les Théosophes, de même que les philosophes anciens et leur élève Paul, qui disait que le corps physique était pénétré, tenu vivant par le *Psyché,* périsprit, pensent que l'homme est une trinité: corps, périsprit, esprit.

Les Bouddhistes qui distinguent ces trois entités, divisent encore le périsprit en plusieurs parties. Toutefois, sur le point d'arriver à la perfection—nirvana—ils n'admettent plus guère qu'une de ces parties: l'Esprit.

Les Grecs faisaient de même, divisant le périsprit en vie et en nature passionelle, ou *Thumos.* Le périsprit est donc lui-même une combinaison: la vitalité physiologique, *Bios;* la nature concupiscible, *Epithumia;* et l'idéalité, *Phren.* Le périsprit est constitué de la substance éthérée qui emplit l'univers, il dérive donc du fluide astral cosmique, qui n'est point l'esprit; car bien qu'intangible, impalpable, ce fluide astral est matière objective, comparativement à l'esprit. Par sa nature complexe, le périsprit peut s'allier assez intimement à la nature corporelle pour échapper à l'influence morale d'une vie plus haute. De même, il peut s'unir assez étroitement à l'esprit pour partager sa puissance, auquel cas son véhicule, l'homme physique, peut paraître un Dieu, même pendant sa vie terrestre. Si une telle union de l'esprit et du périsprit n'existe pas, l'homme n'est point immortel comme entité: le périsprit est tôt ou tard dissocié.

Plutarque dit qu'à la mort, Proserpine sépare le corps de l'âme (périsprit), après quoi cette dernière devient un génie ou *Daïmon,* libre et indépendant. Uue seconde dissolution est à intervenir, sous l'action du bien. *Démètre* sépare le périsprit de l'esprit. Le premier se résoud, avec le temps, en particules éthérées; le second monte, accède aux pouvoirs divins, devient graduellement un pur esprit divin.

Kapila, ainsi que tous les philosophes de l'Orient, faisait peu de cas de la nature périspritale. C'est cette agglomération de particules grossières, émanations humaines douées des imperfections, des faiblesses, des passions, des appétits même humains, et pouvant, dans certaines conditions, de venir objective, que les Bouddhistes appellent *Skandhas,* groupes, les Théosophes, âme, Allan Kardec, le périsprit.

Les Brahmanes et les Bouddhistes disent que l'individualité humaine n'est pas assurée tant que l'homme n'a point quitté, avec le dernier de ces groupes, le dernier vestige de teinte terrestre. De là leur doctrine de la métempsycose, si ridiculisée, mais si peu comprise de nos Orientalistes eux-mêmes. La science enseigne, en effet, que les molécules matérielles composant le corps physique de l'homme sont, par le fait de l'évolution, replacées par la nature dans les formes physiques inférieures. Eh bien, les Bouddhistes ne disent pas autre chose des particules du corps astral; ils prétendent que les groupes semi-materiels du périsprit sont appropriés à l'évolution des formes astrales inférieures, et y accèdent suivant leur degré d'épuration. Par conséquent, tant qu'un homme désincarné contient une seule particule de ces *skandhas*, des *portions* de son périsprit entrent ultérieurement dans le corps astral des plantes et des animaux. Et si l'homme astral est tellement matériel que *Démètre* ne puisse trouver une parcelle d'esprit, alors l'individu est dissous, pièce à pièce, dans le creuset de l'évolution. C'est ce que les Hindous figurent par un passage de 1000 années de durée dans le corps impur des animaux. Les Théosophes sont d'accord, pour le fond, avec ces données.

Pour les Théosophes, les grands caractères, les génies, les poètes, artistes véritables, sont inspirés spirituellement, et ne sont pas— en général du moins—de simples Médiums, instruments passifs dans les mains de leurs guides. Ce sont, au contraire, des âmes (périsprits) richement illuminées, c'est-à-dire possédant l'élément esprit à un haut degré, et pouvant dès lors collaborer avec les Esprits purs, à la spiritualisation, à l'élévation de l'humanité.

En ce qui concerne les phénomènes du périsprit et de la médiumité, nous pensons que le Médium purement passif ne peut discerner les bons esprits des mauvais, qu'il lui faut pour cela devenir médiateur conscient. Nous savons aussi que, si l'homme incarné, fût-il adepte éminent, ne peut lutter en puissance avec les purs Esprits qui, étant libérés de leurs *skandhas*, sont devenus subjectifs aux sens physiques, il peut du moins égaler et même surpasser en matière de phénoménalité, ce que produisent les Médiums ordinaires.

L'enfant, c'est-à-dire un homme non entièrement développé, qui vient à passer dans l'autre monde, peut-il plus y exister, dans des conditions préparées pour les types perfectionnés de son espèce, que la plante ou l'animal?

L'enfant ne possède pour ainsi dire pas encore d'esprit; il n'est qu'âme, et l'éducation n'affecte que sa nature astrale, n'a trait qu'aux choses externes.

Le Cycle de l'homme n'est pas complet tant qu'il n'a point passé par la vie terrestre. Aucun stage d'épreuve ni d'expérience ne peut être sauté: il faut avoir été homme avant que d'arriver Esprit pur.

L'enfant mort est donc une faillite de la nature; il doit revivre de nouveau; le même périsprit subit alors l'épreuve interrompue, à l'aide d'une autre naissance. De même pour un idiot de naissance. *Ce sont les seuls cas de réincarnation humaine.**

Si l'enfant, en effet, qui n'est qu'une dualité, était immortel, pourquois les animaux ne le seraient-ils pas? La trinité seule survit.

À la mort, le périsprit devient le corps extrême, au-dedans se forme un corps plus éthéré, et l'ensemble est plus ou moins ombragé par l'Esprit.

Cependant, les Élémentaires du corps humain ne sont pas toujours dissociés, à la mort corporelle; il se peut que, par un suprême effort, ils puissent retenir du 3-ème élement, et de la sorte, lentement, avec peine, monter de sphère en sphère, rejetant à chaque passage le plus lourd de leur vêtements, revêtant de plus radieuses enveloppes, et débarrassés de toutes particules materielles arriver enfin à la perfection, devenir des *unités,* des Dieux.

Nous avons dit que l'Homme qui n'a pas une étincelle d'esprit divin pour le sauver, après sa mort, ne se distingue guère des animaux.

Il y a de tristes cas de ce genre, non seulement parmi les dépravés, mais aussi parmi les aveugles ou les négateurs quand même. C'est, en effet, la volonté humaine, son pouvoir souverain qui règle en partie la destinée, et si un homme s'obstine à croire à l'annihilation après la mort, elle a lieu. La détermination de la vie physique, du genre de la mort, dépend bien souvent de la volonté. Il est des gens qui échappent, par la seule énergie de leur résolution aux étreintes de la mort, tandis que d'autres succombent à d'insignifiantes maladies. Or, ce qu'un homme fait de son corps, il peut le faire de son corps astral, c'est-à-dire de son périsprit désincarné.

H. P. Blavatsky.

---

*[Consult in this connection *Isis Unveiled,* Vol. I, pp. 346, 347, 351.—*Compiler.*]

FRAGMENTS FROM MADAME BLAVATSKY

[*La Revue Spirite*, Paris, April, 1878]

[*Translation of the foregoing original French text*]

The Saxon Spiritualists are rather confused between the spirit and the périsprit. Perhaps they do not distinguish the one from the other, describing the first by the word soul, the second by spirit. Theosophists do the opposite; for them the spirit properly is *Nous*, the spirit. The périsprit or *Psychê*, is the soul.

Theosophists accept no dogmas, *i.e.*, preconceived ideas or principles, to which everything must be subordinated. They seek truth with wisdom and in good faith, and are willing to accept it from whatever source, even at the cost of the sacrifice of what they have hitherto accepted. Whatever they may teach at the present moment, they are far from thinking that they have settled everything. Such a claim would be that of omniscience; it would be ridiculous. On the day when a new Oedipus shall have found the *complete* solution of that riddle of the ages: "What is man?" on that day the ancient and modern doctrines, the approximations of the Spiritualists themselves, will, like the ancient Sphinx, be flung into the ocean of oblivion.

Theosophists, like the ancient philosophers and their pupil Paul, who said that the physical body was penetrated and kept alive by the périsprit, *Psychê,* consider man as a trinity: body, périsprit, spirit.

The Buddhists, who distinguish these three entities, divide the périsprit still further into several parts. Nevertheless, on the point of approaching perfection—Nirvâna—they hardly admit more than one of these parts: the Spirit.

The Greeks did the same, dividing the périsprit into life and the passional nature, or *Thumos*. The périsprit is thus itself a combination: the physiological vitality, *Bios;* the concupiscible nature, *Epithumia;* and the ideality, *Phren*.

The périsprit is constituted of the ethereal substance that fills the universe, hence it is derived from the cosmic astral fluid, which is not spirit at all, because although intangible, impalpable, this astral fluid is objective matter as compared with spirit. Owing to its complex nature, the périsprit can ally itself intimately enough with the corporeal nature, to escape the moral influence of a higher life. In the same way it can unite closely enough with the spirit to partake of its potency, in which case its vehicle, the physical man, can appear as a God, even during his terrestrial lifetime. If such a union, of the spirit and the périsprit, does not take place, a man does not become immortal as an entity: the périsprit is sooner or later dissociated.

Plutarch says that at death, Proserpine separates the body from the soul (périsprit), after which the latter becomes a genius or *Daïmon,* free and independent. A second dissolution has to occur, under the action of the Good. *Demeter* separates the périsprit from the spirit. The first in time is resolved into ethereal particles; the second ascends, assimilates with the divine powers, and gradually becomes a pure divine spirit.

Kapila, like all the Oriental philosophers, made little of the perisprital nature. It is this agglomeration of gross particles, of human emanations teeming with imperfections, weaknesses, passions, the very human appetites, able, under certain conditions, to become objective, that the Buddhists call *Skandhas,* groups, the Theosophists, soul, Allan Kardec, the périsprit.

The Brâhmaṇas and the Buddhists say that the human individuality is not secure so long as man has not left behind with the last of these groups, the remaining vestige of terrestrial coloring. Hence their doctrine of metempsychosis, so much ridiculed but so little understood by our Orientalists themselves. Science teaches, indeed, that the material molecules that compose the physical body of man are, by the process of evolution, replaced by Nature into lower physical forms. Well, the Buddhists say the very same in regard to the particles of the astral body; they assert that the semi-material groups of the périsprit are appropriated to the evolution of lower astral forms and unite with them according to their degree of refinement. Consequently, so long as a discarnate man contains a single particle of these *skandhas,* some *parts* of his périsprit will have to enter the astral bodies of plants or animals. So if the astral man is composed of such material that Demeter cannot find a particle of spirit, the individual is dissolved, bit by bit, in the crucible of evolution. This is what the Hindus typify by a period of a thousand years spent in the impure bodies of animals. Theosophists are in essential agreement with this idea.

To Theosophists, the great characters, the geniuses, the poets, the true artists, are spiritually inspired, and are not —at least in general—simply mediums, passive instruments in the hands of their guides. They are, on the contrary, souls (périsprits) richly illuminated, *i.e.,* possessing the spiritual element in a high degree, and therefore able to collaborate with pure Spirits for the spiritualization and elevation of mankind.

In what relates to the phenomena of the périsprit and of mediumship, we believe that the purely passive medium cannot discern good spirits from bad, that to do so he must become a conscious mediator. We also know that though the incarnated man, even if a high adept, cannot compete in power with pure Spirits, who, being liberated from their *skandhas* have become subjective to the physical senses, they can at least equal and even surpass in the matter of phenomenalism what is produced by ordinary mediums.

Can a child, *i.e.,* a not completely developed man, who passes into the other world, exist there in the conditions prepared for the perfected types of his species, any more than a plant or an animal?

The child does not yet possess a spirit, so to speak; he is merely a soul, and his education has only affected his astral nature, has only dealt with externals.

The cycle of man is not complete so long as he has not passed through terrestrial life. Not one stage of trial or experience can be skipped; he must have been a man before he reaches the state of pure Spirit.

A dead child then is a failure of nature; it must be born again; the same périsprit must in such a case pass through the interrupted trial by means of another birth. The same for the congenital idiot. *These are the only cases of human reincarnation.*

If the child, indeed, who is only a duality, were immortal, why not the animals also? The triad alone survives.

At death, the périsprit becomes the outermost body; within it is formed a more ethereal body, and the whole is more or less overshadowed by the Spirit.

The elementaries of the human body are, however, not always dissociated at bodily death; it may happen that by a supreme effort they are able to retain some of the third element, and in that way, slowly and with trouble, to ascend from sphere to sphere, throwing off at each step the heavier garment, and becoming clothed in more radiant vestures; finally arriving at perfection, disencumbered of every material particle, and becoming *unities*, Gods.

We said that the man who has not one spark of the divine spirit to save him after death can scarcely be distinguished from the animals.

There are some sad cases of this kind, not alone among the depraved but also among the willfully blind and the out-and-out deniers. It is, indeed, the will of man, his sovereign power, that partly rules his destiny, and if a man persists in believing in annihilation after death, it will take place. The conditions of the physical life, the kind of death, very often depend on the will.

There are some persons who merely by the force of their resolution, escape the embrace of death, while others yield to trifling maladies. Now, what a man can do with his body, he can also do with his astral body, *i.e.*, with his discarnated périsprit.

H. P. Blavatsky.

THE AKHUND OF SWAT

THE FOUNDER OF MANY MYSTICAL SOCIETIES.*

MADAME BLAVATSKY'S DRAMATIC WORD-PAINTING AND GRAPHIC DESCRIPTION OF ABDUL GHAFUR'S REMARKABLE AND EVENTFUL CAREER — ANTAGONISM OF THE SIKHS TO THE MODERN HIEROPHANT — ALMOST SIMULTANEOUS DEATHS OF THE POPES OF ROME AND SAIDU.

Of the many remarkable characters of this century, Ghafur was one of the most conspicuously so.†

If there be truth in the Eastern doctrine that souls, powerful whether for good or bad, who had not time in one existence to work out their plans, are reincarnated, the fierceness of their yearnings to continue on earth thrusting them back into the current of their attractions, then Ghafur was a re-birth of that Felice Peretti, who is known in history as Pope Sixtus V, of crafty and odious memory. Both were born in the lowest class of society, being ignorant peasant boys and beginning life as herdsmen. Both reached the apex of power through craft and stealth and by imposing upon the superstitions of the masses. Sixtus, author of mystical books and himself a practitioner of the forbidden

---

*[This article appeared most likely in the first issue of the New York *Echo* which was started by Charles Sotheran. The cutting of it is pasted in H.P.B.'s *Scrapbook*, Vol. VII, pp. 101-102. An introductory note written by the Editor is dated April 30, 1878, which is the only clue as to the date of the article, although Col. Olcott states in his *Diaries* that the first issue of the *Echo* came out May 3rd. The journal is described as "The Only Secret Society Paper in the World." It was short-lived and its files have never been located.]

†[The inhabitants of Swat—a tract on the Peshawâr border of the North-West Frontier Province of India—are a clan of Yusafzai Pathâns. They are Suni Mohammedans. As their religious leader, the Akhund of Swat, Abdul Ghafur, born in 1794, ruled the tribe for the last thirty years of his life, and died in 1877. He was succeeded by his son Mian Gul, who, however, never possessed the same influence as his father. —*Compiler*.]

sciences to satisfy his lust for power and ensure impunity, became Inquisitor-General. Made Pope, he hurled his anathemas alike against Elizabeth of England, the King of Navarre, and other important personages. Abdul Ghafur, endowed with an iron will, had educated himself without colleges or professors except through association with the "wise men" of Cuttack. He was as well versed in the Arabic and Persian literature of alchemy and astrology as Sixtus was in Aristotle, and like him knew how to fabricate mesmerized talismans and amulets containing either life or death for those to whom they were presented. Each held millions of devotees under the subjection of their psychological influence, though both were more dreaded than beloved.

Ghafur had been a warrior and an ambitious leader of fanatics, but becoming a dervish and finally a Pope, so to say, his blessing or curse made him as effectually the master of the Amîrs and other Mussulmans as Sixtus was of the Catholic potentates of Europe.

Only the salient features of his career are known to Christendom. Watched, as he may have been, his private life, ambitions, aspirations for temporal as well as religious power, are almost a sealed book. But the one certain thing is, that he was the founder and chief of nearly every secret society worth speaking of among Mussulmans, and the dominant spirit in all the rest. His apparent antagonism to the Wahhabees was but a mask, and the murderous hand that struck Lord Mayo was certainly guided by the old Abdul. The Biktashee Dervishes* and the howling, dancing, and other Moslem religious mendicants recognize his supremacy as far above that of the Sheikh-ul-Islam of the faithful. Hardly a political order of any importance issued from Constantinople or Teheran—heretics though the Persians are—without his having a finger in the pie directly or indirectly. As fanatical as Sixtus, but more cunning yet, if

---

*To this day no Biktashee would be recognized as such unless he could claim possession of a certain medal with the seal of this "high-pontiff" of all the Dervishes, whether they belong to one sect or the other.

possible, instead of giving direct orders for the extermination of the Huguenots of Islam, the Wahhabees, he directed his curses and pointed his finger only at those among them whom he found in his way, keeping on the best, though secret, terms with the rest.

The title of Nasr-ed-Dîn (defender of the faith) he impartially applied to both the Sultan and the Shah, though one is a Sunnite and the other a Shiah. He sweetened the stronger religious intolerance of the Osman dynasty by adding to the old title of Nasr-ed-Dîn those of Saif-ed-Dîn (Scimitar of Faith) and Amîr-al-mu'minîn (Prince of the Faithful). Every Amîr-al-Sûrî, or leader of the sacred caravan of pilgrims to Mecca, brought or sent messages to, and received advice and instructions from, Abdul, the latter in the shape of mysterious oracles, for which was left the full equivalent in money, presents and other offerings, as the Catholic pilgrims have recently done at Rome.

In 1847-48 the Prince Mirza, uncle of the young Shah and ex-governor of a great province in Persia, appeared in Tiflis, seeking Russian protection at the hands of Prince Vorontzov, Viceroy of the Caucasus.* Having helped himself to the crown jewels and ready money in the treasury, he had run away from the jurisdiction of his loving nephew, who was anxious to put out his eyes. Popular rumour asserted that his reason for what he had done was that the great dervish, Akhund, had thrice appeared to him in dreams, prompting him to take what he had and share his booty with the protectors of the faith of his principal wife (he brought twelve with him to Tiflis), a native of Kabul. The secret, though, perhaps, indirect influence he exercised on the Begum of Bhopal, during the Sepoy rebellion of 1857, was a mystery only to the English, whom the old schemer knew so well how to hoodwink. During his long career of Machiavellism friendly with the British, and yet striking them constantly in secret; venerated as a new prophet by millions of orthodox, as well as heretic Mussul-

---

*[Prince Mihail Semyonovich Vorontzov (1782-1856), Viceroy of the Caucasus, 1844-56.—*Compiler*.]

mans; managing to preserve his influence over friend and foe, the old "Teacher" had one enemy whom he feared, for he knew that no amount of craft would ever win it over to his side. This enemy was the once mighty nation of the Sikhs, ex-sovereign rulers of the Puñjab and masters of the Peshawar Valley. Reduced from their high estate, this warrior people are now under the rule of a single Mahârâja—of Patiala—who is himself the helpless vassal of the British. From the beginning the Akhund had continually encountered the Sikhs in his path. Scarce would he feel himself conqueror over one obstacle, before his hereditary enemy would appear between him and the realization of his hopes. If the Sikhs remained faithful to the British in 1875, it was not through hearty loyalty or political convictions, so much as through sheer opposition to the Mohammedans, whom they knew to be secretly prompted by the Akhund.

Since the days of the great Nanak, of the Kshatriya caste, founder of the Sikh Brotherhood in the second half of the fifteenth century, these brave and warlike tribes have ever been the thorn in the side of the Mogul dynasty, the terror of the Moslems of India. Originating, as we may say, in a religious Brotherhood, whose object was to make away alike with Islamism, Brâhmanism, and other *isms,* including later Christianity, this sect evolved a pure monotheism in the abstract idea of an ever-unknown Principle, and elaborated it into the doctrine of the "Brotherhood of Man." In their view, we have but one Father-Mother Principle, with "neither form, shape, nor colour," and we ought all to be, if we are not, brothers irrespective of distinctions of race or colour. The sacerdotal Brâhman, fanatical in his observance of dead-letter forms, thus became in the opinion of the Sikh as much the enemy of truth as the Mussulman wallowing in a sensual heaven with his houris, the joss-worshipping Buddhist grinding out prayers at his wheel, or yet the Roman Catholic adoring his jewelled Madonnas, whose complexion the priests change from white to brown and black to suit climates and prejudices. Later on, Arjan, son of Ramdas, the fourth in the succession after Nanak, gathering together the doctrines of the founder and his successor Angad, brought out a sacred volume, called *Adi-Granth,* and largely supplemented it with selections from forty-five Sûtras of the Jainas. While adopting equally the religious figures of the *Vedas* and *Koran,* after sifting them and explaining their symbolism, the *Adi-Granth* yet presents a greater similarity of ideas respecting the most elaborate metaphysical conceptions with those of the Jaina school of Gurus. The notions of Astrology, or the influence of the starry spheres upon ourselves, were evidently adopted from that most prominent school of antiquity. This will be readily ascertained by comparing the commentaries of Abhâyâdeva Sûrî upon the original forty-five Sûtras in the Magadhi or Balabasha language* with the *Adi-Granth.* An old Jaina Guru, who is said to have drawn the horoscope of Ranjit Singh, at the time of his greatest power, had foretold the downfall of the kingdom of Lahore. It was the learned Arjan who retired into Amritsar, changed the sect into a politico-religious community, and instituted within the same another and more esoteric body of Gurus, scholars and metaphysicians, of which he became sole chief. He died in prison, under torture, by the order of Aurungzeb, into whose hands he had fallen, at the beginning of the seventeenth century. His son Govinda, a Guru (religious teacher) of great renown, vowed revenge against the race of his father's murderers, and after various changes of fortune the Afghans were finally driven from the Puñjab by the Sikhs in 1767. This triumph only made their hatred more bitter still, and from that moment until the death of Ranjit Singh, in 1839, we find them constantly aiming their blows at the Moslems. Mahan Singh, the father of Ranjit, had set off the Sikhs into twelve *misls* or divisions, each having its own chief (Sirdar), whose secret Council of State consisted of learned Gurus. Among these were Masters in spiritual Science, and

---

*This valuable work is now being republished by Ookerdhaboy Shewjee, and has been received by the Theosophical Society from the Editor through the President of the Bombay branch. When finished it will be the first edition of the Jaina Bible. *Sûtra-Sangraha* or *Vihiva Pûnnûttee Sûtra,* in existence, as all their sacred books are kept in secret by the Jainas.

they might, if they had had a mind, have exhibited as astonishing "miracles" and divine legerdemain as the old Mussulman Akhund. He knew it well, and for this reason dreaded them even more than he hated them for his defeat and that of his Amîr by Ranjit Singh.

One highly dramatic incident in the life of the "Pope of Saidu" is the following well-authenticated case, which was much commented upon in his part of India about twenty years ago. One day, in 1858, when the Akhund, squatting on his carpet, was distributing amulets, blessings and prophecies among his pious congregation of pilgrims, a tall Hindu, who had silently approached and mingled in the crowd without having been noticed, suddenly addressed him thus: "Tell me, prophet, thou who prophesiest so well for others, whether thou knowest what will be thine own fate, and that of the 'Defender of the Faith,' thy Sultan of Stamboul, twenty years hence?"

The old Ghafur, overcome with violent surprise, stared at his interlocutor, but no answer came. In recognizing the Sikh he seemed to have lost all power of speech, and the crowd was under a spell.

"If not," continued the intruder, "then I will tell thee. Twenty years more and your 'Prince of the Faithful' will fall by the hand of an assassin of his own house. Two old men, one the Dalai Lama of the Christians, the other the great prophet of the Moslems—thyself—will be simultaneously crushed under the heel of death. Then, the first hour will strike of the downfall of those twin foes of truth —Christianity and Islam. The first, as the more powerful, will survive the second, but both will soon crumble into fragmentary sects, which will mutually exterminate each other's faith. See, thy followers are powerless, and I might kill thee now, but thou art in the hands of Destiny, and that knows its own hour."

Before a hand could be lifted the speaker had disappeared. This incident of itself sufficiently proves that the Sikhs might have assassinated Abdul Ghafur at any time had they chosen so to do, and it may be that *The Mayfair Gazette,* which in June 1877, prophetically observed that the rival pontiffs of Rome and Swat might die simultaneously, had heard from some "old Indian" this story, which the writer also heard from an informant at Lahore.

H. P. BLAVATSKY.

THE THEOSOPHICAL SOCIETY

Its Origin, Plan and Aims

[Printed for the Information of Correspondents] *

I. The Society was founded at the City of New York, in the year 1875.

---

*[This is the New York Circular drafted mainly by Colonel H. S. Olcott and which was ready for distribution on May 3rd, 1878. A packet of these was given to Dr. H. J. Billing to take to London, and another to Countess Lydia de Pashkoff to take to Japan. As Col. Olcott points out himself (*Old Diary Leaves,* I, 399-400): "In drafting the New York circular it occurred to me that the membership of, and supervising entities behind, the Society would be naturally grouped in three divisions, *viz.,* new members not detached from worldly interests; pupils, like myself, who had withdrawn from the same or were ready to do so; and the adepts themselves, who, without being actually members, were at least connected with us and concerned in our work as a potential agency for the doing of spiritual good to the world. With H.P.B.'s concurrence I defined these three groups, calling them sections, and sub-dividing each into three degrees. This, of course, was in the hope and expectation that we should have more practical guidance in adjusting the several grades of members than we had had—or have since had, I may add."

Col. Olcott specifically states that the passage beginning: "As the highest development . . ." and ending with: "unseen universes" was written by H.P.B. The important words: "the Brotherhood of Humanity" were here used for the first time, and the Circular is devoid of any mention of Spiritualism or phenomena.

There can be very little doubt of the fact that the inspiring guidance of the Adepts was back of the actual wording of this Circular. It is a document of primary importance in the history of the Theosophical Movement.—*Compiler.*]

II. Its officers are a President; two Vice-Presidents; a Corresponding Secretary; a Recording Secretary; a Treasurer; a Librarian; and Councillors.

III. At first it was an open body, but, later, it was reorganized on the principle of secrecy, experience having demonstrated the advisability of such a change.

IV. Its Fellows are known as Active, Corresponding and Honorary. Only those are admitted who are in sympathy with its objects, and sincerely desire to aid in the promotion of the same.

V. Its Fellowship is divided into three Sections, and each Section into three Degrees. All candidates for active fellowship are required to enter as probationers, in the Third Degree of the Third Section, and no fixed time is specified in which the new Fellow can advance from any lower to a higher degree; all depends upon merit. To be admitted into the highest degree, of the first section, the Theosophist must have become freed of every leaning toward any one form of religion in preference to another. He must be free from all exacting obligations to society, politics and family. He must be ready to lay down his life, if necessary, for the good of Humanity, and of a brother Fellow of whatever race, color or ostensible creed. He must renounce wine, and every other description of intoxicating beverages, and adopt a life of strict chastity. Those who have not yet wholly disenthralled themselves from religious prejudice, and other forms of selfishness, but have made a certain progress towards self-mastery and enlightenment, belong in the Second Section. The Third Section is probationary: its members can leave the Society at will, although the obligation assumed at entrance will continually bind them to absolute secrecy as to what may have been communicated under restrictions.

VI. The objects of the Society are various. It influences its fellows to acquire an intimate knowledge of natural law, especially its occult manifestations. As the highest development, physically and spiritually, on earth, of the Creative Cause, man should aim to solve the mystery of his being. He is the procreator of his species, physically, and having inherited the nature of the unknown but palpable Cause of his own creation, must possess in his inner, psychical self, this creative power in lesser degree. He should, therefore, study to develop his latent powers, and inform himself respecting the laws of magnetism, electricity and all other forms of force, whether of the seen or unseen universes. The Society teaches and expects its fellows to personally exemplify the highest morality and religious aspiration; to oppose the materialism of science and every form of dogmatic theology, especially the Christian, which the Chiefs of the Society regard as particularly pernicious; to make known among Western nations the long-suppressed *facts* about Oriental religious philosophies, their ethics, chronology, esoterism, symbolism; to counteract, as far as possible, the efforts of missionaries to delude the so-called "Heathen" and "Pagans" as to the real origin and dogmas of Christianity and the practical effects of the latter upon public and private character in so-called civilized countries; to disseminate a knowledge of the sublime teachings of that pure esoteric system of the archaic period, which are mirrored in the oldest Vedas, and in the philosophy of Gautama Buddha, Zoroaster and Confucius; finally, and chiefly, to aid in the institution of a Brotherhood of Humanity, wherein all good and pure men, of every race, shall recognize each other as the equal effects (upon this planet)* of one Uncreate, Universal, Infinite, and Everlasting Cause.

VII. Persons of either sex are eligible.

VIII. There are branches of the parent Society in several countries of the East and West.

IX. No fees are exacted, but those who choose may contribute towards the Society's expenses. No applicant is re-

---

*[This parenthesis was written in by H.P.B., according to Col. Olcott's statement.—*Compiler.*]

ceived because of his wealth or influence, nor rejected because of his poverty or obscurity.

Correspondence with the parent body may be addressed to "The Theosophical Society, New York."

[In H.P.B.'s *Scrapbook*, Vol. VII, pp. 113-14, there is a cutting of three columns from the New York *Herald* of May 13, 1878. It is an article written, according to H.P.B's own notation, by Col. H. S. Olcott, and entitled "Muzzling the Indian Press." Its subtitle is: "The Vernacular Press Act for the Suppression of Native Newspapers—Passed at a Single Sitting of the Viceregal Legislative Council, March 14, 1878."

At the end of this cutting, H.P.B. pasted the colored picture of a lion caught in a net, and a mouse gnawing away the net, and wrote the following:]

The despised MOUSE is not always either on hand or willing to save the *Lion*—especially when the beast has too been for so long weaving himself the nets in which he got caught at last.

THE ÂRYA SAMÂJ

ALLIANCE OF THEOSOPHY WITH A VEDIC SOCIETY IN THE FAR ORIENT.*

MADAME BLAVATSKY NARRATES THE HISTORY OF THE BRAHMO-SAMÂJ AND THE ÂRYA-SAMÂJ.—THE CONFLICT OF FAITHS IN INDIA.—WHY THE THEOSOPHISTS NOW RECEIVE THEIR INSTRUCTIONS FROM A HINDU SECRET SOCIETY.

Christendom sends its missionaries to Heathendom at an expense of millions drained from the pockets of would-be pious folks, who court respectability. Thousands of homeless and penniless old men, women and children are allowed to starve for lack of funds, for the sake, perhaps, of one converted "heathen." All the spare money of the charitable is absorbed by these dead-head travelling agents of the Christian Church. What is the result? Visit the prison cells of so-called Christian lands, crammed with delinquents who have been led on to felony by the weary path of starvation, and you will have the answer. Read in the daily papers the numerous accounts of executions, and you will find that modern Christianity offers, perhaps unintentionally but none the less surely, a premium for murder and other heinous crimes. Is anyone prepared to deny the assertion? Remember that, while many a respectable unbeliever dies in his bed with the comfortable assurance from his next of kin, and

---

* [This article was written by H.P.B. for the New York *Echo*, on June 2, 1878, as appears from Col. Olcott's entry of that date in his *Diaries*. The *Echo* was a short-lived publication started by Charles Sotheran, one of the original Founders of the T.S., and the files of which do not seem to be accessible, in spite of a wide-spread search. Col. Olcott's *Diaries* also mention the fact that the first issue of this Journal came out May 3, 1878, or at least was received by him on that date. The actual date on which the present article appeared in print is not definitely known, although it must have been sometime in June of 1878. Its text is copied from the cutting pasted in H.P.B.'s *Scrapbook*, Vol. VIII, pp. 143-44, now in the Adyar Archives.—*Compiler*.]

good friends in general, that he is going to hell, the red-handed criminal has but to believe at his eleventh hour that the blood of the Saviour can and will save him, to receive the guarantee of his spiritual adviser that he will find himself when launched into eternity in the bosom of Christ, in heaven, and playing upon the traditional harp. Why, then, should any Christian deny himself the pleasure and profit of robbing, or even murdering, his richer neighbor? And such a doctrine is being promulgated among the heathen at the cost of an annual expenditure of millions.

But, in her eternal wisdom, Nature provides antidotes against moral as well as against mineral and vegetable poisons. There are people who do not content themselves with preaching grandiloquent discourses, they act. If such books as Higgins' *Anacalypsis,* Inman's *Ancient and Pagan Christian Symbolism,* and that extraordinary work of an anonymous English author—a Bishop, it is whispered—entitled *Supernatural Religion,** cannot awaken responsive echoes among the ignorant masses, who do not read books, other means can be, and are resorted to—means more effectual and which will bring fruit in the future, if hitherto prevented by the crushing hand of ecclesiastical and monarchical despotism. Those whom the written proofs of the fictitious character of Biblical authority cannot reach, may be saved by the spoken word. And this work of disseminating the truth among the more ignorant classes is being evidently prosecuted by an army of devoted scholars and teachers, simultaneously in India and America.

The Theosophical Society has been of late so much spoken about; such idle tales have been circulated about it—its members being sworn to secrecy and hitherto unable, even if willing, to proclaim the truth about it—that the public may be gratified to know, at least, about one portion of its work. This much, we are now permitted to do, and we embrace the opportunity with alacrity, for, unlike our antagonists, the Christians, we are disposed to declare open war and not resort to forgery, intrigue and Machiavellism

---

* [Walter Richard Cassels, 1826-1907. *Vide* Vol. VI, pp. 430-31.]

THE ÂRYA SAMÂJ

to accomplish our ends. The Theosophical Society means, if it cannot rescue Christians from modern Christianity, at least to aid in saving the "heathen" from its influence. It is now in organized affiliation with the Ârya Samâj of India, its Western representative, and, so to say, under the order of its chiefs. A younger Society than the Brâhmo Samâj, it was instituted to save the Hindus from exoteric idolatries, Brâhmanism and Christian missionaries.

The purely Theistic movement connected with the Brâhmo Samâj had its origin in the same idea. It began early in the present century, but spasmodically and with interruption, and only took concrete shape under the leadership of Babu Keshub Chunder Sen in 1858. Rammohun Roy, who may be termed the combined Fénelon and Thomas Paine of Hindustan, was its parent, his first church having been organized shortly before his death in 1833. One of the greatest and most acute of controversial writers that our century has produced, his works ought to be translated and circulated in every civilized land. At his death, the work of the Brâhmo Samâj was interrupted. As Miss Collett says, in her *Brâhmo Year Book* for 1878, it was only in October, 1839, that Debendra Nath Tagore founded the Tattvabodhini-Sabhâ (or Society for the Knowledge of Truth), which lasted for twenty years, and did much to arouse the energies and form the principles of the young church of the Brâhmo Samâj. But, exoteric or open religion as it is now, it must have been conducted at first much on the principles of the Secret Societies, as we are informed that Keshub Chunder Sen, a resident of Calcutta and a pupil of the Presidency College, who had long before quit the orthodox Brâhmanical Church and was searching for a purely Theistic religion, "had never heard of the Brâhmo Samâj before 1858" (see *The Theistic Annual*, 1878, p. 45). Since then the Brâhmo Samâj, which he then joined, has flourished and become more popular every day. We now find it with Samâjes established in many provinces and cities. At least, we learn that in May 1877, "fifty Samâjes have notified their adhesion to the Society and eight of them have appointed their representatives. Native missionaries of the

Theistic religion oppose the Christian missionaries and the Orthodox Brâhmans, and the work is going on livelily. So much for the Brâhmo movement."

And now, with regard to the Ârya Samâj, *The Indian Tribune* of Allahabad uses the following language in speaking of its founder:

> The first quarter of the sixteenth century was no more an age of reformation in Europe than the last of the 19th is in India. Similar causes to those which had operated to bring about a mighty reformation in Europe are, at this moment, working in India. From amongst its own "Benedictines," Swami Dyanand Saraswati has arisen, who, unlike other reformers, does not wish to set up a new religion of his own, but asks his countrymen to go back to the pristine purity and Theism of their Vedic religion. After preaching his views in Bombay, Poona, Calcutta, and the N.W. Provinces, he came to the Puñjab, last year, and here it is that he found the most congenial soil. It was in the land of the five rivers, on the banks of the Indus, that the Vedas were first compiled. It was the Puñjab that gave birth to a Nanak. And it is the Puñjab that is making such efforts for a revival of Vedic learning and its doctrines. And wherever Swami Dyanand goes, his splendid physique, his manly bearing, his erudite discourses, his thundering eloquence, and his incisive logic bear down all opposition. People rise up and say: We shall remain no longer in this state of ignorance, we shall think and act for ourselves, we have had enough of a crafty priesthood and a demoralizing idolatry, and we shall tolerate them no longer. We shall wipe off the ugliness of ages, and try to shine forth in the original radiance and effulgence of our Aryan ancestors.

The Swami is a most highly honoured Fellow of the Theosophical Society, takes a deep interest in its proceedings, and *The Indian Spectator* of Bombay, April 14th, 1878, spoke by the book when it said that the work of Pandit Dyanand "bears intimate relation to the work of the Theosophical Society."

While the members of the Brâhmo Samâj may be designated as the Lutheran Protestants of orthodox Brâhmanism, the disciples of the Swami Dyanand should be compared to those learned mystics, the Gnostics, who had the key to those earlier writings which, later, were worked over into the Christian gospels and various patristic literature. As the above-named pre-Christian sects understood the true esoteric meaning of the Chrêstos allegory, which is now materialized into the Jesus of flesh, so the disciples of the learned and holy Swami are taught to discriminate between the written form and the spirit of the word preached in the *Vedas*. And this is the principal point of difference between the Ârya Samâj and the Brâhmos who, as it would seem, believe in a personal God and repudiate the *Vedas,* while the Âryas see an everlasting Principle, an impersonal Cause in the great "Soul of the universe" rather than a personal Being, and accept the *Vedas* as the supreme authority, though not of divine origin. But we may better quote in elucidation of the subject what the President of the Bombay Ârya Samâj, also a Fellow of the Theosophical Society, Mr. Hurrychund Chintamon, says in a recent letter to our Society:

> Pandit Dyanand maintains that as it is now universally acknowledged that the *Vedas* are the oldest books of antiquity, if they contain the truth and nothing but the truh in an unmutilated state, and nothing new can be found in other works of later date, why should we not accept the *Vedas* as a guide for Humanity? . . . A revealed book or revelation is understood to mean one of two things, viz: (1) a book already written by some invisible hand and thrown into the world; or (2) a work written by one or more men while they were in their highest state of mental lucidity, acquired by profound meditation upon the problems of who man is, whence he came, whither he must go, and by what means he may emancipate himself from worldly delusions and sufferings. The latter hypothesis may be regarded as the more rational and correct.

Our Brother Hurrychund here describes those superior men whom we know as Adepts. He adds:

> The ancient inhabitants of a place near Thibet, and adjoining a lake called Mansovara*, were first called Devneggury (Devanagari) or godlike people. Their written characters were also called Devneggury or Balbadha letters. A portion of them migrated to the North and settled there, and afterwards spread towards the South, while others went to the West. All these emigrants styled themselves Aryans, or noble, pure, and good men, as they considered that a pure gift had been made to humanity from the "Pure Alone." These lofty souls were the authors of the *Vedas*."

---

* [Actually *Mânasa-sarovara.—Compiler.*]

What more reasonable than the claim that such Scriptures, emanating from such authors, should contain, for those who are able to penetrate the meaning that lies half concealed under the dead letter, all the wisdom which it is allowed to men to acquire on earth? The Chiefs of the Ârya Samâj discredit "miracles," discountenance superstition and all violation of natural law, and teach the purest form of Vedic Philosophy. Such are the allies of the Theosophical Society. They have said to us: "Let us work together for the good of mankind," and—we will.

H. P. BLAVATSKY.

SCIENCE

[The cutting of this article is pasted in H.P.B.'s *Scrapbook*, Vol. VII, p. 140, and the text is printed in a lay-out similar to an article by S. Watson, dated May 28, 1878, and published in the *Voice of Truth*, of Memphis, Saturday, June 1st. There is no further identification of its actual source or date.]

As it is claimed to be unphilosophical to enquire into first causes, scientists now occupy themselves with considering their physical effects. The field of scientific investigation is therefore bounded by physical nature. When once its limits are reached, enquiry must stop, and their work be recommenced. With all due respect to our learned men, they are like the squirrel upon its revolving wheel, for they are doomed to turn their "matter" over and over again. Science is a mighty potency, and it is not for us pigmies to question her. But the "scientists" are not themselves science embodied any more than the men of our planet are the planet itself. We have neither the right to demand, nor the power to compel, our "modern-day philosopher" to accept without challenge a geographical description of the dark side of the moon. But, if in some lunar cataclysm one of her inhabitants should be hurled thence into the attraction of our atmosphere, and land, safe and sound, at Dr. Carpenter's door, he would be indictable as recreant to professional duty if he should fail to set the physical problem at rest.

For a man of science to refuse an opportunity to investigate any new phenomenon, whether it comes to him in the shape of a man from the moon, or a ghost from the Eddy homestead, is alike reprehensible.

H. P. BLAVATSKY.

LETTER TO THE EDITOR OF THE "TIFLIS MESSENGER"

[*Translated from the original Russian text.*]*

Dear Sir:

In New York, where many people, who hearing the name of *Tiflis,* will face the serious problem of placing this city in their geographical conceptions—whether at the South Pole or on the White Sea—the newspaper *Obzor* [Review] is not read. This, of course, is *their* bad luck, and does not cast the slightest reflection on the highly unprejudiced and scholarly organ of Mr. Nikoladze. But I, as a Russian, was fortunate to receive a clipping of an editorial in No. 20 of the *Obzor* and to read therein some extremely interesting reminiscences about my unworthy self. The mere fact that such an aesthetical, philological and critical *compendium* of everything that is elegant in the literature of our era, as is the newspaper *Obzor,* has deigned to pay me for this flattering attention, honors me and gives pleasure to the readers in Tiflis.

Allow me, therefore, a distant *half*-compatriot of yours, to express in your respected journal a few words of gratitude, and to make a few remarks directed to your talented *confrère* . . . Having carefully pondered over this little page, as it were, torn from the book of my distant past, which represents me in the clear mirror of honest criticism (in

---

* [This cutting from the Russian newspaper is preserved in one of H.P.B.'s *Scrapbooks* in the Adyar Archives.—*Compiler.*]

my *real* appearance, and not a fancied one), and then, having fathomed the surprisingly profound review of my work *Isis Unveiled,* upon which neither Russia, nor Tiflis, nor even the thoughtful editor of the *Obzor* himself, have ever set eyes—I became pensive, I must confess . . .

It is not the numerous and laudable terms which riveted my attention; others might have been hurt by them, but not I. Oh no! Having lived so many years in America, I have long since become used to newspaper mud-slinging. Here they *bark* louder yet, and even the respected editor of the young *Obzor*—such a valiant expert in this branch of literary art, it would seem—cannot outdo the American press. It made me ponder because, being inclined in my old age to hold to the wise precepts of pagan antiquity, I was reminded of the pronouncement of the Delphic Oracle: "To know yourself (man) as you *are*—in the present, know yourself as you *were*—in the past." Thus I am even grateful to the kind editor who has, in such a timely manner, become the priest of the Delphic Oracle in print. However, as a citizen of the United States, I was hurt for America, which until now has been given priority in the case of new discoveries and practical inventions. The editorial in the *Obzor* has ruined that reputation. All our telephones, phonographs and even "electrical" *men,* have faded before the new and useful discovery of Mr. Nikoladze, namely, the ability to write reviews of books, not on the basis of their actual worth and as a result of honest analysis of the author's ideas, but simply on a practical application of the science of Lavater and Galen,—*i.e.,* by means of physiognomy or *facial fortune-telling,* and phrenology, according to the calendar of Martin Zadeki and Co., at Kiev. This great discovery belongs by rights to the Editor of the *Obzor,* who, as a result of *facial* recollections, has *unveiled* with one stroke of his pen both the unfortunate *Isis* and its no less unfortunate author. Who is unaware of the remarkable ability of Lavater faultlessly to divine and *unveil* the character, talents, vices, and the most intimate traits of anyone he met, for instance, on the street? Lavater, unfortunately, was killed in the days of the French Directorate by the soldiers of Masséna at Zürich;

fate, however, showed its mercy for silly humanity in general, and the victims of the *mercenary* American press in particular, and did not permit the soldiers of Mukhtar Pasha and the Crescent to kill Mr. Nikoladze on the bloody fields of Armenia. It preserved him for the *Obzor,* and so that the great science of "facial fortunetelling" should not perish for lack of a worthy representative. From now on, Russia has found its own Lavater and . . . a new day has dawned in Russian literature. Henceforth, Mssrs. the critics may demand, not the actual published works, but merely the photographs of their authors. In this way the books may be subjected to the careful analysis of the reviewers, by means of their *facial* recollections alone. That will be cheaper and real fine. Clever was old Socrates not to have left any manuscripts; how *bald* and *pug-nosed* they would have appeared to the Editor of the *Obzor,* can be judged from the editorial in No. 20 of his Journal.

One might suppose that if the eyes of the author of *Isis* "were shifting in all directions, carefully avoiding meeting ones own"—it was because of a psychic foreboding of the dangerous Lavaterian abilities of Mr. Nikoladze. Unfortunately I do not remember him personally, and must confess that I never heard about such an unpleasant habit of my "eyes" from anyone else, and have never noticed it myself. It would appear I should ponder more deeply the Socratic precept: "Man, know thyself!"

Further, in the same editorial I learn that, while residing at Kutais, I "fooled local scribblers and cadets." This is very flattering for me personally, but hardly so for the ex-scribblers. Considering that in those peaceful and flourishing days (the sixties) the numerous direct descendants of the reigning princes of Guriya and Imeretia rarely advanced beyond the ranks of cadets and writing clerks, preferring to rush straight from the lower grade benches in the local schools into the embraces of Hymen, and to begin their careers when already bearded, though youthful fathers of families; and furthermore, recollecting that in those distant days I was a mature and rather voluminous lady, and "in addition, with manners which produced a highly unpleasant impression upon the onlooker," it is impossible not to be genuinely sorry for these innocent "fools." With what cold-blooded and merciless satire does Mr. Nikoladze scoff at his compatriots—the illustrious "scribblers and cadets," of the local aristocracy of Kutais.

In conclusion I will permit myself to observe that everything points to the fact that the talented critic, even if he has studied Lavater especially, has nevertheless neglected to acquaint himself with human nature in general. "Artificiality and charlatanry" are weapons only of those who aim at some honor or monetary benefit. Would Mr. Nikoladze dare to say that I or anyone else could possibly have expected anything of that kind in a circle of starving "scribblers and cadets" of Imeretia?

Let us hasten to complete the mystification of the poor *Tiflis Messenger* that was unable to detect the fact that the 64 newspapers and magazines in America which have so far published, and continue to publish, more or less lengthy reviews of *Isis Unveiled,* possibly too laudable, have all, to the very last, been bribed by me. That there are *sixty-four* of them, and those only the ones I have read myself, is easy for me to prove by means of the Scrapbook into which I have pasted them. With such an enormous influence upon the press as I exercise in America, it wouldn't be a bad thing for the Russian government to flirt with me a little, as I might have some influence upon the forthcoming Russian-American progressive and defensive alliance. The press, it would appear is under my thumb in London also. As proof of this I send you a review of *Isis Unveiled* from the London *Public Opinion* of the 29th of December. This journal could also be called *Obzor* [Review]—but of the *public opinion* of Europe, and not the private and prejudiced opinions of its editor. Its specialty is to publish and to hold merely the opinions expressed by the voice of the majority in all matters of criticism, politics, literature and the arts. Would not Mr. Nikoladze like to acquaint himself with the *standing* of the *Public Opinion* of London, where all writers and artists fear it, as they would fire, on account of its impartiality and severity? Its reviewer, apparently, has so little concern with the *personality* of the writer, confining his entire attention to the production itself, that he has more than once called the author of *Isis, Mr. Blavatsky.* I am sending to the editor of the *Tiflis Messenger* the English original for comparison, and ask to be permitted to translate a few lines from the section on *English Literature* in that London review.

[Here follows the Russian translation of the review published in the London *Public Opinion* of December 29, 1877.]

Such is the opinion of one of the most serious among English literary organs concerning my *Isis* and its author, *Mr. Blavatsky.* Many people will of course think that praise of myself is out of place here. But in Tiflis, where many knew me, English is not understood, while everyone sees the Russian *Obzor* of Mr. Nikoladze. Probably he has overlooked the fact that it is quite possible to be the imbodiment of all vices, and physical as well as moral deformity, and yet to be at the same time a good, and even an outstanding writer. The editor of *Obzor* has challenged me with an insulting public declaration, probably because I am located 8,000 miles from him—and I have answered. Will he not favor us now with his estimate of how much, for instance, I had to pay the scholarly journal, *Public Opinion* of London, for its flattering testimonial?

[In H.P.B.'s *Scrapbook*, Vol. VIII, p. 252, there is pasted a cutting from *The Bombay Gazette* of June 18, 1878, entitled "A Wonderful Discovery." It is an account of Dr. Rotura's method of temporarily suspending animal life. At the end of this article H.P.B. added the following remarks:]

NOTE. On the 26th of March 1877 the N. Y. *World* printed [see *Scrapbook*, IV, pp. 49-51] an account of an interview of its reporter with H.P.B., in which she said that the shepherds of Thibet understand how to cause life to be suspended in their domestic animals by manipulating a certain artery in the neck. After a desired time has passed they bring the animals to life again without harm. She used the words, as it appears: "I prophesy to you (the Reporter) that within a year from now scientists will discover how this is done in the case of the lower animals."

[See in this connection H.P.B.'s Letter to the Editor of *La Revue Spirite* of Paris concerning the discovery of Dr. Rotura, published in its issue of December 1879. *Vide* Vol. II of the present Series.]

LETTER TO THE EDITOR OF *L'OPINIONE NAZIONALE*

[*L'Opinione Nazionale*, Firenze, 22 Giugno, 1878]

Nostra Corrispondenza.   Nuova York.

Carissimo Direttore,

Vi spedisco *l'Eco di Nuova York*—nostro Organo locale delle Società secrete—Vi sarà, credo, di speciale interesse che il nostro Presidente come rappresentante le opinioni della nostra Società prende una prominentissima parte coi Repubblicani della Colonia italiana in questo nostro paese nell' inaugurare un monumento a Mazzini.

La cerimonia dello scoprimento avrà luogo al 29 Maggio nel Parco Centrale, e copia de' varii documenti riguardanti codesta funzione vi sarà spedita. La Commissione vorrebbe che io facessi un discorso in lingua russa; ma con tutto l'amore e l'ammirazione che professo per Mazzini ho dovuto rifiutarmi. Detesto far mostra di me sentendomi più atto a vivere nelle selve indiane tra le tigri ed i serpenti che in mezzo a persone in bianchi guanto e con abiti a coda di rondine:

Il giornale italiano *Fanfulla* mi venne assicurato che censurava gl'italiani di America formanti parte di questa Commissione, dichiarandoli una massa di comunisti ed individui di pessima riputazione. Quest'è una bugia infamante. Questi sono repubblicani in cuore, animo e corpo, e quando il nome del Console generale d'Italia cavaliere de Luca è stato proposto ad unanimità, fu fischiato. Ciò si deve attribuire in parte perchè rappresentante un Governo monarchico, al quale Mazzini non si è mai sottoposto; ma principalmente si deve al perchè questo Console era *principalmente* interessato al nefando traffico d'importare dei ragazzi italiani vendendoli ad una vera schiavitù, a suonatori d'organi tedeschi che li facevano morire di fame e di bastone facendo dormire quelle povere creature *l'uno presso l'altro incatenato!* Il fratello H. D. Monachesi, membro della nostra società, americano, di derivazione italiana, forma parte di questa Commissione, fu uno dei più attivi a far crollare il sopradetto traffico, e diverse volte è stato in procinto d'essere ucciso da persone comprate dal Console. Il presidente dissemi che tutti gli associati erano d'accordo con la opinione del signor Monachesi circa il Console de Luca.

La Commissione Mazzini viene presieduta dal Dott. G. Ceccarini e tutti gli altri membri sono rispettabilissimi. È una vera infamia da parte del Console de Luca lo spargere tale calunnia, e ciò non per altro che per dispetto. Come teosofista venite pregato di communicare ciò a quanta onesta gente odia la menzogna e la calunnia, e se è possibile d'inserire in più giornali italiani che potete questi fatti, per lo che vi ho spedito *l'Eco*—Non c'è tempo da perdere: agite.

BLAVATSKY.

LETTER TO THE EDITOR OF *L'OPINIONE NAZIONALE*

[*L'Opinione Nazionale*, Florence, June 22, 1878]

[*Translation of the foregoing original Italian text*]

Our Correspondence.   New York.

My dear Editor,

I am sending to you the *New York Echo*—our local Organ for Secret Societies. It will be, I believe, of special interest to you that our President, as representing the opinions of our Society, is taking a very prominent part with the Republicans of the Italian Colony in this our country in inaugurating a monument to Mazzini.

The ceremony of the unveiling will take place on May 29th in Central Park, and a copy of the various documents regarding this function will be sent to you. The Commission would like me to make an address in the Russian language; but with all the love and admiration that I avow for Mazzini I have had to refuse. I detest making a show of myself, feeling myself more fit to live in the forests of India among tigers and serpents than among persons in white gloves and swallow-tailed coats.

I have been informed that the Italian journal *Fanfulla* has censured the Italians of America forming part of this Commission, declaring them to be a lot of communists and individuals of the worst reputation. This is an infamous lie. They are republicans in heart, soul and body, and when the name of the Italian Consul general, de Luca, was proposed for unanimity, it was hissed. That must be attributed partly to the fact that he represents a monarchial Government, to which Mazzini has never subjected himself; but principally it is due to the reason that the said Consul was *principally* interested in the nefarious traffic of importing Italian boys and selling them to a veritable slavery to players of German organs that made them die of hunger and by the cudgel, making those poor creatures sleep *chained one to the other*! Our brother H. C. Monachesi, a member of our Society, an American of Italian origin, who belongs to this Commission, was one of the most active in overthrowing the above-mentioned traffic, and has been several times on the verge of being killed by persons hired by the Consul. The president told me that all the associates were in agreement with the opinion of Mr. Monachesi concerning Consul de Luca.

The Mazzini Commission is presided over by Dr. G. Ceccarini and all the other members are highly respectable. It is a true infamy on the part of Consul de Luca to spread such a calumny, and for no other reason than spite. As a Theosophist you are asked to communicate this to all those who hate falsehood and calumny, and, if possible, to insert these facts in as many Italian newspapers as you can, for which I have sent you *The Echo*. There is no time to lose: act.

BLAVATSKY.

PARTING WORDS FROM MADAME BLAVATSKY

[*Religio-Philosophical Journal*, Chicago, Vol. XXIV, July 6, 1878, p. 2]

DEAR SIR,—

So far, as I can at present foresee, this will be the last time I shall ask you to print anything over my—to many Spiritualists—loathed signature, as I intend to start for India very soon. But I have once more to correct inaccurate statements. If I had had my choice, I would have preferred almost any other person than my very esteemed friend, Dr. Bloede, to have last words with. Once an antagonist—a bitter and unjust one to me, as he himself admits—he has since made all the amends I could have asked of a scholar and a gentleman, and now, as all who read your valuable paper see, he does me the honor to call me friend. Honest in intent he always is, I am sure, but still a little prejudiced. Who of us but is [not] so, more or less? Duty, therefore, compels me to correct the erroneous impression which his letter on "Secret Societies" (*Journal* of June 15th) is calculated to give about the Theosophical Society. How many "Fellows" we have, how the society is flourishing, what are its operations or how conducted, no one knows or can know, save the presidents of its various branches and their secretaries. Therefore, Dr. G. Bloede, in saying that it has "failed in America, and will fail in Europe," speaks of that of which neither he nor any other outsider has knowledge. If the Society's only object were the study of the phenomena called Spiritual, his strictures would be perfectly warranted; for it is not *secrecy* but *privacy* and exclusiveness that are demanded in the management of circles and mediums. It would have been absurd to make [a] secret society expressly for that purpose. At its beginning the Theosophical Society was started for that sole study, and therefore, was, as you all know, open to any respectable person, who wished to join it. We discussed "Spiritual" topics freely, and were willing to impart to the public the results of all our experiments, and whatever some of us might have learned of the subject in the course of long studies. How our views and philosophy were received—no need to recall the old story again. The storm has hardly subsided; and the total of billingsgate poured upon our devoted heads is preserved in three gigantic scrapbooks whose contents I mean to immortalize some day. When, through the writing and noble efforts of the *Journal* and other spiritual papers, the secret of these varied and vexing phenomena indiscriminately called spiritual will be snatched at last, when the faithful of the Orthodox church of Spiritualism will be forced to give up—partially at least—their many bigoted and preconceived notions, then the time will have come again for Theosophists to claim a hearing. Till then, its members retire from the arena of discussion and devote their whole leisure to the fulfillment of other and more important objects of the Society.

You perceive, then, that it is only when experience showed the necessity for its work to be enlarged, and its objects became various, that the T.S. thought fit to protect itself by secrecy. Since then, none but perjured witnesses, and we know of none, can have told about what we were doing, except as permitted by official sanction and announced from time to time. One of such objects of our society, we are willing to publicly announce.

It is universally known that this most important object is to antagonize Christianity and especially Jesuitism. One of our most esteemed and valued members—once an ardent Spiritualist, but who must for the present be nameless—has but recently fallen a victim to the snares of this hateful body. The nefarious designs of Jesuitism are plotted in secret and carried out through secret agencies. What more reasonable and lawful, therefore, than that those who wish to fight it should keep their own secret, likewise, as to their agencies and plans? We have among us persons in high positions—political, military, financial and social—who regard Christianity as the greatest evil to humanity and are willing to help pull it down. But for them to be able to do much and well, they must do it anonymously. The church—"Triple-headed Snake," as a well-known writer calls it— can no longer burn its enemies, but it can blast their social influence; can no longer roast their bodies, but can ruin their fortunes. We have no right to give our enemy, the church, the names of our "Fellows" who are not ripe for martyrdom, and so we keep them secret. If we have an agent to send to India, or to Japan, or China, or any other heathen country, to do something or confer with somebody in connection with the Society's general plans against missionaries, it would be foolish, nay, criminal, to expose our agent to imprisonment under some malicious pretext, if not death, and even the latter is possible in the faraway East, and our scheme is liable to miscarry by announcing it to the dishonorable company of Jesus.

So, Sir, to sum up in a word, Dr. Bloede has made a great mistake in supposing the Theosophical Society a "failure" in this or any other country. When the society counted three years ago its members by the dozens, it now counts them by the hundreds and thousands. And so far from its threatening in any respect the stability of society or the advancement of spiritual knowledge, the Theosophical Institution which now bears the name of the "Theosophical Society of the Ârya Samâj of India," being regularly chartered by and affiliated with that great body in the land of the Âryas, will be found some day, by the Spiritualists, and all others who claim the right of thinking for themselves, to have been the true friend of intellectual and spiritual liberty—if not in America, at least in France and other countries, where an infernal priesthood thrusts innocent Spiritualists into prison by the help of a subservient judiciary and the use of perjured testimony. Its name will be respected as a pioneer of free thought and an uncompromising enemy of priestly and monkish fraud and despotism.

H. P. BLAVATSKY.

New York, June 17th, 1878.

LA VÉRITABLE MADAME H. P. BLAVATSKY

[*La Revue Spirite*, Paris, octobre, 1878]

L'un de nos amis, homme de lettres et publiciste distingué, avait reçu de l'un de ses confrères de l'Amérique (États-Unis), une lettre concernant les Théosophes: cette lettre nous l'avons inséré, sans nous figurer qu'elle renfermait des erreurs et un récit tant soit peu fantaisiste; une lettre de Madame H. P. Blavatsky nous permet de rectifier ce que nous avons inséré de bonne foi, ce que nous nous empressons de faire comme un devoir et avec plaisir; notre amie nous paraissait surfaite par qui la connait à peine, nous en avons la preuve certaine. Notre religion a été surprise.

Voici, textuellement, la lettre de Madame Blavatsky:

A peine revenue d'un voyage, je trouve dans le numéro de juin dernier de la *Revue Spirite,* un article intitulé «Les Théosophes—Madame Blavatsky». Traduction à peu près fidèle d'une nouvelle publiée l'année dernière dans le *World* de New-York, cet article répète—fort innocemment sans doute—les hallucinations de M. le *Reporter* Américain.

Il existe une race de bipèdes—production à peu près récente de notre siècle à vapeur et iconoclaste par excellence,—que les Académies des Sciences ont jusqu'ici négligé de classifier sous la rubrique de «*Tératologie*», ou science traitant des monstres humains. Les monstres ou *lusus naturae* s'appellent *reporters* ici—comme partout ailleurs—avec cette différence, cependant, que celui du pays de Christophe Colomb et du général Tom-Pouce se distingue de son cousin trans-atlantique, autant que le buffle sauvage des forêts vierges du taureau domestique. Si ce dernier se rend parfois coupable de dégâts commis sur la haie d'un voisin, le premier détruit des forêts entières sur son passage furieux; il rue aveuglément, tue et écrase tout ce qui lui fait obstacle. Avec Messieurs les *reporters* Américains, je ne sais vraiment pourquoi les bons citoyens des États-Unis se donnent seulement la peine de fermer les portes; il n'existe ni serrures assez brevetées, ni secret de famille assez sacré pour les empêcher de se faufiler partout, de fureter, se mêler de tout, et surtout de remplacer la vérité toute nue par la fiction la plus singulièrement habillée dans leurs publications quotidiennes.

Il y a cinq ans que je suis la victime de ces chercheurs de sensations littéraires. Lorsque j'essaye de fermer ma porte au nez de l'un de ces Argus de la presse, il entre par la fenêtre. Balayé de son poste d'observation, il remplace ce qu'il *aurait pu* voir, par ce qu'il n'avait jamais vu, et ce qui n'avait jamais existé! Aussi, ne puis-je, cependant, consentir de gaîté de cœur, à passer aux yeux de vos estimables lecteurs de la *Revue Spirite* pour une complice de ces efforts d'imagination? Quoiqu'en substance l'article traitant de ce que le *reporter* et plusieurs autres personnes ont vu chez moi, un soir, soit assez exacte vers la fin; les détails qui précèdent l'apparition des deux ombres ne le sont guère.

Et d'abord, pour commencer, je ne suis pas *comtesse*, que je sache. Sans oublier qu'il serait plus que ridicule—ce serait *anti-constitutionnel*—à un citoyen ou citoyenne de la République des États-Unis—qui abjure lors de sa naturalisation tout titre de noblesse—de s'en arroger un, surtout lorsqu'il ne lui a jamais appartenu; je suis trop démocrate et j'aime et je respecte assez le peuple, pour que lui ayant voué toutes mes sympathies et cela, sans distinction de race ou de couleur, j'aille m'affubler d'un titre quelconque! J'ai toujours protesté publiquement contre cette tendance si ridicule dans une République comme la nôtre de donner à toute personne étrangère des titres plus ou moins sonores.

Néanmoins—et quoique je ne sois pas *comtesse*, je n'ai jamais eu l'habitude d'offrir des pipes à mes visiteurs.—On peut être démocrate, veuve de tout titre, et ne pas accepter cependant—surtout à mon âge—un rôle ridicule et inconvenant.

En parlant d'âge et quoique les journaux du pays m'eussent voté respectivement et à diverses époques l'âge de 25, 60, 86, 92 et—de 103 ans, je me vois obligée d'assurer à vos lecteurs que je n'ai pas «passé plus de trente ans dans l'Inde». C'est justement mon âge—quoique fort respectable tel qu'il est—qui s'oppose violemment à cette chronologie de fantaisie. Je n'ai pas plus embrassé la «foi Bouddhique» soit «par conviction» ou par autre chose.

Il est vrai que je regarde la philosophie de Gautama Bouddha, comme le système le plus sublime; le plus pur et surtout le plus *logique* entre tout autre. Mais ce système défiguré pendant des siècles par l'ambition et le fanatisme des prêtres est devenu une religion vulgaire; les formes et le culte *exotérique* ou populaire découlés de ce système ressemblent trop à celui de l'église romaine qui en a fait le plagiat servilement pour que je puisse jamais m'y convertir. Ainsi que dans tout système pur et primitif introduit par les grands réformateurs religieux du monde ancien, ses rayons ont trop divergé de leur centre commun—*les Védas des Aryas;* et quoiqu'entre toutes les croyances modernes l'Église Bouddhique soit l'unique qui encourage ses membres à questionner ses dogmes et à rechercher le fin mot de tout mystère qui y est enseigné—j'aime mieux m'en tenir à la source *mère* que de me fier à un des nombreux ruisseaux qui en découlent. «Ne croyez pas ce que je vous dis, rien que pour la raison que c'est *moi,* votre Bouddha qui vous le dis — mais seulement lorsque votre raison ne s'oppose pas à la vérité de mon assertion»—a dit Gautama dans ses *Sûtras* ou aphorismes. Or, et quoique j'admire de toute mon âme la philosophie si élevée de Siddhârta, ou Śakya-Mouni, je m'incline tout autant devant la grandeur morale et la forte logique du Kapila Indou, le grand Âchârya, qui fut cependant l'ennemi le plus acharné du Bouddha. Tandis que ce dernier tenait les *Védas* comme autorité suprême — les Bouddhistes les ont rejeté après coup, lorsqu'il est pourtant prouvé que Gautama, dans sa réforme et protestation contre les abus des rusés Brahmanes, s'est basé entièrement sur le sens ésotérique des grandes Écritures primitives. Donc, si le *reporter*—auteur de l'article en question—eut dit simplement que j'appartenais à la religion qui a inspiré Bouddha, au lieu de me présenter au public comme une Bouddhiste tournant la *Roue de la Loi*—il n'eut dit que la vérité. On peut être Platonicien, sans être nécessairement païen ou idolâtre pour cela; comme on peut rester chrétien sans appartenir à aucune des églises qui se battent depuis dix huit cents ans au nom de l'Homme-Dieu.

Si nos *frères* d'outre-mer s'intéressent à savoir quelle est la religion, ou plutôt le système auquel nous—les Théosophes (de la section intérieure)—adhérons, je suis chargée par le Conseil Administratif de la «*Société Théosophique de l'Arya Samaj des Indes*» de vous le dire—aussitôt que vous nous l'aurez demandé. Nous n'en faisons pas un secret. Seulement —ne nous appelez plus Bouddhistes, car vous commettriez une grave erreur.

Pour en finir je vous assure que je n'ai pas dit la moitié des sottises que l'on m'attribue dans l'article en question. Je n'ai jamais assuré, par exemple, avoir fait *moi-même* l'opération délicate avec les moutons et chèvres du Thibet, pour la simple raison que je ne suis jamais allée dans les endroits montagneux et presque inaccessibles où l'on prétend que ce phénomène de léthargie forcée a lieu. Je n'ai répété que ce qui m'a été assuré, mais personnellement je crois à la possibilité de ce fait—sous certaines réserves cependant. Les possibilités du magnétisme animale sont infinies, et, je crois au Magnétisme—et vous aussi je pense. La dessus, donnons fraternellement la main à travers l'Atlantique, et—ne vous fiez pas trop dorénavant aux articles d'origine américaine.

H. P. BLAVATSKY.

NOTA. Nous acceptons avec empressement, l'exposition du système que les Théosophes préconisent, et nous insérerons ce que notre correspondant voudra bien nous donner; nous aurons tout intérêt à le lire.

THE REAL MADAME H. P. BLAVATSKY

[*La Revue Spirite*, Paris, October, 1878]

[*Translation of the foregoing original French text*]

One of our many friends, a distinguished writer and publicist, received a letter about the Theosophists from one of his confrères in America (United States); we inserted it without imagining that it contained errors and a somewhat fantastic story; a letter from Madame H. P. Blavatsky enables us to rectify what we inserted in good faith, and we hasten to do so as a duty, and with pleasure; our friend seems to us to have been misinterpreted by someone who hardly knows her; we have absolute proof of it. This is rather a surprise to us.

Here is, textually, Madame Blavatsky's letter:

Hardly had I returned from a journey when I found in the June number of *La Revue Spirite* an article entitled "Les Théosophes—Madame Blavatsky," a fairly accurate translation of a story published last year in the New York *World;* this article repeats—quite innocently no doubt—the hallucinations of Mr. American Reporter.

There exists a race of bipeds—the rather recent production of our century of steam and iconoclasm *par excellence*—that the Academies of Science have hitherto neglected to classify under the heading of *"Teratology,"* or the Science treating of human monsters. The monsters or *lusus naturae*, are called *reporters* here—as they are everywhere—but there is this difference, however, that the one of the land of Christopher Columbus and General Tom Thumb differs from his trans-atlantic cousin as much as the wild buffalo of the virgin forest does from the domestic bull. If the latter sometimes becomes guilty of havoc committed on the fence of a neighbor, the former destroys whole forests in his furious career; he rushes blindly and kills and crushes everything that stands in his way. As to Messrs. the American reporters I really do not know why the good citizens of the United States take the trouble to fasten their doors;

there is neither a lock sufficiently patented, nor a family secret sacred enough to prevent them from intruding, from ferreting out, from meddling in everything, and above all from substituting in their daily publication the most strangely dressed-up fiction for the bare truth.

For five years I have been the victim of these hunters for literary sensations. When I try to shut my door in the face of one of these Arguses of the press, he comes in by the window. Swept from his observation post, he substitutes what he *might have* seen by what he never saw at all, and by what never existed; how can I, then, good-naturedly consent to pass in the eyes of the worthy readers of *La Revue Spirite* for an accomplice in these efforts of the imagination? Although in substance the article which treats of what the reporter and several other persons saw in my house one evening, may be accurate enough towards the end, the details that precede the apparition of the two Shades are hardly so.

To begin with I am not a *Countess* so far as I know. Without overlooking the fact that it would be more than ridiculous—it would be *unconstitutional*—in a citizen or citizeness of the Republic of the United States—who abjures all titles of nobility upon being naturalized—to claim one, above all one which never belonged to him or her— I am too democratic, and I love and respect the people sufficiently, having devoted all my sympathy to them, and this without distinction of race or color, to trick myself out in any kind of title! I have always publicly protested against this ridiculous inclination in a Republic like ours of giving every foreigner a more or less high-sounding title.

However—and although I may not be a *Countess*—I have never been in the habit of offering pipes to my guests. One may be a democrat, bereft of every title, and yet not accept —above all at my age—a ridiculous and unseemly rôle.

Speaking of age, and although the newspapers of the country may have voted me respectively and at various times, the ages of 25, 60, 86, 92 and—103 years, I must assure your readers that I have not "passed more than thirty years in India." It is precisely my age—however respectable it may be—that is radically opposed to that fantastic chronology. Neither have I embraced the "Buddhist faith" either "from conviction" or for any other reason.

It is true that I regard the philosophy of Gautama Buddha as the most sublime system; the purest, and, above all, the most *logical* of all. But the system has been distorted during the centuries by the ambition and fanaticism of the priests and has become a popular religion; the forms and the *exoteric* or popular cult proceeding from that system, too closely resemble those of the Roman church which has slavishly plagiarized from it, for me ever to be converted to it. Just as in every pure and primitive system, introduced by the great religious reformers of the ancient world, its rays have diverged too far from their common centre—*the Vedas of the Âryans*; and although among all modern beliefs the Buddhist Church may be the only one to encourage its members to question its dogmas and to seek the last word of every mystery which is taught therein—I much prefer to hold to the *mother* source rather than to depend upon any of the numerous streams that flow from it.

"Do not believe what I tell you just because it is *I*, your Buddha, who says it—but only because your judgment is not opposed to the truth of my assertion"—says Gautama in his *Sûtras* or aphorisms. Now although I admire with all my soul the lofty philosophy of Siddhârtha, or Śâkya-Muni, I bow quite as much before the moral grandeur and the powerful logic of the Hindu Kapila, the great Âchârya, who was, however, the most implacable enemy of the Buddha. While the latter looked on the *Vedas* as the supreme authority—the Buddhists rejected them after all, though it was proved, nevertheless, that Gautama in his reform and protest against the abuses of the wily Brâhmanas, based himself entirely upon the esoteric meaning of the grand primitive Scriptures. Then, if the reporter—the author of the article in question—had simply said that I belonged to the religion that had inspired the Buddha, instead of presenting me to the public as a Buddhist turning the *Wheel of the Law*—he would have spoken nothing but the truth. One can be a Platonist without necessarily being a pagan or an idolater at that, as one may remain a Christian without belonging to any of the Churches which have been fighting one another for eighteen hundred years in the name of the Man-God.

If our trans-atlantic *brothers* are interested in knowing what is the religion, or rather the system to which we—Theosophists (of the inner section)—adhere, I am ordered by the administrative Council of the *"Theosophical Society of the Ârya Samâj of India"* to tell you about it immediately on receipt of your request. We make no secret of it. Only —do not call us Buddhists any more, because you would make a very serious mistake.

In concluding, I assure you that I have not mentioned half the absurdities attributed to me in the article in question. I never asserted, for example, that I *myself* did the delicate operation with the sheep and goats of Tibet, for the simple reason that I never went to the mountainous and almost inaccessible places where the phenomenon of artificial trance takes place, it is said. I only repeated what has been told to me, but personally I believe in the possibility of that act—with certain reservations however. The possibilities of animal magnetism are infinite, and I believe in Magnetism—and you also, I think. On that subject, we fraternally shake hands across the Atlantic, and . . . do not trust too much in future to articles of American origin.

H. P. BLAVATSKY.

NOTE.—We hasten to accept the promised exposition of the system promulgated by Theosophists, and we shall insert whatever our correspondent will kindly send us; we shall be greatly interested in reading it.

[In H.P.B.'s *Scrapbook*, Vol. VII, p. 258, there is pasted a brief cutting entitled "Extreme Measures Advocated." Neither the source, the date, nor the author are stated. It speaks of Charles Sotheran who, declaring himself a labor Socialist, spoke at a mass meeting of strikers and urged them to take extreme measures against the Capitalist exploiters. To this H.P.B. remarked:]

A Theosophist becoming a rioter, encouraging revolution and MURDER, a friend of Communists is no fit member of our Society.

HE HAS TO GO.

[In H.P.B.'s *Scrapbook*, Vol. VII, p. 306, there is pasted the printed copy of the Petition of Bankruptcy against E. Gerry Brown, the former Editor of *The Spiritual Scientist*. In the list of Creditors we find Col. Olcott with $590, and H.P.B. with $150. H.P.B. marked these sums and wrote in red pencil (much faded now) as follows:]

Several hundred more given without asking for a note. H.P.B.

A constant shower of abuse and sneering in *his* paper against [one word illegible] and in their paper too, and bankruptcy to end the whole without a single acknowledgement, excuse or regret.

Such is Elbridge Brown the Spiritualist ! !

[In H.P.B.'s *Scrapbook*, Vol. V, pp. 77-79, there is pasted a cutting entitled "Our Sketches from India," the source and the date of which are unknown. It contains the description of the investiture of several Indian Princes with the Order of the Star of India. At the end of this article H.P.B. wrote in pencil some remarks in Russian. Translated, they read as follows:]

Is it not the remembrance of the year 1857 that compels you to affect such tenderness to the Indian Princes, oh kind men of Albion? In vain . . . When the HOUR STRIKES . . . nothing will stay the hand of Fate!

∴

[These remarks are significantly signed with three dots.]

[In H.P.B.'s *Scrapbook,* Vol. V, p. 81, there is pasted a short cutting of eight lines, the source and the date of which are unknown. It has to do with a certain Dr. Scudder who said that the Oriental nations will never become converted to Christianity until their women first become Christians, and that women can be converted only by the personal agency of women who would go there from Christian countries. Hindu women, it would appear, will not listen to male missionaries. Under this H.P.B. wrote in ink:]

I wish the Rev. may get it . . . Anyhow, the Reverend *fraud* may go to his Christian Hell first. Hindu women will no more listen to female flapdoodle humbugs thanks to the male cheats, who like Scudder go about deceiving the "heathen"—far less *heathen* than themselves.

THE DIARIES OF H. P. BLAVATSKY

[*The superior numbers occurring in the text of the Diaries refer to Compiler's Notes appended at the end of them.*]

[Among the most valuable documents in the Adyar Archives are the many volumes of Colonel H. S. Olcott's *Diaries*. He was in the habit of writing down daily the occurrences of the day, to mention those whom he met and to recount briefly various events that were taking place at the time. He kept such Diaries at least from 1875 on, and almost to the time of his death in 1907. The *Diaries* of 1875-77 mysteriously disappeared years ago, and the Colonel had no idea what could have become of them. For this reason, the *Diaries* for the year 1878 are the first ones available. They are especially interesting because they are the only ones in which H.P.B. wrote. In those days, Col. Olcott had to absent himself on business rather frequently, and during his absences, H.P.B. made all kinds of entries in his *Diary*. When he returned, he resumed writing himself. The 1878 *Diary* gives a vivid picture of the life of H.P.B. and Col. Olcott in the last year of their stay in America, before embarking for India.

Col. Olcott's entries are printed in small type, and only those from October 23rd are included. It has been thought advisable to preserve as much as possible the original punctuation which at times is very ambiguous. No alterations have been made in H.P.B.'s often peculiar abbreviations.]

1878

February 6. Visitors—Hyneman.—Shut up in the room H.P.B. and Isab. Mitchell.[1] Sotheran[2] brings Richard Harte of the N.Y. Echo—insists upon H.P.B. writing an Editorial for Wednesday following. Entrance and visits forbidden. H.P.B. writes her corresp. for Russia.

Letters received: From E.K.[3]—to Moloney[4]—sends back the astral letter. Dr. Bloede, acknowledges his error as to his pitching into H.P.B. for accepting diploma and Sotheran writing his letter to the "Banner."

February 7. H.P.B. writes letters the whole day. At four comes Dr. Bloede,—to dinner Paris, Wimbridge[5] and John Marshall the engraver. Letter from M.˙. Jun.[6] from Boston. Announces return home early on Friday morning. Wimbridge brings the London Illustrated News.—Holkar's and Some One's portraits among others.

2 Letters from N. A. Fadeew[7]—Odessa. H.P.B. 4 feuilletons definitely lost. Asks to write others. Letter from Bundy. Conciliatory and stupid. Package of Sat B'hai[8] from Yarker.

Pope dead.—Panic in England. Russians at Constantinople. Gortchakof hoodwinks Disraeli.—I.˙.[9] ! ! !

February 8. Mol. *home,* brings *grips* from Boston.—Evening—Sotheran. Miss Cowle. [H.S.O.'s entry *after* H.P.B.'s: Miss S. Emma Cowell, 227 East 20th St.] Letter from Davey,—*Spirit of Times,* excusing himself on account of his rheumatism. Holkar's *first* visit. Mol's indignation at the profanation of the Elephanta caves.

February 9. H.P.B. added P.S. to the letter sent to Hurrychund Chintamon.[10] Enquiry about Holkar and Bhurtpur, Letter from Franklin Register. Today St.[11] send *50 copies* ! ! of H.P.B.'s answer to masons. Rel. Ph.[12] full of letters which pitch into O.

February 11. Letters from E. Kislingbury to H.P.B. Letter to Moloney from M. A. Oxon[13] —(reply to his last). Providence Journal sent by Steward (Franklin) with parag. about Masonry. Delivered to W. Mitchell. 2 newsp. to be sent Bombay, Hurrychund. 3 Feuilletons for "Pravda,"[14] Letter and portrait to N. A. Fadeev,—the whole insured.

D. Curtis called at 6—had dinner at 4.—Rosetta working the whole day.—Answered Emily—and N. A. Fadeev. Curtis and Mrs. Mitchell.—Harrisse brought his portrait.[15] Went away at *ten*—and Dr. Wilder[16] came in.—Remained the whole night. Mr. Mitchell came down sick.—1st day of seamstress.

February 12. Letters—from Franklin—sent in clips from papers—and advertisement for H.P.B.'s fight with **Masons.**

1 February "Spiritualist" no 25 January *Spiritualist.* 2d day of seamstress.

Visits evening—Sotheran, Mrs. Winchester.—Mrs. Ames, Mrs. Oliver.—Wimbridge and—Miss Bates. Stopped till 3. —Olcott arrived.—

February 13. Olcott arrived at 8 in the morning. Bothered H.P.B. with fixing bells. Letter from O'Donovan, announces visits. Letter from Wimbridge about l'Inde des Rajahs.[17] H.P.B. went out with I.B.M.

July 8. Went at 10 to Madame Marquette,[18] Spring St. Order to supply her as a witness for H.P.B. Went from there to the City Hall. Presented our naturalization claims. and demanded to be made immediately a "citizen." H.P.B. was made to swear eternal affection, devotion and defence to and of the U. S. Constitution; forswore every particle of allegiance to the Russian Emperor and—was made a "Citizen" of the U. S. of America. Received her naturalization papers and went home happy. Wrote an article for "Vyestnik."[19] H.S.O. came home to dinner and then to Albany by railway on a mutual speculation with Hartmann. Will return — so he says — the day after tomorrow. General Doubleday[20] came just before his departure and remained till 1/2 9. Jenny returned to sleep at 10 with her sister.

July 9. "Press," "World," "Times," etc., speak of H.P.B.'s citizenship. Reporter sent by "Graphic," at 12 to interview the old party. Mrs. and Mr. Shevitch[21] to dinner, also Marble and Wimbridge. Evening,—Clark from Washington and O'Sullivan. Telegraph from H.S.O. notifying of his return from Albany. H.P.B. yielding to O'Sullivan's botherations took a lock of *black hair* from her head and gave it to him.

July 10. H.S.O. turned in at 9. Passport sent from Washington with mistake in the spelling of the name. H.S.O. took it back to the city. Tropical heat, 89 d. at 11 a.m.

August 4. Went to bathe. H.S.O., E. W. Macgrath and

H.P.B. The latter provoked a last farewell admiration from the pious Xtians on the beach by her smoking. Passed the evening with Jennings and Mrs. Cos.....[?] at Gardiner's Hotel. H.P.B. was given "Cocney's" portrait. Went to bed at 1. Wimbridge wrote his letter to Hurrychund.

August 5. Got up at 4 in the morning. H.S.O., H.P.B., Wimbridge and Macgrath took train to New York. A letter from E. K. showing pretensions and being offended with Olcott for what he wrote to her about C. C. Blake.[22] H.S.O. received a letter from Prof. Wyld.[23] Evening to dinner, W. Q. Judge according to orders and Wimbridge. "Indu Prakash" received from India and pamphlet "Answer of Dya Nand Swamee[24] to his critics." An Italian paper from Otho Alexander[25] from Corfu with article on Mazzini's festival and a thrust to the "Fanfulla," by Menelao.[26]

August 6. Olcott gone to Albany. Dictionary received from Odessa. Letters received from Mooljee Thackersey[27] to H.P.B. from Hurrychund Chintamon and Shamajee Chrishnavarma.[28] H. C. sends a whole package of books of the 6 philosophies.—Letter from H.S.O. to H.C. including Wimbridge's letter sent by the latter also. Answer to Mooljee by H.P.B. Evening—Curtis came and began an article on the Swamee and the Arya Samaj. Wimbridge, then Macgrath, and finally Judge who remained to sleep. Macgrath thinks seriously of joining us and going to India.

H.S.O. rec'd from H.C.C. pamphlet on Bhuts and letter.

August 7. Wimbridge to dinner. Evening, Paris and Mr. Tows.

September 11. Wimb. prepared H.P.B.'s portrait for engraving. — Marble dined with us. Then after dinner, McCarthy, Samuels, who wants to join us, Mrs. Morell and Stone (the stony spiritual idiot). Pamphlet received from Hurry C. by a Southern lady—an "old friend" of his. She —a *Christian.*

October 9. All day ringing of the bell. Mrs. C. Daniels came and remained two hours bothering. O'Donovan went on with the sculpting. Mrs. D. made love to O'D. and the latter returned. He dined here. She went away sighing that her husband dies not. Evening. O'D. and W. and H.P.B. alone. Letters to H.S.O. and H.P.B. with portraits and official letter from Lippitt.[29] Consents to accept Fellowship. Write letter the Revd. Ayton, *Oxford,* Vicarage.—Letter from Stainton Moses. Flapdoodle.

Neuralgia ! ! ! Will frighten it off to-night.

October 10. H.P.B. wrote article for Petersburg.—O'Donovan whole day. Mrs. O'Grady came to dinner.—Letter from Rochelle, from van der Linden.[30] Enthusiastic and prepares to send his mite of $1.25 every month to the Arya Samaj. Asks whether he ought not to learn Sanskrit or Pali. Saw Rev. Hoysington the blind lecturer. Agreed with him to preach and stir up the Brahma in the West. Letter from Evans (Philadelph) want to order a Society pin (badge) for himself but is too stingy. Asks how much. Answered, and sent him off to H.S.O.—

Evening. O'Donovan, O'Grady, Wm., Macgrath, Mrs. Daniels and Ayre. Kept them all in the dining room. Wrote article. Mrs. D. brought her picture. Sent a Theos. Circular to Revd. Scudder, Brooklyn, and wrote a greeting in Tamil at a corner of the envelope.

October 11. Article.—O'Donovan and plastering. Made a bunion on H.P.B.'s *nose* on the plaster. Dined here. After dinner Curtis came to finish article on the disposal of Palm's ashes. Wrote in the closet room. Finished article. Began another.

No letter from H.S.O. to W.'s great surprise. Told him that H.P.B. saw one coming, which had an orange and golden atmosphere around it. O'Donovan finished his *bas-relief* and took it home.[31]

Neuralgia ! ! Damn it. All on account of the premature withdrawing and selling off of the carpet. Damn D—.

H.P.B. wrote to Mrs. Corson.[32] No use introducing her to Madame von Vay, as poor Wittgenstein[33] is dead and she is with his family.

October 12. Letter from one who is impudent enough to sign himself M ∴ Junior ! ! ! What next? Prophecy fulfilled. Letter from E.K. sends a circular from Constant in Smyrna and recommends him for a Theosophist. All right. Captain Burton[34] elected *Fellow* of the T.S. of Great Britain. Judge turned up.

Evening: Wilder came and dined. Went away at 9. H.P.B. talked with W. alone till 2 after midnight. He confessed he saw *three distinct* individualities in her. He *knows* it. Does not wish to say so to Olcott for fear H.S.O. will make fun of him ! ! ! ! !

October 13. Jenny went off at 7 leaving to Wim. a parting note. "Called away upon important business. Will be back tomorrow." *No* breakfast—Wim. boiled two eggs and made coffee. *Tom*[35] came at 10. Went off at 1 with Wim. —Wimb. came back at 3. Marble. Prepared cold dinner. At 8 Wim. went away to join Tom at theatre to hear Wilhelmj, the violinist. Louis came. Then Mr., Mrs. and Miss Lackey. H.P.B. wrote answer to the *Sun*, on the infamous editorial which can hurt H.S.O., make Kali[36] pounce on him and Xtians refuse him their money.

Evening. Batchelor, Maynard, Wing. Mrs. Parker[37] brought three Spts. Dr. Pike,—W. H. Pruden and Mrs. E. Hallet from Boston. Pike looking at H.P.B. several times, started and said that no one in the whole world impressed him as much. Once saw in H.P.B. a girl of 16, at another an old woman of 100,—and again a man with a beard ! ! Wim. and Tom returned at 11 from theatre. Tom is here yet with W. and O'Donovan in the dining room chatting and it is ¼ to 4 after midnight. O'Don. brought plaster cast, and it is the portrait of Mrs. Winchester ! ! ! Will correct it tomorrow. Afraid for H.S.O. and his business.

Lackey drunk—evidently.

October 14. Magnificent news! Letters from Massey[38] and Billing.[39] C. C. Blake at the last Theosophical meeting accused *us* of N. Y. and the Arya Samaj of practicing Siva worship—performing the Linga and Sakti Puja ! ! ! What next? Wrote to C. C. M. and Wim. wrote also expressing disgust. Wrote to H.S.O. to come home. H.P.B. wrote to E.K.—and this letter will be the last.

If H.S.O. not ready, *I* have to go.

O'Donovan dined and *demanded* beer.

Evening. Macgrath and his clairvoyant Doctor—a good looking female. Miss Lackey called. H.P.B. wrote to Hurry C. C. and sent copy of Massey's letter. Let him answer.

October 15. H.P.B. wrote to Billing and Thomas—denying the calumny, and calling Carter Blake an "infamous liar." Aired H.P.B. along the streets for two hours.

H.S.O. succeeded in writing a French postal-card. First wrote *mille*, very correctly, then crossed it out and put *mil*, which is not. His first inspiration always better. Sent to H.S.O. Massey's and Billing's letters. ORDERS received for him to create an indignation meeting whether in reality or fancy. On his obeying depends much. H.S.O. expects to get $5,000.

Evening. Curtis and Weisse. Looks ill. H.P.B. is afraid he won't last long. Finished his book and mentions in it three times H.P.B.'s *Isis*; calls it one of the grandest productions of the 19th century.

H.P.B. sent a telegram to Massey, Athenaeum Club, London "*Infernal lie*" ! ! and paid 5 dollars in gold. Money furnished by M∴.

October 16. Letter from H.S.O. Did not yet receive the registered letter with Massey and Billing's letters. Ordered to write to him. M∴ came and raved. Well, I do not wonder.

Wrote the letter to H.S.O. and Ditton.

Tom came and dined before going to theatre.

Evening. Wrote letter of profession of faith to H.C.C. Mrs. Esther Hallet, Dr. Pike, Dr. W. H. Pruden and Miss ———?, a friend of Miss Monachesi. Want to join the T.S.

Took in the afternoon *Isis* to Dunlop's Express Co. with introduction letter from Curtis to Dunlop. Visited W. Q. Judge. Went with him and not having found Dunlop left the Isis to his care. Expressage to Paris only $2.—?? Got an aerial drive there and back. Saw Townsend.

October 17. Letter from Bouton demanding portrait. All ready. Letter from Hoisington and—Hurrychund to Olcott. Marble brought his portrait and dined. Curtis came before and is going to stay all night. Writes article for the *Star* on cremation. *No* letters from H.S.O. Found a postal card in French from—H.S.O. received apparently on Monday, and which Jenny forgot to hand to me. Wimb. found it in the kitchen. O America, oh, servants of America! H.P.B. received a newspaper from Australia *Avoca Mail* with her article translated from Aksakoff on Zöllner and Slade.[40] Sent by Litoner or some such thing.

If H.S.O. does not write we will kill him—the heartless wretch!

October 18. H.P.B.'s article in the *Sun* with stupid editorial. Letters from H.S.O. to Massey and C. C. Blake. Telegraphed for Judge, he came half an hour after that.— Mrs. Daniels came and forced to send a blank application to Hayden the editor in Providence. I wrote to him for $5. Always main chance first. Tom came and upset my rest. Dined. Went away. Paid the $ initiation.

Evening passed with Wimbridge. Blues and crisles for India. Letter from Bloede, congratulating for article in the Sun.

October 19. Letter from E.K. and from H.S.O. to Swamee. H.P.B. wrote her explanation to Massey. A Miss Potter, tall, young, intellectual, daughter of a millionaire came with a card of introduction from E.K., London. Insisted upon seeing me. Lived half her life in Herbert Spencer's family. Knows Huxley and Tyndall. Interested in theosophy, doubts Spiritualism. She and her EIGHT sisters all Materialists. Herbert Spencer read *Isis* and found some beautiful pages and *new original* ideas. She is going to write to him about H.P.B. Says that E.K. is completely under C.C.B.'s influence. Colby and a Spiritualistic *idiot,* both sat three hours. Colby as spoony as sugar. Wants to send us paper to India.

Dinner. Tom and O'Donovan. H.P.B. bad humour. Townsend brought letters from Judge. Sent after Maynard, then they sit till 1 a.m. *Saddarshana Chintanika* came via Bombay and Hong Kong ! ! for H.S.O. and H.P.B. Time we should send them subscription money I should say.

October 20. Article in the *Sun* on the "Baron's Ashes" by Curtis. Sent Hurry C.C., Revd Mohottivati,[41] Otho Alexander, etc. Sent copies of official letters to Hurry C.C., and to Massey our protests. Gave all to Maynard to mail.—Good Fellow.—Marble before dinner. After dinner Mr. and Mrs. Evans from Philadelphia, Mrs. Parker,—Linda Dietz,—Curtis, O'Donovan, Maynard and Tom. Tom bought owl and paid for it. Evans said that H.S.O.'s business proceeded very fairly. He dined at Mathews and has prospect of work for $200. Good job. Linda Dietz wants to join Theosophy. Sent Tom's $5 to Hurry C. by Maynard. Couldn't help telling Wimb. that I felt H.S.O. coming home—his atmosphere very close. He ought to be very near coming. 2 a.m. now, therefore my prophecy is not for Sunday. Well we will see tomorrow. Wimb. thinks not.

October 21. No letter from Mr. Olcott. *Spiritualist* announcing death of Prince E. Wittgenstein, and copying our *Rules* of the Arya Samaj in full, without commentaries.

The *Sun* gives a short thrust to the Baron's ashes but speaks rather flatteringly than otherwise.

Telegram from Moloney.—Means to sleep at home tonight. Therefore I was right to feel the old boy near. Atmosphere does not agree with ME. As for H.P.B. splendid.

Letters from India, from H.C.C. to H.P.B., to Wimb. and H.S.O. Letter from Mooljee to H.P.B. and papers. Dear H.C.C. is he not bamboozled. Books safe. H.S.O. returned from Philadelphia. Has good hopes.

October 22. Instead of going to business at 9—H.S.O. went at 12. Visits came—Mrs. Hallet and Mr. Somebody.— None received. Won't have them. O'Donovan came and had dinner with us. After dinner Harrisse.—H.P.B. left them all in the dining room and retired with H.S.O. in the library to write letters. H.S.O. wrote to Hurrychund and Miss E. Kislingbury. *Narayan*[42] left watch—and in came *Sahib.*[43]

The latter with *orders* from Serapis[44] to complete all by the first days of December. Not to change one particle of Blodget's plans, etc. Well,—H.S.O. is just playing his great final stake.

October 23. And playing it successfully so far. Got names of 13 of best men in N. Y. to a carefully drawn paper which is to be used to help form the Syndicate and to secure the appointment from the alleged President. Sent papers to Blodget for his approval.

Tom Cowell dined with us and was seen to the theatre by Wimb. who went then to the Tile Club.[45]

Evening. Came Mr., Mrs. and Miss Lakey, and a Lieutenant Harkins, 2nd Infantry, U.S.A., who has read Isis and seems a decent sort of fellow.

October 24. Waiting to hear Blodget's decision about change of Syndicate paper.

Went to see Belle and found her poorly. She moves to Orange to live next Tuesday.

Curtis dined with us and worked on article on Mme. Shevitch.

Evening. Received Pall Mall Gazette on Oct. 9 and 11 with C. C. Blake's Jesuitical insult to the Arya Samaj and C. C. Massey's defence of that Society.

H.P.B. wrote H.C.C. about this, enclosing copies of the two paragraphs and of letter today received from Blake accepting Diploma of T.S. of A.S. ! !

She also wrote Blake a stinging letter in reply to same, and sent copy to H.C.C.

I wrote H.C.C. to send Donald Kennedy's Saddarshana Chintanika to care Baring Bros. and Co., London, and postal card to Massey to send Spst of Apr. 12 (fakir portrait) to H.C.C.

Friday October 25. The Syndicate slowly germinates.

O'Donovan, Wimb., H.P.B. and I were at dinner when Jenny brought in a letter from Massey, left at the moment by the postman. Before it came, H.P.B. announced its coming and nature, and when I received it and before the seal was broken she said it contained a letter from Dr. Wyld, and read that too, without looking at it. Massey's 1st page contained a message to me from *the Divine Brother*,[46] so I returned that page to Massey with a narration of particulars and Wimb's certificate added.

H.P.B. wrote letter to Wyld, and others to Carter Blake and C.C.M.

Visitors. Mrs. Barranco and Mr. Thompson—the latter a big, two-fisted *medium*.

October 26. Germination continues.

Received two letters from C.C.M. about Blake matter, one enclosing a letter of B.'s as Jesuitical as possible, and also B.'s second paragraph in P.M. Gazette of 13th.

Evening. Visitors. G. V. Maynard, D. L. Pike (healer), Capt. David Dey, Mrs. Bacon (of Boston), Mrs. Gridley an ex-professional medium, Mrs. Hallett of Boston, and Mons. Frank Daulte, Private Secretary to Chief Justice Daly of the Court of Common Pleas. M. Daulte made application and was initiated into T.S.

October 27. The Sabbath! The Lord's (not Lord Beaconfield's) Day.
"This is the Day the Lord has made.
He calls the hours His own."

Worked like the devil all day at cooking, setting the table, washing dishes, etc.

Wrote H.C.C. more about Blake case, sending him extracts from correspondence bet. Massey and Blake, and C.C.M.'s comments on "the little Brown Man."

H.P.B. wrote Massey and sent copies of the Sun, containing my reply to the Pall Mall Gazette article on the A.S., as well as the Sun's own Editorial of the previous day, to H.C.C. and others.

Evening. Mrs. Daniels, Marble, O'Donovan, Tom, Mr. Shinn. Delivered to Mrs. Daniels her Diploma and also that of D. F. Hayden, Editor of the Providence Press, Prov., R.I. Gave her a paper empowering her to initiate Mr. Hayden.

Shinn and others looked over all the photo. albums.

October 28. Canvassing for Syndicate continued. Good prospects.

Evening. O'Donovan, Wimb., Ranee and I went to Broadway Theatre to see Miss Von Stamwitz in "Messalina, Empress of Rome." Comical.

Afterwards. Wrote letter to Ed., Pall Mall Gazette threatening to publish the story of the little Brown Man if he didn't do the square thing. Also to C.C.M. forwarding the above and requesting him to hand it personally to Greenwood.

October 29. Canvassing continued. Brewster and Co., join Syndicate. Frank Daulte called.

Evening. Went to Union Sq. Theatre to see "Mother and Son." Saw Tom for the first time on the stage. Looked her part well.

Sent photo No. 2 of group to Mohottiwatte Gunananda and Otho Alexander.

October 30. Judge in the morning. All day alone.
Dinner. Tom and Linda Dietz, O'Donovan.
Evening. H.S.O. gone to Philadelphia. H.P.B. remained alone with Charles [47] who purred all the evening near the fire. Wimb. went Tile Club and returned at 1 a.m.

October 31. Ditson—letter and photo sent from Albany. —Judge writes to Dear— wants to know whether his vision of a party come to bribe him into betraying the T.S. was a *reality*. And whether Poodi's bell, who rang his chimes on his upper lip was sent by any of us. Answered both. Went to see Macgrath and Wimb. Came back and found A. Wilder and Prof. Woodward of the Medical College. Latter got enchanted by H.P.B.'s unsophisticated graces and both remained to dinner. Then after dinner came Marquette and took her diploma. Went away. Wimb. sick—got the chills. Daulte came and passed evening, then Batchelor and Tomlinson. No letters.

November 1. A postal card from H.S.O.—When can I get Curtis to write about Sosiosh.[48] No one whole day. Wimb. bad cold, remained at home. Dined alone with him, thank goodness! Evening five double bells *and no one,*— mistake, except another card from H.S.O.; wants his black leather portfolio with certificates. Sent with Wimb. by express. H.P.B. finished her article for *Pravda*.

November 2. H.S.O. writes to say he comes back.— Thus his black portfolio need not be sent to Philadelphia. H.P.B. went to 60th St. 23 to see Mrs. Rhine but found her not for she went to try and get brother to 18th Street at Mr. Pollock—her brother-in-law. Talked with Mrs. Barnett an hour or so, and then H.P.B. returned home on foot through the Park. Lovely day. Sat under the trees near the pond and caught chill.

Came home at 3 and found Belle Mitchell—poor, dear soul! Miss Bates came home. Letter from Hurrychund. Thinks we are going directly and writes but two words. Well... Vediamo!

H.S.O. turned up at 7 and reports good progress. A friend of Wim's, Mr. Gus Petri, came. He is a kind-hearted psychological fellow. Has gift of prophecy and vision. Foretold H.P.B.'s death at sea suddenly. Doubted that she would reach Bombay. Hinted shipwreck for us all, in which Wim and I would be saved and H.P.B. lost! Goak!

November 3. Wrote business letters to further Syndicate affair.

Evening. Tom, Batchelor, O'Donovan, Marble and the Bombay quartette.

November 4. Secured subscriptions of Brewster & Co., and Valentine & Co., T. C. Howell & Co., leather, offered me a consignment of $500 worth of leather. Or that if I got them one order from Bombay or Calcutta they would subscribe.

Evening. Batchelor, Curtis and the Bombay 4.

Today received Curtis's article on Dyanand Saraswati in Rev. Dr. Deems' "Sunday Magazine."

November 5. Silence. Letter from Evans, wants to come on Monday and be initiated. Answered.

Evening.—Dr. Pike.

November 6. Mrs. Thompson came. Sniffled. H.P.B. "guessed" wouldn't buy anything more.

Evening. Wim. went to Tile Club. Alone with Miss Bates.

November 7. Worked all day. Letter from Otho Alexander. Letters from Hurry Ch. Sends portraits of various princes and "Fellows." Holkar's also. Says he grows with every day fonder of H.P.B. Curtis dinner; writes article for Herald on the *four Saviours*.

Evening. Curtis, Harrisse—Daulte brings portrait and self-writing pen.—Jack Passit, gave diploma to him and made him pay $5. Promised to bring rich man to give toward fund of the Arya Samaj.

No letters from *Junior*.

November 8. Letter from Junior—not a damned thing in it. Curtis came at 12 and wrote his article on the 4 *Saviours* for *Herald*. *Lunch*: Letters from Massey—E. K.—declares she will stick by C.C.B. and asks *mercy* for him ! ! She be damned. Massey dissatisfied because the Billings, Wyld and Thomas *won't* have C.C.B. for a Fellow. Letter from Thomas; a good and honest one. Sent both to Hurrychund. Wrote to him—answer.

Evening.—All alone—only Maynard. Worked.

November 9. Body sick and no hot water to bathe it. Nice caboose. Worked all day. Belle Mitchell came and kept company with us for three hours—dear and pure soul.

Letter from Junior. Becomes a lecturer. Aye. Returns Monday. It's time; and leaves half-things undone in Boston. So says—*Senior.*[49]

Evening. The sad Gay lord, from Brooklyn. Assembly of women. Mrs. Haskell with Mrs. Longstreet—a literary lady, —Dr. Pike with Mrs. Mary Don and Mrs. L. L. Denny from Georgia South. Then Mrs. Hallet. Miss Bates saved me by entertaining them.

November 10. Morning.—Maynard called and brought his little girl. Dinner 3.

After dinner Marble,—Curtis,—Pike,—Blackmore, Mrs. Hallet,—Tom.

Evening ditto. Pike fell into a trance and gave flapdoodle. Curtis played at *Manfred*. No *Peck*. Botheration of a cold.

Pike asked Miss B. whether H.P.B. had money; then whether Wim. could lend him some. Having received negative answers to all his questions he departed disgusted.

November 11. Very big cold.—Afternoon at 5 p.m. a man came; would not allow Jenny to announce him and gave no name; forced himself after her, and introduced himself—very strangely. An old, respectable white-haired party. As soon as seated, he mildly declared that he had come to *subpoena* H.P.B. in the Vanderbilt case ! ! H.P.B. told him she did not know the Commodore, *never* saw him. Yet, the old party served her with a paper in which the "people of New York State" commanded the new citizen to appear in the court of the Surrogate and say all she knew; after which he delivered to her on behalf of "the people" a silver dollar, gave hell to Beecher, and said the old Commodore was no better, paid compliments, said that Mr. Lord had charged him to tell H.P.B. that they would give her "plenty of money" *if she helped them* to win the case and—departed.

Evans of Washington did not come.

November 12. Fearful sleepless night on account of the cold and coughing. Got up at 8, sent for a carriage and went 258 Broadway to Lord's office; was received politely and *cuddled;* declared (H.P.B.) she knew nothing; but was asked to *remember,* and *try to think of something* ! ! Was asked to go to court, and *promised* money again.

H.P.B. went to court and produced sensation being seated on witness's chair. William Vanderbilt and lawyers stared at her all the time. Would not swear on the Bible and declared herself a—*heathen.* Disgusted went away. Vanderbilt's lawyer ran after her, and tried to make friends; was sent to Hell. Her carriage was followed by *another carriage.* Will wait developments. Judge at dinner.

Evening Mr. and Mrs. O'Sullivan. Theological and anti-Christian conversation. H.P.B. played a trick on them by suddenly *fainting* to the great dismay of Bates and Wim. Used the greatest willpower to put up the body on its legs.

Letter from C. Daniels. Wants biography for a series of Boston *Index* or something else of articles on H.P.B.

November 13.   Moloney back.
Brought letters from H.C.C. and Shyamjee.—Sick. Answered letters. Miss Bates posted letter to Vera Jelihovsky[50] and H. C. Chintamon. Marble took off the canopy and made himself generally useful.

November 14.   Same.
Curtis at dinner.
Evening. Dr. Pike and Mrs. Hallet. Gaylord came in for a moment. Naray decamped and Morya walked in—broken finger and all. Came with definite orders from Serapis. *Have to go;* the latest from 15 to 20th Dec. Wimb. bothered by lawsuit, very gloomy.

Declared intentions to Bates and Wim. Taffy—Bates going to London before us. On the 1st probably.

O God, O Indra of the golden face! Is this really the beginning and the end!

November 15. Cobb spent the evening with me in the dining-room, but would not see H.P.B.

November 16. Curtis to dine and got points for Sun article on the auction.
Maynard and Dr. Baruch, a mystical Hebrew physician. A strange,

very strange man. Has a prescience as to visitors' death and a spiritual insight as to disease. Old, thin, stooped; his thin, fine, grizzled hair stands out every way from his noble head. Rouges his cheeks to relieve their natural pallor. Has a habit of throwing his head far back and looking up into space, as he listens or converses. His complexion waxen, skin transparent and as thin as tissue paper. Wears thin Summer clothes in the depth of winter, Peculiar habit to say, when answering: "Vell, see he-ere, tee-ar!"

November 17. Visitors evening. Curtis, Dr. Pike, Mrs. Hallet, Mr. Dye (Nibs—the Infant Prodigy), Tom Cowell, Linda Dietz, O'Donovan, M.∴ read the girls' fortunes in cards (?) to their considerable astonishment.

November 18. Letters today from C.C.M., Carter Blake (2), Palmer Thomas, Dr. Wyld (with his photo), O. Alexander, and others.

November 19. To dinner Paris (just back from Colorado) and Marble besides our quartette.

Evening. Mr. and Mrs. Maynard, Mrs. Dr. Edward Bradley, escorted by Batchelor, Curtis and Marble.

Dad pulled out and gave Taffy a lock of hair—the kind that looks to the missionaries like the edge of a thundercloud! Major Poud-hi rang his bell for the first time in months.

November 20. Letter from Mr. Blodget encouraging me about Syndicate and promising that the papers shall be forthcoming from Washington.

H.P.B. received from Revd. W. Ayton, Vicar of Chacombe, Eng., the MSS of his translation of J. Trithemius's prophecies.

Evening: Held the Vedic ceremony of casting the Baron de Palm's ashes into the sea. A highly interesting episode. Our mysterious Hindoo Brother ∴ was present with his helper [...]⁵¹ H.S.O. cast the ashes into the waters of N. Y. Bay at exactly 7:45 p.m.

November 21. Wim. in trouble from a blackmailing lawyer in the matter of the Photo Plate Co.

In Sun, Curtis's description of the ash ceremony of last evening. Evening Telegram copies it and pretends it is its own enterprise that secured it! Taffy⁵² all astral tears from dread of Wim.'s being arrested. Orders from Headquarters to sail on December 7th or 17th, and to pack up at once.

Evening. Mr. Daulte and Batchelor here. The former put $3 silver into Arya Samaj fund.

November 22. Wim. dodging the sheriff's writ and baffling the blackguards who want to lock him up. Curtis dined and worked on his article on the auction at the Lamasery.

Two spiritualists called but were turned off. No other visitors.

Bought Taffy's ticket to Liverpool by the Wisconsin Tuesday next—Price $30.

November 23. Sent third and last photograph to Mohottiwatte Gunananda and Otho Alexander. Mrs. Fowler-Wells called in the evening and confided to us certain designs of old Joe Buchanan which make me laugh. His game is so transparent.

November 24. All hands packing trunks preparatory to Taffy's departure tomorrow evening.

Evening. Mr., Mrs. and Miss Lakey, Batchelor, Mrs. Hallett, Mr. Shinn, Macgrath, 3 Italians (one the friend of Chaille Long).

November 25. Skirmishers to the front! Taffy went aboard ship this evening, and Wim. and I in parting left her in tears. Mr. A. H. Underhill, Freight Manager of the Guion Line was aboard and kindly interfered with the ship's officers to have Taffy well looked after. Two trunks of H.P.B.[53] went by same vessel to L'pool to await our arrival.

O'Donovan and A. Gustam dined with us, and after dinner they two and Wim. and I measured heights of body sitting on the floor backs against wall. I never saw this curious experiment before, and was amused and surprised at the result. Wim's legs were 5 or 6 inches longer than Gustam's and mine, while his body was more than half a head shorter.

November 26. Had a delightful interview with Mrs. Willcox, who feels the same as ever and will be a most useful ally in a certain quarter.

News from Hartmann that Westbook has decided the Albany case in favour of the Receiver. Thus two card prophecies made last evening of Taffy are already fulfilled.

Wrote Mooljee to receive samples of goods shipped by the Syndicate to his care.

November 27. Bright prospects for Syndicate. Had a very valuable talk with Henry Lewis about Reading R. Rd contribution and at his request wrote him a letter to lay before the Reading Board.

Evening. Call from James R. Heenan of the National Assd Press, 145 Broadway, on behalf of the Boston Globe, and gave him the points about the Holmes mediums (?). Batchelor also called. Wim. at Tile Club.

November 28. Thanksgiving Day—and my last in the U.S.

I dined with Emmet R. Olcott[54] at 2 and took the 4½ p.m. boat for Fall River.

Wim. brought Pietri and Macgrath to dinner. H.P.B. had dinner at 3.

Marble turned in, and as Jenny[55] went away made himself as useful as he is ornamental.

Evening. Pietri laid out cards for H.P.B. Prognosticated delay for departure but safe arrival to Bombay. Also death through murder for H.P.B. in 8 years, at the age of 90 (!!). Nothing like clairvoyance.

Mrs. Haskell—and daughter, a Mrs. Parsons, and Dr. Pike. Talked H.P.B. to death.

From 10½ alone with Wim. Go to bed directly.

Paid Jenny 5.

November 29. Morning.—Letters from Mrs. Daniels, a Mr. J. D. Dr. Buck, Cincinnati, 305 Rose St.—wants to join Society (answered and circular sent), and Wilder.

Had seven letters to write and *no* money and *no* stamps. Had to call Sahib.—Got fearfully mad.—Well, it is no fault of mine. Alas! poor "Junior"—if he only knew what he does not know. If he reads this—let him remember—*à bon entendeur salut*. M∴ gave 50 cents for stamps.

Answered the Russian aunt; Buck, Wilder, Daniels—wrote for portraits to Hayden and Brown. Wrote Judge likewise.

Dinner. Enlivened by a telegram from Judge to Wimb. Tells him "to wait for him early in the morning, important news";—perhaps arrest! If so, Wimb. will have to clear out before us to London. Let him go to France.

Evening. Blues—crisles and other piggish feelings.—

Our solitary Curtis—rang dumb-waiter bell at nearly 11. Told that Dana was opposed to having a new article about "the Madam"—and so Curtis took his article on the "Lottery in the Lamasery" to the *World*.

November 30. Belle Mitchell came at 12, and took away the Sahib for a walk and drive. Went to Macy's. Had to materialize rupees. H.P.B. came home at 4. No one at dinner but Paris.

After dinner. Paris signed an application and went off with his violin to a party. Wim. also went off and returned at 2 p.m.

Evening. Maynard—helped the *orphlin* to pass time and made himself generally useful. Mrs. Wells came and brought a heap of Phrenol. Journals.

A letter brought from Judge by Wimbridge from office. H. C. Chintamon writes a declaration of love and sends official letter to the Council through H.P.B. *Snubs* them all very politely.

Letter from E. Kislingbury with *resignation* in it. Too Christian! Too *Blakian* I should say. Oh this villainous brood! When shall we be rid of it!

December 1. About—from 17 to 23 days left. We will see how the *Junior* will be ready!

HIS FATE DEPENDS ON THAT[56]

Morning, H.P.B. in bath, heard H.S.O.'s melodious voice—the Junior had returned from Providence. Got "Tool Company" to sign for $500. Saw Hayden, the latter coming here Saturday.

Furniture and rest *must* be sold or disposed of before the 12th. ORDERS.

Dinner. The faithful Marble turned in. Now O'Donovan and Batchelor. Who next? H.P.B. answered H.C.C. Bombay. He will receive the letter a fortnight before her arrival. All right.

Evening. Mr. and Mrs. Maynard, "Tom," Marble, Batchelor, O'Donovan, Curtis, Col. Chaille Long.

December 2. Letters from H. J. Billing,—Palmer Thomas, and a fool from Chicago—Stanley Sexton, 2 Park Row.—The latter demands to join the T.S. and to take *"three times three"* degrees from the first. Enquires whether H.P.B. saw or felt this magnetic subject's *double* five months ago. The *ass!* Answered all the letters.

Fearful rain. Wimb. did not go to the office but lounged in the arm chair by H.P.B.'s side and slept soundly. H.S.O. gone this morning to Philadelphia. His last and conclusive trip he says. Well—may I.—speed him.[57] Paris at dinner.

Evening. A Mr. Thompson from Montreal, Ex-clergyman

whose eyes were opened to the fraud of Xtianity; who read *Isis,* "learned much in it," and was bound to see its author. Harrisse came, disgusted at Thompson's serious talk, walked off into dining-room and retired early. Found the Rosy Cross Jewel[58] missing from the bureau drawer. *Know who took it.* It will come back.[59] Daulte came in late and put $3 into Arya Samaj fund. Noble man!

December 3. Letters from Evans (Wash.) gushes—flapdoodles and winds up by saying that it is his *kismet* fate to join us in India.

Went for Sahib's errand today.

Marble brought album, and fixed day for auction sale on Tuesday next Dec. 10. Judge at dinner.

Evening. Letter postal card from Miss Ellen Burr—sends 10 copies with Mrs. D's article in. Profession of regret at departure. Curtis, Judge, Wimb., and H.P.B. produces a charm.—Mrs. Wells comes for her talisman; receives it; makes a present of a new book with H.P.B.'s portrait in it as a Lama. Wimb. decorates it with moustache and beard. H.P.B. gives to Mrs. Wells the two vases.

December 4. 10 copies of Hartford *Daily Times* at hand. Gushing and flattering article. Sent copies to Bombay, *London*—(Massey and Thomas), Corfu and Washington to disconsolate Evans. Postal card from Ammi Brown. Will send photo,—if not ready—to India.—Postal card from H.S.O., writes of great success—went last night to Washington. *Vediamo.* Last night Judge slept here. H.P.B. went out for postage stamps—another third row with *Sahib.*

Cheek swollen again. A row with Jenny. Claims $9 owed her by H.S.O. from Wim. and H.P.B. Neither could satisfy her. W. gave her $2, and she swore that her landlord would put her on sidewalk. Can't help it. Somewhat able to get money for *"body"* and our needs—for Jenny—*no orders.*

Wrote to Miss F. E. *Burr* asking for portrait and thanking for papers.

Dinner. Telegram from W. Q. Judge to Wimb. "Motion denied," etc. W. in despair and prison crisles again. Time to clear out.

Evening. Mrs. Haskell of 116 West 29th St. with daughter, a young girl studying medicine; brought a Mrs. Elizabeth K. Churchill from Providence, editorial writer—going *to write us up,* and Miss Alice C. Fletcher, and Dr. Bennett, a *psychic* Doctor (whatever it means). Mrs. Haskell invites H.P.B. after breaking up home to come and sleep at her home and pass a few days with her.—Letters from Hurrychund.

December 5. Judge came early. The only thing he asks Wimb. to do is to keep quiet till his departure; but our Don Quixote *cannot* promise it. Well, if he gets into jail it will be his own fault, and then—good-bye. No waiting. Letter from Junior to M. Has good hopes of making his *entrée* into Bombay with the Govt. seal stamped upon his back side.[60] *Vediamo.* Got samples of ore for M ∴—so much the less trouble for [. . .][61]

Letter from Mrs. Ames. Supplicates to come and see her. Says *her Ned* is overjoyed at the idea. Don't feel like it—don't feel at all!

Taffy in Liverpool, we suppose.—12 days more! Marble came. Carpentering over the broken chair to make it look respectable at the auction sale.

Sale Tuesday next. He passed the whole afternoon preparing all, hanging picture frames and taking notes. Good and honest soul. Wimb. went away after dinner to pack up. H.P.B. remained alone with Marble, then came Daulte and remained till 12.

December 6. A letter from Richard and Boag informing of the arrival from Russia of a parcel. Went down town with Wimb.

Just come from Rich. and Boag. Received Mme. Jelihovsky's book and papers; also letter stating in despair that *no* parcel had arrived yet from America! And this on the 29th of October, five months after it was sent ! ! Olcott has to see, or get insurance money back.

We got cold again, I think. Oh, unfortunate, empty, rotten old body!

After dinner Wimb. was sorely surprised by the arrival

of Sinclair and Moses. Thought they were going to arrest him. They came for a compromise. If he does not make a fool of himself he will be free of all trouble tomorrow.—He plays his *last* card.

Evening. Pike and Hallet. Wimb. went to his office. When at 12 they wanted to go home, the door downstairs could not be opened! Latch and knob were broken. They returned and sat till 2. At last H.P.B. suggested that a policeman should be called through kitchen window, and he broke door and so liberated them. Wimb. came home half past two.

December 7. No letters from H.S.O. A letter from Miss Ellen F. Burr, with a dollar enclosed in it for my portrait. Cannot give hers as it always represents her as *if drunk*. Wants me to write for their paper from India. Have to go and have some made—today.

Letter from Billing—says a voice was heard in their drawing-room which told them there were but four theosoph. in London who should be taught by him theosophy,—when asked who he was—answered: "One of the Brothers from India." Thomas was present.

Judge came this morning. Last night went to Tiflis, and learnt that parcel *was* just received finally, and that Mme. Jelihovsky had sold her bird for 30 roubles! She must have been starving.

Wimb. wound up matters—all safe now. Sold monkey and brought money. H.P.B. with Marble the whole day preparing for auction. Bought a stateroom trunk, 4 doll. Had photos taken $3 a dozen.

Evening. Letters from Otho Alexander, Nicolaides and three for Olcott. Marble, Batchelor and Thompson from Montreal.

December 8. Miss Potter came and she, H.P.B. and Wimb. went all to photographer. H.P.B. was taken with Wim., a *group!!* Miss Potter will call on Tuesday again.

We write from the closet room, anciently occupied by H.S.O. where Marble drove us in under the pretext of auction. Sent *Stars* with Curtis' article on H.P.B.'s lottery to

Hurrychund, Mooljee, Thomas and Otho Alexander, also letter to Vera Jelihovsky.

Pike was first to make his appearance—and welcome; for Jenny went away at three, and Marble drove me nearly crazy fidgeting.

Evening Visitors. Blackmore and Clough—latter wants his diploma. Then Curtis, Maynard with a Captain Hommons (a mystic and seer and a Rosicrucian). Then *Tom*, with Wimb. and O'Donovan, finally Paris—broke gas lamp and carried off lots of rubbish— Marble went to sleep on four chairs with no mattress in dining room.

Tomorrow good-bye all. But — will H.S.O. be ready? That's the question. One, only *one* week more! God help him if he fails . . . . [. . . . .][62]

December 9. Went to bed at four and was aroused at 6—thanks to Marble, who locked the door and Jennie could not get in. Got up breakfasted and went off to meet [. . . .][63]—Battery. Came home at 2. Most infernal row and hullaballoo at auction. All went for a song, as they say in America. If Marble surpassed himself in kindness he did the same in zeal. He sold at auction Levi's,—the landlord's three window shades for 50 cents ! ! !

Curtis came to look out for an article on the sale. Levi the landlord came and demanded his money believing H.P.B. was going away with the furniture. The grocer insulted Jenny and saying that over $100 being due to him he would not trust for one penny more. Elegant.—

Auctioneer took big clock—promised to sell for 60 dollars.

Capt. Hommons came with Maynard,—gave N:[64] the grip and password of the Madagascar [. . . .][65] and therefore was accepted as a Fellow, signed the obligation, paid Maynard $5 initiation to be sent to Hurrychund and went off.

5 o'clock—*Everything gone.* Baron de Palm—adieu.

Evening. Curtis came to write article. Marble prostrated. Wimb. gone office.—Evans from Philadelphia turns up to fetch *me!* Impossible. Suddenly H.S.O. makes his appearance. Bosses and patronises Wimb. at night until the latter becomes raving mad! H.S.O. calls the [. . . .][66] "old horse."

December 10. We breakfast on a board three inches wide. Letter from Daniels and Evans. Article in *Herald* "Mad. *Blavatsky*" appears. A reporter from the Graphic comes to interview H.P.B. Is respectfully begged to go to the devil.

H.P.B. writes to Buck, Cincinnati,—to Ellen Burr, Hartford,—and to Hyde and sends him back his diploma. Two rich Jewesses, Mrs. and Miss Hoymen, produce a sudden siege and force themselves in. She wants to join the Society and signs application.

Evening. H.S.O. lends M ∴. 100 dollars.

December 11. Letters from Miss Burr. Marble flapdoodling all day.

Visitors, visitors, visitors.

H.S.O. lends Morya $100.

Went out on a jamboree with Judge.

December 12. Letters,—from everywhere. H.S.O. goes Orange to Belle, and H.P.B. has teeth extracted and does not go. Send replies and buy things.

Evening.—Curtis comes and invites to Fulton's theatre. Tom at dinner, and brings album. Marble flapdoodles and fidgets—sets me mad. Harrisse after dinner. Dr. Weisse brings his new book on philology and we remain at home. Doulton Fulton and the son of Stephen Pearl Andrews!

H.S.O. does not go to sleep at all and

December 13. [H.S.O.] goes to Menloe Park to Edison[67] about phonograph. H.P.B. sick; telegraphs to Belle Mitchell who comes from Orange and passes day with her.

Visitors, visitors. Articles in all papers. Mrs. Wells is initiated. Mrs. Ames comes with daughter and is also initiated. Curtis. Our photographs brought. Sent to Miss Burr to Thomas and Wyld, England.

Orders—go from Philadelphia. Kali suspects departure and thinks of arresting H.S.O. He receives his regular nomination from the Govt. and appointed commissioner with special passport. He has to go to Phil. on Monday or Tuesday too.

Never return to New York.

Judge and Wim. and H.S.O. and Morya in consultation till 4 a.m.

December 14. H.S.O. gone off early. Wimb. and Judge trying to help H.P.B. Today the trunks *must go.*—They do go—care of Hur. Chund, Bombay. So much the less. Tales feeling a sudden love for H.P.B. sends carriage and boy after her. Positive refusal.—Miss Potter came and wants to join Theosophical. Promises to send $5. *Vediamo.* Marble comes and—H.P.B. falls asleep.

H.S.O. returns with phonograph weiging 100 pounds. General Doubleday came.—Went away as he came. Wimb. on a jamboree with tile club men again. He takes it easy. Poor H.S.O. had barely the time to swallow three spoonfuls of soup and went off. H.P.B. dines alone with Charles purring and Marble jabbering. H.S.O. will have to go to Philadelphia. We send trunks by train on Monday night; and go—when H.S.O. writes he is ready. Wise determination of "old Horse."

Marble—fidgeted and sent telegram to A. C. Wilder. Tile Club gave Wimb. a dinner at *Monico's* Hotel. Wimb. DRANK.

Olcott back at 10— and passed evening writing letters. Sent Edison's photo to Constant [inople], Corfu and London. Phonograph whistles.[68].

December 15. Whole day packing up.

Dinner. Paris, Wimb., Tom, Marbles and Gustam.

Evening. Two Judges—Wm. and John.—The latter initiated. Wilder,—Dr. Weisse, Shin and Ferris, Two brothers Langham, Clough,—Curtis. Griggs came from Connect. to be initiated. O'Sullivan and Johnston of the phonograph. All sent speeches to the Brothers in India. Mrs. Wells, Mrs. Ames and daughter, Maynard, O'Donovan and a painter who came with Mrs. Ames.

Edison was represented by E. H. Johnson.

December 16. Packing up. H.P.B. went to O.'s office and destroyed papers. Changed money into English bank notes. Met at office Maynard, Marble, Griggs. Olcott came home after. Wimb. disappeared till 2 p.m.

Evening. Brosnan, brought presents to Olcott, Wilder, Dr. Gunn and Dr. Campbell, O'Sullivan and wife, Tomlinson, Maynard and wife.

Letters from Massey, Taffy and Billing.

December 17. Great day! Olcott packed up. At 10 he thought going to Phil. At 12 [....][69] stepped in and—as he [H.S.O.] would have no more money coming, and received his last $500 from Reading Co.—he concluded to send him off from New York tomorrow or the day after. Bouton came and gave three copies.—Dr. Weisse brought two copies also for the Bombay and Calcutta papers.

Marble fidgeted but made himself useful. Tom the whole day.

What next? All dark—but tranquil.

CONSUMMATUM EST[70]

Olcott returned at 7 with three tickets for the British steamboat the "Canada." Wrote letters till 11½. Curtis and Judge passed the evening. Maynard took H.P.B. to dinner to his home. She returned home at 9. Maynard made a present of a tobacco pouch. *Charles* lost ! ![71] At nearly 12 H.S.O. and H.P.B. took leave of the chandelier[72] and drove off in a carriage to the steamer, leaving Marble to sleep at home and wait for Wimbridge who was taking leave of Tom until a very late hour.

December 18. Passed last night on the "Canada." Got frozen, sleeping in wet blankets and passed a sleepless night, but S———[73] had the best of us and we did leave the American *soil* on the 17th. H.P.B. in trances of fear for H.S.O. (Kali) and Wimb. (Sinclair) who both had a right to prevent their leaving America—till the moment of departure. Instead of leaving at 11 the steamer left at 2½. Both *Judges* came on board. Curtis, Paris, O'Donovan,

FACSIMILE REPRODUCTION OF ONE OF THE PAGES OF H.P.B.'s DIARY.

Mac Grath, Tom. Maynard brought H.P.B. a silver tankard with the initials—Good fellow. Tom remained with O'Donovan till the last moment. Touching scene. He on deck she waiting on wharf. Poor girl, she really felt for *us*. At last we sailed off at 3,—ran three or four miles and—dropped anchor off Coney Island waiting for tide. H.P.B. who had begun breathing collapsed in fear again for Kali might hearing of H.S.O. departure on the 19th send after him, etc., etc. No *real* fear, but great exhaustion in order to ward off danger from H.S.O.

Evening. Made acquaintance with a Mrs. Wise, Capt. and Mrs. Payton, a Revd. and a young Mr. Wansborough. After tea theological dispute with the Rev.

December 19. Magnificent day. Clear, blue cloudless but —devilish cold. Fits of fear lasted till 11 (the body is difficult to manage—Spirit strong but flesh very weak). At last at 12½ the pilot took the steamer across the Sandy Hook bar. Fortunately we did not get stuck in the sand.

(No danger of that. O.)

All day eating—at 8, 12, 4 and 7. H.P.B. eats like three hogs. Wrote letters to Judge, Billing—London and Brosnan. Wimb. wrote to Tom. Yesterday morning Judge brought to me on the steamer Hurrychund's letter of Nov. 18, the last I will receive from him in America. (How very wise!)

December 20. Still splendid weather, wind abaft, and sea very quiet. Slight motion to ship, but not enough to speak of. Yet H.P.B. the only woman at table.

Last eve after tea had my first set-to with the Revd. Sturge (who has a mouth like a sturgeon). He's an eloquent, oily chap but apparently an easy antagonist to handle. The debate drew from Capt. Payton the admission that missionaries were an unmitigated nuisance. He believed they caused the Sepoy Mutiny.

December 21. Good weather. Little motion. Monotonous and stupid. Several tugs with the Revd. Sturge. Eating all day.

December 22. Weather changed. Wind and gale. Rain and fog. Came pouring into the saloon skylarks [? skylights]. Everyone seasick except Mrs. Wise and H.P.B. Captain Payton and the Revd played piano and Moloney sang songs.

December 23. The same. Only Moloney and Wimb. sick and flapdoodle all day. Weather cleared up.

Evening. After a beautiful day, a fearful gale. Captain telling fearful stories of shipwreck and drowning the whole evening. Mrs. Wise and Mrs. Payton frightened out of their wits.

December 24. Night of tossing and rolling. H.S.O. sick in bed.—Monotonous, stupid, wearisome. Oh for the land —oh for India and home!

COMPILER'S NOTES

[*These Notes correspond with the superior numbers in the text of H.P.B.'s Diaries.*]

[1]Mrs. Isabel B. Mitchell (Isabella Buloid), born Feb. 23, 1835, married in May, 1860, to Wm. H. Mitchell. She was Col. H. S. Olcott's oldest sister for whom he had a deep affection all his life.

[2]Charles Sotheran, one of the original "formers" of the T.S. He was a relative of the London booksellers of the same name. He was also with Sabin & Sons, booksellers in New York, and connected in a literary way with their journal *The American Bibliopolist*. Sotheran had a peculiar temperament. Three mouths after the Society was founded, trouble arose, as Sotheran made inflammatory speeches at a political street meeting and wrote bitterly in the newspapers against H.P.B. and the Society. His resignation was accepted, and, for the sake of protection, the Society was made into a secret body, with signs and passwords. Later on, Sotheran apologized and was taken back into membership. He gave useful help to H.P.B. during the writing of *Isis Unveiled*, and published a small short-lived journal called *The Echo*, in which H.P.B. wrote a couple of articles. After the Founders' departure for India, his name was not again mentioned. See *Bio-Bibliogr. Index* for further data.

[3]Emily Kislingbury.
[4]Nickname which H.P.B. gave to Col. Olcott.
[5]Edward Wimbridge. See *Bio-Bibliogr. Index* for data.
[6]A manner in which Col. Olcott used to refer to himself.
[7]Miss Nadyezhda Andreyevna de Fadeyev (1829-1919), H.P.B.'s favorite aunt, her mother's sister who was only two years her

senior. Many of her letters to H.P.B. are in the Adyar Archives. For a time she was on the Council of the T.S. She remained unmarried and died in Prague, Czechoslovakia.

[8] The "Seven Brothers," a secret organization then existing in India, having as a Ritual something akin to Masonry. John Yarker who issued to H.P.B. her Masonic certificate in the "Rite of Adoption" had evidently a copy of the Sat B'hai ritual and sent it to H.P.B. At the time a ceremony of admission for members of the T.S. was planned, but nothing further was done in this matter.

[9] The Adept-Brother known as Hilarion, Ilarion, and Hillarion Smerdis, who, among other things, collaborated with H.P.B. in the writing of her occult stories.

[10] Hurrichund (or Harichandra) Chintamon was the representative in Bombay of Swâmi Dayânanda Sarasvatî, the head of the Ârya Samâja, founded in 1875. The T.S. in New York joined hands with this organization and for a while diplomas were issued with the words: "The Theosophical Society of the Ârya Samâj of Âryavarta." Later on acute differences occurred, which are outlined in the Supplements to *The Theosophist* of this period, and all association with the Ârya Samâja was severed. A good deal may be found on this subject in Col. Olcott's *Old Diary Leaves*, Volume I.

[11] James M. Stewart, Editor of the *Franklin Register*, Franklin, Mass.

[12] *Religio-Philosophical Journal* published in Chicago, Ill.

[13] "M. A. (Oxon.)" was the pseudonym of Rev. William Stainton Moses (or Moseyn) (1840-92), at one time Editor of the Spiritualistic magazine *Light*, and a very good friend of the Founders. Consult Col. Olcott's *Old Diary Leaves*, Vol. I on this subject. See also the *B.-B. Index*, s. v. Moses.

[14] *Pravda* (Truth) was a daily newspaper published at Odessa, Russia, 1877-80. Its Editors-Publishers were Joseph Dolivo-Dobrovolsky and K. E. Rosen. Starting in early 1878, H.P.B. wrote for it a number of "Letters," under the general title "From Across the Sea, from Beyond the Blue Ocean."

[15] Monsieur Harrisse was a Frenchman in New York with whom the Founders were on friendly terms. He was an amateur artist. One evening H.P.B. asked him to draw the head of a Hindu chieftain, as he should conceive one to look. Evidently with the unspoken help of H.P.B. who sat near him, Harrisse produced in black and white crayons the first portrait of Master M. ever drawn. After the portrait was finished, the cryptograph signature of the Master was precipitated upon it. *Vide* Col. Olcott's *Old Diary Leaves*, I, 370-72, for a full account of the circumstances involved.

[16] Dr. Alexander Wilder (1823-1908), well-known physician and a deep scholar of Classical languages and philosophies. Collaborated in the production of *Isis Unveiled*. See the *Bio-Bibliographical Index* for comprehensive sketch of his life and work.

[17] Most likely the then recently published work by Louis Rousselet entitled *l'Inde des Rajahs. Voyage dans l'Inde Centrale*, Paris, 1875.

[18] Dr. L. M. Marquette, a woman-physician, who met H.P.B. in Paris in 1873, when she stayed with her cousin Nicholas von Hahn and his friend M. Lequeux, and who knew her intimately. *Vide* Col. Olcott's *Old Diary Leaves*, I, 27-28, for Dr. Marquette's testimonial in regard to H.P.B.'s character.

[19] *Russkiy Vestnik* (Russian Messenger), very well-known Russian monthly Journal published in Moscow. It was founded by the outstanding journalist and political leader M. N. Katkov, in 1856. It was in this journal that appeared for many years H.P.B.'s Series "From the Caves and Jungles of Hindostan," "The Enigmatical Tribes of the Azure-Blue Hills," and "The Durbâr in Lahore."

[20] Gen. Abner Doubleday (1819-93), a prominent figure in the Civil war days and founder of baseball. He was Vice-President of The Theosophical Society and a close friend of H.P.B., Col. Olcott and W. Q. Judge. See *Bio-Bibliographical Index* for further data.

[21] Mrs. Helene von Schewitsch was an early friend of H.P.B.'s. She was an author and socialite, born at Munich, March 21, 1845, as the daughter of Baron von Dönniges (also spelt Tönniges); her mother was a cultured Jewish lady. Helene was first married to a Rumanian Boyar, Janko von Racowitza who died soon; then to the actor Siegwart Friedman from whom she was divorced; then to Serge von Schewitsch, a Russian; this was about 1875. Unfortunately, Helene committeed suicide at Munich, October 3, 1911. She also seems to have been the cause of Lasalle's duel and death. In spite of being a very erratic and temperamental individual, she was deeply interested in Theosophy and wrote about her experiences with H.P.B. in a most friendly and understanding way. See her work entitled *Wie Ich Mein Selbst Fand* (C. H. Schwetschke und Sohn, Berlin, 1901; 2nd ed., M. Altmann, Leipzig, 1911) published under her name of von Schewitsch. An English translation by Cecil Mar was published by Constable & Co., London, 1910, under the title of *Princess Helene von Racowitza. An Autobiography*. Pages 349-355, and 391 concern H.P.B. Excerpts from the original German work have been published in translation in *The Theosophical Review*, Vol. XXIX, January, 1902, pp. 386-88, 470-71.

[22] Dr. C. Carter Blake seemed for a time to be devoted to Theosophical work, but was a member of the Jesuit order when he joined the T.S. He was expelled from the Society at a later date. See *The Mahatma Letters*, etc., Letter No. LIV, in this connection.

[23] Dr. George Wyld of Edinburgh.

[24] Swâmi Dayânanda Sarasvatî of the Ârya Samâja in India.

[25] Otho Alexander, an early member of the T.S. resident in Corfu, Greece.

²⁶Pasquale Menelao, President of the Corfu Lodge of the T.S. which was founded in 1877.

²⁷Mooljee Thackersey. Col. Olcott mentions meeting him on one of his early travels before he had met H.P.B. The Founders started corresponding with him in 1877.

²⁸Pandit Shamji Krishnavarma was a man of stirling worth and great integrity of character. He was born in 1857 and was at one time connected with the Ârya Samâja. It was he who sent to the Founders in New York an English translation of the Samâja's Rules, which led them to rescind the Resolutions of the Council to amalgamate the T.S. with Swâmi Dayânanda's Society. Shortly after the Founders settled in Bombay, Krishnavarma left India for Oxford, England, accepting the position of Oriental Lecturer of Balliol College. Before taking this decision, he had a serious consultation with H.P.B. and Col. Olcott. Within an incredibly short time, he had mastered Greek and Latin and passed difficult examinations in Law and Political Economy. He was appointed Lecturer in Sanskrit, Marâthî and Gujarâtî and assisted Prof. Sir Monier Monier-Williams who had originally sponsored his arrival. Upon his return to India, he was appointed to the Dewanship of the State of Junagadh. (See *The Theos.*, IV, Nov., 1882, p. 27 and Supplement to June, 1883, p. 12; V, Suppl. to Oct., 1883, p. 14; and XVI, March, 1895, pp. 403-04).

²⁹General Francis J. Lippitt (1812-1902), a distinguished American military man and Lecturer on Law. Was a friend of Lafayette and of De Toqueville whom he assisted in the preparation of his works. He was an ardent Spiritualist and a great friend of the Founders. See the *B.-B. Index*, s. v. LIPPITT.

³⁰C. H. Van der Linden and Peter van der Linden, father and son, who joined together and remained loyal members of the T.S. in America to the time of their death.

³¹A reproduction of this plaque appears as frontispiece in Col. Olcott's *Old Diary Leaves*, Vol. I, but this illustration is of a copy in bronze now at Adyar, evidently copied from the original plaster. H.P.B.'s name in Tamil was most likely added when this copy was made in India.

³²Caroline Rollins Corson, wife of Prof. Hiram Corson of Cornell University, Ithaca, N. Y., both of whom were close friends of H.P.B.'s in the early days. She was born in France and educated in her native country and in Germany. Aside from translation work, she also wrote some valuable articles on Faust, Machiavelli, Victor Hugo and others.

³³Prince Emil-Karl-Ludvigovich von Sayn-Wittgenstein. See *Bio-Bibliogr. Index* for data.

³⁴Captain Sir Richard Francis Burton (1821-90), British explorer and Orientalist, celebrated translator of the so-called "Arabian Nights."

³⁵Nickname for Col. Olcott's wife. She was Mary Epplee Morgan.

³⁶"Tom" was Miss Sarah Cowell of New York, an actress.

daughter of the Rev. Richard U. Morgan, D.D., rector of Trinity parish, New Rochelle, N. Y., whom the Colonel married April 26, 1860.

[37] Described by Col. Olcott in his *Diary* as "the Irish Lady who agitates for Women's Rights, etc."

[38] Charles Carleton Massey was an English Barrister-at-Law and litterateur keenly interested in Spiritualism. He was one of the ablest metaphysicians in England and a lucid and scholarly writer on psychic subjects. He visited the U.S.A. in 1875, and went to Chittenden, Vt. to verify for himself Col Olcott's accounts of the Eddy phenomena. Massey became one of the original "formers" of the T.S. However, after several years of friendship, differences arose between him and the Founders. He resigned when the Society for Psychical Research attacked H.P.B. and gave allegedly damaging evidence against her. He died in 1905. See *Bio-Bibliogr. Index* for further data.

[39] Dr. Harry J. Billing.

[40] This is A. N. Aksakov's article entitled "The Scientific Hypothesis Respecting Mediumistic Phenomena," translated by H.P.B. and published in the *Avoca Mail and Pyrenees District Advertiser* of Australia, August 27, 1878.

[41] Rev. Mohottiwatte Gunânanda, Buddhist Chief Priest of Dipaduttama Vihâra, at Colombo, Ceylon, and a member of the General Council of the T.S.

[42] An Adept-Brother spoken of by H.P.B. as "the Old Gentleman." He contributed a great deal of material during the production of *Isis Unveiled*. There exists only one letter from him preserved in the Adyar Archives. It is written in red pencil and its facsimile may be found in *Letters from the Masters of the Wisdom*, Second Series, No. 24, as well as in C. Jinarâjadâsa's booklet, *Did Madame Blavatsky Forge the Mahatma Letters*, Adyar, 1934, p. 43. This Adept was living near Arcot, not far from Madras, when H.P.B. and Col. Olcott saw him about April 30, 1882. A letter to *The Theosophist* from him, refuting the accusations of Swâmi Dayânanda Sarasvatî against the Founders, appears in the June, 1882, Supplement, pp. 6-8. It is dated "Tiruvallam Hills, May 17," and signed "One of the Hindu Founders of the Parent Theosophical Society."

[43] Most likely Master M. H.P.B.'s entry hints very plainly at the little understood fact of the overshadowing of her consciousness by the higher consciousness of Initiates.

[44] The Adept-Brother known by the name of "Serapis" belonged to the Egyptian Section of the Brotherhood and was very active in the initial stage of the Theosophical Movement. A considerable number of original letters from him to Col. Olcott have been preserved.

[45] The members of the Tile Club were artists who met monthly at each other's studios and painted designs on tiles supplied by the host, whose property they became.

[46] This phrase does not occur anywhere else, and it is not known what particular Adept is referred to.

⁴⁷H.P.B.'s cat. In a later entry the disappearance of Charles is alluded to with consternation.
⁴⁸More correctly *Saoshyant*, one of the Saviours to come, according to the Zoroastrain religion, the other two being Oshêdar Bâmî and Oshêdar Mâh.
⁴⁹Most likely Master M.
⁵⁰Madame Vera Petrovna de Zhelihovsky, H.P.B.'s sister. She was born in 1835 and died 1896. She was a very well-known authoress in Russia specializing in children's stories.
⁵¹Apparently the cryptograph of an initiate; very similar to the one which appears in H.P.B.'s letter to A. P. Sinnett, No. XI, p. 20, of the well-known volume of letters.
⁵²Nickname for Miss Rosa Bates.
⁵³One of these trunks is now at Adyar, still in good condition.
⁵⁴Emmet Robinson Olcott, one of Col. Olcott's brothers, who was born October 12, 1846.
⁵⁵Jenny was the maid.
⁵⁶These words are written in red pencil, in large letters, and in a handwriting which C. Jinarâjadâsa thought to be that of Master Serapis. There is by their side a short sentence in red also and signed by the symbols of which H.P.B. says in a letter "the Old Gentleman your Narayan."
⁵⁷The "I.—" most likely stands for Master Ilarion.
⁵⁸There is some evidence that this jewel had originally belonged to Cagliostro.
⁵⁹There is a short letter from Master Serapis in which he says that "the *lost one* is restored in its proper place. The gueburs made it invisible out of malice." *Vide* Letter No. 22 in *Letters from the Masters of the Wisdom*, Second Series.
⁶⁰Colonel Olcott arrived at Bombay bearing official credentials from the U.S. Government as a Commercial Commissioner.
⁶¹Symbol for Master Narayan.
⁶²Words in a script that has not been identified.
⁶³Symbol for an Adept whom H.P.B. went to meet at "The Battery," a point in New York harbor.
⁶⁴Word illegible.
⁶⁵Symbol for either an Adept or a Lodge.
⁶⁶Symbol for Master Narayan. The incident about calling him "old horse" is related by Col. Olcott in *Old Diary Leaves*, Vol. I, pp. 247-48.
⁶⁷Thomas Alva Edison (1847-1931), the famous inventor and scientist, who became a member of the T.S.
⁶⁸As far as is known, this photograph must have been brought to Bombay when the Founders went to India.
⁶⁹Name undecipherable.
⁷⁰As the facsimile shows, there is over this entry a large symbol in red pencil, an arrow pointing down to a circle containing a cross, and

the signature of Master Narayan at the side. *"Consummatum est"* (It is finished, or accomplished) is written in large letters, in blue pencil, and underlined. It is not certain whether these two words are in H.P.B.'s handwriting or not.

[71] A reporter writing in the New York *Sun* of December 19, 1878, had this to say: "Charles in the meantime had been sent to a good Theosophist's house, but had disappeared from the basket *in transitu,* and has not been seen since. 'I don't know where he is,' said the Hierophant [H. S. Olcott], 'but I presume we will find him in Bombay when we get there'."

[72] The words "took leave of the chandelier" are underlined in blue.

[73] Most likely Master Serapis.

APPENDIX

NOTE ON THE TRANSLITERATION OF SANSKRIT

The system of diacritical marks used in the Bibliographies and the Index (with square brackets), as well as in the English translations of original French and Russian texts, does not strictly follow any one specific scholar, to the exclusion of all others. While adhering to a very large extent to Sir Monier-Williams' *Sanskrit-English Dictionary*, as for instance in the case of the *Anusvâra*, the transliteration adopted includes forms introduced by other Sanskrit scholars as well, being therefore of a selective nature.

It should also be noted that the diacritical mark for a long "a" was in the early days a circumflex, and therefore all of H.P.B.'s writings embody this sound in the form of "â." No change has been made from this earlier notation to its more modern form of the "macron," or line over the "a." Such a change would have necessitated too many alterations, and almost certainly would have produced confusion; therefore the older usage has been adhered to throughout.

GENERAL BIBLIOGRAPHY

(With Selected Biographical Notes)

The material contained in the following pages is of necessity a selective one, and is intended to serve three purposes: (a) to give condensed information, not otherwise readily available, about the life and writings of some individuals mentioned by H. P. B. in the text, and who are practically unknown to the present-day student; (b) to give similar data about a few well-known scholars who are discussed at length by H. P. B., and whose writings she constantly quotes; and (c) to give full information regarding all works and periodicals quoted or referred to in the main text and in the Compiler's Notes, with or without biographical data of their authors. All such works are marked with an asterisk (*).

Âdi-Granth. Sacred book of the Sikh Gurus. It is an important compilation of the utterances of the early Vaishnava saints or *Bhagats*. It is from them that Nânak, the founder of the sect, took his doctrines, and each of the 31 *râgs* forming the body of the *Granth*, is followed by utterances of the saints, chiefly of Kâbir, while the conclusion of the book contains more verses by the same authors, as well as by the celebrated Sûfî, Shêkh Farîd of Pâkpattan. The *Âdi-Granth* was compiled about 1600 by Arjân, the fifth Guru; it is written in a special Sikh script, the *Gurmukhi*, and sets forth the Sikh creed in its original pietistic form, before it assumed its militant character. The texts are in various dialects and even partly in Persian. *Vide* Ernst Trumpp, *The Âdi-Granth or Holy Scriptures of the Sikhs*, London, 1877.

Agrippa von Nettesheim, Henry Cornelius (1486-1535). German writer, soldier, physician and magician. For many years in the service of Maximilian I, the German King who sent him, 1510, on a diplomatic mission to England. From 1511 to 1518, he was in Italy in the service of William VI of Monferrato and of Charles III of Savoy. His early interest in the occult sciences brought him into open conflict with the Church at Dôle, Pavia and Metz. He practiced medicine in Cologne, Geneva, Freiburg and Lyon for short periods, until Margaret, Duchess of Savoy and regent of the

Netherlands, appointed him archivist and historiographer to the Emperor. Eventually he went to France where he was arrested for some disparaging words about the queen-mother, but was soon released. He was married three times and had a large family. Agrippa's famous *De occulta philosophia,* which brought him into antagonism with the Inquisition, was written about 1510, partly under the influence of the author's friend, John Trithemius, then abbot of Würzburg, but its publication was delayed until 1531, when it appeared at Antwerp (also Lugduni: Fratres Beringo, 1533. 3 vols.). His other principal work is *De incertitudine et vanitate scientiarum, etc.* (Antwerp, 1531), wherein he denounces the accretions of theological Christianity. He also wrote *De nobilitate et praecellentia feminei sexus* (Coloniae, 1532). An edition of his works was publ. at Leyden in 1550, with several later editions.

*Aitareya-Brâhmaṇa. See HAUG.

AKSAKOV, ALEXANDER NIKOLAYEVICH. Russian author, philosopher and prominent figure among writers on Spiritualism. He was born May 27/June 8, 1832, in the village of Repyevka, Gorodishchensky uyezd, Province of Penza, on the estate of his father, Nikolay Timofeyevich, brother of Serguey Timofeyevich, the author of the renowned *Family Chronicle.* His mother was Catherine Alexeyevna Panov, of an old aristocratic family of the Province of Simbirsk. He was educated in the Alexander Lyceum of St. Petersburg, and on graduation in 1851, entered service in the Ministry of the Interior. Appointed on a Statistical Expedition, he spent some time in the Provinces studying religious dissidents. In 1855-56 he attended courses at the Faculty of Medicine at Moscow University, but soon after resumed his service to the State in the Department of Governmental Properties. He retired from Government service in 1878 with the rank of Actual Civil Councillor.

From his early years, Aksakov was interested in problems of theology and philosophy, and, while still in the Lyceum, came in contact with the teachings of Swedenborg; this was his introduction to a philosophical outlook whereby he endeavored to establish an empirical basis for his belief in the spiritual destiny of mankind. As a result of his studies, he published the following works: 1) *On Heaven, the World of Spirits, and Hell, as Seen and Heard by E. Swedenborg,* Leipzig, 1863; 2) *The Gospel according to Swedenborg,* Leipzig, 1864; 3) *The Rationalism of Swedenborg, etc.,* Leipzig, 1870.

This latter work led him to the sphere of Spiritualism which absorbed his interest in the second half of the sixties. It is in the writings of Andrew Jackson Davis that he found the clearest exposition of his own attitude, and so he proceeded to publish in Germany a series of German translations from Davis' works: *Der Reformator*, Leipzig, 1867; *Der Zauberstab*, ditto, 1868; *Die Principien der Natur*, ditto, 1869; *Der Arzt*, ditto, 1873. His special interest lay in the study of such psychic phenomena as would provide evidence for the existence of a spiritual Principle in man. In so doing, Aksakov found a most sympathetic interest in Professor Butlerov, the renowned Russian chemist, who openly declared his belief in the reality of mediumistic phenomena.

During this period of his life, Aksakov translated into Russian a large number of works, among which should be mentioned:

1) *Manual of Magnetotherapy*, of Count F. von Szapary. Trans. from the French, St. Petersburg, 1860.

2) *Experimental investigation of Spiritualism*, of R. Hare. Trans. from the English, Leipzig, 1866.

3) *Spiritualism and Science*. Investigations of Crookes' Psychic Force. St. Petersburg, 1872.

4) *Outline of the History of the Committee on Mediumism of the Physical Society at the St. Petersburg University*, St. Petersburg, 1883.

5) *Monument to Scientific Prejudice*. The conclusions of the committee on Mediumism, St. Petersburg, 1883.

He also wrote several monographs on Hellenbach and d'Assier and their works. He published in German several of the works mentioned above, adding to the list two works by A. R. Wallace. As far as is known, Aksakov himself paid all the expenses connected with this vast literary output.

In 1874, Aksakov founded at Leipzig a monthly called *Psychische Studien* dedicated to the investigation of little known psychic phenomena. This periodical continued to be published until 1934, having changed its name to *Zeitschrift für Parapsychologie* in 1925. A perusal of the contents of the early volumes of this publication shows it to have been by far one of the most outstanding periodicals on the subject published at the time.

Aksakov's personal views concerning Spiritualism are clearly outlined in his Preface to his first edition of *Spiritualism and Science* (St. Petersburg, 1872), from which it appears that he made a clear distinction between observed facts and the theories current at the time to account for them. The basis and chief purpose of his literary activity was to observe and to record *facts* of genuine mediumism, entirely devoid of any theory or hypothesis, or religious and sectarian bias. He contended that a scientific approach to this subject would require an array of scientifically established *facts,* and that in due course of time some plausible theory, or a series of them, would emerge to justify facts on some reasonable basis. These views are further outlined in the January, 1878, issue of his periodical. It is evident, therefore, that the views of Aksakov on this whole subject were very closely allied to H.P.B.'s attitude towards the known facts and genuine manifestations of the mediums of her time. She found in Aksakov a splendid ally, and they both aroused rabid enmity on the part of those whose minds had crystallized on mere theories, in the various factions of the Spiritualistic and Spiritistic movement.

At a later time, Aksakov published the following works:

1) *Spiritism,* by K. R. E. von Hartmann. Trans. by A. M. Butlerov, 1887.

2) *A. M. Butlerov on Mediumism.* With a portrait of the author and reminiscences of N. P. Wagner, 1889.

3) *Forerunners of Spiritism for the last 250 Years* [Russian text]. St. Petersburg: V. Demakov, 1895; 513 pp.

4) *A Case of partial dematerialization of the body of a medium.* Trans. from the French, Boston, 1898.

5) *Animism and Spiritism* [Russian text], 2nd ed., St. Petersburg: V. Demakov, 1901. 679 pp.; German tr., Leipzig, 1894; French tr., Paris, 1906.

Aksakov died in 1903, after a long and extremely useful life in the cause of scientific research on little known lines, and in a field suspect by official science. Most of his work along these lines had to be located in Germany, on account of the enmity existing then in Russia against anything pertaining to this field of research.

ALDEN, WILLIAM LIVINGSTON. American author, b. at Williamstown, Mass., October 9, 1837; d. in 1908. Graduated from Jefferson College, Penna., 1858; married, 1865, Agnes M. McClure; admitted to New York Bar, 1860; practiced until 1865; leader-writer on New York *World, Times, Graphic,* etc., until 1885; U.S. Consul-General at Rome, 1885-89; leader-writer on Paris *Herald,* 1890-93; since then resided in London (61, Clondesdale Road, S.W.). Works: *Canoe and Flying Proa,* 1878.—*Domestic Explosives,*

1877.—*Life of Columbus*, 1881.—*Cruise of the "Ghost"*, 1882.— *New Robinson Crusoe*, 1888.—*The Moral Pirates*, 1904.—*Told by the Colonel*, 1893.

Alden was present at the meeting of September 8, 1875, when the organization of The Theosophical Society was proposed; he was also present at the meeting of October 16th. He did not remain a member for any length of time, however, and in 1881 ridiculed the Society in the newspapers. As a writer, he had considerable repute for caustic and humorous criticisms upon current topics. Consult Col. Olcott's *Old Diary Leaves*, I, pp. 123-24, for the account of a curious experience which Alden had at New York in 1874.

Appleton Cyclopaedia of Biography.

BABINET, JACQUES. French physicist, b. at Lusignan, March 5, 1794; d. Oct. 21, 1872. Studied at École Polytechnique in Metz. After a short time in an artillery regiment, became professor of physics at Lycée Saint-Louis, then at Collège de France. Entered the Académie des Sciences in 1840. Works: *Résumé complet de physique*, etc., Paris, 1825.—*Sur la mesure des forces chimiques*, etc. He was a talented journalist and an imaginative writer.

BEAUMARCHAIS, PIERRE AUGUSTIN CARON DE (1732-99). *Le Barbier de Séville*, 1775.—*Le Mariage de Figaro*, 1778.

BORELLI, GIOVANNI ALFONSO. Italian physiologist and physicist, b. at Naples in 1608; d. in Rome, Dec. 31, 1679. Appointed professor of mathematics at Messina, 1649, and at Pisa, 1656. Returned to Messina, 1667, and retired to Rome in 1674, where he lived under the protection of Christina, Queen of Sweden. His best known work is *De motu animalium* (1680-81), in which he explains the movements of the animal body on mechanical principles. In a letter published under the pseudonym of Pier Maria Mutoli in 1665, he was the first to suggest the idea of a parabolic path for a comet; among his many astronomical works is his *Theoria mediceorum planetarum ex causis physicis deducta* (Florence, 1666), in which he considered the influence of attraction on the satellites of Jupiter.

BREWSTER, SIR DAVID. Scottish physicist, and one of the founders of the British Association; b. at Jedburgh, Dec. 11, 1781; d. at Allerby, Feb. 10, 1868. He made his name by a series of investigations on the diffraction of light, the results of which he contributed from time to time to *Philosophical Transactions* and other scientific journals. From 1859 on, Brewster was principal of Edinburgh University, and succeeded J. J. Berzelius as one of the eight "foreign associates" of the Institute of France. In addition to his *Treatise on Optics* (1831) and other works, he edited the *Edinburgh Encyclopaedia* (1808-30) and was one of the leading contributors to the 7th and 8th ed. of the *Encyclopaedia Britannica*.

BROWN, ROBERT, JR. (1844-?). **The Great Dionysiak Myth*, London, 1877.—**Poseidôn*: A Link between Semite, Hamite, and Aryan, being an Attempt to trace the cultus of the God to its sources, etc., London, 1872. 8vo.

BUCHANAN, JOSEPH RODES (1814-99). See Vol. VI, pp. 429-30, for a biographical sketch.

BÜCHNER, LUDWIG. German philosopher and physician, b. at Darmstadt in 1824; d. at Darmstadt, May 1, 1899. Studied at Giessen, Strasbourg, Würzburg and Vienna. Became, 1852, lecturer in medicine at the Univ. of Tübingen, where he published his great work, *Kraft und Stoff* (1855). The extreme materialism of this work excited so much opposition that he was compelled to give up his position. Retired to Darmstadt where he practiced as a physician. He wrote also: *Natur und Geist*, 1857.—*Aus Natur und Wissenschaft*, 1862 and 1884.—*Darwinismus und Socialismus*, 1894.

BUCKLE, HENRY THOMAS (1821-62). **History of Civilization in England*. Vol. I in 1857; Vol. II in 1861.

BUTLEROV, ALEXANDER MIHAYLOVICH. Renowned Russian chemist, founder of the so-called "Butlerov School," b. Aug. 25/Sept. 6, 1828, at Chistopol', Province of Kazan'; died Aug. 5/17, 1886, on his estate of Butlerovka in the same Province. He was the son of a lieutenant-colonel of modest means and was educated at home and in the Gymnasium of Kazan', before entering the physio-mathematical department of the Kazan' University. His unusual capacities resulted in a rapid progress in his studies and a generous recognition on the part of his teachers. His University appointed him to its Staff to teach chemistry and physical geography. In 1854 he became Doctor of Chemistry at Moscow University and was retained there to teach Chemistry. During three separate trips abroad, Butlerov spent considerable time studying the progress of chemistry in Europe, and establishing personal relations with a number of outstanding scientists, such as Bunsen, Kekule and others. His scientific research laid the foundation of chemistry in Russia and coincided with the first marked development of organic chemistry in Europe.

It is of special interest to students of Theosophy to note his intense interest in Spiritualistic and allied phenomena. He became versed in the subject and approached it from the purely scientific viewpoint. On his initiative, there was organized in St. Petersburg in 1871 the first scientific Committee for the investigation of mediumistic phenomena, which included Professors Ovsyannikov, Chebishev and Zion. He was also very active in the formation of another Committee for the same purpose, suggested by Prof, Mendeleyev and made up of members of the Physical Society at the University of St. Petersburg. He was a constant contributor to the Spiritualistic journal *Rebus* for which H.P.B. wrote. His articles on the general subject of mediumship and psychic manifestations were published at St. Petersburg in 1889, with reminiscences by his life-long friend and co-worker, Prof. N. P. Wagner.

CAESAR, GAIUS JULIUS (102 ?-44 B.C.). *Commentarii de bello Gallico*, written in 51 B.C. Loeb Classical Library.

CASSELS, W. R. (1826-1907), *Supernatural Religion*, etc. London, 1874. 2 vols,; Vol. III in 1877. Many editions.

COBB, JOHN STORER. English barrister and Doctor of Laws; at one time Editor of the *New Era* magazine, the organ of the Reformed Jews in New York. Was a leader in the Cremation Movement. He assisted in the formation of The Theosophical Society, and was elected its Recording Secretary. In 1878 he was sent as Presidential Agent by the Council of the T.S. in New York, to assist in the formation of the British Theos. Society. He seems to have lost interest soon after and was heard of no more.

COLEMAN, CHARLES. *The Mythology of the Hindus*, with Notices of Various Tribes inhabiting the two Peninsulas of India and the neighboring Islands, etc. 3 pt. London, 1832, 4to.

COLEMAN, WILLIAM EMMETTE. American author and lecturer, b. at Shadwell, Va., June 19, 1843. As a boy of twelve, was assistant librarian in the Richmond Public Library, and at sixteen became interested in various reformatory movements of the country and became a Spiritualist. For a time he was a stage manager and actor; later was reconstruction clerk at the military headquarters at Richmond, and after 1874 held a civilian position in the quartermaster's department, U.S. Army. Settled in San Francisco in 1880. Lectured widely on scientific subjects and was especially interested in Oriental religions and languages, publishing a large number of papers. He also wrote two extended works: *Darwinism and Spiritualism* (1877), and *Spiritualism—Cui Bono?* (1878), in an attempt to place Spiritualism on a scientific basis. For some peculiar reason, Coleman opposed Theosophy and H. P. Blavatsky from the very first, and published a number of articles trying to expose H.P.B. as a literary fraud. It appears that he was preparing a larger work for publication, *Theosophy Unveiled*, intended to be a complete analysis of it as a mere humbug; but no such work has ever been published. While a few of Coleman's strictures have some small justification in fact, and cannot be completely rejected, his arguments are shallow and his facts often confused.

COOKE, JOSIAH PARSONS (1827-94). * *The New Chemistry*, 1872; 2nd. ed., London, 1874. See Vol. IX, p. 240, for biogr. sketch.

CORSON, EUGENE ROLLIN (1855-?), **Some Unpublished Letters of Helena Petrovna Blavatsky*. With an Introduction and Commentary. London: Rider & Co. [1929], 255 pp., facs. & ill.

CORSON, HIRAM. American educator and author, b. in Philadelphia, Pa., Nov. 6, 1828; d. at Ithaca, N. Y., June 15, 1911. Received his earliest schooling in the home of his parents, Joseph Dickinson and Ann Hagey Corson. His father, a mathematician of exceptional ability, trained him in mathematical thought; and it was not until Hiram was fifteen that he was sent to the Treemount Seminary at Norristown, Pa., where, at the classical and mathematical school of the Rev. Dr. Samuel Aaron, and later at the classical school of the Rev. Dr. Anspach, at Barren Hill, Pa., he spent five years in study, distinguishing himself both in mathematics and the knowledge of Latin and Greek.

In the Fall of 1849, Hiram went to Washington, D.C., where he utilized his knowledge of stenography by connecting himself with the reporting corps of the United States Senate, for a time serving also as private secretary to Senator Lewis Cass. In the Summer of 1850 he became connected with the library of the Smithsonian Institution, then under the vigorous direction of the distinguished bibliographer, Prof. Charles Coffin Jewett. Under the direction of the latter, Hiram received a thorough training in bibliography and library management; he also attended for some seven years the literary and scientific courses given there by outstanding men of science. Stimulated by these, he gave all his leisure to the study of great literature—English, French and German. His marriage, in Sept., 1854, to Caroline Rollin, a lady of French birth and European education, deeply interested in literature, strongly stimulated his literary trends.

In 1859, moving with his family to his native city, he became a public lecturer on English literature, drawing to his audiences many cultivated people. He became widely known and liked. In 1864 Princeton conferred on him the degree of Master of Arts; and in the following year Girard College in Philadelphia elected him to its chair of moral science, history and rhetoric. Soon after he accepted the more congenial professorship of rhetoric and English literature in St. John's College at Annapolis, Md. In 1870, he became associated with Cornell University, where he taught until 1903, when he was made professor emeritus, after a long and most fruitful career.

"It is with his work as a teacher of English literature that Prof. Corson is most familiarly associated, and by it he will perhaps be longest remembered. Possessed not only of a great breadth of culture and a rare discrimination, but of a voice of exceptional range and singular sympathetic power, he has been an interpreter and inspirer of no usual order . . . For more than a generation of human life he stood foremost among his colleagues as a spokesman of the higher interests of the soul; and in every class which went out from Cornell he kindled something of his own noble love of literature, of his sensitiveness to the ideal, of his contempt for the merely material in act and life . . . However appreciative of the old, no one was ever more impatient of mere convention . . . No venerable imposture escaped his scorn; no seer-eyed heresy failed of his welcome." (W. T. Hewett, *Cornell University, A History*, 1905, Vol. II, pp. 39-40.)

In the many books which Prof. Hiram Corson wrote or edited, he dealt with most of the great phases of English letters. Among his works, the following should be mentioned as being, each one of them, examples of deep learning and noble aim: *Handbook of Anglo-Saxon and Early English* (1871); *The University of the Future* (1875); *An Introduction to the Study of Robert Browning's Poetry* (1886); *An Introduction to the Study of Shakespeare* (1889); *A Primer of English Verse*, etc. (1892); *The Aims of Literary Study* (1895).

Prof. Corson did not limit his attention purely to letters; he was a zealous opponent of slavery, publicly deprecated many aspects of organized religion, and was deeply apprehensive of the social effects of concentrated wealth.

On July 15, 1874, Corson's only daughter died and the blow was devastating. Hiram Corson found no comfort in the religion of the Churches and gradually turned to Spiritualism for some sign and assurance of the continued existence of his child. He later became convinced of that and his belief in Spiritualism became firmly established. He read Col. Olcott's articles in the New York *Daily Graphic* about the manifestations at the Eddys' homestead at Chittenden, Vt., and also H.P.B.'s articles attacking Dr. Beard. He wrote to H.P.B. to learn the real facts and to know more about her. From this casual contact their mutual friendship grew, and after some spirited correspondence, the Corsons invited H.P.B. to visit their home in Ithaca, N. Y. The invitation was accepted and H.P.B. spent a few weeks with them in the Fall of 1875. The Corsons lived at that time in the Richardson Cottage, on Heustis Street, prior to the time when they occupied Cascadilla Cottage, where Hiram Corson died and where many of his books are dated.

It is at Ithaca that H.P.B. started to write *Isis Unveiled* in earnest, although the very beginning of it may have been already laid before she left New York. She wrote about twenty-five closely written foolscap pages a day, with no access to any books except those in the extensive library of the Corsons, which had no relation to her subject anyway. After H.P.B. returned to New York, a few additional letters were exchanged with the Corsons, but apparently, for one reason or another, their mutual friendship cooled. Some light is thrown on this subject by Eugene Rollin Corson, their son.

Caroline Rollin Corson, Prof. Corson's wife, was pre-eminently social by nature; she adopted with full heart her husband's country, and brought to him not only a rare intellectual sympathy, but to the little world of his colleagues and students a breadth of travelled experience, a refinement and grace of manner, a knowledge of books and men, and a facile charm of conversation which made their home a center of culture. She also became interested in Spiritualism, but only moderately; it never possessed her as it did Hiram Corson. She had accepted the loss of her daughter with composure and resignation, and her interest in H.P.B. was more in the woman herself than in her doctrines and mission. She was not interested in Occultism; on the contrary, she was greatly opposed to it. Eventually, she entered the Catholic Church, where she apparently found comfort, and she died May 21, 1901, at a convent in Rochester where she was in the habit of going at odd times for rest and retreat.

It would appear that Prof. Corson, being then a thorough believer in Spiritualism, could not accept either H.P.B.'s strictures on this Movement or her explanations concerning the phenomena of the séance-room; nor was he any better pleased with certain utterances of Col. Olcott in his lectures. Corson sided with the Spiritualists and published in the *Banner of Light* of Boston, Mass., some accusations against H.P.B.'s good faith. According to his son, Prof. Corson "was quite too hasty in his revulsion of feeling; he later realized it and was quite willing to admit it. His sorrow and his state of mind at the time may well explain the error he had fallen into . . . My father followed the future history of the Theosophical Society with great interest; he bought H.P.B.'s books as well as a number of works which were the direct outcome of the Society in India."

The last preserved letter between H.P.B. and the Corsons was written to Mrs. Corson and dated from New York, August 28, 1878. There is no further evidence of any direct contact between them.

Prof. Corson's Spiritualistic views have been expressed by him in a book entitled *Spirit Messages* which was published posthumously in 1911.

Sources: H. Corson, *Corson Family* (1906); *N.Y. Times*, June 16, 17, 1911; Murray E. Poole, *A Story Historical of Cornell University*, etc. (1916); W. T. Hewett, *Cornell University*, etc. (1905); Eugene Rollin Corson, *Some Unpublished Letters of Helena Petrovna Blavatsky*. Introd. and Commentary (1929).

Cox, Edward William. English Serjeant-at-Law, b. at Taunton, 1809; d. November 24, 1879. Eldest son of Wm. Charles Cox, manufacturer at Mill Hill, Middlesex, and Harriet, daughter of William Upcott of Exeter. Educated at the college school of his native town; called to the bar at the Middle Temple, May 5, 1843, but practiced little as a barrister. Recorder of Helston and Falmouth, 1857-68, and recorder of Portsmouth from the latter date to his death; chairman of the second court of Middlesex sessions, from 1870 to the end of his life. Established the *Law Times*, April 8, 1843, to which he thereafter devoted the greater part of his time. Became proprietor of *The Queen, a Lady's Newspaper*, started in 1861, and later established a journal known as *Exchange and Mart*. Issued several other papers, and was the author of a large number of legal works, the most important of which, *The Law and Practice of Joint-Stock Companies,* ran to six editions.

Cox married first, in 1836, Sophia, daughter of William Harris, surgeon in the royal artillery; and later, 1844, Rosalinda Alicia, daughter of J. S. M. Fonblanque.

On February 22, 1875, Cox founded in London the Psychological Society of Great Britain, for the systematic investigation of mediumistic and related phenomena, which were included under the term "psychological." Its membership included W. Stainton Moses, Walter H. Coffin, C. C. Massey, Hensleigh Wedgwood, all of whom later served on the first Council of the Society for Psychical Research. When Cox died, his Society was dissolved, Dec. 31, 1879. Members of this body of "rationalists" ascribed the phenomena of the *séance*-room to unconscious action of the normal faculties of the medium, not to the work of the spirits of the dead. Cox, well known as a leading English investigator of these phenomena before founding his Society, suggested the term "Psychic Force" to designate the origin of the mediumistic and related phenomena. He regarded spirit and matter as basically one, with interchange from one to the other; and the soul as a composition whose substance "is vastly more refined than the thinnest gas." The Psychic Force was the faculty of the soul which is the effective agent of all mental and physical spiritualistic manifestations.

In the interest of his Society, Cox published several treatises of originality and vigor, such as: *What Am I?* (1874). — *The Mechanism of Man* (1876).—*Spiritualism Scientifically Examined;* etc., a booklet issued in 1872.

Together with A. R. Wallace, Chas. Bradlaugh, Dr. James Edmunds, Cox had been a member of the Committee deputed by the London Dialectical Society to investigate the phenomena of Spiritualism in January, 1869. The work of Cox and of his Society represented a reaction against the prevailing passive acceptance by believers of the notion that spirits of the dead were the prime agents in the phenomena.

(Sources: *Times,* Nov. 26, 1879, p. 8; *Law Times,* Nov. 29, 1879, pp. 73, 88; *Illustrated London News,* March 5, 1859, p. 221; and Dec. 6, 1879, pp. 529, 530 (with portrait); S. C. Hall's *Retrospect of a Long Life,* 1883, II, 121-26; Hatton's *Journalistic London,* 1882, pp. 208-11; *Proceedings,* Psychological Society, 1875-79.)

DARWIN, CHARLES ROBERT (1809-82). *On the Origin of Species by Means of Natural Selection, or the Preservation of Favoured Races *in the Struggle for Life.* Published on November 24, 1859, the entire edition of 1250 copies being exhausted on the day of issue.

DAVIS, ANDREW JACKSON. American Spiritualist and Seer, b. in Blooming Grove, Orange Co., N. Y., August 11, 1826; d. Jan. 13, 1910. He was the son of Samuel Davis, a stern, poverty stricken shoemaker, given to drink, and totally uneducated, as was also Andrew's mother, a woman with a weak body but strong visionary powers. During the summer months, the father eked out his living by hiring himself out as a farm-laborer. The family moved frequently from one small town to another without seeming to better themselves. Some time prior to 1842, they settled at Poughkeepsie, N. Y., whence Andrew was later to receive his name of "the Poughkeepsie Seer." The young lad was an undersized, delicate boy, with next to no education, and in childhood of no conspicuous ability. His academic training consisted of a total of five months schooling acquired at different periods of a few weeks each. In 1841 he was apprenticed to a shoemaker named Armstrong, and worked at that trade for about two years. Incapable of really learning the trade, he became employed by a merchant in a general store, but he was a failure at this occupation also. In his later boyhood, Davis' latent psychic powers began to develop. He heard voices in the field—gentle voices which gave him good advice and comfort. Clairvoyance followed clairaudience, and the ability to see visions of various kind.

In 1843, a certain Professor Grimes came to Poughkeepsie to lecture on animal magnetism; he attempted to put Davis into a trance, but the experiment failed; a few weeks later, however, William Levingston, a local tailor and amateur mesmerizer, succeeded in "magnetizing" him. The result was such a rare clairvoyance that Levingston gave up his own business and devoted his efforts to Davis, using his powers for the diagnosis and the cure of disease. The human body became transparent to Davis' inner sight, and each organ stood out clearly and with a special radiance of its own which was dimmed by disease. His ministrations were not confined to those who were in his presence, as he was able to diagnose cases at considerable distance. In this earlier phase of Davis' psychic experiences he had no immediate memory when he returned from trance of what his impressions had been; being registered, however, on a certain level of his inner consciousness, he was able to recall them at a later date.

In March, 1844, a very strange episode occurred in his life. He was suddenly possessed by some power which led him to take off on a rapid journey in a condition of trance. He found himself among wild mountains and claimed to have met two venerable men with whom he held intimate and inspiring exchanges upon medicine and morals. Either prior to or during this experience, he had wandered into the Catskill Mountains and was later found some forty miles from home. Davis claimed that he had met Galen and Swedenborg during this episode.

By 1845 Davis felt urged to turn from healing to writing. He selected as magnetizer Dr. S. S. Lyon, a physician then practicing in Bridgeport, Conn., and the Rev. Wm. Fishbough of New York, as reporter and scribe. Both men gave up their practices and followed the "call." No money and no publicity of any kind was involved in this matter, which makes it that much more remarkable. From Nov. 28, 1845, to Jan. 25, 1847, Davis delivered while in a state of trance one hundred and fifty-seven lectures, which were carefully taken down *verbatim* and, after a minimum of editing, were published in the Summer of 1847 in the shape of a large octavo volume of nearly eight hundred closely printed pages, under the title of *Principles of Nature, Her Divine Revelations, and A Voice to Mankind.*

Among those who frequently attended the circle while this work was being dictated, was the Rev. Dr. George Bush, Professor of Hebrew in the University of New York, and a well-known Swedenborgian. He writes:

> "I can solemnly affirm that I have heard Davis correctly quote the Hebrew language in his lectures, and display a knowledge of geology which would have been astonishing in a person of his age, even if he had devoted years to the study. He has discussed, with the most signal ability, the profoundest questions of historical and biblical archaeology, of mythology, of the origin and affinity of language, and the progress of civilization among the different nations of the globe . . ."

The opening of the second part of this work will illustrate the nature of the subject and the phraseology used to describe it:

> "In the beginning the Univercoelum was one boundless, undefinable, and unimaginable ocean of Liquid Fire! The most vigorous and ambitious imagination is not capable of forming an adequate conception of the height and depth and length and breadth thereof. There was one vast expanse of liquid substance. It was without bounds—inconceivable—and with qualities and essence incomprehensible. This was the original condition

of Matter. It was without forms, for it was but *one* Form. It had not motions, but it was an eternity of Motion. It was without parts, for it was a Whole. Particles did not exist, but the Whole was as *one* Particle. There were no suns, but it was one Eternal Sun. It had no beginning, and it was without end. It had not length, for it was a Vortex of one Eternity. It had not circles, for it was one Infinite Circle. It had not disconnected power, but it was the very essence of all Power. Its inconceivable magnitude and constitution were such as not to develop forces, but Omnipotent Power.

"Matter and Power were existing as a Whole, inseparable. The *Matter* contained the substance to produce all suns, all worlds, and systems of worlds, throughout the immensity of Space. It contained the qualities to produce all things that are existing upon each of those worlds. The *Power* contained Wisdom and Goodness, Justice, Mercy, and Truth. It contained the original and essential Principle that is displayed throughout immensity of Space, controlling worlds and systems of worlds, and producing Motion, Life, Sensation, and Intelligence, to be impartially disseminated upon their surfaces as Ultimates."*

From these opening sentences Davis traces the evolution of the Universe, which he terms *Univercoelum,* by a gradual process of differentation into vast systems of suns, moving in concentric circles of inconceivable magnitude round the Great Eternal Centre. Later he describes the particular solar system to which we belong, and the gradual progression through geological cycles of our own planet. He seems to be as much at home in chemistry as in the realm of marine fauna or the history of fossils. In a lecture of March, 1846, he gives a fairly accurate description of an eighth planet which was not identified until September of the same year by Leverrier and Adams, and was given the name of Neptune.

Such was the beginning of Davis' psychic revelations which extended eventually over some twenty-six works in all and became known as the "Harmonial Philosophy." Among these should be mentioned: *The Great Harmonia,* 1850-52; *The Philosophy of Spiritual Intercourse,* 1856; *The Penetralia,* 1856. In some of these and other works, Davis displayed a remarkable prophetic power. He correctly described the automobile, the typewriter and flying machines. He also gave a description of certain belts or sheaths surrounding the earth, which are closely similar to present-day

---

*34th Amer. ed., Boston, 1876, pp. 121-22.

scientific discoveries of the magnetic belts around our globe. He also gave a very precise and minute description of the manner in which the dying person leaves his worn-out body.

Before he reached the age of twenty-one, Davis attained a state when he needed no second person to induce his trance, but could do so himself. Eventually, he attracted the attention of many earnest people, Edgar Allan Poe being one of his visitors.

The object of life for Davis was to qualify for advancement in the tremendous universal scheme of things, and the best method of human advancement was purification and self-control. The return to a simple life and to simple beliefs and a primitive brotherhood were essential. Money, alcohol, lust, violence and priestcraft were the chief impediments to racial progress. Davis consistently lived up to his own professions. His view of the general social order was along lines of idealistic Socialism, infused with the highest moral code. He preached social reconstruction and spiritual regeneration. The main source of information concerning his views and the story of his early life is his own Autobiography, *The Magic Staff;* published as early as 1857, this gives only a picture of his early years.

Davis' literary output was enormous, and it stands to reason, of course, that his writings contain a great many errors, misconceptions, and somewhat confused ideas often expressed in very complicated language. This is always so in the case of natural-born visionaries and sensitives, and it is for the student himself to seek in the midst of much trivial material gems of truth and pearls of wisdom which abound in Davis' philosophy of life. The Spiritualistic movement has attempted for years to identify Davis with it; yet it is obvious that his conceptions and his word-descriptions were vastly different from anything that has ever come through ordinary mediums; nor did he have any of the common Spiritualistic beliefs in regard to manifestations and the appearances in *séance*-rooms. His writings deserve a close study, especially by those who are interested in the earliest attempts on the part of the Teachers to introduce into the Western world long-forgotten ideas concerning the true nature of the Universe and Man. It may be stated, without fear of contradiction, that Davis' writings contain scattered ideas and conceptions reminiscent of *The Secret Doctrine*, especially with regard to the origin and evolution of worlds. Even the language of some of the passages is akin to later installments of the Esoteric Philosophy. While it would be rash and unwise to consider Davis in the light of a trained occultist, which he certainly was not, and never claimed to be, yet he should be reckoned among those rare figures of extreme spiritual and psychic sensitivity whose inner Ego can at times become attuned to invisible Realities and channel into the brain—in a condition of trance and not self-consciously, however—pictures impressed upon the Âkâśic waves.

It is therefore no great wonder that H.P.B. would have had such profound respect for Andrew Jackson Davis, whom she considered to be a Seer, and whose warnings against intercourse with unprogressed entities in the astral world she quoted more than once.

DEUTSCH, IMMANUEL OSCAR MENAHEM. German Orientalist, b. of Jewish extraction at Neisse, Oct. 28, 1829; d. at Alexandria, May 12, 1873. Studied at the Univ. of Berlin and became a Hebrew and classical scholar. Appointed, 1855, assistant in the British Museum Library. He worked intensely on the *Talmud* and contributed more than 190 papers to *Chambers' Encyclopaedia*. He is the author of a famous article on the *Talmud* in the *Quarterly Review* for October, 1867, which was translated into many European languages.

DICKENS, CHARLES JOHN HUFFAM (1812-1870). *Little Dorrit,* 1857. —*Edwin Drood,* 1870.

DOUBLEDAY, ABNER. American military man, b. at Ballston Spa, N.Y., June 26, 1819; d. at Mendham, N. J., Jan. 26, 1893. Son of Ulysses Freeman and Hester Doubleday, his father being representative in Congress. Educated at Cooperstown, N. Y. and privately. While at school, invented the game of baseball, 1839. This claim was thoroughly investigated by a commission set up in 1907, and of which Col. A. G. Mills, a leader in U. S. amateur sports, was chairman. The commission substantiated the claim and showed that Abner Doubleday devised the diagram of bases and positions for players in 1839. As a result of this, the National Baseball Hall of Fame was established at Cooperstown.

Doubleday graduated in 1842 from the U. S. Military Academy at West Point, being commissioned as brevet second lieutenant in the 3rd U.S. Artillery. As second lieutenant of 1st U. S. Artillery, he served with Gen. Zachary Taylor in the Mexican War, being engaged in the battle of Monterey and in operations connected with Buena Vista. In 1854-55 he was engaged against the Apache Indians, and from 1856 to 1858 against the Seminole Indians in Florida. He was in active service throughout the Civil War, 1861-65. He was second in command at Fort Sumter, and aimed the first gun fired in its defence, April 12, 1861, when attacked by the Confederates. In May, 1861, he was made major of the 17th U. S.

Infantry, and went into service with Gen. Patterson's campaign column in the valley of the Shenandoah. In August, 1861, he was assigned to the command of the artillery defences of Washington, and on Feb. 3, 1862, of all the defences there, being appointed brigadier-general of Volunteers.

In the following May, Abner Doubleday joined McDowell's column at Fredericksburg, Va., and in August reinforced the Federal troops fighting at Cedar mountain. He withdrew on Aug. 19th, with the remainder of Pope's army, to hold the line of the Rappahannock against the advance of the Confederates under Gen. Lee. He drove the opposing forces across the river and checked the advance of Stonewall Jackson at Gainsville. He was engaged in the battle of Manassas, Aug. 29 and 30, 1862, and succeeded to the command of Hatch's division on the latter day. He commanded a division in the army of the Potomac, Sept. 16, 1862-July 1, 1863. At Antietam he held the extreme right and opened the battle. For his gallantry in this action he was made brevet lieutenant-colonel in the regular army. On Nov. 29, 1862, he was appointed a major-general of Volunteers. He fought in the battles of Fredericksburg and Port Conway and was sent on July 1, 1863 to Gettysburg by Gen. Reynolds to reinforce Buford's cavalry. After considerable losses inflicted on the opposing forces, he was forced back to Cemetery Ridge, south of Gettysburg. On the third day of the battle, Gen. Pickett's charge struck Gen. Webb's division on the right of Doubleday's command. In advancing, the charging column exposed their right flank, and Gen. Doubleday's front line struck the vulnerable point and disordered the enemy's advance to such an extent that they were easily repulsed. When Reynolds fell, Doubleday commanded the field until the arrival of Gen. Howard. His heroic work at Gettysburg is commemorated by a bronze statue unveiled on the battlefield Sept. 25, 1917.

On March 11, 1865, he was made brevet colonel, and March 13, brigadier-general and major-general for services rendered. In August of the same year he was mustered out of Volunteer service and assumed his position as lieutenant-colonel in the regular army. From May, 1866, to November, 1867, he was in command of the post at Galveston, Texas, and later was on duty as colonel at Fort McKavett, Texas.

Doubleday retired from the regular army December 11, 1873. Apart from his military career, he was an able engineer, and in 1870 obtained a charter in San Francisco for the first cable railway ever built. He published *Reminiscenses of Forts Sumter and*

Moultrie in 1860-61 (1876), *Chancellorsville and Gettysburg* (1882), a pamphlet with maps, *Gettysburg Made Plain*, and articles in periodicals on army matters, water supply for cities and other topics. He was married in Washington, D.C., January, 1853, to Mary, daughter of Robert Hewitt, a lawyer of Baltimore. He is buried at the National Cemetery, Washington, D.C.

Very soon after the formation of the Theosophical Society he joined its ranks, attended its meetings and became a staunch friend of the Founders. After the departure of the latter for India, Doubleday was made the President *pro tem* in U.S.A., with W. Q. Judge as Secretary. A gift from him of over seventy books to the Aryan Branch of the T.S. in New York became the nucleus for a later large library.

It has been stated that Doubleday translated into English Éliphas Lévi's *Dogme et Rituel de la Haute Magie* and his *Fables et Symboles*; it is not known what became of these translations. Another unfinished and most likely lost work of his was a complete Index and Digest of the early issues of *The Theosophist*. It is a great pity that this labor has not been preserved as it should have been for the benefit of later students. On April 17, 1880, Doubleday was elected Vice-President of the Theosophical Society, and the official letter to this effect came from India bearing H.P.B.'s signature. He was associated with the Aryan T.S. in New York until his death. All in all, Abner Doubleday was a very remarkable man and will be long remembered.

DUPOTET DE SENNEVOY, BARON JULES (1796-1881). See for biographical sketch Vol. VII, p. 368.

EDDY BROTHERS. Horatio and William Eddy were primitive folk farming a small holding at the hamlet of Chittenden, near Rutland, Vermont. An observer described them as "sensitive, distant and curt with strangers, looking more like hard-working rough farmers than prophets or priests of a new dispensation, with dark complexions, black hair and eyes, stiff joints and a clumsy carriage." They seem to have been at feud with some of their neighbours and were not liked by them. The curious phenomena of materialization which took place at the homestead became widely known and aroused great curiosity. Guests who came to observe and investigate, found accommodations and were boarded in a large room with food as simple as their surroundings. For this board, the Eddys charged a low rate, but they do not seem to have made any profit from their psychic demonstrations.

The ancestry of the Eddy Brothers was rather interesting. Not only was there an unbroken record of psychic powers extending over several generations, but their grandmother four times removed had been burned as a witch as a result of the Salem trials of 1692. When young, the Eddy Brothers were persecuted and even tortured by their fanatical father, in order to stop the phenomena which were taking place; their mother, herself a strong psychic, was unable to stop this brutality. Later on, the father tried to make some money out of the powers of his two sons by hiring them out as mediums. This only added to their unfortunate plight.

The best account of the mediumship of the Eddy Brothers is the one by Colonel Henry Steel Olcott. The *Daily Graphic* of New York sent him to Chittenden to report his findings for that paper; this was in October, 1874. The result of his ten-week's stay in Vermont was a series of fifteen remarkable articles which appeared in October and November, 1874, in the New York *Daily Graphic*. It is on the basis of these articles that Col. Olcott prepared his work entitled *People from the Other World* which was published, profusely illustrated by Alfred Kappes and T. W. Williams, by the American Publishing Company, Hartford, Conn., in 1875.

The Eddy Brothers seem to have covered just about the whole range of physical mediumship; however, it was William Eddy's mediumship which took the form of materializations, while Horatio gave *séances* of quite a different character. Some visitors, among them a Dr. Beard of New York, tried to show up the alleged "tricks" of the Eddy Brothers, but to no avail; they were genuine mediums for physical manifestations as evidenced by several of the most careful observers, notably Col. Olcott himself.

ELEAZAR I (Lazar, Eleazar ben Shammua'). See for biogr. sketch Vol. VI, p. 433.

ELPHINSTONE, MOUNTSTUART. Scottish statesman and historian, b. in 1779; d. Nov. 20, 1859. Having received an appointment in the civil service of the East India Company, he reached Calcutta in 1796. Appointed, 1801, assistant to the British resident at Poona, at the court of the peshwa. When war broke out, he acted as virtual aide-de-camp to General Wellesley. Appointed, 1804, British resident at Nagpur, and in 1808 as first British envoy to the court of Kabul. He became, 1810, resident at Poona. Played important role in the conflict with the Marâthâs. Appointed, 1819, lieutenant-governor of Bombay, where he remained until 1827, his principal achievement being the compilation of the "Elphinstone Code." He may be regarded as the founder of the system of State education in India.

He returned to England in 1829. Chief works: *An Account of the Kingdom of Caubul, and its dependencies in Persia, Tartary, and India*, etc., London, 1815.—*The History of India*, London, 1841, embracing the Hindu and Mohammedan periods.—*The Rise of British Power in the East*, London, 1858.

ENNEMOSER, JOSEPH. Austrian medico-philosophic writer, b. Nov. 15, 1787, at Hintersee, Tirol; d. at Egern, Sept. 19, 1854. After fighting against the French in 1809 and again in 1813-14, he took his M.D. at Berlin in 1816, and was appointed professor of medicine at the Univ. of Bonn, 1819. Practiced at Insbruck, 1837-41; moved to Münich where he became widely known by his use of hypnotism. His chief work is: *Der Magnetismus in seiner geschichtlichen Entwickelung*, 1819; 2nd ed., 1844; partial Engl. trans. 1854.—He also wrote: *The History of Magic*, transl. from the German by Wm. Howitt (1792-1879), London, 1854, 2 vols.

FELT, GEORGE H. A New York engineer and architect, brilliant and possessing genius, regarding whose life and career almost nothing seems to be known. He lectured on "The Lost Canon of Proportion of the Egyptians, Greeks and Romans" at the gathering held on September 7, 1875, when the formation of the Theosophical Society was proposed; he continued the same subject Sept. 13th. For a short time he acted as Vice-President, but soon drifted out of the Society. J. W. Bouton intended publishing a large volume outlining Felt's discoveries, but this venture apparently did not eventuate, and only a most elaborate prospectus of this forthcoming work survives. Consult Col. Olcott's *Old Diary Leaves*, Vol. I, for details about Felt's ideas and claims.

FLINT, CHARLES RANLETT (1850-1934), *Memories of an Active Life*. New York and London: G. P. Putnam's Sons, 1923. xviii, 349 pp.

FOLGER, ROBERT B., *The Ancient and Accepted Scottish Rite, in Thirty-three Degrees*, etc. A full and complete history with an appendix . . . New York, 1862; 2nd ed., N.Y., 1881.

FRIEDENTHAL, KARL RUDOLF. Prussian statesman, b. at Breslau, Sept. 15, 1827; d. March 6, 1890. Industrialist. In German Reichstag, 1867-81; in 1870 also in Prussian House of Representatives; Minister of Agriculture, 1874-79. Belonged to the Liberal Center Party.

GALATINUS (PIERRE GALATIN or GALATINO). French theologian and scholar of the late 15th and early 16th century, b. in small town of Pouille (whence his name) of poor and obscure parents. Joined Order of St. Francis; was at Otrante when the Turks laid siege to the city. Sent to Rome where he perfected himself in Greek and Oriental languages. Selected to teach theology and philosophy to his co-brothers of the Order. Upon return to Naples, chosen as "définiteur" of the Province of Bari. Called to Rome by Leon X, and appointed his "pénitencier." Was still at Rome as late as 1539. His only work is: *Opus de arcanis catholicae veritatis,* etc., Ortona, 1518, fol., the 1st ed. of which is very scarce; left at Rome some 15 volumes of MSS, which are in the Vatican Library.

GORCHAKOV, PRINCE ALEXANDER MIHAYLOVICH. Russian statesman, b. July 16, 1798; d. at Baden-Baden, March 11, 1883. Educated at the lyceum of Tsarskoye Selo. Entered foreign office under Count Nesselrode. When German confederation was re-established in 1850, he was appointed Russian minister to the Diet and established close personal ties with Bismarck. Transferred to Vienna during the Crimean War. Appointed, 1856, minister of foreign affairs in place of Nesselrode. Became Chancellor and was, for a time, the most powerful minister in Europe. At the congress of Berlin, 1878, at the end of the Russo-Turkish campaign, the aged chancellor held nominally the post of first plenipotentiary, but left to Count Shuvalov the odium for the concessions which Russia had to make to Great Britian and Austria.

GOUGENOT DES MOUSSEAUX, Le Chevalier HENRY-ROGER. French writer, b. at Coulomniers (Seine-et-Marnes), April 22, 1805; d. Oct. 5, 1878. Trained in diplomacy. Served at the Court of King Charles X. Retired to his native town during revolution of 1830, and devoted himself to archaeological, religious and spiritistic studies. Ardent Catholic and prolific writer, whose passion for accumulating factual data from the civilizations of the past was used to great advantage by H.P.B. in her discussions of magic. Works: *Dieu et les Dieux,* Paris: Laguy frères, 1854. 8vo. Often considered as his chief work.—*Moeurs et pratiques des démons.* Paris, 1854; 2nd rev. ed., Paris, 1865.—**La Magie au xixme siècle, ses agents, ses vérités, ses mensonges.* Paris: H. Plon, E. Dentu, 1860. 8vo; augm. ed., Paris, 1864.—*Les hauts phénomènes de la magie, précédés du spiritisme antique.* Paris: H. Plon, 1864. 8vo.—*Le Juif, le Judaïsme et la Judaïsation des peuples chrétiens.* Paris: H. Plon, 1869. 8vo.; 2nd ed., Paris, 1886. Very scarce. This work produced a veritable sensation abroad and was translated into various languages.

**Guide to Theosophy, A.* Collection of Selected Articles. Published by Tookaram Tatya, Bombay, 1887.

THE HOUSE AT 302 WEST 47TH STREET, NEW YORK

This drawing was made by Mr. Knapp of Cincinnati, Ohio, and was published in *The Path*, Vol. VIII, November, 1893, with this description: "The illustration shows the narrow front porch of the house facing Eighth avenue .... The entrance to the apartments is down on 47th Street under the rear suites of rooms. H.P.B. had the flat which begins in the middle of the building, running to the front on Eighth avenue and being immediately over the shop .... Her writing-room was in front, taking in the corner window and the next two over the shop ..."

This flat became known as the "Lamasery"; it is here that much of *Isis Unveiled* was written, and where it was finished.

WILLIAM QUAN JUDGE
1851-1896
(Consult the *Bio-Bibliographical Index* for a comprehensive biographical outline.)

GUIDO OF AREZZO. Italian musician who lived in the 11th century, also known as Guido Aretinus, Fra Guittone, and Guy of Arezzo. Has been called the father of modern music. Of his life very little is known. He first appears in history as a monk in the Benedictine monastery of Pomposa, where he taught singing and invented a new educational method. Envy and jealousy drove him away and he went to Arezzo; received, about 1030, an invitation to Rome from Pope John XIV; the latter became his first pupil in Rome. Later, his former superior induced him to return to Pomposa. At one time he worked in the Benedictine monastery of St. Maur des Fosses where he invented his novel system of notation and taught the brothers to sing by it. There is no room for question as to the importance of his musical reforms and innovations. There is little doubt that the names of the first six notes of the scale, *ut, re, mi, fa, sol, la,* still in use in France and Italy, were introduced by him. They were derived from the first syllables of six lines of a hymn to St. John the Baptist. One of his most important treatises is the *Micrologus Guidonos de disciplina artis musicae.*

GUILLEMAIN DE SAINT-VICTOR, LOUIS, **Handbook of the Women Freemasons or the True Freemasonry of Adoption.*

HALLEY, EDMUND. English astronomer, b. in London, Oct. 29, 1656; d. Jan. 14, 1742. Educated at Queen's College, Oxford. Studied astronomy in his school days, publishing, 1676, a paper on planetary orbits. Went to St. Helena to make observations in the Southern hemisphere. Upon returning to England, began a friendship with Newton, which resulted in the publication of the *Principia*, the expense being borne by Halley. Observed the comet of 1682, calculated its orbit, and predicted its return in 1757. Succeeded Flamstead as astronomer-royal, 1720. Made innumerable contributions to the science of astronomy. Principal works: *Catalogus stellarum australium*, London, 1679.—*Synopsis astronomiae cometicae*, Oxford, 1705.—*Astronomical Tables*, London, 1752.—Translated the work of Apollonius from the Arabic which he learned with this end in view.

HAMMOND, WILLIAM ALEXANDER H. American physician, b. at Annapolis, Aug. 28, 1828; d. at Washington, Jan. 5, 1900. Son of a physician; studied at Harrisburg and graduated in medicine at New York Univ., 1848; Practiced at Philadelphia Hospital; then was Ass. Surgeon of the Army; 1859, Prof. of physiology and anatomy at Baltimore Univ.; 1860 went back to the Army, serving in Gen. Patterson's Hdqrts.; 1862, became Brig.-General and Surgeon-Gen. of the Army. Founded the Army Medical Museum. Resigned in 1864, went to New York and became Prof. of Psychiatry and nervous diseases at College of Physicians and Surgeons; in 1874, held chair in these subjects at the Medical Faculty in New York. Chief works: *The Medical and Surgical History of the Rebellion.—On Sleep and Its Derangements*, Philadelphia, 1869.—*Physics and Physiology of Spiritualism*, Philad., 1870.

HARDINGE-BRITTEN, MRS. EMMA (? -1899). An English woman who in her youth had gone to New York with a theatrical company, and had remained there with her mother. Being strictly Evangelical, she was strongly repelled by what she considered the unorthodox views of the Spiritualists, and fled in horror from her first *séance*. In 1856, she was again brought into contact with the subject, and received proof which made it impossible for her to doubt any longer. She soon discovered that she was herself a powerful medium. One of the best attested cases in the early history of Spiritualism was that in which she received intimation that the mail steamer *Pacific* had gone down in mid-Atlantic with all aboard; she was threatened with prosecution by the owners of the ship for repeating what had been told her by an alleged returned spirit of one of the crew. The information, however, proved to be correct, and the vessel was never heard of again. Eventually the young lady became a prominent orator, writer and traveller in the cause of Spiritualism. She returned to England in 1866, where she wrote her work: *Modern American Spiritualism* (New York, 1870). Mrs. Emma Hardinge married a second time in 1870 and became Mrs. Britten. Dr. W. Britten was also a Spiritualist. For many years, Mrs. Britten travelled the length and breadth of the United States proclaiming the doctrines of Spiritualism amid much opposition, for she was militant and anti-Christian in her views. Some adherents of Spiritualism have considered her as the female St. Paul of that movement. In 1878, she and her husband went together to New Zealand as missionaries of the cause, and stayed there several years. During this period, Mrs. Britten wrote her *Faiths, Facts and Frauds of Religious History*.

One of the most important contributions of Mrs. Britten to the history of modern Spiritualism is her large work entitled *Nineteenth Century Miracles* (Manchester, 1883) which is copiously documented and illustrated with rare portraits. It is in this work (pp. 296 and 441) that occurs an account of the formation of The Theosophical Society in which both the Brittens took part from the very first.

In 1876, while still working in America, Mrs. Britten published in New York a work called *Art Magic; or, Mundane, Sub-Mundane and Super-Mundane Spiritism*. She affirmed that this work had been written by an Adept of her acquaintance whom she had first met in Europe, and for whom she was but acting as "Translator" and "Secretary." His name, she said, was Chevalier Louis. This work, whatever may have been its actual origin, deals with some of the subjects outlined later at far greater length in *Isis Unveiled*, but contains also a great many errors and curious misstatements. We refer the student to the fascinating and important chapter XII of Col. H. S. Olcott's *Old Diary Leaves*, Vol. I, wherein the author gives the full background concerning this strange work. This account is well worth a careful perusal.

Mrs. Britten published also *Ghost Land; or Researches into the Mysteries of Occultism* (Boston, 1876) and founded the magazine *The Two Worlds* at Manchester, England. She left an indelible mark upon modern Spiritualism.

Mrs. Britten left the Theosophical Society fairly soon, although she had some contact with its leaders until 1890. Her reputation was somewhat clouded, however, when she joined Prof. Coues and others in spreading the calumny that *Isis Unveiled* had been written by Baron de Palm. Unfortunate and needless as such circumstances are, and however much they may be regretted, they seem to occur from time to time in many lives otherwise dedicated to truth, as far as it can be realized; and there can hardly be any doubt that Mrs. Britten's endeavor was to voice a great many spiritual ideas and noble precepts for the benefit of others, even though her own personal Karman led her to do so through a purely psychic movement where truth and error are often sorely confused.

HARE, ROBERT. American chemist, b. at Philadelphia, Jan. 17, 1781; d. May 15, 1858. His father, also Robert, served in the Pennsylvania legislature and was trustee of Pennsylvania University. Robert was educated at home and studied chemistry under James Woodhouse. For some years he managed his father's brewery, devoting his spare time to chemical research. Discovered, 1801, the oxy-hydrogen blow-pipe, source of the highest degree of heat then known, which led to the founding of the platinum industry. At this time he formed a close friendship with Benjamin Silliman which became almost a partnership in research. Elected, 1816, Prof. of Chemistry at the Univ. of Penna. His greatest interest was in electricity; he invented the calorimeter and the deflagrator for generating a high electric current; we owe to him also the use of the mercury cathode in electrolysis, and new methods for the analysis and synthesis of gases.

Hare was a vigorous contributor to the *American Journal of Science*. On his retirement in 1847, he gave his collection of apparatus to the Smithsonian Institution and was elected honorary member of that body. Apart from his various scientific papers and pamphlets, he published under the pen-name of "Eldred Grayson" a novel, *Standish the Puritan* (1850). Hare was one of the first eminent men of science who, setting out to expose the delusions of Spiritualism, became firm believers instead. This happened in 1853. Being a strong sceptic himself, he experimented for himself, and like William Crookes at a later date, devised apparatus to use with the mediums. He embodied his research in his work, *Experimental Investigation of the Spirit Manifestations*, etc. (New York: Partridge & Brittan, 1855, 460 pp., 2 portraits). This report led to a disgraceful persecution of one who was, with the exception of Agassiz, the best known man of science in America. The professors of Harvard passed a resolution denouncing him and his "insane adherence to a gigantic humbug." He had already resigned his chair, but suffered much in loss of reputation. The American Association for the Advancement of Science howled him down also, and placed themselves on record that the subject of Hare's research was unworthy of their attention.

Sources: E. F. Smith, *The Life of Robert Hare* (1917), and *Chemistry in America* (1910); Henry Simpson, *The Lives of Eminent Philadelphians* (1859).

HAUG, DR. CARL FRIEDRICH, **Die Allgemeine Geschichte*, Stuttgart, 1841.

HAUG, MARTIN. German Orientalist, b. at Ostdorf, Württemberg; d. at München, June 3, 1876. Studied Oriental languages, especially Sanskrit, at Tübingen and Göttingen, and in 1854 settled as *privatdozent* at Bonn. Removed to Heidelberg, 1856, where he assisted Bunsen in his literary work. Went out to India in 1859, where he became superintendent of Sanskrit studies and professor of Sanskrit at Poona. The result of his researches into Zend literature was a volume of *Essays on the Sacred Language, Writings and Religion of the Parsees*, Bombay, 1862. Having returned to Stuttgart in 1866, he was called to München as professor of Sanskrit and comparative philology in 1868. Haug also edited, translated and explained **The Aitareya Brâhmanam of the Rigveda*, Bombay, 1863, 2 vols.

HIGGINS, GODFREY (1773-1833). **Anacalypsis, an Attempt to Draw Aside the Veil of the Saitic Isis*, etc. 2 vols. London: Longman, etc., 1836. Very scarce.

HOME, DANIEL DUNGLAS. Scottish Spiritualistic medium, b. near Edinburgh, March 20, 1833. When nine years old, was taken by aunt to the USA. Became converted to Spiritualism in 1850, and for the next five years gave *séances* in New York and elsewhere; sent to Europe, 1855, by friends who provided the means for it; his *séances* in Europe aroused very considerable interest and were attended by a great many notables. Home subsisted until 1858 on the bounty of his friends. In August, 1858, he married Alexandrine (Sasha) de Kroll and settled in Russia with wealthy relatives. His wife, however, died in 1862 and Home's finances became again unsettled. In 1866 he was adopted by a wealthy widow, Mrs. Lyon, who provided him with money; she got tired of him after a while and sued him for the recovery of her "gifts." The Court gave judgment in her favor. In 1870-72, Home had a series of sittings with Sir Wm. Crookes. He married in 1871 another Russian woman of means, and spent a number of years on the European continent. He died at Paris, June 2, 1886 after a long and painful illness. As a medium, he was connected with all known forms of manifestation, and was never detected in any fraud. His phenomena are the best attested in the history of Spiritualism. His two works are: *Incidents in My Life.* Series 1, 2. London: Longman, Green, 1863-72. 8vo.; 2nd ed., Ser. 1. London, 1864. 8vo.; 5th ed., with Introd. by Judge Edmonds. Ser. 1. New York, 1864. 8vo.—*Light and Shadows of Spiritualism.* London, and New York: G. W. Carleton & Co., 1877. 483 pp. (pp. 301-28 concern H. S. Olcott); 2nd ed. London, 1878.

In spite of some statements to the contrary, H.P.B. did not know Home personally and never met him. Cf. *Collected Writings*, Vol. VI, pp. 73 and 289-90; also *The Mahatma Letters to H. P. Sinnett*, p. 37, where it says that ". . . Home—the medium . . . He is the bitterest and most cruel enemy O. and Mad. B. have, though he has never met either of them . . ."

For further information about Home, consult the following works: Madame D. Home. *D. D. Home. His Life and Mission.* London: Trübner & Co., 1888. 8vo. viii, 428. Also Dutton & Co., 1921.— *The Gift of D. D. Home,* by the same author. London: Kegan Paul & Co., 1890. 8 vo. viii, 388.— Horace Wyndham, *Mr. Sludge, The Medium.* London, 1937. xii, 307.—Jean Burton, *Heyday of a Wizard.* New York: Alfred A. Knopf, 1944.

HOOKE, ROBERT. English experimental physicist, b. at Freshwater, Isle of Wight, July 18, 1635; d. in London, Mch. 3, 1703. After 1655, was employed and patronized by the Hon. Robert Boyle.

Appointed, 1662, curator of experiments to the Royal Society, of which he was elected a Fellow in 1633. Appointed, 1665, professor of geometry in Gresham college. Secretary to the Royal Society, 1677-83, and published in 1681-82 the papers read before that body under the title of *Philosophical Collections*. His optical investigations led him to adopt the undulatory theory of light; he was the first to state clearly that the motions of the heavenly bodies must be regarded as a mechanical problem; and he approached the discovery of universal gravitation. Unfortunately, he was a man of irritable temper and made some virulent attacks on Newton and other men of science.

HORROCKS, JEREMIAH. English astronomer, b. in 1619 at Toxteth Park, near Liverpool. Student at Emmanuel College, Cambridge, 1832-35; then tutor at Toxteth, studying astronomy in his spare time. He calculated that, contrary to the prediction in Kepler's Rudolphine Tables, a transit of Venus would occur on November 24 (old style), 1639. This was a Sunday, and Horrocks, acting at the time as curate of Hoole, rushed from his clerical duties just in time to see the transit actually take place. This was the first transit of Venus to be observed. A brilliant young man, to whom are due several important contributions to astronomical knowledge, he died in his 22nd year, Jan. 3, 1641.

HURRYCHUND CHINTAMON. *Commentary on the Bhagavad-Gîtâ.*

HYSLOP, JAMES HENRY. American educator, b. at Xenis, O., August 18, 1854, d. June 17, 1920. Son of Robert Hyslop; graduated at the Univ. of Wooster, O., 1877; Ph.D., Johns Hopkins, 1887; married, Oct. 1, 1891, Mary Fry Hall, Philadelphia, Penn.; taught in the University of Lake Forest, Ill.; Smith College, Northampton, Mass.; Bucknell Univ., Lewisburgh, Penna.; and Columbia Univ., where he was Prof. of Logic and Ethics. Works: *Elements of Logic*, 1892.—*Ethics of Hume*, 1893.—*Elements of Ethics*, 1895.—*Syllabus of Psychology*, 1899.—Articles and Reviews in various magazines and the *Proceedings* of the Society for Psychical Research, and later, as his interest in psychic research developed: *Science and a Future Life*, 1905.—*Enigmas of Psychic Research*, 1906.—*Psychic Research and the Resurrection*, 1908.—*Psychic Research and Survival*, 1913.—*Life after Death*, 1918.—*Contact with the Other World*, 1919.

Hyslop was present at the meetings of September 8 and October 16, 1875, when The Theosophical Society was proposed and organized, but he later lost interest in it.

INMAN, THOS., *Ancient and Pagan Christian Symbolism, etc. London, 1869; 2nd ed., N.Y., 1871.

IVINS, WILLIAM MILLS. Distinguished American lawyer, b. at Upper Freehold, N. J., April 22, 1851; d. in New York, July 23, 1915. Son of Augustus and Sarah (Mills) Ivins. Graduated in 1869 from Adelphi Academy, Brooklyn, N.Y. Studied at Columbia law school and was admitted to the Bar in 1873. Began law practice as a member of the Brooklyn firm of Bergen & Ivins and during that period represented H.P.B. in her lawsuit against Clementine Gerebko. (*Vide* pp. 83-84 of the present volume.)

During 1885-88, Ivins was judge advocate general of New York state. He was a close student of municipal government, and in 1881-82 was to a large extent acting mayor of New York under Wm. R. Grace. As Chamberlain of the city, he fought a courageous battle for various municipal reforms, and exposed corrupt conditions. In 1907-09, was Chairman of a committee which prepared a Charter for New York city, known as the Ivins Charter, which became a model for other city charters. A formidable courtroom opponent, he won a number of important law cases and took part in political campaigns on the side of much-needed reforms. A many-sided man, Ivins was interested in botany, biology, general philosophy, assembled an extensive library on Napoleon which was given to Columbia University after his death, and wrote several works on legal matters. He was married to Emma Laura Yard; they had five children. (*Vide* pp. 95-100 of the present volume for further information on Ivins and the "Hiraf" Club.)

JACOLLIOT, LOUIS (1837-1890). *La Bible dans l'Inde. Vie de Jezeus Christna. Paris, 1869. 8vo. Translated as *The Bible in India*. Hindoo origin of Hebrew and Christian Revelation. London, 1870. 8vo.

JENNINGS, HARGRAVE (1817?-1890), *The Rosicrucians, their Rites and Mysteries. London, 1870. 8vo.; 2nd ed., rev., corr. and enl., London, 1879; 3rd ed., newly rev., 1887.

JINARÂJADÂSA, C. (1875-1953). *Letters from the Masters of the Wisdom. 1881-1888. Transcribed and Compiled by C. J. First Series. With a Foreword by Annie Besant. Adyar, Madras: Theosophical Publishing House, 1919. 124 pp.; 2nd ed., 1923; 3rd ed., 1945; 4th ed., with new and addit. Letters (covering period 1870-1900), 1948.—*Second Series. Adyar: Theos. Publ. House,

1925; Chicago: The Theos. Press, 1926. 205 pp., facs.—**Did Madame Blavatsky Forge the Mahatma Letters?* Adyar: Theos. Publ. House, 1934. 52 pp. with 30 ill.

JUDGE, WILLIAM QUAN. One of the chief Founders of The Theosophical Society. The life of Mr. Judge is so indissolubly involved in the history and development of The Theosophical Society, that to outline the one is almost identical to outlining the other. We limit ourselves here to the lesser known facts of Mr. Judge's early life, prior to his meeting H.P.B. and Col. Olcott.

The son of Frederick H. Judge and Mary Quan, William Quan Judge was born in Dublin, Ireland, April 13, 1851, and spent his early childhood in a country where material adversity often found compensation in its natives' awareness of the silent forces of nature. At the age of seven a serious illness struck the lad and the doctor informed the family gathered at his bedside that William was dead. But before grief could overwhelm the would-be mourners, to everyone's amazement the boy revived. His recovery was slow, however, but during the year of his convalescence, he began to show an interest in mystical subjects. Unaware of his ability to read, the family found him engrossed in books dealing with Mesmerism, Phrenology, Magic, Religion and similar subjects.

The Judge family came to the U.S.A. when William was thirteen, sailing on the Inman Liner "City of Limerick," which arrived in New York on July 14, 1864. The mother had already died at the birth of her seventh child in Ireland, and the father had to assume the double responsibility of educating and providing for the children. After a brief stay at the Old Merchant's Hotel on Courtland St., and later on Tenth St., New York, the family finally settled in Brooklyn, N.Y.

Hardship was no stranger to the Judge household, but William managed to finish his schooling before going to work. He eventually became a clerk in the Law Office of George P. Andrews, who later became Judge of the Supreme Court of New York, and developed an interest in the legal profession, for which he soon began to prepare himself. His father died soon after. On coming of age, William became a naturalized American citizen in April, 1872, and was admitted to the State Bar of New York one month later. His industry, natural shrewdness and inflexible persistence commended him to his clients and he became, as time went on, a specialist in Commercial Law.

In 1874, Judge married a school teacher, Ella M. Smith of Brooklyn (who died April 17, 1931), by whom he had a daughter who succumbed to diphtheria in infancy. The marriage was not successful; his wife, a strict Methodist at the time, not only did not share his later theosophical interests, but opposed them, both on personal and religious grounds. The loss of their child added to the unhappiness of their family life, especially so since Judge was very fond of children, who responded to his affection.

It was in the Fall of 1874, shortly after his marriage, that Judge came in contact with H. P. Blavatsky. According to Olcott, he was then serving in the Law office of E. Delafield Smith, U.S. Attorney for the Southern District of New York. After reading Col. Olcott's articles in the New York *Daily Graphic* (published in March, 1875, as a work entitled *People from the Other World*) outlining his experiences at the Eddy Homestead at Chittenden, Vt., where some weird Spiritualistic *séances* were being held, he wrote to the Colonel asking for an introduction to Madame Blavatsky. Eventually the desired invitation came, and resulted in an association that was to last throughout their lives.

Judge became a frequent visitor at H.P.B.'s apartment, at 46 Irving Place, New York, where the founding of the Theosophical Society was soon to take place. According to Col. Olcott, one evening, after a lecture by a New York architect, George H. Felt, on "The Lost Canon of Proportion of the Egyptians, Greeks and Romans," Olcott wrote on a scrap of paper: "Would it not be a good thing to form a Society for this kind of study?"—and gave it to Judge. H.P.B. read the note and nodded assent. (H. S. Olcott, *Old Diary Leaves*, I, 118).

A new life now commenced for the young lawyer, and his association with H.P.B. and Col. Olcott brought him his greatest opportunity. His youth and his sense of insecurity, both material and spiritual, prevented him at first from taking full advantage of the gifts thus laid before him, but in his struggle with himself, beset as he was, with adverse financial and domestic difficulties, he developed an inner strength which later was to marshal into activity all his hidden powers.

We do not have any information as to whether W. Q. Judge participated at all in the preparation of *Isis Unveiled*, the writing of which at the time demanded much of H.P.B.'s energy. His younger brother, however, John H. Judge, rendered valuable service in the matter of preparing H.P.B.'s manuscript for the printer, by copying a good portion of the work. This was not an easy task, for typewriters were unknown in those days, and it was necessary to prepare manuscripts for publication by means of handwritten copy. Young John H. Judge met H.P.B. when he was only seventeen years of age; he had a great admiration for H.P.B. and considered it a signal privilege to assist her in her literary task. John H. Judge visited the Point Loma Theosophical Headquarters in California on August 25, 1914, and related these facts to the body of students gathered to receive him.*

Strangely enough, a short time before the actual publication of H.P.B.'s first work, some disruption occurred in the relations between H.P.B. and W. Q. Judge, possibly due to some occult test. Writing about it, Olcott says: "During that year of interregnum [which he places at between July 16, 1877 and Aug. 27, 1878] Mr. Judge did not visit us, owing to a difficulty between Mme. Blavatsky and himself, nor did she write to him nor he to her, his only letters being addressed to me. This is mentioned merely by way of explaining why his name does not appear at that period in either of the Minute Books or in 'Old Diary Leaves' . . . When between us three were re-established, and continued down to the death of H.P.B."†

W. Q. Judge's position as one of the three chief Founders of the Theosophical Society—questioned as it has been by some ignorant critics—is amply substantiated by both Col. Olcott and H.P.B. In the light of their emphatic statements to this effect, there can be no doubt on the subject.‡

---

*Cf. Râja-Yoga Messenger, Point Loma, Calif., Vol. X, No. 10, October, 1914, pp. 16-17.

†Historical Retrospect, etc., p. 19.

‡Consult the following sources: Letter from H.P.B. to Judge, Ostende, July 27, 1886; also one dated August 22, 1886; H.P.B.'s Letter to the Second Convention of the American Section, T.S., April, 1888; Report on above Convention, The Theosophist, IX, July, 1888, pp. 620-621; H.P.B.'s Letter to Richard Harte, dated London, Sept. 12, 1889; H.P.B.'s "Preliminary Explanation" to E. S. Instruction No. III, quoting Master's own words; Richard Harte in The Theosophist, XI, Suppl., to December, 1889, p. xlii; Statement published in Lucifer, VIII, June, 1891, pp. 319-20; The Theosophist, XII, July, 1891, p. 634; Col. Olcott in The Theosophist, XII, Sept., 1891, p. 707; Col. Olcott's words in The Path, VI, Nov., 1891, p. 260; Allan Griffiths in Lucifer, IX, Nov., 1891, p. 259; Annie Besant in her Circular Letter to the Blavatsky Lodge, March 11, 1892. All the above-mentioned passages are quoted in Theosophia, Los Angeles, Calif., Vol. XVII, Spring, 1961.

When H.P.B. and Olcott left the U.S.A. for India, December 17, 1878, the small group of Theosophists was left in the hands of the Acting President, Major-General Abner Doubleday, of Civil War fame, and W. Q. Judge. The Society had largely been conducted as a "literary salon" with H.P.B. as the main attraction. The vacuum she left behind could not be filled either by Doubleday or Judge. During the years immediately following the removal of the Founders to India, Judge was left very much alone both by H.P.B. and the Masters. The golden days when Judge could visit the *Lamasery,* as H.P.B.'s apartment in New York was called, seemed gone for ever. Judge wrote rather despairingly to Olcott, complaining that he was being left out in the cold. This situation was undoubtedly connected with his trials as a probationary chela. He asked for news about the Masters, just anything. It is from the period of 1879-82 that Judge's correspondence with Dâmodar K. Mâvalankar dates. The replies of the latter revealed to Judge a more intimate relationship between Master and pupil than he had ever hoped for himself, and this made Judge his fervent admirer and life-long friend. In the series entitled "A Hindu Chela's Diary," Judge paraphrases Dâmodar's mystical experiences, as described in his letters to him.*

In a letter to Dâmodar dated June 11, 1883, Judge writes: "I have your last. On the back is written in red pencil 'Better come M ∴' . . ."† It was in 1884, which year marked the turning-point in Judge's career, that he undertook his long wished for journey to India. He went via Paris where he arrived March 25, 1884.‡ When H.P.B., Col. Olcott and party arrived in Paris, March 28th, Judge was on hand to meet them.†† According to some of his published letters,‡‡ Judge was ordered by the Masters to stay there and help H.P.B. in writing *The Secret Doctrine,* which at that time was still envisioned as a new version of *Isis Unveiled* —a plan abandoned later. Judge worked for and with H.P.B., both in Paris and at Enghien, where they stayed for a while in May as guests of Count and Countess Gaston d'Adhémar. He also

---

*Consult Sven Eek, *Dâmodar and the Pioneers of The Theosophical Movement,* Adyar, 1965, pp. 78-100.

†Original letter is in the Adyar Archives. The letter from Dâmodar referred to has been lost.

‡*The Word,* XV, April, 1912, pp. 17-18.

††Olcott, *Old Diary Leaves,* III, 86.

‡‡*The Word, ibid.*

was in London for a few days during H.P.B.'s hurried trip there in early April. Judge left Paris for India at the end of June, arriving in Bombay July 15th, where he lectured the 18th on "Theosophy and the Destiny of India." After lecturing at Poona, Hyderâbâd, Secunderâbâd and Gooty, he reached Adyar August 10th. His brief stay at Adyar seems to be shrouded in somewhat of a mystery, which we may never be able to unravel for lack of adequate documentation.

It was during Judge's stay at Adyar that the *Christian College Magazine* of Madras published the article "The Collapse of Koot Hoomi," with fifteen forged letters purporting to have been written by H.P.B. That period was one of grave anxiety and serious trouble, and the atmosphere at Adyar must have been electrically charged. We do not know exactly when Judge left Adyar on his return trip to New York, but he does state himself that he was in London in November, 1884, on his way home via England.*
It was on November 1st, 1884, that H.P.B. and party left London and boarded the steamer at Liverpool, on their way to India via Alexandria and Port Said. Olcott, on the other hand, sailed from Marseilles for Bombay on October 20, arriving at his destination November 10th.† From the above it follows that Judge left Adyar at about the time when both H.P.B. and Olcott were en route to Adyar from Europe. Considering the routes used in those days, it is most likely that their steamers met each other somewhere in the Mediterranean, but no information has ever come to light on this subject, nor any hint as to why Judge left Adyar so soon and without waiting for the Founders' arrival. There is no information either on a meeting between Judge and Dâmodar and what the former thought of him after personally contacting him.

Judge sailed for the U.S.A. from Liverpool, November 15, 1884, on the British steamer *SS Wisconsin*, and reached New York November 26th.‡ It was on that voyage that A. E. S. Smythe, future President of the Canadian Theos. Society, met him for the first time.††

The fact, however, that Judge's visits to H.P.B. and to Adyar marked the beginning of his exceptionally successful work for the Society would indicate that he derived inspiration from his journey.

---

*Judge's pamphlet entitled *Light on the Path and Mabel Collins*.
†Olcott's original *Diaries*.
‡Lloyd's of London records.
††*Canadian Theosophist*, XX, April, 1939, p. 35.

Upon his return to New York, Judge found his financial prospects greatly improved. He joined the law firm in which Olcott's brother worked, and thus he was able to devote more time to the Society.

Col. Olcott graphically describes the inner change which had taken place in Judge. He says: ". . . Mr. Judge felt what you may call the 'divine afflatus' to devote himself to the work and to pick up the loose threads we had left scattered there in America and carry on. The result shows what one man can do who is altogether devoted to his cause."*

In reviewing the situation in America, Judge realized that a radical change was needed in the administration of the Society, if it were to make any headway. Consequently, he wrote to H.P.B. and Olcott suggesting that an American Section be formed. This was done in June, 1886, with Judge elected as permanent General Secretary. The new Section soon prospered under his vigorous leadership and new branches were chartered all over the country.

Judge's despondency and immaturity of earlier years seemed entirely gone. He soon attracted to himself devoted workers who gladly carried out his plans. Olcott comments again: ". . . His brain was fertile in good practical ideas, and to his labours almost exclusively was due the rapid and extensive growth of our movement in the United States; the others, his colleagues, but carried out his plans."†

In April, 1886, Judge started his magazine *The Path* which was to become the backbone of Theosophical publicity in the U.S.A. As there were few qualified writers at the time in America, Judge wrote a great many articles himself. He did so under a number of pseudonyms, such as *An American Mystic, Eusebio Urban, Rodriguez Undiano, Hadji Erinn, William Brehon* and others. His style was simple and direct, and he dealt with a variety of theosophical and allied subjects. H.P.B.'s admiration of this journal was very marked, and she referred to it as "pure Buddhi."

In the Summer of 1888, Judge published *An Epitome of Theosophy*, a gem of succinct presentation of the chief tenets of the Ancient Wisdom. In a much shorter form it had previously appeared as a Theosophical "Tract," and was also published in *The Path* (Vol. II, Jan., 1888). So wide spread was its circulation at the time, that the Theosophical Publication Society in England

---

*Proceeding, First Annual Convention of the T.S. in Europe, London, July, 1891, p. 49.
†*Old Diary Leaves*, IV, 508.

published the expanded version which Judge wrote specifically for that purpose.

In 1889 Judge started a smaller magazine intended for inquirers which he called *The Theosophical Forum*.* His answers to questions submitted are models of concise expression founded on a deep knowledge of technical Theosophy. He also contributed articles to *The Theosophist* and to *Lucifer* which H.P.B. started in London in the Fall of 1887.†

Judge's understanding of the Indian philosophy found expression in an excellent interpretation of *The Yoga Aphorisms of Patañjali* which was produced with the assistance of James Henderson Connelly and published in New York in 1889.

In 1890 Judge published *Echoes from the Orient*, a broad outline of Theosophical tenets which originally appeared in *Kate Field's Washington*, under the pseudonym of "Occultus."

In the same year appeared a rendering of the *Bhagavad-Gîtâ*, based mainly on the translation of J. Cockburn Thomson, but with valuable commentaries in footnotes. He also wrote further Notes or Commentaries in *The Path*, and these were published later in book form.

In the latter part of 1891, appeared Judge's *Letters That Have Helped Me*, a series of letters written by him to "Jasper Niemand" (Mrs. Julia ver Planck, later Mrs. Archibald Keightley) which had originally appeared in *The Path*. Much later, namely in 1905, there was published at New York a second series of Letters compiled by Jasper Niemand and Thomas Green. Both series have been repeatedly reprinted.

In 1893 Judge published *The Ocean of Theosophy*, which in

---

*A monthly of only eight pages at first, and not exceeding twelve pages later, it ran from April, 1889, through April, 1895, seventy issues in all. A New Series was inaugurated in May, 1895, slightly larger in size, and running through June, 1898; at this time another change in format took place, and the journal was published at Flushing, N. Y. under H. T. Hargrove and later A. H. Spencer, from July, 1898 through April, 1905. This later Series is very scarce today.

†Many of Judge's articles have been published in book form by The Theosophy Company of Los Angeles, London and Bombay. The first collection is entitled *Vernal Blooms* and appeared in 1946; the second is entitled *The Heart Doctrine* and was issued in 1951. Other of Judge's articles have been published from time to time in pamphlet form by various Theosophical groups.

subsequent years became one of the Theosophical classics, running through innumerable editions.

Judge was also instrumental in publishing a large number of *Oriental Department Papers* consisting of Sanskrit and other Oriental Scriptures specially translated for this Department by Prof. Manilal Dvivedi and Chas. Johnston. He also issued from June, 1890, through March, 1894, the *Department of Branch Work Papers* containing valuable suggestions for Theosophical work and study. Both of these series of Papers are now quite scarce.

Approximately in 1894-95, Judge supplied the current edition of Funk & Wagnalls' *The Standard Dictionary* with definitions of Theosophical terms, and was announced therein as a specialist on the subject.

A number of articles and essays from Judge's active pen appeared in *The Irish Theosophist, The Pacific Theosophist, The New Californian, The Vahan,* and the *Proceedings* of various Theosophical Congresses and of the World's Fair Parliament of Religions in 1893. His literary activity was outstanding, particularly considering that it was limited to a period of hardly ten years (reckoned from the founding of *The Path*), during which Judge was often ill.

In December, 1888, Judge was in Dublin, Ireland, and there is evidence that he went from there to London and assisted H.P.B. in the formation of the Esoteric Section.* On December 14 of that year H.P.B. issued a special order appointing Judge as her "only representative for said Section in America" and as "the sole channel through whom will be sent and received all communications between the members of said Section and myself [H.P.B.,]" and she did so "in virtue of his character as a chela of thirteen years standing."†

The same year Judge was appointed by Col. Olcott as Vice-

---

*The Path, III, March, 1889, p. 393.

†The text of this document was originally published in an undated E.S.T. Circular, issued almost immediately after May 27, 1891, the date on which a full meeting of the E.S. Council, appointed by H.P.B., was held at the Hdqrts. of the T.S. in Europe, 19 Avenue Road, London, England, following H.P.B.'s passing. The original is in the Archives of the former Point Loma Theos. Society, and a facsimile thereof may be found in Vol. X of the *Collected Writings*, p. 194.

President of the Theosophical Society, and in 1890 was officially elected to that office, the rules having been changed.

The special trust and confidence reposed in Judge by H.P.B. may be better understood if the psychological mystery connected with him is born in mind, a mystery which is better known in the Orient and which had remained completely unknown in the West until recent times. As explained by C. A. Griscom, one of Judge's friends and co-workers,

"It was the good fortune of a few of us to know something of the real Ego who used the body known as Wm. Q. Judge. He once spent some hours describing to my wife and me the experience the Ego had in assuming control of the instrument it was to use for so many years. The process was not quick nor an easy one and indeed was never absolutely perfected, for to Mr. Judge's dying day, the physical tendencies and heredity of the body he used would crop up and interfere with the full expression of the inner man's thoughts and feelings. An occasional abruptness and coldness of manner was attributable to this lack of co-ordination. Of course Mr. Judge was perfectly aware of this and it would trouble him for fear his real friends would be deceived as to his real feeling. He was always in absolute control of his thoughts and actions, but his body would sometimes slightly modify their expression . . . Mr. Judge told me in December 1894, that the Judge body was due by its Karma to die the next year and that it would have to be tided over this period by extraordinary means. He then expected this process to be entirely successful, and that he would be able to use that body for many years, but he did not count upon the assaults from without, and the strain and exhaustion. This, and the body's heredity, proved too much for even his will and power. Two months before his death he knew he was to die, but even then the indomitable will was hard to conquer and the poor exhausted, pain-racked body was dragged through two months in one final and supreme effort to stay with his friends."*

In this connection, the following passage from one of H.P.B.'s letters to Judge, written from Ostende on October 3, 1886, is of great interest:

"The trouble with you is *that you do not know the great change* that came to pass in you a few years ago. Others have

---

*Letters that have Helped Me, Vol. II, pp. 119-20.

COL. HENRY STEEL OLCOTT
1832-1907
This photograph, taken in the early days of The Theosophical Society,
is preserved in the Adyar Archives.

DR. ALEXANDER WILDER
1823-1908
(Consult the *Bio-Bibliographical Index* for a biographical outline.)

occasionally their *astrals* changed and replaced by those of Adepts (as of Elementaries) and they influence the *outer*, and the *higher* man. With you, it is the NIRMANAKAYA not the 'astral' that blended with your astral. Hence the dual nature and fighting."*

The fact referred to in both of these excerpts is what is known as *Tulku*, a technical Tibetan term which describes the condition when a living Initiate or High Occultist sends a portion of his consciousness to take embodiment, for a longer or shorter period of time, in a neophyte-messenger whom that Initiate sends into the outer world to perform a duty or to teach. There are many degrees of this condition, and most of its mysteries remained under the seal of secrecy until the present century, and are even today but very imperfectly understood among students of the Movement. It is this teaching which provides the key to the many apparent contradictions in the character of Messengers and Chelas as witnessed in the history of the Movement for many years past.†

In a forthright letter dated from London, Oct. 23, 1889, H.P.B. spoke of Judge as being *"part of herself since several aeons"* and wrote to him saying:

"The Esoteric Section and its life in the U.S.A. depends on W.Q.J. remaining its agent and what he is now. The day W.Q.J. resigns, H.P.B. will be virtually dead for the Americans.

"W.Q.J. is the *Antaskarana* between the two *Manas*(es) the American thought and the Indian—or rather the trans-Himalayan Esoteric Knowledge."‡

With H.P.B.'s death, May 8, 1891, a great cohering and vitalizing influence was removed from the public activity of the T.S. At first, the shock of her physical disappearance momentarily united all in seeming solidarity, but the contest of strong wills which had existed in the Society for some time past could only be delayed temporarily.

On May 13th Judge sailed for London. He attended the Convention of the European Branches of the T.S., July 9-10, under

---

*The Theosophical Forum, Point Loma, Calif., Vol. III, August 15, 1932, p. 253.

†This subject, and cognate Tibetan doctrines associated with *Tulku*, as well as *Āveśa*, are treated at length in the recently published work by Geoffrey A. Barborka entitled *H. P. Blavatsky, Tibet and Tulku*, The Theosophical Publishing House, Adyar, Madras, India, 1966.

‡*The Theosophical Forum*, Vol. III, June, 1932, where it was published from the original in the Archives of the Point Loma T.S. Facsimile in *Theosophia*, Vol. VII, March-April, 1951.

Olcott's chairmanship; Annie Besant had arrived a few days after H.P.B.'s death. It is during that period in London that the Esoteric Section was placed under the joint Outer Headship of Judge and Annie Besant. Judge returned to the U.S.A. on August 6th.

In January 1892, less than a year after H.P.B.'s passing, Col. Olcott, an ailing man at the time, resigned the Presidency of the T.S. in Judge's favor, and prepared to devote his remaining years to the writing of his memoirs and to other literary work. There is strong evidence, however, that illness and fatigue were not the only reasons for this action. Among other and more compelling reasons, was one connected with the E.S. Olcott had originally opposed its formation, but yielded when learning that the Masters themselves had ordered H.P.B. to organize such a Section. Eventually, after H.P.B. had gone, the leading members of the Blavatsky household in London began to look to Judge and Annie Besant for leadership and direction. Olcott himself has written: "Every possible thing was done to reduce my position to that of a cipher or figurehead; so I met the thing half way with my resignation."* There is more to this story, however, than has ever appeared in print.

When Olcott's resignation came up for discussion and action before the Blavatsky Lodge of London, Annie Besant, as President thereof, addressed a strong letter to the membership of that Lodge, dated March 11, 1892, expressing her candid view that "the present Vice-President, and remaining Co-Founder of the Society, William Quan Judge, is the most suitable person to guide the Society, and one who cannot with justice be passed over." This was an unqualified endorsement of Judge as the future President of the T.S.†

At the Annual Convention of the American Section held at Chicago, April 25, 1892, Judge's election to the Presidency was unanimous; this decision, however, was accompanied by an unanimous Resolution, strongly supported by Judge, that Olcott should revoke his resignation due to go into effect on May 1st.

The European Section did not hold its Convention in London until July, 1892, at which time Judge was unanimously elected President, the European members having understood that Olcott's decision to resign was final. The situation was further complicated and uncertain because Olcott himself had intimated in May 1892

---

*Old Diary Leaves, IV, p. 428.

†Full text of this Letter may be found in Sven Eek's *Dâmodar*, etc., p. 115.

that his resignation was still an open question "dependent upon the contingencies of my health and the proof that my return to office would be for the best interest of the Society."

The Indian Section, as early as February of that year, had unanimously agreed to recommend that the Presidential office should not be filled during the lifetime of Olcott, but that his duties be performed, if necessary, by the Vice-President acting as Pres. of the T.S. Thus the Indian members were not actually called on to vote.

Col. Olcott had also raised an objection to Judge's assuming the Presidency immediately, demanding that Judge first resign his post as General Secretary of the American Section, as otherwise this would give him three votes out of five on the General Council.

On August 21st, 1892, Olcott issued an Executive Circular in which he stated that on February 11th of that year "the familiar voice of my Guru chided me for attempting to retire before my time . . ." He also pointed out that on April 20th Judge had cabled him from New York that he was not then able to relinquish the Secretaryship of the American Section and wrote him enclosing a transcript of a message he had also received "for me" [Olcott] from a Master that "it is not time, nor right, nor just, nor wise, nor the real wish of the ∴ that you should go out, either corporeally or officially." His communication ended with the following statement:

". . . I revoke my letter of resignation and resume the active duties and responsibilities of office; and I declare William Q. Judge, Vice-President, my constitutional successor and eligible for duty as such upon his relinquishment of any other office in the Society which he may hold at the time of my death."*

Judge, in a Notice to the members of his own American Section, gave an unqualified endorsement to this latest development and expressed his satisfaction. This action alone, if nothing else, throws a flood of light upon the nobility of his character.

The year 1893 was marked by an event which showed the great impact that Theosophical publicity had made in America. It spelled out Judge's high point of success when, at his suggestion, the Theosophical Society was invited to participate in the Parliament of Religions held at Chicago during the World's Fair. Dis-

---

The Path, Vol. VII, October, 1892, pp. 235-36.

tinguished representatives of Oriental religions were chosen from the ranks of the T.S. Hevavitarana Dharmapala, the resuscitator of Buddhism in Asia, came from Ceylon; Prof. G. N. Chakravarti represented Brahmanism, bringing credentials from three Brahmanical Sabhâs. He was Professor of Mathematics at the University of Allâhâbâd (ancient Prayâga), and a member of the T.S. Branch in that city. Judge organized the Theosophical meetings, and officially represented Col. Olcott; he, with Annie Besant, stimulated the Congress with their clear exposition of the ancient teachings. The sessions were held on September 15, 16 and 17, and were attended by overflow audiences.

It so happened that Annie Besant was especially strongly impressed by the personality of Chakravarti, and from that time on her opinions became colored by his point of view. Playing on her desire for occult powers, Chakravarti "captured" Mrs. Besant in less than two months. Judge watched his growing ascendency over her mind with anxiety, as he intuitively felt that a subtle attempt was being made then to divert her efforts from the genuine line of occultism into a sectarian offshoot. He became more uneasy when, on Mrs. Besant's return to England with the party that included Chakravarti, she prepared to go to India on a long lecture tour, and he warned her that it was not an auspicious time to go. Before leaving, she spent some time in London during which she saw a good deal of the Brâhmana; the latter left for India shortly before Mrs. Besant and Countess Wachtmeister started for the Orient.

A vivid light is thrown upon this very critical period in the history of the T.S. by Dr. Archibald Keightley, a successful physician, a staunch supporter of H.P.B., and a most reliable student. In the protest he made in defence of Judge in 1895, there occurs the following passage. After giving instances of Chakravarti's psychic ability to throw a glamour over individuals or groups, he writes:

"I lived at Headquarters [London] during Mr. Chakravarti's visit there and knew from Mrs. Besant, from him and from personal observation, of his frequent magnetisation of Mrs. Besant. He said he did it to 'co-ordinate her bodies for work to be done.' To a physician and a student of occultism, the magnetisation of a woman advanced to the critical age of midlife, a vegetarian, an ascetic, by a man, a meat-eater, one of full habit, large appetite and of another and dark race, is not wise. The latter magnetism will assuredly overcome the former, however excellent the intentions of both persons. And I soon saw the mental effect of this in Mrs. Besant's entire change of view, in other matters besides those of H.P.B. and Mr. Judge."*

It should be borne in mind here that for a number of years during the mission of H.P.B., both in India and later, there existed a growing antagonism on the part of certain groups of proud Indian Brâhmanas against the divulging by her of esoteric truths to the "outcastes," truths which they considered their jealously guarded secret knowledge to which they believed they had exclusive rights. Even individuals such as Subba Row fell victims to this inbred feeling, apparently oblivious of the fact that H.P.B.'s actions were taken on direct orders of her Teachers. Brahmanical orthodoxy was entrenched in its age-old exclusiveness, and, even though its votaries could not suppress the work of the Theosophical Society, they could at least make repeated attempts to distort its teachings and foil its main objectives. Even Col. Olcott repeatedly fell under the same subtle and pernicious influence, and had to be severely taken to task by H.P.B., as many of her letters to him plainly show. The Allâhâbâd Branch of the T.S. was a hotbed of this Brahmanical exclusiveness and haughtiness, as is conclusively shown by the message which Master M. ordered H.P.B. to convey to A. P. Sinnett with regard to the Prayâga Branch—one of the most important pronouncements from the Teachers.†

Approximately at this time in the life of Judge we see the gradual emergence of a simmering enmity against him on the part of those whose secret jealousy and lust for personal power made them a sounding board for nefarious influences the real nature of which they obviously did not realize. Judge's own declaration that he was in personal touch with the Masters and received communications from them, both for his own use and for transmission to others, became fruitful soil upon which the thorny weeds of enmity could grow. In some instances such feelings can be readily understood, but to find both Olcott and Annie Besant among these, proves both the subtle nature of the temptation and their lack of intuition. While making complimentary statements about Judge in print, they obviously indulged in vastly different feelings behind the scenes. This is not intended as a cheap accusation. The situation prevailing at the time should serve as a lesson. An imperative need for all students of the occult is to

---

*The Path, X, June, 1895, pp. 99-100.
†The Mahatma Letters, etc., Letter No. 134, dated from Dehra Dun, November 4, 1881.

constantly bear in mind that dedicated workers, pledged disciples, and even merely sincere aspirants, wholeheartedly engaged in Theosophical work, are tested, tried, and disciplined at every turn by the sudden *exteriorization* of their pent up and delayed Karman, an occult law stressed by H.P.B. herself. This is a process of purification which nothing can stop or set aside, until the disciple has worked off his negative karmic tendencies and has risen above his weaknesses into the pure air of impersonal spirituality. Unless this fact is understood, no satisfactory explanation can ever be found for the recriminations, accusations, abuses and injustices which occurred at the time to embitter Judge's last remaining years. While explaining their nature, the above occult law never justifies wrong action or thought for which every student is fully responsible.

It would be inadvisable to give a full account of the so-called "Judge Case" within the scope of the present outline. All pertinent data on the subject may be obtained by the perusal of *The Theosophist, The Path* and *Lucifer* for approximately the years 1893-96, and the following three main sources of information issued at the time: *The Case Against W. Q. Judge* (London: Theos. Publ. Society, 1895) published by Annie Besant and prepared by her at the request of Olcott; *Reply by William Q. Judge*, read by Dr. A. Keightley on behalf of Judge before an informal meeting of the T.S. Convention at Boston, Mass., on April 29, 1895, and published in pamphlet form; and *Isis and the Mahatmas* published by Judge in London in 1895, and dealing mainly with the attack published in the *Westminster Gazette*.

The accusations against Judge grew mainly out of a number of documents which Walter R. Old, at one time a devoted worker in H.P.B.'s household in London, and Sidney V. Edge, brought to Adyar in December, 1893, and which purported to prove that Judge had been misusing the names and handwritings of the Masters to bolster his own personal aims. Olcott considered the documents incriminating. Acting on a formal request of Annie Besant, who by then was at Allâhâbâd with Prof. Chakravarti, Olcott wrote to Judge, Feb. 7, 1894, offering him two alternatives: (1) resignation from all offices, in which case only a general public explanation would be made; (2) to have a Judicial Committee convened as provided for in the Constitution of the Society. In the latter case, the proceedings would be made public. Judge decided in favor of the second alternative, and cabled March 10th in reply to Olcott: "Charges absolutely false. You can take what proceedings you see fit; going to London in July." The Judicial Committee met in London on July 10th, 1894, to consider the six charges which had been drawn by Annie Besant.

The basic charges were that Judge had been untruthful in claiming uninterrupted teaching from, and communication with, the Masters from 1875 to the present time; and that he had sent messages, orders and letters as if sent and written by Masters.

Judge challenged the Committee's jurisdiction in the case, pointing out that "the President and Vice-President could only be tried as such by such Committee, for official misconduct—that is misfeasances and malfeasances."* The Judicial Committee found itself also face to face with its own limitations, on the very basis of the T.S. Constitution, as it could not try anyone within the T.S. on questions of personal beliefs. Upon motion duly made, the charges were dismissed, and Olcott, concurring with this, made the following historically important statement:

> "Mr. Judge's defense is that he is not guilty of the acts charged; that Mahatmas exist, are related to our Society, and in personal connection with himself [Judge]; and he avers his readiness to bring many witnesses and documentary proofs to support his statements. You will at once see whither this would lead us. The moment we entered into these questions we should violate the most vital spirit of our federal compact, its neutrality in matters of belief. Nobody, for example, knows better than myself the fact of the existence of the Masters, yet I would resign my office unhesitatingly if the Constitution were amended so as to erect such a belief into a dogma: everyone in our membership is as free to disbelieve and deny their existence as I am to believe and affirm it. For the above reason, then, I declare as my opinion that this inquiry must go no farther; we may not break our own laws for any consideration whatsoever."†

In retrospect, it seems most curious that any kind of special Judicial Committee should have been required to convene, with all the attendant expenses of long journeys, in order to arrive at a conclusion which anyone could have readily arrived at by carefully consulting the Constitutional basis of the T.S.

In a sudden *volte face*, symptomatic of the many confused trends of thought fighting for supremacy at the time, Annie Besant stated:

Old Diary Leaves, V, p. 191. *The Path*, Vol. IX, Aug., 1894, p. 161.
†Olcott, *op.cit.*, V, pp. 186-87. From the Minutes of the Judicial Committee of the Theosophical Society, July 10, 1894.

"For some years past persons inspired largely by personal hatred for Mr. Judge, and persons inspired by hatred for the Theosophical Society and for all that it represents, have circulated a mass of accusations against him, ranging from simple untruthfulness to deliberate and systematic forgery of the handwritings of Those Who to some of us are most sacred. The charges were not in a form that it was possible to meet, a general denial could not stop them, and explanation to irresponsible accusers was at once futile and undignified . . . I regard Mr. Judge as an Occultist, possessed of considerable knowledge and animated by a deep and unswerving devotion to the Theosophical Society. I believe that he has sometimes received messages for other people in one or other of the ways that I will mention in a moment, but not by direct writing by the Master nor by his direct precipitation; and that Mr. Judge has then believed himself to be jusified in writing down in the script adopted by H.P.B. for communications from the Master, the message psychically received, and in giving it to the person for whom it was intended, leaving that person to wrongly assume that it was a direct precipitation or writing by the Master himself—that is, that it was done *through* Mr. Judge, but done *by* the Master."*

When this entire period is carefully viewed in retrospect, many of the issues at stake appear rather childish and immature against the background of additional information on certain occult subjects which has become available since the publication in 1923 of *The Mahatma Letters to A. P. Sinnett.* Had the information contained therein on the rationale behind the sending of letters and messages by the Mahâtmans, either by precipitation or otherwise, been available at the time, it is quite possible that responsible officials could have stemmed the tide of recrimination which enveloped the Society for years.

Even then several partial explanations on this subject were available in some of the writings of H.P.B., but somehow or other they had either not been consulted or simply forgotten. Portions of several of the Letters written by the Masters to Sinnett had been copied by several of the officials and placed in the hands of a few, carefully selected people; it is a wonder that certain other excerpts from them, bearing upon the matter of messages and

---

*Olcott, *op.cit.*, Vol. V, pp. 195-96, 200-201. From the Statement by Annie Besant read at the Third Session of the European Convention of the T.S., July 12, 1894.

precipitations, had not been equally dealt with, thus avoiding a great deal of unnecessary trouble.

The following two statements, among others, should be borne in mind. Master K. H. wrote to Sinnett:

> "In noticing M's [Master Morya's] opinion of yourself expressed in some of his letters—(you must not feel altogether so sure that because they are in *his* handwriting, they are written by him, though of course every word is sanctioned by him to serve certain ends)—you say he has 'a peculiar mode of expressing himself to say the least'."*

On another occasion, Master K. H. explained:

> "Very often our very letters—unless something very important and secret—are written in our handwritings by our chelas."†

In the light of the above passages, what becomes of the accusation that Judge, while transmitting admittedly genuine messages from the Masters, yet gave them "a misleading material form,"‡ meaning the handwriting used by Judge on those occasions?

The judicial verdict of the Committee was received with mixed feelings. The charges had been met on legal grounds, but human emotions are never satisfied with merely legal decisions, and so Judge's guilt or innocence was to be decided rather by public opinion than otherwise. The minds of important officials in the Society were already made up for reasons which were not necessarily expressed in official sessions of Councils and Committees.

On September 27, 1894, Walter R. Old, then Treasurer and Recording Secretary of the T.S., sent in his resignation being "unable to accept the official statement with regard to the inquiries held upon the charges preferred against the Vice-President of the T.S."†† This was of course his privilege; but he went one fatal step further. He published in the *Westminster Gazette* the entire series of papers in the so-called Judge Case which had been entrusted to him by Col. Olcott. This breach of faith precipitated a number of recriminations, accusations and emotion-whipped opinions as if Pandora's box had been suddenly opened. Charges and counter charges followed. At the Adyar Annual Convention, in December, 1894, Judge who was still Vice-President of the T.S.,

---

**The Mahatma Letter*, etc., p. 232; 3rd ed., p. 229.
†*Op.cit.*, p. 296; 3rd ed., 291.
‡*Lucifer*, XIV, Aug., 1894, pp. 459-60.
††*Old Diary Leaves*, V, p. 256.

was slandered, and Col. Olcott, occupying the Chair, unfortunately did nothing to improve the prevailing Theosophical climate. Annie Besant renewed her charges against Judge and was supported by others. It soon became obvious that no satisfactory agreement could be reached between the contending parties. The final outcome of this unfortunate state of affairs was the decision of the American Section, the largest of the three then existing Sections, to become an independent body as "The Theosophical Society in America," under the Presidentship of Judge. This became a fact at the Boston Convention on April 28-29, 1895, by a majority vote of 190 against 9.

A large number of the English lodges took a similar course. Some lodges and individual members in Continental Europe and Australia withdrew at a later date and affiliated with the Society in America. Judge expressed the general feeling in these words:

> "The Unity of the Theosophical Movement does not depend upon singleness of organization, but upon similarity of work and aspiration; and in this we will 'KEEP THE LINK UNBROKEN'."*

Judge's health had long been very poor. He had contracted Chagres fever in South America which had had debilitating effect on him. Later tuberculosis set in. During the Parliament of Religions he was at times unable to speak above a whisper, and he had many premonitions of death. The concerted enmity of some of his former co-workers must have contributed a great deal in depleting his physical resistance and he passed away on March 21, 1896, at about nine o'clock in the morning, at his New York home, in the presence of Mrs. Judge, E. T. Hargrove and an attending nurse.

KAPILA. *The Aphorisms of the Sânkhya Philosophy of Kapila, with illustrative extracts from the Commentaries. Text and Translation by James R. Ballantyne. Allâhâbâd: Presbyterian Mission Press, 1852, 1854, 1856; 3rd ed., London, Trübner & Co., 1885.

KHUNRATH, HENRY (b. about 1560). *Amphitheatrum Sapientiae Aeternae solius verae, Christiano-Kabbalisticum, divinomagicum, etc., an unfinished work which appeared after his death with preface and conclusion by Erasmus Wohlfahrt. Hanoviae: Giulielmus Antonius, 1609. fol. 2 pts. French transl., Paris: Chacornac, 1898. 2 Vols. 8vo. 12 plates. See also Vol. V (1883), pp. 376-77, of the present Series.

---

*Report of the American Convention, 1895, p. 24.

KNORR VON ROSENROTH, BARON CHRISTIAN (1636-1689). *Kabbalah denudata. Vol. I, Sulzbach, 1677-78; Vol. II, Frankfurt: J. D. Zunneri, 1684.

LARA, D. E. DE. A learned old gentleman of Portuguese-Hebrew extraction who was present at the meeting of September 8, 1875, when the Theosophical Society was formed. Both H.P.B. and Col. Olcott had great affection for him. He seems to have remained a member till he died, but very little is known about his life and work.

LÉVI ZAHED, ÉLIPHAS. Pseudonym of Alphonse-Louis Constant, renowned French occultist and writer. He was born February 8, 1810, in a poor family; his father was Jean-Joseph Constant, a shoemaker, and his mother, a very pious woman of considerable intelligence, was Jeanne-Agnès Beaucourt. The life of Éliphas Lévi—who is much better known by this literary pseudonym—can very definitely be divided into three distinct epochs. During the first of these, his associations were religious and clerical. He received his early education in a school for boys established by the Abbé J.-B. Hubault Malmaison in Paris, and partook of his first communion at the age of twelve. Partly because of his own inclination, and partly as a result of the influences he was subjected to at the time, he was given a "push" in the direction of a clerical profession. In October, 1825, he entered the Seminary of Saint-Nicolas du Chardonnet, to complete his classical studies and familiarize himself with Hebrew. He graduated in 1830 and went to the College of Issy, to study literature; from there he moved to the Seminary of Saint-Sulpice where he showed considerable talent for poetry, a talent which he used throughout his life. In December, 1835, he became an assistant deacon, received his tonsure, and took very strict vows which included celibacy. This must have been the result of youthful enthusiasm at an age when, as he himself has said, he was unaware of life's experiences. While giving lessons to young girls, he became enamored of one Adèle Allenbach. Eventually he had to confess this to his superior, and the result was that he never was ordained and left the Seminary in June, 1836. His father had already died, and his poor mother, deeply shocked by what her son had done, committed suicide.

There followed years during which Alphonse-Louis eked out a livelihood by drawing, painting, and literary work, for all of which he had real talent. His closest friends were Flora Tristan and Alphonse Esquiros, well-known writers of the day. Within himself there was a constant struggle between early tendencies to a life of retirement and meditation, and more worldy inclinations which assailed his peace of mind and thwarted his plans. In July, 1839, yielding to his early tendencies, he went to the Benedictine monastery of Solemnes, planning to remain there permanently. He was totally disappointed in the way of life he encountered there, although his stay was productive of some good results, as he wrote there his *Le Rosier de Mai* (Paris: Gaume, 1839) a book of canticles and legends. He had occasion to dip into the writings of the Gnostics, the early Fathers of the Church, Cassien, and even Madame Guyon, all of whom influenced his mind very considerably. He left Solemnes with little but recommendations, and returned to Paris with no definite plan in view.

It is approximately at this time that begins the second epoch of his life, partially overlapping the first. After brief periods during which he got some work supervising studies in religious schools, he met Le Gallois, an Editor, who enthusiastically decided to publish his manuscript entitled *La Bible de la Liberté*, a work which he had written in a spirit of great rebelliousness and in his search for freedom from oppression. As this work was dangerous to the Church, the clerics sought to bribe him with money, to consent to stop the book's publication. They did not succeed, however, and the work was placed on sale at Versailles, on Feb. 13, 1841. An hour later, most of the copies were confiscated by the authorities and Alphone-Louis himself was arrested in early April, 1841, hailed into Court for attacking public and religious morals, and sentenced to eight months in prison and a three hundred franc fine. While in prison, he discovered the writings of Swedenborg, another mystic who exercised a very marked influence upon his mind. He was helped in prison by his friend Flora Tristan who brought him additional food.

Leaving the prison of Sainte-Pélagie in April, 1842, Alphonse-Louis began another two years of wandering and mental uncertainty. He engaged in some painting of murals, and tried for a while to reinstate himself with the clergy. Under the name of Beaucourt, he stayed at Choisy and Évreux, living there in the Seminary and distinguishing himself by his eloquence. Unfavorable publicity in the newspapers, probably due to his enemies among the clergy, ruined his stay there and he left. At this time, he was studying the writings of Lully, Agrippa and Postel, and wrote another work entitled *La Mère de Dieu* (Paris: Gosselin, 1844).

It was in the Fall of 1844 that Alphonse-Louis forsook his clerical garb, and apparently renounced the vows he had taken.

The emotional side of his life, denied all expression through the years of strenuous religious discipline, was in a turmoil. He had an affair with a Mlle. Eugénie C. which resulted in a son born three months after he was married in a civil ceremony to Mlle. Naomi Cadiot, July 13, 1846, a girl who was considerably younger than he. This marriage lasted some seven years during which his wife was very helpful to him in various difficult circumstances. He seems to have paid no attention whatsoever to the fate of his natural son until many years later.

In 1846, he published *La Voix de la famine* (Paris: Ballay aine, 1846. 8vo), a work which was interpreted as instigating class warfare, and which landed him in prison again; while sentenced for one year and a fine of one thousand francs, he managed to leave after six months, mainly due to his wife's exertions.

In 1848, he founded a paper entitled *La Tribune du peuple*, and wrote a number of pamphlets, most of which contained very radical ideas, which of course did not help him in his rather strained circumstances. While political in nature, these pamphlets reflected a very high idealism and an inner revolt against the injustices of the times. On the side, he was doing some interior decorating of an artistic nature, was rebuilding furniture and renovating old vases. In 1850, he met the renowned Abbé Migne, and was commissioned by him to prepare for his enormous Patrological Series the *Dictionnaire de littérature chrétienne* (Migne, 1851, 4to), which forms Vol. VII of his *Nouvelle encyclopédie théologique*.

In the course of his married life, he had four children, all of whom died in infancy. In 1853, his wife, infatuated by another man, ran away—a circumstance which left a deep wound in Alphonse-Louis' heart which was never entirely healed.

In the Spring of 1854 he went to London, met Bulwer-Lytton and engaged with him in some magical evocations, such as one of Apollonius of Tyana, concerning which H.P.B. writes in the present Volume. In 1855 he founded with Charles Fauvety *La Revue philosophique et religieuse*, a monthly which lasted some three years or so. It is at about this time of his life that Éliphas Lévi—as he now signed himself—began publishing in serial installments his *Dogme et Rituel de la haute magie* which appeared in book form in 1856 (Paris, Germer-Baillière). Another "subversive" piece of literature, a poem this time, landed him in prison once more, but he was pardoned by Napoleon III.

In 1859 and 1861 respectively, appeared from the same publisher two other works by Éliphas Lévi, namely, *l'Histoire de la magie* and *La Clef des grands mystères*—works which brought him considerable prestige, reputation and esteem; this was a rather peaceful period in his life during which a growing number of disciples and followers, among people of power and wealth in Paris, helped him financially as well.

For a short time in 1861, he became a Freemason in the Lodge called *Rose du parfait silence,* but he quit on becoming disgusted with what he found therein.

He made another trip to London and most likely had a considerable influence on the studies of Bulwer-Lytton, as the latter's work, *A Strange Story,* definitely reflects.

In 1865, Éliphas Lévi published *La Science des esprits.*

His wife, after some years of absence, suddenly sued him, and in January, 1865, a Civil Court annuled his marriage, as having been contracted by a cleric, this being against the laws of the land. This fact, if nothing else, goes to show that Éliphas Lévi was never "defrocked," as has been wrongly stated by a number of writers.

The period of 1869-70 was one of creative effort but also of failing health. Éliphas Lévi had a bad heart which troubled him more and more.

In 1870, his fortunes sustained another blow on account of the Franco-Prussian War. Most of his income stopped and he was very hard up. After the Commune, in July, 1871, he went by invitation to visit his great friend, Madame Mary Gebhard, at Elberfeld, Germany, and stayed there about two months. This, of course, was before Mary Gebhard had met H.P.B., and at a time when she had found in Éliphas Lévi's works what she had been looking for. She remained his staunch disciple until his death, and used to travel to Paris once a year to see him.* She received from him the original manuscript of *Les Paradoxes de la Haute Science* (Paradoxes of the Highest Science). By consulting Vol. VI, pp. 257-63, of the present Series, the reader will find a comprehensive exposition of the background connected with this manuscript, and how it was finally published with comments by Master

---

*Vide Vol. VI of H.P.B.'s *Collected Writings* where, on pp. 434-36, will be found a comprehensive account of the Gebhard Family. Mary Gebhard was born in Dublin in 1832, and for a time was educated in the Convent of Sacré Cœur in Paris.

K. H. Madame Gebhard contributed to the pages of *The Theosophist* (Vol. VIII, Jan., 1886, pp. 241-42) some brief "Personal Recollections of Éliphas Lévi," which, unfortunately give a somewhat inaccurate picture of this remarkable man.

As the years went by, Éliphas Lévi continued to write and some of his unpublished MSS were copied by different people from among his immediate pupils. A number of these fragments found their way into the hands of Theosophists, probably through Baron Spedalieri, one of his pupils, and were published in English translation at various times in the early volumes of *The Theosophist*.

Eventually Éliphas Lévi's heart condition brought about dropsy, and he died quietly on May 31, 1875. The Catholic clergy promoted a story that he had recanted and received communion before his death—a story which has been denied by his closest friends who knew the circumstances. He was interred at the Cemetery of Ivry, but in 1881 was placed in a common grave the location of which is not known.

Three other works from the pen of Éliphas Lévi were published posthumously. These are: *Le Livre des Splendeurs; Le Grand Arcane* (Paris: Chamuel, 1896; 2nd ed., 1921); and *Le Livre des Sages* (Paris: Chacornac, 1913).

Most of the chief works mentioned above have been translated at various times into foreign languages, and received world-wide distribution, so that the writings of Éliphas Lévi have become very well known throughout the world.

H.P.B. had a very considerable regard for Éliphas Lévi and his learning, but warned her students against accepting literally some of his teachings. According to her, he expounded "the true Hermetic Philosophy in the rather coarse language of the Jewish Seers and for the benefit of a Christian-born public"; to her he was "undoubtedly a great occultist," but "being a charming and witty writer," has "more mystified than taught in his many volumes on magic." Under no circumstances did she look upon him as an initiate or a practical occultist.

For a comprehensive and rather detailed account of Éliphas Lévi's life and work, consult Paul Chacornac, *Éliphas Lévi: 1810-1875. Rénovateur de l'occultisme en France.* Paris: Chacornac Frères, 1926. xviii, 300 pp., ill.

LIVY (TITUS LIVIUS) (59 B.C.-A.D. 17). *History of Rome* (Ab urbe condita libri); was in 142 books and told the story of Rome from the arrival of Aeneas in Italy down to the death of Drusus, younger brother of the Emperor Tiberius, in A.D. 9. Of these books only 35 are extant. *Loeb Classical Library.*

LIPPITT, GENERAL FRANCIS J. Born in Providence, R.I., July 19, 1812; d. in 1902. Son of Joseph F., and Caroline S. Lippitt. Graduated from Brown, 1830. Captain 1st N.Y. volunteers in Mexican War; served in Civil War as Colonel 2nd Calif. Inf. and Bvt. Brig.-Gen. U.S. volunteers. Married, Sept. 25, 1865, Mrs. Pickering Dodge. Counsel for U.S. in Dpt. of Justice, 1877-82. Was guest of Lafayette at La Grange, 1832, and present at his burial, 1834. Assisted De Toqueville in preparing his *La Démocratie aux États-Unis,* 1834. Attached to American Legation in Paris, 1834-35. Member, State Constitutional Convention, Calif., 1894. Lecturer at Boston Univ. Law School, 1873-74, and at Naval War College, Newport, 1896, 1897, 1900. Author of several military works, law treatises and musical compositions.

General Lippitt was greatly interested in Spiritualism, and became an intimate friend of both Col. Henry S. Olcott and H. P. Blavatsky in the very early days of The Theosophical Society in the U.S.A. Strangely enough, he does not refer to this association in his *Reminiscences* (Providence, R.I.: Preston and Rounds Co., 1902) written "for his Family, his near relatives and intimate friends." In 1888, Gen. Lippitt published a pamphlet under the title of *Physical Proofs of Another Life.* A few years prior to this, a rich Spiritualist, Henry Seybert, died at Philadelphia, Pa., leaving a considerable sum of money by will to the University, on condition that a committee of respectable and impartial scientists should be formed to investigate the mediumistic phenomena and report upon the same. The trust was accepted, the committee appointed, and their report appeared in due time. It was most unsatisfactory. Thousands of intelligent men and women could have done the work, and done what this committee did not do—given the facts of mediumship as they are. Among a host of indignant protests appeared Gen. Lippitt's pamphlet, able, conclusive and scathing. In the words of Col. Olcott: "General Lippitt is a gentleman held in high esteem throughout America for his blameless character and excellent scholarship, as well as for his courageous support of his convictions. The present pamphlet, which embraces a series of letters to the Seybert Commission, embodying narratives of highly interesting personal tests and experiences with phenomena, is worthy of his literary reputation, and shows how different might have been the report if the members of the Commission had cared as much to get at the truth of spiritualism as to boycott it." (*The Theosophist,* Vol. X, Nov. 1888, p. 132.)

A number of letters written by H.P.B. to Gen. Lippitt during the period of March to July, 1875, exist in the Adyar Archives. Presumably Gen. Lippitt returned them to Col. Olcott after H.P.B.'s death in 1891. They have been published in the Series known as *H.P.B. Speaks,* Vols. I and II (Adyar: Theos. Publ. House, 1950 and 1951). During this period, H.P.B. resided in Philadelphia, and the letters contain most interesting information concerning her views about the mediums of the day and the character of Spiritualism.

LORIS-MELIKOV, COUNT MICHAEL T. (1826-88). See for biogr. sketch Vol. II, footnote to art. "Armenians."

LUNDY, DR. JOHN PATTERSON (1823-92). *Monumental Christianity, or the Art and Symbolism of the Primitive Church as Witnesses and Teachers of the one Catholic Faith and Practice.* New York: J. W. Bouton, 1876. xviii, 453 pp.

LURIA, ISAAC BEN SOLOMON (1534-1572). *Commentarius in librum Zeniutha. Tractatus de revolutionibus animarum.* Contained in the Second Volume of C. Knorr von Rosenroth's *Kabbala Denudata,* Frankfurt, 1684 (Vol. I was publ. at Sulzbach, 1677-78).

MACKENZIE, KENNETH ROBERT HENDERSON (?-1886). Prominent Mason known as "Cryptonymus." *The Royal Masonic Cyclopaedia of History, Rites, Symbolism and Biography,* London, 1877 [1875-77]. 8vo.

MACKEY, ALBERT GALLATIN (1807-1881). *Encyclopaedia of Freemasonry.* Edited by Robert I. Clegg. Chicago: The Masonic History Co., 1929.

Mânavadharmaśâstra (Laws of Manu). Text critically edited by J. Jolly. London: Trübner & Co., 1887. Trübner Oriental Series. —Transl. by G. Bühler. Oxford: Clarendon Press, 1886. SBE XXV.

MARSHALL, WM. S., Lieut.-Col. *A Phrenologist Among the Todas, or the Study of a Primitive Tribe in South India.* London: Longmans, Green & Co., 1873. xx, 271, ill.

MASSEY, CHARLES CARLETON. English Barrister and Writer, b. Dec. 23, 1838 at Hackwood Park, Basingstoke, the residence of his granduncle, Lord Bolton; died of heart failure March 29, 1905. His father, an MP, was Under Secretary for the Home Office and

Chairman of Committees during the administration of Lord Palmerston, and later Minister of Finance for India. C. C. Massey was educated at Westminster School. He studied law, was called to the bar and quickly gained a flourishing practice; however, he threw it over, to devote himself to the study of philosophy and psychology, especially the investigation of psychic phenomena. Only once did he return to the bar in later years, and it was to take up the defense of Dr. Henry Slade at his famous trial in London; he did so without fee when he became convinced that the medium had been treated unfairly by Prof. Ray Lankester. Massey never married and most of his work was of a literary kind. He translated into English Prof. Zöllner's report on his experiments with Slade and published it under the title of *Transcendental Physics* (London, 1880), a work which was reviewed at length by H.P.B. in *The Theosophist* (Vol. II, Feb., 1881, pp. 95-97). He also translated E. von Hartmann's *Spiritism*, and translated and annotated Baron Carl du Prel's learned work on *The Philosophy of Mysticism* (London, Redway, 1889, 2 vols.).

Massey became in 1882 one of the Founders of the Society for Psychical Research. Sir William F. Barrett who convened the meeting at which the Society was organized says: ". . . It was in his rooms we used to meet for consultation and Committee work, and to his generous hospitality and ungrudging expenditure of time we were constantly indebted. [Massey was] a profound student of philosophy and psychology, and one of the most original and suggestive thinkers I have ever known . . ." (S.P.R. *Journal*, Vol. XII, pp. 95-96). Although Massey was on the first Council of the S.P.R. in 1882, he resigned from it in October, 1886, remaining, however, a member of the S.P.R. until a couple of years before his death. He contributed a number of important papers to the publications of the Society. As to his own ideas, Massey was convinced that the phenomena of Spiritualism neither afforded nor could ever afford evidence of what we mean by immortality. He believed that self-realization can be attained only through what he called the "process of the Cross," self-surrender and spiritual realization.

Massey was also one of the chief organizers of the British Theosophical Society, which held its first meeting at 38, Great Russell St., London, on June 27, 1878. Massey was chosen as President and Miss E. Kislingbury as Secretary.

As is evidenced from a number of letters written by H.P.B. to various people, she had a very high regard for C. C. Massey and his sterling qualities, even though they did not always see eye to eye with each other.

(Consult: *Thoughts of a Modern Mystic. A Selection from the Writings of the late C. C. Massey.* Ed. by Prof. W. F. Barrett, London, 1909.)

MAYER, ALFRED MARSHALL (1836-97). *The Earth a Great Magnet*: a Lecture, etc. New Haven, Conn., 1872. 8vo.

MAYO, RICHARD SOUTHWELL BOURKE, SIXTH EARL OF (1822-72). Born in Dublin, educated at Trinity College. After travels in Russia, entered Parliament and was chief secretary for Ireland, 1852-66. Appointed Viceroy of India, 1869, where he consolidated the frontiers and re-organized the finances, putting India on a paying basis. He promoted irrigation projects, railways, forestry. Assassinated by a convict while inspecting convict settlements on Andaman Islands.

MENDELEYEV, DMITRIY IVANOVICH. Russian chemist, the youngest of a family of seventeen, b. at Tobolsk, Siberia, Feb. 7, 1834; d. at St. Petersburg, Feb. 2, 1907. Attended the gymnasium of his native town; studied science at St. Petersburg, was graduated in chemistry, 1856, subsequently becoming *privatdozent*. Became, 1863, prof. of chemistry in the technological school at St. Petersburg, and three years later succeeded to the chair in the University. Resigned professorship, 1890, and became director of the Bureau of Weights and Measures.

Mendeleyev's name is best known for his work on the *Periodic Law*. His Periodic Tables of Elements embodies in its conception an aspect of the Sevenfold Nature of the Universe; it has stood the test of time and was fully supported by the most recent developments of atomic physics. It still remains a corner stone of modern science. H.P.B. herself refers to it on various occasions throughout her writings. [Cf. *The Secret Doctrine*, II, 627.]

Mendeleyev's best known work is *The Principles of Chemistry*, 1868-70 (Engl. ed., 2 vols., 1905), which has gone through many subsequent editions in various languages. The author was considered one of the finest teachers of his time.

Peculiarly enough, Mendeleyev assumed a very prejudiced attitude towards Spiritualistic manifestations and his astute scientific mind failed to do justice to the subject when it came up for investigation before a scientific committee.

MILL, JAMES (1773-1836). *The History of British India*. London: Baldwin, Cradock, and Joy, 1817. 3 vols.; also 1848.

MOLIÈRE (JEAN BAPTISTE POQUELIN—1622-73). *Tartuffe, 1664.

MONACHESI, HERBERT D. American newspaper reporter, Italian by birth and of very psychic temperament. He was responsible for a very lucid article regarding the original programme of the T.S. published in the Sunday Mercury of New York in 1875. He seems to have dropped out very soon after, and no further information about him has been found.

MOSES, WILLIAM STAINTON. English clergyman and medium, b. at Donington, Lincolnshire, Nov. 5, 1839; d. in 1892. Known for many years to Spiritualists all over the world under the pseudonym of "M.A., Oxon." His father was headmaster of the Grammar School in his native town. At Bedford Grammar School, which he entered when sixteen, he carried off several prizes. He matriculated at Exeter College, Oxford, 1858, taking a third class in Classical Moderations in 1860. Shortly before his final examination his health broke down and he was compelled to go abroad for a year, visiting among other places Mount Athos. Having turned his thoughts toward the ministry, he was ordained, and from 1863 to 1870 acted as curate, first in the Isle of Man and later in the West of England. Towards the end of this period his health again failed, and an affection of the throat compelled him to give up parish work. In 1870 he came to London, and took up his residence with his friends, Dr. and Mrs. Stanhope Speer, acting as tutor to their young son. The following year he obtained an appointment as English master in University College School, which he held until 1889, when failing health forced him to retire. In his last years he suffered from extreme depression and nervous prostration, as well as severe neuralgic pains. The immediate cause of his death was Bright's disease. In his various capacities he discharged his duties efficiently and conscientiously, and retained the respect and warm regard of those he came in contact with.

It was in 1872 that Stainton Moses contacted Spiritualism through the reading of R. Dale Owen's book, *The Debatable Land*. He visited various mediums, sat in many private circles, and soon developed strong mediumistic powers of his own, which manifested themselves first in physical phenomena and later in automatic writing. He rapidly came to the front of the Spiritualistic movement, took a leading part in founding the British National Association of Spiritualists, served on the Council of the Psychological Society, and, until 1886, on that of the Society for Psychical Research, when he resigned from that body because of the Society's attitude towards Eglinton and other public mediums. From 1884 to his death he was also President of the London Spiritual Alliance. He also acted for many years as Editor of the magazine *Light*.

While Stainton Moses was an exponent of almost all the various phases of mediumship, he is best known for his automatic writings excerpts from which were published under the title of *Spirit Teachings* (London: The Psychological Press Ass'n, 1883; also as "Memorial Edition," London, 1894). They began in March, 1872, and continued for about ten years. The teachings given in the published volume are supposed to emanate from an entity who calls himself + Imperator and delivers orations of a rather noble-minded type and in flowing language.

Other works of Stainton Moses are: *Psychography*, London, 1878; *Spirit Identity*, 1879; and *The Higher Aspects of Spiritualism*, 1880.

The first contact between Stainton Moses and Col. Olcott took place in April, 1875, when he wrote to the Colonel about his recently published book. A close friendship developed, not only with the Colonel but with H.P.B. whom Moses held in very high regard. A more complete account of this association may be found in H. S. Olcott's *Old Diary Leaves*, I, 60, 300-329, where many highly interesting facts are brought out. Students should also consult *The Mahatma Letters to A. P. Sinnett*, for various passages wherein the identity of Moses' "controls" is hinted at.

From what Col. Olcott says, it would appear that a rather lively exchange of correspondence went on for several years between Moses and the Founders. While Moses' own letters are in the Adyar Archives, the letters of the Colonel and of H.P.B. have never been located, in spite of considerable search having been made in the Spiritualistic Archives and Libraries of London, where the papers of Stainton Moses are deposited.

Sources: *Dictionary of National Biography*; "Records of Private Séances," *Light*, 1892, 1893; "The Experiences of W. Stainton Moses," by F. W. H. Myers, in *Proceedings*, S.P.R., Vols. IX and X; Podmore, *Modern Spiritualism*.

Mosheim, Johann Lorenz von. German evangelical theologian, b. at Lübeck, October 9, 1684; d. at Göttingen, Sept. 9, 1775. Cofounder of the Göttingen University, and its Chancellor, 1747. Regarded as the founder of modern Church history. Chief works: *Institutiones historiae ecclesiasticae*, 1726; German ed., 1769-78 in nine vols.; Engl. tr. by Archibald Maclaine, New York, 1880.—*Institutiones historiae christianae majores*, 1763.

Mousseaux. See Gougenot des Mousseaux.

Müller, Max [Friedrich Maximilian] (1823-1900). *Chips from a German Workshop.* London: Longmans, Green & Co., 1867-75. 4 vols.

**New American Cyclopaedia*, 1858-63, 16 vols.; edited by Geo. Ripley and Chas. A. Dana. New edition, as *American Cyclopaedia*, 1873-76, 16 vols., was prepared by the same editors.

Newton, Henry Jotham. American manufacturer and inventor, b. at Hartleton, Pa., Feb. 9, 1823; d. in New York, Dec. 23, 1895; younger son of Dr. Jotham and Harriet (Wood) Newton, both originally from Connecticut. When the father, a young physician of promise, died within a year of his son's birth, the mother returned to her father's home in Somers, Conn. Henry was sent to school there and afterwards finished at the Literary Institute of Suffield. He was then apprenticed for four years to Whittlesey Brothers, piano makers of Salem, Conn. His progress was so rapid that in three years he became a member of the firm. Five years later, 1849, he went to New York where he associated himself with Ferdinand Lighte in the piano business. In further association with the Bradbury Brothers, the firm soon won a leading place in the trade. In 1858 Newton retired with a competency, which he invested so judiciously in New York real estate that he died a millionaire. Early freed for the rest of his life to devote himself to his various hobbies, the chief of which was photography, he worked under the guidance of Chas. A. Seely, publisher of the *American Journal of Photography*; he outfitted a laboratory in his own home and engaged in innumerable experiments. He became known as "the father of the dry-plate process," and was a pioneer in the preparation of ready-sensitized paper and the production of the paraffin paper process. For a long time he was Treasurer of the American Photographical Society, and after 1867, Chairman of the Photographic Section of the American Institute of the City of New York.

A scientific interest in spirit photography led Newton to the study of Spiritualism; he exposed a number of fraudulent mediums, including the famous Etta Roberts, by apparatus and tests which he originated. His faith in the truths of Spiritualism remained unshaken, however, and for the last twenty years of his life he was President of the First Society of Spiritualists in New York.

Newton became one of the original "formers" of The Theosophical Society in 1875 and its Treasurer for the first few years. He was directly involved, together with Col. Olcott, in arranging for the first scientific cremation in America, when, on Dec. 6, 1876, the body of Baron de Palm was cremated in Washington, Penna. He had been the executor of the Baron's Will, and the event received nation-wide publicity, interestingly described by Col. Olcott in Vol. I of his *Old Diary Leaves*. Newton, however, did not accept H.P.B.'s explanation of Spiritualistic phenomena, and was greatly disturbed by what he read in *Isis Unveiled*. He later resigned from the T.S. with considerable bitterness.

Newton's wife, Mary A. Gates, of Wetherfield, Conn., whom he married in 1850, was an accomplished musician and shared her husband's unorthodox views and interests. They had two daughters. Newton was run over and killed by a street car during an evening rush hour as he was crossing Broadway between 22nd and 23rd Streets, then "the most dangerous spot in New York."

In the opinion of Col. Olcott (*The Theos.*, XIV, Nov., 1892, p. 72), Newton was "a man of dauntless moral courage, most tenacious of his opinions and, having been for many years a firm Spiritualist, withdrew from our Society when he found that neither Mr. Felt nor H.P.B. were going to show him either an adept or an elemental . . ."

NIEBUHR, BARTHOLD GEORG. German statesman and historian, b. at Copenhagen, Aug. 27, 1776; d. at Bonn, Jan. 2, 1831. Studied at Univ. of Kiel; became private secretary to Count Schimmelmann, Danish minister of finance; in 1799, entered state service. Chief director of the National Bank from 1804 to 1806, when he took a similar appointment in Prussia. In 1810, was made royal historiographer and professor at Berlin University, and two years later published two volumes of his *Römische Geschichte* (Engl. transl., 1847-51). In 1816, while on his way to Rome to take up post as ambassador, discovered in the cathedral of Verona the long-lost *Institutes* of Gaius. While in Rome, he discovered and published fragments of Cicero and Livy, and collaborated with Cardinal Mai and von Bunsen. He retired in 1823 and went to Bonn.

Niebuhr's *Roman History* (to which he added a 3rd vol. in 1832) counts among epoch-making historical works for its momentous influence on the general conception of history.

OLCOTT, HENRY STEEL. President-Founder of The Theosophical Society. Born at Orange, N. J., August 2, 1832. Eldest son of Henry Wyckoff Olcott and Emily Steel who were married October 19, 1831, and had six children. Henry Steel married Mary Epplee Morgan, April 26, 1860, her father being the Rev. Richard U.

Morgan, D.D., Rector of Trinity Parish, New Rochelle, N. Y. They had three sons and a daughter; the youngest son and daughter died in infancy.* Olcott's two surviving sons kept in contact with him even after his divorce and his identification with the Theosophical Society. His sister, Isabella (Belle) Buloid (married in 1860 to William Hinckley Mitchell of New York), remained his staunchest friend throughout his life.

Around 1630 a number of well-to-do Puritan families had migrated to New England from their homeland. Two men by the name of Thomas Olcott are known to have settled in the New World at this time. One was a prosperous farmer, but he lived in Boston. The earliest record of him dates from 1630. The other whom Col. Olcott believed was most probably his American ancestor was first heard of in 1635. He then lived in Newtown (now Cambridge, Mass.). In June of that year he left for Hartford, Conn., where he became a prosperous merchant. He founded a center for trade and commerce for the Colony of Connecticut.

Col. Olcott was greatly interested in genealogy and did a good deal of research, particularly in regard to his own ancestors. He came across a book by Nathaniel Goodwin (1782-1855) entitled *The Descendants of Thomas Olcott*, etc., published at Hartford, Conn. in 1845, giving detailed biographical information concerning the Puritans and early settlers. Col. Olcott edited and published a new edition of this book at Albany, N. Y. in 1874, in which he included various pertinent information he had gathered himself. He also investigated the English progenitors of his family, but did not find any absolute proof that any of the six families he traced were his ancestors. There were different names which doubtless indicated a close relationship, such as Alcock, Alcocks, Alcocke, Allcocks, Allcox, Alcot, Alcott, Ollcot, Olcot, and Olcott. The Heraldic Crests consisted of a cock standing on a crown, a globe or a single bar, in some cases crowing and in others silent.†

One of these possible ancestors was Nathan Alcock, who received his medical degree in 1737 and became an M.D. in 1741 at Jesus

---

*The four children were: Morgan, b. Jan. 20, 1861; William Topping, b. June 11, 1862; Henry Steel, b. March 20, 1864; and Bessie, b. June 21, 1868.

†Consult also the work of Mary Louisa Beatrice Olcott entitled *The Olcotts and their Kindred from Anglo-Saxon times through Roncésvalles to Gettysburg and after*. 2nd ed., New York: National Americana Publications, 1956; 315 pp., ill., bibliography.

College, Cambridge. The man whom Olcott himself believed was his most likely ancestor was Dr. John Alcock who was born at Beverley, Yorkshire, about 1430, and died Oct. 1, 1500. He was Dean of Westminster, Bishop of Rochester and Worcester, and in 1486 succeeded the celebrated Morton as Bishop of Ely. He founded in 1486 a school at Kingston-upon-Hull, and in 1496 Jesus College at Cambridge, which he established on the site of the former convent of St. Radigund.

The family name was a corruption of two Saxon words: *eald* (German *ald*, *alt*) meaning old, and *coc*, a male bird. The coat of arms used by Thomas Olcott consisted of three cocks' heads, showing similarity to that of the von Hahn family from which H.P.B. was descended. Olcott later placed a bas-relief over the door of the Western Library at Adyar combining the two symbols.

Limited finances curtailed Olcott's education. His father's business failed in 1851, thus compelling Henry to take up farming. He had studied at the College of the City of New York and later at Columbia University. He now worked a small farm on a share basis for two years, then returned to New York where he devoted himself to the scientific study of agriculture. When most young men are beginning their career, Olcott had already won, at the age of twenty-three, international recognition as an outstanding scientist of agriculture for his work on the Model Farm of Scientific Agriculture at Newark, N. J. He became cofounder with Henry C. Vail, of the Westchester Farm School, near Mt. Vernon, N. Y., which pioneered the present system of agricultural education in the U.S. based on the Swiss model, and was the only private school exclusively devoted to agriculture. His work attracted the attention of the Greek Government which offered him the chair of Agriculture at the University of Athens, an honour which he declined. His research in sorgum, just then imported into the U.S.A., and his recognition of its economic importance, resulted in the publication of his first book, *Sorgho and Imphee, the Chinese and African Sugar-Canes* (New York: A. O. More, 1858), which ran through seven editions, was ordered to be placed in the libraries of the State of Illinois and prescribed as a school text. The Government of the United States offered Olcott the Directorship of Agriculture, and two private owners offered him the managership of two immense properties; Olcott declined these offers, as he preferred to carry on independently.

In 1858, Olcott paid his first visit to Europe, aimed at the improvement of agriculture, and his Report of what he saw was published in the 1858-64 edition of Appleton's *New American Cyclopaedia*.* Recognized as an expert, he became the American correspondent of the well-known *Mark Lane Express* and Associate Agricultural Editor of the famous New York *Tribune*. This phase of Olcott's life concluded with the outbreak of the American Civil War.

On December 2nd, 1859, Olcott was present at the hanging of John Brown at Charlestown, Va. This man had been a fervent advocate for the abolition of slavery, but had taken matters into his own hands in occupying a small town with a band of his followers. He was captured and sentenced to be hanged. The Virginians were determined that no Northerner should witness the hanging, but the New York *Tribune* wanted someone on the spot. Olcott volunteered to go. When he got to Charlestown, he realized he had forgotten to claim his trunk which had a New York label with his initials. Baggage had to be examined by the Provost Marshal. The situation was desperate but fortunately a young officer who was a brother Mason recognized a secret sign which Olcott gave and fetched the trunk from the Court House. Some fourteen years later, Olcott wrote a spirited account of what he had witnessed, which is a masterpiece of reportorial writing.†

Olcott's passion for liberty drove him to enlist in the Northern Army; he went through the whole of the North Carolina Campaign under General Burnside, and was invalided to New York, having contracted dysentery, which periodically plagued him later in life. As soon as he recovered, he prepared to start again for the front, but the Government, noting his great ability and courage, chose him

---

*Edited by George Ripley and Charles A. Dana. Olcott's article therein is entitled "Agricultural Schools"; it may be found in Vol. I of this *Cyclopaedia*, and gives a rather comprehensive account of the history of such Schools in Europe and America.

Olcott also wrote *Outlines of the first Course of Yale Agricultural Lectures*, with an Introduction by John A. Porter. New York: C. M. Saxton, Barker & Co., 1860; 186 pp.

†Col. Olcott's account is entitled "How We Hanged John Brown." It was published in the weekly Magazine *New India*, New Series, November 17, 1928. It is evident from the text itself that the account was penned fourteen years after the event. In spite of considerable research, it has not been possible to ascertain which American newspaper or magazine published it in the first place, or what was the source from which *New India* republished it.

to conduct an inquiry into fraud, corruption and graft at the New York Mustering and Disbursing Office. He was made Special Commissioner of the War Department. Every means was tried to stop his resolute investigation, but neither bribes nor threats could check the determined young officer in his conduct of a campaign more dangerous than in combat. He fought through four years of opposition and calumny, and rounded up every criminal, sending the worst one to Sing Sing for ten years. The Government expressed its appreciation on this occasion by writing that the "conviction was as important to Government as the winning of a great battle," and rewarded Olcott by promoting him to the rank of Colonel.

Soon the Navy Department applied for the use of Olcott's services, to eradicate abuses in the Navy Yards. With resolute and unsparing zeal he cleansed the Department, and reformed the system of accounts. The extent of the Government's appreciation of his work is seen in the letter Col. Olcott received from the Secretary of the Navy, wherein he writes:

"I wish to say that I have never met with a gentleman entrusted with important duties, of more capacity, rapidity, and reliability than have been exhibited by you throughout. More than all, I desire to bear testimony to your entire uprightness and integrity of character, which I am sure have characterized your whole career, and which to my knowledge, have never been assailed. That you have thus escaped with no stain upon your reputation, when we consider the corruption, audacity and power of the many villains in high position whom you have prosecuted and punished, is a tribute of which you may well be proud, and which no other man occupying a similar position and performing similar services in this country has ever achieved."

Col. Olcott received similar acknowledgements from the Judge Advocate-General of the Army and other Officials.

Resigning his Commission in 1865, Olcott devoted himself to the study of Law. The New York Bar Association confirmed in a recent letter that he was admitted to the Bar in May of 1868. On the other hand, the University of New York, in a letter dated April 16, 1964, stated that there is no record of where Olcott studied Law. They suggested that he probably studied in some law office and was admitted to the Bar on the strength of his work and experience. With his customary energy, Olcott grappled with the intricacies of barely formulated insurance law, codifying anarchic practices. He became a specialist in Customs, Revenue and Insurance cases, and soon acquired a large and prosperous clientele. The Treasury of the City of New York retained him as its attorney to handle large suits against the City. As Secretary of the first National Insurance Convention, he prepared Notes which were published in two volumes. They have served as a standard work on insurance and the *Insurance Journal's* opinion was that "no addition to insurance literature more valuable than this compact octavo has yet been published." He drafted an insurance statute which was accepted by ten States of the Union and enacted into law. The Life Mutual Insurance Company of New York also retained him to represent the insurance profession in the State Legislature.

In spite of his preoccupation with agriculture, Government duties and legal work, Olcott felt a deep fascination for the occult and mystical. He had followed with keen interest various psychic phenomena, such as those connected with the Steel Sisters, from 1851 onwards; he studied whatever books were available on the subject of mesmerism, hypnotism and allied research, and discovered that he had himself a certain amount of mesmeric power which he once successfully tried on the daughter of a friend who was about to undergo a dental operation. But his interest in such matters occupied but a subordinate position to his professional duties until, in 1874, his attention was attracted to some remarkable Spiritualistic phenomena.

One day in July of 1874, while working in his New York law office, Olcott had a sudden urge to investigate contemporary Spiritualism. He purchased a copy of the Boston *Banner of Light* and read in it the account of the curious phenomena which were then taking place at the Eddy farmhouse in the township of Chittenden, Vt., and decided to go there to see for himself. He secured an assignment as special reporter for the New York *Sun*, for that purpose and left for Chittenden. After a brief stay there he wrote articles which created a sensation and were republished by other leading papers of the country.

Upon his return to New York, Olcott was persuaded by the New York *Daily Graphic* to return to Chittenden and to write a series of articles for that paper, with sketches to be made by an artist. Olcott returned to the Eddys' Homestead Sept. 17th; his articles appeared twice a week for twelve weeks, and the papers containing his stories were sold for as much as a dollar a copy. A number of Publishers competed for the right to put these reports in book form, and they were finally published in March, 1875, under the title of *People from the Other World* by the American Publishing Company of Hartford, Conn., illustrated by Alfred Kappes and T. W. Williams.

Olcott stayed at Chittenden until early November, 1874, and, as is well known, met H.P.B. who had come there on October 14th accompanied by a French Canadian lady.*

Such was the background of the future President-Founder of The Theosophical Society. Olcott brought to his Theosophical task an unsullied record of public service, a keen capacity, a great ability to work, and an altruism which H.P.B. declared at a later date she had never seen equalled outside the Âsrama of the Masters.

Col. Olcott's life-story from 1874 on is almost identical with the history of the T.S. itself, from its founding to his death in 1907. His many journeys and the chief events in his Theosophical career, from 1874 to after H.P.B.'s passing in May of 1891, are chronologically listed (with source references) in the special Chronological Surveys appended to every Volume of the *Collected Writings*, and therefore will not be repeated here. A few special points, however, require elucidation, as they cannot be clearly outlined in any brief Chronological Survey.

The role played by Col. Olcott in the production of *Isis Unveiled* is fully explained in the Introductory portion of the edition of this work which is part of the present Series of *Collected Writings*. The *Letters from the Masters of the Wisdom*, First and Second Series, transcribed and annotated by C. Jinarâjadâsa, should also be consulted for various sidelights on the early period of Theosophical work in U.S.A.

During that period Col. Olcott had many problems to solve other than those of a Theosophical nature. His wife did not approve of his new activities, as they obviously interfered with his professional work as a breadwinner for the family. On the eve of his departure for India he evidently lost a fee of ten thousand dollars for some legal work, which he might have salvaged had he remained in America.

When Col. Olcott was about to leave for India, he received from the President of the U.S. a signed letter to all American Ambassadors and Consuls, while the Secretary of State had issued to him a special diplomatic passport, charging him with the duty

---

*Olcott, *Old Diary Leaves*, I, 1-5, 10.

of promoting cultural and other relations between the U.S. and other countries of the world.

On Indian soil, Col. Olcott found poverty, disease and ignorance, and plunged at once into far flung activity aimed at an over-all regeneration of India. He travelled—both alone and with H.P.B.—far and wide lecturing to thousands of people; he organized the first Swadeshi Exhibition of Indian arts and crafts, urging the people to protect their national arts and industries; he founded a school for the Panchamas, the untouchables, the first one of its kind in India; he gave a great impetus to the revival of Sanskrit, established a unique Library at Adyar and started collecting palm-leaf manuscripts which today number 15,000 or more. He pleaded for the reformation of social life become decadent with age and aroused the patriotism of the people, which resulted in the formation of the Indian National Union in 1884, changed the following year to the Indian National Congress in which A. O. Hume was so active. A considerable number of his lectures on the great religions and allied subjects were issued as *A Collection of Lectures on Theosophy and Archaic Religions* (publ. by A. Theyaga Rajier, F.T.S., Madras, 1883. 218 pp.); a revised and enlarged ed. under the title of *Theosophy, Religion and Occult Science* was published by Geo. Redway in London in 1885.*

Olcott's contribution towards the revival of Buddhism in Ceylon is one of the most significant by-products of his Theosophical activity, repercussions of which are heard even today in various parts of the Buddhist world.

We should bear in mind that in the second half of the nineteenth century, the British, following the Portuguese and Dutch domination, had firmly established themselves in Ceylon and their

---

*Col. Olcott's literary activity was very considerable. Most of his contributions were in the nature of articles and essays on a great variety of occult and theosophical subjects, published in the early days in the *Spiritual Scientist* of Boston, Mass., and the London *Spiritualist*, and from October, 1879, in the pages of *The Theosophist*. A few scattered articles and reviews appeared in other, non-theosophical journals. Olcott also translated into English Adolphe d'Assier's renowned work *l'Humanité posthume* under the title of *Posthumous Humanity. A Study of Phantoms* (London: Geo. Redway, 1887), to which he added an Appendix showing the popular beliefs current in India respecting the *post-mortem* vicissitudes of the human entity.

language, religion and customs had taken firm root. People used English for their routine work and thought it degrading to use Sinhalese or Tamil. Education in missionary schools was geared to produce clerks for Government service and British mercantile firms. Local cottage industries and paddy cultivation—the mainstay of earlier economy—were regarded as inferior occupations. Ancient dagobas and vihâras were in ruins. In order to obtain a post in the Government service one had to embrace Christianity. Except for two or three pirivenas, there were only two Buddhist schools. Western customs took precedence over Sinhalese, and Western modes of dress were considered a sign of respectability. Native customs and traditions were eclipsed and their value ignored.

After the arrival of H.P.B. and Olcott in Ceylon, in 1880, and the formation of the first branch of the T.S., things began to change in a very extraordinary manner. Shortly after the commencement of their work, a marked transformation in the national life of the country took place, in the form of a resurgent love for the native religion, language and culture. This was mainly due to the Buddhist school-movement, the Sinhalese newspaper *Sarasavi Sandaresa* and the English journal *The Buddhist* which had been started. On his three successive trips to Ceylon, Olcott organized educational institutions where Buddhist children would not be forced to study Christianity and attent chapel services. Ananda College for boys and Musaeus College for girls are the result of his inspiration, and he invited educated men and women from America and Europe to come to serve in these institutions. From this small beginning there grew a vast educational movement directed by the Buddhists themselves. Through Olcott's initiative they obtained Government grants, such as were given to schools of other faith. Today there are over 400 Buddhist schools in Ceylon, and portraits of Col. Olcott hang in each of them. In 1962, the Ceylonese Government introduced legislation to nationalize the schools, and most of them now are operated by the State.

So many years after, it is difficult to picture the tremendous vigor and persistence of Col. Olcott in this work. Accompanied by an interpreter, usually D. B. Jayatileke (later, Sir and Chief Minister of the Ceylon Government), and the young Hewavitarne Dharmapâla, he jounced through jungle roads by bullock cart at night and lectured to the villagers during the day, collected funds for schools and roused the spirit of the people to a national rebirth along various lines.

His most outstanding work for the sake of Buddhism was the writing of a *Buddhist Catechism* which was first published in

Sinhalese on July 24, 1881. It was acceptable to the various sects of the religion and became a standard text for teaching Buddhism to children on approved lines—a book that has gone through more than fifty editions in English and possibly an equal number in various languages of the Buddhist countries of Asia.

In his defence of Buddhists in Ceylon, Olcott established friendly relations with the British Governor, Sir Arthur Gordon, later Lord Stanmore, who was sympathetic and helped redress various grievances which were brought to his attention. Later Col. Olcott, representing the Ceylonese Buddhists, went to London to obtain various reforms from the Secretary of State for the Colonies, where he was highly successful. The declaration of the Vesâkha, May Full Moon Day, as a public holiday in Ceylon, was directly due to Col. Olcott's efforts.

Another great service to Buddhism was rendered by Col. Olcott's two very successful visits to Japan, during which he addressed thousands of people. As a result of these trips, he was able to formulate Fourteen Fundamental Propositions as a basis of union between all the schools of Buddhism—a Code of Conduct which was unanimously approved at a Buddhist Congress at Adyar in 1891.

Another most valuable achievement was the designing of a flag for the Buddhists from the colors traditionally known as those in the aura of Gautama the Buddha. In due time this flag came to symbolize the unity of the entire Buddhist world. It was adopted as the common flag of Buddhism by the World Fellowship of Buddhists which met for the first time in Ceylon in 1950, and its acceptance was confirmed by the Fellowship meeting in Japan in 1952. It is now used in some sixty countries during festivities of various kinds.

Small wonder that the people of Ceylon should honor the day of Col. Olcott's passing every year as a holiday, and that during his lifetime seven leading Buddhist Priests of Ceylon should have given him a Letter of Authorization to admit people to Buddhism, an honor never before or since conferred upon a Westerner!

As has often been the case with many prominent students of occultism and active workers in the Cause, Olcott's character exhibited some curious contradictions and marked duality. He had some striking limitations, one of them being his long established habit of judging from externals. He shared with other "Yankees" an innate love "to show off" upon occasion, and his remarkable organizing ability made him prone at times to exaggerate the organizational aspect of the Movement to the disadvantage of the underlying spirit. In one of the most important letters received by him from K.H., he is flatly warned against permitting his suspicions and resentment against some of H.P.B.'s "follies" to bias his intuitive loyalty to her. He is reminded that *"With occult matters she has everything to do . . . . . She is our direct agent . . ."**

The careful perusal of the correspondence between Olcott and H.P.B. over a period of years would show any impartial student that Olcott often misunderstood H.P.B.'s motives and aims, instead of suspending judgment when his mind was temporarily confused. When Olcott permitted himself to be influenced by subtle forces emanating from insidious origins through Brahmanical channels, he imagined that a "Blavatsky cult" or something of that nature was about to be established within the Movement and set about to counteract it. This proved to be quite superfluous. The impact on him of the Coulomb troubles resulted in his trying to play down the existence of both the Masters and occult phenomena, a fact which was pointed out by K.H. in a message to H.P.B.†

On the positive side of Olcott's character, we must bear in mind his many outstanding and rare qualities which are not frequently met with. No one knew more about these than H.P.B. herself. On several distinct occasions, she came out forcefully in defence of Olcott. "It would be desirable for the cause of theosophy and truth," she said, "were all the critics of our President in general, less learned, yet found reaching more to the level of his all-forgiving good nature, his thorough sincerity and unselfishness.‡ Further on in the same manuscript she says that

> ". . . 'truth does not depend on show of hands'; but in the case of the much-abused President-Founder it must depend on the show of *facts*. Thorny and full of pitfalls was the steep path he had to climb up alone and unaided for the first years. Terrible was the opposition outside the Society he had to build—sickening and disheartening the treachery he often encountered within the Head-Quarters. Enemies gnashing their teeth in his face

---

*Letter received on board the *SS Shannon*, Aug. 22, 1888. Cf. *Letters from the Masters of the Wisdom*, First Series, Letter 19.

†*Ibid., Second Series*, pp. 68-69, quoting an excerpt from a memorandum in H.P.B.'s handwriting in the Adyar Archives.

‡"The Original Programme of The Theosophical Society," a Manuscript signed by H.P.B. and dated by her Ostende, Oct. 3rd., 1886. Cf. *Collected Writings*, Vol. VII, pp. 135 *et seq.*

around, those whom he regarded as his staunchest friends and coworkers betraying him and the Cause on the slightest provocation. Still, where hundreds in his place would have collapsed and given up the whole undertaking in despair, he, unmoved and unmovable, went on climbing up and toiling as before, unrelenting and undismayed, supported by that one thought and conviction that he was doing his duty. What other inducement has the Founder ever had, but his theosophical pledge and the sense of his duty toward THOSE he had promised to serve to the end of his life? There was but one beacon for him—the hand that had first pointed to him his way up: the hand of the MASTER he loves and reveres so well, and serves so devotedly though occasionally perhaps, unwisely . . . . . for cleverer in administrative capacities, more learned in philosophy, subtler in casuistry, in metaphysics or daily life policy, there may be many around him; but the whole globe may be searched through and through and no one found stauncher to his friends, truer to his word, or more devoted to real, practical theosophy—than the President-Founder; and these are the chief requisites in a leader of such a movement—one that aims to become a Brotherhood of men . . ."

Col. Olcott was a natural healer; he had that gift from early youth, and had studied mesmerism in the then available works which were mainly from French sources. When he travelled up and down India, he rediscovered that power within himself which had remained latent and unused for many years. He began to heal the sick and to alleviate their sufferings. His success was phenomenal, and hundreds of people trailed behind him seeking relief. This of course contributed substantially to his success in publicizing the work and the teachings of the Society. After some years, his vitality began to ebb due to the immense strain upon his natural powers, and his Teacher ordered him to cease his ministrations.

When in 1888 H.P.B. organized the Esoteric Section, Col. Olcott at first opposed its formation because he feared it would become an empire within an empire and would militate against the basic principles of the Theosophical Constitution. His attitude—which theoretically had some justification—was modified when he received a Letter from Master K.H. while on his way to Europe, but his doubts on this subject were never altogether resolved. His own individual relation to the E.S. is fully clarified by the following passage from the *E.S.T. Circular* of November 1894, entitled

BIBLIOGRAPHY 515

"By Master's Direction" wherein on page 3 W. Q. Judge writes:

". . . . Colonel Olcott is the old standard-bearer, and has been the medium for teaching, himself having Chelas whom he has instructed, but always on the lines laid down by the Master through H.P.B. ∴ He was selected by the Master to do a certain and valuable work not possible for anyone else, and he was never taken into the E.S. by a pledge, for, like myself, he was in the very beginning pledged directly to the Master."

Col. Olcott's own testimony is quite explicit. On September 13, 1890, he wrote from Adyar:

"The Esoteric Section was created by Mdme. Blavatsky with my concurrence, to gather together under a common bond of pupilage all such of our Colleagues as were anxious to study the Esoteric Philosophy under Mdme. Blavatsky's teachership. Already nearly 1,000 persons, scattered over the world have enrolled themselves in her list. She is the Chief of that Section— as Mr. Harte truly says—and its sole Manager; to her alone her pupils have to look for results. After watching results for a whole year and finding a great satisfaction expressed with her teachings I consented last summer while in London,* to be her intermediary for Asiatic countries, to forward documents and correspondence. This is all my connection with the Section, and this in my private, not my public capacity. The Society is quite neutral in all such matters."†

Circumstances connected with Olcott's attempted resignation from the Presidency of the T.S., some time after H.P.B.'s passing, and the vicissitudes of the so-called "Judge Case" have already been explained in the biographical outline of Judge's life and work to which the reader is referred for the chief facts of that period.

Olcott's lecturing and administrative activities continued practically unabated for a number of years beyond the lifetime of H.P.B. He travelled widely, promoted the cause of Buddhism and the growth of the Theosophical Society, and kept in constant touch with a great variety of people throughout the world. His executive

---

*This is an error. H.P.B.'s appointment of Col. Olcott as confidential agent for the E.S. in Asiatic countries is dated London, December 25, 1889.

†*Madras Times,* Sept. 15, 1890. Letter addressed to the Editor of the *Indian Daily News.*

abilities continued to be felt everywhere, yet the passing of H.P.B. meant a lessening of his contact with the Adept-Brothers who by then communicated but rarely with anyone—a circumstance which should be regarded as a natural closing of a temporary cycle of direct contact between them and their most promising agents and pupils.

Soon after H.P.B.'s death Olcott decided to begin publishing in *The Theosophist*—the oldest Theosophical Journal—monthly installments of a historical outline intended to describe the formation of the T.S., his early association with H.P.B. in the U.S.A., and the gradual growth of the Movement. The first installment of these reminiscences which were to be entitled *Old Diary Leaves* appeared in *The Theosophist*, Vol. XIII, March, 1892, and the First Series was concluded in Vol. XV, September, 1894, with the description of the Founders' departure for India.* An "Oriental Series" began the very next month, and the consecutive installments of this historical outline continued with great regularity into the years of the twentieth century, and were eventually published in book form, running into six volumes.

Rightly or wrongly, Olcott felt that a strong tendency to hero-worship was setting in with regard to H.P.B., and one of the main objectives of his outline was to counteract it. In doing so, he allowed himself to deal rather flippantly with certain phases and aspects of H.P.B.'s life and character, and laid himself open to severe criticism for having "belittled" his old colleague and friend. Certain passages of the First Series were construed by some of his co-workers as irreverent and were resented by them to such an extent that when Olcott asked Countess Wachtmeister to have the First Series published as a book by the H.P.B. Press in London, she refused unless he expunged portions distasteful to her. This he declined to do, and the volume was published in 1895 by G. Putnam's Sons, London and New York.†

Old Diary Leaves, in spite of many shortcomings and errors, must be considered Col. Olcott's *magnum opus*. Without this work, little would have been known of the history of the Theosophical Society. Most of the text was written several years after the events described, but on the basis of his personal *Diaries,* now in the

---

*A second edition of Vol. I appeared in 1941, published this time, as was the case with all the later volumes, by The Theosophical Publishing House, Adyar, Madras, India.

†J. Ransom, *Short History of The Theosophical Society,* p. 294.

Adyar Archives. Volume One, however, was largely written from memory as his *Diaries* for the period of 1874-78 had mysteriously vanished. Nevertheless, the first volume remains the most important and well written of them all.

When in 1906 Col. Olcott visited America for the last time, he wrote to an old friend, most likely William Mitchell, the husband of Belle Mitchell, Olcott's sister, who had passed away in 1896, suggesting a long-delayed visit together. Olcott was rather sad and depressed when they met. He felt very keenly the absence of H.P.B. and, realizing his own infirmities and advancing age, experienced loneliness and homesickness. In the course of the conversation, the subject of William Quan Judge was brought up and Olcott's friend asked him whether he did not mourn him at all. To quote from the narrative:

" 'Yes, yes,' he interrupted, 'I know how you feel about him and always have felt.' Then, taking my hand in his, he gave my face a searching glance, before he answered, in a manner subdued and most impressive:

" 'We learn much and outgrow much, and I have lived much and learned more, particularly as regards Judge.' ...

" 'I know now, and it will comfort you to hear it; that I wronged Judge, not wilfully or in malice; nevertheless, I have done this and I regret it.'. . . . ."*

On September 25, Olcott embarked for India. When the ship was outside Genoa, Italy, he had a fall which injured his right knee and caused severe bruises. He was carried ashore and taken to a hospital where he stayed for twenty-eight days. He continued his voyage to India on November 7th, going first to Colombo, Ceylon, and later, on December 3rd, to Adyar.

The physicians declared him seriously ill with heart trouble and evidently did not hold out much hope for recovery. He set about his most important tasks, but early in February, 1907, had to remain in bed. He passed away on the 17th of February, at 7:17 a.m.

Some of those who attended him just before his passing testified to the appearance of three of the Adept-Brothers around his deathbed, which, as usual, is something which can neither be proved nor disproved. It is, however, safe to say that the passing of the

---

*The Word, New York, Vol. XXII, October, 1915, pp. 7-19, where an anonymous account was published under the title of "Colonel Olcott: A Reminiscence."

old warrior could not have remained unnoticed by his superiors whom he served so well.

As a superb organizer, devoted to his Teachers and to the interests of the Society which he left behind, Col. Olcott is undoubtedly the man to whom we owe the world-wide structure of the organized Movement. Without his dynamic activities, the esoteric work of H.P.B., the direct Messenger of the Adept-Brothers, would not have been as potent as it proved to be. Col. Olcott's figure is better known in the Buddhist world than it is in the West, although time helps to bring him into correct historical perspective even in the Occident.

On February 17, 1962, on the fifty-fifth anniversary of Col. Olcott's passing, tribute was paid to him at the United Nations Headquarters in New York by Dr. G. P. Malalasekera, permanent representative of Ceylon to the United Nations, who lighted a lamp of the type lit in thousands of homes throughout Ceylon, when yearly he and his work are honoured with religious ceremonies through the length and breadth of the Island. The flame of the lamp stands as a symbol of the love and gratitude which the Buddhist people feel for the man who restored their privileges and their right to a Buddhist education, and renewed their national consciousness which today has created a new and independent nation.*

Offering flowers and burning incense, thousands of Ceylonese meditate on this yearly occasion and pray:

> "May the merit we have gained by these good deeds pass on to Col. Olcott, and may he gain happiness and peace."

OWEN, ROBERT DALE. Statesman, social reformer and author, b. at Glasgow, Scotland, Nov. 9, 1801; d. at his Summer home on Lake George, N. Y., June 24, 1877. Eldest son of Robert Owen and Ann Caroline Dale. Mother was the daughter of David Dale, proprietor of the cottonmills at New Lanark, where Robert Owen was beginning to put into practice his theory of social reform. Almost the whole of Robert Dale Owen's life was spent in the U.S., and was shaped by his father's influence. Possessed of much of his father's gift for original and liberal thought in social matters, he added to it a practicality and patience all his own. Instructed in New Lanark school and by private tutors until the age of eighteen when for four years he attended the progressive in-

---

*New York *Herald Tribune*, February 18, 1962.

stitution of Philipp Emanuel von Fellenberg, at Hofwyl, Switzerland, where his beliefs in human virtue and social progress were strengthened. Upon returning to his father's cottonmill community, he took charge of the school and managed the factories in his father's absence. Came to the U.S. with his father, November, 1825, where Robert Owen established a community at New Harmony, Ind., as an experiment in social reform. Robert Dale busied himself with teaching and editing the *New Harmony Gazette*. After the experiment failed, in the Spring of 1827, he became interested in another somewhat similar venture, the Nashoba (near Memphis, Tenn.) community founded by Frances Wright and devoted to the gradual emancipation of slaves. He went to Europe with her, meeting a number of prominent personalities. Back in the U.S., he engaged for about two years in the work of the "Free Enquirers," a group opposed to organized religion and advocating liberal divorce laws, industrial education and a more equal distribution of wealth. In June, 1829, he moved to New York and devoted much of his time to editing the *Free Enquirer*; he took active part in various social and industrial reforms, meeting some degree of success as well as many obstacles. The work which he did in New York, promoting lectures, educational and health centers, and free-thinking publications, corresponded closely to the activities of his father, whom he joined in England in 1832. For a while, father and son were co-editors of *The Crisis*, but Robert Dale soon returned to New Harmony and began a different cycle in his varied life. He served three terms in the Indiana legislature (1836-38) and was elected to Congress in 1842 as a Democrat, serving two terms (1843-47), but was defeated for a third. In 1845 he introduced the bill under which the Smithsonian Institution was constituted and insisted that the work of the Institution should include popular dissemination of knowledge as well as investigation. In 1853, President Pierce appointed Robert Dale Owen *chargé d'affaire* at Naples, and two years later made him minister. It was in Italy that Owen became seriously interested in Spiritualism, publishing later his two works on this subject: *Footfalls on the Boundary of Another World* (1860), and *The Debatable Land between This World and the Next* (1872).

When Owen returned to America in 1858, he became one of the leading advocates of emancipation. His letter to the President, dated Sept. 17, 1862, published with letters to Chase and Stanton in a pamphlet, *The Policy of Emancipation* (1863), was credited by Secretary Chase with having "had more influence on him

[Lincoln] than any other document which reached him on the subject." In 1863, Owen was appointed chairman of a Committee to investigate the conditions of the freedman, out of which study grew his volume, *The Wrong of Slavery* (1864), an understanding treatment of the whole problem. Owen was opposed to the immediate enfranchisement of the Negro, advocating a plan whereby the suffrage should be granted freedmen after a period of ten years.

Besides the works already mentioned, Owen was the author of: *Pocahontas: A Historical Drama* (1837); *Beyond the Breakers* (1870), a novel; and many pamphlets on questions of public interest. In 1873-75, he contributed a number of autobiographical articles to the *Atlantic Monthly*. The first of these (Jan.-Nov., 1873), covering his first twenty-seven years, were published in book form under the title, *Threading My Way* (1874).

Owen was married twice: on April 12, 1832, to Mary Jane Robinson, who died in 1871; and on June 23, 1876, to Lottie Walton Kellogg.

(Sources: Autobiogr. sketches, as mentioned above; G.B. Lockwood, *The New Harmony Movement* (1905); F. Podmore, *Robert Owen: A Biogr.* (2 vols., 1906); L. M. Sears, "Robert Dale Owen as a Mystic," *Ind. Mag. of Hist.*, March, 1928.]

PANCOAST, DR. SETH. Born in Darby, Penna., July 28, 1823; d. in Philadelphia, Dec. 16, 1889. American physician, anatomist and Kabalist, descended from one of the settlers who came to America with William Penn; son of Stephen Pancoast, a paper manufacturer, and Anna Stroud. Preliminary education in local schools; first few years of adult life spent in business; began study of medicine when he was twenty-seven years old, in Oct., 1850, at the Univ. of Pennsylvania, from which he was graduated M.D. in 1852. Became Prof. of Anatomy in the Female Medical College of Pennsylvania; resigned, however, at the end of first year, to become Prof. of Anatomy at the Pennsylvania Medical College, in which position he continued until 1859 when he became Prof. Emeritus.

Apart from his medical work, Pancoast became greatly interested in Kabalistic literature, in which field he became a noted scholar and built up what was considered to be the largest library of books dealing with the occult sciences ever assembled in U.S.A. at the time. He blended his Kabalistic studies with his medical knowledge, producing several rather remarkable works, such as: *The Kabbala; or the True Science of Light*, New York: R.

Worthington, 1877 and 1883; this book is said to have been the first written in English which attempted to explain the 10 Sephiroths and other similar subjects. It was followed by *Blue and Red Light: or, Light and Its Rays as Medicine*, 1877, which, while dealing with the therapeutic value of light, has a great deal of Kabalah in it also.

Dr. Pancoast was married three times: first, to Sarah Saunders Osborn; second, to Susan George Osborn; third to Carrie Almena Farnald; his family included children by all three wives. He was elected Vice-President of The Theosophical Society and remained a member until his death. He also wrote for Spiritualistic papers under the pseudonyms of "Lex" and "Lex et Lux." H.P.B. always spoke with great respect of his erudition, but when, as Col. Olcott says (*The Theos.*, XIV, Nov., 1892, p. 72), "it came to putting theory to the test, by evoking the unseen elemental races which guard the threshold of knowledge, he confessed he lacked courage, though she [H.P.B.] frequently offered to assist in the ceremonies and, if necessary, face the worst of the phantoms alone."

PARACELSUS, THEOPHRASTUS BOMBAST VON HOHENHEIM (ca. 1490-1541). **Astronomia magna: oder die gantze Philosophia sagax der grossen und kleinen Welt*. Gedruckt bei Martin Iechler, in Verlegung Hieronymus Feyerabends, Frankfurt, 1571. First ed. in British Museum 531.n.23.

PASHKOV, COUNTESS LYDIA ALEXANDROVNA DE. Russian woman-writer and traveller of the middle 19th century. She was *née* Glinsky and had been first married to Teleshov. She travelled extensively in Egypt, Palestine and Syria, and was at one time correspondent of the Paris *Figaro*. Most of her works were written in French. Among them may be mentioned: *La pension Vera Glinsky.—Un divorce en Russie.—Moeurs Russes* (St. Petersburg, 1876-77).—*En Orient. Drames et Paysages* (St. Petersburg, 1879).

Once when she was travelling between Baalbek and the river Orontes, probably around 1872, the Countess met H.P.B. and her caravan. They camped together near Deir Mar Maroon between the Lebanon and the Anti-Lebanon. That night a Syrian ascetic who accompanied H.P.B. evoked the astral picture of an old priest who had been connected with the ancient temple, ruins of which were in the vicinity. They were also shown the place as it was when the temple stood there; a vast city spread then far and wide over the plains.

H.P.B. and Countess de Pashkov travelled together for a while, and various curious phenomena took place at the command of H.P.B.

See H. S. Olcott, *Old Diary Leaves,* I, 334-35, for a quotation from the New York *World* of April 21, 1878, and *The Theosophist,* Vol. V, April, 1884, p. 168.

PHILLIPS, WENDELL. American orator, writer and reformer, b. in Boston, Mass., Nov. 29, 1811; d. Feb. 2, 1884. Inherited not only a superb physique and family traditions of a high order, but also ample means. Educated at the Boston Latin School; graduated from Harvard, 1831. After three years at the Harvard Law School, he was admitted to the bar and opened an office in Boston, but was never enthusiastic about his profession. In 1837, he married Ann Terry Greene who soon became an invalid, but their domestic life was quite happy; they had no children.

Phillips early became identified with the anti-slavery movement, and was greatly encouraged in this by his wife. His great opportunity presented itself on Dec. 8, 1837, at a public meeting held in Faneuil Hall to protest against the murder of Elijah P. Lovejoy, the abolitionist editor, at Alton, Ill. Phillips listened in the audience while James T. Austin, attorney general of the commonwealth, compared the assassins of Lovejoy to the Revolutionary patriots; then he responded with a stirring indictment of the outrage. His passionate eloquence caught the imagination of the audience which responded with cheers. Thus, at the age of twenty-six, he took his place in the front rank of the anti-slavery movement. His ability as an orator and his family prestige, as well as his charm and persuasive power, made him invaluable as a champion. Disregarding hostility from various quarters, he devoted himself to advocating other moral causes as well, such as prohibition, reform in penal methods, votes for women, and the labor movement. His denunciation of the moneyed corporations and his urging of the laboring class to organize to further its own interests were regarded by some as aberrations of a noble mind. Actually, Phillips had an unusually clear perception of national trends and was ahead of his time. He also showed himself as an uncompromising critic of academic conservatives. An omnivorous reader and a thorough scholar, he knew how to impart his knowledge in a simple and appealing way. He was an aristocratic-looking man, with a rich, persuasive voice and a graceful, self-assured manner. Like many other men who have stirred their country to eliminate evils of various kind, Phillips was frequently sharp of tongue and sometimes unfair to his opponents, but he was courageous, self-sacrificing and magnanimous, and has been called the "Knight-Errant of Unfriended Truth."

Among his many orations and speeches, there is one that stands out especially; its subject is "The Lost Arts" on which he spoke more than two thousand times. It is a speech which H.P.B. thought very highly of, and quoted from upon numerous occasions. It outlines some of the knowledge possessed by the Ancients and now lost.

POE, EDGAR ALLAN (1809-49). *Nevermore.

*Preamble and By-Laws of The Theosophical Society. Pamphlet dated October 30, 1875, and printed in New York.

RANDOLPH, P. B. See *Appendix* in Volume III of this Series.

READE, W. WINWOOD (1838-1875), *The Veil of Isis. London: Chas. J. Skeet, 1861. 250 pp.

*Rigveda.—Rigveda-Samhitâ. Ed. by Max Müller (Samhitâ and pada texts in nâgarî). 2nd ed., London: Trübner & Co., 1877. 2 vols. 8vo.—Transl. by Müller and Herman Oldenberg. Oxford: Clarendon Press, 1891, 1897. SBE XXXII, XLVI.

ROSSETTI, GABRIELE PASQUALI GIUSEPPE (1783-1854), *Disquisitions on the antipapal spirit which produced the reformation; its secret influence on the literature of Europe in general, and of Italy in particular. Transl. from the Italian by Miss Caroline Ward. London: Smith Elder & Co., 1834.

ROUSSELET, LOUIS (1845-1929), *l'Inde des Rajahs. Voyage dans l'Inde Centrale, Paris, 1875; Engl. transl. as *India and its Native Princes.* London, 1878.

SALVERTE, ANNE-JOSEPH EUSÈBE BACONNIÈRE DE (1771-1839). French politician and writer who was born and died in Paris. *Des Sciences Occultes; ou, Essai sur la magie, les prodiges et les miracles. Paris: Sédillot, 1829. 2 vols.; 2nd ed., Paris: J. B. Baillière, 1843. —Transl. with Notes by Anthony Todd Thomson as *The Occult Sciences. The Philosophy of Magic, Prodigies and Apparent Miracles.* London: A. Bentley, 1846; New York: Harpers, 1847, 1855.

SCHWARZENBERG, PRINCE FRIEDRICH ZU. Catholic ecclesiastic, b. at Vienna, April 6, 1809; d. March 27, 1885. Became a priest, 1833; Prince Archbishop of Salzburg, 1836; Cardinal, 1842; and Prince Archbishop of Prague, 1850. Occupied himself with trying to secure greater freedom of Church from State in Germany and Austria.

*Sepher Yetzirah. See Vol. VIII, p. 415, for particulars.

SHAKESPEARE, JOHN. English Orientalist, b. at Lount, August, 1774; d. 1858. Son of a small farmer; educated at a school kept by a clergyman who brought him to the notice of Marquis of Hastings, the lord of the manor; the latter sent him to London to learn Arabic. About 1805, he was appointed to an Oriental professorship at Royal Military College, Marlow; in 1809, he became professor of Hindustani in training college for cadets opened by the East India Co.; retired in 1829. He was a very frugal man, unmarried, and set money aside. Chief works: *Hindustani Grammar*, 1813; 6th ed., 1855.—**A Dictionary: Hindustani and English*, 1817, 4th ed., 1849 (with Engl.-Hind. added).—*Introd. to the Hindustani Language*, 1845.

SHAKESPEARE, WILLIAM (1564-1616), *Macbeth, 1605-06.

SHAMJI KRISHNAVARMA. See p. 437 in the present Volume.

SHIMON BEN YOḤAI. See Vol. VII, pp. 269-70, for particulars about his life and work.

SIMMONS, CHARLES EZRA. American physician, specializing in gynecology, b. at Troy, N. Y., Aug. 16, 1840; d. in New York, May 3, 1918. Son of Joseph Ferris and Mary Sophia Gleason, and great grandson of Albertus Simon, who was of Dutch extraction and settled in the colony of Rensselaerswyck, N. Y., on the Hudson River. His brother was a prominent New York financier. After three years at Williams College, 1857-60, Chas. Simmons entered Beloit College, Wis., where he graduated in 1861. He then spent a year at the University of Göttingen, Germany, and in 1862-63 studied at Jefferson medical college in Philadelphia; then he went to the college of physicians and surgeons at Columbia Univ., where he was graduated M.D., 1864. Thereafter he practiced at Troy and New York City where he had one of the largest practices. He was Commissioner of charities and corrections of New York, 1885-95. He was a man of energy and courage, a lover of people and animals, kindly in manner, and acquired a great many friends. He was a member of a great many medical and other societies. In 1865, he had married Sarah Ruby, daughter of Jacob Gould, a banker, a founder of Rochester, N. Y. and its first mayor. They had one son and two daughters.

Dr. Simmons, though an Episcopalian, was interested in various progressive movements; he was present at the formation of the Theos. Society, and became for a time one of its Councillors.

SINNETT, ALFRED PERCY (1840-1921). *Incidents in the Life of Madame Blavatsky. London: George Redway, 1886, xii, 324 pp.; 2nd ed., London: Theos. Publ. House, 1913, 256 pp. Somewhat abbreviated.—*The Letters of H. P. Blavatsky to A. P. Sinnett, and Other Miscellaneous Letters. Transcribed, Compiled and with an Introduction by A. T. Barker. New York: Frederick A. Stokes Co., 1924. xvi, 404 pp.—*The Mahatma Letters to A. P. Sinnett, 3rd & rev. ed., Adyar, Theos. Publ. House. 1962.

SLADE, DR. HENRY. American medium principally known in connection with his slate-writing, and familiar to the mediumistic circles in Michigan as early as 1860. It was not, however, until his selection by the Blavatsky-Olcott committee that he first came to prominence. Information as to his birth and early life is lacking; he died in a private hospital in Michigan, in September, 1905.

Suspicions of fraud expressed by some of the observers at his *séances* have never been substantiated. On the other hand considerable testimony exists in corroboration of the genuineness of Slade's mediumistic phenomena. In his paper, "The Possibility of Mal-Observation in Relation to Evidence of the Phenomena of Spiritualism," read at a General Meeting of the Society for Psychical Research, July 5, 1886, C. C. Massey recounts a phenomenon produced by Slade in New York and witnessed by him in company with Col. Olcott, on the 14th of October, 1885. The phenomenon consisted in a chair, found to be free of all attachments, being raised and moved about, at Massey's request, while the medium at a distance remained immobile and simultaneously observed. In the words of Massey: "No mediumistic phenomenon that I have witnessed has made stronger or more lasting impression upon me than this one" (*Proceedings*, S.P.R., Vol. IV, p. 81). Among those who came to acknowledge the reality of phenomena exhibited in Slade's presence were Dr. Alfred Russel Wallace, Serjeant Edward W. Cox, Dr. C. Carter Blake, Dr. George Wyld, Miss Kislingbury (in 1876, Secretary to the British National Association of Spiritualists), Prof. Zöllner and his colleagues Fechner, Weber and Scheibner. In Russia, Grand Duke Constantine, Prof. Butlerov and A. N. Aksakov were among those converted to belief by experiments with Slade.

SOLOVYOV, VSEVOLOD S. (1849-1903). *A Modern Priestess of Isis. Translated from Russian into English (somewhat abridged) by Walter Leaf. London: Longmans, Green, and Co., 1895. See Vols. VI, p. 446, and VII, pp. 332-34, for particulars about Solovyov and his writings.

SOTHERAN, CHARLES. Author, Bibliographer and Scholar, b. at Newington, Surrey, England, July 8, 1847; d. in New York in 1902. Son of Charles and Frances Elise (Hirst) Sotheran, and relative of the famous London Booksellers of the same name. Educated in England in private schools and St. Marie's College, Rugby. Married Mrs. Alice (Hyneman) Rhine, Oct. 17, 1893. Came to the U.S.A. in 1874, and began reportorial work on the New York *World*. Was literary Editor of the New York *Recorder* and *Star*, and Editor of the New York *Echo*, a short-lived journal which he published for a time. Was connected with Sabin and Sons, Booksellers in New York, in the editing of their journal, *The American Bibliopolist*. Later he was connected editorially with several other journals both in U.S.A. and England. Sotheran was a prominent Mason and representative in U.S.A. of the Swedenborgian Rite. He was the author of the following works: *Alessandro di Cagliostro, Impostor or Martyr?*, 1875; *Percy Bysshe Shelley as a Philosopher and Reformer*, New York, 1876; *Horace Greeley, and Other Pioneers of American Socialism*, N. Y., 1892 and 1915; *The Theatres of New York*, 1893. Also numerous separate bibliographies.

His rather fiery temperament kept him and his friends in a turmoil. He took active part in the founding of the Theosophical Society, but only three months later made some inflammatory speeches at a political street meeting, to which H.P.B. strongly objected. Sotheran resigned from the T.S. in a huff, but six months later apologized for various critical and unfriendly remarks he had made, and was reinstated. This episode, however, should not prejudice the reader against Sotheran. He was a remarkable man in more ways than one, and his role in the work of the Society in its early stages of growth should not be judged by the above mentioned unfortunate episode. We have a source of interesting information about Sotheran as a man and thinker in Mrs. Laura C. Langford-Holloway's account entitled "Helena Petrovna Blavatsky: a Reminiscence," published in *The Word*, New York, Vol. XXII, December, 1915, pp. 136-153, wherein she writes as follows:

". . . Knowing as I did of the friendship existing between herself [H.P.B.] and Mr. Chas. Sotheran, one of the ablest newspaper writers ever in New York, a man of broad culture and a rarely noble character, I have sometimes wondered that her biographers have not manifested more interest in the man and his services to her. Mr. Sotheran was a member of the Rosicrucian Society, a Mason of exalted rank, and a writer versed in the history of all Oriental systems of religious thought. He was the originator of the word "Theosophy," as the name for the new society, and he it was who introduced to Madame Blavatsky the scholarly men whose names are mentioned in connection with *Isis Unveiled*. He was the most influential champion Madame Blavatsky possessed while living in New York, and he was an ideal friend—royally true and unvaryingly helpful. He was eager that she should be identified with the circle of literary people about her, for he felt a real admiration for her great mental ability, and desired that others should appreciate her. A spirit of self-depreciation that decreased her influence, he had noted, and this he tried to help her overcome. It was a defect in her character, this tendency to underrate her ability, and he urged her to combat it. He had little success in this effort, for she cared not at all for her accomplishments and only sought recognition in her occult work.

"It was often asserted—on what basis of proof I never knew —that Mr. Sotheran was acquainted with one, at least, of the Brotherhood of Adepts, and was, in some way, identified with their broad aims for the betterment of the race. And it was generally understood that he had met Madame Blavatsky abroad, and knew of the task she was undertaking in this country. He, at least, held an exalted view of her genius, and urged her to write, and deprecated her interest in religious "fads" as he characterized spiritism. He opposed public *séances* in an uncompromisingly bitter way. So strong was his hostility to the subject, that he would never engage in conversation on it, or kindred themes. Nor did he ever concur in the claim that Madame Blavatsky's position required that she should investigate the matter thoroughly.

"His attitude was that she was a genuine occultist, with reasonable powers of mind, and had been trained to use them. And he often asserted that occultism was a noble study, and one about which the West did not know anything whatever.

"The services of this man to the Theosophical Society in its beginnings have never been justly recognized. He was a helper, without whom the work of society organization, of research work in connection with *Isis Unveiled*, of securing a publisher for this work, and then of having it properly placed before the public, would not have been half so efficiently performed.

"Mr. Sotheran knew New York, and had a position among men that was unique. His life was singularly free of entanglements; he was most fortunately situated to enjoy his advantages as a man of great ability and attainments, of ample financial resources, a bachelor, and one of a group of New Yorkers who lent character and dignity and prestige to the best circle of society.

"He was an admitted occultist, but was opposed to the prominence given occult phenomena on the ground that it could but add to the burdens imposed by the ignorant upon those who demonstrated laws they could not master. And he deplored the tendency of many about Madame Blavatsky to have her become the miracle-worker of the age. He spoke of her intellectual ability as of far greater value to the new Society than any mere psychic power she possessed, and he tried to counteract the influence of those who, appreciating her less, would have had her waste her time upon phenomena. A wise friend he was, and a true prophet, for he counseled her to discourage those who expected her to entertain them with signs and wonders, and to insist upon the serious study of the hidden forces of nature . . ."

This description, while showing ignorance of certain facts which pertain to the orders received by H.P.B. from her Superiors to work for a time with the outward Spiritualistic Movement, gives nevertheless an interesting picture of Sotheran's many-sided character and should be recorded here for posterity.

STEWART, BALFOUR (1828-87). *The Sun and the Earth. In Science Lectures for the People. Fourth Series, 1872-73, delivered in Manchester, England.

*Talmud. Vide Vol. VIII, p. 416, for comprehensive data. Also art. by I. O. M. Deutsch in the Quarterly Review for October, 1867.

TAPPAN, CORA L. V. (later Tappan-Richmond). American trance-medium of considerable renown. Under her maiden name of Scott she had very early made her appearance in the Spiritualistic Movement. At the age of thirteen she was already addressing audiences in Wisconsin; three years later she went to New York, and from that time onwards she became famous throughout the States as a Spiritualist lecturer. In 1873 she came to England, receiving there also an enthusiastic welcome. Her lectures and her poetry are supposed to have been delivered under spirit-inspiration. They show some degree of eloquence and surpass those of other trance-mediums in coherence and intelligence.

TEXTOR DE RAVISI, BARON ANATOLE-ARTHUR. French Catholic Orientalist, b. at Bourges, 1822; d. in Paris, 1902. Actively engaged, 1847-52, in the colonization of the Island of Réunion, and in 1853-63 in devoloping the maritime commerce of Karikal, India; was for a while Governor of that city, but resigned in 1864 and became engaged in financial transactions. Works: *Architecture hindoue*, etc., 1870-7-1.—*Âme et corps, d'après la théologie égyptienne*.

VARLEY, CROMWELL FLEETWOOD. Electrical engineer, b. at Kentish Town, London, England, April 6, 1828; d. at Cromwell House, Bexley Heath, Kent, Sept. 2, 1883. He was the son of Cornelius Varley, watercolor-painter, and was named after two of his ancestors, Oliver Cromwell and General Fleetwood. He was educated at St. Saviour's, Southwark. After leaving school he studied telegraphy, and was engaged in 1846 by the Electric and International Telegraph Co. in whose employ he remained until 1868, when he retired, spending much of his time producing new inventions.

The first improvement he introduced in telegraphy was the "killing" of the wire by giving it a slight permanent elongation; next he devised a method of localizing the faults in submarine cables; in 1854, he patented the double current key and relay, by which it became possible to telegraph from London to Edinburgh direct; then came the polarized relay, and his translating system for use in connection with the cables of the Dutch lines. In 1870, he patented an instrument called cymaphen, for the transmission of audible signals, and it is claimed for him that it contained the essentials of the modern telephone. Thus, one year before the date of the Bell patent, namely in 1870, music was transmitted by this instrument from the Canterbury Music Hall in Westminster Bridge Road to the Queen's Theatre in Long Acre over an ordinary telegraph wire with complete success.

Varley's name is chiefly remembered in connection with the Atlantic cable; the first cable, laid in August, 1858, was a failure. Varley conceived the idea of making an artificial line composed of resistances and condensers, which should exactly represent the working conditions of a submarine cable. This paved the way to further and successful attempts at Trans-Atlantic telegraphy. In 1871, Varley was elected a fellow of the Royal Society. He is the author of various technical papers on electricity, etc., mainly in the *Philosophical Transactions* and the *Electrician*.

By his first wife, from whom he was divorced, Varley had two sons and two daughters; his second wife was Jessie, daughter of Captain Charles Smith of Forres, Scotland. His two brothers, Frederick Henry and Samuel Alfred, were also inventors. Varley was buried at Christ Church, Bexley.

Varley's interest in Spiritualism dates from about 1850. He undertook experiments which showed that the phenomenon of table-rapping was not due to any detectable electrical or magnetic force. He later developed an electrical control designed to detect any attempt by the medium to leave his or her assigned position under cover of *séance*-room darkness; this was used in the investigation of Florence Cook and other mediums (see *The Spiritualist*, London, March 20, 1874); Varley maintained in this connection that his apparatus showed that Miss Cook was not only in the dark chamber while "Katie King" was in sight, but also perfectly quiescent. Varley testified before the Dialectical Society in 1869, relating his positive success with D. D. Home. He himself experienced numerous psychic manifestations in his own home, believed himself to be possessed of mesmeric healing power, and observed a number of apparitions. His wife demonstrated clairvoyance and prophetic trance.

(Rf.: *Times*, Sept. 3 and 11, 1883; *Engineering*, Sept. 7, 1883; *Telegraphic Journal*, Sept. 15, 1883; *Report on Spiritualism of the Committee of the London Dialectical Society*, etc. London: Longmans, Green, Reader and Dyer, 1871, pp. 157-72.)

VENTURA DI RAULICA. See Vol. VII, p. 400 for information.

*Vihiva Pûnnûttee Sûtra or Bhâgvatî Sutra. Publ. by Ookerdhaboy Shewjee, Bombay, 1877.

VISHNU BAWA BRAHMÂCHÂRI. *An Essay in Marâthî (unidentified).

VOLNEY, CONSTANTIN FRANCOIS CHASSEBEUF, COMTE DE. French *savant*, b. at Craon (Maine-et-Loire), Feb. 3, 1757; d. in Paris, April 25, 1820. Was at first surnamed Boisgirais from his father's estate, but assumed the name of Volney. Spent some four years in Egypt and Syria, publishing his *Voyage en Égypte et en Syrie* in 1787. Was a member of both the States-General and of the Constituent Assembly. In 1791 appeared his *Les Ruines, ou méditations sur les révolutions des empires,* an essay on the philosophy of history. Volney tried to put his politico-economic theories into practice in Corsica. He was thrown into prison during the Jacobin triumph, but escaped the guillotine. He went to the U.S.A., 1795, where he was accused of being a French spy, and returned to France, 1798. He was not a partisan of Napoleon, but served him in the senate. Became a member of the Institute, 1795.

WACHTMEISTER, COUNTESS CONSTANCE (1838-1910). **Reminiscences of H. P. Blavatsky and "The Secret Doctrine."* London: Theos.

Publ. Soc.; New York: *The Path*; and Madras: Theos. Soc., 1893. 162 pp. *Vide* Vol. VI, p. 448, in the present Series, for detailed biographical data.

WAGNER, PROF. NIKOLAY PETROVICH (1829-1907). See Vol. VI, p. 449, for biographical data.

WESTBROOK, JUDGE R. B. No definite information is available about him. He was for a time a Professor of Philology at a British University, it would seem. He was made one of the Councillors of the T.S., and became a Vice-President of it in 1877. H.P.B. had a high regard for him, but it is not clear what became of him at a later date.

WILDER, DR. ALEXANDER. Distinguished physician, author and Platonic scholar, b. at Verona, Oneida Co., N.Y., May 14, 1823; d. at Newark, N.J., September 8, 1908. Descendant of a New England family which came from Lancaster, England, to Massachusetts Bay in 1638. Sixth son of Abel and Asenath (Smith) Wilder, and the eighth child of a family of ten. Educated at first in the common schools of New York state. Being precocious beyond years, started teaching school at fifteen, studying by himself the higher branches of mathematics and the classics, to which were added later French, Hebrew and political science. The circumstances of the deaths of several of his father's family demolished his confidence in current medical methods, and he began studies in medicine, in order to render himself as far as possible independent of physicians. Meantime, he worked at farming and type-setting, reading medicine with local physicians, and was awarded in 1850 a diploma by the Syracuse Medical College. Became then a general practitioner, lecturing for about two years on anatomy and chemistry in the college. After several assignments as Editor of various dailies, he settled in New York City and became, 1858, a member of the editorial staff of the *Evening Post* with which he remained connected for thirteen years. Despite his repeated refusals, Dr. Wilder was made to accept in 1873 a professorship of physiology in the Eclectic Medical College of New York, but left there in 1877 on account of internal dissensions and dishonest practices beyond his control. From 1878-83, he taught psychology at the U. S. Medical College, until it went out of existence by a decision of the courts. In 1876, he became secretary of the National Eclectic Medical Association, and held the office until 1895, meantime editing and publishing nineteen volumes of its *Transactions*, besides contributing extensively to its literature. However, to quote Dr. Wilder's own words: "... my observation of medical colleges is not favorable to them as schools of morals or as promoters of financial probity. The more there is professed, the less it seems to be believed ... physicians boasted loudly then, as now, of being a learned body and invoked special legislation to protect them from competitors ..." He allowed himself to become for a while a subject in such experimentations, and had abundant reasons, as he says himself, to regret this. He was influenced to a very considerable extent by the study of Swedenborg, and later by the writings of General Hitchcock on Alchemy and Hermetic Philosophy. He experienced a number of radical changes in his religious views, identified himself for a time, together with his brothers, with several religious movements of a revivalist kind, but finally grew out of them and into a sphere of spiritual freedom, and became an outstanding—yet, unfortunately, not well recognized—exponent of Platonism and the Hermetic Philosophy. A strong individuality brings with it into life a forgotten knowledge of its real work, but it takes often many years to bring it out into the open.

In 1882, Dr. Wilder attended the School of Philosophy at Concord, Mass., and a year later took part in the organization of the American Akademé, a philosophic society holding meetings at Jacksonville, Ill. He edited its journal for four years, contributing many monographs on such subjects as: "The Soul," "Philosophy of the Zoroasters," "Life Eternal," "Creation and Evolution," and others. He also made a translation from the Greek of the Dissertation of Iamblichus *On the Mysteries of the Egyptians* (orig. publ. in *The Platonist;* issued in book form in 1911 by The Metaphysical Publ. Co., New York).

Dr. Wilder wrote a number of most scholarly and illuminating articles in *The Evolution,* a Journal published in New York, on such subjects as: "Bacchus the Prophet-God" (June, 1877), "Paul, the Founder of Christianity" (Sept., 1877), "Paul and Plato," and others. He contributed philosophical essays to *The Metaphysical Magazine* of New York around 1894-95, and wrote extensively on various metaphysical and Platonic subjects for *The Word,* from 1904 on. One of the most valuable pamphlets issued by him is entitled *New Platonism and Alchemy*: A Sketch of the Doctrines and Principal Teachers of the Eclectic or Alexandrian School; also an Outline of the Interior Doctrines of the Alchemists of the Middle Ages (Albany, N.Y., 1869). H.P.B. quoted many passages from the various writings mentioned above, and expressed her delight over the attitude of Dr. Wilder towards the subjects of which they treat.

In addition to various essays on medical subjects, such as Thought, Cerebration, the Ganglionic Nervous System, Vaccination as a medical fallacy, and others, Dr. Wilder wrote a *History of Medicine* (New Sharon, Main: New England Eclectic Publ. Co., 1901. 946 pp. Index), and contributed invaluable Notes and Comments to special editions of the works of other scholars, such as: *Ancient Symbol-Worship* by Westropp and Wake (Boston, 1874); *Symbolical Language of Ancient Art and Mythology* by R. Payne Knight (New York, 1876).

Dr. Wilder contributed a good deal of material to the section of *Isis Unveiled* entitled "Before the Veil," the circumstances of which are fully explained in the Introductory chapter to the edition of that work forming an integral part of the present Series. He was a staunch friend of both H.P.B. and Col. H. S. Olcott, and had a very high regard for their work. Dr. Wilder was a tall man, spare of person, with a massive head and piercing eyes; he spoke fluently, was an omnivorous reader, and possessed a remarkable memory. His many-sided writings should some day be compiled into a uniform edition and published for the benefit of present-day scholars who are quite unaware of his intuitive insight into so many different regions of thought.

WIMBRIDGE, EDWARD. An English architect in New York, who with Miss Rosa Bates accompanied the Founders to India. He was an artist and carved on wood the first cover of *The Theosophist* in October, 1879. He also etched on copper a portrait of H.P.B. When Miss Bates quarrelled with Emma Coulomb and the Founders, and left them, Mr. Wimbridge went with her. "Since then, a furniture-manufacturing business, for which I helped him, along with the late K. N. Seervai, to find the capital, enriched him, but I have never heard that his thirst for spirituality, survived the shock. He made the best furniture in India, however." (H. S. Olcott in *The Theosophist*, Vol. XIX, Aug., 1898, p. 703.) He died at Bombay, May 13, 1898.

WINDTHORST, LUDWIG (1812-1891). German Catholic statesman at Hanover, and leader of the Party of the Center; Minister of Justice, 1862-65; elected to Reichstag in 1867.

WITTGENSTEIN, PRINCE EMIL-KARL-LUDWIG VON SAYN-. (Spelled with only one "t" in Russia.) Russian Lieutenant-General who belonged to a Princely House (now extinct) which was a branch of the

German family Sayn-Wittgenstein-Barleburg. He was born in 1824. In 1845, he accompanied Prince Alexander of Hesse to the Caucasus; in 1848, he took part in the war against Denmark; then entered Russian service, and soon became aide-de-camp to Prince Vorontzov, Viceroy of the Caucasus, where he took part in the military operations. In 1862, he was attached to the Grand-Duke Konstantine Nikolayevich in Warsaw, Poland. During the Turkish War with Russia, 1877-78, he was in the suite of the Emperor. He died in 1878. He was a close friend of H.P.B. and her family, and became one of the earliest and most earnestly interested members of the T.S. As appears from an Editorial Note by H.P.B. in *The Theosophist* (Vol. IV, March, 1883, pp. 141-42), Prince von Wittgenstein received, for some reason or other, special protection from the Brothers in times of great danger.

Aside from poetry, he wrote *Kavalerie-Skizzen* (Darmstadt, 1859) and *Deutschland in die Schranken* (Darmstadt, 1860).

YARKER, JOHN (1833- ?), *Notes on the Scientific and Religious Mysteries of Antiquity*, etc., 1872; 2nd ed., New York: J. W. Bouton, 1878.

ZHELIHOVSKY, VERA PETROVNA DE, younger sister of H. P. Blavatsky, b. at Odessa, Southern Russia, April 17/29, 1835; d. May 5/18, 1896. She was first married to Nikolay Nikolayevich de Yahontov (1827-58) which accounts for the fact that some of her writings are signed with the letter "Y"; some years after the death of her husband, she married Vladimir Ivanovich de Zhelihovsky. She had two sons by her first marriage, and one son (who died in infancy) and three daughters by the second. (For details consult the Genealogical Table in the present Volume.)

As the years went by, she became widely known in Russia and some European countries as a writer of children's stories, and as an unusually clever contributor to various Russian periodicals. At certain periods in her life, her financial circumstances were strained, and she was able to supplement her slim income by writing, which in her day was not an easy thing for a woman in Russia to do. She was a person of great courage and tireless energy.

Among her many stories, some of which appeared serially in Russian magazines and others were later published in book-form, the following may be mentioned: *Prince Iliko: Young Caucasian Prisoner; In a Tatar Hangout; Caucasian Legends* (St. Petersburg, 1901); *Adventures* (1898); *Stars: Christmas Stories for Children;*

The Czar and the Cossack (Moscow, 1904); *Spring Dawn* (St. Petersburg, 1904); *Yermolov in the Caucasus* (St. Petersburg, 1889).

Those especially interested in H.P.B.'s family background, are grateful to her sister for having written a most valuable and authentic biographical sketch of their mother, under the title of "Helena Andreyevna von Hahn: Romantic Writer." It was published in the well-known Journal *Russkaya Starina* (Russian Old Days), Vol. 53, March, 1887, pp. 733-66, and should sometime be published in English.

Madame de Zhelihovsky published several essays concerned with H.P.B.'s life; these should be considered an important source material, as she kept a diary and was very careful about her statements and their chronological sequence. The most valuable of these writings is her serial article entitled "The Truth about H. P. Blavatsky" (Pravda o Yelene Petrovne Blavatskoy) which appeared in the journal called *Rebus* (Vol. II, 1883: Nos. 40, 41, 43, 44, 46, 47, 48) and was later circulated in pamphlet form. It deals with H.P.B.'s early years and recounts a number of interesting psychic experiences. It is from this account that A. P. Sinnett quotes at considerable length in his *Incidents in the Life of H. P. Blavatsky* (London and New York, 1886). He is in error, however, with regard to his source of information, and this error should be corrected.

When Sinnett was writing his account of H.P.B.'s life, a project with which H.P.B. herself was by no means in sympathy, he pressed her for various information and data. H.P.B. therefore translated into English most of her sister's story above referred to, in order to provide Sinnett with the facts which he sought. As stated by Sinnett himself (p. 6 of the Introductory to his book), H.P.B.'s sister had recently revised and corrected her story specifically for the purpose in view. It appears that "the *Rebus* . . . was committed deeply to certain rigid views concerning the origin and cause of such phenomena as those with which it dealt. This led to some mutilation of the narrative at the time of its publication, but the authoress has now endeavoured to restore it as far as possible to its proper shape, with the help of the original manuscript, which she had preserved, and from which portions missing from the periodical have now been translated."

H.P.B.'s translation is quite lengthy; it is in her own handwriting and is preserved in the Archives of the Theosophical Society at Adyar, India. It may be said to be an almost exact translation of the printed Series to which have been added those passages which, apparently, the Editor of *Rebus* thought fit to eliminate. In addition, H.P.B. has added here and there some sentences of her own and a few footnotes, a fact which is quite obvious from their context and style, one or two of them being even signed "Translator." Some of the sheets on which H.P.B. wrote have various notes scribbled and crossed out on their reverse side; however, after close scrutiny, these have been proved to be duplications, draft-translations, and occur in a far better form in the main text.

When some short excerpts from this translation were published in *The Theosophist* (Vol. XLVII, March and May, 1926), C. Jinarâjadâsa stated in a prefatory note that he had received it from Miss Francesca Arundale; it may well be that the latter got it from Sinnett while in London, and if so, that would account for the fact that this translation of Vera Petrovna's text is not complete in the Archives; the beginning of the story is missing, and the MS starts from that part which tells about H.P.B.'s father and his "Voltairian" tendencies. Writing to Sinnett, H.P.B. refers to this translation and incidentally identifies the source of the material (See *The Letters of H. P. Blavatsky to A. P. Sinnett,* pp. 149, 155).

While Sinnett does mention the *Rebus* essay by its actual title, he also refers to certain "Personal and Family Reminiscences" put together by Madame de Zhelihovsky and from which he intends to quote, but actually did not. Vera Petrovna de Zhelihovsky wrote in 1884 an entirely different series of articles entitled "The Inexplicable or the Unexplained: From Personal and Family Reminiscences." These were also published in the *Rebus* (Vol. III, Nos. 43-48; Vol. IV, Nos. 4-7, 9-11, 13-14) and consist of an outline of various mediumistic and psycho-mental phenomena which took place in the life of the author in Russia. Some of them are quite remarkable, and to some extent similar to those which took place in H.P.B.'s early youth. The Series gives some interesting sidelights about various members of the family, among them Peter A. von Hahn, H.P.B.'s and Vera's father. But there are very few references to H.P.B., and the Series does not contain any of the material wrongly ascribed to it by Sinnett. H.P.B. herself makes a passing reference to this Series in her *Letters to Sinnett*, pp. 155-56, and briefly quotes from it. Beyond that one quoted passage, this later Series is not included in Sinnett's book.

Another outline of H.P.B.'s life and character was written by her sister for the *Russian Review* (Russkoye Obozreniye) under the title of "H. P. Blavatsky: A Biographical Sketch," and appeared in November and December, 1891 (Vol. VI, pp. 242-94, 567-621). It has considerable historical value. It appeared in French in the pages of the *Nouvelle Revue* of 1892, and was almost completely translated into English and published in *Lucifer* (Vols. XV and XVI, Nov., 1894—April, 1895).

Another biographical sketch in Russian was appended to the Russian edition of H.P.B.'s *Mysterious Tribes of the Blue Hills* and *The Durbâr in Lahore* (St. Petersburg: V. I. Gubinsky, 1893). It was translated into English by Kirk and Lieven and published in *The London Forum* (incorp. *The Occult Review*), Vols. LX, LXI, LXII, Dec., 1934-July, 1935.

We have two other accounts from the pen of Vera Petrovna which are of great interest; they deal with her own early years in Russia, and provide fascinating glimpses into the family background and the customs of the day. One of them is entitled *When I was Small* (Kak ya bila malen'koy) and is an account of her childhood up to her seventh year (2nd rev. and enl. ed., St. Petersburg: A. F. Devrient, 1894, 269 pp., fig.), and another is *My Adolescence* (Moyo otrochestvo), a continuation of the subject into later years (St. Petersburg: Ed. Off. of "Readings for Children," 1893, 295 pp.; 3rd ed., ca. 1900; 4th ed., 1902). Many of H.P.B.'s own rather vague dates and facts pertaining to her early years can be verified or corrected by these two books.

Valuable accounts concerning some of H.P.B.'s startling occult phenomena are provided by Vera Petrovna in her articles in *Rebus*, July 15 and 22, 1884; also No. 50 of 1884; *Novosti i Birzhevaya Gazeta*, June 13 and 20, 1889; and her outspoken reply to V. S. Solovyov's hostile book, her own title being *H. P. Blavatsky and a Modern Priest of Truth* (St. Petersburg, 1893).

A most cordial affection existed throughout the years between H.P.B. and her sister Vera. If Madame de Zhelihovsky did not always understand the real "H.P.B.," she nevertheless always trusted her and defended her to the very last. It has been said that the mental suffering which she experienced when Solovyov attacked H.P.B. broke down her health and hastened her death. She felt very keenly the injustices under which W. Q. Judge suffered and defended him whenever she could do so. She travelled several times to Western Europe to visit H.P.B. and their reunions meant always a great deal to both of them.

Zohar, or *Midrash ha-Zohar* and *Sepher ha-Zohar*. See Vol. VII, p. 402, for complete data about Hebrew text and translations.

ZÖLLNER, JOHANN K. F. (1834-82). *Wissenschaftliche Abhandlungen.* Leipzig, 1878-81. 4 vols. *Vide* Vol. V, pp. 265-67, for bio-bibliographical data.

INDEX

INDEX

[References to definitions of terms are in italics]

A

Abdul Ghafur, character and activities of, 369 *et seq.*
Abdul-Hamid, 259.
Abhâva, and padârtha, 332.
Abhâyâdeva Sûrî, Commentaries of, 373.
Adam, as Tree of Life, 288.
Adams, Chas. F., 98.
Adept(s): connected with T.S., 375 fn.; cryptograph of, 421, 439; doppelgängers of, 242; guard nature's secrets, 108; moral courage of, 102;—psychologist working through disembodied soul, 352; surpass mediums in phenomena, 363(367).
Adi-Granth, sacred volume of Sikhs, 373; 443.
Afghans, and Sikhs, 373.
Agardi, Endreinek: on de Lassa, 160-61; pupil of Master M., 162.
Aged of the Aged, 112.
Agrippa, Cornelius: 138; biogr., 443-44.
Ain-soph, and Sephira, 111-12.
Aitareya-Brâhmana, on doctrine of evolution and earth, 227.
Ajñâna, *336.*
Aksakov, A. N.: 1, 2, 210, 211, 212, 213, 413; instructs H.P.B. to select mediums for Russian investigation, 91, 94, 264; noble defender of spiritual cause, 204; on a new Commission for investigating Spiritualism, 213; on geometrical figures, 359, 360; on Zöllner's experiments with Slade, 314-315; report and protest of, on Russian investigation, 205 *et seq.;* biogr., 444-46.
Albertus Magnus, 138.
Alchemists, 106.
Alden, Wm. L., biogr., 446-47.
Alexander, Otho, of Corfu, 409, 414, 418, 427, 436.
Alexander II: and Turkish barbarities, 256-57; character of, 259, 262.
Alexandrian School, 141.
Allen, Judge, and the Holmeses, 69.
Allgemeine. See Haug, C.F.
Al Rezi Pasha, 14, 19, 23.
American Bibliopolist, and Sotheran, 121.
Amicis, Pietro d', 137.
Amîr-al-Mu'minîn, as a title, 371.
Amîr-al-Sûrî, as a title, 371.
Amphitheatrum. See Khunrath.
Anacalypsis. See Higgins.
Analogy: law of, and harmony, 289; only rule of evidence accepted by Theosophists, 296.

542   BLAVATSKY: COLLECTED WRITINGS

Analysis, unemotional, of facts, 300.
Anania, instant death of, 159.
Anastasis, Paul on, 293.
Ancient. See Folger.
Ancient. See Inman.
Ancients, knowledge of, and modern science, 116; reliability of, 232.
Angad, Sikh teacher, 373.
Angels, handed down mysterious doctrines, 110.
Animals: absorb particles of excarnate men, 294-95; and real meaning of metempsychosis, 362-63(366-67); Dr. Rotura and suspension of life in, 389-90.
Anima Mundi, or Svabhavat, 293.
Animus, ethereal substance of the soul, 292-93.
Annihilation: and role of will, 298-99; belief in, and after-death states, 364(368); of soul, 284, 287, 288-89, 295; of destruction, 333-34.
Anthony, Senator, 306.
Antidotes, Nature provides, against moral poisons, 380.
Anvaya, *336.*
Apocalypse, Cabalistic treatise, 132, 223.
Apollonius of Tyana: a mediator, 299; magical evocation of, by Éliphas Lévi, 144 *et seq.*
Apparitions: child—, and Dr. Monck, 351; occult facts behind, 35.
Appleton's Cyclopaedia of Biography, on James Mill's work, 240.
Ardahan, siege of, 255, 258.
Arjan, Sikh teacher, 372, 373.
Art Magic. See Hardinge-Britten.
Arts, lost, 231.

Ârya Samâj: 409, 410, 411, 414, 415, 418, 421, 425; nature of its ideas, 382-84; T.S. as Western representative of, 381.
Ashes, Baron de Palm's, cast into the sea, 421.
Asiatic Journal, 241.
Asmodeus, and Satan, 111.
Astral: emanations of circle and medium, and materialized spirits, 286; fluid compared with spirit, 361(366); man feeds, forms of lower kingdoms, 294-95, 363(367); interchanges, 351-52.
Astral Light: and first envelope of the soul, 284; everything impressed on, 268; pictures in the, and phantasmas, 299.
Astrology, and the *Adi-Granth,* 373.
Atom(s): becomes a man or living soul, 334; each, imbued with vital principle and *latent* spark of divine life, 330-31; indestructible, 299.
Atrya, and Hilarion, 90.
Attractions, interplanetary magnetic, and gravitation, 244.
Auction, at the "Lamasery," 428.
Aurungzeb, tortures Arjan, 373.
Authority, nature of, 116.
Avatars, 328.
Avoca Mail, H.P.B.'s translation in, 413, 438.
Ayton, Rev., 410, 421.

B

Babinet: denies levitation, 243, 245; biogr., 447.
Babouches, 182.
Bacon, Roger, 138.
Badagas, and Todas, 357.

INDEX 543

Bakshish, 180.
Balaam, ass of, contrasted with modern ones, 222.
Balabasha, language, 373.
Balbadha, letters or Devanagari, 383.
Banner of Light, 134 *et seq.,* 289, 290.
Barbarities, of Turks, 255 *et seq.,* 262.
Barber. See Beaumarchais.
Barborka, G. A., *H. P. Blavatsky, Tulku and Tibet,* 481 fn.
Baruch, Dr., mystical Hebrew physician, 420-21.
Bashi-Bazouks, atrocities of, 255.
Basilideans, 105.
Basilio, Don, 128 & fn.
Bates, Miss Rosa, goes to London, 420, 422, 426.
Bath-Kol, 229.
Beard, Dr. Geo. M.: 135, 136, 189, 223; absurd claims of, 224-25; H.P.B.'s views about, and challenge to, 36 *et seq.,* 47 *et seq.*
Beaumarchais, *Barber of Seville,* 128 fn., 447.
——, *Marriage of Figaro,* 128 fn., 447.
Beecher, Rev., 244.
Belgrade, H.P.B. in, 14(19), 165.
Bellachini, S., on Slade's phenomena, 316-17.
Bennett, Mrs., a cheat, 220.
Bertrand, Sergeant, and corpses, 286.
Besant, Annie, on formation of T.S., 123.
Bhagavad-Gîtâ, various spellings of, 250.
Bible, fictitious character of authority of, 380.
Bible. See Jacolliot.
Billing, Dr. H. J.: 246, 375 fn., 411, 412, 424; hears a Brother's voice, 427.

Bios: and périsprit, 361(365); and psychê, etc., 292.
Bismarck, involved in controversy over Slade, 317.
Blake, Dr. Carter-: 409, 412, 424, 436; accuses Founders, 411.
Blavatsky, H. P.: able to get money for "body" only, 425; age of, acc. to reporters, 397 (401); aims at demonstrating Spiritualism mathematically, 199; amusing remarks about her nose, 319; an occultist, 34; and monument to Mazzini, 390-91(391-92); and Olcott as twin "Theosophical gorgons," 320; and the Russian protest, 217 *et seq.;* ascribed psychological powers she never had, 324, 328; asked by Aksakov to select mediums for Russia, 91, 94; at Kutais, 387; at Mentana, 55 fn.; at Northport, L.I., 56, 83-85; at Odessa in 1870, 263; auction at her home, 428; buys trunks, 427; calumniated by Home, 198; can detect cheating in mediums, 141; cat of, lost, 431, 440; compares herself to a bramble-bush, 302; confused with Nathalie Blavatsky, 204; could produce phenomena at will, 73; date of arrival in N.Y., 224 & fn.; date of Amer. citizenship, 224 fn., 408; declines to make public address, 390(392); defends Eddys, 189-90; defends Olcott, 188; defends reality of magic, 134 *et seq.;* defends Spiritualism, 67; defends validity of Masonic diploma, 307 *et seq.;* defines character of reporters, 396(400-01); denies misstatements about herself, 54; Diaries of, 406-33; discusses mediums

Holmes, 59 *et seq.*; earliest writings not identified, 1-2; "eats like three hogs," 433; endorses Slade as genuine medium, 223; faints and has difficulty coming to, 420; familiar with magic, 144; family background of, xxvi *et seq.*; friend and champion of mediums, 190; gets aerial drive, 412; goes on errand for Sahib, 425; goes out with Judge, 429; goes to meet a Brother, 428; goes to Tiflis astrally, 427; has cold again, 426; has courage of her opinions, 358; has father's photo, 44; has group-photo taken, 427; horoscope of, lxxiv; has teeth extracted, 429; helped by M. in production of phenomena, 73; helps to draft Circular on T.S., 375 fn.; helps wounded Russian soldiers, 313; heterodox Spiritualist, 135; homesick for India, 434; in Belgrade, 14(19), 165; intends to immortalize her *Scrapbooks*, 394; lawsuit of, 56, 83-85; leaves Sandy Hook, 433; life-story of, from birth to 1874 xxvi-lii; light of truth as beacon of her life, 127; makes fun of critics, 324; martyrdom of, begins, 90; meaning attached by, to term Spiritualism, 74; meets Master bodily, 3-4; member of Grand Lodge, 142; never a medium except in earliest youth, 203; not a Countess, 397 (401); not a medium, 73, 143, 198; not a Spiritualist, 140; not a *Western* Mason, 308; not an exoteric Buddhist, 398(402); Notes on the Diaries of, 434-40; on clairvoyance, 423; only "she-Cabalist" in America, 189; on plight of Spiritualism, 47-49; ordered to tell truth about phenomena, 90; overshadowed by Adepts, 414, 438; portrait of, as a lama, 425; presented with part of father's medal by "spirit," 43, 44, 203-04; produces a charm, 425; protects honest mediums, 141; protests on being slandered and gives warning, 247-49; reads unopened letter, 415; receives message in Russian through Slade, 224; receives papers from sister, 426; regards philosophy of Gautama Buddha as most sublime system, 398(402); relatives of, in Turko-Russian War, 255 *et seq*; ridicules Nikoladze, 385 *et seq.*; role of, in manifestations at the Eddys, 35; Russian writings of, 313; sails for India, 431, 433; sells monkey, 427; sent on purpose from Paris to America, 73; slandered by mediums, 190-91; smokes on the beach, 408; strolls through park, catches chill, 417; subpoenaed in Vanderbilt case, 419-20; taken for a drive by Mrs. Mitchell, 423; takes out lock of *black hair* from her head, 408, 421; takes photo, 427; three distinct individualities in, 411; translates art. by Wagner, 90; translates Olcott's articles, 2 & fn.; true Spiritualist, 192; trunks of, at Adyar, 422, 430, 439; under orders, 73; visits Judge, 412; warns mediums, 212-13; witnesses of, are living men, 284; witnesses recovery of stolen property phenomenally at Cawnpoor, 275-77; writes Aksakov on *Isis*, 264.

——, *Isis Unveiled*: 358, 412; R. Brown on, 323; date of publication, 264; on Elementals and

Elementaries, 266, 281; on reincarnation of children, etc., 298; original title of, altered, 237 fn., 302; partly written at Ithaca, N. Y., 452; reviewed by *Public Opinion*, 388; H. Spencer read, 413; on Todas, 357; A. R. Wallace on, 323; criticized and praised by reviewers, 323.

——, *Notebook*: Travel-Impressions from Hungary, 11-17(17-22); Notes on above, 22-25.

——, *Scrapbooks*: 247 fn., 369 fn., 379 fn., 384; H.P.B. calls out apparitions at Eddys, 53; H.P.B. meets Olcott, 34; H.P.B. never overwhelmed, 44; in Adyar Archives, 29; letter from E. G. Brown, 45; ordered to expose Dr. Child, 75 fn.; on abuse by W. E. Coleman, 319; on *Art Magic*, 238; on Atrya & Hilarion, 90; on A. von Vay & elementals, 281; on Baron de Palm, 214, 233; on being abused, 313; on being slandered, 249 fn.; on Rev. Bellow, 121; on Mrs. Bennett, 220-21; on Dr. Bloede, 143, 260; on E. G. Brown as a medium, 271; on E. G. Brown's bankruptcy, 404; on E. G. Brown's character, 88; on Brown's ingratitude, 95; on "Cave of the Echoes," 338 fn.; on Circular from Brotherhood of Luxor, 87; on Mrs. Compton, 137 fn.; on Crookes and phenomena, 194; on Elementals, 123; on embryonic man, 124; on Englishmen and the future fateful hour for India, 404-05; on Felt, 193; on First *Occult Shot*, 101 fn.; on formation of T.S., 121, 122; on "ghosts," 44; on Mrs. Holmes and orders from M., 120-21; on Home's anonymous letters, 220; on Home's mediumship, 203, 204; on E. Kislingbury, 271; on lion and mouse, 378; on Masonic diploma, 281; on Mind's return and Nous, 233; on Moloney, 277; on Monachesi's art., & wisdom of India, 133; on Nana Sahib, 337; on Olcott and Dr. Gardiner, 72; on Olcott as future Hanuman, 194; on orders from Serapis to write art., 119; on orders received from T. B. to tell truth about phenomena, 89-90; on orders to establish T.S. and choose Olcott, 94-95, 124; on Peebles and Spiritualists, 264, 290; on phenomenalism and P. C. Mittra, 282; on *Preamble of T.S.*, 150; on *Providence Journal*, 306; on Dr. Rotura's discovery, 389-90; on Scheol, 187 fn.; on Dr. Scudder and Hindu Women, 405; on searching mediums, 278; on Sotheran's political activities, 403-04; on Sotheran, 193, 290; on Spirits as ignoramuses, 143 fn.; on T.S. as a secret Society, 194; on F. Thomas' art. on Spiritualism, 214;

——, *Sketchbook*: analysis of contents, 3-11; Legend of the Night Flower, 6-7(7-8); on nature & adeptship, 4, 5; on Woman's happiness, 5.

——, *Theosophical Glossary*, on Spiritualism, 74.

Blavatsky, Nathalie, gossips about, and Home, 204.

Blavatsky, N. V.: died, acc. to H.P.B., 54; marriage of H.P.B. to, 55.

Blavatsky. See Barborka, G. A.

Bloede, Dr.: 143, 199, 201, 203, 204, 260, 324, 413; from antagonist turns friend, 393, 406.
Blood, of Saviour and crimes, 380.
Bobileff, Mr. 207.
Boehm, clerical deputy, 317.
Bombay Gazette, The, on Rotura, 389.
Books: hint about certain, as sources of mediaeval Cabala, 132; influence of, and of spoken word, 380; on Cabala difficult to understand, 131; reviewed by physiognomy, 386 *et seq.*
Books of Hermes, taught evolution, 232.
Borelli: anticipated Newton, 243; biogr., 447.
Boston Herald: 220; and Home, 195.
Bouton, J. W., 237 fn., 264, 431.
Boyle, 243.
Boys, traffic in Italian, by Consul de Luca, 390-91 (392).
Brahmâ, 239, 244, 333.
Brâhmans, Dravida, and Peebles, 305.
Brâhmo-Samâj: and personal God, 383; its origin and purpose, 381.
Brâhmo Year Book, 381.
Brain: catches glimpses of the "eternal thought," 268; neurine of, and child, 297.
Brédif, 89, 90, 212, 316.
Brewster, David: denies miracles, 242; biogr., 447-48.
British, tribunal not Jesuitical, 225.
Brotherhood(s): as offshoots of Occultism, 105; has records and doctrines that cannot be revealed to profane, 306; location of, secret for present, 113; occult, 103; of Asia Minor and Cabalistic MS., 105, 106; of Humanity and the T.S., 377.
Brothers, story about the, by P. Davidson, 162.
Brown, E. Gerry: appointed sole deputy for selection of mediums, 91, 94, 120; as a medium, 271; contacts H.P.B., 45-46; goes bankrupt, 404; H.P.B. on character of, 88; ingratitude of, 95; on Brotherhood of Luxor, 85; on Oriental Spiritualists, 90.
Brown, John, and Olcott, 506.
Brown, Robert, opinion of, on *Isis Unveiled,* 323.
——, *Poseidon,* 323, 448.
——, *The Great Dionysiak Myth,* 323, 448.
Buchanan, J. R., 272, 448.
Büchner, 37, 448.
Buck, Dr. J. D., applies for fellowship, 423.
Buckle, H. T., *Hist. of Civil. in England,* and H.P.B., 2; 448.
Buddha: based himself on esoteric meaning of the *Vedas,* 398 (402); errors of Wm. Jones about, 239; philosophy of Gautama, the purest and most logical, 398 (402).
Buddhism: exoteric and pure, 398 (402); Olcott's role in reviving, 510-12.
Buddhists: bhikkus wear yellow, 240 fn.; on molecules after death, 362(366); on the périsprit and spirit, 361(365); rejected the *Vedas* at a later period, 398(402).
Buguet, 196.
Bulwer-Lytt*on, Zanoni,* 100.
Burnouf, 251.
Burr, Miss Ellen F., 425, 427, 429.
Burton, Capt. R. F.: 411, 437; and H.P.B., 358.
Butlerov, A. M.: protests, 210 212, 213, 215; biogr., 448-49.

INDEX

C

Cabala (Kabalah): and implicit faith, 130; axiom of the, 334; def. by Lévi, *130;* elements of the, 130; genuine and Mosaic, contrasted, 110-11; intentional slang of, 131; meaning of term, 111; New Testament, easiest, 114; only existing copy preserved, 105, 106; Oriental, the most secret, 106; problems of Jewish, 113; relation of Jewish, to Chaldean, 150; textbook of secrets of Nature, 102; three Magi borrowed from the, 129.

Cabalists: and Rosicrucians, 105; become and are not made, 106-07; do not tell one *how* to do, 131.

Caesar, believed in augurs, etc., 232.

———, *Commentaries,* Huxley on, 231; 449.

Cagliostro: 137; last of Rosicrucians, 104, 141, 161; maligned, 310; may be seen again, 161.

California, Atrya and Hilarion in, 90.

Calphurnia, Caesar's wife, 232.

SS Canada, Founders sail on, 431.

Carbonari, and occultism, 107 fn.

Carpenter, Dr. W. B.: 224, 354, 356; limited view of, on Hindu phenomena, 272 *et seq.*

Cassels, W. R. *Supernatural Religion,* etc., 380, 449.

Castro, Adolpho de, and H.P.B., 1.

Catherine, Princess, murdered, 163.

Catherine II, 92.

Catholic World, on Home, 197.

"Cave of the Echoes," magical evocation in, 346 *et seq.*

Cawnpoor, phenomenon by a gosâin at, 275-77.

Ceccarini, Dr. G., and the Mazzini Commission, 391(392).

Century, 19th, age of destruction, 221.

Chabutara, police-house, 275.

Charles, H.P.B.'s cat, 416, 431, 438, 440.

Chaturhôtri Mantra, on evolution of Earth, 227.

Child: a soul, not a spirit, 363 (367); an animal at first, 297; dead, a failure of nature, must be reborn, 298, 363(368); influence of elementaries on, 285; only a duality, 364(368).

Child, Dr.: H.P.B. ordered to expose, 58 *et seq.,* 75 *et seq.,* 75 fn.; letter of, to *Daily Graphic,* 80-81.

Childs, G. Washington, 242.

Chinese, characteristics of, 108, 109.

Chips. See Müller, Max.

Chittenden, H.P.B. and Olcott at, 34.

Choate, J. M., medium, 278.

Chrêstos, and Jesus of flesh, 383.

Christ: a c t u a l existence of. doubted, 140 fn.; cures Mary of Magdala, 140.

Christian, Theology particularly pernicious, 377.

Chistianity: fetishism of, 333; greatest evil to humanity, 394; object of T.S. is to antagonize, 394; offers premium for crimes, 379-80; T.S. saves heathen from, 381.

Christians, prophesy about, 374.

Christna. See Krishna.

Church: plagiarized from exoteric Buddhism, 398(402); rites and ceremonies of, stem from Occultism, 118; triple-headed snake, 394.

Cicero: 232; *divinum quiddam* of, 229.

Circle(s): magnetic, and will power, 352-53; story of the luminous, 177 *et seq.*
Citizenship, American, of H.P.B., 408.
Clairvoyance, absurd information through, 92-93.
Clairvoyants, trained, and materializations, 267.
Clarke, W. H., at the Holmeses, 64.
Cobb, J. S., 311, 420, 449.
Colby: 413; foolish words about magic, 135 *et seq.*
Coleman, Chas., *The Mythology of the Hindus*, 241, 449.
Coleman, Wm. E.: 238; abuses H.P.B., 318; dishonest dealings of, 322; invites controversy, 321-22; biogr., 449-50.
Colleges, for neophytes of secret science, 103.
Collett, Miss, *Brâhmo Year Book*, on Brâhmo Samâj, 381-82.
Cologne Gazette, on Turkish barbarities, 256.
Colville, W. J., 277.
Commentaries, See Caesar.
Commentary. See Hurrychund, C.
Compensation, Law of, 200.
Compton, Mrs.: an electric battery, 137; transfiguration of, 339.
Conception, and astral light, 284-85.
Confucius, compared to Christ and Buddha, 108-09.
Consciousness: evolution of, into intellectual self-consciousness, 334; latent spirit and distinct, 331.
Consummatum est, 431, 439-40.
Cooke, J. P., *The New Chemistry*, on wave theory of light, 243; 450.
Corbyn, Geo., and Masonry, 281.
I Corinth., on things of the spirit, 294, 297.

Corpuscular, and wave theories of light, 243-44.
Corson, E. R., *Some Unpubl. Letters of H.P.B.*, 46; 450.
Corson, Hiram: 46; on Olcott's address, 193; biogr., 450-53.
Courage, moral, which fires the heart of true adept, 102.
Cowell, Miss S. Emma (Tom), 407, 411.
Cox, Sergeant E. W.: 214, 224; biogr., 453-54.
Cremation: earliest idea of, 278; of de Palm, 214, 233.
Crimes, Christianity offers premium for, 379-80.
Croquet, at Windsor, 253-54.
Crookes, Sir Wm.: 222, 272, 273, 274; on levitation, 244.
Cross, key to Heaven in Egyptian symbolism, 129.
Croucher, J., on the soul, 290, 296.
Cubical stone, symbol of Deity, 200.
Curtis: 407, 409, 410, 412, 417, 418, 419, 423, 427, 428, 429, 431; dodges sheriff, 421.
Cuttack, "wise men" of, 370.
Cuvier, and the mammoth, 230.
Czechs, protest Pope's discourse, 260.

D

Daemon est Deus inversus, 200.
Daily Graphic, 1, 2, 32, 44, 64, 68, 80, 81.
Daily Times (Hartford, Conn.), 425.
Daimon (Daimonion): of Socrates, 229; périsprit after death is a, 362(366); soul as, 294.
Damascus, oracle from, 181 *et seq.*

INDEX

Damiani, G., 337.
Dâmodar, and Judge, 475.
Darwin, *On the Origin of Species*: and H.P.B., 2; 454-55.
Dasyus, astral, 336.
David, a Cabalist, 111.
Davidson, Peter, tale of, about the Brothers, 162.
Davis, A. J.: and "Diakka," 117, 269; biogr., 455-59.
Dayânanda Sarasvatî: 409; character of, 382-83.
Death: and belief in annihilation, 364(368); avoidance of, depends on will, 299, 364(368); fear of, 115; mysterious, of assassins, 173; instant, at remote control, 158, 159; périsprit after physical, 364(368); second, acc. to Lévi, 329; second, acc. to Plutarch, 294, 362(366).
Debendro Nath Tagore, 381.
Deity, and Justice, 200.
Delessert, inspector of Police, 151 *et seq.*
Demeter: and périsprit, 362(366), 363(367); and second death, 294.
Dervishes: Biktashee, 370 & fn.; errors about, fakirs and svâmis, 240-41; story of the, and the magic mirror, 177 *et seq.*
Descartes, on nature of light, 243.
Deuteronomy, 111.
Deutsch, I.: eulogizes *Talmud*, 132 fn.; biogr., 459.
Devachan, state of bliss for monad, 36.
Devanagari [Devanâgarî], 241.
Devas, and Dayus, 336.
Devil, and God, 200.
Dharma-Khanda, 252.
Dharmapala, H., 511.
Dhoti, loin cloth, 244, 274.
Dhyânânta. *336.*
Diakka, 82, 117, 135, 140, 187, 283.

Dialectical Society, 211.
Dickens, Chas., *Edwin Drood*: and H.P.B., 2; 459.
——, *Little Dorrit*, 75, 459.
Did Mad. Blavatsky, etc. See Jinarâjadâsa.
Dimension: fourth, 314; fourth, and Pythagorean Tetraktys, 360.
Disquisitions. See Rossetti, G.
Ditson, Dr. G. L., 246.
Divine Brother, 415.
Divinum quiddam, of Cicero, 229.
Dogma, and faith are pillars of Theology, 304.
Dogme. See Lévi.
Doppelgängers, of adepts, 242.
Double: story about murder by the astral, of medium, 163 *et seq.*, 173 fn.
Doubleday, Gen. A.: 408, 430, 436; biogr., 459-61.
Dravida, Brâhmans, 305.
Duad, and Unity, 200.
Du Potet, 137, 166, 461.
"Dweller," Elementary, 117.

E

Earth: fourth planet, its role, 112; *Vedas* on evolution of, 227.
Earth-bound: elementaries and phenomena, 286; fiendish revenge of an, soul, 352; guides, 270; Khunrath on, elementaries, 287.
Earth. See Mayer, A. M.
Echo (N.Y.): 390(391), 391 (392), 406; publ. by Sotheran, 369 fn., 379 fn.
Eddy Brothers: apparitions at the, during H.P.B.'s stay, 31-34, 53; H.P.B. defends the, 36 *et seq.*; biogr., 461-62.

Eddy, William, genuine medium, 35, 351.
Edison, Thos. A.: Olcott sees, about phonograph, 429; represented by E. H. Johnson, 430.
Edmonds, Judge, 48.
Edward I, and R. Lully, 107 fn.
Edwin Drood. See Dickens.
Ego: as astral man and animals, 294-95; or self-being, *336.*
Egyptian, adept, 87.
Eidola, materialized, 293.
Eleazar, Rabbi, and the *Zohar:* 110; 461.
Elementals: and A. von Vay, 281; and conception, 284-85; and elementaries, 268-69, 284, *330;* and invisible world, 73; and phenomena, 285; determine temperament of child, 285, 287; form astral body of infants, 298; role of, in evocation story, 352.
Elementary(ies): 191; and elementals contrasted, 268-69; and phenomena, 285-86; are usually earth-bound guides, 270; attracted to vicious parents and their offspring, 285; human, 284, 285; Khunrath on, 286-87, 329; Lévi on, and second death, 329-30; malice of, towards people, 141, 142; nature of, spirits, 112; not all, are annihilated, 298; of human body may ascend after death, 364(368); or Diakka, 135, 140.
Elements: four primary, 330; occult, and conception, 285.
Elephanta, Caves of, 407.
Elphinstone, M. biogr., 462-63.
——, *Kingdom of Kabul:* on fakirs, etc., 239; 463.
——, *The History of India,* 239, 463.
Emanations, ten and Sephira, 112.
Encyclopaedia. See Mackey.

Ennemoser: 139; biogr., 463.
Epithumia: and périsprit, 361 (365); or concupiscible nature, 292.
Equilibrium, of opposites, 200.
Esoteric Section: and Olcott, 514-15; W. Q. Judge assisted H.P.B. in forming the, 479.
Esprits malin, 135.
Essenes: Jesus trained by the, 106; knowledge of, 116.
Ether: and gravitation, 244; Leibnitz on, 243; Webster on, 244.
Eve, and Psychê, 128-29.
Evil: and Duality, 200; endless, 112.
Evocation, of Apollonius of Tyana, 144 *et seq.*
Evolution: double, must be accepted, 233; of man and of horse, 228-30; of spirit, 230; of the Earth acc. to *Vedas,* 227; taught in *Books of Hermes,* 232.
Exodus, on witches, 140.

F

Fadeyev, Miss N. A. de: 253, 313, 407, 434-35: letter from H.P.B. to, 424 fn.; sends box to H.P.B. from Russia, 4; testimony of, about A. Mitrovich, 10, 11 fn.
Fadeyev, Gen. R. A. de, 255 fn.
Faith: and dogma are pillars of Theology, 304; implicit, and the Cabala, 130.
Fakirs: errors about, dervishes and svâmis, 240-41, 244; levitation of, 244; phenomena of, 354.
Fales, Wm. S., 84, 95, 96, 98, 99.
Fanfulla, on Mazzini, 390(392), 409.

INDEX 551

Fellger, Dr. A., physician, 59.
Felt, Geo. H., 122, 123, 193, 463.
Fern, I. F., an occultist, 45.
Fire-philosophers, 105, 111.
Firman, and Home, 198, 201, 202.
Flint, C. R., *Memories of an Active Life*: on H.P.B.'s lawsuit, 84-85; on the "Hiraf" Club, 96-99; 463.
Fluctibus, Robertus de (Fludd), 131, 138.
Folger, R. B., *The A. and A. Scottish Rite*, on validity of rites, 309-10; 463.
Folliol-Crenwille, 23.
Force: and Will, 334; transforming medium's appearance, 137.
Fossils, and the Spiritualists, 230.
France, destinies of, 107 fn.
Franklin Register, 306, 307 fn., 311, 312, 407, 435.
Freemasons, 126, 131. See Masonry.
Friedenthal: and "miracles," 317; biogr., 463.
Frosya, 166 et seq.

G

Galatinus, 131, 463-64.
Gardiner, Dr., and Olcott, 72, 301.
Garibaldi, H.P.B. not on Staff of, 55 fn.
Gebhard, Mary, and É. Lévi, 494-95.
Geluk-pa, Order of, and yellow hats, 240 fn.
Geniuses: not m e d i u m s, 363 (367); spiritually inspired, 295.
Geometrical, figures and fourth dimension, 359-60.
Gerebko, Clementine: 54; H.P.B.'s business-connection with, 55-56, 83-85.

Ghebers, 118.
G. K., 89.
Gnomes, sylphs, etc., 284 *et seq.*
Gnostics: and later Gospels, 382; Ophites and Basilideans, 105.
Goblins, elementary, 111.
God: contradictory ideas of Christians about, 333; Hugo on, 199; man can become a, 73; spirit means both, and alcohol, 332; symbol of harmony, 199-200.
Gods, on reviling the, 237.
Golden Gate: between two worlds, 191; leading to Infinite Truth, 130.
Golos, art. by Mendeleyev, 217.
Good, and Evil, 200.
Go-pâla, cowherd, 356.
Gopura, 355-56.
Gorchakoff, Prince, 259, 464.
Gosain [Gosâin]: 241; performs phenomenon at Cawnpoor, 275-77.
Gospoja P—, 166 *et seq.*
Gougenot des Mousseaux, H. R.: 139; biogr., 464.
———, *La magie*, etc., on Home and de Ravignan, 196.
Govinda, Sikh guru, 373.
Gravitation: nature of, 242-43; various scientists on, 243.
Gray, Dr., 244.
Great Dionysiak. See Brown, R.
Greek, ideas about constitution of man, 292-93.
Guegidze, Michalko, a servant, 32.
Guide to Theosophy, on formation of T.S., 123, 464.
"Guides:" and "controls" unreliable, 284, 295; as earth-bound elementaries, 270.
Guido of Arezzo: 154; biogr., 465.
Guillemain de Saint-Victor, *Handbook of the Women Freemasons*: on adoptive masonry, 312; 465.

Guppy, Mrs., medium, 272.
Guriya, and Imeretia, 387.
Guru-Brâhmans, generations of trained, 267.

H

Hahn, Nicholas von, H.P.B.'s cousin, 436.
Hahn, Col. Peter A. von, dies at Stavropol', 83.
Halley: 243; biogr., 465.
Hallock, Dr., 226.
Hammond, Dr.: 245; biogr., 465-66.
Handbook. See Guillemain.
Hardinge-Britten, Emma: biogr., 466-67.
——, *Art Magic*: 143; how many printed, 238; 467.
——, *Nineteenth Century Miracles*: on formation of T.S., 122; 466.
Hare, R.: 213; biogr., 467-68.
Harmony: God a symbol of, 200; Home and, 201; law of, and analogy, 289; touchstone of truth, 296.
Harrison, W. H., 290 fn.
Harrisse, Mons.: 414, 429; portrait of Master by, 407, 435.
Hartmann, 332.
Haug, C. F., *Allgemeine Geschichte*: on Chinese, 109; 468.
Haug, Martin: on *Vedas*, 227; biogr., 468.
Haynau, J. J., 22.
Herald (N.Y.), art. in, 429.
Hermann, juggler, 316.
Hermetic Philosophers: books of, difficult to understand, 131; magicians and giants of intellect, 138; price exacted for following in their footsteps, 128; proved what they claimed, 138.

Herodotus, 232.
Higgins, G., *Anacalypsis*, 380, 468.
Hilarion (Illarion); 407, 424, 435; and Atrya, 90; story of, about de Lassa, 161-62.
Hilton, and the Jews, 262.
Hindustani, 241.
Hindustani-English Dict. See Shakespeare, J.
Hinrichs, Fred. W.: 96, 97-98; letter from, to Jinarâjadâsa on "Hiraf" Club, 99-100.
"Hiraf," art. on Rosicrucianism, 99-100.
"Hiraf" Club, historical background of, 95-100.
History. See Livy.
Hist. of Civil. See Buckle.
Hist. of Diplomacy. See Horvath.
History of India. See Elphinstone and Mills, J.
Holloway-Langford, Laura: and Olcott, 517, 526; unpubl. MS. of, 2.
Holmes, Mr. and Mrs.: 422; and their mediumship, 59 *et seq.*, 75 *et seq.*; caught cheating, 120-21; exposure of, and H.P.B.'s role, 73.
Home, D. D.: a renegade, 197; and anonymous letters, 220; assails Leymarie, 195; beseeches di Raulica, 196; calumniates H.P.B., 198; demonized, 196; distorts harmony, 201; doubts H.P.B.'s mediumship, 203; never met H.P.B., 469; statements of, unreliable, 245; twice tried for swindling, 204.
——, *Incidents in my Life*: on advice of his spirit-mother, 198; untruthful, 196-97; upholds Catholic clergy's conspiracy, 202.
Hommons, Capt., a Rosicrucian, 428.

Homo, genus, and the horse, 229-30.
Hooke, R.: 243; biogr., 469-70.
Horrocks, J.: 243; biogr., 470.
Horse: and Orohippus, 229; and Protohippus, 230.
Horvath, J., *Hist. of Diplomacy*, 23.
Howitt, W., 139.
Hugo, Victor, on God, 199.
Human, nature same through the ages, 130.
Humanity, Brotherhood of, 377.
Hungary, H.P.B.'s Travel-Impressions from, 11-17(17-22).
Hurrychund, C.: 407, 409, 426, 433: data on, 435; on the *Vedas*, 383; snubs the Council, 424.
———, *Commentary on the Bhagavad-Gîtâ*: on exoteric and esoteric knowledge, 306; 470.
Huss, John, 260.
Huxley: contrasted with Slade, 228; New York lectures on evolution, 226 *et seq.*; on human testimony, 231; surprise of, about U.S.A., 225.
Huygens, on nature of light, 243.
Hyneman, Leon, 312.
Hyslop, J. H., biogr., 470-71.

I

Iconoclasm, of scientists, 243.
Idiots, congenital, and reincarnation, 298, 364(368).
Illarion. See Hilarion.
Illuminati, 108, 111.
Illustrated Weekly, The, Turguenyev's poem in, 253.
Imagination, and materialized forms, 267.

Imeretia, and Guriya, 387, 388.
Immortality: conditional, 293, 298; of atoms, 331; of soul, 102.
"Impossible," and "never" should be erased as terms, 109.
Incantations, magical effects of, 352-53.
Incidents. See Home.
Incidents. See Sinnett.
l'Inde. See Rousselet.
Indépendence Belge, and H.P.B., 1.
India: future fateful hour for, 404; magic in, 141-42; women of, and Christianity, 405.
Indian Spectator, The, on Dayananda Sarasvati, 382.
Indian Tribune, The, on Dayananda Sarasvati, 382.
Inductive, method, 230.
Initiates, hard to catch, leave no trace behind, 161.
Initiation, ordeals and trials of, 115.
Inman, Thos., *Ancient and Pagan Christian Symbolism*, 380, 471.
Inquisition, danger to Hermeticists, 131.
Intelligences, ten and Sephira, 112.
Interviews, H.P.B. on reporters', 237.
Isis, lifting veil of, 115, 118.
Israelites. See Jews.
Iśvara-Bhava [Îśvara-Bhâva], 335.
Italians, in U.S.A. and Mazzini, 390-91(391-92).
Ivins, Wm. M.: 1, 95, 97, 98, 99; on H.P.B.'s lawsuit, 84; biogr., 471.
Iyam, earth, 227.
Izvertzoff, story about, and the magical evocation of the Shaman, 339-53.

J

Jacolliot, L., on levitation, 244.
———, *The Bible in India*: 240; 471; on *Bhagavad-Gîtâ* and Krishna, 249 *et seq.*
Jadar-Christna, 251.
Jâdûgar, conjurer, 275.
Jadupati [Yadupati], 251.
Jainas, Sûtras of, 373 & fn.
James, on sensual nature, 297.
Janmotsar, festival of, 250.
Jehovah, originated with Moses, 110.
Jennings, H., *The Rosicrucians*: 104 fn., 105; 471; ablest book on symbols, 126.
Jenny, H.P.B.'s maid, 423, 425, 428.
Jesuitism, object of T.S. is to antagonize, 394.
Jesuits, and Home, 195 *et seq.*
Jesus: a Cabalist, 129; and Chrêstos, 383; trained by Essenes, 106.
Jews, condition of, in Russia, 262-63.
Jezeus Christna. See Krishna.
Jinarâjadâsa, C., *Did Mad. Blavatsky Forge*, etc., 438.
———, *Letters from the Masters*, etc.: 87; 471-72; on the lost Rosy Cross jewel, 439.
Jiva-Bhava [Jîva-Bhâva], 335.
Jones, Elder, 261.
Jones, Sir Wm., errors of, 239.
Journalism: heliocentric, 241; recrimination is soul of American, 322.
Jude, on psychical nature, 297.
Judge, John H.: goes on board to take leave of Founders, 431; helps with *Isis Unveiled*, 473; initiated into T.S., 430.
Judge, Wm. Q.: 413, 416, 426, 427; goes on board to take leave of Founders, 431; goes out with H.P.B., 429; H.P.B. visits, 412; in consultation with Master M., 430; life-story and writings of, 472-90; telegraphs Wimbridge, 423; to dinner, 409, 410, 425.
Justice, nature of, 200.

K

Kabak, saloon, 263.
Kabbalah. See Knorr.
Kali (Mrs. Olcott), 411, 437.
Kalindjikoulosek, 179.
Kama-rupa [Kâma-rûpa], M. appearing in, 90.
Kaniya [Kanyâ], Sign of Virgo, 252.
Kant, 332.
Kapila: 296, 332; despised psychical nature, 294; H.P.B.'s regard for, 398(402); on périsprit, 362(366); *Sûtras* of, 302-03.
Karageorgević, Alexander, 164 & fn.
Karapapahs, 258.
Karikal, 251.
Katardži, Maria, 165 fn.
Kepler, on magnetic nature of sun, 243.
Keshub Chunder Sen, and Brâhmo Samâj, 381.
Khunrath, H., 138, 330.
———, *Amphitheatrum Sap. Eternae*: on elementaries, 286-87, 298, 329; 490.
Kiev, full of Jews, 263.
King, John: 60; H.P.B. brings out face of, 73.
King, Katie: 57 *et seq.*; and Holmes discussed, 75 *et seq.*; and Miss F. Cook, 190; biography of, 63 fn., 65, 66; H.P.B. brings out face of, 73.
Kingdom. See Elphinstone.

Kislingbury, Emily: 271, 324, 406, 409, 410, 412, 413, 414, 418; Coleman misrepresents, re Olcott, 320; on loss of spirituality, etc., 288-89; resigns, 424.
Kittara, Prof., interested in Spiritualism, 213.
Knorr von Rosenroth, C., *Kabbalah denudata*, 131-32 & fn., 145 fn., 491.
Knowledge: always respected, 138; true, retarded by men of science, 24.
Kolozsvár (Cluj), and E. Agardi, 161.
Koran, 181, 373.
Kossuth, 325.
Kotwal, chief of Police, 275.
Kotzebue, Count Paul, 263.
Krishna [Krishṇa]: 356; derivation and spellings of, 250-52; washes feet of Brâhmans, 261.
Kutais, H.P.B. at, 387.

L

Lachaud, counsel for Leymarie, 195.
Lamas, do not wear yellow robes, 240 fn.
Lampsakano, errors of, 239-41.
Lancaster, and Lankester, 222.
Language(s): limitations of Western, in regard to metaphysics, 332, 360; symbolic, of highpriests, 131; symbolic, very ancient, 126.
Lankester, and Slade, 228.
Lankester-Donkin, alliance and Slade, 222 *et seq.*, 318.
Lao-tse, 108.
Larvae, 293, 330.
Lassa, story of Vic de, 151 *et seq.*
Lavater, and Nikoladze, 386-88.
Laws, immutable, govern universe, 296-97.

Leadership, Founders did not offer, to Spiritualism, 322.
Leibnitz, on planetary motions, 243.
Letters. See Jinarâjadâsa.
Letters. See Sinnett.
Lévi, Éliphas: a magician, 139; and term "elementary," 265, 299; defines Cabala, *130;* Home defames grave of, 198; on Christian Cabalistic Scriptures, 132; biogr., 490-95.
——, *Dogme et Rituel*, etc.: 283; on afterdeath condition of the soul, 288; on elementaries and second death, 329-30; on evocation of Apollonius of Tyana, 144 *et seq.*; on occult elements in conception, 285.
——, *La Science des esprits*: 283; on vampirism, necromancy and mediumship, 286.
Levitation: and opposite polarities, 244; of fakirs and tables, 243, 244; witnessed by H.P.B., 352.
Leymarie: 225; assailed by Home, 195, 198, 201; victim of Jesuits, 195, 198-99; unjustly sentenced, 202.
Liberal Christian, The, and formation of T.S., 121-23.
Light, wave and corpuscular theories of, 243.
Linden, van der, 410, 437.
Lippit, Gen. F. J.: 410, 437; biogr., 496-97.
Litolff, Henri, 22-23.
Little Dorrit. See Dickens.
Livy, *History*, and Niebuhr, 232, 495-96.
Lodge(s): of adepts divided into Sections, 107; H.P.B. a member of the Grand Lodge, 142; secret, in Asia Minor, 105; 106; mysterious events connected with, 107 fn.
Logos, or Verbum, 129.

Long, Col. Chaille, 422, 424.
Longfellow, not a Spiritualist, 282.
Loris-Melikoff, 258, 259.
Louis, Chevalier, and *Art Magic*, 467.
Love: a nightmare, 5; spiritual, as attraction, 36.
Luca, de, Italian Consul in N.Y. traffics in boys, 390-91(392).
Lucifer, on formation of T.S., 123.
Lully, Raymond: 138; supplies Edward I with funds, 107 fn.
Lundy, Rev. J. P., *Monumental Christianity*: on washing disciples' feet, 261; 497.
Luria, Isaac b. S., *Treatise on the Revolutions of the Souls*: 154 & fn.; 497; on three kinds of spirits, 330.
Luxor; Brotherhood of, 85; Circular from, 85-88; Section of Grand Lodge composed of *living* mortals, 142-43.

M

M.˙. Jn., *i.e.*, Olcott, 407, 410.
Macbeth. See Shakespeare.
Mace, J., Comm. of Police, 195.
MacKenzie, K., *Royal Masonic Cyclop.*: on Brotherhood of Luxor, 87; on various rites, 309; 497.
Mackey, A. G., *Encyclop. of Freemasonry*: on adoptive masonry, 312; 497.
Madagascar, password of, 428.
Madonnas, change color acc. to climate, 372.
Magic: and esoteric Theurgy, 139; and will power, 150; as a science, 137; ceremonial, and elementaries, 287; course of, 141; does exist, 141; H.P.B. defends reality of, 134 *et seq.*; is psychology practically a p p l i e d, 324; performance of, by a Shaman, 346 *et seq.*; performance of Dervishes, 177 *et seq.*; relation to Spiritualism, 101-02; White and Black, 117, 118, 141; White or sacred, 139.
Magicians: ancient High Priests were, 139; control spirits, 137; Dervishes at work, 181 *et seq.*
Magie. See Gougenot.
Magiism, 126.
Magnetism: and gravitation, 244; current of, in a circle, 352-53; possibilities of animal, are infinite, 399(403).
Mahan Singh, 373.
Mahatma Letters. See Sinnett.
Man: atom becomes a, 334; a trinity, 331, 361(365); can assume any shape, 227; can become a God, 73, 293; can surpass in phenomena average "spirits," 296; cycle of, incomplete without terrestrial life, 363 (367); elementary, reborn on our planet, 112; evolution of, and of horse, 228-29; inner, and astral light, 284; must be one before becoming a spirit, 298; riddle of, and Oedipus, 361(365); triune nature of, 292-94, 298.
Mânasa-sarovara, lake of, and the Âryans, 383.
Mand, of Todas, 356.
Mango-tree, phenomenal growth of, 273-74.
Manifestations: and other spirits than excarnate humans, 283; nature of objective, 294; subjective and objective, 293.
Mantras, and evolution of Earth, 227.
Manu, 296.
Manu, Laws of, 240, 497.
Marble, Mortimer: 246, 409, 411,

INDEX 557

413, 414, 419, 427, 428, 430; faithful, 424; fixes day for auction, 425; good and honest soul, 426; most active at auction, 428.

Markoff, V., letter of, on Commission's work, 216-17.

Marquette, Dr. L. M., 246, 408, 436.

Marriage. See Beaumarchais.

Marshall, Wm. E., *A Phrenologist Among the Todas*: unreliable, 353, 354; 497.

Martyrdom: fate of genuine students of Hermeticism, 128; rare now, 102.

Marvins, Dr., 136.

Maskelyne, and Cooke, jugglers, 274.

Masonry: adoptive, 311, 312; Geo. Corbyn and, 281; corpse without Eastern philosophy, 310; H.P.B. and, 281, 289, 307 *et seq.*

Massey, C. C.: 326, 327, 411, 438; letter from, read by H.P.B. unopened, 415; biogr., 497-99.

Master(s): and portrait by Harrisse, 407, 435; appearing in kama-rupa, 90; H.P.B. meets, bodily, 3-4; M. and H.P.B.'s phenomena, 73; M. borrows $100 from Olcott, 429; M. brings orders to found Society, 73; M. dissatisfied, 412; M. forbids H.P.B. to help Mrs. Holmes, 120-121; M. furnishes $5, 412; M. gives money for stamps, 423; M. in consultation with Judge, Wimbridge and Olcott, 430; M. probably "Sahib," 414; M. reads fortunes in cards, 421; orders Circular of Luxor to be issued, 87; present at casting of de Palm's ashes into sea, 421; Serapis, 87; voice of, heard by Billing, 427.

Materialism, and Spiritualism, 73.

Materialists, and evolution, 228-31.

Materializations; nature of, 266-67; role of elementaries in, 286; role of H.P.B. in the, at the Eddys, 35.

Matter, universe called forth out of pre-existing, 268.

Mayer, A. M., *The Earth a Great Magnet*: 244; 497.

Mayfair Gazette, The, on Abdul Ghafur, 374-75.

Mayo, murder of Lord: 370; biogr., 499.

Mazzini, monument to, and H.P.B., 390-91 (391-92).

McClellan, David, 309.

Mediator: conscious, and mediums, 295, 363 (367); of ancient days, 299-300.

Medium(s): and shells, 35; and Russian investigation, 205 *et seq.*; at the mercy of elementary spirits, 141; attitude of Roman Church towards, 197; breathe in emanations of corpses, 286; considered possessed by ancients, 140; contrasted with mediators, 295; controlled by spirits of many kinds, 199; could be cured in Temples, 140; evolved man can surpass, in phenomena, 363 (367); geniuses are not, 363 (367); H.P.B. mediumistic in earliest youth, 203; H.P.B. not a, 73, 191; irresponsible, 267, 300; may be directed by Adepts in psychic science, 289; passive, cannot discern good spirits from bad, 295, 363 (367); should be searched, 278; slander H.P.B., 190-191; s p u r i o u s, try to swindle, 119-20; stand on shaky ground, 303-04; testing, by occult methods, 201; to be selected for Russia, 91, 120; transformed

into another shape by *force*, 137; worst enemies of, are mediums, 190.
Mediumship: and vampirism, 286; H.P.B. never practiced, 198; malpractices of, 269-70; of Sibyls and Pythonesses guided by High Priests, 139; phenomena of, 351-52.
Memories. See Flint.
Mendeleyev, D. I.: and Committee of St. Petersburg, 91, 205 *et seq.*, 215 *et seq.*; biogr, 499.
Mendenhall, and Luxor, 142.
Menelao, Pasquale, of Corfu, 409, 437.
Mentana, H.P.B. at, 55 fn.
Mercury (N. Y.), 53, 54.
Mercy, and justice, 200.
Mesmer, 137.
Mesmeric, exhalations and spiritualistic manifestations, 294.
Mesmerism, powers of, 159-60.
Mesmerizer(s): l e a r n e d, are magicians, 137; French, entrances sensitive, 168 *et seq.*
Metanoia, *293.*
Metempsychosis, real meaning of, *362-63 (366-67), 294-95.*
Metz, Rev. F., and the Todas, 353.
Mian Gul, 369 fn.
Mill, James, *The Hist. of British India,* on fakirs, 240, 499.
Mind: as phren, 292; cannot return to earth after joining nous, 233.
Miracle(s): not a violation of law, 137; occultists deny, 242.
Miracle Club, 88.
Mirville, de, 139.
Mirza, Prince, and Pr. Vorontzov, 371.
Misl, division of Sikhs, 373.
Missionaries: blot upon Christianity, 379-80; caused Sepoy mutiny, 433.

Mitchell, Isabel B.: 406, 417, 419, 434; comes to see H.P.B., 429; moves to Orange, 415.
Mitrovich, Agardi and Teresina: 9-10; testimony about, from N. A. de Fadeyev, 10, 11 fn.
Mittra, Peary Chand, on Spiritualism, 282.
Modern Priestess. See Solovyov.
Mohammedans, 369 fn., 370, 371, 372. See Mussulmans.
Mohottiwatte, G., 414, 416, 422, 438.
Molecules, material and astral, enter plants and animals, 362-63 (366-67).
Molière, *Tartuffe,* 38.
Moloney: nickname for Olcott, 277, 406, 420; sings on board, 434.
Monachesi, H. D.: 246; and Consul de Luca, 391(392); data on, 500; defines original programme of Founders, 133.
Monck, Dr., and child-apparition, 351.
Montecchi, and Capuletti, of the 19th century, 128.
Monumental. See Lundy.
Moon, man from the, and science, 384-85.
Morphy, Paul, 325.
Moscow Vedomosty, 263.
Moses: initiated in Egypt, 110; responsible for Jehovah myth, 110.
Moses, Wm. Stainton ("M. A. Oxon."): 291, 407, 434; challenges from, 302 *et seq.*; biogr., 500-01.
Mosheim: 105; biogr., 501.
Mukhtar Pasha, lies of, 258.
Müller, F. Max, and spelling of Indian terms, 250.
———, *Chips,* etc.: on Wm. Jones and *Vedas,* 239; 502.

INDEX 559

Mussulmans: prophesy about, 374; secret societies among, and Abdul Ghafur, 370. See Mohammedans.
Mysteries: ancient, and Spiritualists, 118; mixed with fables and fiction, 105; of Samothrace, 141.
Mythology. See Coleman.

N

Nana Sahib, 275.
Nanak, and Sikhs, 372.
Narayan: called by Olcott "old horse," 428, 439; "leaves watch" to *Sahib,* 414, 420; letter from, 438; message from, 439; signature of, in Diary, 431, 439-40; symbol of, 426.
Nasr-ed-Dîn, as title, 371.
Nations, unknown to history, 104.
Nature: provides antidote against moral poisons, 380; secrets of, 102, 108.
Necromancy: 74; and the Roman Church, 197.
Nègre, Marconis de, 309.
Nepal, metaphysical schools of, 268.
Neurine, of brain and child, 297.
Nevermore. See Poe.
New American Cyclopaedia, on Todas, 357-58, 502.
Newark Daily Journal, 214.
New Chemistry. See Cooke.
Newton, H. J.: pays with Olcott for de Palm's cremation, 233; biogr., 502-03.
Newton, Sir I.: 242; anticipated by Borelli, 243.
Nicholas, Grand Duke, 257.
Niebuhr: biogr., 503; butchers Livy's *History,* 232.

Night-Flower, Legend of the, 6-7 (7-8).
Nikoladze, on H.P.B.'s book, 385 *et seq.*
Nîlgiri Hills, 357.
Nineteenth. See Hardinge-Britten.
Nir-Narrain, sect, 241.
Nirvana [Nirvâṇa]: and Sahajânanda, 335; progress towards, 294, 298.
Nivritti, and pravritti, 268.
Notebook. See Blavatsky.
Notes, etc. See Yarker.
Nous: 298; and psychê in Paul, 292; at second death, 294; no return of mind after joining, 233; or ruach, 299; or spirit and psychê, 361(365); union of soul and, 293; whisperings of our, 335.
Novoye Vremya, on séances with Slade, 315.

O

Obrenović, Prince Miloš (1780-1860), 23, 164 fn.
Obrenović, Prince Mihailo (1823-68): 23; murder of, 163, 164 fn.
Obrenović, Pr. Milan (1854-1901), 165 fn. IV, Pr. Milan, 165 fn.
Obsession, and mediumship, 140.
Obzor: insults H.P.B., 389; on H.P.B. and her book, 385 *et seq.*
Occult, training in schools, 267.
Occult Sciences: superficial knowledge of, dangerous, 127; world not prepared for, 73.
Occultism: believes in immutability of nature's laws, 242; book-learning in, insufficient, 103; book-study of, and journey to Orient, 133; Chaldean, and offshoots, 107 fn.; Colleges of, exist t o d a y, 103; denies miracles, 242; dual in nature,

117; East as cradle of, 103; gave rise to Church rites, 118; is essence of Spiritualism, 295; mysterious lever of intellectual forces, 128; or ancient Spiritualism, 199; origin of most of what we know, 116; *practical*, 103, 106-107, 126; science of sciences, double-edged weapon, 101; sects of, guilty of heresies, 104; works on, written for the few, 132.

Occultist: duty of, towards Science and Theology, 128-29; must be ready for persecution, 128; must not scorn public opinion, 129; must unlearn all he knew before, 128; well-nigh insurmountable difficulties to become practical, 130.

Odessa, H.P.B. witnesses uprising in, 263.

O'Donovan: 410; sculpting H.P.B.'s head for plaque, 409-10.

Oedipus: and enigma of Sphinx, 127, 291; and riddle of man, 361(365).

Olcott, Emmet R., Col. Olcott's brother, 422.

Olcott, H.S.: and Buddhism, 510-12; and H.P.B. as Hermetic Science Twins, 187; and John Brown, 506; and the E.S., 514-15; appointed Commissioner of Government, 429; art. of, on ancients, 88; as M. Jun., 407, 410; buys tickets, 431; calls a Brother "old horse," 429; chosen to form T.S., 94-95; destroys papers prior to leaving, 431; fate of, depends on being ready, 424, 439; first inspiration of, always better, 412; gets samples of ore for M., 426; goes to Orange, 429; goes to Philad., 416, 425; goes to see Edison, 429; Government credentials of, 426, 439; had access to store of knowledge, 302; idea of cremation and, 278; in Boston, 72; in consultation with M., 430; in danger, 433; investigates Holmeses, 60; Kislingbury on, and Coleman's falsehood, 320; lends $100 to M., 429; life-story and writings, 503-18; nicknamed Moloney, 406; on crisis in Spiritualism, 95; on de Palm, 233; on Indian Press, 378; on physical phenomena, 292; on Mrs. Thayer's phenomena, 121, 122; promotes Syndicate, 415, 416, 418, 421, 422; rabid Spiritualist, 34; receives message from Divine Brother, 415; receives orders for indignation meeting, 412; returns from Philadelphia, 414; rushes into print, 328; seasick, 434; sings on board, 434; throws out worthy hints, 303; *unselfish* Spiritualist, 188; wife of, thinks of arresting him, 429, 431, 433.

——, *Diaries*: 379 fn.; entries in, 415-16, 417-18, 420-22.

——, *Old Diary Leaves*: on E. G. Brown, 46; on Circular of Brotherhood of Luxor, 87; on first Circular about T.S., 375 fn.; on formation of T.S., 122, 123; on H.P.B.'s "First Occult Shot," 100; on H.P.B.'s land, 83 fn.; on "old horse" incident, 439; on de Palm's burial, 214; Vol. I of, written from memory, 123; writing of, 516-17.

——, *People from the Other World*: 2, 32, 462, 509; date when published, 321 & fn.; on H.P.B.'s mediumship, 203; on Mrs. Compton, 339; reviewed by Wagner, 212.

INDEX 561

Old Diary Leaves. See Olcott.
"Old horse" incident, 428, 430.
Oliver, J. F., 246.
Ookerdhaboy Shewjee, publ. Jaina Bible, 373 fn.
Ophites, offshoots of, 105.
l'Opinione Nazionale, Editor of, a Theosophist, 391(392).
Orders: to go from Philadelphia, 429; to leave Dec. 18, 431: to sail for India, 415, 420, 421; to sell furniture, 424.
Orient, journey to the, might open doors to mysteries, 133.
Oriental, philosophy and Spiritualism, 270.
Origin. See Darwin.
Orohippus, and horse, 229.
O'Sullivan, and black lock of H.P.B.'s hair, 408.
Otechestveniya Zapisky, on Spiritualism, 217.
d'Ourches, Count, 160-61.
Outflowing, and inflowing, 113.
Owasso, control of Slade, 225, 316.
Owen, R. D.: 53, 59; and Holmes, 60 *et seq.*; defended by H.P.B., 68; biogr., 518-20.

P

P***, 89.
Padârtha, and abhâva, 332.
Palm, Baron de: 428; ashes cast into sea, 421; H.P.B. on, 214, 233.
Pancoast, Dr. Seth: 123; biogr., 520-21.
Parabrahma [Parabrahman], *335.*
Paracelsus, 106, 131, 138, 141.
——, *Philosophia sagax,* on astral light and inner man, 284, 521.
Parker, Mrs. S., 411, 414.
Parker, Theodore, humbugging spirit, 135.

Pashkoff, Countess L. de: 375 fn.; biogr., 521-22.
Path, The, letter of H.P.B. in, 224 fn.
Pathâns, clan of Yusafzai, 369 fn.
Paul I, Emperor, 92-93.
Pavlovsky, Military College, 93.
Pedactyl, horse and Huxley, 228, 232.
Peebles, Dr. J. M.: 264, 269, 282, 290; is enjoined secrecy by Brâhmans, 305.
Pentateuch, symbols of, and Moses, 111.
People. See Olcott.
Peretti, Felice. See Sixtus V.
Périsprit: after death becomes outermost body, 364(368); and skandhas, 362(366); as psyché, 361(365); Greek division of, 361(365); nature and source of, 361-62(365-66); reincarnation of the, of dead child, 363(368); union of, with spirit makes man a god, 362(366).
Petty, boys, 205.
Phantasma, 293, 299.
Phantoms: real, evoked by Slade, contrasted with opaque, 223-24.
Phasma, 293, 299.
Phenomena: and other spirits than excarnate humans, 283; and starting of T.S., 393-94; learn what they are and what they are not, 274; man can produce, greater than mediums, 296; must be defended, 45; role of elementaries in, 285-86; witnessed by strangers, 246.
Phenomenalism, not true Spiritualism, 282.
Philadelphia Inquirer, and biogr. of Katie King, 63 fn.
Philalethes, Eugenius, 138.
Phillips, W.: lecture on Lost Arts, 231 & fn.; biogr., 522-23.
Philosophers. See Hermetic.

Philosophia. See Paracelsus.
Philos. of Magic. See Salverte.
Phonograph, 429, 430, 439.
Phren: and périsprit, 361(365); as mens or mind, 292.
Phrenologist. See Marshall.
Physiognomy, and r e v i e w i n g books, 386 *et seq.*
Pico della Mirandola, 131.
Planetary, spirits inspire men, 295.
Pliny, 232.
Plutarch, on afterdeath states, 294, 362(366).
Pneuma: and Demeter, 295; or nous and second death, 294.
Poe, E., *Nevermore,* 60.
Polarities, and levitation, 244.
Pope, blesses Moslems, 259-60.
Popular Science Monthly, 272, 322.
Portraits, "spirits" as, of dead people, 34.
Poseidon. See Brown, R.
Possession, and mediumship, 140.
Potter, Miss, 413.
Power(s), hidden, in man which can make a god of him, 73; inherent in man, 273-74; *real,* and the people, 130.
Prague, protest of Czechs in, against Pope, 260.
Pratt, Judge C. E., 54, 84.
Pravda (Odessa): 407, 417, 435; H.P.B.'s writings in, 313.
Pravritti, and nivritti, 268.
Preamble and By-Laws of T.S., 150, 523.
Precipitations, nature and rationale of, *488-89.*
Pretences, false, of scientists, 226 *et seq.*
Principle: everlasting, and the Ârya Samâj, 383; one indefinable, and its correlations, 334; pure, 112.
Programme, original, of Founders, 133.

Propagandism, sacred flame of, 102.
Prophecy of Ezekiel, Cabalistic treatise, 132.
Prophets, Schools of, still extant, 302.
Proserpine: and the daïmon, 294; and the périsprit, 362(366).
Protest, by Russians against Report on Spiritualism, 217-20.
Protohippus, 230.
Providence Journal, 306, 407.
Psychê: and Eve, 128-29; and nous in Paul, 292; compound nature of, 292-93; parts of, indestructible, 299; dissolution of, and second death, 294; or périsprit, 361(365); same, must be reborn in case of dead child, 298.
Psychical, nature, 297, 298.
Psychological, science to be studied by Theosophists, 339.
Psychology: magic is, practically applied, 324; a debatable land, 228-29.
Psychophobia, in Russia, 210-11, 212, 216.
Public Opinion, dangerous Hydra, 129-30.
Public Opinion (London), on *Isis Unveiled,* 323, 388.
Puñjab [Pañjâb], 372, 373, 382.
Pythagoras: on nature of light, 243; penetrates the mysteries, 360; Tetraktys of, and fourth dimension, 360.
Pythoness, guided by High Priest, 139.

Q

Quarterly Review. See Deutsch.

INDEX

R

Rakas, shrines, 263.
Rammohun Roy, outstanding leader, 381.
Ramsay, on Tennessee, 231.
Ramsgate, and H.P.B., 3-4.
Randolph, P.B., 269.
Ranjit Singh, 373, 374.
Ravignan, Father, 196, 201.
Rayleigh, Lord, cautious observer, 224.
Reade, W. W., *The Veil of Isis*, 273 fn., 523.
Rebus, 338 fn.
Red, hats, 240 fn.
Regazzoni, 137.
Reincarnation: and metempsychosis, *294-95*; of child, 298; of children and congenital idiots, 363-64(367-68).
Religio-Philosophical Journal, 75, 77, 92, 142.
Religions, originated in *Vedas*, 398(402).
Reminiscences. See Wachtmeister.
Reporters: H.P.B.'s definition of *396(400-01)*; misquote H.P.B., 237, 242; New York, 225.
Revolution of the Souls. See Loria.
Revues des Deux Mondes: and H.P.B., 1; on Babinet, 243.
Revue Spirite, La, 195, 396(400), 397(401).
Rig-Veda, teaches evolution, 232, 523.
Rites, Christian, and symbolism, of occult origin, 118.
Robinson, James C., 98.
Rolling-pot, phenomenon of the, 276.
Roman Church: and Home, 196-97; and necromancy, 197; attitude of, towards mediums and "spirits," 197.
Rope, knots tied in, 314-15.
Ros, meaning dew, 105.

Rosencrantz, role of, 105-06.
Rosicrucians: do not exist any longer, 104; had to struggle alone, 115; offshoots of, 105; Oriental, 107; origin of the, 105-06; term should be restricted to one sect only, 104.
Rosicrucians. See Jennings, H.
Rosicrucianism, art. on, by "Hiraf," 99-100.
Rossetti, G., *Disquisitions*, etc.: on symbolic language, 126; 523.
Rosy Cross, seventh rule of, 103, 115.
Rosy Cross Jewel, lost, 425, 439.
Rotura, Dr., on suspending life in sheep and goats, 389-90, 399 (403).
Rousselet, L., *l'Inde des Rajah*, etc., 408, 436, 523.
Royal. See MacKenzie, K.
Ruach, or nous, 299.
Russian(s): chairman of Scientific Comm. coming to America, 212-13; Comm. on Spiritualism a disgrace, 210-11, 215 *et seq.*; compared with the English, 355; investigation of Spiritualism, 204 *et seq.*; Protest of, against Mendeleyev's Report, 217-20.
Russkiy Vestnik, 408, 436.
Russo-Turkish War, 253 *et seq.*

S

Saddarshana Chintanika, 414, 415.
Saffar Ali Bek, 32.
Sahajânanda, perfect bliss, *335*.
Sahib: gives stamps, 423; H.P.B. goes on errand for, 425; relieves Narayan, 414; row with, about stamps, 425; taken for a drive by Mrs. Mitchell, 423.
Saidu, Pope of, 374.

Saif-ed-Dîn, as title, 371.
Saint-Germain, Count de: 141; a living mystery, 109; autographed MS. of, 107 fn.; predicts French Revolution, 107 fn.
St. Paul: on anastasis, 293; on triune man, 292.
St. Petersburg: Committee of, for Spiritualistic investigation, 91, 94; new Comm. from Medical Society, 213; University of, and its investigation, 120, 204 *et seq.*, 210-11, 212-13.
St. Petersburg Vedomosty: 204, 216; Aksakov's art. in, 359; on séances with Slade, 315 *et seq.*
Salverte, *Des Sciences occultes*: on evolution, 232; 523.
Samothrace, mysteries of, 141.
Sankey, D., hymn by, 187 fn.
Sargent, Epes, fooled by medium, 220-21.
Sarpa-râjñî, 227.
Sat B'hai, secret organization in India, 311, 407, 435.
Saxon, Mr., 189.
Scheol, 187 & fn.
Schewitsch, Helene von: 408, 415; biogr., 436.
Schools: of Prophets still extant, 302; psychological training, 267.
Schopenhauer, helps to understand Theosophy, 332.
Schuyler, Mr. 255.
Schwartzenberg, P r i n c e : 260; biogr., 523.
Science: and scientists, 221, 384-85; colleges for neophytes of secret, 103; iconoclasm of, 243; of discerning spirits, 139; modern, and knowledge of ancients, 116; past of, a Potter's Field of exploded superstitions, 221; prejudices of, 221-22; secret, 101, 103; Theology and Occultism, 128.

Science. See Lévi, É.
Sciences. See Salverte.
Scientists: are not science itself, 384; are runaways, 109; data of, as uncertain as those of Spiritualists, 230; prejudiced, 221; Russian, prejudiced, 210-11, 215 *et seq.;* should investigate any new phenomenon, 385; unfair and biased, 232-33.
Scîn-lâc, spectral form, evocation of, 171 & fn.
Scriptures, Hebrew and hidden signs, 115.
Scrutator, term analysed, 327.
Secrecy: and privacy in study of phenomena, 393; enjoined upon Peebles by Brâhmans, 305; in connection with work of T.S., 395.
Sects, occult, guilty of heresies, 104.
Seers: generations of trained, 267; trained, on elementals, 268; where are the, 303; who are the, 289.
Self-discipline, results of, 299.
Selger, Dr., 81.
Sepher Yetzirah, 131, 524.
Sephira, and Ain-soph, 111-12.
Sepoy Mutiny: and Abdul Ghafur, 371; caused by missionaries, 433.
Serapis: Adept of Egyptian Section, 438; and date of sailing, 431; on the lost Jewel, 439; orders to leave for India, 415, 420.
Serpents, Queen of the, 227.
Seymour, Sanctuary of, 309.
Shakespeare, John, *Hindustani-English Dict.*: 241; on gopura, 356; biogr. of author, 524.
Shakespeare, Wm., *Macbeth*, 170.
Shaman, evocation by a, 346 *et seq.*

Shamji, Krishnavarma: 409; biogr., 437.
Shaw, Miss May, medium, 267.
Shedim, four classes of intermediate spirits, 111.
Shells: and Devachan, 36; and mediums, 35; magnetic attraction of, 36.
Sheppard, Jesse, medium, 92.
Shield, story of the magic, 177 *et seq.*
Shimon ben Yochai, and *Zohar*, 110-11.
Shishac, and Śâkya, 239.
Showers, Mrs., medium, 355.
Sibyls, guided by High Priests, 139.
Siddhârtha, lofty philosophy of, 398(402).
Sikhs: enemies of Abdul Ghafur, 372; religious principles of the, 372-73.
Simmons, Chas. E., biogr., 524.
Simmons, Mr., partner of Slade, 224, 315, 316.
Simulacra, spirit-forms mere, 160.
Sinnett, A. P., *Incidents,* etc.: 525; on H.P.B.'s arrival in New York, 224 fn.; on mediums, shells and H.P.B.'s role in manifestations, 35.
——, *The Letters of H. P. Blavatsky,* etc.: 525; on Mitrovich, 11; on the Story of the Double, 173 fn.
——, *The Mahatma Letters,* etc.: 525; K.H. on H.P.B.'s art. on triune nature of man, 300.
Sirdar, chief of a *misl*, 373.
Sixtus V, Pope, compared with Abdul Ghafur, 369-70.
Skandhas: 296; and animal forms, 294-95; and peregrinations of molecules, 362(367); are the périsprit, 362(366); def. *294;* spirits liberated from, 363(367).
Sketchbook. See Blavatsky.

Slade, Dr. H.: 274; contract with, 211, 216; contrasted with Huxley, 228; evokes *real* phantoms, 223; genuine medium, 223; golden hour of, 225; pretended exposure of, and Lankester-Donkin alliance, 222 *et seq.;* Russian message to H.P.B. through, 224; triumph of, 314 *et seq.;* biogr., 525.
Slanders, H.P.B. and, 247-49.
Smith, Deacon Richard, 241.
Socrates: 300, 387; daïmonion of, 229.
Solomon, a Cabalist, 111, 115.
Solovyov, V.S., *A Modern Priestess of Isis*: on H.P.B. and Dickens, 2; on *Isis,* 264 & fn.; 525.
Some Unpublished. See Corson, E. R.
Sorcery, *137.*
Sosiosh [Saoshyant], 417.
Sotheran, Chas.: 121, 193, 194, 324; abused H.P.B. but amends, 290; and title of *Isis,* 237 fn.; and Yarker, 311-12; as labor socialist, 403-04; biogr., 433, 525-28; learned member of Rosae Crucis, 126; publ. *Echo,* 369 fn.
Soul(s): afterdeath condition of, acc. to Lévi, 288; atom becomes a living, or man, 334; disembodied, and adept-psychologist, 352; first envelope of the, and astral light, 284; mind and nous, 233; nature of, acc. to "Zeus," 287-88; potential annihilation of, 284; three kinds of, taught by Jews, 330; union of, and nous, 293.
Spencer, H.: 266; read *Isis,* 413.
Spheres, seven, and ours, 112.
Spirit: evolution of, 230; *latent,* in every atom, 330-31; meaning both God and alcohol, 332; misuse of term, 292-93; must be

recognized for real expansion of science, 233; or Nous, 361 (365); state of pure, attained only through experience as a man, 363(367).

Spirits: adjuged demons by R. Church, 197; and elementals, 73; as portraits of dead people, 34; belief in agency of, foolish, 53; can be commanded, 140; disembodied, not elementary, 112, 142; elementary, their nature, 112, 141; -forms as mere simulacra, 160; high Planetary, inspire men, 295; Hindu views about, 336; humbugging, and Diakkas, 134, 140; inferior nature of materialized, 335-36; land of, *terra incognita* to Spiritualists, 192; larvae as materialized, 293; materialized, and astral emanations, 286; never descend into our sphere, 36; of many kinds and mediums, 199; other than excarnate human, involved in phenomena, 283; pure, attracted by harmony, 201; pure, rarely descend to our sphere, 140.

Spiritual: agencies associated with material life, 295; body and psychê, 293; genuine, substances, 223-24; sight developed in pagodas, 289.

Spiritual Scientist, 122.

Spiritualism: ancient, or occultism, 199; and communication between worlds, 118; and materializations, 267; and phenomenalism, 282; contest of, with Theosophy, 301; crisis for, 194 *et seq.*; defended by H.P.B., 67; East may send nurses to take care of, 117; Founders did not offer leadership to, 322; H.P.B.'s attitude towards, 190-92; H.P.B. practical follower of Eastern, 110; magic and sorcery, *137*; malpractices of, 269-70; meaning of term acc. to H.P.B., 74; plight of modern, 47-49; reason for H.P.B.'s identification with, 73; relation of, to magic, 101-02; Russian investigation of, 204 *et seq.*, 210-11; 215 *et seq.*; school of magic or controllable, 353; should be a true philosophy, 304; true, degraded by followers, 305; unconscious magic, 295; spread of true, helped by antagonists, 223; will become a science, 110; will progress only when illumined by Oriental Philosophy, 270; will triumph over opposition, 113-14.

Spiritualist(s): and evolutionists, 228 *et seq.*; anthropomorphic ideas of, 333; as neophytes of mysteries, 118; Circular about, from Brotherhood of Luxor, 85-88; data of, uncertain, 230; debase name of spirit, 296; def., *140*; H.P.B. a true, 192; persecuted by clergy, 394, 395; Saxon, confuse spirit and périsprit, 361(365); *true*, has no fear of death, 115; warned by H.P.B. about a Russian scientist, 212-13.

Spiritualist, The: 53, 271, 281, 282, 284, 305, 313, 330, 337, 359, 414; H.P.B. pays tribute to, 290 fn.

Standard (London), on Turkish barbarities, 257.

Star (N.Y.), 413, 427.

Stavropol': H.P.B.'s father dies at, 83; his grave at, 43, 44.

Stewart, Balfour, *The Sun and the Earth*, 244, 528.

Stewart, James M., 407, 435.

Strygis, elementary spirits, 145 fn.

Sturge, Rev., 433.

INDEX 567

Substance(s) : ethereal, filling universe, as source of périsprit, 361(366); genuine spiritual, contrasted with opaque phantoms, 223-24.
Summerland, 192.
Sun: Kepler on magnetic nature of, 243; nature of, key to gravitation, 243.
Sun (N.Y.): 189, 233, 239, 241, 261, 323, 413, 414; infamous editorial in, 411; Olcott's art. on Mrs. Thayer, 121, 122.
Sun. See Stewart, B.
Sunday Herald, 203.
Sunday Mercury, The (N.Y.), 54, 133.
Supernatural. See Cassels.
Survival, of the fittest, 297.
Sûtra-Sangraha, of Jainas, 373.
Sûtras, of Gautama Buddha, 398 (402).
Sûtras. See Kapila.
Svabhavat; or Anima Mundi, 293; pre-existing matter, 268.
Svâmis: errors about, fakirs and dervishes, 240-41, 245.
Swat: Akhund of, 369 *et seq.*; location of, 369 fn.
Swedenborg, E., a seer but deluded, 304.
Syeverniy Vestnik, on Turkish barbarities, 257.
Symbols, Christian, derived from ancients, 129.

T

Taffy. See Bates, Rosa.
Talismans, mesmerized, of Pope Sixtus V, 370.
Talmud, 132 & fn., 528.
Tarboosh, 181.
Tartuffe. See Molière.
Tatmos, girl-sensitive from Damascus, 181 *et seq.*

Tattvabodhini-Sabhâ, 381.
Temple, destruction of second, and Cabala, 110-11.
Teratology, should include reporters, 396(400).
Ternary, as Cabalistic symbol, 129 fn.
Tertullian, 300.
Tetraktys, and fourth dimension, 360.
Textor de Ravisi: on Krishna, 251-52; biogr., 528-29.
Thackersey, Mooljee, 409, 422, 437.
Thayer, Mary Baker, her flower apports, 121, 122.
Theft, objects of, recovered phenomenally, 275-77.
Theistic Annual, The, 381.
Theologians, revile the gods, 237.
Theology: Christian, particularly pernicious, 377; dogma and faith as pillars of, 304; Science and Occultism, 128.
Theosophic, seminary, 110.
Theosophical Society: affiliated with Ârya Samâj, 395; as a secret society, 193-94; Circular drafted by Olcott and H.P.B. on objects of, 375-78 & fn.; has no dogmas, 304; historical background of, 121-24; made into secret body, 376, 393-95; members of, sworn to secrecy, 380; most important object of the, 394; object of, cleansing of Spiritual truth, 306; ordered formed by M., 73; orders to found, and choose Olcott, 94-95; pioneer of free thought, 395; statement by Committee of the, 245-46; s e c r e t organization, 245-46; the "formers" of the, 124; three Sections of, 375 fn., 376; to aid in saving heathen from Christianity, 381.

Theosophist, The, 162, 163, 173 fn., 338 fn.
Theosophists: adhere to facts, 304; essential beliefs of, 334-35; have no dogmas, 304, 361 (365); not infallible, 300, 304; tread path worn by footsteps of sages, 291.
Theosophy: adversely received by public, 394; and true Spiritualism, 74.
Theravâda School, and yellow robes, 240 fn.
I Thessalonians, on man as a trine, 292.
Theurgy, esoteric, is magic, 139.
Thomas, Fred, unfair art. by, 214.
Thought: T.S. pioneer of free, 395.
Thumos: and périsprit, 361(365); passional nature, 292.
Thury: 223; on levitation, 244.
Tibet, lamas of, and their robes, 240 fn.
Tiflisskiy Vestnik: 388, 389; H.P.B.'s writings in, 313.
Tile Club, 415, 438.
Time, and timelessness, 335.
Tiriêri, of Todas, 356.
Todas: 353; customs and character of, 356-58.
Toes, evolution of, 229.
Topčider, murder at, 164 fn.
Trance: of Damascus girl, 182 *et seq.;* of sensitive, 168 *et seq.*
Tree-trick, performed by fakirs, 273-74.
Tribune (N.Y.), 322.
Truth: Cause of, 199; cleansing of spiritual, object of T.S., 306; hurricane of, imminent, 116; light of, beacon of H.P.B.'s life, 127; to help readers to seek the, 136; various means of disseminating, 380; will triumph over all opposition, 114.
Tsong-kha-pa, 240 fn.

Tuitit Bey: 87; orders from, 89.
Tulku, doctrine of, 481.
Turguenyev, I.S., poem of, 253-54.
Turks, barbarities of, 255 *et seq.,* 262.
Tyndall, 225.

U

Unity, and Duad, 200.
Universal Masonry, Yarker in, on adoptive masonry, 311-12.
Universe: called forth out of pre-existing matter, 268; material and invisible, governed by same laws, 296-97.
Unknown, object of terror to people, 130.

V

Vampirism, and necromancy, 286.
Vanderbilt, H.P.B. subpoenaed in, case, 419-20.
Varley, C.F.: 31; biogr., 529-30.
Vartamana, 335, 336.
Vaughan, Thos., 106, 109.
Vay, A. von: 410; on *Isis* and elementals, 281.
Vâyu, lord of airy regions, 227.
Vedas: 373; and Dayânanda Sarasvatî, 383; and Wm. Jones, 239; Âryans as authors of, 383; Buddha based himself on esoteric meaning of, 398(402); common center of all religions, 398(402); Haug on age of, 227.
Veil of Isis, The: magus lifting the, 329; original title of H.P.B.'s first book, 237 fn., 302.

INDEX

Ventura di Raulica, 196.
Verbum, or Logos, 129.
Verulam, Lord, on superstition and natural causes, 233.
Vestnik Yevropy, art. of Wagner, 90.
Vihiva Pûnnûttee Sûtra, 373 fn., 530.
Virchow, and Slade, 317-18.
Virgin Mary, appears in Maringen, 317.
Vishama, *336*.
Vishnu Bawa Brahmachâri, on padârtha and abhâva, 332, 530.
Vlasto, Solon J., 246.
Vlukolak (vukodlak), evil spirits, 168, 169.
Voice of Truth, 384.
Volney: 251; biogr., 530.
Vorontzov, Prince M.S.: 55; and Prince Mirza, 371.
Vourdalaki. See Vlukolak.
Vučić, 164 fn.
Vyatireka, *336*.

W

Wachtmeister, Countess C., *Reminiscences*, etc.: on H.P.B.'s Sketchbook, 4; 530-31.
Wagner, N. P.: 89, 90, 215, 223, 531: champions phenomena, 212; reviews Olcott's book, 212, 216.
Wahhabees, 370-71.
Wallace, A. R.: 223, 224, 272, 273, 274; on *Isis*, 323.
Wand, seven-jointed, and magical feats, 150.
Warner, Dr., 244.
War of Roses, 222.
Washing, disciples' feet, 261.
Wave Theory, and corpuscular theory of light, 243-44.

Wellesley, Col., and Turkish barbarities, 256-57.
Westbrook, R. B., 246, 531.
White, Eliza: medium, 58 *et seq.*; and Mr. Owen, 61.
Whitney, Prof., 250.
Wiggin, Rev. J. H., 121, 122.
Wilder, Dr. A.: 407, 411, 417, 423, 435; biogr., 531-33.
Will, and Force, 334.
Will power: and escape from death, 299, 364(368); and magical feats, 150; magician can form circle by, 352-53; sovereign power, 364(368).
Willis, and persecutors, 211.
Wimbridge, E.: 407, 409, 411, 413, 414, 422, 423, 430, 431; afraid of prison, 425, 426; drunk, 430; makes portrait of H.P.B. for engraving, 409; plays his last card, 427; winds up matters safely, 430; biogr., 533.
Windsor, croquet at, 253-54.
Windthorst, and "miracles," 317, 533.
Wissenschaftliche Abhandlungen, 315. See Zöllner.
Witte, A. Y. de: 255 fn.; on Turkish barbarities, 258 & fn.
Witte, K. A. de, 255 fn., 258 fn.
Witte, S. Y. de, Prime Minister, 258 fn.
Witte, Y. F. de, 258 fn.
Wittgenstein, Prince: 220, 410; death of, 414; biogr., 533-34.
Wodan (Odin), and Buddha, 239.
Woldrich, Dr., on Elementaries, 265 *et seq.*
Wong Chin Foo, 248.
Word, influence of books and spoken, 380.
World (N.Y.): 239, 244, 246, 278, 396(400), 423; and Rotura's experiments on goats, 389, 399 (403).

Worship, exoteric, falls before fact and logic, 305.
Wren, 243.
Wyld, Dr. George, 409, 436.

X Y Z

Yadavas, Yadu, 251.
Yahontov, R. N. de, 255 fn.
Yarker, John: and H.P.B.'s Masonic diploma, 308 et seq., 311-12.
——, *Notes on the Scientific*, etc.: 311; on degradation of Masonry, 310-11; on Rites of Grand Orient, 309; 534.

Yellow, robes of bhikkus, 240 fn.
Youmans, Prof. 255.
Zadecki, Martin, calendar of, 386.
Zanoni. See Bulwer-Lytton.
Zeitung des Judenthums, Das, and H.P.B., 1.
"Zeus," a cabalist, on nature of the soul, 287-88.
Zhelihovsky, Vera P. de: 258 fn., 420; H.P.B. helps, financially, 313; package for, arrives, 427; package for, lost, 426; sells her bird, 427; biogr. and writings, 534-37.
Zohar: 131, 538; and Shimon ben Yohai, 110-11.
Zöllner: 413, 538; on four-dimensional beings and experiments with Slade, 314-15, 360.